Point/Counterpoint focuses on areas of controversy or disagreement within human resource management, offering the arguments for and against a position, along with some conclusions that leave room for interpretation by the student.

Outsourcing (Ch. 1)
Too Much Human Resources Regulation? (Ch. 3)
Wages and Conditions in Foreign Plants (Ch. 4)
Selecting for Fit versus Skills (Ch. 7)
360-Degree Feedback (Ch. 8)
What Should Be the Basis for Compensation? (Ch. 11)
Team versus Individual Incentives (Ch. 12)
Are Labor Unions Still Needed? (Ch. 14)

 Human Resources Legal Brief describes specific legal issues that are especially important and relevant to the chapter topic. Relevant laws and regulations are discussed throughout the text, but this section calls attention to issues that either are the focus of significant public interest or are so important that they are likely to dominate human resource practice in the future.

On-the-Job Injuries as Crimes (Ch. 1)
Child Labor and International Business (Ch. 4)
An End to Age Discrimination Lawsuits? (Ch. 8)
Stock Options as Incentives (Ch. 12)
Legislating Domestic Partner Benefits? (Ch. 13)
The Merits (?) of Diversity Training (Ch. 16)
When Is Temporary Permanent? (Ch. 17)

 Human Resources Around the Globe discusses human resource practices from outside the United States, offering a useful background for students who will be working in a global economy.

Nike Shoots Itself in the Foot (Ch. 2)
Toyota Wants Only the Best (Ch. 4)
To the Four Corners... (Ch. 6)
Teaching Language Skills for a Global Workforce (Ch. 9)
International Assignments and Career Development (Ch. 10)
Global Benefits: Similarities and Differences (Ch. 13)
Too Little Diversity? (Ch. 16)

 Human Resources Fad, Fashion, Or Fact? discusses an emerging trend, practice, or idea that may become a long-lasting element of effective human resource management, or may prove to be just the latest fashion and lose popularity in the future. Students are invited to reach their own conclusions based on the facts presented.

Location, Location, Location (Ch. 2)
Home Safety for Telecommuters (Ch. 3)
Labor Shortage? What Labor Shortage? (Ch. 5)
The Fine Print: Hiring Through Handwriting Analysis (Ch. 7)
Training—Valuable Investment or a Waste of Money? (Ch. 9)
The New Career Model . . . or a Model for Failure? (Ch. 10)
Minimum Wage . . . But Which One? (Ch. 11)
Pay for Morale? (Ch. 12)
Changing Relationships between Management and Labor (Ch. 14)
An Eye for an Eye . . . (Ch. 17)

 Human Resources Tech Talk discusses how technology has affected human resource practices.

Using Intranets to Enhance Communication (Ch. 2)
Recruiting with the Web (Ch. 6)
Computerized Employee Screening? You Bet! (Ch. 7)
Transforming the Technician (Ch. 10)
Negotiating Salaries on the Web (Ch. 11)
Too Much Technology? (Ch. 15)

 Human Resources in the Twenty-first Century identifies a trend or practice the authors see as growing, then discusses why it is expected to become more common in the future.

Can You Take It with You? (Ch. 3)
Easy Come, Easy Go! (Ch. 5)
Training for the MTV Generation (Ch. 9)
Taking It with You (Ch. 13)
Emerging Trends in Unionization (Ch. 14)
Building the Perfect Work Environment (Ch. 15)
Will the Glass Ceiling Ever Be Shattered? (Ch. 16)

Human Resource Management

Human Resource Management

Angelo S. DeNisi

Texas A & M University

Ricky W. Griffin

Texas A & M University

Houghton Mifflin Company

Boston   New York

■ *To Adrienne, my wife, my friend, and my partner in life (ADN)*
For Glenda, my one constant (RWG)

Executive Editor: George Hoffman
Senior Associate Editor: Susan M. Kahn
Senior Project Editor: Fred H. Burns
Senior Production/Design Coordinator: Jennifer Meyer Dare
Manufacturing Manager: Florence Cadran
Marketing Manager: Melissa Russell

Cover design: Rebecca Fagan
Cover images: (top) © Steven Edson-Photonica; (bottom) © Minoru Toi-Photonica

Photo and cartoon credits appear on page 557.

Printed in the U.S.A.

Library of Congress Catalog Number: 99-72015

ISBN: 0-395-68512-5

1 2 3 4 5 6 7 8 9 — DOW — 04 03 02 01 00

PART ONE   An Overview of Human Resource Management   1

1   The Nature of Human Resource Management 2

PART TWO   The Environment of Human Resource Management   33

2   The Strategic Human Resource Environment 34

3   The Legal Environment 68

4   The Global Environment 102

PART THREE Staffing the Organization   135

5   Human Resource Planning and Job Analysis 136

6   Recruiting Human Resources 168

7   Selecting and Placing Human Resources 194

PART FOUR   Enhancing Motivation and Performance   229

8   Performance Management 230

9   Training, Development, and Organizational Learning 264

10   Career Planning and Development 296

PART FIVE   Compensating and Rewarding the Workforce   323

11   Basic Compensation 324

12   Incentives and Performance-Based Rewards 354

13   Employee Benefits and Services 380

PART SIX   Managing the Existing Workforce   405

14   Managing Labor Relations 406

15   Managing the Work Environment 438

16   Managing the Diverse Workforce 474

17   Managing New Employment Relationships 500

Appendix 1   Human Resource Information Systems 529

Appendix 2   Data and Research in Human Resource Management 537

CONTENTS

PREFACE XXV

PART ONE   An Overview of Human Resource Management   1

Chapter 1   The Nature of Human Resource Management   2

EVOLUTION OF THE HUMAN RESOURCE FUNCTION 5
   Origins of the Human Resource Function 6
   Personnel Management 8

CONTEMPORARY HUMAN RESOURCE MANAGEMENT 9
   Human Resource Management Tasks and Functions 10
   The Human Resource Management System 15

GOALS OF HUMAN RESOURCE MANAGEMENT 17
   Facilitating Organizational Competitiveness 17
   Enhancing Productivity and Quality 18
   Complying with Legal and Social Obligations 19
   Promoting Individual Growth and Development 19

THE SETTING FOR HUMAN RESOURCE MANAGEMENT 20
   Human Resource Management: Line versus Staff Management
      Perspectives 20
   Human Resource Management: Smaller versus Larger
      Organization Perspectives 23
   Human Resources as a Center of Expertise 24

HUMAN RESOURCE MANAGERS 26
   Professionalism and Human Resource Management 26
   Careers in Human Resource Management 27

CHAPTER SUMMARY 27

REVIEW AND DISCUSSION QUESTIONS 28

CLOSING CASE: Enterprise Builds on People 28

BUILDING HUMAN RESOURCE MANAGEMENT SKILLS 30

ETHICAL DILEMMAS IN HUMAN RESOURCE MANAGEMENT 30

HUMAN RESOURCE INTERNET EXERCISE 31

■ *The Lighter Side of HR* 6

■ *Human Resources Legal Brief: On-the-Job Injuries as Crimes* 10

■ *Point/Counterpoint: Outsourcing* 12

PART TWO   The Environment of Human Resource Management   33

Chapter 2   The Strategic Human Resource Environment   34

THE STRATEGIC CONTEXT OF HUMAN RESOURCE MANAGEMENT 36
  The Influence of Organizational Purpose and Mission 38
  The Influence of the Top Management Team 39

CORPORATE, BUSINESS, AND FUNCTIONAL STRATEGIES 40
  SWOT Analysis and Human Resource Management 40
  Corporate Strategy and Human Resource Management 41
  Business Strategy and Human Resource Management 45
  Functional Strategies and Human Resource Management 48

HUMAN RESOURCE STRATEGY FORMULATION 48
  The Impact of Organization Design 50
  The Impact of Corporate Culture 51
  The Impact of Technology 53
  The Impact of the Workforce 54

HUMAN RESOURCE STRATEGY IMPLEMENTATION 55
  Individual Processes and Human Resource Management 55
  Interpersonal Processes and Human Resource Management 58

EVALUATING THE HUMAN RESOURCE FUNCTION IN
  ORGANIZATIONS 60

CHAPTER SUMMARY 61

REVIEW AND DISCUSSION QUESTIONS 62

CLOSING CASE: Blending Strategy and People at Chaparral Steel 62

BUILDING HUMAN RESOURCE MANAGEMENT SKILLS 64

ETHICAL DILEMMAS IN HUMAN RESOURCE MANAGEMENT 65

HUMAN RESOURCE INTERNET EXERCISE 66

  ■ *The Lighter Side of HR* 43

  ■ *Human Resources Around the Globe: Nike Shoots Itself in the Foot* 47

  ■ *Human Resources Fad, Fashion, or Fact? Location, Location, Location* 50

  ■ *Human Resources TechTalk: Using Intranets to Enhance Communication* 59

Chapter 3   The Legal Environment   68

THE LEGAL CONTEXT OF HUMAN RESOURCE MANAGEMENT 70
  The Regulatory Environment of Human Resource Management 70
  Basic Areas of Legal Regulation 71

EQUAL EMPLOYMENT OPPORTUNITY 72
  Discrimination and Equal Employment Opportunity 73
  Protected Classes in the Workforce 75

Equal Employment Opportunity Legislation 77
Enforcing Equal Employment Opportunity 82

LEGAL ISSUES IN COMPENSATION 87
Legal Perspectives on Total Compensation 87
Legal Perspectives on Other Forms of Compensation 88

LEGAL ISSUES IN LABOR RELATIONS 89
Unionization and the Law 89
Collective Bargaining and the Law 89

EMERGING LEGAL ISSUES IN HUMAN RESOURCE MANAGEMENT 90
Employee Safety and Health 90
Emerging Areas of Discrimination Law 92
Employment-at-Will 94
Ethics and Human Resource Management 95

EVALUATING LEGAL COMPLIANCE 96

CHAPTER SUMMARY 97

REVIEW AND DISCUSSION QUESTIONS 97

CLOSING CASE: *Seinfeld* and Sexual Harassment 98

BUILDING HUMAN RESOURCE MANAGEMENT SKILLS 99

ETHICAL DILEMMAS IN HUMAN RESOURCE MANAGEMENT 100

HUMAN RESOURCE INTERNET EXERCISE 100

■ *The Lighter Side of HR* 71

■ *Point/Counterpoint: Too Much Human Resources Regulation?* 83

■ *Human Resources Fad, Fashion, or Fact? Home Safety for Telecommuters* 91

■ *Human Resources In the Twenty-first Century: Can You Take It with You?* 95

Chapter 4   **The Global Environment 102**

THE GROWTH OF INTERNATIONAL BUSINESS 105

GLOBAL ISSUES IN INTERNATIONAL HUMAN RESOURCE
MANAGEMENT 107
International Human Resource Management Strategy 107
Understanding the Cultural Environment 109
Understanding the Political and Legal Environment 111

THE HUMAN RESOURCE FUNCTION IN INTERNATIONAL BUSINESS 115
General Human Resource Issues in International Business 115
Specific Human Resource Issues in International Business 117

DOMESTIC ISSUES IN INTERNATIONAL HUMAN RESOURCE
MANAGEMENT 120
Local Recruiting and Selection Issues 120
Local Training Issues 121
Local Compensation Issues 122

MANAGING INTERNATIONAL TRANSFERS AND ASSIGNMENTS 123
  Selecting Expatriates 123
  Training Expatriates 125
  Compensating Expatriates 126

INTERNATIONAL LABOR RELATIONS 128

CHAPTER SUMMARY 129

REVIEW AND DISCUSSION QUESTIONS 130

CLOSING CASE: Human Resources and International Mergers 130

BUILDING HUMAN RESOURCE MANAGEMENT SKILLS 132

ETHICAL DILEMMAS IN HUMAN RESOURCE MANAGEMENT 132

HUMAN RESOURCE INTERNET EXERCISE 133

■ *Point/Counterpoint: Wages and Conditions in Foreign Plants* 112

■ *Human Resources Around the Globe: Toyota Wants Only the Best* 122

■ *The Lighter Side of HR* 116

■ *Human Resources Legal Brief: Child Labor and International Business* 114

PART THREE   Staffing the Organization 135

Chapter 5 Human Resource Planning and Job Analysis 136

STRATEGIC IMPORTANCE OF HUMAN RESOURCE PLANNING 138

JOB ANALYSIS AND HUMAN RESOURCE PLANNING 139
  Purposes of Job Analysis and Human Resource Planning 139
  Linking Job Analysis with Human Resource Planning 141

THE JOB ANALYSIS PROCESS 142
  Determining Information Needs 142
  Selecting Job Analysis Methods 143
  Responsibilities for Job Analysis 144

JOB ANALYSIS METHODS 145
  Collecting Job Analysis Data 145
  Specific Job Analysis Techniques 147
  Job Descriptions and Job Specifications 151

THE HUMAN RESOURCE PLANNING PROCESS 152
  Forecasting the Supply of Human Resources 152
  Forecasting the Demand for Human Resources 155
  Using the Human Resource Information System 158
  Matching the Supply of and Demand for Human Resources 159

DEVELOPING FOLLOW-UP ACTION PLANS 159
  Planning for Growth 160
  Planning for Stability 161
  Planning for Reductions 161

EVALUATING THE HUMAN RESOURCE PLANNING PROCESS 162

CHAPTER SUMMARY 163

REVIEW AND DISCUSSION QUESTIONS 163

CLOSING CASE: One Way to Select the Next CEO 164

BUILDING HUMAN RESOURCE MANAGEMENT SKILLS 165

ETHICAL DILEMMAS IN HUMAN RESOURCE MANAGEMENT 165

HUMAN RESOURCE INTERNET EXERCISE 166

■ *Human Resources in the Twenty-first Century: Easy Come, Easy Go!* 156

■ *Human Resources Fad, Fashion, or Fact? Labor Shortage? What Labor Shortage?* 160

Chapter 6 **Recruiting Human Resources 168**

GOALS OF RECRUITING 170
   The Organization's Goals in Recruiting 170
   The Prospective Employee's Goals in Recruiting 171

SOURCES FOR RECRUITING 172
   Internal Recruiting 172
   External Recruiting 172

METHODS OF RECRUITING 175
   Methods for Internal Recruiting 175
   Methods for External Recruiting 177
   Techniques for External Recruiting 178

REALISTIC JOB PREVIEWS 183

JOB CHOICE FROM THE PROSPECTIVE EMPLOYEE'S
   PERSPECTIVE 184

ALTERNATIVES TO RECRUITING 185
   Overtime 185
   Temporary Workers 186
   Employee Leasing 187
   Part-Time Workers 187

EVALUATING THE RECRUITING PROCESS 188

CHAPTER SUMMARY 188

REVIEW AND DISCUSSION QUESTIONS 189

CLOSING CASE: The Recruiter's Edge 189

BUILDING HUMAN RESOURCE MANAGEMENT SKILLS 191

ETHICAL DILEMMAS IN HUMAN RESOURCE MANAGEMENT 191

HUMAN RESOURCE INTERNET EXERCISE 192

■ *Human Resources Around the Globe: To the Four Corners . . .* 174

■ *Human Resources TechTalk: Recruiting with the Web* 182

■ *The Lighter Side of HR* 184

Chapter 7 Selecting and Placing Human Resources 194

THE SELECTION PROCESS 196
Steps in Selection 196
Responsibilities for Selection 198

BASIC SELECTION CRITERIA 199
Education and Experience 199
Skills and Abilities 200
Personal Characteristics 201

POPULAR SELECTION TECHNIQUES 202
Applications and Background Checks 203
Employment Tests 205
Work Simulations 210
Personal Interviews 211
References and Recommendations 213
Physical Examinations 213

SPECIAL SELECTION METHODS FOR MANAGERS 215
Assessment Centers 215
Networks and Contacts 216

SELECTION TECHNIQUE RELIABILITY AND VALIDITY 216
Reliability 217
Validity 217
Single- versus Multiple-Predictor Approaches 219

THE SELECTION DECISION 220
Job Offer and Negotiation 220
Determining Initial Job Assignments 222

EVALUATING SELECTION AND PLACEMENT ACTIVITIES 222

CHAPTER SUMMARY 223

REVIEW AND DISCUSSION QUESTIONS 224

CLOSING CASE: Hiring High-Risk Employees Can Pay Off
for Business 224

BUILDING HUMAN RESOURCE MANAGEMENT
SKILLS 226

ETHICAL DILEMMAS IN HUMAN RESOURCE
MANAGEMENT 226

HUMAN RESOURCE INTERNET EXERCISE 227

■ *Point/Counterpoint: Selecting for Fit versus Skills* 202

■ *Human Resources TechTalk: Computerized Employee Screening?
You Bet!* 206

■ *The Lighter Side of HR* 208

■ *Human Resources Fad, Fashion, or Fact? The Fine Print: Hiring through
Handwriting Analysis* 214

PART FOUR   Enhancing Motivation and Performance   229

Chapter 8   Performance Management   230

WHY ORGANIZATIONS CONDUCT PERFORMANCE APPRAISALS 232
   Importance of Performance Appraisal 232
   Goals of Performance Appraisal 235

THE PERFORMANCE APPRAISAL PROCESS 236
   The Role of the Organization 236
   The Role of the Rater 238
   The Role of the Ratee 239
   Who Performs the Performance Appraisal? 239

METHODS FOR APPRAISING PERFORMANCE 244
   Ranking Methods 245
   Rating Methods 246

UNDERSTANDING THE LIMITATIONS OF PERFORMANCE APPRAISAL 250

PERFORMANCE MANAGEMENT AND PROVIDING FEEDBACK 252
   The Feedback Interview 252
   Archiving Performance Management Results 253

PERFORMANCE MANAGEMENT FOLLOW-UP MEASURES 255

EVALUATING THE PERFORMANCE APPRAISAL AND MANAGEMENT
   PROCESSES 256

CHAPTER SUMMARY 257

REVIEW AND DISCUSSION QUESTIONS 258

CLOSING CASE: Accelerated Performance Reviews May Improve Retention 258

BUILDING HUMAN RESOURCE MANAGEMENT SKILLS 260

ETHICAL DILEMMAS IN HUMAN RESOURCE MANAGEMENT 261

HUMAN RESOURCE INTERNET EXERCISE 261

■ *Human Resources Legal Brief: An End to Age Discrimination Lawsuits?* 234

■ *The Lighter Side of HR* 238

■ *Point/Counterpoint: 360-Degree Feedback* 243

Chapter 9   Training, Development, and Organizational Learning   264

PURPOSES OF TRAINING AND DEVELOPMENT 266
   The Nature of Training 266
   The Nature of Development 267
   Learning Theory and Employee Training 268

NEW-EMPLOYEE ORIENTATION 270
   Goals of Orientation 270
   Basic Issues in Orientation 271

ASSESSING TRAINING AND DEVELOPMENT NEEDS 273
    Needs Analyses 273
    Setting Training and Development Goals 274
    In-House Programs versus Outsourced Programs 275

DESIGNING TRAINING AND DEVELOPMENT PROGRAMS 276
    Outlining and Defining Training and Development Program Content 276
    Selecting Training and Development Instructors 278

TRAINING AND DEVELOPMENT TECHNIQUES AND METHODS 279
    Work-Based Programs 279
    Instructional-Based Programs 281
    Training Technology 283

MANAGEMENT DEVELOPMENT 284
    Special Needs for Management Development 284
    Special Techniques for Management Development 284
    Organization Development 284

EVALUATING TRAINING AND DEVELOPMENT 287

CHAPTER SUMMARY 290

REVIEW AND DISCUSSION QUESTIONS 291

CLOSING CASE: Boeing Trains for the Future 291

BUILDING HUMAN RESOURCE MANAGEMENT SKILLS 292

ETHICAL DILEMMAS IN HUMAN RESOURCE MANAGEMENT 293

HUMAN RESOURCE INTERNET EXERCISE 294

■ *Human Resources Around the Globe: Teaching Language Skills for a Global Workforce* 277

■ *Human Resources in the Twenty-first Century: Training for the MTV Generation* 282

■ *The Lighter Side of HR* 284

■ *Human Resources Fad, Fashion, or Fact? Training—Valuable Investment or a Waste of Money?* 288

Chapter 10 Career Planning and Development 296

THE NATURE OF CAREERS 298
    The Meaning of Career 298
    Traditional Career Stages 299
    Emerging Career Stages 300

HUMAN RESOURCE MANAGEMENT AND CAREER DEVELOPMENT 302
    Organizational Perspectives on Careers 302
    Individual Perspectives on Careers 304

CAREER PLANNING AND CAREER MANAGEMENT 304
    The Importance of Career Planning 304
    The Consequences of Career Planning 306
    Limitations and Pitfalls in Career Planning 307

CAREER MANAGEMENT FOR NEW ENTRANTS 308
    Early-Career Issues 309
    Coping with Early-Career Problems 309

CAREER MANAGEMENT FOR MIDCAREER EMPLOYEES 310
    Midcareer Issues 310
    Coping with Midcareer Problems 310

CAREER MANAGEMENT FOR LATE-CAREER EMPLOYEES 313
    Late-Career Issues 314
    Coping with Late-Career Problems 315

CAREER DEVELOPMENT ISSUES AND CHALLENGES 315
    Career-Counseling Programs 315
    Dual-Career and Work-Family Issues 316

EVALUATING CAREER MANAGEMENT ACTIVITIES 317

CHAPTER SUMMARY 317

REVIEW AND DISCUSSION QUESTIONS 317

CLOSING CASE: Retaining Valued Employees through Multiple Career Paths 319

BUILDING HUMAN RESOURCE MANAGEMENT SKILLS 320

ETHICAL DILEMMAS IN HUMAN RESOURCE MANAGEMENT 321

HUMAN RESOURCE INTERNET EXERCISE 322

   ■ *Human Resources Fad, Fashion, or Fact? The New Career Model . . . or a Model for Failure?* 301

   ■ *Human Resources Around the Globe: International Assignments and Career Development* 306

   ■ *Human Resources TechTalk: Transforming the Technician* 312

PART FIVE Compensating and Rewarding the Workforce 323

Chapter 11 Basic Compensation 324

DEVELOPING A COMPENSATION STRATEGY 326
    Basic Purposes of Compensation 326
    Wages versus Salary 328
    Strategic Options for Compensation 328
    Determinants of Compensation Strategy 332
    Pay Surveys and Compensation 333

DETERMINING A WAGE AND SALARY STRUCTURE 336
    Job Evaluation and Job Worth 336
    Establishing Job Classes 341
    Establishing a Pay Structure 341
    Pay for Knowledge and Skill-Based Pay 342

WAGE AND SALARY ADMINISTRATION 344
    Managing Compensation 344
    Determining Individual Wages 345

Pay Secrecy 346
Pay Compression 347

EVALUATING COMPENSATION POLICIES 347

CHAPTER SUMMARY 348

REVIEW AND DISCUSSION QUESTIONS 349

CLOSING CASE: Working by the Hour at General Motors and Wal-Mart 349

BUILDING HUMAN RESOURCE MANAGEMENT SKILLS 351

ETHICAL DILEMMAS IN HUMAN RESOURCE MANAGEMENT 351

HUMAN RESOURCE INTERNET EXERCISE 352

■ *Human Resources Fad, Fashion, or Fact? Minimum Wage . . . But Which One?* 331

■ *Human Resources TechTalk: Negotiating Salaries on the Web* 334

■ *Point/Counterpoint: What Should Be the Basics for Compensation?* 343

■ *The Lighter Side of HR* 346

Chapter 12 Incentives and Performance-Based Rewards 354

PURPOSES OF PERFORMANCE-BASED REWARDS 356
Rewards and Motivation 356
Rewards and Performance 358
Rewards and Other Employee Behaviors 359

MERIT COMPENSATION SYSTEMS 360
Merit Pay Plans 360
Limitations of Merit Compensation Systems 361
Skill- and Knowledge-Based Pay Systems and Merit 362

INCENTIVE COMPENSATION SYSTEMS 363
Incentive Pay Plans 363
Other Forms of Incentives 364
Limitations of Incentive Compensation Systems 365

TEAM AND GROUP INCENTIVE REWARD SYSTEMS 366
Team and Group Pay Systems 366
Other Types of Team and Group Rewards 367
Limitations of Team and Group Reward Systems 368

EXECUTIVE COMPENSATION 369
Standard Forms of Executive Compensation 369
Special Forms of Executive Compensation 370
Criticisms of Executive Compensation 372

NEW APPROACHES TO PERFORMANCE-BASED REWARDS 374

CHAPTER SUMMARY 375

REVIEW AND DISCUSSION QUESTIONS 376

CLOSING CASE: Continental's Remarkable Turnaround 376

BUILDING HUMAN RESOURCE MANAGEMENT SKILLS 377

ETHICAL DILEMMAS IN HUMAN RESOURCE MANAGEMENT 378

HUMAN RESOURCE INTERNET EXERCISE 379

- *Human Resources Fad, Fashion, or Fact? Pay for Morale? 359*

- *The Lighter Side of HR 365*

- *Point/Counterpoint: Team versus Individual Incentives 367*

- *Human Resources Legal Brief: Stock Options ad Incentives 371*

Chapter 13 **Employee Benefits and Services 380**

BASIC CONSIDERATIONS IN INDIRECT COMPENSATION
AND BENEFITS 382
Purposes of Indirect Compensation and Benefit
Programs 384
Legal Considerations 386

MANDATED PROTECTION PLANS 387
Unemployment Insurance 388
Social Security 388
Workers' Compensation 389

OPTIONAL PROTECTION PLANS 390
Insurance Coverage 390
Private Pension Plans 390

PAID TIME OFF 392

OTHER TYPES OF BENEFITS 394

CAFETERIA-STYLE BENEFIT PLANS 398

EVALUATING INDIRECT COMPENSATION AND BENEFIT
PLANS 399

CHAPTER SUMMARY 400

REVIEW AND DISCUSSION QUESTIONS 401

CLOSING CASE: Flexible Benefits Are All the Rage 401

BUILDING HUMAN RESOURCE MANAGEMENT SKILLS 402

ETHICAL DILEMMAS IN HUMAN RESOURCE MANAGEMENT 403

HUMAN RESOURCE INTERNET EXERCISE 403

- *The Lighter Side of HR 383*

- *Human Resources Around the Globe: Global Benefits: Similarities and
  Differences 384*

- *Human Resources in the Twenty-first Century: Taking It with You 392*

- *Human Resources Legal Brief: Legislating Domestic Partner Benefits 396*

PART SIX Managing the Existing Workforce 405

Chapter 14 Managing Labor Relations 406

THE ROLE OF LABOR UNIONS IN ORGANIZATIONS 408
Historical Development of Unions 408
Legal Context of Unions 411
Union Structures 415

TRENDS IN UNIONIZATION 415
Trends in Union Membership 417
Trends in Union-Management Relations 418
Trends in Bargaining Perspectives 419

THE UNIONIZATION PROCESS 421
Why Employees Unionize 421
Steps in Unionization 422
Decertification of Unions 423

THE COLLECTIVE BARGAINING PROCESS 425
Preparing for Collective Bargaining 425
Setting Parameters for Collective Bargaining 425

NEGOTIATING LABOR AGREEMENTS 426
The Negotiation Process 426
Barriers to Effective Negotiation 428
Resolving Impasses 429

ADMINISTERING LABOR AGREEMENTS 431

CHAPTER SUMMARY 432

REVIEW AND DISCUSSION QUESTIONS 433

CLOSING CASE: AMR and Its Pilot Problems 433

BUILDING HUMAN RESOURCE MANAGEMENT SKILLS 435

ETHICAL DILEMMAS IN HUMAN RESOURCE MANAGEMENT 435

HUMAN RESOURCE INTERNET EXERCISE 436

■ *Point/Counterpoint: Are Labor Unions Still Needed?* 412

■ *Human Resources in the Twenty-first Century: Emerging Trends in Unionization* 416

■ *Human Resources Fad, Fashion, or Fact? Changing Relationships between Management and Labor* 420

Chapter 15 Managing the Work Environment 438

EMPLOYEE RIGHTS IN THE WORKPLACE 440
The Meaning of Employee Rights 440
Preserving Employee Rights 442

THE ROLE OF DISCIPLINE IN ORGANIZATIONS 442
Discipline, Punishment, and Development 442
The Dysfunctional Employee 443

MANAGING THE DISCIPLINE SYSTEM 444
    Documenting Disciplinary Actions 445
    Approaches to Discipline 445

THE PHYSICAL ENVIRONMENT 449
    Hours of Work 449
    Illumination, Temperature, and Office and Work Space Design 450

EMPLOYEE SAFETY AND HEALTH 451
    Common Workplace Hazards and Threats 453
    Organizations and OSHA 454
    Controlling Accidents at Work 455
    Controlling Occupational Diseases 456

JOB DESIGN IN THE WORKPLACE 457

HEALTH AND STRESS MANAGEMENT PROGRAMS 461
    Causes of Stress at Work 461
    Consequences of Stress at Work 464
    Wellness Programs in Organizations 466
    AIDS in the Workplace 467

CHAPTER SUMMARY 468

REVIEW AND DISCUSSION QUESTIONS 469

CLOSING CASE: Safety Comes to Georgia-Pacific 469

BUILDING HUMAN RESOURCE MANAGEMENT SKILLS 471

ETHICAL DILEMMAS IN HUMAN RESOURCE MANAGEMENT 471

HUMAN RESOURCE INTERNET EXERCISE 472

■ *Human Resources in the Twenty-first Century: Building the Perfect Work Environment* 450

■ *Human Resources TechTalk: Too Much Technology?* 463

■ *The Lighter Side of HR* 465

Chapter 16 **Managing the Diverse Workforce** 474

THE NATURE OF WORKFORCE DIVERSITY 476
    The Meaning of Workforce Diversity 476
    Trends in Workforce Diversity 476

DIVERSITY MANAGEMENT VERSUS EQUAL EMPLOYMENT OPPORTUNITY 478
    Similarities among People at Work 479
    Differences among People at Work 479
    Identical Treatment versus Equitable Treatment 479

BASIC DIMENSIONS OF DIVERSITY 481
    Age Distributions 481
    Gender 482
    Ethnicity 482
    Disability 484
    Other Dimensions of Diversity 485

THE IMPACT OF DIVERSITY ON ORGANIZATIONS 486
    Diversity and Social Change 486
    Diversity and Competitiveness 486
    Diversity and Conflict 488

MANAGING DIVERSITY IN ORGANIZATIONS 490
    Individual Strategies for Dealing with Diversity 490
    Organizational Strategies for Dealing with Diversity 491

THE MULTICULTURAL ORGANIZATION 494

CHAPTER SUMMARY 495

REVIEW AND DISCUSSION QUESTIONS 496

CLOSING CASE: The Avon Way 496

BUILDING HUMAN RESOURCE MANAGEMENT SKILLS 497

ETHICAL DILEMMAS IN HUMAN RESOURCE MANAGEMENT 498

HUMAN RESOURCE INTERNET EXERCISE 499

■ *Human Resources in the Twenty-first Century: Will the Glass Ceiling Ever Be Shattered?* 484

■ *Human Resources Around the Globe: Too Little Diversity?* 488

■ *The Lighter Side of HR* 489

■ *Human Resources Legal Brief: The Merits (?) of Diversity Training* 493

Chapter 17 **Managing New Employment Relationships 500**

THE NATURE OF EMPLOYMENT CONTRACTS 502
    Employment at Will 502
    The Nature of Psychological Contracts 503
    Psychological Contracts and Employee Rights 506
    The Nature of Social Contracts 507

MANAGING KNOWLEDGE WORKERS 508
    The Nature of Knowledge Work 509
    Knowledge Worker Management and Labor Relations 510

MANAGING LOW-SKILL WORKERS 511

OUTSOURCING 513

CONTINGENT AND TEMPORARY WORKERS 514
    Trends in Contingent and Temporary Workers 514
    Advantages and Disadvantages of Using Contingent and Temporary Workers 514
    Managing Contingent and Temporary Workers 516

MANAGING NEW FORMS OF WORK ARRANGEMENTS 518
    Managing Alternative Work Schedules 519
    Managing Alternative Work Sites 521

CHAPTER SUMMARY 523

REVIEW AND DISCUSSION QUESTIONS 523

CLOSING CASE: Temps, Temps, Temps Everywhere! 524

BUILDING HUMAN RESOURCE MANAGEMENT SKILLS 525

ETHICAL DILEMMAS IN HUMAN RESOURCE MANAGEMENT 526

HUMAN RESOURCE INTERNET EXERCISE 527

■ *Human Resources Fad, Fashion, or Fact? An Eye for an Eye . . .* 505

■ *The Lighter Side of HR* 517

■ *Human Resources Legal Brief: When Is Temporary Permanent?* 518

Appendix 1 **Human Resource Information Systems 529**

WHAT ARE HUMAN RESOURCE INFORMATION SYSTEMS 530
    The Nature of Information Technology 530
    Human Resource Information Systems 531

POTENTIAL USES OF HUMAN RESOURCE INFORMATION SYSTEMS 532
    Human Resource Functions 532
    Record Keeping and Report Generation 532

ISSUES AND CONCERNS IN THE USE OF HUMAN RESOURCE INFORMATION
    SYSTEMS 534
    Legal Issues 534
    Ethical Issues 535

CONCLUSIONS 535

Appendix 2 **Data and Research in Human Resource Management 537**

DETERMINING CAUSAL RELATIONSHIPS 537

COMMON HUMAN RESOURCE RESEARCH ISSUES 540
    Samples and Sampling 540
    Measurement Issues 541
    Statistical Issues 542

OTHER TECHNICAL ISSUES IN HUMAN RESOURCE RESEARCH 545
    Validity Generalization 545
    Utility Analysis 546

GLOSSARY 549

PHOTO AND CARTOON CREDITS 557

NAME INDEX 559

ORGANIZATION AND PRODUCT INDEX 564

SUBJECT INDEX 569

Angelo S. DeNisi

Angelo S. DeNisi is the B. Marie Oth Professor of Business at Texas A&M University, where he also serves as director of the Center for Human Resource Management and director of the M.S. program in human resource management. After receiving his Ph.D. in industrial/organizational psychology from Purdue University, Angelo taught at Kent State University, the University of South Carolina, and Rutgers University before moving to Texas A&M. He has taught human resource courses at the undergraduate and graduate levels, including courses for M.B.A., M.S., and Ph.D. students. He has also taught classes and conducted seminars on various human resource topics in Singapore, Jerusalem, Hong Kong, Santo Domingo, and Jakarta. He is a fellow of the Academy of Management and has served as editor of the *Academy of Management Journal,* a member of the Board of Governors, and the chair of the Human Resources Division. He is also a fellow of The Society for Industrial and Organizational Psychology (SIOP) and is the current SIOP president. In addition, he served on the Board of Governors of the Southern Management Association. His research interests include performance appraisal, job analysis, and work experiences of persons with disabilities. His research has been funded by such organizations as the National Science Foundation and the Army Research Institute, and has appeared in such journals as the *Academy of Management Journal, Journal of Applied Psychology, Psychological Bulletin, Journal of Personality and Social Psychology,* and *Industrial and Labor Relations Review.* He has also published a book about his research entitled *Cognitive Approach to Performance Appraisal: A Program of Research.*

Professor DeNisi has received a number of honors over the years, including being named Honorary Professor, Department of Management, City University of Hong Kong; External Examiner, Human Resource Consulting/Management, Nanyang Business School, Nanyang Polytechnic University, Singapore. His research has also been honored, including winning awards such as The William Owens Award for the Outstanding Publication in Industrial and Organizational Psychology, 1998; Outstanding Publication in Organizational Behavior, Organizational Behavior Division of the Academy of Management, 1997; and Best Paper in Organizational Communications, Organizational Communications Division of the Academy of Management, 1992.

Ricky W. Griffin

Ricky W. Griffin is the Lawrence E. Fouraker Professor of Management and head of the Department of Management at Texas A&M University. He formerly served as director of the Center for Human Resource Management at Texas

A&M. His research interests include workplace aggression and violence, executive skills and decision making, and workplace culture. Ricky's research has been published in such journals as *Academy of Management Review, Academy of Management Journal, Administrative Science Quarterly,* and *Journal of Management.* He has also served as editor of *Journal of Management.* Ricky has served the Academy of Management as chair of the Organizational Behavior Division. He has also served as president of the Southwest Division of the Academy of Management and on the board of directors of the Southern Management Association. Ricky is a fellow of both the Academy of Management and the Southern Management Association. He is also the author of several market-leading textbooks. In addition, his texts are widely used in dozens of countries and have been translated into numerous foreign languages.

Welcome to the Land of Change.

If you're familiar with the major businesses in your area, you've probably observed first-hand how dramatically the business environment has changed in recent years. These changes have had a significant impact on the practice of human resource management. What's more, business forecasters predict that the roles of employees, managers, and human resource professionals are likely to see more changes in the decades ahead. Thus, students taking Human Resource Management now will enter a business environment in a few years that requires the ability to apply principles of effective management—and effective human resource practices—to a variety of changing and challenging situations. Helping students meet this test is the goal of this book.

What's Different About Our Text?

Our book primarily differs from others in the field in its approach: its coverage of important topics that are covered briefly, if at all, in other texts; its special features; and its representation of the real human resource issues that will have an impact on students throughout their careers in business. *It is our point of view that all future managers need to understand human resource issues, and this assumption has guided everything we have done in this book.*

As we begin the twenty-first century, it's becoming absolutely clear that the effective management of a firm's human resources is a major source of competitive advantage and may even be the single most important determinant of a firm's performance long-term. This book is designed to be a tool to help teach future managers about the importance of human resource management and provide some ways to manage those resources more effectively. At the same time, we are aware that not everyone who takes a course in human resource management will become a human resources manager. Many management students are required to take a human resources course, even though they plan to work in some other area of management, and some business students take one because they have some vague notion that "managing people" might be important. These students all deserve the best we can give them.

So as we were writing this book, we thought about the thousands of students we have taught in human resources courses over the years. And we considered what today's students most need in order to function effectively in an environment characterized by changes in the traditional models of work as well as the role of human resources and its relationship to management. You'll find our responses to these challenges outlined below.

Our Book in a Nutshell

We can summarize the approach of this text in a sentence:

This book provides the traditional material students need to know, prepares them for the challenges they need to understand, and engages them in the

*process of actively considering the impact of effective human resource manage-
ment on companies and employees.*

There are many other technical details that we could have included and that a
future human resources manager probably needs to know. Those students,
though, will take many other human resources courses in the future, so they
will have the opportunity to learn those technical skills. But *all* managers will
have to manage people, and many managers will find themselves in a position
to be a "consumer" of human resource management. When a manager has
problems dealing with people, he or she must usually ask for some expert advice. At that point, a human resources manager is consulted, and that manager
will make some recommendations. The operating manager must then decide if
these recommendations make sense and should be adopted. This requires the
manager to understand something about the theories underlying various
human resource practices, and to know something about the difference between good practices and simply popular—or even bad—practices. The well-
informed operating manager will need to know what kinds of questions to ask
the human resources manager, and what kinds of answers to expect in return.

Examples:

A typical manager does not need to know in great detail the various pieces of
civil rights legislation. He or she DOES need to have some basic notion about
the law, however, and what types of practices *might* get the company into trouble. Likewise, the typical manager does not need to know how to validate a test
or how to conduct a job analysis, but she or he does need to know whether the
evidence for validity or the information from the job analysis makes any sense.
Furthermore, as more human resource functions are either outsourced or
tasked to some center of expertise, the manager needs to have some basis for
evaluating the proposals or projects that are submitted. At the very least, the
typical manager needs to know what questions should be asked of the internal
or external consultant, to make sure that the consultant has considered the relevant issues.

*It is our goal to educate future managers well enough to make them better,
more informed consumers of human resource practices.*

Emerging Topics, Special Features

To prepare students to deal with the human resource challenges they will face
in the workforce, we have identified several key topics emerging as critically
important, and devoted a separate chapter to each. These include:

- The new relationships between employees and their organizations
- The management of diversity
- The global environment for human resources
- The organizational environment for human resource activities

We have also developed a number of special features to bring human resource management to life and engage students in exploring issues, considering trends, and asking thoughtful questions. Our discussion of each topic is

firmly grounded in theory and research. But at the same time, the variety of cases, exercises, and features brings a perspective to the discussion of these topics that you won't find in other texts.

Every chapter includes . . .

- An opening real-world case highlighting a recent event, issue, or trend that illustrates a major point or theme in the chapter.
- A more detailed closing case with questions to guide discussion.
- "The Bottom Line" at the end of most major sections, explaining the relevance or importance of the topic to the general manager.
- A "Chapter Summary" and "Review and Discussion Questions" to help students review, test, and apply what they have learned.
- "Ethical Dilemmas in Human Resource Management"—scenarios that present a situation related to the chapter material which poses an ethical dilemma. Students are asked to discuss what they believe would be the response of most managers.
- A "Human Resource Internet Exercise" directing students to the Web site of a company or organization or to search the Web for information about some topic illustrating how organizations are really approaching issues discussed in the chapter.
- "Building Human Resource Management Skills"—exercises that require the student to apply the information from the chapter to a specific problem.

Other features appear throughout the book where relevant . . .

- "Human Resources Fad, Fact, or Fashion?" discusses an interesting emerging trend, practice, or idea which may become a long-lasting element of effective human resource management, or may prove to be just the latest fad and lose popularity in the future. The student is invited to reach his or her own conclusion based on the facts presented.
- "Point/Counterpoint" features focus on areas of controversy or disagreement within human resource management, offering the arguments for and against a position, along with some conclusions that leave room for interpretation by the student.
- "Human Resources in the Twenty-first Century" sections identify a trend we see as growing, then discuss why the trend or practice is expected to become more common in the future when students are ready to move into management.
- "Human Resources Legal Briefs" describe specific legal issues that are especially important and relevant to the chapter topic. Relevant laws and regulations are discussed throughout, but this section calls attention to legal issues that either are the focus of significant public interest or are so important that they are likely to dominate human resource practice in the future.
- "Human Resources Around the Globe" discusses noteworthy human resource management practices from outside the United States, offering a useful background for students who will be working in an increasingly global economy.
- "Human Resources TechTalk" discusses how technology has affected human resource practices.
- "The Lighter Side of HR" reinforces important points made in the chapter with amusing cartoons.

What's Covered, How, and Why

The first section of the text is a chapter that details "The Nature of Human Resource Management." It begins with a brief history of the human resource function but quickly comes to a discussion of the function in contemporary organizations, including the various relationships firms have with their human resource functions, as well as the new role of the human resource function. We show that role as helping companies to be more competitive while insuring a reasonable work setting for employees (including the opportunity to personal growth), and assuring that all this is accomplished within the constraints of the law.

The remainder of the text is organized into five sections: the Environment of Human Resource Management; Staffing the Organization; Enhancing Motivation and Performance; Compensating and Rewarding the Workforce; and Managing the Existing Workforce. Each section consists of three (or, in the final part, four) chapters that deal with the kinds of issues students need to understand.

"The Environment of Human Resource Management" establishes the background against which human resource activities unfold. Here we deal with the role of organizational factors in determining how human resources should be managed, emphasizing the importance of having the human resource function support and help further the firm's strategic goals. We also introduce the reader to the variety of laws and regulations that relate to how we are able to deal with human resource problems that might arise, and we also discuss differences in managing human resources in other countries, as we establish the global environment in which most organizations now exist.

"Staffing the Organization" covers how organizations plan for future human resource needs and then recruit potential applicants for the jobs they will have available. In this section we also deal with some of the more technical aspects of how an organization might go about selecting among those applicants without violating the law. The next two sections deal with ways to enhance performance and motivation. In these sections we discuss how to develop performance appraisal systems and how an organization can use appraisal information to help improve employee performance. The chapter on training and development includes information on how to evaluate any training and development program and also deals with larger scale organizational changes that might be needed. The chapter on careers makes the case for strategic career planning on the part of both the organization and the employee.

The next three chapters cover compensation and benefits. Here we deal not only with basic compensation issues such as job evaluation and establishing a compensation structure, but also with some of the issues involved in developing a system of skill-based or knowledge-based pay. We also discuss various plans and approaches for linking pay to performance and point out the strengths and weaknesses of several of these approaches. Finally, we discuss the role of employee benefits in compensation, and ways in which benefit plans can be used to develop some form of competitive advantage for a firm.

The final section, Managing the Existing Workforce, should help readers understand some issues that will grow in importance as they advance through the workforce. In this section we discuss the importance of both the physical and the psychological environment in which an employee works, along with ways to improve both. We cover traditional topics such as union-management relations, but we also include a number of less traditional topics that we believe are vitally important.

Specifically, in Chapter 15 we cover the importance of employee rights, how these rights relate to disciplinary programs in organizations, and general health and safety issues. We also look at the growing importance of wellness programs at work, the available evidence concerning their effectiveness, and the ways in which jobs can be redesigned to make them more motivating. Finally, we discuss some of the issues associated with AIDS in the workplace, and how an organization might form a policy for dealing with AIDS-related issues.

Chapter 16 deals with the increasingly important topic of managing diversity. We make a special point of presenting what is actually known about the specific impacts of workplace diversity on organizational operations, as distinguished from what is merely speculation.

Chapter 17 explores issues associated with new employment relationships, such as the different types of contracts at work (including psychological contracts), how they have been changing, and the effects of these changes on employees. We also look at several topics not often covered in human resources texts: the problems of managing high-tech employees, especially in a strong economy; problems with managing a temporary workforce; and the issues involved in managing employees who work at different locations (including home) or on different schedules. It is clear that organizations are adopting new technologies as a means of competing, and that high-tech workers will become more common, as will the challenges associated with them. Likewise, many organizations are trying to cushion their permanent workers from the vagaries of the economy by hiring temporary workers when demand is high. As this trend continues to gain popularity, it becomes critically important for managers to understand the advantages and disadvantages of employing temporary workers so that they can better decide if this route is best for their company or department. Finally, new technologies at work have made telecommuting a more common arrangement, and changing needs and desires have made alternative work schedules more common. How well do these arrangements work? This chapter attempts to provide some solid information for the manager contemplating these possibilities.

An Effective Teaching and Learning Package

We are pleased to provide several supplements to help both instructors and students.

- *Student and Instructor Web Sites.* Student and instructor Web sites provide additional information, guidance, and activities that will help enhance the concepts presented in the text. The student site includes the Internet exercises from the text (with updates as necessary), hyperlinks to the companies highlighted in each chapter, links to sites of general human resource interest, interactive application exercises, and ACE self-tests. The instructor site provides downloadable versions of the lecture outlines from the Instructor's Resource Manual that can be edited or used as is, PowerPoint slides, and the Video Guide.
- *Instructor's Resource Manual with Test Bank.* This resource includes for each chapter the list of learning objectives, a detailed lecture outline, suggested answers to all text questions and end-of-chapter activities, and the test bank. The Test Bank includes both recall and application oriented multiple-choice, essay, short-answer, and scenario-based questions.

- *Computerized Test Bank.* With this Windows program, the instructor can select questions and produce test masters for easy duplication. The program gives instructors the option of selecting their own questions or having the program select them. It also allows instructors to customize tests by creating new questions, editing existing ones, and generating multiple versions of tests.
- *PowerPoint Slides.* PowerPoint slides that are downloadable from the instructor Web site provide an effective presentation tool for lectures and include an outline of the text chapters and selected figures and key term definitions.
- *Color Transparencies.* Full color transparencies illustrate major topics in the text. Two types of transparencies are included: highlights of key figures from the text and additional images that can be used to enhance lecture presentation.
- *Video Package.* To illustrate important concepts from the text, real-world video examples from leading organizations are provided. The video segments run from 10 to 20 minutes to allow time for classroom discussion. The Video Guide (available on the Web site) provides suggested uses, teaching objectives, an overview, and issues for discussion for each video segment.

A Final Word

We have attempted to outline the specific approaches and features that distinguish our text from others you may have used or seen. Most of the differences aren't apparent from a quick look at the Contents, but they will be obvious to you as you browse through this book. We believe that both instructors and students will benefit from our efforts to create a text that prepares tomorrow's managers to understand the basic principles of good human resource management, and to be effective and thoughtful partners in creating and implementing successful human resource policies.

Acknowledgments

A project such as this is never just the result of one or two people's efforts. There are many people who have contributed to this book, in different ways, over the years. First, we must thank the many (indeed, more than we would like to admit) students who have taken our classes over the years. They endured the process of climbing a learning curve as we learned how and what to teach, and they were the "guinea pigs" whenever we decided to try new ideas or approaches. But, more than that, authors form ideas about how a text should be written only by spending a lot of time observing students using other texts. So, to all the students who complained about the texts we assigned them, we apologize and hope that this book will better meet students' needs, challenge their minds, and engage their interest.

Our colleagues have also helped us form ideas through discussions, as well as through the feedback they provided over the years. These discussions and conversations were critical for crystallizing the concepts that appear in this book. Other feedback from colleagues helped develop better writing skills and allowed each of us to be able to communicate our ideas more clearly. Therefore, we thank all those colleagues from the University of Houston, Purdue University, the University of Missouri, Kent State University, the University of South

Carolina, Rutgers University, and, of course, Texas A&M University. Somewhere along the line, though, some people played an even greater role in guiding and developing our ideas. We must therefore specifically thank and acknowledge the efforts and help of our mentors John Ivancevich and Ernest McCormick.

As we actually started writing this book, a number of other people played a role that should be acknowledged. We want to thank the reviewers of this text for spending time reading drafts of chapters and providing useful feedback for us on how to make them better. In particular, we want to thank

Paula Becker Alexander
Seton Hall University

Debra A. Arvanites
Villanova University

Sheila R. Baiers
*Kalamazoo Valley
Community College*

Janet C. Barnard
*Rochester Institute of
Technology*

Jennifer Carney
(MBA candidate)
Georgia State University

Robert R. Cordell
*West Virginia University at
Parkersburg*

Barbara J. Durkin
SUNY, College at Oneonta

Maureen J. Fleming
The University of Montana

Donald G. Gardner
University of Colorado

Carol B. Gilmore
University of Maine

Audrey Guskey
Duquesne University

Barbara L. Hassell
University of North Texas

Micki Kacmar
Florida State University

Alice E. Nuttall
*Kent State University,
Tuscarawas Campus*

Stephen Owens
Western Carolina University

Robert Paul
Kansas State University

Alex Pomnichowski
Ferris State University

Paul R. Reed
Sam Houston State University

Joan B. Rivera
West Texas A&M University

Rebecca A. Thacker
Ohio University

Charles N. Toftoy
*George Washington
University*

J. Bruce Tracey
Cornell University

Carolyn Wiley
*The University of Tennessee
at Chattanooga*

We also want to thank the professionals at Houghton Mifflin, especially Susan Kahn, Kathy Hunter, George Hoffman, Fred Burns, Jennifer Meyer Dare, Marcy Kagan, and Linda Hadley, who at various times encouraged, threatened, supported, and browbeat us to get the book finished and to make it the best we could. We hope you are pleased with the final product.

Finally, we must thank family and friends for their support through the entire process. These are the folks who had to listen to brilliant ideas (even when they weren't so brilliant) and our complaints about unreasonable reviewers (who truly weren't) and those editors who kept pressuring us to get the book finished (who really did). Without their help, this book would never have been completed. We are especially indebted to Glenda Griffin and Adrienne Colella, who play the multiple roles of wives, partners, collaborators, colleagues, and best friends. It is with all our love, respect, and appreciation that we dedicate this book to them.

Angelo DeNisi
Ricky W. Griffin

PART ONE

An Overview of Human Resource Management

CHAPTER 1
The Nature of Human
Resource Management

1

The Nature of Human Resource Management

CHAPTER OUTLINE

Evolution of the Human Resource Function
Origins of the Human Resource Function
Personnel Management

Contemporary Human Resource Management
Human Resource Management Tasks and Functions
The Human Resource Management System

Goals of Human Resource Management
Facilitating Organizational Competitiveness
Enhancing Productivity and Quality
Complying with Legal and Social Obligations
Promoting Individual Growth and Development

The Setting for Human Resource Management
Human Resource Management: Line versus Staff Management Perspectives
Human Resource Management: Smaller versus Larger Organization Perspectives
Human Resources as a Center of Expertise

Human Resource Managers
Professionalism and Human Resource Management
Careers in Human Resource Management

CHAPTER OBJECTIVES

After studying this chapter you should be able to:

■ Summarize the evolution of the human resource function in organizations.

■ Characterize contemporary human resource management in terms of its basic tasks, functions, and systems.

■ Identify and discuss the fundamental goals of human resource management in organizations.

■ Discuss the responsibilities for human resource management in terms of staff and management functions and describe the human resource management department.

■ Discuss human resource managers in terms of professionalism and careers.

Southwest Airlines is one of the most successful firms in the world today. Unlike other major airlines, however, Southwest flies no international routes, serves no meals on any of its flights, subscribes to no computerized reservation systems, has no preassigned seating or business or first-class compartments, and refuses to transfer bags to other airlines. Yet it also boasts the lowest costs and highest profits and regularly has the highest levels of efficiency, productivity, and customer satisfaction in the airline industry today.

One key to Southwest's success is Herb Kelleher, its co-founder and CEO. Kelleher is both respected and liked by his employees and is affectionately known to them as "Uncle Herbie." From the company's earliest days, Kelleher decided to make his employees feel like part of the team. For example, Southwest has a policy that no employee will be laid off. Kelleher also shares all relevant operating information about the firm with his employees, offers innovative compensation and advancement opportunities, and stresses employee involvement in every phase of Southwest's operations. One popular book, *The 100 Best Companies to Work for in America*, recently recognized Southwest as one of the ten best companies to work for, *Fortune* magazine has suggested that Kelleher may be the best CEO in America, and one recent survey has suggested that Southwest is the single best place to work in America.

What does it take to work for Southwest Airlines? Obviously, candidates need the skills necessary to perform the job for which they are being considered. But beyond

"Working here is truly an unbelievable experience. They treat you with respect, pay you well, and empower you. They use your ideas to solve problems. They encourage you to be yourself. I love going to work."

(unidentified Southwest Airlines employee)*

technical skills successful applicants must also demonstrate the capacity to get along with others, to be a team player, and to be willing to pitch in wherever needed. In return for these qualities, Southwest provides a stimulating and enjoyable work environment, reasonable pay, good benefits, opportunities to advance, and job security.

Southwest's approach to dealing with its employees has paid big dividends. They view themselves as part of Kelleher's team and strive to work together in the best interests of the company. The firm has the lowest turnover in the industry—around 6 percent—and a workforce committed to flexibility and innovation. For example, it is not uncommon to find Southwest pilots helping to check in passengers or ticket agents helping to unload luggage. During the Persian Gulf crisis in 1990–1991, more than one-third of the airline's employees took a voluntary pay cut to help offset higher jet fuel prices. And during a recent Southwest company picnic, employees presented Kelleher with a new Harley-Davidson motorcycle as a token of their affection.

Robert Levering and Milton Moskowitz, "The 100 Best Companies to Work for in America," *Fortune*, January 12, 1998, pp. 84–95 (*quote on p. 84); "Scrappy Southwest Reaches Coast in One Stop," *Wall Street Journal*, April 22, 1997, pp. B1, B2; "Southwest Airlines Charts a High-Performance Flight," *Training & Development*, June 1995, p. 39; Kenneth Labich, "Is Herb Kelleher America's Best CEO?" *Fortune*, May 2, 1994, pp. 44–52; "Southwest Airlines Makes Flying Fun," *USA Today*, September 22, 1998, p. 4E.

■ **Human resources** are the people an organization employs to carry out various jobs, tasks, and functions in exchange for wages, salaries, and other rewards.

■ **Human resource management** is the comprehensive set of managerial activities and tasks concerned with developing and maintaining a qualified workforce—human resources—in ways that contribute to organizational effectiveness.

Herb Kelleher clearly recognizes the value of people in the success of his business. If Southwest needs a new airplane or a new computer system for managing its flight operations, it can just buy them. Neither of these assets can give the firm a sustained competitive advantage, however, because Delta, United, or American can easily buy precisely the same equipment. But the people who work for Southwest have an unusual relationship with their employer and provide the firm with a rare and valuable set of resources that its competitors cannot easily duplicate or sustain. Indeed, the quality and character of these human resources set Southwest apart from other airlines.

Regardless of their size, mission, market, or environment, all organizations strive to achieve their goals by combining various resources into goods and services that will be of value to their customers. Financial resources such as ownership investment, sales revenues, and bank loans are used to provide capital and to cover expenses necessary to conduct business. Material resources such as factories, equipment, raw materials, computers, and offices play an important role in the actual creation of goods and services. And information resources about consumers and the firm's competitive environment help managers make decisions, solve problems, and develop strategies. But no resources are more vital to an organization's success than are its human resources.[1]

An organization's **human resources** are the people it employs to carry out various jobs, tasks, and functions in exchange for wages, salaries, and other rewards. The chief executive officer responsible for the overall effectiveness of the organization, an advertising manager responsible for creating newspaper ads, an operations manager sent to open a new manufacturing facility in Brazil, a financial analyst who manages the organization's cash reserves, and the custodian who cleans the offices after everyone else goes home are all human resources. And in his or her own way, each is a vital ingredient that helps determine the overall effectiveness—or lack of effectiveness—of the organization as it strives to accomplish its goals and objectives. At Southwest Airlines, Herb Kelleher, along with the firm's pilots, flight attendants, ground staff, maintenance workers, and myriad other employees constitute the firm's human resources.

Human resource management refers to the comprehensive set of managerial activities and tasks concerned with developing and maintaining a qualified workforce—human resources—in ways that contribute to organizational effectiveness. As we will see, organizations that once paid only lip service to human resource issues are increasingly recognizing the dramatic impact that effective human resource management can have in all areas of an organization. Indeed, effective human resource management is becoming a vital strategic concern for most organizations today.[2]

An organization's human resources are clearly among its most important assets as it strives to distinguish itself from its competitors and to effectively accomplish its goals and meet the expectations of its various constituents. Consider, for example, MindSpring Enterprises, the fourth-largest Internet service provider in the United States. MindSpring, based in Atlanta, has a deliberate strategy of hiring only the best talent available and focusing a lot of that talent on providing high-intensity customer service. Largely as a result of people like those pictured here, the company is growing by leaps and bounds and has achieved an exceptionally high rate of profitability for a firm in this extremely competitive industry.

In this chapter we explore the nature of human resource management in a way that provides a useful framework for the more detailed discussions that follow in subsequent chapters. We begin by briefly tracing how human resource management has evolved to its present role in modern organizations. We then look at contemporary human resource management more closely. The goals of the human resource management function are then identified and discussed. Next we examine how the responsibilities for human resource management are shared as staff and management functions. The human resource department in different kinds of organizations is then discussed. Finally, we focus on professionalism and career development of human resource managers.

EVOLUTION OF THE HUMAN RESOURCE FUNCTION

Although people have always engaged in business, the practice of management itself has been of special interest and concern for only about a hundred years or so.[3] Many early businesses were small enterprises and farms run by families interested only in supporting themselves and in providing security for family members. The Industrial Revolution of the eighteenth century, however, sparked a greater interest in business growth and expansion, and large-scale business operations began to emerge throughout Europe and the United States. As these businesses grew and became increasingly complex, owners began to step aside and turn the operation of their firms over to full-time professional managers. And even those owners who remained in control of their businesses still found it necessary to rely on other managers to oversee a portion of the operations. This transition, in turn, resulted in greater awareness of the various functions of management that were necessary for long-term organizational success.[4]

Although a few management pioneers and writers like Robert Owen, Mary Parker Follette, and Hugo Munsterberg recognized the importance of people in organizations, the first serious study of management practice—during the early years of the twentieth century—was based on scientific management.[5] **Scientific management**, in turn, was concerned with how to structure individual jobs so as to maximize efficiency and productivity. The major proponents of scientific management, such as Frederick Taylor and Frank and Lilian Gilbreth, had backgrounds in engineering and often used time-and-motion studies in which managers relied on stopwatches to teach workers precisely how to perform each task that made up their jobs. In fact, scientific management was very concerned with every motion a worker made and provided many examples of how changes in movements or in the placement of some piece of equipment increased productivity.

"The Lighter Side of HR," however, illustrates in humorous form an argument made by critics of scientific management—that labor would use the production standards established by management as a way to work even more slowly! Other critics argued that individual workers were generally valued only in terms of their capacity to perform assigned tasks as efficiently and as productively as possible. Still, scientific management helped augment the concepts of assembly-line production, division of labor, and economies of scale that really gave birth to the large businesses that transformed domestic and international economies throughout the twentieth century.[6]

■ **Scientific management**, one of the earliest approaches to management, was concerned with how to structure individual jobs to maximize efficiency and productivity.

Some people might think that the popularity of workplace comic strips such as *Dilbert* and *Cathy* is a recent phenomenon. But in reality the workplace has been a source of comic humor for more than a century, dating back to political and editorial cartoon features often centered on labor and labor–management conflicts. This cartoon, for example, is from early in the twentieth century. It depicts how some critics of scientific management thought that labor might be able to use Taylor's time-and-motion study ideas against management. The bricklayers in the cartoon, for example, have apparently been successful in getting work rules approved that allow them five minutes between motions. They are now waiting for the timer to hit the five-minute mark again so that they can perform their next task!

MODERN BRICK–LAYING IN CHICAGO.

Origins of the Human Resource Function

As businesses such as General Motors (started in 1908), Bethlehem Steel (started in 1899), Ford Motor Company (started in 1903), Boeing (started in 1916), and the other industrial giants launched during this era expanded rapidly and grew into big companies, they obviously needed to hire more and more workers. Ford, for example, increased its manufacturing capacity from 800 cars per day in 1910 to 9,109 cars per day by 1925.[7] At the same time, its workforce also increased from fewer than two hundred workers to several thousand workers. And this same pattern of growth and hiring was being repeated in hundreds of other businesses across dozens of industries. Businesses needed more workers to perform the operating jobs that produced ever-greater quantities of products. In the early days of this business explosion, the so-called foreman, or first-line supervisor, usually hired new workers. Office workers were also needed, so people with titles such as "office manager" hired clerks and secretaries.

As these businesses became more complex and as their hiring needs became more complicated, however, the task of hiring new employees became too time consuming for a first-line supervisor or office manager to perform. In addition, these supervisors and managers had extra administrative duties to perform. For example, in 1913 Ford was paying its unskilled employees $2.34 per nine-hour day. Because the pay was so low and the work both monotonous and tiring, the firm was experiencing turnover of almost 400 percent per year. That is, the firm was having to replace its average worker four times each year. Thus Ford was hiring workers to fill new jobs while also hiring workers to replace

As noted in the text, in 1913 Ford was paying workers like these $2.34 per nine-hour day. But because this wage was so low and the work so boring, the average worker only stayed on the job for a few months before seeking better opportunities. But very shortly after this photograph was taken, Ford revolutionized by boosting pay to a minimum of $5 a day and shortening the workday itself to 8 hours. As a result, turnover dropped sharply and Ford could have its pick of the droves of workers who showed up looking for jobs. This trend, in turn, led directly to the creation of what would eventually evolve into one of the first "personnel" departments anywhere.

others who had left. In 1914 Henry Ford made a bold move to more effectively attract and retain higher-quality workers by boosting the firm's pay to a minimum of $5 for an eight-hour day.[8] This action attracted a groundswell of new job applicants and almost overwhelmed first-line supervisors who were then hiring new employees while overseeing the work of existing ones.

As a result of growth and complexity, most large businesses, including Ford, started to hire their employees through newly created specialized units. Ford, for example, called this unit the "employment department." Although these units were initially created to hire new employees, they soon began to help manage the existing workforce as well. For example, the emergence and growth of large labor unions like the United Auto Workers and the passage of the Fair Labor Standards Act in 1938 (which established a minimum wage) and the National Labor Relations Act in 1935 (which dealt with unionization procedures) made it necessary for businesses to have one or more managers represent the interests of the business to organized labor and to administer the growing number of laws and regulations that were governing labor practices.

Meanwhile, other developments, many taking place in other parts of the world, provided organizations with some of the tools they would need to better manage these employment processes. For example, in England the work of Charles Darwin popularized the ideas that individuals differed from each other in ways that were important. In France the work of Alfred Binet and Theophile Simon led to the development of the first intelligence tests, and during World War I several armies tried using these tests to better assign soldiers to jobs. These attempts at staffing continued in the private sector after the war, and by 1923 *Personnel Management*, a seminal book by Scott and Clothier, was already spelling out how to match a person's skills and aptitudes with the requirements of the job.

Another important ingredient in the origin of the human resource function during this period was the so-called **human relations era**, which emerged following the **Hawthorne studies**. Between 1927 and 1932 the Western Electric Company sponsored a major research program at its Hawthorne plant near Chicago. This research, conducted by Roethlisbeger and Mayo, revealed for perhaps the first time that individual and group behavior played an important role in organizations and that human behavior at work was something managers really needed to understand more fully. One of the Hawthorne studies suggested, for example, that individual attitudes may have been related to performance, and another suggested that a work group may have established norms to restrict the output of its members.[9] Prior to these studies, many managers paid virtually no attention to their employees as people, but instead viewed them in the same way they viewed a machine or a piece of equipment—as an economic entity to be managed dispassionately and with concern only for resource output.

Stimulated by the Hawthorne findings, managers began to focus more and more attention on understanding the human character of their employees. It was during this era, for example, that Abraham Maslow popularized his **hierarchy of human needs**.[10] Douglas McGregor's well-known **Theory X** and **Theory Y** framework also grew from the human relations movement.[11] The basic premise of the human relations era was that if managers could make their employees more satisfied and happier, they would work harder and be more productive. Today researchers and managers alike recognize that this viewpoint was overly simplistic and that both satisfaction and productivity are complex phenomenon that affect and are affected by many different things. Nonetheless, the increased awareness of the importance of human behavior during this period helped organizations to become even more focused on managing their human resources. These organizations saw effective management of human resources as a means of potentially increasing productivity and, incidentally, as a way of slowing the growth of unionism, which was beginning to gain popularity.

Personnel Management

As businesses grew increasingly large, they began to create specialized units to cope with their hiring needs, to deal with government regulations, and to provide a mechanism for dealing with behavioral issues. During the 1930s and 1940s these units gradually began to be called **personnel departments** (the word *personnel* was derived from an old French word that meant "persons"). They were usually set up as special, self-contained departments charged with the responsibility of hiring new workers and administering basic human resource activities like pay and benefits. The recognition that human resources needed to be managed and the creation of personnel departments also gave rise to a new type of management function—**personnel management**.[12] The manager who ran the personnel department was called the **personnel manager**.

During this period personnel management was concerned almost exclusively with hiring first-line employees—production workers, sales clerks, custodians, secretaries, blue-collar workers, unskilled labor, and other operating employees. Issues associated with hiring, developing, and promoting managers and executives did not surface until later.

Personnel management took another step forward in its evolution during World War II. Both the military and its major suppliers developed an interest

Margin notes:

- The **human relations era** supplanted scientific management as the dominant approach to management during the 1930s.

- The human relations era was instigated by the **Hawthorne studies**.

- Abraham Maslow's **hierarchy of human needs** was developed during the human relations era.

- Douglas McGregor's **Theory X** and **Theory Y** framework grew from the human relations movement.

- **Personnel departments**, specialized organizational units for hiring and administering human resources, became popular during the 1930s and 1940s.

- **Personnel management**, a new type of management function, grew from the recognition that human resources needed to be managed. The **personnel manager** ran the personnel department.

in matching people with jobs. That is, organizations wanted to optimize the fit between the demands and requirements of the jobs that needed to be performed and the skills and interests of people available to perform them. Psychologists were consulted to help develop selection tests, for example, to assess individual skills, interests, and abilities. During the 1950s the wartime lessons were adapted for use in private industry. New, more sophisticated techniques were developed, especially in the area of testing, and companies also began to experiment with more sophisticated reward and incentive systems. In addition, labor unions became more powerful and demanded a broader array of benefits for their members. At the same time, government legislation expanded and continued to add complexity to the job of the personnel manager.

Still, from its inception until the 1970s, personnel management was not seen as a particularly important or critical function in most business organizations. Although many other managers appreciated personnel management as a necessary vehicle for hiring new operating employees, it was also seen primarily as a routine clerical and bookkeeping function—placing newspaper ads to recruit new employees, filling out paperwork on those employees after they were hired, and seeing that everyone got paid on time.

While other organizational units like marketing, finance, and operations grew in status and perceived importance, the personnel department of most organizations was generally relegated to the status of a "necessary evil" that had to be tolerated but which presumably contributed little to the success of the organization. Its offices were often drab and poorly equipped, for example, and located away from central activity areas of the organization. And personnel managers themselves were often stereotyped as individuals who could not succeed in other functional areas and who were assigned to personnel either because the organization had nothing else they could do or as a signal that the individual was not a candidate for promotion to a higher-ranking position.

CONTEMPORARY HUMAN RESOURCE MANAGEMENT

Over time, however, the role of human resource management changed dramatically and became much more important in most organizations.[13] Perhaps the first major stimulus for this increase in importance was the passage in 1964 of the Civil Rights Act. This law made it illegal for employers to consider such factors as gender, religion, race, skin color, or national origin in making employment-related decisions. The 1964 Civil Rights Act, combined with several subsequent amendments, executive orders, and legal decisions, made the processes of hiring and promoting employees within the organization far more complex than ever before.

Organizations quickly realized that those responsible for hiring and promoting employees needed to fully understand the legal context within which they functioned. For example, ethical and moral issues aside, improper or inappropriate hiring practices left the organization open to lawsuits and other legal sanctions, accompanied by large fines, judgments, and new expenses. (We discuss the 1964 Civil Rights Act and related regulations more fully in Chapter 3.) And as discussed in the "Human Resources Legal Brief," legal issues continue to add uncertainty and complexity to the work of all managers. Specifically, although it might not seem logical that an accident at work could be

On-the-Job Injuries as Crimes

 For years the law has recognized that organizations could be held legally responsible for injuries their employees suffer at work, especially when those injuries resulted from unsafe or hazardous working conditions. But such offenses were seen exclusively as torts, remediable by fines and similar monetary penalties.

But recently, some attorneys and courts have taken the position that organizations and/or their agents can also be criminally liable for injuries at work. For example, Jorge Torres worked for Morton International's plant in Long Beach, California. He was buried alive in 1994 when a sixty-ton mountain of salt opened beneath him like quicksand, sucking him to the bottom of a storage bin. The local district attorney charged Morton and two of the firm's supervisors with manslaughter for failing to provide Torres with a platform from which to work.

"These are not accidents. They knew that they had created illegal [working] conditions which were dangerous."

(Scott Harshbarger, former attorney general of Massachusetts)*

Similarly, the state of Massachusetts recently charged the owner of a scrap-metals plant with manslaughter after one worker was pulled into a shredding machine and another was crushed by a loading truck. Prosecutors charged that the owner had ignored warnings to provide adequate safety procedures for his workers. Several other states have taken similar actions in recent times.

Whether or not this trend will continue, of course, will depend on how the courts interpret the relevant laws and how those initial rulings stand up to appeal. One thing is sure, however: managers everywhere must pay closer attention to how their actions and decisions affect others. Failure to do so can be accompanied by major surprises—and maybe time in jail.

References: "Treating on-the-Job Injuries as True Crimes," *Wall Street Journal*, February 26, 1997, pp. B1, B8 (*quote on page B1); "Deadly Accidents in Quarries on Rise," *USA Today*, July 8, 1998, pp. 1A, 2A.

viewed as a crime, some recent court decisions suggest otherwise! And most organizations would classify workplace safety as a human resource issue.

Human Resource Management Tasks and Functions

As human resource management was becoming more important because of the increasingly complex legal environment, many managers were beginning to recognize that human resource management had important strategic implications for the organization as well. During the 1960s and 1970s, for example, international competition grew rapidly, and all organizations found it more important than ever to use their resources wisely and to capitalize on their full value. Rapid advances in technology and communication also dictated that managers carefully assess every facet of their operation to ensure that they were being as efficient and as productive as possible. Yet, at the same time, there was increasing concern over what was called "quality of work life" issues. While managers were becoming increasingly concerned with ways to improve productivity and competitiveness, they also began to realize that workers needed to feel that their jobs were a source of personal satisfaction and growth.[14] Successful organizations were those that could maximize effectiveness and make work more meaningful and fulfilling.

As noted earlier, human resources are any organization's most important resource. Hiring the right people and then equipping them with the right skills and abilities can substantially affect the quality and quantity of whatever goods or services the organization produces. And properly motivated and committed employees can add immeasurable value to an organization's bottom line. Given the shift in competitiveness, then, top executives in most firms began to see that human resource management practices and policies significantly affected their ability to formulate and implement strategy in any area and that other strategic decisions significantly affected the firm's human resources as well.

It was only natural, therefore, for human resource management to be elevated to the same level of importance and status as other major functional areas of the firm.[15] The top human resource executive at most companies today has vice-presidential or executive-vice-presidential status and is a fully contributing member of the firm's executive committee, the executive body composed of key top managers that makes major policy decisions and sets corporate strategy. Although a few managers and organizations still use terms like *personnel management* or *employee relations*, most progressive and forward-looking firms now use the term *human resource management* to better reflect the sophistication and maturity of the function. In keeping with this trend, we also use the human resource management terminology throughout this book. Some organizations have already gone beyond this terminology and use specialized terminology that better fits their culture. The top human resource executive at Southwest Airlines, for example, has the title of vice president for people. Similarly, Wal-Mart uses the title senior vice president of people for its top human resource executive.

The 1980s and 1990s brought some other changes to the human resource management function as well. Many firms found that they were not able to compete well in the new, global marketplace. Some of these firms went out of business or were acquired by other, more successful firms as a wave of mergers and acquisitions began in the United States. After the merger of two firms (or the takeover of one by another), there was often not the same need for as many employees, and many workers lost their jobs. Those firms that could not compete, and that were not acquired by some other company, closed down, and yet more workers lost their jobs. Finally, those firms that were struggling to be competitive often concluded that they could be more efficient with fewer employees, and we saw the beginning of an era of downsizing, rightsizing, or reengineering. Whatever it was called, there were fewer and fewer jobs around. Note, however, that a no-layoff policy is one of the major features of management at Southwest Airlines.

Worker displacement not only made the job of the human resource manager more difficult but also had a more profound, direct effect on this function in many organizations. As these organizations looked for new ways to be competitive and reduce costs, they looked for activities within the company that could be done more efficiently by outsiders. For example, it became common for companies to fire their cleaning and maintenance employees and hire an outside cleaning firm to save money. But it also became somewhat common for companies to reduce the size of their human resource management staffs and turn to outside help for specific projects. This practice, commonly known as **outsourcing**, has resulted in smaller human resource staffs within companies, and more reliance on outside consultants to provide the services that those staffs once provided. Thus while the importance of human resource management activities is growing, the importance of human resource departments may be shrinking. But regardless of whether the work is done by internal employees or is outsourced to consultants, the activities carried out by human resource managers is indeed growing in importance. The specific pros and cons of outsourcing are noted in "Point/Counterpoint."

■ **Outsourcing** is the practice of hiring external vendors to provide basic human resource management services for an organization, based on the vendors' ability to perform the services more efficiently than the organization itself can.

POINT/COUNTERPOINT   Outsourcing

 Outsourcing refers to an organization's contracting with an outside provider for services formerly provided inside the organization. Typically, the organization determines its core functions and then outsources all other activities. In some cases all human resource activities are outsourced, but more typically, only activities that are fairly routine, such as enrolling employees in benefits programs, or even administering those programs, are outsourced.

POINT . . . **Outsourcing makes sense for organizations because . . .**	COUNTERPOINT . . . **But on the other hand, outsourcing could be a problem because . . .**
The need for full-time, permanent employees is reduced.	Higher-paid jobs within large corporations will be replaced by low-paying jobs with vendors.
Jobs that deal with routine and dull tasks are eliminated from the organization.	Organizations will have fewer entry-level jobs, making it more difficult for some people to start careers.
Fewer employees are working in marginal jobs where satisfaction might be low.	Employees providing outsourced services will have fewer benefits and less security.
When budgets get tighter, costs can be reduced by dropping programs, but no permanent employees will lose their jobs.	No new human resource managers will be gaining important experience to replace those managers dealing with strategic issues when necessary.
Managers in human resources can spend their time dealing with larger, strategic issues that are better suited to their abilities.	An activity that is outsourced can no longer be a source of competitive advantage, as many other organizations who use the same vendor will have the same programs.
Vendors who provide services for a number of organizations can provide those services less expensively than if the organization provides the services itself.	Fewer employees will feel committed to their organizations.

So . . .   It probably makes sense for an organization to outsource certain activities, especially those that are totally routine, that can be performed more efficiently by outside vendors, and that are not seen as a potential source of competitive advantage. However, an organization must also recognize the downsides to outsourcing so that it is not the solution to all human resource problems. It is especially critical to ensure that some new managers are always gaining experience and are ready to move up to the level of "strategic" decision making when they are needed.

Figure 1.1 shows the major tasks and functions that make up contemporary human resource management. This figure also represents the framework around which this book is organized. As you can see, one set of tasks and functions, covered in Part Two of the book, involves the environment within which human resource management is to occur. To function effectively within the environment, most experts agree that it is necessary to adopt a strategic perspective on human resource management.[16] That is, all aspects of the human resource management system should be coordinated, and together they should support the strategic goals of the organization. We discuss strategic human resource management in more detail in Chapter 2.

As noted earlier, the legal environment of human resource management has contributed significantly to its current importance to organizations. Organizations that do not understand the legal environment are almost certain to encounter difficulties in virtually every aspect of human resource management.

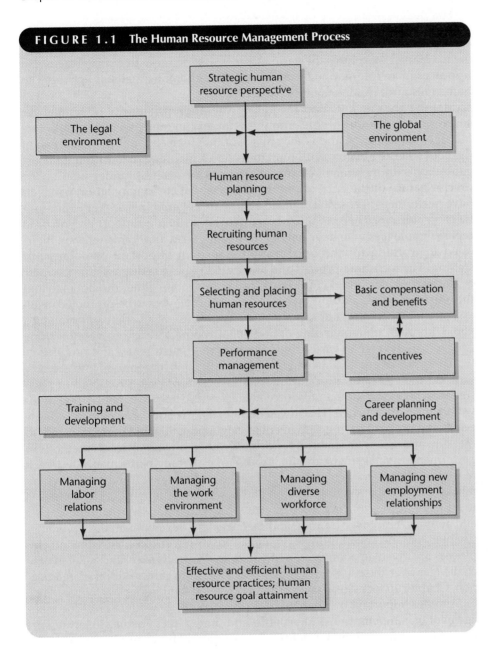

FIGURE 1.1   The Human Resource Management Process

Understanding the legal environment begins with equal employment opportunity and requires a complete understanding of both protected classes in the workforce and what organizations must do to ensure that everyone has the same chances for success in the workplace. In addition, all managers must understand and consider numerous special legal issues regarding compensation, benefits, labor relations, working conditions, training practices, and other related areas of human resource management. Chapter 3 covers these and other legal issues confronting human resource managers today.

Still another vital dimension of the environment of human resources is the international context in which the organization functions. Large multinationals like Ford, Sony, and Unilever clearly have numerous international human resource issues to manage. But many smaller firms are also venturing into foreign markets. Even purely domestic firms may find themselves buying from, selling to, and/or competing with businesses in other countries. Thus all managers today must have an appreciation of the international business environment. Chapter 4 explores the various issues associated with managing human resources in an international company and with taking a global approach to human resource management.

Staffing the organization (acquiring the appropriate mix of human resources needed by the organization) is another fundamental human resource management function and is the subject of the three chapters in Part Three of the book. Staffing begins with human resource planning (determining the organization's future human resource needs) and job analysis (understanding the precise nature of the current and future jobs that the organization needs to have performed). These and related issues are covered in Chapter 5. Because most organizations need to hire new employees, either to support growth or to replace employees who have left, recruiting qualified applicants who are interested in working for the organization is also an important component of staffing. The recruiting process and associated issues are discussed in Chapter 6. The actual selection of employees for various jobs—either outsiders to join the organization as new employees or current employees to be promoted or reassigned—involves the appropriate and effective use of a variety of techniques and a thorough understanding of both legal and performance-related factors. Chapter 7 is devoted to various selection and placement issues and processes.

After employees have been given their initial job assignment and are performing their jobs (or after current employees have been promoted or reassigned to new jobs), human resource managers also help to enhance their motivation and performance. The three chapters in Part Four are devoted to these issues and topics. The first step in enhancing motivation and performance is to measure and assess the current performance of employees. Various methods of performance management and the process of providing performance feedback to employees are among the topics discussed in Chapter 8. Another fundamental element in enhancing motivation and performance in most organizations is to train employees to work more effectively by providing them with new skills and abilities. Employee training and management development are covered in Chapter 9. Many contemporary organizations also work to ensure that all employees are given an adequate opportunity to grow, advance, and take on new challenges over the course of a potentially long-term career with the organization. Chapter 10 focuses on several career development issues.

Another important component of the human resource function is the management of compensation and benefits, and these topics are the subject of Part Five. All employees who work for an organization, for example, expect to receive basic compensation for their contributions to the organization. A variety of issues and considerations regarding basic wage and salary administration are introduced and discussed in Chapter 11. Further, given that many employees will work harder if they believe that their efforts will lead directly to additional rewards, many organizations today offer various incentives to their employees and often base certain rewards on actual performance. Chapter 12 covers a variety of both traditional and innovative incentives and performance-based rewards. Beyond wages, salaries, and incentives, most organizations also provide various benefits to their employees. Chapter 13 is therefore devoted to employee benefits and services.

The ongoing management of the existing workforce, covered in the four chapters of Part Five, is also at least the partial responsibility of human resource managers. Organized labor—unions and other labor groups—is a critical element in this set of tasks and functions. As we will see in Chapter 14, understanding the unionization process, the process of collective bargaining, and the processes of negotiating and administering labor agreements are vital parts of labor relations. Chapter 15 focuses on a variety of issues associated with the work environment, including discipline, grievances, and conflict in organizations. An array of other issues associated with the work environment, including employee rights, employee safety and health, quality-of-life programs, and health and stress management programs, is also covered in Chapter 15.

Many organizations today are also confronting the need to understand and manage diversity in their workforce. The modern workforce is becoming more and more diverse in terms of gender, ethnicity, age, and so forth. Although it is important to treat people fairly and to avoid any form of discrimination, it is also important for organizations to recognize and appreciate differences among people. Workforce diversity is thus the topic of Chapter 16. Finally, because of the dynamic nature of human resource management, its practitioners must also be ever alert to new issues, challenges, and opportunities. Chapter 17 introduces and discusses some of these important contemporary human resource challenges. Key topics include workplace and workforce transitions, such as organization change, technology, participation and empowerment, changes in job assignments and/or job responsibilities, termination, and retirement, as well as the use of contingent workers (part-time employees, temporary workers, contract workers, and so forth).

The Human Resource Management System

The preceding section discussed the various tasks and functions of human resource management from the perspective of discrete, self-contained activities. In reality, however, these tasks and functions are highly interrelated and do not unfold in a neat and systematic manner. Each of the various tasks and functions can affect and/or be affected by any of the other tasks and functions. And most basic human resource functions are practiced on an ongoing and continuous basis. For example, on any given day a human resource manager may need to help develop a recruiting strategy for hiring new sales representatives, set the base starting salary for a newly hired engineer, approve a pay raise for another engineer, negotiate with a vendor for a particular new employee benefit, oversee a training program for employees transferring to a new plant, resolve a union grievance about working hours, and terminate a problem employee.

Indeed, it is truly appropriate to think of human resource management as a system. A system is an interrelated set of elements functioning as a whole. A **human resource management system**, then, is an integrated and interrelated approach to managing human resources that fully recognizes the interdependence among the various tasks and functions that must be performed. This viewpoint is illustrated in Figure 1.2. The basic premise of this perspective is that every element of the human resource management system must be designed and implemented with full knowledge and understanding of, and integration with, the various other elements. For example, basic compensation levels may affect training needs, and training, in turn, affects selection criteria and initial job placement decisions. If starting wages are relatively low, the organization will not be able to hire highly skilled workers and may therefore need to provide more up-front training. And if training can be provided only in some skill areas, current proficiency in other required skills becomes a selection criterion.

■ A **human resource management system** is an integrated and interrelated approach to managing human resources that fully recognizes the interdependence among the various tasks and functions that must be performed.

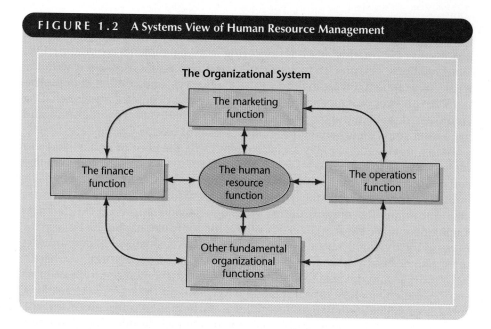

FIGURE 1.2   A Systems View of Human Resource Management

Figure 1.2 also illustrates another useful systems-based perspective on human resource management. Many systems themselves comprise subsystems—systems within a broader and more general system. By viewing the complete, overall organization as a system, human resource management then can be conceptualized as a subsystem within that more general organizational system. As Figure 1.2 shows, the human resource management subsystem both affects and is affected by the other functional subsystems throughout the organization. This perspective can help reinforce the idea that human resource management must be approached from the same strategic vantage point afforded the other areas within the organization. A failure to do so can result in unanticipated consequences, poor coordination, and less effective performance.

For example, if the organization makes a strategic commitment to dramatically increase the quality of its products or services, it will almost certainly need to use a number of mechanisms to do so. Among other things, the organization will need to hire more qualified new workers and to provide more training to both new and current workers. Even with the most sophisticated equipment and technology available, quality gains will be limited unless the people who run that equipment and who use that technology are sufficiently skilled to do so in the proper ways. Similarly, if the financial function of an organization dictates that major cost cutting be undertaken, some portion of those costs may come from the human resource area. Thus human resource managers may need to reduce the size of the workforce, attempt to renegotiate labor contracts at a lower rate, defer payment of some benefits, and so forth.

The increasing globalization of business also reinforces the need to view the human resource management function from a systems perspective. That is, human resource managers must take a global perspective in managing people. Within the borders of their own country, human resource managers must consider the social norms, individual expectations, and so forth that shape worker behaviors. Cross-national assignments for managers are also an important consideration for many businesses today. Thus the global perspective on human resource management includes the need to understand domestic similarities and differences in managing human resources in different countries and the role of international assignments and experiences in the development of human resource skills and abilities.

THE BOTTOM LINE All managers should recognize and appreciate the fact that human resource management is no longer a mere set of clerical tasks performed in a vacuum. Instead, the human resource function is a vital and integral component of the effective management of any enterprise. Moreover, the tasks and functions of human resource management are most appropriately viewed from an interrelated systems perspective.

GOALS OF HUMAN RESOURCE MANAGEMENT

Although we have already defined human resource management, it is also both important and useful at this juncture to more specifically identify and discuss the basic goals of human resource management in modern organizations.[17] Figure 1.3 illustrates the four basic goals of the human resource management function in most organizations today.

Facilitating Organizational Competitiveness

All organizations have a general set of goals and objectives that they try to accomplish. Regardless of the time horizon or the level of specificity involved in these goals, they are generally all intended to promote the organization's ability to be competitive in its efforts to fulfill its purpose or mission. For example, business organizations like Microsoft, Wal-Mart, Nestlé, and Toyota exist primarily to make a profit for their owners. Thus their goals and objectives usually deal with sales or revenue growth, market share, profitability, return on investment, and so forth. Other organizations exist for different purposes, and so they have goals other than increased profitability. Educational organizations like Ohio State University, Houston Community College, and the St. Louis Independent School District have their unique purpose, for example. And the same can be said for health care organizations like the Mayo Clinic, governmental organizations such as the U.S. Postal Service and the state of Missouri's Revenue Department, charitable organizations like the United Way, and so forth.

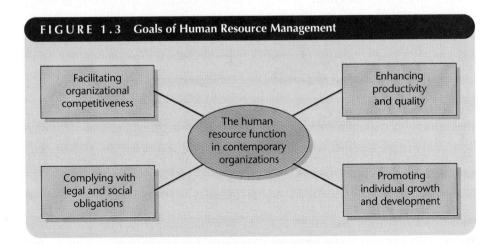

FIGURE 1.3 Goals of Human Resource Management

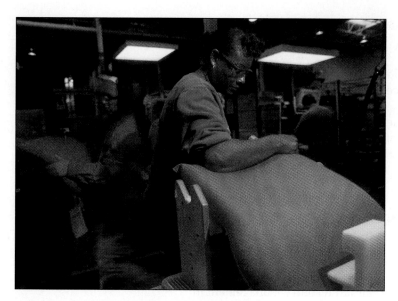

One important goal of resource management is enhancing productivity and quality in the organization. For example, Herman Miller recently opened a new manufacturing plant in Holland, Michigan designed to make office furniture faster and cheaper, but with higher quality, than ever before. To realize the plant's full potential, human resource managers had to first take steps to better understand the skills and abilities workers would need in the new plant and then recruit and hire workers who possessed those skills and abilities. This Miller employee is stapling fabric to the back of a seat cushion. Because of the higher productivity and quality in the plant, these chairs are among the most profitable sold by the company.

■ **Productivity** is an economic measure of efficiency that summarizes and reflects the value of the outputs created by an individual, organization, industry, or economic system relative to the value of the inputs used to create them.

■ **Quality** is the total set of features and characteristics of a product or service that bear on its ability to satisfy stated or implied needs.

Even though people often associate competitiveness only with businesses, each of these other types of organizations must also be managed effectively and compete for the right to continue to work toward fulfillment of its purpose. For example, a state university that misuses its resources and does not provide an adequate education for its students will not be held in high regard and will come under pressure from the state legislature, students, and other constituents. Similarly, a hospital that does not provide technical support for its doctors or adequate health care for its patients will find those doctors and patients increasingly less interested in using its facilities.

Given the central role that human resources play in organizational effectiveness, it is clear that the organization needs to employ those individuals most able to help accomplish its goals and thus to remain competitive. The human resource management function in any organization must therefore have as one if its basic goals the clear understanding of how the organization competes, the kinds of human resources necessary to promote its ability to compete, and the most appropriate methods for attracting and developing those human resources.[18] This goal relates clearly to the strategic perspective developed more fully in Chapter 2.

Enhancing Productivity and Quality

A related but somewhat more narrow concern for most organizations in the world today are the issues, hurdles, and opportunities posed by productivity and quality. **Productivity** is an economic measure of efficiency that summarizes and reflects the value of the outputs created by an individual, organization, industry, or economic system relative to the value of the inputs used to create them.[19] **Quality**, meanwhile, is the total set of features and characteristics of a product or service that bear on its ability to satisfy stated or implied needs.[20] In earlier times many managers saw productivity and quality as being inversely related, thinking that the best way to be more productive was to lower quality and, therefore, costs. But today most managers have come to realize that productivity and quality usually go hand in hand. That is, improving quality almost always increases productivity.

Organizations around the world have come to recognize the importance of productivity and quality to their ability not only to compete but also to survive. But actually improving productivity and quality takes a major and comprehensive approach that relies heavily on human resource management. Among other things, an organization that is serious about productivity and quality may need to alter its selection system to hire different kinds of workers. And it will definitely need to invest more in training and development to give workers the necessary skills and abilities to more productively create high-quality products and services and use new and different types of rewards to help maintain motivation and effort among its employees. Thus human resource management also has the goal in most organizations of helping to enhance productivity and quality through a variety of activities and tasks.

Complying with Legal and Social Obligations

A third fundamental goal of the human resource management function today is to ensure that the organization is complying with and meeting its legal and social obligations. We noted earlier the impact of the 1964 Civil Rights Act and other regulations on hiring and on various related human resource management practices and activities. More recently, the Americans with Disabilities Act is having a major impact on human resource management. It is clearly important that organizations stay within the relevant legal boundaries in all dealings with their employees. An organization that does not comply with government regulations and various legal constraints risks huge financial penalties, as well as considerable negative publicity and damage to its own internal corporate culture.

Beyond the strict legal parameters of compliance, however, more and more organizations today are also assuming at least some degree of social obligation to the society within which they operate. This obligation extends beyond the minimum activities necessary to comply with legal regulations and calls for the organization to serve as a contributing "citizen." Such efforts might include outreach programs to help attract individuals—often from minority populations—who may lack the basic skills necessary to perform meaningful jobs or even the divestiture of holdings in countries with poor records on human rights. These activities are becoming increasingly important as financial management firms offer investment funds that specialize in socially responsible organizations, and corporate social performance (CSP) is often considered another dimension of organizational performance.[21]

Promoting Individual Growth and Development

Finally, a fourth goal for human resource management in most contemporary organizations is to help promote the personal growth and development of their employees.[22] As a starting point this goal usually includes basic job-related training and development activities. But in more and more organizations, it is increasingly going far beyond basic skills training. Some firms, for example, now offer basic courses in English, math, and science for their employees. Many organizations also include some provision for career development—helping people understand what career opportunities are and are not available to them and how to best pursue those opportunities. Formal mentoring programs are also commonly being used to help develop women and minorities for advancement in the organization.[23]

Individual growth and development may also focus on areas that do not directly relate to job responsibilities. For example, some organizations provide stress management programs to help their employees cope with the anxieties and tensions of modern life. Wellness and fitness programs are also becoming more common as organizations seek new and different ways to help their employees remain physically, mentally, and emotionally fit and better prepared to manage their lives and careers. Still another common area for continuing education is personal financial planning, which may even include assistance in writing a will or planning for retirement.

THE BOTTOM LINE   The human resource function has four fundamental goals to pursue: facilitating organizational competitiveness, enhancing productivity and quality, complying with legal and social obligations, and promoting individual growth and development. Although it may occasionally be necessary to make short-term tradeoffs among these goals, human resource managers should keep all four goals in mind as they develop and implement plans and activities.

THE SETTING FOR HUMAN RESOURCE MANAGEMENT

As organizations continue to change and adapt to new challenges, the settings in which human resource activities take place can also change. The traditional model, where all human resource activities resided in a separate human resource department, is becoming rare. Instead, we are seeing human resource activities carried out by both line and staff managers. Furthermore, we are seeing differences in the way human resource management operates in larger versus smaller companies. We will explore some of these different settings.

Human Resource Management: Line vs. Staff Management Perspectives

■ **Line managers** are directly responsible for creating goods and services.

Organizations historically divided their managers into two groups, line management and staff management, and human resource management was traditionally considered to be a staff function. **Line managers** were directly responsible for creating goods and services. That is, their contributions to the organization could be directly assessed in terms of their actual contributions and costs to the organization's bottom line. The performance of a sales manager whose unit costs $500,000 per year to support (for salaries, administration, and so forth) and generates $3.5 million per year in revenue can be evaluated this way. Operations managers, financial managers, and marketing managers were generally considered to have line functions.

■ **Staff managers** are responsible for an indirect or support function that would have costs but whose bottom-line contributions were less direct.

Staff managers, on the other hand, were responsible for an indirect or support function that would have costs but whose bottom-line contributions were less direct. Legal, accounting, and human resource departments were usually thought of as staff functions. Their role was to support line management's efforts to achieve organizational goals and objectives. Today, however, many organizations have blurred this distinction. New forms of organization design and a trend toward smaller staff units have shifted traditional work arrangements, for example.[24] As a result, although human resource activities are still often seen as staff functions, line managers now often have responsibility for human resource management. Understanding how human resource management can exist in either setting helps shed light on the way in which human resource managers interact with other managers.

Any organization that has a human resource department assigns that unit staff (or support) functions with staff (or support) responsibility.[25] The human resource department is usually given specific responsibility for certain functions and shares responsibility for others. The most common specific responsibility assigned to the human resource department is legal compliance. The de-

Human resource management activities take place in a rich and sometimes challenging array of settings. Consider Wal-Mart, which built its domestic reputation in large part on friendly and helpful customer service. As the retailing giant moves aggressively into foreign markets, its human resource managers face new challenges. For example, the company recently purchased a chain of 95 stores in Germany and is converting them to Wal-Marts. Because German clerks are notorious for being cranky and providing little customer service, Wal-Mart managers will have to pay extra attention in their hiring, compensation, and training in this new environment.

partment is expected to keep abreast of all local, state, and federal laws that affect human resource practices and to monitor court cases and decisions that might modify or extend those laws. Human resource managers are also usually expected to maintain data and records to show how the organization has attempted to maintain compliance. In larger organizations a separate human resource unit is also often created for the sole purpose of dealing with organized labor. Usually called the labor relations department, this unit handles labor contract negotiations and administers labor agreements after they have been accepted.

The human resource department also takes primary responsibility in most organizations for recruiting potential new employees for entry-level positions and for the initial screening of applicants for those positions. Similarly, human resource managers generally design the organization's basic compensation and benefits system. They also design the performance appraisal system, basic training and development programs, incentive and performance-based reward systems, and discipline and grievance systems. Increasingly, human resource managers have also gotten involved with total quality management efforts and their organization's international activities.

In the more modern, strategic view of human resource management, the human resource department is also responsible for coordinating the various human resource management activities and for ensuring that they are consistent with corporate strategy. In fact, given the trend mentioned earlier (and which will be discussed in subsequent chapters) of outsourcing many human resource management functions, in some organizations this coordination has become the *primary* role for human resource management departments in some firms. In many of these organizations, activities formerly carried out by the human resource management department are either subcontracted to outside firms (which can presumably carry them out more efficiently with less expense) or are performed by line managers.

Management positions that were once called line positions are more likely to be called **operating managers** today. These are the managers who are

■ **Operating manager** is an increasingly popular term for someone previously called a line manager.

overseeing the acquisition of other kinds of resources, the transformation of those resources into goods and services, and the sale and distribution of those goods and services to customers. Even in organizations that continue to have specialized human resource managers to handle some of the human resource duties, operating managers are increasingly expected to participate in the human resource management function. Therefore, between trends toward outsourcing and trends toward moving human resource management functions to line or operating managers, the traditional human resource department is becoming less critical for modern organizations.

Increasingly, therefore, operating managers are expected to recognize, appreciate, and follow the various legal constraints imposed on the organization, even though compliance may technically be the responsibility of the human resource department. For example, it is inadvisable to ask a job applicant certain questions regarding personal plans or activities (e.g., Are you planning to start a family soon? or What type of position does your husband/wife have?). Such questions, even when asked innocently, may be the basis for discrimination, can damage the career prospects of the applicant, and can cost the firm money in the form of a lawsuit or legal settlement if actual discrimination is later demonstrated. Thus all operating managers need to understand the legal framework within which they function.

In fact, in many organizations where self-managed work teams are common, almost all human resource activities are the responsibility of the team leader and the team members themselves. In such cases the team leader and members may be responsible for designing and implementing their own human resource practices and policies. However, they will likely rely on a human resource manager to provide assistance and advice.

But even as the lines of distinction between human resource managers as staff and operating managers blur, the potential for conflict between the staff and operating managers still exists. This conflict usually stems from their basic interdependence and the limits that each can impose on the other. Operating managers, for example, may view the myriad legal regulations for hiring new employees as unnecessary and burdensome and vent their frustrations at the human resource managers who try to ensure compliance. Likewise, human resource managers may become frustrated when operating managers do not take such regulations seriously or do not follow them in an appropriate manner. And although each can be of benefit to the other, taking advantage of that benefit requires extra time. For example, a human resource manager who needs input from an operating counterpart to design a training program may become frustrated at the additional time and effort needed to get that information and perhaps may wish that she or he had never asked for the information.[26]

Clearly, then, human resource managers and operating managers must work closely together. Each has valuable expertise and information that can be of benefit to the other. Moreover, each is likely to need the expertise and information that the other can provide to carry out his or her own job most effectively. And finally, the two sets of managers must work together closely if they are to achieve the full and complete potential that resides in the human resources of their organization. Human resource management is truly a shared responsibility and must be approached from that perspective. When conflict does arise, both parties need to work productively to get it resolved and to proceed to work together as partners with the same ultimate set of goals and objectives. Some organizations avoid these problems by having operating managers perform human resources functions. Other organizations avoid these problems by out-sourcing many human resources activities. But in those remaining organizations where a traditional human resources department still exists, resolution of the conflict between staff and operating managers is essential for human resources managers to become strategic partners in the organization.

Human Resource Management: Smaller versus Larger Organization Perspectives

As noted earlier, responsibilities for carrying out human resource functions may reside in an entirely separate organizational unit, most often called the human resource department. Not all small organizations have such depart-ments, however.

Human resource management in smaller organizations   Most small organiza-tions still use operating managers to handle basic human resource functions. In the case of a franchised operation, such as a single McDonald's or Subway restaurant, or an individual retail outlet, such as a Gap or Limited clothing store, the store manager generally hires new employees, schedules and tracks working hours for employees, and disciplines problem employees. The fran-chiser or home office, in turn, generally suggests or mandates hourly wages, provides performance appraisal forms for local use, and may handle payroll services as well.

A small independent business is generally operated in the same way, with the owner or general manager handling human resource duties. Payroll and other basic administrative activities may be subcontracted out to businesses in the local community that specialize in providing such services for other local organizations. Relatively little training is provided in small organizations such as these, and other human resource issues are relatively straightforward. More-over, very small organizations are exempt from many legal regulations (again, we cover this topic more fully in Chapter 3). Thus a single manager can usu-ally handle the human resource function in smaller firms without too much difficulty.

Human resource management in larger organizations   As the firm grows be-yond a certain size, however, a separate human resource unit becomes a virtual necessity. At first the manager who had been handling the human resource du-ties may delegate them to a special assistant or even to an individual human resource manager. But when an organization reaches a size of around 200 to 250 employees, it generally establishes a self-contained human resource de-partment. Although there is no standard approach, a firm of this size might be expected to have one full-time manager and a single secretary or assistant in its human resource department. These individuals handle all of the firm's human resource administration activities and functions.

As the organization continues to grow, however, more assistance is needed to staff the human resource department, and so that department grows as well. Indeed, in very large organizations human resource functions are likely to be handled by specialized subunits. For example, large firms might have one de-partment to handle recruiting and selection, one to handle wage and salary administration, one to handle training and development, and still another to handle labor relations. Figure 1.4 shows, in simplified form, how Texas Instruments has organized its human resource function.

Human Resources as a Center of Expertise

Because of shifting perspectives regarding staff and line managers and the dynamic nature of both management in general as well as human resource management in particular, it is becoming increasingly useful to conceptualize human resources as a **center of expertise** in an organization. That is, everyone in the organization should recognize human resource managers as the firm's most critical source of information about employment practices, employee behavior, labor relations, and the effective management of all aspects of human resources. This view of human resource management is illustrated in Figure 1.5, which builds on and extends from the systems view of human resource management presented earlier in Figure 1.2.

When a firm maintains a traditional human resource function, this logic is obvious—the human resource department and human resource managers are explicitly responsible for these things and must ensure that their activities are consistent with and appropriately support other functions within the organization. And because human resource departments are also being viewed more and more as cost centers, with the goal of providing clear and measurable financial benefits to the organization, it is especially important that others in the organization recognize and value the contributions made by the human resource department.[27]

But even if the organization does not have a traditional human resource department or if many human resource functions have been outsourced, human resource managers should still be seen by other managers as experts—the best source of information—in all aspects of the organization having anything to do with employees. At a general level, for example, human resource should be able to offer assistance to other managers who need to enhance the motivation of their employees, plan for an impending layoff, or prepare workers to use new technology. More specifically, even if various functions like recruiting, selection, and/or hourly compensation services are being outsourced, human resource managers need to be the critical evaluators of which vendors to use,

■ Human resource management as a **center of expertise** is a perspective arguing that everyone in the organization should recognize human resource managers as the firm's most critical source of information about employment practices, employee behavior, labor relations, and the effective management of all aspects of human resources.

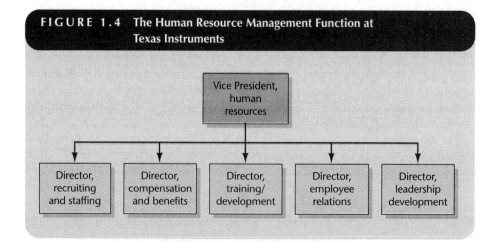

FIGURE 1.4   The Human Resource Management Function at Texas Instruments

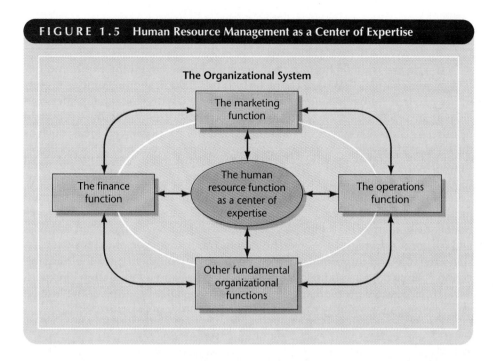

FIGURE 1.5   Human Resource Management as a Center of Expertise

which new services to buy, and so forth. That is, human resource managers should continue to be responsible for evaluating, reviewing, and improving outsourced practices. And finally, at a strategic level human resource managers must provide the big-picture perspective on the management of the organization's human resources. For example, human resource managers should be able to address questions about how outsourced practices integrate with other in-house human resource practices? Are the various outsourced and in-house practices consistent? And do outsourced and in-house practices mutually reinforce and support each other?

Given the obvious importance of human resources as a center of expertise, then, we have adopted this conceptualization as a recurring theme throughout this book. Thus our fundamental goal is to provide future and present managers with the information and skills they need to recognize human resource management as a critical center of expertise. For the future and present human resource manager, we will equip you with the perspective and point of view to be a provider of expertise regarding the full array of human resource activities, functions, and responsibilities. For the future and present manager in other areas of the organization, we will equip you with the perspective and point of view to understand and effectively utilize the expertise that resides in human resources regardless of the form or structure an organization uses for human resource management.

THE BOTTOM LINE   The nature and process of human resource management are in a continuing state of flux. Factors and forces such as organizational role (line versus staff emphasis, for example), organizational size (smaller versus larger organizations), and the mix of outsourced versus in-house practices continue to affect all areas of human resource management. But the human resource function in general, and human resource managers in particular, should remain a critical center of expertise in organizations.

H U M A N   R E S O U R C E   M A N A G E R S

S o who are today's human resource managers? Given the rapid and dynamic changes that have characterized this field, it should come as no surprise that human resource managers represent a diverse set of professionals with a variety of backgrounds, experiences, and career objectives. A human resource executive today needs to understand many specialized areas, such as the legal environment, the process of change management, and labor relations. In addition, contemporary human resource executives must possess general management skills and abilities reflecting conceptual, diagnostic, and analytical skills. Increasingly, for example, many companies are also expecting their human resource managers to have a fundamental understanding of other functional areas, such as marketing and operations, and knowledge about business and corporate strategy. Moreover, human resource managers must fully understand the role and importance of the human resource function for their organization.[28] Thus both a solid educational background and a foundation of experience are necessary prerequisites for success, especially in terms of the human resource manager's ability to function within a center of expertise.[29]

Professionalism and Human Resource Management

Accompanying the shifts and changes in human resource functions and importance has been a greater emphasis on professionalism, reflected by a clear and recognized knowledge base and a generally understood way of doing business. No longer are human resource managers looked upon as second-class corporate citizens. And more and more organizations are including a stint in human resources as a normal step on a person's way to the top. Senior human resource executives in large firms earn six-figure salaries and receive the same sorts of perquisites once reserved only for executives of operating units. For example, the average base salary for a top regional or division human resource manager with generalist responsibilities is around $94,100. In very large organizations, meanwhile, the top human resource executive usually earns $200,000 or more, plus additional income from incentives.[30] The demand for talented human resource executives continues to grow. For example, the number of new human resource positions grew by more than 30 percent in 1997 compared to 1996.

Many human resource managers today belong to the Society for Human Resource Management (SHRM), the field's largest professional association. SHRM publishes professional journals that enable members to stay abreast of the newest developments in the field, sponsors workshops and conferences, and so forth. To help establish human resource management as a recognized profession, SHRM has created the Human Resource Certification Institute, or HRCI. The HRCI has aspirations of becoming the recognized symbol of accreditation in much the same way as the accounting profession uses the CPA exam to designate individuals who have formally achieved basic minimal competencies in prescribed areas.

The HRCI currently has two levels of accreditation. To become a professional in human resources, a manager must have four years of professional experience and pass an examination covering the basic body of human resource knowledge (having a college degree in an appropriate field such as human resource management or industrial/organizational psychology reduces the experience requirement to two years). To become a senior professional in human resource management, an individual must pass the same exam and have eight years of professional experience. Moreover, the three most recent years of experience must be at a policymaking (senior executive) level in an organization.

Careers in Human Resource Management

Career opportunities in human resource management are expected to continue to grow and expand. One obvious way to enter this profession is to get a degree in human resource management (or a related field) and then to seek entry-level employment as a human resource manager. Alternative job options may be as the human resource manager for a small firm or as a human resource specialist in a larger organization. Some universities also offer specialized graduate-degree programs in human resource management. For example, a master of science or master of business administration degree with a concentration in human resource management is likely to lead to a higher-level position in an organization than would a bachelor's degree alone.

Another route to human resource management is through line management. As described earlier, more and more firms are beginning to rotate managers through the human resource function as part of their own personal career development program. Thus even people who go to work in marketing or finance may very well have an opportunity at some point to sample central human resource management responsibilities. Regardless of the path taken, however, those interested in human resource management are likely to have a fascinating, demanding, and rewarding experience as they help their organization compete more effectively through the power of the people who make up every organization in every industry in every marketplace in the world today.

THE BOTTOM LINE Human resource management is becoming increasingly professional, both in its orientation and in the preparation required of its practitioners. Moreover, positions in human resource management continue to expand in scope, responsibility, and compensation.

Chapter Summary

Human resource management is a relatively new functional area in many organizations. As today's large organizations began to emerge around one hundred years ago, they found it necessary to establish specialized units to handle hiring and the administration of current employees. These units were usually called personnel departments and were headed by personnel managers. The original personnel function is now more commonly called human resource management and generally enjoys much more respect and significance in organizations than was the case in earlier times.

Contemporary human resource management deals with a variety of complex and strategic issues. The basic tasks and functions of human resource managers today include adopting a strategic perspective, understanding their environmental context,

staffing the organization, enhancing motivation and performance of employees, conducting the ongoing management of the existing workforce, and meeting other challenges. An integrated human resource management system, supported by an electronic information system, typifies the human resource function in most companies today.

Human resource management generally has four basic goals to pursue. These goals are facilitating organizational competitiveness, enhancing productivity and quality, complying with legal and social obligations, and promoting individual growth and development. Although the human resource manager's focus may vary among the goals during any specific period of time, all are important.

Line, or operating, managers and staff, or specialized human resource, managers typically share the responsibility for effective human resource management. Both sets of managers must work to deal with the conflict that often occurs. The owner or general manager still often handles human resource management in smaller firms, but as organizations grow they usually establish separate human resource departments. As the organizational boundaries of human resource management have changed and blurred, especially in terms of outsourcing alternatives, the human resource function is increasingly seen as a center of expertise.

Today's human resource managers are becoming more and more professional in both their training and their orientation toward their work. Various career paths are also available for people wanting to work in the human resource function. Regardless of approach or career path, however, human resource managers need a broad and thorough knowledge of all aspects of the organization if they are to make meaningful contributions.

Review and Discussion Questions

1. Identify five examples of human resources in your college or university.

2. Summarize the evolution of the human resource function in organizations.

3. Summarize the basic ideas underlying the human resource management system concept.

4. What are the goals of human resource management?

5. Who is responsible for human resource management?

6. Why do you think human resource management (or personnel) was previously held in such low esteem in many organizations?

7. Do you think human resource management would have become more important even if laws

such as the 1964 Civil Rights had never been passed? Why or why not?

8. Identify several things that might happen if an organization fails to recognize that its human resource management practices make up an interrelated system.

9. Do you think some human resource management goals are more important than others? Why or why not? What implications might be drawn if a particular manager felt that certain goals were indeed more important than others?

10. Do you think a large company today could function without a human resource department?

Closing Case

Enterprise Builds on People

When most people think of car-rental firms, the names Hertz, Avis, National, Budget, and Alamo usually come to mind. But in the last few years, Enterprise Rent-A-Car has overtaken all of these industry giants and today stands as both the largest and the most profitable business in the U.S. car-rental industry.

Jack Taylor started Enterprise in St. Louis in 1957. Taylor had a unique strategy in mind for Enterprise, and that strategy has been remarkably successful from the firm's earliest days. Most car-rental firms like Hertz and Avis are located in or near airports. Their customers are business travelers and people who fly for vacation and then need transportation when they arrive. But Enterprise goes after a different customer. Specifically, the firm seeks to rent cars to individuals whose own cars are being repaired, who are driving on vacation, or who for some other reason simply need an extra car for a few days.

Enterprise got its start by working with insurance companies. A standard feature in many automobile insurance polices is the provision of a rental car when one's own personal car has been in a wreck or has been stolen. Firms like Hertz and Avis charge relatively high daily rates because their customers need the convenience of being near an airport and/or their expenses are being paid by their employer. These rates are often higher than insurance companies are willing to pay, however, so insurance company customers often end up footing part of the bill themselves. In addition, airport locations are also often inconvenient for people seeking a replacement car while theirs is in the shop.

But Enterprise locates its agencies in downtown and suburban areas, near where many people live. The firm also provides local pickup and delivery service in most areas. In addition, it usually negotiates exclusive contract arrangements with local insurance agents. As a result, Enterprise gets the agent's referral business while guaranteeing lower rates more in line with insurance-coverage rates.

One key to Enterprise's success has been its human resource strategy. The firm carefully targets a certain kind of individual to hire: its preferred new employee is a college graduate from the *bottom* half of the graduating class, and preferably one who was an athlete or actively involved in campus social activities. The rationale for this unusual academic standard is actually quite simple. Managers do not believe that especially high levels of achievement are necessary to perform well in the car-rental industry, but having a college degree nevertheless demonstrates intelligence and motivation. In addition, because interpersonal relations are important to its business, Enterprise wants people who were social directors or high-ranking officers of social organizations such as fraternities or sororities. Athletes are also desirable because of their competitiveness.

Once hired, these new employees at Enterprise are often shocked at the performance expectations placed on them by the firm's higher-level managers. New employees generally work long, grueling hours for what many see as relatively low pay. And all Enterprise managers are expected to jump in and help wash or vacuum cars when the agency gets backed up.

So what are the incentives for signing on with Enterprise? For one thing, it's an unfortunate fact of life that many college graduates with low grades often struggle to find work. Thus a job at Enterprise is still better than no job at all! Moreover, the firm does not hire outsiders for other than entry-level jobs—every position is filled by promoting someone already inside the company. Thus Enterprise employees know that if they work hard and do their best, they may very well succeed in moving up the corporate ladder at a growing and successful firm.

Case Questions

1. Are there other industries in which Enterprise's approach to human resource management might work?

2. Does Enterprise face any risks from its human resource strategy?

3. Would you want to work for Enterprise? Why or why not?

Sources: "Enterprise Takes on Rent-A-Wreck," *Business Wire,* May 11, 1998, p. 5111281; Brian O'Reilly, "The Rent-a-Car Jocks Who Made Enterprise #1," *Fortune,* October 28, 1996, pp. 125–128; "It Only Hertz When Enterprise Laughs," *Business Week,* December 12, 1994, p. 44; Ron Lieber, "First Jobs Aren't Child's Play," *Fast Company,* June 1999, pp. 154–171; "Enterprise Takes New Direction," *USA Today,* October 28, 1999, p. 3B.

Building Human Resource Management Skills

Purpose: This exercise serves as an icebreaker at the beginning of the course and gets students to think about how human resource management will affect them personally.

Step 1: Your instructor will divide the class into small groups of four to five students. Group members should first introduce themselves to each other.

Step 2: Group members should write their majors and career objectives on a sheet of paper and place the sheets so that everyone can read them.

Step 3: Working as a group, respond to the following questions and ideas:

1. How does human resource management affect each academic major and set of career objectives represented in the group?

2. How would you feel about starting your career in a human resource department?

3. How would you feel about taking a position in human resources later in your career?

4. What specific skills and abilities do you believe are most important for someone who wants to work in human resources?

5. What do you expect from the human resource department at the organization where you begin your career?

Step 4: Each group should select one member to serve as its representative. Your instructor may ask each representative to summarize her/his group's responses to these questions either verbally or in writing.

Step 5: Reconvene with your group and discuss areas of agreement and disagreement among the various groups and group members.

Ethical Dilemmas in Human Resource Management

Assume that you are a top human resource executive for a large privately held company. Your specific area of responsibility is managing all aspects of compensation and benefits for the company; you report to the executive vice president of administration. This individual, in turn, is from the finance department and oversees human resources, finance, and environmental regulation and shows little interest in human resources per se as long as things are going smoothly.

The firm employs more than twenty thousand workers, has operations in fifteen countries, and has a long and stable history of growth and profitability. The owners of the firm, the descendants of the original founder, are not actively involved in management and express satisfaction with the firm's current and projected financial performance. Indeed, all components of financial performance are excellent and the firm is widely respected for the quality of its management. The owners also have often expressed an interest in protecting their workers and maintaining as much job security as possible. The firm has not been forced to lay off any of its employees in more than twenty years.

About a year ago you read some research extolling the benefits of outsourcing. You have been quietly looking into how outsourcing might benefit your company. Your findings are troubling, and you are now trying to decide how to proceed. Specifically, you have determined that outsourcing parts of the firm's human resources function could yield some modest savings for the firm. Unfortunately for you, compensation and benefits also seem to be the area most conducive to outsourcing.

On the one hand, as a manager you feel obligated to consider anything that might lower costs and/or improve financial performance of the firm. And outsourcing does seem almost certain to improve financial performance, albeit only in relatively small ways. Thus if you present your findings to your boss, the firm and its owners will benefit. On the other hand, if outsourcing were to be implemented, you estimate that approximately fifteen employees would lose their jobs and your own position would be substantially diminished in importance.

Questions

1. What are the ethical issues in this situation?

2. What are the basic arguments for and against outsourcing in this situation?

3. What do you think most managers would do? What would you do?

Human Resource Internet Exercise

 Robert Levering and Milton Moskowitz recently published a best-selling book entitled *The 100 Best Companies to Work For in America*. They base their discussion on extensive reviews of the human resource practices of many different firms. Listed below, in alphabetical order, are the ten organizations considered to be the very best places to work.

Beth Israel Hospital Boston
Delta Air Lines
Donnelly
Federal Express
Fel-Pro
Hallmark Cards
Publix Super Markets
Rosenbluth International
Southwest Airlines
USAA

Use a search engine to locate the Web page addresses for these firms. Visit their sites and see what information they contain that is relevant to prospective employees. Use the information you find to answer the questions that follow.

Questions

1. What specific information on each Web page most interested you as a prospective employee?

2. Based solely on the information you located, which company scores best, in your mind, as a potential employer?

3. What are the advantages and disadvantages to both employers and individuals seeking employment to using the Internet as a potential recruiting tool?

Notes

1. Thomas A. Stewart, "A New Way to Think about Employees," *Fortune*, April 13, 1998, p. 169; Jeffrey Pfeffer, "Producing Sustainable Competitive Advantage through the Effective Management of People," *Academy of Management Executive*, February 1995, pp. 55–69; Peter Cappelli and Anne Crocker-Hefter, "Distinctive Human Resources Are Firms' Core Competencies," *Organizational Dynamics*, Winter 1996, pp. 7–22.

2. See Charles R. Greer, *Strategy and Human Resources* (Englewood Cliffs, N.J.: Prentice-Hall, 1995) for an overview of the strategic importance of human resources.

3. Daniel Wren, *The Evolution of Management Thought*, 4th ed. (New York: Wiley, 1994).

4. Thomas A. Mahoney, "Evolution of Concept and Practice in Personnel Administration/Human Resource Management (PA/HRM)," *Journal of Management*, Vol. 12, No. 2, 1986, pp. 223–241.

5. Frederick W. Taylor, *Principles of Scientific Management* (New York: Harper and Brothers, 1911).

6. Oliver E. Allen, "'This Great Mental Revolution,'" *Audacity*, Summer 1996, pp. 52–61.

7. J. M. Fenster, "How General Motors Beat Ford," *Audacity*, Fall 1992, pp. 50–62.

8. Wren, *The Evolution of Management Thought*.

9. Elton Mayo, *The Human Problems of an Industrial Civilization* (New York: Macmillan, 1933).

10. Abraham Maslow, "A Theory of Human Motivation," *Psychological Review*, July 1943, pp. 370–396.

11. Douglas McGregor, *The Human Side of Enterprise* (New York: McGraw-Hill, 1960).

12. James H. Dulebohn, Gerald R. Ferris, and James T. Stodd, "The History and Evolution of Human Resource Management," in Gerald R. Ferris, Sherman D. Rosen; Darold T. Barnum (eds.), *Handbook of Human Resource Management* (Cambridge, Mass.: Blackwell Publishers, 1995), pp. 18–41.

13. Robert R. Blake, "Memories of HRD," *Training & Development*, March 1995, pp. 22–28.

14. Richard A. Starkweather and Cheryl L. Steinbacher, "Job Satisfaction Affects the Bottom Line," *HRMagazine*, September 1998, pp. 110–112.

15. Randall S. Schuler, "Repositioning the Human Resource Function: Transformation or Demise?" *Academy of Management Executive*, August 1990, pp. 49–60.

16. For example, see John E. Delery and D. Harold Doty, "Modes of Theorizing in Strategic Human Resource Management: Tests of Universalistic, Contingency, and Configurational Performance Predictions," *Academy of Management Journal*, August 1996, pp. 802–835.

17. Dave Ulrich, "A New Mandate for Human Resources," *Harvard Business Review*, January–February 1998, pp. 124–133.

18. Brian Becker and Barry Gerhart, "The Impact of Human Resource Management on Organizational Performance: Progress and Prospects," *Academy of Management Journal*, August 1996, pp. 779–801; Russell A. Eisenstat, "What Corporate Human Resources Brings to the Picnic: Four Models for Functional Management," *Organizational Dynamics*, Autumn 1996, pp. 7–22.

19. John W. Kendrick, *Understanding Productivity: An Introduction to the Dynamics of Productivity Change* (Baltimore: Johns Hopkins, 1977).

20. Ross Johnson and William O. Winchell, *Management and Quality* (Milwaukee: American Society for Quality Control, 1989).

21. Samuel B. Graves and Sandra A. Waddock, "Institutional Owners and Corporate Social Performance," *Academy of Management Journal*, August 1994, pp. 1034–1046.

22. Rudy M. Yandrick, "Help Employees Reach for the Stars," *HRMagazine*, January 1997, pp. 96–100.

23. Michelle Martinez, "Prepared for the Future," *HRMagazine*, April 1997, pp. 80–87.

24. Susan Brooks, "Managing a Horizontal Revolution," *HRMagazine*, June 1995, pp. 52–58.

25. Stephanie Overman, "A Day in the Life of a HR Generalist," *HRMagazine*, March 1993, pp. 78–83.

26. See Martha I. Finney, "The Catbert Dilemma," *HRMagazine*, February 1997, pp. 70–76 for an interesting discussion of the relationship between human resource managers and other managers in organizations.

27. Brian D. Steffy and Steven D. Maurer, "Conceptualizing and Measuring the Economic Effectiveness of Human Resource Activities," *Academy of Management Review*, Vol. 13, No. 2, 1988, pp. 271–286.

28. Lotte Bailyn, "Patterned Chaos in Human Resource Management," *Sloan Management Review*, Winter 1993, pp. 77–86.

29. Martha Finney, "Degrees That Make a Difference," *HRMagazine*, November 1996, pp. 74–82; Bruce Kaufman, "What Companies Want from HR Graduates," *HRMagazine*, September 1994, pp. 84–90.

30. *Fortune*, March 2, 1998, p. 221.

PART TWO

The Environment of Human Resource Management

CHAPTER 2
The Strategic Human Resource Environment

CHAPTER 3
The Legal Environment

CHAPTER 4
The Global Environment

2

The Strategic Human Resource Environment

CHAPTER OUTLINE

The Strategic Context of Human Resource Management
The Influence of Organizational Purpose and Mission
The Influence of the Top Management Team

Corporate, Business, and Functional Strategies
SWOT Analysis and Human Resource Management
Corporate Strategy and Human Resource Management
Business Strategy and Human Resource Management
Functional Strategies and Human Resource Management

Human Resource Strategy Formulation
The Impact of Organization Design
The Impact of Corporate Culture
The Impact of Technology
The Impact of the Workforce

Human Resource Strategy Implementation
Individual Processes and Human Resource Management
Interpersonal Processes and Human Resource Management
Evaluating the Human Resource Function in Organizations

CHAPTER OBJECTIVES

After studying this chapter you should be able to:

■ Describe the strategic context of human resource management.

■ Identify three types of strategy and relate each to human resource management.

■ Discuss human resource strategy formulation and relevant organizational factors.

■ Describe the human resource strategy implementation context.

■ Discuss the processes through which human resource strategy is implemented.

■ Discuss how the human resource function in organizations can be evaluated.

For the past several years Starbucks Corporation has been the highest profile and fastest growing food and beverage company in the United States. Howard Schultz bought Starbucks in 1987 when it was still a small mail-order operation. Schultz promptly reoriented the business away from mail-order sales and emphasized retail coffee sales through the firm's coffee bars. Today, Starbucks is not only the largest coffee importer and roaster of specialty beans but also the largest specialty coffee bean retailer in the United States.

What are the keys to Starbucks' phenomenal growth and success? One important ingredient is its well-conceived and implemented strategy. Starbucks is on a phenomenal growth pace, opening a new coffee shop somewhere almost every day. But this growth is planned and coordinated at each step of the way through careful site selection. And through its astute promotional campaigns and commitment to quality, the firm has elevated the coffee-drinking taste of millions of Americans and fueled a significant increase in demand. Another key to Starbucks' success is its near-fanatical emphasis on quality control and operations efficiencies. For example, milk must be heated to precise temperatures before it is used, and every espresso shot must be pulled within twenty-three seconds or else discarded. And no coffee is allowed to sit on a hot plate for more than twenty minutes. Schultz also refuses to franchise his Starbucks stores, fearing a loss of control and a potential deterioration of quality.

The people who work for Starbucks have also played a major role in the firm's success. Managers at each store have considerable autonomy over how they run things, as long as each location follows the firm's basic principles. Starbucks also uses a state-of-the-art communica-

"One reason a lot of youths don't find corporate America so attractive is because of the IBM image: I'll become a blue suit. Starbucks makes you feel like a partner."

(Karen Hunsaker,
Starbucks employee)*

tion network to keep in contact with its employees. The firm hires relatively young people to work in its restaurants, and the starting hourly wage at Starbucks is somewhat higher than it is for most entry-level food services jobs. The company offers health insurance to all of its employees, including part-timers, and also has a lucrative stock-option plan for everyone in the firm. A state-of-the art information system allows every employee to keep abreast of what's happening in the company.

Its phenomenal growth rate notwithstanding, Starbucks is also continually on the alert for new business opportunities. One area of growth is into international markets. In 1996 Starbucks opened its very first coffee shops outside the United States—two in Japan and another in Singapore. By the end of 1998, there were fifty-four Starbucks stores in Asia. International expansion has subsequently become a major growth area for the firm, and its goal is to have five hundred sites in Europe by the year 2003. Another growth area for the company is through brand extension with other companies. For instance, the firm has collaborated with Dreyer's to distribute five flavors of Starbucks coffee ice cream to grocery freezers across the country. Starbucks has also collaborated with Capital Records on two Starbucks jazz CDs available in its stores. And Redhook Brewery even uses Starbucks coffee extract in its double black stout beer!

"Brewing a British Coup," *USA Today*, September 16, 1998, pp. 1D, 2D; Jennifer Reese, "Starbucks—Inside the Coffee Cult," *Fortune*, December 9, 1996, pp. 190–200 (*quote on p. 196); "Starbucks Does Not Live by Coffee Alone," *Business Week*, August 5, 1996, p. 76; "Grounds for Success," *Entrepreneur*, May 1998, pp. 120–126; "Reheating Starbucks," *Business Week*, September 28, 1998, pp. 66–70.

Starbucks has achieved undeniable success through an astute combination of strategy, control, and human resources. Under the leadership of Howard Schultz, the firm has been on a phenomenal growth and expansion pace, with everything dictated by an overarching strategy. Precise operations systems and control standards ensure consistent product quality, and highly motivated people throughout the organization keep everything running according to plan. Take away any of the three elements—strategy, operations, and motivated people—and both the company and its remarkable performance would not look the same. Indeed, more and more managers today are recognizing the important linkages that exist among strategy, operations, and human resource management. Further, a strategic orientation to human resource management provides a useful and effective perspective on how to best create these linkages.

Thus this chapter is devoted to the strategic human resource environment. The first section discusses the strategic context of human resource management in terms of the organization's purpose, mission, and top management team. The next section focuses on corporate, business, and functional strategies and their relationship with human resource management. We then address the increasingly important area of strategic human resource management, first in terms of its formulation and then its implementation. Important organizational characteristics that affect and are affected by these processes are also described. Finally, we provide a framework for how organizations evaluate the human resource function.

THE STRATEGIC CONTEXT OF HUMAN RESOURCE MANAGEMENT

Human resource management does not occur in a vacuum but, instead, occurs in a complex and dynamic milieu of forces within the organizational context.[1] A significant trend in recent years has been for human resource managers to adopt a strategic perspective of their job and to recognize the critical linkages between organizational strategy and human resource strategy. Figure 2.1 illustrates the framework we will use to describe strategic human resource management. As the figure shows, this process starts with an understanding of the organization's purpose, mission, and influence of the top management team and ends with the human resource manager serving as a strategic partner to the operating divisions of the organization. That is, under this new view of human resource management, the human resource manager's job is to help operating managers achieve their strategic goals by serving as a center of expertise for all employment-related activities and issues.

Furthermore, once we adopt this view of the human resource function, it becomes difficult to discuss the one "best" way to carry out that function. Traditionally, managers discussed the newest and presumably the best ways to interview candidates or to select personnel, as well as the best models for compensation and performance appraisal. But when we begin to consider the role of the human resource department as being that of a strategic partner, working toward the organization's strategic goals, it no longer makes sense to talk about the single best way to do anything. Instead, an organization must adopt human resource practices that are consistent with its strategic goals and

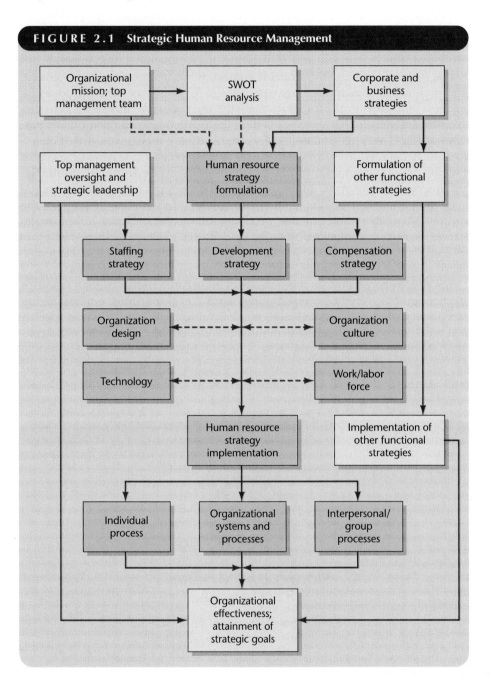

FIGURE 2.1   Strategic Human Resource Management

missions and with the other factors we discuss throughout this chapter. Therefore, an organization must choose human resource practices that fit with its strategy and mission, and so the best practices for one firm may not be the best for another. We will try to remind the reader of this fact throughout the book, but we recognize that this issue can be a source of frustration. Students and managers alike often want to know what will work best in a particular organization. Within the context of a strategic view, however, the best solution or practice will depend on various characteristics of the organization. Thus what is best will depend on factors such as strategic goals and top management values. There are few, if any, simple answers once we recognize the strategic role of human resource management.

The Influence of Organizational Purpose and Mission

■ An organization's **purpose** is its basic reason for existence.

■ An organization's **mission** is a statement of how it intends to fulfill its purpose.

An organization's purpose and mission are among the most fundamental contextual forces that define the strategic context of human resource management. An organization's **purpose** is its basic reason for existence. The purpose of a business is to earn profit for its owners; the purpose of a university is to discover and disseminate new knowledge; the purpose of a museum is to preserve artifacts and historic relics. An organization's **mission** is how its managers have decided to fulfill its purpose. That is, a mission statement specifies how the organization intends to manage itself to most effectively pursue the fulfillment of its purpose. A mission statement attempts to specify the unique characteristics and strengths of an organization and identifies the scope of the business's operations in particular products and markets.[2] Figure 2.2 shows the Starbucks mission statement. Note the prominence given to the firm's employees as the very first "guiding principle." This statement—and its placement—clearly conveys the importance that Starbucks places on its employees.

Both its purpose and its mission affect an organization's human resource practices in some obvious ways. A university, for example, must employ highly educated faculty members to teach courses and to conduct research in specialized areas. A civil-engineering firm must employ people who understand construction and structural engineering; a natural history museum needs people who understand history and science; a marketing firm needs employees with sales expertise. But even finer gradations can also be drawn within each type

FIGURE 2.2   Starbucks' Corporate Mission Statement

STARBUCKS MISSION STATEMENT

To establish Starbucks as the premier purveyor of the finest coffee in the world while maintaining our uncompromising principles as we grow.

The following five guiding principles will help us measure the appropriateness of our decisions:

- Provide a great work environment and treat each other with respect and dignity.

- Apply the highest standards of excellence to the purchasing, roasting and fresh delivery of our coffee.

- Develop enthusiastically satisfied customers all of the time.

- Contribute positively to our communities and our environment.

- Recognize that profitability is essential to our future success.

Courtesy—Starbucks Coffee Company.

of organization, as defined by their respective missions. For example, an oil-exploration firm like Shell needs petroleum engineers, whereas an electronics firm like Intel needs electrical engineers, and a construction firm like Bechtel needs civil engineers.

Moreover, mission statements often provide subtle cues as to the importance the organization places on its human resources. Many progressive firms today, like Starbucks, for instance, make some reference to the importance of their human resources in their mission statement. Southwest Airlines, Wal-Mart, and Compaq Computer also stress the value of their employees in their mission statements. But some firms do not explicitly refer to employees in their mission statements. Although most of these firms do, of course, really value the people who work for them, the lack of specific reference to those people might indicate that human resources are somehow not seen as being as important to the organization as other issues and goals. Although mission statements make a public commitment to some course of action (such as valuing human resources), we must recognize that, of course, in some cases the language of a mission statement is intended to placate a group of stakeholders, such as employees, rather than to truly signal an organization's priorities.[3]

Top managers play a key role in setting the tone for the kind of relationship an organization will have with its employees. For example, Patricia Gallup is the CEO of PC Connection, a very successful New Hampshire firm that sells computers and computer peripherals through mail order. Although the firm employs almost 1,000 people, she knows virtually all of them by name. Her office is centrally located in the middle of the company's facilities; her door is always open, and anyone can drop by at any time to discuss problems or ideas. And at least partially as a result, PC Connection is widely recognized as a great place to work.

The Influence of the Top Management Team

The **top management team** of an organization refers to the group of senior executives responsible for the overall strategic operation of the firm. Common organizational positions that are assumed to be part of the top management team include the chairperson of the board of directors, the chief executive officer (CEO), the chief operating officer (COO), and the president. Other members of the top management team generally include the senior executive (usually having the title of vice president) responsible for each major functional area within the organization. For example, the senior vice presidents responsible for marketing, finance, and human resource management are all likely to be considered part of an organization's top management team.

The top management team sets the tone for the organization and plays a major role in shaping its culture (as discussed later in this chapter). Some top management teams have a clear vision of where they want the firm to go and how they think it should get there. They also do a good job of articulating this vision throughout the organization. In this case middle and lower-level managers know what is expected of them and can direct their efforts and the efforts of members of their division, department, or team toward this common goal. Other top management teams, however, present an ambiguous, contradictory, or vague vision of where they see the organization headed. As a result, other managers in these organizations may be unsure how to proceed and unable to communicate effectively with their own employees as well.[4] In fact, views of leadership that emphasize the importance of personal charisma in leaders tend

■ The **top management team** of an organization refers to the group of senior executives responsible for the overall strategic operation of the firm.

to suggest that effective leaders need both a clear vision and a means of communicating that vision. In this latter case, the organization is less likely to be successful if the top managers are unable to accomplish both these goals.[5]

Although top managers sometimes use speeches and proclamations to articulate the organization's vision and purpose, their behavior more commonly communicates their true personal values and beliefs and thus those of the organization. Herb Kelleher knows many Southwest Airlines employees by name and insists that they call him Herb. Sam Walton personally visited every Wal-Mart store at least once a year and spoke with all employees via the firm's satellite telecommunications network almost every week. His successor, David Glass, still carries on that tradition. Employees who work for leaders like these recognize the importance of each person's work and that senior management values their efforts. In contrast, some top managers try to insulate themselves from lower-level members of the organization. These managers seldom visit work locations and treat their employees with disdain. James Dutt, a former CEO of Beatrice Foods, once told a subordinate that if his wife and children got in the way of his working twenty-four hours a day, seven days a week, he should get rid of them.[6]

THE BOTTOM LINE Many organizations today attempt to adopt a strategic orientation toward human resource management. The organization's purpose and mission provide the foundation for such a strategic context. The influence of the top management team is also pervasive in most organizations.

CORPORATE, BUSINESS, AND FUNCTIONAL STRATEGIES

As indicated in the preceding section, top managers are responsible for the strategic operations of their firms. The key to strategic operations, in turn, is developing and implementing effective strategies. These strategies may be at the corporate, business, and/or functional level—including the human resource function.[7] (In addition to strategy formulation, as shown earlier in Figure 2.1, the top management team of the organization provides oversight and strategic leadership for the organization on a continuous and ongoing basis.) It should be clear by now, therefore, that functional strategies should be consistent with and supportive of corporate strategy.

SWOT Analysis and Human Resource Management

■ Strategies are typically formulated through a process involving a **SWOT analysis**.

The first step in formulating strategy is what some managers call a **SWOT analysis**. SWOT is an acronym that stands for strengths, weaknesses, opportunities, and threats. The idea behind a SWOT analysis is for managers in the firm to carefully assess both the opportunities and threats that exist in a firm's environment and the strengths and weaknesses that exist within the organization. The managers then attempt to use the firm's strengths to capitalize on environmental opportunities and to cope with environmental threats. Strengths are also used to offset weaknesses within the organization. Human resources play a fundamental role in SWOT analysis because the nature and type of people that work within an organization and the organization's ability to attract new talent represent significant strengths or weaknesses. Likewise, a surplus or a scarcity of talented and capable people in the external labor market also represents important environmental opportunities and threats.[8]

Many organizations formulate strategy at three basic levels: the corporate level, the business level, and various functional levels. **Corporate strategy** is the set of strategic alternatives that an organization chooses from as it manages its operations simultaneously across several industries and several markets. **Business strategy** is the set of strategic alternatives that an organization chooses from in order to most effectively compete in a particular industry or market. Finally, **functional strategies** consider how the firm will manage each of its major functions, such as marketing, finance, and human resources. Strategies at all three levels, however, impact on the human resource management function under the strategic approach to human resource management.

Corporate Strategy and Human Resource Management

Using the results of their SWOT analysis, most organizations develop a corporate strategy from one of two perspectives. One perspective focuses on a single overarching grand strategy for the firm, and the other is based on diversification.

Grand strategy   A **grand strategy** is a single overall framework for action that the top management team develops at the corporate level.[9] It is most commonly used when a business chooses to compete in one market or in only a few very closely related markets. When a business has identified a unique niche and is successfully expanding aggressively within that particular market niche, it is pursuing what experts call a *growth strategy*. As the term suggests, a growth strategy focuses on the growth and expansion of the corporation. During the 1990s, for example, Home Depot increased its number of outlets by 25 percent per year, clearly a growth strategy.[10] Starbucks has also been using a rapid growth strategy as it continues its geographic and brand expansion.

A key challenge for human resource managers when firms are using a growth strategy is recruiting and training large numbers of qualified employees to help operate growing operations. Home Depot, for instance, hires dozens of new management trainees each year, along with hundreds of new retail associates and other operating employees to staff its new stores. Human resource managers at Home Depot are responsible for recruiting and hiring these people, orienting and training them, and making their initial job assignments. Similarly, Starbucks hires dozens of new employees each month. The firm's human resource managers run continuous training programs to teach these new employees the precise methods for brewing coffee and maintaining quality control in all other areas of their job responsibilities. Thus in both firms the human resource function focuses its activities on ways to help the organization achieve its corporate goals.

We should also note, though, that when organizations view the human resource area as a true strategic partner, they also use input from human resource managers in their initial formulation of corporate strategy. So, for example, when Home Depot's top managers decided to pursue a growth strategy, the firm's top management team likely consulted with the human resource management team to ensure that the latter group had the capability to attract and train the large number of new employees needed to implement the anticipated growth. In other words, a true partnership requires the parties to consult with and support each other.

■ **Corporate strategy** is the set of strategic alternatives that an organization chooses from as it manages its operations simultaneously across several industries and several markets.

■ **Business strategy** is the set of strategic alternatives that an organization chooses from in order to most effectively compete in a particular industry or market.

■ **Functional strategies** consider how the firm will manage each of its major functions, such as marketing, finance, and human resources.

■ A **grand strategy** is a single overall framework for action that the top management team develops at the corporate level.

An organization's corporate, business, and functional strategies clearly impact human resource management in a variety of ways. Consider, for example, the recent success enjoyed by Greyhound, the venerable bus company. Greyhound has substantially expanded its route structure, focusing specifically on carrying passengers back and forth between the United States and Mexico. This one segment of the market is estimated to exceed $200 million a year and is growing at an annual rate of 20 percent. As a result of this new focus, Greyhound has had to hire more bilingual drivers and train those drivers in a variety of legal issues associated with transporting passengers across national boundaries.

A growth strategy can also be pursued externally through the acquisition of other businesses, mergers, or joint ventures. A major initial challenge for human resource managers in this situation will be determining how to merge two existing workforces into a single cohesive and integrated unit. In some cases, for example, there will be unnecessary duplication of employees, and choices will have to be made about which overlapping employees to retain, which to transfer, and which to lay off. Similarly, it is very likely that the two firms will be using different human resource philosophies for such things as training practices, promotion policies, and so forth. Hence human resource decision makers must decide which practices to retain and which to discard. When The Walt Disney Company acquired ABC, among the first questions that had to be answered was who would manage various parts of the new enterprise and how would the human resources of two firms be integrated into one new operation. In fact, there is reason to believe that the failure to integrate different strategies and cultures may be an important factor in the failure of some mergers and acquisitions.[11] Furthermore, since there is always a great deal of concern and speculation over what will happen to employees, the entire merger or acquisition process must be managed relative to its impact on employees. Failure to do so can result in undue stress, the loss of valued employees, and long-lasting morale problems in organizations.[12] "The Lighter Side of HR" clearly illustrates the depth of issues associated with a merger or acquisition.

A second grand strategy that organizations sometimes are forced to adopt, at least in the short run, is called a *retrenchment* or a *turnaround strategy*. This happens when an organization finds that its current operations are less than effective. For example, a firm might find that its dominant products are in declining markets, its technology is rapidly becoming obsolete, or it is in some other way not performing as well as it should. Major changes are usually needed to rectify these kinds of problems. In most of these cases, organizations go through a period of *downsizing* (or *rightsizing*, as some managers prefer to call it) in an effort to get back on the right track. They close operations, shut down factories, terminate employees, and take other actions to scale back current operations and reduce their workforce. Their ultimate goal is to be able to take the resources that are generated as a result of these steps and reinvest them into other more promising products and markets.

Downsizing has become a common response to competitive problems. As more employees find their jobs at risk, the traditional *psychological contract* between the organization and the employee is changing. No longer can employees feel certain of keeping their jobs as long as they perform well, and the increased uncertainty makes it more difficult for employees to fully commit to their organizations. As a result of these problems, human resource managers clearly need to be involved when the organization is eliminating jobs and/or decreasing the size of its workforce. They need to help manage the process so that employees continue to feel attached to and committed to the organization. In addition, human resource managers must help ensure that decisions about who is to be let go be made for job-related reasons, as opposed to reasons that might reflect or suggest bias or illegal discrimination. Similarly, human resource managers can help optimize the transition process for displaced workers through such practices as

The Lighter Side of HR
Mergers and acquisitions are a common element of many corporate strategies today, but blending two different organizations into one is seldom as easy as its sounds at first. Indeed, as humorously illustrated here, joining two companies together is in some ways very much like a marriage or similar bonding between two people. Human resources managers often play key roles in such functions as they work to blend people and human resource systems from two different organizations into one.

"Do you, Scofield Industries, take Amalgamated Pipe?"

equitable severance packages and outplacement counseling. A few years ago International Harvester declared bankruptcy and was reborn as Navistar, a much smaller operation. Throughout all phases of this process, human resource managers were involved in making decisions about which employees would be most valuable to the new enterprise and how best to retain them.

A final grand strategy some firms use is a stability strategy. A *stability strategy* essentially calls for maintaining the status quo. A company that adopts a stability strategy plans to stay in its current businesses and intends to manage them as they are already being managed. The organization's goal is to protect itself from environmental threats. A stability strategy is frequently used after a period of retrenchment or after a period of rapid growth. When the firm is using a stability strategy, human resource managers play a major role in determining how to best retain the firm's existing employees when the firm can offer little in the way of advancement opportunities, salary increases, and so forth.

Diversification strategy   Another widely used approach to corporate strategy is diversification.[13] A corporation that uses the **diversification strategy** usually makes the decision to own and operate several different businesses. For example, General Electric, one of the most successful practitioners of this

■ A **diversification strategy** is used by companies that are adding new products, product lines, or businesses to their existing core products, product lines, or businesses.

strategy, owns a variety of businesses that manufacture aircraft engines, industrial products, major appliances, and technical products. It also owns the NBC television network and has financial services and insurance businesses as well.

Sometimes the various businesses owned by a corporation are related to one another in some way. This strategy is called *related diversification*.[14] The basic underlying assumption for using related diversification is that the corporation can achieve synergy among the various businesses it owns. For example, The Limited operates more than a dozen retail chains, including Express, Victoria's Secret, Structure, Bath & Body Works, and Abercrombie & Fitch. A single group of buyers supplies all of the firm's chains, a single development operation seeks new locations for all chains, and so forth. This type of organization often adopts a policy of rotating managers across the various businesses in order for them to develop an overall managerial perspective on the whole firm. A manager might start out with Express, get promoted to a new position at Bath & Body Works, and then move into yet another position with Abercrombie & Fitch. The related aspects of the businesses presumably make such cross-business transfers easier. Moreover, since the markets for each business are similar, the firm can develop relatively uniform procedures for selection, compensation, training, and so forth.

Sometimes, however, an organization decides to expand into products or markets that are unrelated to its current ones. This approach is called *unrelated diversification*. A firm that pursues a strategy of unrelated diversification attempts to operate a number of unique businesses in different, unrelated markets. General Electric, as already noted, owns businesses that compete in a variety of unrelated areas. The basic logic behind unrelated diversification is that a company can shield itself from the adverse impact of business cycles, unexpected competition, and other economic fluctuations. Since the various businesses are presumably unrelated, a downturn or setback in one does not necessarily suggest a corresponding downturn or setback in another.

Human resource executives in a firm that uses unrelated diversification must approach the human resource function in a way that is very different from that of their counterparts in a firm that uses related diversification. Managers in the first situation typically remain within a single business unit as they progress up the corporate ladder. Moreover, given that each unrelated business is likely to have its own unique hiring, compensation, and training needs—as dictated by its own competitive environment—these functions will likely be customized and decentralized to each business. Thus while the career tracks and compensation packages for managers at Express and Victoria's Secret will likely be very similar to one another, the career tracks and compensation packages for managers at NBC and GE Appliance may be quite dissimilar. The NBC compensation packages, for instance, will more closely resemble those at ABC and CBS, whereas the GE Appliance compensation packages may be more like those at Whirlpool and Maytag.

Organizations that use the diversification approach for managing their corporate strategy must also work to ensure close coordination between their corporate human resource functions and the human resource functions within each of their businesses or divisions. Essentially, the corporate human resource group must interface with three sets of constituents. One set of constituents is the top management team, or corporate management. Second, corporate human resources can also be involved in representing the firm in its interactions with such external constituents as the government, labor unions, and benchmark companies (companies to which the organization compares itself). And third, corporate human resources can also be involved with the division management, division human resources, and the employees of each division or business owned by the corporation.[15]

Business Strategy and Human Resource Management

As noted earlier, decisions must also be made as to how to best compete in each market where a firm operates. This question determines business strategy. A diversified corporation must therefore develop a business strategy for each of its operating units.[16] Two different approaches can be used to develop a business-level strategy.

The adaptation model   One approach to business strategy is called the **adaptation model**.[17] This model suggests that managers in an organization should try to match its strategy with the basic conditions of its environment. Different levels of environmental complexity and change are expected to be most appropriately matched with different forms of strategy. The three basic strategic alternatives from which managers should select are the defender strategy, the analyzer strategy, and prospector strategy.

A *defender strategy* is assumed to work best when a business operates in an environment with relatively little uncertainty and risk and high degrees of stability. The goal of the defender is to identify for itself a relatively narrow niche in the market and to then direct a limited set of products or services at that niche. Although defenders may compete with other firms aggressively, the primary approach here is to guard and to secure the company's position within an existing market. Thus while defenders monitor trends and developments outside their chosen domain, they focus primarily on their existing environment. Hershey Foods is a good example of a defender. The firm concentrates almost exclusively on the confectionery market. Another good example of a defender is Wrigley, the venerable chewing-gum company. Human resource managers in organizations using a defender strategy are most likely to recruit and seek to retain stable employees who exhibit high levels of commitment and loyalty to the firm.

A second type of strategy used in this approach is the prospector strategy. The *prospector strategy* anchors the other end of the continuum. This strategy works best when the environment is dynamic, is growing, and has considerable uncertainty and risk. Prospectors are advised to always be on the alert for discovering and capitalizing on new ideas and opportunities. They focus on new products and markets and try to avoid a long-term commitment to any single type of technology, using multiple technologies instead. This approach makes it easier for the organization to shift from one product market to another very easily. General Electric is a good example of a prospector. As noted earlier, the firm owns everything from a jet engine business to a television network. For the right opportunity the firm will buy any business that might be for sale or sell any business it currently owns. Human resource managers in organizations using the prospector strategy may prefer to recruit and retain entrepreneurial employees who are highly flexible and who are more dedicated to their craft or profession than to the organization itself.

The *analyzer strategy* falls between the extremes of the defender and prospector. The analyzer strategy is most appropriate in relatively stable

■ The **adaptation model** is one popular approach to business strategy.

conditions with some moderate degree of uncertainty and risk. An analyzer tries to identify and take advantage of new markets and products while maintaining a nucleus of traditional core products and customers. Disney is a good example of an analyzer. The firm cautiously moved into television and video markets a few years ago, has expanded its movie division, and is currently investing in electronic games and virtual-reality products, but takes each step slowly and only after careful deliberation. Human resource managers in firms that pursue this strategy may seek to recruit and retain employees who might be moderately entrepreneurial and flexible, but who will also be quite dedicated and loyal to the organization.

The adaptation model also identifies a fourth strategic alternative called the reactor. However, the *reactor* is really seen as a strategic failure and is not held up as a model that any firm should emulate. A reactor is a firm that either improperly ignores its environment or else attempts to react to its environment in inappropriate ways. During the early 1980s Kmart was guilty of using the reactor strategy. It failed to keep pace with Wal-Mart, for example, and spread itself too thin by investing heavily in specialty retailing. Human resource managers in organizations that are functioning as reactors may lack a clear understanding of exactly what qualities they are seeking in their employees. And indeed, this lack of understanding may very well contribute to the firm's poor performance.

> ▨ The **competitive strategies** framework suggests that three basic strategies are appropriate for a wide variety of organizations in diverse industries.

Competitive strategies   The other dominant approach to business-level strategies identifies three **competitive strategies** that are presumed to be appropriate for a wide variety of organizations in diverse industries.[18] These strategies are differentiation, cost leadership, and focus.

> ▨ A company that uses a **differentiation strategy** attempts to develop an image or reputation for its product or service that sets it apart from the competition.

A company that uses a **differentiation strategy** attempts to develop an image or reputation for its product or service that sets it apart from the competition. The differentiating factor may be real and/or objective, such as product reliability or design, or it may be more perceptual and/or subjective, such as fashion and appearance. Regardless of its basis, however, a firm that successfully differentiates its products or services from those of its competitors can charge higher prices for those products or services, thereby earning a larger profit. Rolex and BMW are firms that have successfully used a differentiation strategy. Human resource managers contribute to the successful use of a differentiation strategy by recruiting and retaining employees who can perform high-quality work and/or who can provide exemplary customer service. Likewise, employee training will likely focus on quality improvement, and reward systems may be based on factors such as quality of work and customer satisfaction.[19]

> ▨ A **cost leadership strategy** focuses on minimizing the costs as much as possible.

A **cost leadership strategy** focuses on minimizing the costs as much as possible. This approach allows the firm to charge the lowest possible prices for its products, thereby presumably generating a higher overall level of revenue. Low cost may be achieved through production efficiencies, distribution efficiencies, or product design efficiencies. Timex and Hyundai are examples of businesses that have successfully used a cost leadership strategy. Human resource contributions here focus on recruiting and retaining employees who can work as efficiently and productively as possible. On the other hand, more-experienced employees may demand higher wages, so it might also be possible to reengineer jobs to require minimal skills and then to select employees who can perform the jobs but who may not remain long with the organization. Fast-food restaurants often control labor costs with this type of an approach.

Nike Shoots Itself in the Foot

One of the most compelling issues facing many international businesses today is the ethics of moving production to countries where labor costs are low, thus reducing overall production costs. And Nike, the U.S. sports apparel giant, often finds itself at the center of that controversy. About 75 percent of Nike's production is done in Indonesia, China, and Vietnam to capitalize on lower labor costs in those countries. But with low costs often come difficult issues.

For example, in March 1997 a U.S.-based labor group released a report condemning Nike for its labor practices in Vietnam. One charge was that fifty-six women were forced to run laps around the factory for wearing nonregulation shoes; twelve women reportedly fainted and had to be hospitalized. Another charge was that workers were being paid subminimum wages. Nike expressed distress when the news was released and promised a full investigation.

To help deal with the situation, Nike hired Andrew Young, the civil rights leader, former mayor of Atlanta, and former U.S. ambassador to the United Nations, to

"While Nike claims it is trying to monitor and enforce its code of conduct, its current approach to monitoring and enforcement is simply not working."

(Thuyen Nguyen, Vietnam Labor Watch)*

study and report on conditions at its overseas plants. His seventy-five-page report, unfortunately, generated even more controversy. Young basically concluded that Nike's overseas operations were in fine shape and that human rights were not being violated. For example, he found that Nike plants were clean, adequately ventilated, and well lit and that there was no pattern of widespread or systematic abuse.

But virtually ignored in Young's report was the issue of wages. His argument was that he lacked the skill to assess pay in a global economy. Moreover, he argued, Nike's pay practices are the same as dozens of other multinational firms—paying people the prevailing wages within their own country. But critics argued that Young—and Nike—missed the point. They contend that companies that pay the local minimum are exploiting people and that giant corporations should be doing more to raise standards of living by paying more than minimum wages.

Sources: "Nike to Take a Hit in Labor Report," *USA Today*, March 27, 1997, p. 1A, 2A (*quote on p. 2A); "Nike Hasn't Scrubbed Its Image Yet," *Business Week*, July 7, 1997, p. 44.

Training may emphasize efficient production methods, and reward systems may be based more on quantity than on quality of output. One popular approach to reducing costs today is to move production to countries where labor costs are lower than in the home country. The potential pitfalls of this approach, however, are illustrated in "Human Resources Around the Globe."

Finally, the **focus strategy** is undertaken when an organization tries to target a specific segment of the marketplace for its products or services. This focus may be toward a specific geographic area, a specific segment of the consuming population based on ethnicity or gender, or some other factor that serves to segment the market. Within that focus a firm may attempt to either differentiate or to cost lead its products or services. Fiesta Mart is a Houston-based grocery store chain that has prospered by focusing its marketing on the large number of immigrants, especially Hispanics, who live in the Southwest. These stores sell Mexican soft drinks, corn husks for wrapping tamales, and many other products that are not carried in general-purpose grocery stores. The key human resource goal in this instance is recruiting and retaining employees who understand the focal market. For example, Fiesta Mart must recruit, hire, and retain employees who really understand the products they are selling and who speak Spanish, the language of most of its customers.

■ The **focus strategy** is undertaken when an organization tries to target a specific segment of the marketplace for its products or services.

Functional Strategies and Human Resource Management

The third level of strategy formulation and implementation is the functional level. Functional strategies address how the organization will manage its basic functional activities, such as marketing, finance, operations, research and development, and human resources. Thus it is at this level that human resource strategy formulation formally begins to take shape. It is clearly important that a human resource functional strategy be closely integrated and coordinated with corporate, business, and other functional strategies. Indeed, without such integration and coordination, organizational competitiveness will clearly suffer.[20]

And much of our discussion throughout the remainder of this text explicitly or implicitly addresses the human resource function from a contextual perspective that includes other fundamental business functions. As shown earlier in Figure 2.1, human resource strategy is, of course, our primary concern. Keep in mind, however, that other functional strategies are also developed and, as shown in the figure, combine with the human resource strategy and top management strategic leadership to determine the firm's overall performance.

THE BOTTOM LINE   Organizations select from an array of corporate, business, and functional strategic alternatives. Human resource managers need to have a clear understanding of exactly which strategies the firm's top managers have chosen and ensure that their own efforts are consistent with and provide support for those strategies. To the extent that the human resource function is seen as a strategic partner and/or a center of expertise, of course, its managers should also be actively involved in the formulation of corporate and business strategies, as well as other functional strategies.

HUMAN   RESOURCE   STRATEGY   FORMULATION

Using the organization's overarching corporate and business strategies as context, managers can then, as noted earlier, formally develop the firm's human resource strategy. As illustrated in Figure 2.1, this strategy commonly includes three distinct dimensions—a staffing strategy, a development strategy, and a compensation strategy. These dimensions are shown in more detail in Figure 2.3.

Staffing refers to the set of activities used by the organization to determine its future human resource needs, to recruit qualified applicants interested in working for the organization, and to then select the best of those applicants as new employees. Obviously, however, this process can be undertaken only after a careful and systematic strategy has been developed to ensure that staffing activities mesh appropriately with other strategic elements of the organization. For example, as already noted, if the business is employing a growth strategy, the staffing strategy must be based on the aggressive recruiting and selection of large numbers of qualified employees. But if retrenchment is the expectation, the staffing strategy will focus instead on determining which employees to retain and how to best handle the process of terminating other employees.

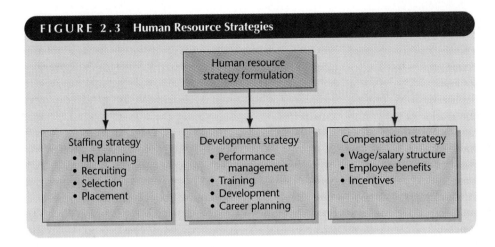

FIGURE 2.3 Human Resource Strategies

Similarly, human resource managers must also formulate an employee development strategy for helping the organization enhance the quality of its human resources. This strategy usually involves performance management, the actual training and development of employees and managers, and career planning and development for appropriate employees. As with staffing, the development strategy must be consistent with corporate and business strategies. For example, if an organization is using a differentiation strategy, the firm will need to invest heavily in training its employees to produce the highest-quality products and/or provide the highest-quality service. Further, performance management must focus on recognizing and rewarding performance leading to improved quality. But if cost leadership is the strategy of choice, the firm may choose to invest less in training (helping to keep overall costs low) and orient what training is offered toward efficiency and productivity-improvement methods and techniques.

And third, the compensation strategy must likewise complement the firm's other strategies. Basic compensation, performance-based incentives, and employee benefits and services, the basic components of the compensation strategy, must be congruent with their relevant strategic contexts to be effective. For example, if a firm is pursuing a strategy of related diversification, its compensation system must be geared to, first, rewarding those employees whose skills allow them to move across businesses and, second, be flexible enough to facilitate those same cross-business transfers. If a manager moves from one division to another, for instance, that manager's pension plan should be readily "portable" to the new assignment. If the firm is using unrelated diversification, on the other hand, compensation may instead be focused on depth of knowledge and skills. Hence the firm may choose to pay a premium salary to a highly talented expert with unusual skills relevant to one of the firm's business. The ability of this expert to move across businesses is less important and thus not likely to be a factor in compensation.[21] "Human Resources Fad, Fashion, or Fact?" describes an interesting approach some high-tech firms are using in an effort to more effectively staff, develop, and compensate their employees.

When attempting to formulate the human resource strategy, as well as its three basic components, human resource managers must also account for other key parts of the organization. These components are important because they affect both how strategies are formulated and how they are implemented. Four

---

Location, Location, Location

Firms in the high-tech industry often face cutthroat competition for new workers. A chronic shortage of qualified workers has been the primary catalyst for this competition. Workers find that they can hop from job to job in search of better perks and higher pay. And because these firms tend to be clustered in California's Silicon Valley, Seattle, Boston, Denver, Dallas, and Austin, firms competing for the same workers are across the highway or around the corner from one another. And because the workers mingle with each other during their leisure time, they are keenly aware of both new job opportunities and prevailing wage rates.

But a few firms have attempted to deal with labor competition by locating in relatively isolated, out-of-the-way places. Gateway Computers, for example, was one of the first to succeed with this strategy by setting up shop in North Sioux City, South Dakota. Another success has been Great Plains Software, founded in 1981 by former farmer Doug Burgum. Today, Great Plains is regularly cited as a great place to work and an especially well-managed firm.

The logic behind these kinds of locations is often related to workforce issues. Although workers certainly pre-

"Here, you can work a lot, leave, be with your kids in 5 minutes and be at a movie in 10 minutes. The work-life balance is easier to achieve."

(Doug Burgum, CEO of Great Plains Software, based in Fargo, North Dakota)*

fer the hip urban environments of Austin or Seattle, some others prefer the peace and quiet of smaller venues. These people see smaller communities as a nice alternative for raising a family, for example, and as a way to escape from the traffic, crime, and higher costs of most urban environments. The firms find that although they may have to work harder to convince workers to relocate to their isolated settings, the people who do are more stable and likely to remain with the firm for a longer period of time.

Of course, not everyone believes that this strategy is a good one. Although critics acknowledge the benefits of lower turnover, they also point to the higher costs of recruiting and the difficulties in managing growth. And as one piece of evidence, they can now point to the fact that while Gateway kept its manufacturing facility in South Dakota, the firm recently moved its corporate headquarters to San Diego. The reason? As the company continued to grow, it was having trouble convincing qualified managers to move to North Sioux City.

References: "High-Tech Firms Go Rural," *USA Today,* August 4, 1998, pp. B1, B2 (*quote on page B1); "Small Towns Find Ways to Create Their Own Jobs," *Wall Street Journal,* September 23, 1998, p. T1.

---

of the most critical components are organization design, the corporate culture, technology, and labor and the workforce.[22]

The Impact of Organization Design

■ **Organization design** refers to the framework of jobs, positions, clusters of positions, and reporting relationships among positions that are used to construct an organization.

Organization design refers to the framework of jobs, positions, groups of positions, and reporting relationships among positions that are used to construct an organization.[23] One form of organization design used by many smaller and/or newer organizations is the *functional design* (this design is also called the *U-form organization,* with the *U* representing "unitary"). The organization groups its members into basic functional departments such as marketing, finance, and operations. Thus the top of the organizational chart is likely to reflect positions for vice president of marketing, finance, operations, research and development (R&D), and human resources. To operate effectively, this form of organization requires considerable coordination across departments. Senior management is usually expected to provide this coordination. A U-form organization will typically have a single human resource department responsible for organizationwide human resource functions and activities, and the human resource manager and department will work with all other functional areas across the firm.

A second form of organization design used today is the *conglomerate*, or *H-form design* (the *H* stands for "holding company"). A conglomerate design is used when an organization has implemented a strategy of unrelated diversification. The corporation itself is essentially a holding company that results from this unrelated diversification. Because the various businesses that make up the organization are unrelated to the others, each functions with a high degree of autonomy and independence. A corporate-level staff usually plays a key role in coordinating the activities of the various divisions. For example, human resource management is a common staff function in an H-form organization. But each of the unrelated businesses within the corporation will also have its own human resource department that functions with relative autonomy within that specific business. The corporate-level staff will provide broad and general oversight and will link business-level issues with corporate-level issues.

A third form of organization design that is fairly common today is the *divisional* or *M-form organization* design (the *M* stands for "multidivisional"). The divisional design looks similar to the H-form design except that in the former the businesses are closely related to one another. The M-form design is especially popular because of the presumed synergies that can result from related business groupings. In an M-form organization, coordination is usually decentralized down to the various operating companies where the work is actually being performed. Although M-form organizations may have a corporate human resource staff, most of the basic human resource functions are handled within each division.[24] The primary function of the corporate-level human resource department will be to facilitate synergy across businesses.

In recent years many organizations have been moving toward yet another form of organization design. Although this new design has no precise name, the popular press often refers to it as the *flat organization*, or the *horizontal corporation*. Such an organization is created by eliminating levels of management, reducing bureaucracy, using very wide spans of management, and relying heavily on teamwork and coordination to get work accomplished. Horizontal corporations are presumed to be highly flexible and to provide a great deal of opportunity for adaptation, fewer managers, and greater levels of empowerment on the part of subordinates. The human resource function in these organizations is likely to be diffused throughout the organization such that operating managers take on more of the responsibility for human resource activities, with a somewhat smaller human resource staff providing basic services and playing more of a consultative role.

The Impact of Corporate Culture

The culture of the organization also affects how it formulates and implements its human resource strategy. An organization's **culture** refers to the set of values that help its members understand what the organization stands for, how it does things, and what it considers important.[25] Culture is a complex and amorphous concept that defies objective measurement or evaluation. Nevertheless, because it is the foundation of an organization's internal environment, culture plays a major role in shaping managerial behavior and is a strong element in how the organization manages its human resources.

■ An organization's **culture** refers to the set of values that help its members understand what the organization stands for, how it does things, and what it considers important.

An organization's culture is a critical ingredient to its success. Many younger workers today are attracted to companies that provide opportunities for fun and allow them the freedom to express their own individuality. These opportunities, meanwhile, are often manifested through the firm's culture. The offices at Excite, shown here, clearly project the kind of cultural image that is likely to appeal to today's workers—casual, relaxed, and open and adorned with personal photos, mementos, and souvenirs.

The importance of culture   An organization's culture plays a very important role in determining how well the organization will be able to achieve its goals and how well the members of the organization will be able to function together. Culture is an intangible characteristic of an organization that cannot be seen or objectively measured. However, its force permeates an entire organization and affects virtually every aspect of individual behavior within an organization; thus culture has clear implications for human resource management. Although there is no such thing as an ideal culture, a strong and well-articulated culture enables people within the firm to know what the organization stands for, what it values, and how to behave with regard to the organization.[26] The human resource department often plays a key role in helping new employees learn about the culture through orientation.

The determinants of culture   A number of forces shape an organization's culture. One of the most important forces is the founder of the organization. Organizations that have strong-willed and visionary founders often find that the remnants of that founder's vision remain a central part of their culture. Walt Disney's influence is still found throughout the corporation that bears his name. Likewise, even though Sam Walton died a few years ago, his values and approach to doing business will likely remain a part of Wal-Mart for decades to come. As an organization grows, its culture is modified, shaped, and refined through other forces. These forces include symbols, stories, slogans, heroes, and ceremonies. Shared experiences also play a role in determining and shaping the culture of an organization. Team members who work long hours together to develop a major new product like the new Ford Thunderbird or who jointly experience a major crisis like dealing with the NBA strike frequently develop a common frame of reference and become a more cohesive work group.

Managing culture   Once created, culture can be very hard to change, but it can still be managed effectively. The key point is for managers to recognize the importance of culture and take appropriate steps to transmit the nature of that culture to others in the organization. For current organizational employees culture can be communicated through training, consistent behavior, and other organizational activities. For newcomers culture is most likely to be transmitted via orientation, training, and the telling and retelling of stories and corporate history. Sometimes something as simple as a slogan can be used to manage culture. For example, Schwinn, the venerable bicycle company, has been attempting to change its corporate culture. One of the mechanisms for enacting this change is the adoption of a new slogan: "Established 1895. Re-established 1994."[27]

Human resource managers may find that, depending on the circumstances, corporate culture may either facilitate or impede their work. If the firm has a strong and well-understood culture that seems attractive to people, human resource managers will often find it easier to attract and retain the most qualified employees. Southwest Airlines and Starbucks fall into this category, with each of these firms receiving large numbers of applications from prospective employees. And like other managers in these firms, the human resource managers have a clear understanding of what the organization stands for and how they are expected to contribute. But if the firm is perceived as having a weak or unattractive culture, fewer people may be interested in working there and its human resource managers may be unclear of their own role and mission.

The nature of the firm's culture also plays another important role in affecting human resource strategy. Specifically, if an organization has a strong culture and wishes to maintain it, one major means available for doing so is to select people who have values consistent with that culture. We discuss the role of "fit" later in the book, but for now it is important to note that some organizations select employees who best fit the organization's culture and image, even though they are not necessarily the most qualified of all applicants. In other words, these organizations might select individuals who are qualified enough to do the job, but who also share the values and beliefs of the firm's culture.

The Impact of Technology

The impact of technology also plays a key role in the formulation and implementation of the firm's human resource strategy. At the broadest level of analysis, an organization's technology can be described in terms of manufacturing versus service. **Manufacturing** is a form of business that combines and transforms resources into tangible outcomes that are then sold to others.[28] For example, General Motors buys raw materials, products, and parts from other companies and combines these to create cars and trucks that are then sold to individuals around the world. Manufacturing once dominated the U.S. economy. Foreign competition, however, has greatly reduced the importance of manufacturing relative to its once lofty position in the U.S. economy.

The other general form of technology is service operations. A **service** organization transforms resources into an intangible output and creates time or place utility for its customers.[29] For example, American Express sells few tangible products. Instead, the financial services company facilitates travel and credit purchase transactions for customers and thus provides time and place utility. The service sector now represents almost 75 percent of the U.S. economy and is responsible for almost 90 percent of all new job creation.[30]

The human resource function in manufacturing businesses is likely to be quite different from the same function in service businesses. Among other things, for example, the criteria used for hiring employees, the methods used for training employees, the reward system used to compensate employees, and labor relations with unionized employees are all likely to vary between these forms of organizational settings. Other aspects of technology are also important for human resource management. For example, automation—the process of designing work so that it can be completed or almost completely performed

■ **Manufacturing** is a form of business that combines and transforms resources into tangible outcomes that are then sold to others.

■ A **service** organization transforms resources into an intangible output and creates time or place utility for its customers.

by machines—is an important consideration. omputers and manufacturing, as well as robotics, are also important technological elements that affect human resource management. Rapid changes in technology play a major role in human resource management in terms of training, as well as selection, compensation, and other areas and functions.

The Impact of the Workforce

Labor trends and workforce composition also are an important part of the organizational environment of human resource management. Unionization, collective bargaining, and other labor issues are also especially relevant.

Workforce trends and issues   A number of changes in the workforce continue to emerge and affect human resource management. Decades ago the workforce in the United States was primarily male and primarily white. Now, however, the workforce is much more diverse in numerous ways.[31] For example, in earlier times most people followed a fairly predictable pattern of entering the workforce at a young age, maintaining a stable employment relationship for the period of their work lives, and then retiring at a fairly predictable age of sixty-five. But today these patterns and trends have changed. For example, the average age of the U.S. workforce is gradually increasing and will continue to do so.

A number of factors have contributed to this pattern. First, the baby-boom generation continues to age. Declining birth rates among the post-baby-boom generation are simultaneously accounting for a smaller percentage of new entrants into the workforce. Improved health and medical care also contributes to an aging workforce. People are simply able to maintain a productive work period for a longer time today. And finally, mandatory retirement ages have been raised or dropped altogether, allowing people to remain in the workforce for a longer period of time.

Gender differences in the workforce also play an important role. More and more women have entered the workforce, and their presence is felt in more and more occupational groupings that were traditionally dominated by men. By the year 2000 the composition of the workforce in the United States is predicted to be almost 50 percent female. Nevertheless, some critics still claim that a glass ceiling exists in some organizations. A *glass ceiling* refers to a transparent barrier that keeps women from progressing to higher levels in the organization. We explore this concept and related points more fully in Chapter 3.

Changing ethnicity is also reflected in the workforce today. The percentage of whites in the workforce is gradually dropping while the percentage of Hispanics in the workforce is climbing at an almost comparable rate. The percentage of blacks and Asians in the workforce is also growing but at a much smaller rate. In addition to age, gender, and ethnicity, other diversity forces are also affecting the workforce. For example, country of national origin is an important diversity dimension. Employees with disabilities and physically challenged employees now constitiute an important part of the workforce. And many others dimensions of diversity such as single-parent status, dual-career couples, gays and lesbians, people with special dietary preferences, and people with different political ideologies and viewpoints are each playing an important role in organizations today. We cover diversity more fully in Chapter 16.

Unionization and collective bargaining issues   Unionization and collective bargaining issues are also an important part of the organizational environment in which human resource management takes place. *Labor relations* is the process of dealing with employees who are represented by an employee association, usually called a union. Union membership in the United States has been gradually declining for the last several years but remains an important force in many industries. Furthermore, the success of the teamsters in their strike against United Parcel Service (UPS) in 1997, as well as other high-profile strikes such as the ones at General Motors and Northwest Airlines in 1998, may well encourage unions to renew their efforts to organize more workers. In any case unions can play an important role in formulating and implementing human resource strategy. For example, if management and union leaders do not work together, the union can be a major obstacle to making significant workplace changes. But on the other hand, a strong union can facilitate the same type of change if its leaders and the firm's management are working together productively. We cover unionization and collective bargaining in detail in Chapter 14.

THE BOTTOM LINE   Human resource management must be approached in a systematic and strategic manner. Formulating a human resource strategy encompasses the determination of staffing, development, and compensation strategies. In addition, the human resource manager must consider the impact of organization design, corporate culture, technology, labor trends, and the composition of the workforce.

HUMAN RESOURCE STRATEGY IMPLEMENTATION

After human resource managers have formulated their strategy—taking into consideration organization design, culture, technology, and the workforce—they can turn their attention to its actual implementation. As shown in Figure 2.1, strategy implementation involves the actions of individual employees (as manifested through various individual processes), groups of employees (as manifested through various interpersonal and group processes), and organizational systems and processes. Figure 2.4 illustrates these processes in more detail.

Individual Processes and Human Resource Management

Individual processes generally determine the performance effectiveness exhibited by each employee in a firm. The starting point for understanding individual processes is the psychological contract that an organization has with its employees. A **psychological contract** is the overall set of expectations held by an individual with respect to what he or she will contribute to the organization and what the organization, in turn, will provide to the individual.[32] Individuals see themselves as contributing their time, energy, effort, experience, and talent and expect to receive compensation, benefits, security, challenge, opportunities for promotion, and similar forms of rewards. Properly established and maintained psychological contracts are a fundamental starting point in ensuring that employees are committed to working toward organizational goals and contributing to organizational effectiveness by implementing the strategies that managers have developed.

■ A **psychological contract** is the overall set of expectations held by an individual with respect to what he or she will contribute to the organization and what the organization, in turn, will provide to the individual.

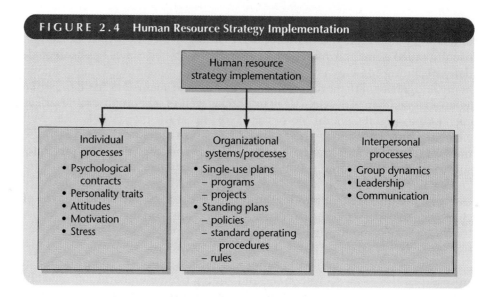

FIGURE 2.4 Human Resource Strategy Implementation

Human resource managers play an especially key role in how psychological contracts are formed and perceived. For example, it is usually human resource managers who explain to new employees how the compensation system and benefits programs work, when and how their performance will be evaluated, what to expect in terms of promotion and career opportunities, and so forth. And when the organization finds it necessary to change its agreements with its workers, human resource managers usually play a key role in communicating these changes to workers and are often seen by workers as the cause of such changes.[33] We explore psychological contracts more fully in Chapter 17.

Individual personality traits are also an important part of individual processes in an organization. Personality is the relatively stable set of psychological attributes or traits that distinguish one person from another. Some organizations believe that one or more particular personality traits may relate to how well an employee can perform a certain job or type of job. Self-esteem and agreeableness, for example, may be important traits for someone who will be working in a job that requires regular contact with the public. Conscientiousness may be an important trait for a worker who will be responsible for encoding and communicating critical information to other managers on a regular basis. Tolerance for ambiguity might be important for people who will be working in a job setting with little structure and guidance. Human resource managers are usually responsible for determining the best way to measure relevant personality traits in job applicants and for being able to verify that those measures—as well as the underlying traits—do indeed relate to job performance.

Attitudes also play an important role in implementing strategy in an organization. If people have positive attitudes toward their work and organization, they will be more committed to making contributions to organizational effectiveness and in helping achieve strategic goals. Workers with negative attitudes, on the other hand, are less likely to make this commitment and may be more inclined to be absent frequently and/or to seek employment elsewhere. Human resource managers are often called on to help other managers assess the attitudes of their workers by developing attitude surveys, administering those surveys to employees, and then interpreting and evaluating the results.

Perhaps the most important individual process in organizations, however, is motivation. Motivation is the set of forces that cause people to behave in certain ways and is a major determinant of individual performance. And again, motivational processes are clearly linked to the human resource function in any organization. For example, consider the motivational process that relates to equity perceptions. The equity theory of motivation suggests that a key ingredient in employee motivation is the extent to which people perceive that they are being treated equitably by their organizations, especially relative to other people. The human resource manager can contribute to perceptions of equity by, for example, clearly communicating to employees the precise basis used to determine compensation. If employees know, for example, that a particular salary level is a direct function of a college degree and four years of experience, they can objectively relate that fact to how other employees are compensated. On the other hand, if they have no real basis for understanding the company's compensation structure, they are more likely to attribute it to favoritism, office politics, or a similar subjective source.

Another important perspective on motivation is the expectancy theory. The expectancy theory suggests that motivation depends on how much we want something and how likely we think we are to get it. If people believe that certain behaviors (such as high-quality work behavior) will lead to specific valued outcomes (like a pay increase or praise from their supervisor), they are likely to try to exhibit those behaviors. But if they see little or no linkage between a behavior and a valued outcome, they may see little reason to exhibit the behavior. Human resource managers can capitalize on this perspective by trying to learn more about the goals that motivate individual workers and then helping those workers see how they can attain their goals by hard work and sustained contribution to the organization.

A final part of motivation is the reinforcement process. Reinforcement suggests that behavior that results in pleasant consequences is more likely to be repeated and that behavior that results in unpleasant consequences is less likely

A psychological contract represents the fundamental relationship between an employee and an organization. In today's fast-paced environment characterized by near-constant change and high turnover among employees, the psychological contracts between skilled craftspeople and their employers is especially important. For example, this worker is very carefully shaping the front end of a prototype for a new model of automobile. The exacting work can only be done by highly trained human hands and a careful eye. The organization, in return for this artistic diligence, allows the worker to take the time to do the job right and rewards the worker with appreciation and recognition of a job well done.

to be repeated. Thus when employees who work hard and help meet goals are recognized and rewarded for their efforts, they will likely continue to work hard. But if their hard work and effort is ignored or undervalued, they will choose different behaviors in the future. Human resource managers can play an important role in ensuring that rewards are linked to performance and that unacceptable behaviors like sexual harassment or excessive absenteeism result in unpleasant consequences such as a reprimand.

Still another important individual process in organizational settings is stress. Stress is a person's adaptive response to a stimulus that places excessive psychological or physical demands on that person. Important considerations for human resource managers include an understanding of the causes of stress, the processes by which stress affects individuals, and how organizations and individuals can better cope with stress in organizational settings. Human resource managers are increasingly being asked to help employees learn to cope with stress.

Interpersonal Processes and Human Resource Management

Of course, little behavior in organizations takes place in isolation. More typically, people work in a social context with coworkers, supervisors, and/or subordinates. Thus interpersonal processes are also important factors for human resource managers to understand. For example, many organizations today are grouping workers into work teams. Human resource managers may play an important role in deciding how these groupings occur and in helping to manage group dynamics after teams are formed. Thus an understanding of role structures within groups, group norms, cohesiveness, interpersonal communication, and interpersonal conflict can help the human resource manager better utilize the dynamics of teams and other groups as they work toward various strategic goals.

Leadership is also an important priority for many organizations. Most experts believe that effective leadership is vitally important to organizational success, yet they cannot agree on how to define, measure, or predict leadership. Human resource managers are expected to help identify potential leadership qualities among existing employees and to then help structure procedures for developing and enhancing those qualities. Obviously, then, these managers must have a basic understanding of leadership to help the organization achieve its goals.

A final important interpersonal process that is directly related to the implementation of human resource strategy is communication. Communication is the process by which two or more parties exchange information and share meaning. Written communication, oral communication, and nonverbal communication are pervasive in organizations. Electronic mail has become an especially important area of communication in recent years. In many organizations the human resource department is responsible for coordinating communication among employees through newsletters, bulletin boards, and so forth. The "Human Resources Tech Talk" box describes how some firms today are using so-called intranets to facilitate communication among employees. Clearly, then, human resource managers need to understand how to enhance communication to make sure that their efforts are indeed helping to implement their strategies.

Using Intranets to Enhance Communication

An "intranet" is essentially a miniature Internet created by and operated within the boundaries of a particular company or organization. Moving human resource functions onto the company intranet can improve service to all employees, help the human resource department interact with employees more effectively, and reduce many routine administrative costs. Employees with virtually any employment-related question—upcoming holiday work schedules, benefit options, training opportunities, for example—can use the company intranet to access the information they want, when and where they need it. And their questions are answered without requiring personal service, which is costly and often unnecessary.

Many companies have eliminated printing and distribution costs for employee manuals by replacing them with electronic versions. Other ways to decrease costs across the organization include switching from paper to

"Once you have an intranet, it's amazing how much you get done at work."

(Michele Wolpe, manager of communications, Silicon Graphics)*

electronic forms to request anything from vacation days to reallocating 401(K) holdings to annual benefits enrollment. In addition to the cost savings, many employees appreciate the ability to quickly and privately find out about changes that affect their lives.

Employers that effectively integrate human resource content into a company-wide intranet—rather than a stand-alone human resource site—provide a seamless and intuitively logical medium for employees to interact with the company and among themselves in a comfortable, relevant, and logical way. The benefits of this approach can be seen both in dollars added to the bottom line and in intangible, but vital, assets such as increased information sharing and improved morale.

Source: Martha Finney, "Harness the Power Within," *HR Magazine*, January 1997, pp. 66–74 (*quote on page 69); Patricia Gray, "How to Become Intranet Savvy," *HR Magazine*, December 1997, pp. 66–71.

Human resource managers must obviously have a keen understanding of both individual and interpersonal processes to be effective. For one thing these behavioral processes play a major role in determining the relative effectiveness of various human resource functions such as compensation, rewards, performance appraisal, and training and development. For another, all managers need to understand and appreciate these behavioral processes to better understand the actions of those with whom they work. And finally, human resource managers are often charged with the responsibility to develop and implement programs aimed at improving various behavioral processes. For example, the managers may be asked to overhaul the reward system to boost motivation and productivity, to develop training programs that teach workers how to cope with stress, or to help identify ways to improve interpersonal communication or resolve interpersonal conflict.

THE BOTTOM LINE Successfully implementing human resource strategy generally relies on various individual and interpersonal processes in the organization. Key individual processes include psychological contracts, individual personality traits, employee attitudes, motivation, and stress. Interpersonal processes include group behavior, leadership, and communication. Human resource managers are also often involved in various efforts to understand, direct or focus, or change these individual and interpersonal processes and must therefore have a thorough knowledge of each one, as well as an understanding of the interrelationships among them.

EVALUATING THE HUMAN RESOURCE FUNCTION IN ORGANIZATIONS

Evaluating the effectiveness of the human resource function has emerged as an important trend in recent years. Human resource management was historically seen as an organizational cost or expense. That is, the organization budgeted a certain amount of money to spend on the management of its human resource function. As long as the human resource manager stayed within this budget, things were generally assumed to be fine. More recently, however, many organizations have come to view human resource management in a different light. Specifically, because so many human resource management functions can now be subcontracted or outsourced to external vendors, as discussed in Chapter 1, organizations are paying more attention to the actual costs and value of an in-house human resource management function. Further, a variety of approaches are being used in an attempt to measure the costs and benefits of specific human resource functions. Line managers may even be given the option of choosing to use the corporation's human resource department for various functions or to subcontract those functions to external vendors. We deal with the evaluation of specific human resource functions at the conclusion of many chapters in this book.

In addition to the evaluation of specific human resource functions, however, another recent trend has been toward evaluating entire systems of human resource activities. Some evidence suggests that organizations that adopt certain sets of human resource practices tend to be more successful than organizations that adopt different sets of practices. Although the specific practices under investigation differ somewhat from study to study—practices that have been termed, for example, **high-performance work systems**—evidence seems to be mounting that organizations that follow these more "enlightened" practices in human resources are actually more profitable than other organizations.[34] In this view human resource practices are seen as competitive activities that may allow a firm to utilize its human resources in ways that create a stronger competitive advantage relative to other firms.

■ **High-performance work systems** rely on a set of best practices to use human resources to gain a meaningful competitive advantage.

This perspective also suggests a new approach to the evaluation of human resource activities. Rather than show how a specific human resource practice (for example, using certain types of tests to select new employees) results in higher levels of productivity, this approach suggests that "bundles" of human resource practices are related more clearly to a firm's performance. This view even implies that organizational strategy and human resource practices are not really related at all, because all organizations will be more competitive if they adopt the right set of practices. A number of issues remain, of course—for example, we need to better understand exactly *how* these practices may lead to improved performance, and we need to come to some agreement about exactly what practices can be considered as part of a high-performance work system. But these issues aside, firms that adopt practices such as those illustrated in Table 2.1 may potentially outperform other firms.[35]

These examples are derived from several research studies and are typical of what are often suggested as high-performance work activities. They are also, unfortunately, quite broad and cover numerous elements. For example, as we will see in Chapter 8, formal performance appraisals can take many forms. Although it may be better to have *some* formal appraisal than to have none at all, it is also likely to be true that different types of appraisal systems will lead to

TABLE 2.1	Human Resource Practices That May Lead to Improved Firm Performance

Self-Directed Work Teams

Attitude surveys

Information sharing (e.g., newsletters)

Contingent pay

Favorable selection ratio (i.e., many applicants for each opening)

Formal performance appraisal

Social events

different outcomes. Likewise, although it might be preferable to make pay contingent on *something*, exactly what pay should be contingent on is probably important as well. Therefore, perhaps the reason that these practices are sometimes advocated as "best," without regard to strategic goals, is because they are so broad. Further, perhaps these practices are actually *too* broad in basic terms to be really useful to organizations; thus if the practices were defined more narrowly, we might well find that their success does depend on the organization's strategy. In general, however, there is reason to believe that an organization can be more competitive if it adopts these practices, and this attitude represents a new way of evaluating a firm's human resource practices.

THE BOTTOM LINE Organizations and managers are appropriately focusing attention on the evaluation of various functions and activities, including human resource management. But much remains to be learned before any definitive conclusions can be reached regarding either which practices to evaluate or how to best evaluate them.

Chapter Summary

The strategic context of human resource management plays an important role in determining the effectiveness of not only the human resource function but also the entire organization. Understanding the organization's purpose and mission guide human resource managers as they formulate their strategy. They must also recognize the role of the top management team.

Top managers use SWOT analysis to formulate corporate, business, and functional strategies. As part of this process, the current status of an organization's human resources can be a critical organizational strength or weakness. Corporate strategy considers which markets or businesses the firm intends to address, whereas business strategy deals with competitive issues within a particular market or business. The firm's human resource strategy is an important functional strategy that must be integrated with marketing, finance, operations, and other relevant functional strategies.

The process of formulating human resource strategy results in separate but consistent strategies for staffing, employee development, and compensation. Further, to enact human resource strategy effectively, it must be closely coordinated with the particular form of organization design the firm adopts, the culture it creates, the technologies it employs, and a variety of workforce characteristics.

The implementation of human resource strategy requires an understanding of fundamental individual and interpersonal behavioral processes. Individual processes include psychological contracts, individual personality traits, employee attitudes, motivation, and stress. Interpersonal processes include group behavior, leadership, and communication.

Further, managers should attempt to evaluate the effectiveness of the human resource function and its role in helping the organization attain its strategic goals. This evaluation usually focuses on specific human resource practices. However, recent evidence suggests that bundles of so-called best practices may also be a viable approach.

Review and Discussion Questions

1. Discuss the influence of organizational purpose, organizational mission, and the top management team on human resource strategy.

2. Distinguish between corporate, business, and functional strategies. How does each general level of strategy relate to human resource management?

3. Specify the circumstances under which a firm's human resources might be seen as an organizational strength as part of a SWOT analysis. Specify the circumstances under which human resources might be seen as a weakness.

4. Discuss how the specific corporate strategies relate to human resource management.

5. Discuss how the specific business strategies relate to human resource management.

6. What would be the advantages and disadvantages to an individual who accepts a job as a human resource manager in a firm that is in the midst of a retrenchment corporate strategy? How about a reactor business strategy?

7. If you were hired as a human resource manager in a large firm in which the human resource function was poorly integrated with other functional areas, what steps might you take to improve this integration?

8. Explain how an organization's design, culture, technology, and workforce issues are related to human resource management.

9. How does the firm's human resource strategy interact with other functional strategies and with the strategic leadership of top management to affect organizational effectiveness?

10. Why is it important for all managers to understand behavioral forces in organizations? Why might it be especially important for human resource managers to understand these forces?

Closing Case

Blending Strategy and People at Chaparral Steel

Although few people may have heard of Chaparral Steel Corporation, the company enjoys a stellar reputation as one of the most effective firms in the steel industry. Chaparral was founded in 1973 in a small town south of Dallas and today enjoys annual sales of almost $500 million. In earlier times most steel companies were large, bureaucratic operations like U.S. Steel (now USX) and Bethlehem Steel. However, increased competition from low-cost foreign steel firms—especially those in Japan and Korea—has caused major problems for these manufacturers with their high overhead costs and inflexible modes of operation.

These competitive pressures, in turn, have also led to the formation of so-called minimills like Chaparral. These minimills are consciously designed to be much smaller and more flexible than the traditional steel giants. Because of their size, technology, and flexibility, these firms are able to maintain much lower production costs and to respond more quickly to customer requests. And today Chaparral is recognized as one of the best of this new breed of steel companies. For example, although most mills produce one ton of steel with an average of 3 to 5 hours of labor, Chaparral produces a ton with less than 1.4 hours of labor. Chaparral has also successfully avoided all efforts to unionize its employees.

Since its inception, Chaparral has been led by Gordon Forward. Forward knew that for Chaparral to succeed with what was then a new strategic orientation in the industry it would also need to be managed in new and different ways. One of the first things he decided to do as a part of his new approach was to systematically avoid the traditional barriers that tend to be created between management and labor, especially in older industries like steel. For example, he mandated that there would be neither reserved parking spaces in the parking lot nor a separate dining area inside the plant for managers. Everyone dresses casually at the work site, and people throughout the firm are on a first-name basis with one another. Workers take their lunch and coffee breaks whenever they choose, and the coffee is even provided free for everyone!

Forward also insisted that all employees be paid on a salary basis—no time clocks or time sheets for anyone, from the president down to the custodians. Workers are organized into teams, and each team selects its own "leader." The teams also interview and select new members, as needed, and are responsible for planning their own work, setting their own work schedules, and even allocating vacation days among themselves. And teams are also responsible for implementing any disciplinary actions that need to be taken toward a member.

Forward clearly believes in trusting everyone in the organization. For example, when the firm recently needed a new rolling mill lathe, Chaparral budgeted $1 million for the purchase and then put the purchase decision in the hands of an operating machinist. This machinist, in turn, investigated various options, visited other mills in Japan and Europe, and then recommended an alternative piece of machinery costing less than half of the budgeted amount. Forward also helped pioneer an innovative concept called "open book management"—any employee at Chaparral can see any document, record, or other piece of information at any time and for any reason.

Chaparral also recognizes the importance of investing in and rewarding people. Continuous education is an integral part of the firm's culture, with a variety of classes being offered all the time. For example, one recent slate of classes included metallurgy, electronics, finance, and English. The classes are intended to be of value to both individual workers and to the organization as a whole. The classes are scheduled on site and in the evening. Some include community-college credit (there are tuition charges for these classes, although the company pays half the cost), and others are noncredit only (these classes are free). Forward has a goal that at any given time at least 85 percent of Chaparral's employees will be enrolled in at least one class.

Everyone also participates in the good—and bad—times at Chaparral. For example, all workers have a guaranteed base salary that is basically adequate, but which, by itself, is below the standard market rate. In addition, however, each employee gets a pay-for-performance bonus based on his or her individual achievements. Finally, companywide bonuses are paid to everyone on a quarterly basis. These bonuses are tied to overall company performance. The typical bonuses increase an employee's total compensation to a level well above the standard market rate. Thus hard work and dedication on everyone's part means that everyone can benefit.

Case Questions

1. Describe the strategic context of human resource management at Chaparral Steel.

2. How do organization design, corporate culture, technology, and workforce issues relate to human resource management at Chaparral?

3. What are the apparent roles of individual and interpersonal processes at Chaparral?

Sources: John Case, "HR Learns How to Open the Books," *HRMagazine*, May 1998, pp. 70–76; John Case, "Opening the Books," *Harvard Business Review*, March–April 1997, pp. 118–129; Brian Dumaine, "Chaparral Steel: Unleash Workers and Cut Costs," *Fortune*, May 18, 1992, pp. 88; Ricky W. Griffin and Ronald J. Ebert, *Business Essentials*, 2nd ed. (Englewood Cliffs, N.J.: Prentice-Hall, 1998), p. 119.

Building Human Resource Management Skills

Purpose: The purpose of this exercise is to enhance your appreciation of the linkages among human resource strategy and corporate, business, and other functional strategies.

Step 1: Your instructor will divide the class into small groups of four or five members each. Read the introductory scenario below and then proceed through the remaining steps in order. Develop brief, overview answers to the various questions.

The Situation: Your group has just been hired as the top management team for a midsize firm. The firm has been floundering in recent years—market share and profits have dropped, morale is low, and the firm's stock price is at an all-time low. The board of directors has come to realize that a retrenchment is needed to turn the firm around. Thus the board fired the old team, hired your team, and has given you total responsibility for the anticipated turnaround. The facts are as follows: your firm has been making home appliances such as refrigerators, stoves, and microwaves. Ten years ago the company had 20 percent of the market, had annual revenues of $500 million, and had a workforce of fifteen thousand employees. Today the company has 7 percent of the market, annual revenues of less than $300 million, and a workforce of 14,500. (No new employees have been hired in three years, but few have left.) As a first step the board wants your group to trim the workforce, improve product quality, and develop a better marketing strategy. Longer term, the board wants the firm to diversify into other, less competitive markets.

Step 2: Identify three fundamental human resource strategy issues, challenges, and opportunities currently facing your firm.

Step 3: Fast forward five years: your turnaround has been successful. The firm has increased its market share to more than 15 percent, sales are more than $450 million, and the workforce has been trimmed. Things are looking bright, but your team and the board believe that it is still a bit soon to launch a diversification effort. Identify three fundamental human resource strategy issues, challenges, and opportunities facing your firm now.

Step 4: Fast forward another five years: your firm has continued to prosper and has just launched a diversification program. The core business now has almost 25 percent of the home-appliance business, sales are approaching $750 million, and the workforce has grown to almost twenty thousand employees. As first steps in diversification, the firm has bought another firm that makes home-electronic products (televisions, stereos, and so on) and is starting its own new small-appliances business (can openers, coffee makers, and so on). Identify three fundamental human resource strategy issues, challenges, and opportunities facing your firm now.

Step 5: Fast forward another five years: your firm has continued to prosper and now sees itself as a mature, diversified home-products company. In addition to the businesses already noted, your company also now owns businesses that make telephones and related communication equipment (facsimile machines, copiers), run cable-related television operations (regional cable television companies, pay-per-view businesses), and sell automotive accessories (CD players, portable facsimile machines). But your management team believes that the firm has now entered a period of stability. Little new growth is foreseen, for instance, and the company wants to maintain its status quo for the next few years. Identify three fundamental human resource strategy issues, challenges, and opportunities facing your firm now.

Step 6: Report your ideas and suggestions through whatever form your instructor assigns (in-class presentations, written notes to be turned in, general discussion).

Ethical Dilemmas in Human Resource Management

 Assume that you are a project manager in the human resource department for a large manufacturing business. All told, your firm's human resource department employs about 120 people. As part of a strategy calling for related diversification, the firm has recently announced a merger with one of its largest competitors. That firm has about one hundred people in its human resource department. Your firm will be the dominant partner in the merger, controlling 56 percent of the new enterprise.

Your boss just informed you that you will be responsible for developing plans to integrate the two human resource departments during the merger. The boss estimates that the new, combined department will need about 160 people, necessitating a layoff of about 60 people. Your most critical task, therefore, will be to decide who stays and who has to leave. Your boss has given you clear and unambiguous written instructions that you are to select the best people possible from the two current departments, regardless of current affiliation. However, after giving you these instructions, your boss also said softly, "Of course, we should try to take care of as many of our own people as we can."

Questions

1. What are the ethical issues in this situation?

2. What criteria might you find it necessary to use in making decisions?

3. What are your personal feelings about how to prioritize individual employees in a situation like this?

Human Resource Internet Exercise

 AT&T maintains what it calls a "Factbook" on the Internet. Its Web address is **http://www.att.com/factbook/**. The Factbook includes a wide array of information about the firm, its mission, its strategy, and other elements of its operations. It also has information about careers and jobs at AT&T.

Visit the Web site and read and study the information that you find. Focus especially on information regarding the firm's strategy and its human resource. Use the information you find to answer the following questions.

Questions

1. What relationships, if any, do you see between AT&T's corporate or business strategies and its human resource strategy?

2. This chapter suggests that overall strategy affects human resource strategy and that human resource strategy also affects overall strategy. Can you make any inferences about which of these two viewpoints AT&T seems to have adopted?

3. If AT&T changed its corporate or business strategies, would it necessarily have to change its human resource strategy? Why or why not?

Notes

1. Charles R. Greer, *Strategy and Human Resources* (Englewood Cliffs, N.J.: Prentice-Hall, 1995). See also David P. Lepak and Scott A. Snell, "The Human Resource Architecture: Toward a Theory of Human Capital Allocation and Development," *Academy of Management Review*, Vol. 24, 1999, pp. 31–48.

2. See Charles W. L. Hill and Gareth R. Jones, *Strategic Management: An Integrated Approach*, 4th ed. (Boston: Houghton Mifflin, 1998).

3. Janine Nahapiet and Sumantra Ghoshal, "Social Capital, Intellectual Capital, and the Organizational Advantage," *Academy of Management Review*, Vol. 23, 1998, pp. 242–266.

4. Catherine M. Daily and Charles Schwenk, "Chief Operating Officers, Top Management Teams, and Boards of Directors: Congruent or Countervailing Forces?" *Journal of Management*, 1996, Vol. 22, No. 2, pp. 185–208.

5. S. A. Kirkpatrick and Edwin A. Locke, "Direct and Indirect Effects of Three Core Charismatic Leadership Components on Performance and Attitudes, *Journal of Applied Psychology*, Vol. 81, 1996, pp. 36–51; see also Harry G. Barkema and Luis R. Gomez-Mejia, "Managerial Compensation and Firm Performance: A General Research Framework," *Academy of Management Journal*, Vol. 41, 1998, pp. 135–145.

6. Shelly Brauch, "The 100 Best Companies to Work For in America," *Fortune*, January 11, 1999, pp. 118–144; Hugh Menzies, "The Ten Toughest Bosses," *Fortune*, April 21, 1980, pp. 62–74.

7. Hill and Jones, *Strategic Management: An Integrated Approach*.

8. Brian Becker and Barry Gerhart, "The Impact of Human Resource Management on Organizational Performance: Progress and Prospects," *Academy of Management Journal*, August 1996, pp. 779–801.

9. Kenneth Andrews, *The Concept of Corporate Strategy*, rev. ed. (Homewood, Ill.: Dow Jones-Irwin, 1980).

10. "Go-Go Goliaths," *Business Week*, February 64, 1995, pp. 64–70.

11. David M. Schweiger and James P. Walsh, "Mergers and Acquisitions: An Interdisciplinary View," in Kenneth Rowland and Gerald Ferris (eds.), *Research in Personnel and Human Resource Management*, Vol. 8 (Greenwich, Conn.: JAI Press, 1990), pp. 41–107.

12. David M. Schweiger and Angelo DeNisi, "Communications with Employees Following a Merger: A Longitudinal Field Study," *Academy of Management Journal*, Vol. 34, 1991, pp. 110–135.

13. Hill and Jones, *Strategic Management: An Integrated Approach*.

14. Jay Barney and Ricky W. Griffin, *The Management of Organizations* (Boston: Houghton Mifflin, 1992).

15. Russell A. Eisenstat, "What Corporate Human Resources Brings to the Picnic: Four Models for Functional Management," *Organizational Dynamics*, Autumn 1996, pp. 7–21.

16. John O. Whitney, "Strategic Renewal for Business Units," *Harvard Business Review*, July–August 1996, pp. 84–98.

17. Raymond E. Miles and Charles C. Snow, *Organizational Strategy, Structure, and Process* (New York: McGraw-Hill, 1978).

18. Michael Porter, *Competitive Strategy* (New York: Free Press, 1980).

19. Robert L. Cardy and Gregory H. Dobbins, "Human Resource Management in a Total Quality Organizational Environment: Shifting from a Traditional to a TQHRM Approach," *Journal of Quality Management*, Vol. 1, No. 1, 1996, pp. 5–20.

20. Henry Mintzberg, "Patterns in Strategy Formulation," *Management Science*, October 1978, pp. 934–948.

21. Edilberto F. Montemayor, "Congruence between Pay Policy and Competitive Strategy in High-Performing Firms," *Journal of Management*, Vol. 22, No. 6, 1996, pp. 889–912.

22. Peter Bamberger and Avi Fiegenbaum, "The Role of Strategic Reference Points in Explaining the Nature and Consequences of Human Resource Strategy," *Academy of Management Review*, October 1996, pp. 926–958.

23. Richard L. Daft, *Organization Theory and Design*, 6th ed. (Cincinnati, Ohio: South-Western, 1998).

24. John Purcell and Bruce Ahlstrand, *Human Resource Management in the Multidividual Company* (Oxford: Oxford University Press, 1994).

25. Terrence E. Deal and Allan A. Kennedy, *Corporate Cultures: The Rights and Rituals of Corporate Life* (Reading, Mass.: Addison-Wesley, 1982).

26. Jay Barney, "Organizational Culture: Can It Be a Source of Sustained Competitive Advantage?" *Academy of Management Review*, July 1986, pp. 656–665.

27. "Pump, Pump, Pump at Schwinn," *Business Week*, August 23, 1994, p. 79.

28. Paul M. Swamidass, "Empirical Science: New Frontiers in Operations Management Research," *Academy of Management Review*, October 1991, pp. 793–814.

29. Richard B. Chase and Warren J. Erikson, "The Service Factory," *The Academy of Management Executive*, August 1988, pp. 191–196.

30. Brian O'Reilly, "The New Face of Small Business," *Fortune*, May 2, 1994, pp. 82–88.

31. Taylor H. Cox and Stacy Blake, "Managing Cultural Diversity: Implications for Organizational Competitiveness," *Academy of Management Executive*, August 1991, pp. 45–56.

32. Denise Rousseau, "Changing the Deal While Keeping the People," *Academy of Management Executive*, February 1996, pp. 50–61.

33. Elizabeth Wolfe Morrison and Sandra L. Robinson, "When Employees Feel Betrayed: A Model of How Psychological Contract Violation Develops," *Academy of Management Review*, January 1997, pp. 226–256; Sandra Robinson, Matthew Kraatz, and Denise Rousseau, "Changing Obligations and the Psychological Contract," *Academy of Management Journal*, 1994, Vol. 37, No. 1, pp. 137–152.

34. Mark A. Huselid, "The Impact of Human Resource Management Practices on Turnover, Productivity, and Corporate Financial Reporting," *Academy of Management Journal*, Vol. 38, 1995, pp. 635–672.

35. Brian Becker and Barry Gerhart, "The Impact of Human Resource Management on Organizational Performance: Progress and Prospects," *Academy of Management Journal*, Vol. 39, 1996, pp. 779–801.

3

The Legal Environment

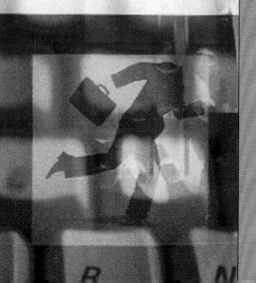

CHAPTER OUTLINE

The Legal Context of Human Resource Management
The Regulatory Environment of Human Resource Management
Basic Areas of Legal Regulation

Equal Employment Opportunity
Discrimination and Equal Employment Opportunity
Protected Classes in the Workforce
Equal Employment Opportunity Legislation
Enforcing Equal Employment Opportunity

Legal Issues in Compensation
Legal Perspectives on Total Compensation
Legal Perspectives on Other Forms of Compensation

Legal Issues in Labor Relations
Unionization and the Law
Collective Bargaining and the Law

Emerging Legal Issues in Human Resource Management
Employee Safety and Health
Emerging Areas of Discrimination Law
Employment-at-Will
Ethics and Human Resource Management

Evaluating Legal Compliance

CHAPTER OBJECTIVES

After studying this chapter you should be able to:

■ Describe the legal context of human resource management.

■ Identify key laws that prohibit discrimination in the workplace and discuss equal employment opportunity.

■ Discuss legal issues in compensation.

■ Discuss legal issues in labor relations.

■ Describe several emerging legal issues in human resource management.

It's a fact of life in the coaching profession that job security is a tenuous thing. For the most part, if teams win enough games, the coaches keep their jobs. But if teams struggle and fail to meet expectations, the coaches usually take the fall. It's also a fact of life, however, that most of the laws that govern employment relationships at Exxon, Microsoft, and other businesses also apply to the New York Yankees baseball team, the Notre Dame football program, and other professional and college athletic programs. And the University of Notre Dame recently learned this lesson the hard way!

The job of head coach at Notre Dame is clearly one of the most stressful jobs in the world. The loyalty and dedication of Fighting Irish fans is legendary, and these fans expect—indeed, demand—nothing but the best from their team. Only a top national ranking and major post-season bowl appearance define success for the team, with the consistent goal of contending for the national championship. And every Fighting Irish game is nationally televised and extensively covered in major media outlets across the country, so the team, its players, and its coaches are always in the public eye.

The latest head coach at Notre Dame is Bob Davie. Davie was the team's former defensive coordinator under Lou Holtz and was awarded the top spot when Holtz retired after the 1996 season. At the time of the changeover, the football team's performance was already declining, and Davie knew he had to do something quickly to get things back on track. One of his first priorities was to review his coaching staff, a process that ended with the firing of Joe Moore, the team's sixty-four-year-old offensive line coach, on December 2, 1996.

Moore subsequently filed a lawsuit against Notre Dame, claiming that the basis for his termination was age discrimination. Davie and Notre Dame, for their part,

"Let's face it—he's 64 years old."

(Notre Dame football coach Bob Davie)*

contended that age had played no role in Moore's termination, so the case eventually wound its way to the courtroom. The primary basis for Moore's claim of age discrimination was comments Davie had made about the firing that included key references to Moore's age. For example, Davie told a former graduate assistant, "Let's face it—he's 64 years old."

The university, meanwhile, argued that Moore was fired because of his abusive behavior toward some of the players. In addition, defense attorneys argued, Davie had heard that Moore was planning to retire in another year or two and so was just trying to maintain continuity in his coaching staff. Unfortunately for the defense, U.S. District Judge Allen Sharp subsequently informed the jury that continuity is not a legitimate reason for termination, especially if the individual is expected to retire soon.

When the jury handed down its verdict in July 1998, Notre Dame and Bob Davie were indeed found to have violated the Age Discrimination in Employment Act. Moore was awarded $42,935.28 in back pay; that amount was then doubled by the additional jury finding that Notre Dame had knowingly disregarded the law. The university was also ordered to pay for Moore's legal and related court costs. All in all, then, this case resulted in another big loss for the Irish. University officials, Davie, and Irish fans everywhere only hope that when the spotlight turns back to the gridiron that team members can put all this behind them and get back to their winning ways.

"Jury: Notre Dame Guilty of Age Discrimination," *Charlotte Observer*, July 16, 1998, pp. 1B, 8B (*quote on page 8B); "Notre Dame Found Guilty of Age Discrimination," Associated Press, July 15, 1998; "Jury Finds Notre Dame Guilty," *Houston Chronicle*, July 16, 1998, p. 10.

Like virtually every other organization today, the University of Notre Dame must adhere to the laws and regulations that govern its employment practices. In general, organizations try to follow such laws and regulations for a variety of reasons. One reason is an inherent commitment in most organizations to ethical and socially responsible behavior. Another is to avoid the direct costs and bad publicity that might result from lawsuits brought against the organization if those laws and regulations are broken. Throughout the trial, for example, Notre Dame was a popular topic in the media, with most experts agreeing that the university's image was clearly tarnished. As we will see, failure to follow the law, even if due to a well-intentioned misunderstanding, can be enormously costly to an organization.

As we noted in Chapter 1, the proliferation of laws and regulations affecting employment practices in the 1960s was a key reason for the emergence of human resource management as a vital organizational function. Managing within the complex legal environment that affects human resource practices requires a full understanding of that legal environment and the ability to ensure that others within the organization understand it as well.[1] This chapter is devoted to the legal environment of human resource management. We first establish the legal context of human resource management. We then focus on perhaps the most important area of this legal context, equal employment opportunity. Two subsequent sections introduce legal issues in compensation and in labor relations. A variety of emerging legal issues are then introduced and discussed. We conclude by summarizing ways that many organizations evaluate their own legal compliance.

THE LEGAL CONTEXT OF HUMAN RESOURCE MANAGEMENT

Various forces shape the legal context of human resource management. The catalyst for modifying or enhancing the legal context may be legislative initiative, social change, or judicial rulings. Governmental agencies pass laws that affect human resource practices, for example, and the courts interpret those laws as they apply to specific circumstances and situations. Thus the regulatory environment itself is quite complex and affects a variety of different areas within the human resource management process.[2]

The Regulatory Environment of Human Resource Management

The legal and regulatory environment of human resource management in the United States emerges as a result of a three-step process, starting with the actual creation of new regulation. This regulation can come in the form of new laws or statutes passed by national, state, or local government bodies but, in reality, generally starts at the national level. State and local regulations are more likely to extend or modify national regulations than they are to create new ones. The courts also play a role in dictating federal regulation. In addition, as we will see later, the president of the United States can also create regulations that apply to specific situations.

The second step in the regulation process is the enforcement of these regulations. Occasionally the laws themselves provide for enforcement through the creation of special agencies or other forms of regulatory groups. In other situations enforcement might be assigned to an existing agency, such as the Department of Labor. The court system also interprets laws that the government passes and provides another vehicle for enforcement. To be effective, an enforcing agency must have an appropriate degree of power. The ability to levy fines or bring lawsuits against firms that violate the law are among the most powerful tools provided to the various agencies charged with enforcing human resource regulations.

The third step in the regulation process is the actual practice and implementation of those regulations in organizations. That is, organizations and managers must implement and follow the guidelines that the government has passed and that the courts and regulatory agencies attempt to enforce. In many cases following regulations is a logical and straightforward process. In some cases, however, a regulation may be unintentionally ambiguous or be interpreted by the courts in new ways. Regardless of the clarity of the regulation, the actual process of implementing and demonstrating adherence to it may take an extended period of time. Thus organizations are sometimes put into the difficult position of being unsure of how to follow a particular regulation and/or need an extended period of time to achieve full compliance. "The Lighter Side of HR" further highlights this point!

> **The Lighter Side of HR**
>
> The regulatory environment of human resource management imposes numerous constraints on organizations. Laws regarding employment practices have become so complicated in recent years that many employers are unsure of their own rights when it comes to hiring or terminating employees. For example, a firm that uses discriminatory practices can be sued for not hiring someone or for firing a current employee. But the firm can also be liable if it should reject or fire someone but fails to do so! Not surprisingly, then, many employment decisions today are routinely reviewed by human resource experts and/or attorneys. And the opinions of these experts and attorneys often determine whether or not someone will be hired or fired.

"I've been speaking to my attorneys, Larson, and this time we think we've got you fired."

Basic Areas of Legal Regulation

Regulations exist in virtually every aspect of the employment relationship. As illustrated in Figure 3.1, equal employment opportunity law intended to protect individuals from illegal discrimination is the most fundamental and far-reaching area of the legal regulation of human resource management. Indeed, in one way or another, virtually every law and statute governing employment relationships is attempting to ensure equal employment opportunity in some way or other. In addition, however, certain related areas of regulation have an identity beyond equal employment opportunity. As also shown in Figure 3.1, these include protection against illegal discrimination against current employees with regard to performance appraisal, promotion opportunities, and various other dimensions of the employment relationship. In addition, several related legal issues warrant separate discussion.

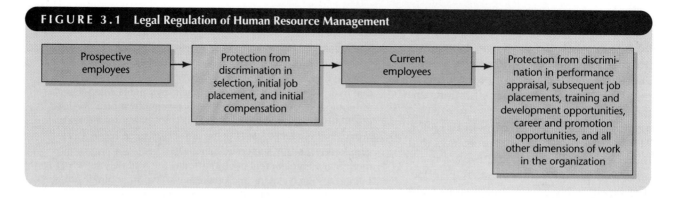

FIGURE 3.1   **Legal Regulation of Human Resource Management**

Prospective employees → Protection from discrimination in selection, initial job placement, and initial compensation → Current employees → Protection from discrimination in performance appraisal, subsequent job placements, training and development opportunities, career and promotion opportunities, and all other dimensions of work in the organization

THE BOTTOM LINE   All managers need to understand the basic legal context of human resource management. Specifically, they should be familiar with the regulatory environment of human resource management as well as the basic areas of legal regulation that affect their actions. Serving as the center of expertise in areas related to the legal context in general and legal regulation in particular is especially important for an organization's human resource function.

EQUAL EMPLOYMENT OPPORTUNITY

Some managers assume that the legal regulation of human resource management is a relatively recent phenomenon. In reality, however, even though the specific context for most current issues goes back only to the early 1960s, concerns about equal opportunity can actually be traced to the Thirteenth and Fourteenth Amendments to the Constitution of the United States. The Thirteenth Amendment, passed in 1865, abolished slavery, and the Fourteenth Amendment, passed in 1868, made it illegal for government to take the life, liberty, or property of individuals without due process of law. The Fourteenth Amendment goes on to specifically prohibit states from denying equal protection to their residents.

The Fourteenth Amendment originally applied only to black citizens of the United States but was eventually broadened by various judicial decisions and interpretations to include other groups such as Asians and other immigrants. Most recently it has been applied to the concept of reverse discrimination, wherein white citizens argue that they have been discriminated against by agencies going too far in their efforts to provide equal opportunity to minorities.[3] It is also important to note, however, that the Fourteenth Amendment relates only to so-called state actions. That is, it applies only to the actions of governments or to private groups deemed to be state agents and thus does not specifically apply to private employers.

The Reconstruction Civil Rights Acts of 1866 and 1871 extended protection offered to people under the Thirteenth and Fourteenth Amendments. For example, the Reconstruction Civil Rights Act of 1866 granted all persons in the United States the same property rights as its white citizens then held. The Reconstruction Civil Rights Act of 1871 granted all U.S. citizens the right to sue in federal court if they believe they have been deprived of their civil rights. Even though these laws are more than one hundred years old, they still form the basis for federal court actions that involve the payment of compensatory and punitive damage.[4]

Discrimination and Equal Employment Opportunity

The basic goal of all equal employment opportunity regulation is to protect people from unfair or inappropriate discrimination in the workplace.[5] Interestingly, most laws passed to eliminate discrimination do not explicitly define that term. It is also instructive to note that discrimination per se is not illegal. Whenever one person is given a pay raise and another is not, for example, the organization has made a decision to differentiate the first person from the second. As long as the basis for this discrimination is purely job related, however, such as on the basis of performance or seniority, and is applied objectively and consistently, such actions are legal and appropriate. Problems arise, though, when differentiation among people is not job related, and in such cases the resulting discrimination is illegal. Various court decisions and basic inferences from the language of various laws suggest that **illegal discrimination** is what results from behaviors or actions by an organization or managers within an organization that cause members of a protected class to be unfairly differentiated from others. (We discuss protected classes later.) Figure 3.2 shows various kinds of illegal discrimination.

Disparate treatment **Disparate treatment** discrimination exists when individuals in similar situations are treated differently and when the differential treatment is based on the individual's race, color, religion, sex, national origin, age, or disability status. For example, if two people with the same qualifications for the job apply for a promotion and the organization decides whom to promote based on one individual's religious beliefs, the individual not promoted is a victim of disparate treatment discrimination. To prove discrimination in this situation, an individual filing a charge must demonstrate that there was a discriminatory motive. Specifically, the individual must prove that the organization intended consciously to discriminate against that individual in one or more aspects of an employment relationship.

One circumstance in which organizations can legitimately treat members of different groups differently is when a **bona fide occupational qualification** (**BFOQ**) exists for performing a particular job such that sex, age, or other personal characteristic legitimately affects a person's ability to perform the job. For example, a producer casting a new play or movie can legally refuse to hire an older person to play a role that is expressly written for a very young person.

> ▨ **Illegal discrimination** is what results from behaviors or actions by an organization or managers within an organization that cause members of a protected class to be unfairly differentiated from others.

> ▨ **Disparate treatment** discrimination exists when individuals in similar situations are treated differently and when the differential treatment is based on the individual's race, color, religion, sex, national origin, age, or disability status.

> ▨ A **bona fide occupational qualification** (**BFOQ**) is a characteristic without which a person cannot perform the job effectively. These might include race or sex for some jobs, or might include minimum visual ability or strength.

FIGURE 3.2 **Forms of Illegal Discrimination**

There are actually very few BFOQs, however. For example, it is illegal for a restaurant to hire only young, attractive people as servers based on the argument that that's what its customers prefer. In fact, customer and/or client preference can *never* be the basis of a BFOQ. Therefore, an organization relying on a BFOQ to eliminate certain individuals from consideration must be sure that it is using necessary—not just preferred—criteria for selecting individuals.

■ **Disparate impact** discrimination occurs when an apparently neutral employment practice disproportionately excludes a protected group from employment opportunities.

Disparate impact   A second form of discrimination is disparate impact. **Disparate impact** discrimination occurs when an apparently neutral employment practice disproportionately excludes a protected group from employment opportunities. For example, suppose an organization gives all applicants an employment test before making selection decisions and then uses scores from that test to decide whom to hire. In addition, while the organization may not have any apparent discriminatory hiring practices against women, further suppose that the employment test is structured so that most women generally perform more poorly than do men on the test. This would be an example of disparate impact in that the organization has no direct intention to discriminate against women, but the use of a particular employment practice results in discrimination against women. In this situation intent to discriminate is irrelevant.

One of the first instances in which disparate impact was defined involved a landmark court case, *Griggs v. Duke Power*. Following passage of Title VII (discussed more fully later), Duke Power initiated a selection system that required new employees to have either a high school education or a minimum cutoff score on two specific personality tests. Griggs, a black male, filed a lawsuit against Duke Power after he was denied employment based on these criteria. His argument was that neither criteria was a necessary qualification for performing the work he was seeking. After his attorneys demonstrated that those criteria disproportionately affected blacks and that the company had no documentation to support the validity of the criteria, the courts ruled that the firm had to change its selection criteria on the basis of disparate impact.[6]

The important criterion in this situation is that the consequences of the employment practice are discriminatory, and thus the practice in question has disparate (sometimes referred to as adverse) impact. In fact, if a plaintiff can establish what is called a *prima facie* case of discrimination, the company is considered *guilty* of discrimination unless it can prove its innocence. This situation doesn't mean that the company is automatically guilty, but it does mean that the burden of proof rests with the company to defend itself, rather than with the plaintiff's trying to prove discrimination. It is therefore extremely important to understand how one establishes such a prima facie case.

■ The **four-fifths rule** suggests that disparate impact exists if a selection criterion (such as a test score) results in a selection rate for a protected class that is less than four-fifths (80 percent) of that for the majority group.

Although there are several ways to establish such a case, the most common approach is the so-called **four-fifths rule**. Specifically, the courts have ruled that disparate impact exists if a selection criterion (such as a test score) results in a selection rate for a protected class that is less than four-fifths (80 percent) of that for the majority group. For example, if an employment test results in 60 percent of the white applicants for a job being hired but only 30 percent of the Hispanic applicants being hired, disparate impact is likely to be ruled because Hispanics are being hired at a rate that is less than four-fifths than that of whites. Again, the organization using the test is not automatically guilty, but it would be required to prove that its differential selection rate of whites versus Hispanics was not due to discrimination.

Pattern or practice   The third kind of discrimination that can be identified is pattern or practice discrimination. **Pattern or practice discrimination** is similar to disparate treatment but occurs on a classwide basis. That is, rather than discriminating against a single member of a protected class, the organization guilty of pattern or practice discrimination is discriminating against all members of a protected class. Title VII of the 1964 Civil Rights Act (again, discussed more fully later) gives the attorney general of the United States express powers to bring lawsuits against organizations thought to be guilty of pattern or practice discrimination. Specifically, Section 707 of Title VII states that such a lawsuit can be brought about if there is reasonable cause to believe that an employer is engaging in pattern or practice discrimination. A good example of disparate treatment discrimination allegedly occurred several years ago at Shoney's, a popular family-oriented restaurant chain with operations and locations throughout the South. A former assistant manager at the firm alleged that she was told by her supervisor to use a pencil to color in the *o* in the Shoney's logo on employment applications turned in by black applicants. The presumed intent of this coding scheme was to eliminate those applicants from further consideration.[7]

> ■ **Pattern or practice discrimination** is similar to disparate treatment but occurs on a classwide basis.

To demonstrate pattern or practice discrimination, the prosecution must prove that the organization intended to discriminate against a particular class of individuals. A critical issue in practice or pattern lawsuits is the definition of a statistical comparison group or a definition of the relevant labor market. A labor market consists of workers who have the skills needed to perform the work and who are within reasonable commuting distance to the organization. Clearly, the definition of the labor market is a major issue, then, in resolving lawsuits brought under pattern or practice discrimination suits.

Retaliation   A final form of illegal discrimination that has been occasionally identified in some organizations is retaliation for "participation and opposition." Title VII states that it is illegal for employers to retaliate against employees for either opposing a perceived illegal employment practice or participating in a proceeding that is related to an alleged employment practice. If an employee's behavior fits the legal definition of participation and/or opposition and the organization takes some measure against that particular employee, such as a reprimand, demotion, or termination, the employee can file a lawsuit against the organization under Title VII.[8]

Protected Classes in the Workforce

At various times in the past, many organizations and their managers have been guilty of one or more forms of discrimination, as just described. The basis of this discrimination was typically a stereotype, belief, or prejudice about classes of individuals. For example, common stereotypes at one time were that black employees were less dependable than white employees, that women were less suited to certain types of work than were men, and that disabled individuals could not be productive employees. Based on these stereotypes, many organizations routinely discriminated against blacks, women, and disabled people. Figure 3.3, for example, illustrates recruiting advertisements from earlier times with explicit or implicit discriminatory statements. Such ads would create major problems if an organization tried to use them today!

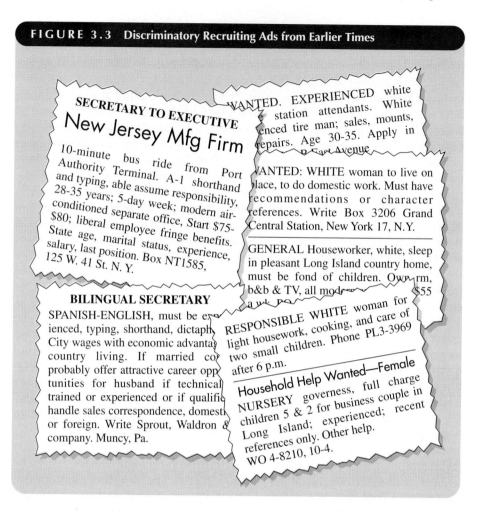

FIGURE 3.3   **Discriminatory Recruiting Ads from Earlier Times**

■ A **protected class** consists of all individuals who share one or more common characteristic as indicated by that law.

To combat this discrimination, laws have been passed to protect various classes or categories of individuals. While varying from law to law, a **protected class** consists of all individuals who share one or more common characteristic as indicated by that law. The most common characteristics used to define protected classes include race, color, religion, gender, age, national origin, disability status, and status as a military veteran. As we will see, some laws pertain to a variety of protected classes, while others pertain to only a single protected class. Class definition generally involves first specifying the basis of distinction and then specifying which degree or category of that distinction is protected. For example, a law may prohibit discrimination on the basis of gender—a basis of distinction—and then define the protected class as females. This does not mean that an organization can discriminate against men, of course, but the law was almost certainly passed on the assumption that most gender-based discrimination has been against women and thus it is women who need to be protected in the future.

At the same time, an important issue that emerges is the extent to which an organization can give preferential treatment to members of a protected class. While exceptions can be made in certain circumstances, by and large the intent of most equal employment opportunity legislation is to provide fair and equitable treatment for everyone, as opposed to stipulating preferential treatment for members of a protected class.[9] This issue does become a bit complicated, though, and so we will return to it later.

Equal Employment Opportunity Legislation

A large body of legal regulation has been created in an effort to provide equal employment opportunity for various protected classes of individuals. The major laws and related regulations that constitute this body are discussed more fully in this section.

Title VII of the Civil Rights Act of 1964   The most significant single piece of legislation specifically affecting the legal context to human resource management to date is **Title VII of the Civil Rights Act of 1964**. The passage of this law was a direct result of the civil rights movement of the early 1960s. Congress passed the Civil Rights Act and President Lyndon Johnson signed it in 1964 as a way to ensure that equal opportunities are made available to everyone. Title VII of the Civil Rights Act states that it is illegal for an employer to fail to hire, refuse to hire, or discharge any individual or to in any other way discriminate against any individual with respect to any aspect of the employment relationship on the basis of that individual's race, color, religious beliefs, sex, or national origin. The law also makes it illegal to segregate, limit, or classify employees or applicants for employment in any way that could deprive an individual of equal employment opportunities, or that could lead to such deprivation.

The law applies to all elements of the employment relationship, including compensation, employment terms, working conditions, and various other privileges of employment. Title VII applies to all organizations with twenty or more employees working twenty or more weeks a year and that are involved in interstate commerce. In addition, it also applies to state and local governments, employment agencies, and labor organizations. Title VII also created the Equal Employment Opportunity Commission, or EEOC, to enforce the various provisions of the law (we discuss the EEOC later).

Executive Order 11246   Because President Johnson believed that Title VII of the 1964 Civil Rights Act was not comprehensive enough, he subsequently issued **Executive Order 11246**. This order prohibits discrimination based on race, color, religion, sex, or national origin for organizations that are federal contractors and subcontractors. Executive Order 11246 specifically states that employers who receive more than $10,000 from the federal government must take **affirmative action** to ensure against discrimination in its hiring and retention practices. The executive order also specifies that organizations with contracts greater than $50,000 must develop a written affirmative action plan for each of their organizational units within 120 days of the beginning of the contract. Executive Order 11246 is enforced by the Office of Federal Contract Compliance Procedures, or OFCCP, also discussed later.

Executive Order 11478   President Richard Nixon issued **Executive Order 11478**. This executive order requires the federal government to base all of its own employment policies on merit and fitness and specifies that race, color, sex, religion, and national origin should not be considered. The order also extends to all contractors and subcontractors doing business worth $10,000 or more with the federal government.

■ **Title VII of the Civil Rights Act** states that it is illegal for an employer to fail to hire, refuse to hire, or discharge any individual or to in any other way discriminate against any individual with respect to any aspect of the employment relationship on the basis of that individual's race, color, religious beliefs, sex, or national origin.

■ **Executive Order 11246** prohibits discrimination based on race, color, religion, sex, or national origin for organizations that are federal contractors and subcontractors.

■ **Affirmative action** represents a set of steps, taken by an organization, to actively seek qualified applicants from groups underrepresented in the workforce.

■ **Executive Order 11478** requires the federal government to base all of its own employment policies on merit and fitness and specifies that race, color, sex, religion, and national origin should not be considered.

The Americans with Disabilities Act of 1990 forbids discrimination on the basis of disability and requires reasonable accommodation for disabled employees so long as it doesn't impose an unreasonable burden on the organization. Howard Samuels, an employee of Analog Devices in Wilmington, Massachusetts, is learning sign languages on company time and at company expense. Once the company learned he was losing his hearing, steps were taken to organize the class for Samuels and several other workers.

■ **The Equal Pay Act of 1963** requires that organizations provide men and women who are doing equal work the same pay.

The Equal Pay Act of 1963   **The Equal Pay Act of 1963** requires that organizations provide the same pay to men and women who are doing equal work. The law defines equality in terms of skill, responsibility, effort, and working conditions. Thus an organization cannot pay a man more than it pays a woman for the same job on the grounds that, say, "he needs the money more because he has a bigger family to support." Similarly, organizations cannot circumvent the law by using different job titles for essentially the same work, such as a school district giving a man the title of assistant superintendent and a woman the title of curriculum coordinator. If the work is essentially the same, then pay differentials on the basis of difference in titles alone is illegal.

This regulation does not mean, of course, that men and women must be paid the same if there are legitimate job-related reasons for pay differences. For example, a man may be paid more than a woman doing the same job if there are legitimate organizational practices to support such a differential. For example, suppose a firm gives a 5 percent seniority raise every year. A man who has worked for the firm for ten years may, therefore, legitimately be paid more than a woman who has worked there for only five years. Of course, for these practices to be legal the organization must also be paying the woman more than it is paying another man who has worked in the organization for only two years. Other potential differences in pay might be made on the basis of merit, quantity or quality of performance, or any other work- or performance-related factor.

■ The **Age Discrimination and Employment Act (ADEA)** prohibits discrimination against employees over the age of forty.

The Age Discrimination and Employment Act   The **Age Discrimination and Employment Act (ADEA)** was passed in 1967 and amended in 1986. The ADEA prohibits discrimination against employees over the age of forty. The

ADEA is very similar to Title VII of the 1964 Civil Rights Act in terms of both its major provisions and the procedures that are followed in pursuing a case of discrimination. Moreover, like Title VII, enforcement of the ADEA is the responsibility of the EEOC.

The ADEA was passed in response to a disquieting trend that was noticed at some organizations in the early 1960s. Specifically, these firms were beginning to overtly discriminate against older employees when the firms found it necessary to lay off people or to otherwise scale back their workforce. By targeting older workers who tended to have higher pay because of their seniority with the firm, companies were substantially cutting their labor costs. In addition, there was some feeling that organizations were also discriminating against older workers in their hiring decisions. The specific concern here was that organizations would not hire people in their forties or fifties because (1) firms would have to pay those individuals more because of their experience and salary history and (2) those individuals would have a shorter potential career with the organization. Consequently, some organizations were found to be guilty of giving preferential treatment to younger workers over older workers.

In recent years age-bias lawsuits have actually started to decline. For example, the number of age-related claims filed with the EEOC declined from 19,809 in 1993 to 15,785 in 1997. Several explanations have been suggested for this trend. For one thing, low unemployment in the 1990s has simply forced employers to retain as many qualified employees as possible. For another, some organizations seem to be more sensitive about age-related issues today and are thus less likely to take inappropriate or illegal actions against older workers.[10]

The Vocational Rehabilitation Act of 1973   The **Vocational Rehabilitation Act of 1973** requires that executive agencies and subcontractors and contractors of the federal government receiving more than $2,500 a year from the government engage in affirmative action for disabled individuals. The Employment Standards Administration of the Department of Labor was assigned the role of enforcing the Vocational Rehabilitation Act of 1973.

The Vietnam Era Veterans' Readjustment Act of 1974   The **Vietnam Era Veterans' Readjustment Act of 1974** is very similar to the 1973 Vocational Rehabilitation Act. The 1974 law requires that federal contractors and subcontractors take affirmative action toward employing Vietnam-era veterans. Vietnam-era veterans are specifically defined as those serving as a member of the U.S. armed forces between August 5, 1964, and May 7, 1975. Enforcement of the Vietnam Era Veterans' Readjustment Act was assigned to the Office of Federal Contract Compliance Procedures, or OFCCP.

The Pregnancy Discrimination Act of 1978   As its name suggests, the **Pregnancy Discrimination Act of 1978** was passed to protect pregnant women from discrimination in the workplace. The law requires that pregnant women be treated the same as any other employees in the workplace. Therefore, the act specifies that a woman cannot be refused a job or promotion, be fired, or otherwise be discriminated against simply because she is pregnant (or has had an abortion). She also cannot be forced to leave employment with the organization as long as she is physically able to work. Finally, the Pregnancy Discrimination Act specifies that if other employees have the right to receive their jobs back after a leave, then this benefit must be accorded to pregnant women as

■ The **Vocational Rehabilitation Act of 1973** requires that executive agencies and subcontractors and contractors of the federal government receiving more than $2,500 a year from the government engage in affirmative action for disabled individuals.

■ The **Vietnam Era Veterans' Readjustment Act of 1974** requires that federal contractors and subcontractors take affirmative action toward employing Vietnam-era veterans.

■ The **Pregnancy Discrimination Act of 1978** was passed to protect pregnant women from discrimination in the workplace.

well. In one recent high-profile case, actress Hunter Tylo won a $5 million judgment against the producers of the television show *Melrose Place* after they used her pregnancy as a basis for writing her out of the show.[11]

■ The **Civil Rights Act of 1991** makes it easier for individuals who believe that they have been discriminated against to take legal action against organizations and provides for the payment of compensatory and punitive damages in cases of discrimination under Title VII.

The Civil Rights Act of 1991   The **Civil Rights Act of 1991** was passed as a direct amendment to Title VII of the Civil Rights Act of 1964. Several decisions by the U.S. Supreme Court that essentially redefined parts of the 1964 act led to this amendment. The Civil Rights Act of 1991 essentially restored the force of the Civil Rights Act of 1964, which had been reduced by these decisions. The Civil Rights Act of 1991 makes it easier for individuals who believe that they have been discriminated against to take legal action against organizations.

It also provides, for the first time, the potential payment of compensatory and punitive damages in cases of discrimination under Title VII. Title VII itself, as originally passed, provided only for compensation for back pay. But the new law also limits the amount of punitive damages that can be paid to someone. Depending on the size of the organization, the allowable damage range is from $50,000 to $300,000 for each instance of violation of the law. Further, punitive damages can be paid only if the employer intentionally discriminates against someone or if the employer discriminated with malice or reckless indifference to an individual's federally protected rights.

This law also enables employees of U.S. companies working in foreign countries to bring suit against those companies for violation of the Civil Rights Act. The only exception to this provision is the situation in which a country has laws that specifically contradict some aspect of the Civil Rights Act. For example, Muslim countries often have laws limiting the rights of women. Foreign companies with operations in such countries would almost certainly be required to abide by local laws. As a result, a female employee of a U.S. company working in such a setting would not be directly protected under the Civil Rights Act. However, her employer would still need to fully inform her of the kinds of discriminatory practices she might face as a result of transferring to the foreign site and then ensure that when this particular foreign assignment is completed her career opportunities will not have been compromised in any way.

The Civil Rights Act of 1991 has had a number of very important effects. For one thing, because of the potential payoff for a successful discrimination suit, it has dramatically increased the number of suits that individuals have filed against businesses. This increase in lawsuits has dramatically clogged the EEOC to the point where it has several thousand pending cases that it simply does not have time to process. For example, during the three years ending September 1994, the number of backlogged, unresolved cases in the hands of the EEOC more than doubled.[12] A second effect of the Civil Rights Act of 1991 has been to make organizations even more aware than they were before of the need to avoid any instance of discrimination in the employment relationship.

■ The **Americans with Disabilities Act of 1990** (ADA) prohibits discrimination based on disability in all aspects of the employment relationship such as job application procedures, hiring, firing, promotion, compensation, and training, as well as other employment activities such as advertising, recruiting, tenure, layoffs, leave, and fringe benefits.

The Americans with Disabilities Act of 1990   The **Americans with Disabilities Act of 1990 (ADA)** is one of the newest significant pieces of equal employment opportunity legislation to affect human resource management. The ADA was passed in response to growing criticisms and concerns about employment opportunities denied to people with various disabilities. For example, one survey found that of 12.2 million Americans not working because of disabilities, 8.2 million would have preferred to work. Similarly, another survey found that almost 80 percent of all managers surveyed rated the overall performance of their disabled workers to be good to excellent. In response to these trends and pressures, the ADA was passed to protect individuals with disabilities from being discriminated against in the workplace.[13]

Specifically, the ADA prohibits discrimination based on disability in all aspects of the employment relationship such as job application procedures, hiring, firing, promotion, compensation, and training, as well as other employment activities such as advertising, recruiting, tenure, layoffs, leave, and fringe benefits. In addition, the ADA requires that organizations make reasonable accommodations for disabled employees as long as the accommodations themselves do not pose an undue burden on the organization. The act initially went into effect in 1992, covering employers with twenty-five or more employees. It was expanded in July of 1994 to cover employers with fifteen or more employees.

The ADA defines a disability as a mental or physical impairment that limits one or more major life activities, a record of having such an impairment, or being regarded as having such an impairment. Clearly included within the domain of the ADA are individuals with such disabilities as blindness, deafness, paralysis, and similar handicaps. In addition, the ADA covers employees with cancer, with a history of mental illness, or with a history of heart disease. The act also covers employees regarded as having a disability, such as individuals who are disfigured, or who for some other reason an employer feels will prompt a negative reaction from others. In addition, the ADA covers mental and psychological disorders, such as mental retardation, emotional or mental illness, and learning disabilities. On the other hand, individuals with substance abuse problems, obesity, and similar non-work-related characteristics are not covered by the ADA.[14] But because the ADA defines disabilities in terms of limitations on life activities, myriad cases continue to be raised. For example, in recent years workers have attempted to claim protection under the ADA on the basis of alcoholism, depression, and dental problems! All told, more than eighteen thousand claims were filed with the EEOC in 1997 arguing that individuals had experienced discrimination on the basis of a disability.[15]

The Family and Medical Leave Act of 1993   The **Family and Medical Leave Act of 1993** was passed in part to remedy weaknesses in the Pregnancy Discrimination Act of 1979. The 1993 law requires employers having more than fifty employees to provide up to twelve weeks of unpaid leave for employees after the birth or adoption of a child; to care for a seriously ill child, spouse, or parent; or in the case of an employee's own serious illness. The organization must provide the employee with the same or a comparable job upon the employee's return.[16]

The law also requires the organization to pay the health care coverage of the employee during the leave. However, the employer can require the employee to reimburse these premiums if the employee fails to work after the absence. Organizations are allowed to identify key employees, specifically defined as the highest paid 10 percent of their workforce, on the grounds that granting leave to these individuals would cause serious economic harm to the organization. The law also does not apply to employees who have not worked an average of twenty-five hours a week in the previous twelve months.[17]

Clearly, then, a substantial body of laws and regulations governs equal employment opportunity. Many people argue, of course, that all of these laws and regulations are necessary. Without them organizations might either

■ The **Family and Medical Leave Act of 1993** requires employers having more than fifty employees to provide up to twelve weeks of unpaid leave for employees after the birth or adoption of a child; to care for a seriously ill child, spouse, or parent; or in the case of an employee's own serious illness.

intentionally or unintentionally revert to former employment practices that led to illegal discrimination against large numbers of people. On the other hand, some critics argue that the regulatory environment has grown too complex. They point to the myriad and occasionally contradictory rules and regulations that have created a "bureaucratic jungle" that is just too hard to navigate. The arguments on both sides of this issue are highlighted in "Point/Counterpoint."

Enforcing Equal Employment Opportunity

The enforcement of equal opportunity legislation generally is handled by two agencies: the Equal Employment Opportunity Commission, or EEOC, and the Office of Federal Contract Compliance Procedures, or OFCCP. The EEOC, a division of the Department of Justice, was created by Title VII of the 1964 Civil Rights Act and is now responsible for enforcing Title VII, the Equal Pay Act, and the Americans with Disabilities Act. The EEOC has three major functions: (1) investigating and resolving complaints about alleged discrimination, (2) gathering information regarding employment patterns and trends in U.S. businesses, and (3) issuing information about new employment guidelines as they become relevant.

The first function is investigating and resolving complaints about alleged discrimination in the workplace. Figure 3.4 illustrates the basic steps that an individual who thinks that she or he has been discriminated against in a promotion decision might follow to get the complaint addressed. In general, if an individual believes that she or he has been discriminated against, the first step in reaching a resolution is to file a complaint with either the EEOC or a corresponding state agency. The individual has 180 days from the date of the incident to file the complaint. The EEOC will dismiss out of hand virtually all complaints that exceed the 180-day time frame for filing. After the complaint has been filed, the EEOC assumes responsibility for investigating the claim. The EEOC can take up to sixty days to investigate a complaint. If the EEOC either finds that the complaint is not valid or does not complete the investigation within a sixty-day period, the individual has the right to sue in a federal court.

If the EEOC believes that discrimination has in fact occurred, its representative will first try to reach reconciliation between the two parties without taking the case to court. Occasionally, the EEOC may enter into a *consent decree* with the discriminating organization. This consent decree is essentially an agreement between the EEOC and the organization that stipulates that the organization will cease certain discriminatory practices and perhaps implement new affirmative action procedures to rectify its history of discrimination.

On the other hand, if the EEOC cannot reach an agreement with the organization, two courses of action may be pursued. First, the EEOC can issue a "right to sue letter" to the victim, which simply certifies that the agency has investigated the complaint and found potential validity in the victim's allegations. Essentially, that course of action involves the EEOC giving its blessings to the individual to file suit on his or her own grounds. Alternatively, in certain limited cases the EEOC itself may assist the victim in bringing suit in federal court. In either event, however, the lawsuit must be filed in federal court within three hundred days of the alleged discriminatory act. The courts follow this guideline very strictly, and many valid complaints have lost standing in court because lawsuits were not filed on time. As already noted, the EEOC has recently become backlogged with complaints stemming primarily from the passage of the newer Civil Rights Act, which makes it easier to file suit. One recent court case that involved the implementation of a discriminatory seniority sys-

POINT/COUNTERPOINT   Too Much Human Resources Regulation?

Human Resources and the Law: As should be clear to you, many laws deal with the human resource management function. Since the 1960s and the passage of the Civil Rights Act, the number of new regulations and guidelines has increased at an alarming rate. As you may be aware, a backlash has begun to develop against some of these regulations. Some of the criticism began when President Reagan publicly joked about OSHA safety regulations regarding how to use a ladder, and more recently many people of all races have begun speaking out against affirmative action, suggesting that it leads to reverse discrimination. Is there too much regulation in the human resource field? Do these regulations sometimes put organizations at a competitive disadvantage?

POINT ... There is too much regulation of Human Resources activities because ...	COUNTERPOINT ... But without continuing these regulations, there will be problems such as ...
Too many individuals are members of protected classes so that no one is really protected.	Everyone is protected by nondiscrimination laws, not only protected-class members.
The laws against discrimination have already done their job, so women and minorities can effectively compete for any job.	Women still earn less than 80 percent of what men do (on average), and the poverty rate among African-Amercans is still several times higher than it is for white Americans.
Continuing such regulations, especially in light of recent improvements, actually results in reverse discrimination. This trend is most obvious under quota systems.	Reverse discrimination is illegal. Quotas are considered reverse discrimination unless imposed by court order.
Organizations should have the right to select whomever they believe is the most qualified—not to do so would be in violation of stockholder expectations.	Nothing in the law or in any court decision would force an organization to hire less-qualified individuals. It is important to realize that *qualified* means "able to do the job." A hiring system based on racism would actually be harmful to a firm's effectiveness.
No one can understand the complex regulations, which often make no sense and which may even contradict each other.	The laws are complex and court decisions suggest interpretation that may be contradictory, but the same could be said for all the other laws we have. Should we abandon them all?

So ...   There are many misconceptions about antidiscrimination legislation. Quotas and reverse discrimination are illegal under the law, although it may sometimes seem as though organizations are discriminating against majority-group applicants and employees. The law simply requires organizations to *not* discriminate against persons who are members of a protected class. In fact, such discrimination would actually result in less-qualified persons being hired. The key, however, is to focus on the level of performance predicted by a test score, not on the test score itself. When viewed in this light, the goals of the law and the goals of the organization are not in conflict.

tem was settled in such a way that amended Title VII to provide exceptions to the three-hundred-day deadline for filing a lawsuit.

The EEOC recently announced a new policy for prioritizing pending complaints to help clear its backlog and to provide better enforcement of the law. When a new complaint is filed, a case officer quickly reviews it and makes a

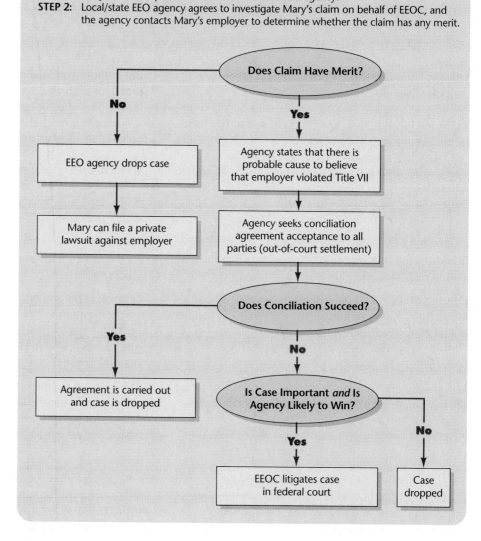

FIGURE 3.4 Investigating and Resolving a Discrimination Complaint

MARY SMITH believes she has been discriminated against at work. She was passed over for a promotion to supervisor, and believes it was because she was a woman, rather than because she was unqualified. Specifically, all candidates for promotion must be approved by their immediate supervisor, and most of these supervisors are older white men who have been heard to say that women should not be promoted. In fact, almost no women have been promoted to supervisor in this organization. What can Mary do?

STEP 1: Mary files a complaint with her local or state EEO agency.
STEP 2: Local/state EEO agency agrees to investigate Mary's claim on behalf of EEOC, and the agency contacts Mary's employer to determine whether the claim has any merit.

judgment as to its merits. Cases that appear to reflect a strong likelihood of discrimination are then given higher priority than are cases that appear to have less merit. Even higher priority is given to cases that appear to have the potential for widespread or classwide effects.[18]

The second important function of the EEOC is to monitor the hiring practices of organizations. Every year all organizations that employ one hundred or more individuals must file a report with the EEOC that summarizes the number of women and minorities that organization employs in nine job categories. The EEOC tracks these reports to identify potential patterns of discrimination that it can then potentially address through class-action lawsuits.

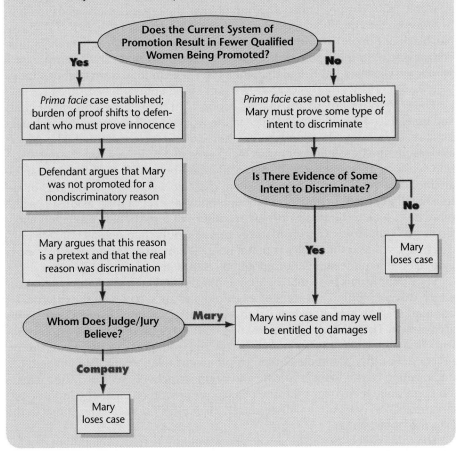

FIGURE 3.4 (Continued)

Once the case goes to court, and assuming that Mary and EEOC believe they have a case of disparate treatment, the process goes through several more crucial steps.

STEP 3: Mary tries to establish a *prima facie* case of discrimination.

The third function of the EEOC is to develop and issue guidelines that help organizations determine whether their decisions are violations of the law enforced by the EEOC. These guidelines themselves are not laws, but the courts have generally placed great weight on them when hearing employment discrimination cases. One of the most important sets of guidelines is the uniform guidelines on employee selection procedures developed jointly by the EEOC, the U.S. Department of Labor, the U.S. Department of Justice, and the U.S. Civil Service Commission. These guidelines summarize how organizations should develop and administer selection systems so as not to violate Title VII. The EEOC also frequently uses the Federal Register to issue new guidelines and opinions regarding employment practices that come about as a result of newly passed laws.[19] This practice has been particularly important in recent years as a result of the passage of the ADA.[20]

The other agency primarily charged with monitoring Equal Employment Opportunity legislation is the Office of Federal Contract Compliance Procedures. The OFCCP is responsible for enforcing the executive orders that cover companies doing business with the federal government. Recall from our earlier discussion that businesses with federal contracts of more than $50,000 cannot discriminate on the basis of race, color, religious beliefs, national origin, or gender for any of their employment practices, and that these businesses must have a written affirmative action plan on file.[20]

■ A **utilization analysis** compares the racial, sex, and ethnic composition of the employer's workforce to that of the available labor supply.

An affirmative action plan generally has three basic elements. The first element is called the utilization analysis. A **utilization analysis** compares the racial, sex, and ethnic composition of the employer's workforce to that of the available labor supply. For each group of jobs, the organization needs to identify the percentage of its workforce with a particular characteristic (for example, black or female) and identify the percentage of workers in the relevant labor market with that same characteristic. If the percentage in the employer's workforce is considerably less than the percentage in the external labor supply, then that minority group is characterized as being underutilized.

The second part of an affirmative action plan is the development of goals and timetables for achieving balance in the workforce concerning those characteristics, especially where underutilization exists. Goals and timetables generally specify the percentage of protected classes of employees that the organization seeks to have in each group and the date by which that percent can be attained. It is important to recognize that these goals and timetables do not automatically constitute quotas. A quota would involve setting aside a specific number of jobs to be filled only by members of a particular protected class. Goals and timetables are considerably more flexible than quotas. The idea underlying goals and timetables is that if no discriminatory hiring practices exist, then over time underutilization should be eliminated.

For example, suppose that a particular organization finds that for a particular job category, only 25 percent of its employees are women. In the external labor market, however, 40 percent of those seeking positions in comparable jobs are women. Thus the organization appears to have an underutilization problem. This underutilization might have resulted from past discriminatory hiring practices or other anomalies in the employment relationship. However, if the organization ceases to discriminate and begins to actively seek qualified female job applicants, then, over time, the percentage of women currently in those underutilized job categories will gradually rise until it reflects conditions in the external labor market.

The third part of the affirmative action program is the development of a list of action steps. These steps specify what the organization will do to actually reduce underutilization. Common action steps include making extra efforts in communicating job openings to women and minorities, recruiting at schools that predominantly cater to a particular protected class, participating in programs that are designed to improve employment opportunities for underemployed groups, and taking all necessary steps to remove inappropriate barriers to employment.

The OFCCP conducts yearly audits of government contractors to ensure that they have been actively pursuing their affirmative action goals. These audits involve examining a company's affirmative action plan and conducting site visits to determine how individual employees perceive the company's affirmative action policies. If the OFCCP finds that its contractors or subcontractors are not complying with the relevant executive orders, then it may notify the EEOC, advise the Department of Justice to institute criminal proceedings, or request that the secretary of labor cancel or suspend contracts with that organization. This latter step is the OFCCP's most important weapon, since it has a clear and immediate impact on an organization's revenue stream.

It is also possible that organizations other than those falling under OFCCP jurisdiction might institute affirmative action plans. Courts have often demanded that organizations found guilty of past discrimination institute such plans to remedy the past discrimination. In fact, there have been cases where the courts imposed a hiring quota on an offending organization. In these cases the company was forced to hire specific numbers of protected class members over a specified period of time. It is important to remember, however, that these instances are rare and have a clearly specified time limit. In general, affirmative action does *not* mean that an organization must hire a certain number of employees from protected classes. In fact, such quota systems, where not imposed by a court order, are considered a form of **reverse discrimination** and are themselves considered illegal.

Although the EEOC and the OFCCP are the two primary regulatory agencies that enforce equal employment legislation, various other government agencies and components come into play. The Department of Labor and the Department of Justice, for example, are both heavily involved in the enforcement of equal employment opportunity legislation. The U.S. Civil Service Commission is also actively involved in monitoring compliance in government organizations where civil service jobs exist. In addition, the U.S. judicial system plays an important role in enforcing all human resource management legislation.

■ **Reverse discrimination** refers to any practice that has disparate impact on members of nonprotected classes. Thus, for example, quota systems that require an organization to hire a certain number of black females would be considered as reverse discrimination relative to white males unless the system was dictated by a court order.

THE BOTTOM LINE Equal employment opportunity is the central part of the legal context of human resource management. Managers need to have clear and specific knowledge about the various forms of illegal discrimination, the protected classes in the workplace, and the fundamental and relevant laws and related regulations that affect their organization. In addition, managers need to be familiar with the various agencies that enforce equal employment legislation.

L E G A L   I S S U E S   I N   C O M P E N S A T I O N

As noted earlier, most employment regulations are designed to provide equal employment opportunity. However, some legislation goes beyond equal employment opportunity and really deals more substantively with other issues. One such area concerns legislation involving compensation. We introduce this legislation here and return to it in Chapter 11.

Legal Perspectives on Total Compensation

Over the years the federal government has passed several laws dealing with total compensation. The most far-reaching of these has been the Fair Labor Standards Act. **The Fair Labor Standards Act (FLSA),** passed in 1938, established a minimum hourly wage for jobs. The rationale for this legislation was to ensure that everyone who works would receive an income sufficient to meet basic needs. The first minimum wage was 25 cents an hour. Of course, this minimum wage has been revised many times and is currently $5.15 per hour.

The FLSA was amended in 1990 to permit a subminimum training wage equal to the greater of $3.35 per hour, or 85 percent of the minimum wage. Employers are permitted to pay this subminimum wage to any new employee who is under the age of twenty for a period of up to ninety days. The rationale for this amendment was that organizations would be motivated to hire more younger employees and to provide them with training because they could pay

■ **The Fair Labor Standards Act**, passed in 1938, established a minimum hourly wage for jobs.

Ever since the passage of the Fair Labor Standards Act in 1938 workers in the United States have had the protection of a minimum hourly wage. Over time, however, the purchasing power of this wage drops because of inflation, and workers sometimes have to wait until Congress raises the minimum wage before their purchasing power can catch up with actual prices. The state of Washington recently took steps to correct this problem by passing a law that automatically adjusts its minimum wage each year based on inflation rates. As a result, minimum wage earners like this waitperson will have less uncertainty about the purchasing power of their wages in the future.

them a lower wage for this initial period of time. Interestingly, this amendment also causes a dilemma for managers in some situations—the FLSA amendment clearly provides an incentive for hiring more young workers, yet the firm is still forbidden from discriminating against older workers because of the ADEA!

The FLSA also formally defined for the first time the workweek in the United States as forty hours per week. It further specifies that all full-time employees must be paid at a rate of one and a half times their normal hourly rate for each hour of overtime work beyond forty hours in a week. This hourly rate includes not only the base wage rate but also components such as piece-rate payment and bonuses. Note, however, that the law makes no provision for daily work time. Thus, while a normal workday might be thought of as eight hours, an employer is actually free to schedule, say, ten or twelve hours in a single day without paying overtime, just as long as the weekly total does not exceed forty hours.

Not all employees are covered by the FLSA. Although several factors are used to determine who is covered, the primary distinguishing characteristic is the basis for payment. The FLSA primarily covers workers who are called nonexempt, which refers to occupations where individuals are paid on an hourly basis. Exempt employees (which refers to the fact that they are literally exempt from the minimum wage and overtime provisions of the FLSA), on the other hand, include executive, professional, administrative, and outside sales employees who are generally paid on a monthly or annual basis. The determination of exempt status depends on job responsibilities and standards. Moreover, the actual determination of whether or not a job is exempt is a fairly complicated process. A number of criteria are used to determine whether or not an individual's job is exempt from the FLSA.[22]

■ The **Employee Retirement Income Security Act of 1974,** or **ERISA,** was passed to guarantee a basic minimum benefit that employees could expect to be paid upon retirement.

Legal Perspectives on Other Forms of Compensation

Another important piece of legislation that affects compensation is the **Employee Retirement Income Security Act of 1974,** or **ERISA.** This law was passed to protect employee investments in their pensions, and to ensure that employees would be able to receive at least some pension benefits at the time of retirement or even termination. ERISA does not mean that an employee must receive a pension but, rather, is meant to protect any pension benefits to which the employee is entitled. (This will be discussed in somewhat more detail in Chapter 16.) ERISA was passed in part because some organizations had abused their pension plans in their efforts to control costs, or to channel money inappropriately to other uses within the organization, or due entirely to corruption.

THE BOTTOM LINE Government regulations cover virtually every aspect of employee compensation. All managers, therefore, need to have a basic understanding of the legal context of pay, working hours, and benefits. Human resource managers, further, need a complete and thorough understanding of these issues.

LEGAL ISSUES IN LABOR RELATIONS

Another area of human resource management where various government regulations are extremely important is labor relations. The term *labor relations* generally refers to the formal and legal relationship between an organization and some or all of its workers who have formed and joined a labor union. We introduce these regulations here and then cover them in more direct relation to unions in Chapter 14.

Unionization and the Law

The National Labor Relations Act, or **Wagner Act**, was passed in 1935 in an effort to control and legislate collective bargaining between organizations and labor unions. Prior to this time, the legal system in the United States was generally considered to be hostile to labor unions. The Wagner Act was therefore passed in an effort to provide some sense of balance in the power relationship between organizations and unions. The Wagner Act described the process through which labor unions could be formed and the requirements faced by organizations in dealing with those labor unions. The Wagner Act served to triple union membership in the United States and granted labor unions significant power in their relationships with organizations.

Following a series of crippling strikes, however, the U.S. government concluded that the Wagner Act had actually shifted power too much in the favor of labor unions. Businesses, as a result, had been placed at a significant disadvantage. As a result of this imbalance, Congress subsequently passed the **Taft-Hartley Act** in 1947 and the **Landrum-Griffin Act** in 1959. Both of these acts regulate union actions and their internal affairs in a way that puts them on equal footing with management and organizations.

■ **The National Labor Relations Act**, or **Wagner Act**, was passed in an effort to control and legislate collective bargaining between organizations and labor unions.

■ The **Taft-Hartley Act** and the **Landrum-Griffin Act** regulate union actions and their internal affairs in a way that puts them on equal footing with management and organizations.

Collective Bargaining and the Law

Collective bargaining is the process used to negotiate a labor contract between a union and management. Each of the laws noted above, as well as several other sets of regulations, precisely govern the steps involved in this negotiation process and carefully spell out what each side can and cannot do. Given the complexities of this process, we discuss it in detail in Chapter 14.

THE BOTTOM LINE   Several important laws govern relationships between organizations and labor unions. Given both the complexities and the significance of these relationships and the importance of good labor relations, most larger organizations use dedicated specialists to handle union-related issues. All managers, however, need to understand the basic legal context of labor relations.

EMERGING LEGAL ISSUES IN HUMAN RESOURCE MANAGEMENT

In addition to these established areas of the legal regulation of human resource practices, several emerging legal issues are likely to become more and more important in the future. These include employee safety and health; various emerging areas of discrimination law, employee rights, and employment-at-will; and ethics and human resource management.

Employee Safety and Health

Employee safety and health are becoming increasingly important issues for organizations and employees. Indeed, "Human Resources Fad, Fashion, or Fact?" highlights some interesting ideas that have recently surfaced regarding employee safety and health issues outside the traditional workplace. **The Occupational Safety and Health Act of 1970**, also called **OSHA**, is the most comprehensive piece of legislation ever passed regarding worker safety and health in organizations. OSHA granted the federal government the power to establish and enforce occupational safety and health standards for all places of employment directly affecting interstate commerce. The Department of Labor was given power for applying the standards and enforcing the provisions of OSHA. The Department of Health was given responsibility for conducting research to determine the criteria for specific operations or occupations and for training employers to comply with the act. OSHA also makes provisions through which individual states can substitute their own safety and health standards for those suggested by the federal government.

The basic premise of OSHA is that each employer has an obligation to furnish each employee with a place of employment that is free from hazards that cause or are likely to cause death or physical harm.[23] This regulation is known as the *General Duty Clause*. OSHA is generally enforced through inspections of the workplace by OSHA inspectors. An inspection might be instigated at the specific request of an employee, or it may come about because the Department of Labor has targeted certain industries or special hazards. Some firms are also randomly chosen for OSHA inspections out of a nationwide pool.

These inspections are conducted by specially trained agents of the Department of Labor called compliance officers. A compliance officer usually arrives at a workplace unannounced, presents his or her credentials to management,

■ **The Occupational Safety and Health Act of 1970**, also called **OSHA**, grants the federal government the power to establish and enforce occupational safety and health standards for all places of employment directly affecting interstate commerce.

Home Safety for Telecommuters

 It's an interesting convergence of legal and social trends. Influenced primarily by the Occupational Safety and Health Act (OSHA), many organizations today are paying close attention to hazards and unsafe conditions in the workplace. At the same time, though, more and more people are moving into telecommuter roles in which they do a portion of their work at home. So since many employees are working at home, what kinds of obligations does an organization have to ensure that people who are working at home enjoy the same protections there as they do in the office or factory? What happens, for example, if an employee falls down stairs while going to his or her basement home office? Or what happens if a worker develops carpal tunnel syndrome because of a poorly configured workstation at home?

Many legal experts contend that the same protections that apply at work also apply to people who are working in their homes. As a result, most companies that allow

"In order to be a telecommuter, you have to have approved lights, desk, chair, computer pads, you name it."

(Bobbie Collins, manager at Merrill Lynch)*

telecommuting are paying more attention to home office safety for their workers. For example, AT&T provides its telecommuters with equipment, tips on how to avoid injuries, and, if the employee wants, a free home office safety inspection. Merrill Lynch requires inspections of home offices and mandates that telecommuters go through a two-week training program.

But not everyone thinks these practices are beneficial. Some workers, for example, see home inspections by their employers as an invasion of their privacy. And some employers complain that the extra costs of monitoring safety in workers' homes would be so high that they are considering banning or cutting back on telecommuting opportunities for their workers. Who knows where all this will lead? Only time—and the courts, no doubt—will tell.

References: "Working at Home Raises Job Site Safety Issues," *USA Today*, January 29, 1998, p. 1B (*quote on p. 1B); Jonathan Segal, "Home Sweet Office?" *HRMagazine*, April 1998, pp. 119–129.

informs the employer of the reasons for the inspection, and describes the general procedures necessary to conduct the investigation. The OSHA inspector can review the organization's records of death, injuries, and illnesses; can conduct a tour of the premises accompanied by a company representative; can interview employees; and can hold a closed conference to discuss findings and discuss time frames for correcting any potential violations that he or she has observed.[24]

If an OSHA compliance officer believes that a violation has occurred, a citation is issued to the organization. The organization is required to post this citation in a prominent place near the location of the violation even if the organization intends to contest it. Nonserious violations may be fined up to $1,000 for each incident. Serious violations or willful and repeated violations may be fined up to $10,000 per incident. A compliance officer has the right to adjust fines downward if the employer has no prior history of violations and/or the organization is relatively small.

In addition to these civil penalties, willful violations that result in the death of an employee may also be subject to criminal penalties. Fines can be as high as $20,000, and an employer or agent of the organization can actually be imprisoned. In addition, criminal charges can be filed against anyone who falsifies records that are subject to OSHA inspection or anyone who gives advance notice of an OSHA inspection without permission from the Department of Labor. An organization that receives an OSHA citation has fifteen days to contest it.

Emerging Areas of Discrimination Law

Managers must also be familiar with several emerging areas of discrimination law. One area of particular importance today relates to the ADA as discussed earlier in this chapter. Recall that the ADA requires that organizations cease to discriminate against employees on the grounds of disability and make reasonable accommodation to meet the disability requirements of qualified employees. However, the ADA is both so vast in scope and so complex in nuance that many organizations are having a difficult time determining how to best comply with its various guidelines.

One important set of issues relates to the definition of a disability. As noted earlier, the ADA defines disability as a physical or mental impairment that substantially limits one or more of the major life activities of an individual, (2) a record of such an impairment, or (3) being regarded as having such an impairment. But the concept of physical or mental impairment is interpreted broadly. For example, it includes physiological disorders and conditions, cosmetic disfigurements, and anatomic losses affecting one or more of several body parts, as well as any mental, physical, or physiological disorder. Clearly, the law applies to individuals who are confined to wheelchairs, who are visually impaired, and/or who have similar physical disabilities. At the same time, however, psychological disabilities make the provision and application of the ADA more complicated.

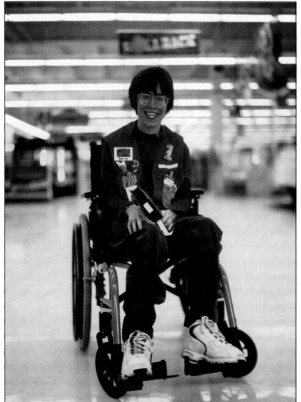

A continuing legal issue today in many organizations relates to the concept of "reasonable accommodation" for disabled workers as required by the ADA. Ginny Lockwood, shown here, works as a greeter in a New York Wal-Mart store. Because of the nature of this job, the organization has to make little or no accommodation for Lockwood. But if Wal-Mart wanted to use a mobility-impaired worker as a checker or stocker, significantly greater accommodation would be necessary. The question in this situation thus centers around whether Wal-Mart is meeting the test of the ADA simply by providing a job to a disabled individual or if additional steps are required.

In addition, the reasonable accommodation stipulation adds considerable complexity to the job of human resource managers and other executives in organizations. Clearly, for example, organizations must provide wheelchair ramps and sufficiently wide hallways to accommodate individuals confined to a wheelchair. At the same time, however, providing accommodations for other disabilities may be more complex. Using a psychological example again, it might be necessary for an organization to provide on-site psychological support systems for individuals who have such disabilities. In an example that is relevant for selection activities, if an applicant for a job takes an employment test, fails the test (and so is not offered employment), and then indicates that he or she has a learning disability (for example) that makes it difficult to take paper-and-pencil tests, the organization would likely be required to either find a different way to administer the test or allow the applicant to take the test a second time before making a final decision.

At present, because of the complexities and vagaries of the law, the EEOC is not taking a very firm stance regarding the enforcement of the ADA. Instead, its current focus is primarily on the issuance of guidelines and interpretations to allow organizations to more effectively comply. The U.S. Supreme Court did take a major step toward clarifying the ADA in mid-1999, however. In a landmark decision, the Court ruled that individuals who can correct or overcome their disabilities through medication or other means are not protected by the ADA. For example, if a worker can correct his or her vision by wearing corrective lenses but prefers not to do so, an employer no longer must make accommodation for that individual.[25] All things considered, the ADA is likely to have a profound influence on human resource management practices for a long time to come.

Another emerging issue on discrimination deals with AIDS in the workplace. While AIDS is considered a disability, under the ADA, the AIDS situation itself is sufficiently severe that it notes special discussion. Employers cannot legally require an AIDS test or any other medical examination as a condition for making an offer of employment. However, after an offer of employment has been extended, organizations can make that offer contingent on the individual's taking a physical examination. If an individual is found to be HIV positive, an employer cannot discriminate against that job applicant in a hiring decision (that is, the offer of employment cannot be withdrawn). However, many health insurance plans exclude preexisting conditions from coverage and to the extent that such a clause exists in the employer's health insurance plan, a new employee with AIDS may not be covered with the insurance.

Essentially, organizations must follow a certain set of guidelines and employ common sense when dealing with AIDS-related issues. For example, organizations must treat AIDS like any other disease that is covered by law, they must maintain confidentiality of all medical records, they cannot discriminate against a person with AIDS, they should strive to educate coworkers about AIDS, they cannot discriminate against AIDS victims regarding training or consideration for promotion in the organization, and they must accommodate or make a good-faith effort to accommodate AIDS victims.

Yet another emerging area of discrimination law involves sexual harassment. Sexual harassment has long been a problem in organizations and has been held to be a violation of Title VII of the Civil Rights Act of 1964. However, the importance of sexual harassment was brought to center stage during a 1991 confirmation hearing for Supreme Court Justice Clarence Thomas. Sexual harassment is defined by the EEOC as unwelcome sexual advances in the work environment. If the conduct is indeed unwelcome and occurs with sufficient frequency to create an abusive work environment, the employer is responsible for changing the environment by warning, reprimanding, or perhaps firing the harasser.[26]

The courts have ruled and defined that there are two types of sexual harassment. One type of sexual harassment is **quid pro quo harassment**. In this case the harasser offers to exchange something of value for sexual favors. For example, a male supervisor might tell or imply to a female subordinate that he will recommend her for promotion or provide her with a salary increase in exchange for sexual favors. The other, more subtle, type of sexual harassment is the creation of a **hostile work environment**. For example, a group of male employees who continually make off-color jokes and lewd comments and perhaps decorate the work environment with inappropriate photographs may create a hostile work environment for a female colleague to the point where she is uncomfortable working in that job setting. As noted, it is the organization's responsibility to deal with this sort of problem.[27]

■ **Quid pro quo harassment** sexual harassment occurs when the harasser offers to exchange something of value for sexual favors.

■ **Hostile work environment** sexual harassment is more subtle and results from a climate or culture that is punitive toward people of a different gender.

Although most sexual harassment cases involve men harassing women, many other situations of sexual harassment can be identified as well. Sometimes women harass men, and sometimes there is same-sex harassment. And indeed, several recent cases involving same-sex harassment have focused new attention on this form of sexual harassment.[28] Regardless of the pattern, however, the same rules apply: sexual harassment is illegal, and it is the organization's responsibility to control it.

Employment-at-Will

■ **Employment-at-will** is a traditional view of the employment relationship that holds that both employer and employee have the mutual right to terminate an employment relationship at any time, for any reason, and with or without advance notice to the other.

The concept of employment-at-will dates back to early employment relationships in England. The basic premise of **employment-at-will** is that both employer and employee have the mutual right to terminate an employment relationship at any time, for any reason, and with or without advance notice to the other. Specifically, the idea is that an organization employs an individual at its own will and can therefore terminate that employment at any time for any reason. Over the last two decades, however, some employees have begun to challenge the employment-at-will doctrine by filing lawsuits against their former employers on the grounds of what is called wrongful discharge.[29]

The legal basis of these lawsuits ranges from the various pieces of civil rights legislation discussed earlier to specific clauses in union contracts. Union contracts, for example, frequently specify the steps that must be followed before an organization can terminate the employment of a given individual or employee. Some lawsuits have argued that the same process must be accorded to all employees whether they are union members or not. Numerous tort-based lawsuits in the last several years have served to constrain or minimize the employment-at-will provisions in certain circumstances. For example, the courts have ruled that employees may not be fired for exercising rights that are protected by law. In the past, for example, some organizations were guilty of firing workers who filed worker compensation claims or who took excessive time off to serve on jury duty.

Another instance of how employment-at-will can be overturned is when there is an express or implied guarantee of continued employment. For example, sometimes the organization may have a stated policy that employees cannot be dismissed except for good cause. It follows logically, then, that this policy constitutes an implied contract and that an employee who is dismissed without good cause has grounds for a lawsuit. The courts have also ruled that organizations must deal in good faith with their employees. For example, an organization that asks an employee to undergo an extended and rigorous training program and then terminates the employment of that person prior to the completion of the training might be violating a good-faith relationship.

Another emerging issue related to employment-at-will relates to employee knowledge. The courts have long held that an employee with secret and proprietary technical knowledge, such as chemical formulas for a revolutionary new fertilizer or electronic specifications for a new computer module, could not simply resign and then turn that information over to a competitor. But in recent years this issue has been extended to areas such as general organizational practices, strategies, and business plans. With the continued evolution of information technology, this issue, as discussed more fully in "Human Resources in the Twenty-first Century," promises to become increasingly important to human resource managers responsible for recruiting and hiring new executives.

Can You Take It with You?

 As knowledge and information come to play increasingly important roles in organizations around the world, more and more companies are wondering how to manage knowledge and information access and control. An especially important emerging issue today, and one that promises to become even more important in the years to come, has to do with high-level trade secrets held by key executives who leave a company. If the executive in question is moving to a different industry or starting a new business in an unrelated area, the company may have few concerns. But what if he is going to work for a major competitor? Or what if she has actually been recruited by another firm specifically because of her insider knowledge? Increasingly, these cases are ending up in the courtroom.

For example, when the head of Campbell's U.S. soup business left for a position at H. J. Heinz, Campbell's sued Heinz because the executive had been specifically recruited to help Campbell's biggest competitor upgrade its own soup business. The eventual settlement allowed the executive to work instead for Heinz's tuna and pet-food businesses for two years before being allowed to work in the soup business. Similar issues arose when Dow Chemical recruited fifteen managers from General Electric's plastics business, when a high-ranking Eastman Kodak executive was recruited by rival Fuji Film, and when a PepsiCo soft-drink executive was recruited by the bever-

"So what does a company do when an executive studies up on confidential information just before he departs for a competitor?"

(Alan Sklover, New York attorney specializing in employment law)*

age unit at Quaker Oats. Each of these cases ended up in court.

One recent case highlighted even more complicated issues. Bayer AG of Germany sued General Electric because GE had recruited a senior executive from Bayer's medical technology business. Bayer's suit alleged that the executive actually went out of his way to gain new insights and acquire new information about Bayer's plans and technologies before departing. The case was eventually settled out of court but still raises major issues for managers to consider.

So what can individual managers and employers do to maintain both individual freedom and corporate propriety? For one thing, employers often require key executives to sign legal agreements that they will not directly compete with the company in the future and/or will not disclose sensitive information to others. An executive being recruited by another firm, then, should be sure to inform suitors of any such existing agreements. For another, the employee should also take care to not seek new information after taking another job and be sure to both turn over copies of sensitive documents and not maintain personal copies. But no system is fail-safe. After all, a person's memory can't be erased!

References: "Secret Suits: What Did He Know?" Wall Street Journal, January 19, 1998, p. B1; "What's in Your Head Can Hurt You," Fortune, July 20, 1998, p. 153.

Ethics and Human Resource Management

Another important and related issue for all managers, not just human resource managers, is ethics. Ethics are a separate concept from the law but are also closely intertwined. **Ethics** refer to an individual's beliefs about what is right and wrong and what is good and bad. Ethics are formed by the societal context in which people and organizations function. In recent years there has been an increased emphasis on ethical behavior and ethical conduct on behalf of managers and organizations. The basic premise is that laws are passed by the government to control and dictate appropriate behavior and conduct in a society. Moreover, ethics serve much the same purpose because of their premise about what is right and what is wrong.

But ethics and law don't always precisely coincide. For example, it may be perfectly legal for a manager to take a certain action, but many observers might find that action unethical. For example, an organization undergoing a

■ **Ethics** refer to an individual's beliefs about what is right and wrong and what is good and bad.

major cutback might be able to legally terminate a specific employee who is nearing retirement age. But if that employee has a long history of dedicated service to the organization, many people would consider termination to be of questionable ethics. Managers from every walk of the organization must take steps to ensure that their behavior is both ethical and legal. To accommodate this situation, some organizations develop codes of conduct or ethical statements that are an attempt to publicly communicate their stance on ethics and ethical conducts.

THE BOTTOM LINE The legal context of human resource management continues to evolve and change, and new issues continue to emerge. Thus managers need to be familiar with existing regulations while they continue to monitor current developments, pending legislation, and court decisions. The human resource function should play an especially important part in this process as partial fulfillment of its center of expertise role.

EVALUATING   LEGAL   COMPLIANCE

Given the clear and obvious importance as well as the complexities associated with the legal environment of human resource management, organizations must comply with the laws and regulations that govern human resource management practices to the best of their ability. The assurance of compliance can best be done through a three-step process. The first step is for managers to have a clear understanding of the laws that govern every aspect of human resource management. That is, human resource managers and other managers alike must understand and be intimately familiar with the various laws that restrict and govern their behavior vis-a-vis their employees.

Second, organizations should rely on their own legal and human resource staffs to answer questions and to periodically review procedures. Virtually all larger organizations have a legal staff consisting of trained professionals in various areas of the legal environment of business. A human resource manager or other manager with a legal question regarding a particular employment issue or practice might be well advised to consult with the firm's attorney about the legality of that particular action.

And third, organizations may also find it useful to occasionally engage in external legal audits of their human resource management procedures. This procedure might involve contracting with an outside law firm to review the organization's human resource management systems and practices to ensure that they are complying with all appropriate laws and regulations. Such an external audit will, of course, be expensive and somewhat intrusive into the organization's daily routine. However, when properly conducted, an external audit can go a long way toward keeping an organization out of trouble.

THE BOTTOM LINE Managers should carefully monitor the extent to which they and their organization complies with all relevant laws affecting employment relationships. Knowing the laws, regularly reviewing procedures, and periodically auditing compliance can all help keep the organization out of legal trouble while simultaneously insuring the most effective use of the firm's human resources.

Chapter Summary

The legal context of human resource management is shaped by a variety of forces. The first step in this process is the creation of new regulation. The second step is the enforcement of those regulations. The third step is the actual practice and implementation in organizations of those regulations. Regulations exist in virtually every aspect of the employment relationship.

The basic goal of all equal employment opportunity regulation is to protect people from unfair or inappropriate discrimination in the workplace. Illegal discrimination results from behaviors or actions by an organization or managers within an organization that cause members of a protected class to be unfairly differentiated from others. Four basic kinds of discrimination are disparate treatment, disparate impact, pattern or practice discrimination, and retaliation. Depending on the specific law, a protected class consists of all individuals who share at least one characteristic as indicated by that law.

The major laws and related regulations that affect equal employment opportunity include Title VII of the Civil Rights Act of 1964, Executive Order 11246, Executive Order 11478, the Equal Pay Act of 1963, the Age Discrimination and Employment Act (ADEA), the Vocational Rehabilitation Act of 1973, the Vietnam Era Veterans' Readjustment Act of 1974, the Pregnancy Discrimination Act of 1979, the Civil Rights Act of 1991, the Americans with Disabilities Act of 1990, and the Family and Medical Leave Act of 1993. The enforcement of equal opportunity legislation generally is handled by the Equal Employment Opportunity Commission (EEOC) and the Office of Federal Contract Compliance Procedures (OFCCP.)

The most far-reaching law dealing with total compensation is the Fair Labor Standards Act, passed in 1938. This law established a minimum hourly wage for jobs. Another important piece of legislation that affects compensation is the Employee Retirement Income Security Act of 1974, or ERISA.

The National Labor Relations Act, or Wagner Act, was passed in 1935 in an effort to control and legislate collective bargaining between organizations and labor unions. Congress subsequently passed the Taft-Hartley Act in 1947 and the Landrum-Griffin Act in 1959 to regulate union actions and their internal affairs.

Several related areas of human resource management are also affected by laws and associated legal issues. These include employee safety and health, (especially as related to the Occupational Safety and Health Act), various emerging areas of discrimination law (especially sexual harassment), employment-at-will, and ethics and human resource management.

Review and Discussion Questions

1. Describe the process through which the legal context of human resource management is created.

2. Summarize the role of the Thirteenth and Fourteenth Amendments to the U.S. Constitution in terms of equal employment opportunity.

3. What is illegal discrimination? What is legal discrimination?

4. Identify and summarize the various forms of illegal discrimination.

5. Identify and summarize five major laws that deal with equal employment opportunity.

6. Why is most employment regulation actually passed at the national level, as opposed to the state or local level?

7. Which equal employment opportunity laws will likely affect you most directly when you finish school and begin to look for employment?

8. Which equal employment opportunity law do you think is most critical? Which do you think is least critical?

9. Which equal employment opportunity law do you think is the most difficult to obey? Which do you think is easiest to obey?

10. In the case of a conflict between a legal and an ethical consequence of a human resource decision, which do you think should take precedence?

Closing Case

Seinfeld and Sexual Harassment

What role could a popular television show possibly play in a major sexual harassment lawsuit? As it turns out, a pretty big one! The show in question is *Seinfeld*, one of the most popular situation comedies in television history. The specific incident that occurred took place in the corporate headquarters of Miller Brewing Company and involved Jerold MacKenzie, a fifty-five-year-old, nineteen-year Miller executive, and Patty Best, his secretary.

The incident occurred in 1993. The *Seinfeld* episode involved a story in which the show's main character, Jerry Seinfeld, meets and starts dating an attractive woman. It later turns out that he cannot remember her name but does recall that it rhymes with a part of the female anatomy. He subsequently spends the rest of the episode running through different possible names for his friend. She finally dumps him when she realizes that he doesn't know her name. After she leaves, he learns that her name is Delores.

Mr. MacKenzie apparently found the show to be especially funny. The next day at work he made a point of bringing it up for discussion with Ms. Best, who indicated that she had not seen the show. As he began to describe the show for her, she apparently indicated to him that she didn't want to discuss it. Mr. MacKenzie persisted, however, and continued to push her to discuss it with him. When he couldn't bring himself to actually say the name of the female body part, however, he ended up making a photocopy of a dictionary page containing the word and giving it to Ms. Best.

Ms. Best later testified that she became quite upset and reported to Miller's human resource department that Mr. MacKenzie had sexually harassed her. She also indicated that he had also harassed her on earlier occasions as well. A few days later, Mr. MacKenzie was summoned to a meeting with a group of Miller attorneys and a senior human resource manager. Mr. MacKenzie was asked about the *Seinfeld* incident and acknowledged that it had happened as Ms. Best had reported. He also indicated that he saw it as simply office conversation and that Ms. Best had not seemed to be bothered or upset at the time of the conversation.

The next day, a senior corporate executive visited Mr. MacKenzie and told him that he was being terminated for unacceptable management performance. The incident with Ms. Best was identified as a major part of the final decision to terminate MacKenzie's employment with Miller, but he was also told that it was part of a pattern of poor decisions that had already attracted the attention of senior managers. Mr. MacKenzie indicated surprise but left without too much discussion.

As time passed, however, Mr. MacKenzie gradually began to feel that he had been mistreated. Finally, in 1997 he reached the point where he really felt compelled to take some action. After consulting with his attorney, he filed a lawsuit against Miller Brewing Co., the executive who had made the decision to terminate him, and Ms. Best. Among his charges were wrongful discharge and libel. After hearing both sides of the case, a jury of ten women and two men decided that he was right. Indeed, the jury so strongly believed that Mr. MacKenzie was a victim, rather than a sexual harasser, that it awarded unusually large judgments, including punitive damages, of $24.5 million against Miller, $1.5 million from Ms. Best (this award was later dropped because of a legal technicality), and slightly more than $600,000 from the executive who had terminated him.

Case Questions

1. Do you think Mr. MacKenzie's actions constituted sexual harassment? Why or why not?

2. Do you think Miller's termination of Mr. MacKenzie was justified? Why or why not?

3. What is your opinion of the jury's decision?

Sources: "The *Seinfeld* Firing," *Wall Street Journal*, May 11, 1998, p. A20; "Ex-Miller Executive Wins Award in '*Seinfeld*' Case," *Wall Street Journal*, July 16, 1997, p. B13.

Building Human Resource Management Skills

Purpose: Affirmative action was created as a way of directly and proactively attracting more qualified members of protected classes into the workforce. While most people believe that affirmative action has served a useful function, some people now believe that it is no longer needed. Specifically, they argue that companies today recognize the importance of hiring the best people possible and will continue to seek out those individuals on their own, without the overarching pressure of formal affirmative action. Advocates of affirmative action, however, believe that it is still necessary to meet its original objectives. The purpose of this exercise is to give you additional insights into the arguments surrounding affirmative action.

Step 1: Your instructor will divide the class into groups of seven members each. Using a random procedure, divide your group into two subgroups of three members each and a moderator.

Step 2: One subgroup will develop a set of arguments as to why affirmative action is still a necessary and important component of equal opportunity employment. The other group will develop a set of arguments as to why affirmative action is no longer a necessary and important component of equal employment opportunity.

Step 3: Reconvene as a group of seven. The moderator will randomly select one side to present its case first. That group has three minutes to make its case. The second group will then take three minutes to make its case and one additional minute to rebut the first group. Finally, the first group will have one minute to rebut the arguments made by the second group.

Step 4: The moderator will then summarize the relative persuasiveness of each group regarding the affirmative action issue. The moderator should feel free to add any personal thoughts about the issue that were not mentioned by either group.

Step 5: Develop a brief summary of the arguments made by both groups. Using the format suggested by your instructor, share these arguments with the rest of the class.

Ethical Dilemmas in Human Resource Management

 Assume that you are a human resource manager in a large manufacturing plant. The following facts summarize an important situation:

1. A potential safety hazard has been identified in a section of the factory.

2. You strongly recommended to the plant manager that this safety hazard be corrected immediately.

3. The plant manager agrees that the problem is a priority, although not one that is as important as you seem to believe.

4. The manager's plans are to reduce the number of people who work in the area as much as possible and then correct the safety hazard next month when the plant will be shut for a week while some new technological equipment unrelated to the safety hazard is installed.

5. Trying to correct the problem now would indeed be very expensive, adding several thousand dollars to the cost of correcting the problem next month when the plant is closed.

This morning you went to your health club for your daily workout. While getting dressed in the locker room, you inadvertently overheard a conversation between two people outside the locker area. It seems that one is an OSHA inspector. This individual told his friend that he was scheduled to make an unannounced visit to a nearby manufacturing plant later in the week for an inspection. You were not trying to eavesdrop, and you didn't hear the entire conversation. However, based on what you did hear, you are almost certain that your plant will be inspected.

Questions

1. What are the ethical issues in this situation?

2. What are the pros and cons for keeping this information to yourself versus telling your plant manager what you heard?

3. What do you think most managers would do? What would you do?

Human Resource Internet Exercise

 One of the most critical issues facing all human resource managers today is compliance with various legal regulations. This Web site summarizes most current lawsuits in federal courts involving claims of discrimination of various forms: http://www.law.cornell.edu/topics/employment.html

Visit this Web site and select any two categories of pending lawsuits. Then visit those locations and review some of the lawsuits. Choose two lawsuits from each area that seem interesting to you (for a total of four). Write up a brief description of each lawsuit. Then describe the potential implications for you, as a future human resource manager, of each potential outcome of the lawsuits.

Questions

1. How useful is the Internet in keeping human resource managers informed about legal actions that may affect them?

2. Does relying on the Internet for legal information pose any risks?

3. What other legal information would you like to see on the Internet?

Notes

1. David Israel, "Learn to Manage the Legal Process," *HRMagazine*, July 1993, pp. 83–89.
2. "HR and the Government," *HRMagazine*, May 1994, pp. 43–48. See also J. Ledvinka, *Federal Regulation of Personnel and Human Resource Management* (Boston: Kent, 1982).
3. "Damned If You Do, Damned If You Don't," *Forbes*, December 15, 1997, pp. 122–133.
4. Jon M. Werner and Mark C. Bolino, "Explaining U.S. Court of Appeals Decisions Involving Performance Appraisal: Accuracy, Fairness, and Validation," *Personnel Psychology*, Spring 1997, pp. 1–24.
5. See Philip E. Varca and Patricia Pattison, "Evidentiary Standards in Employment Discrimination: A View toward the Future," *Personnel Psychology*, Summer 1993, pp. 239–250.
6. *Griggs v. Duke Power Company*, 401 U.S. 424 (1971).
7. "Culture of Racial Bias at Shoney's Underlines Chairman's Departure," *Wall Street Journal*, December 21, 1992, p. A1.
8. "Flood of 'Retaliation' Cases Surfacing in U.S. Workplace," *USA Today*, February 10, 1999, pp. 1A, 2A.
9. "When Quotas Replace Merit, Everybody Suffers," *Forbes*, February 15, 1993, pp. 80–102.
10. "As Workers Grow Older, Age-Bias Lawsuits Decline," *USA Today*, June 26, 1998, p. B1.
11. "Recent Suits Make Pregnancy Issues Workplace Priorities," *Wall Street Journal*, January 14, 1998, p. B1; "Pregnant Workers Clash with Employers over Job Inflexibility," *Wall Street Journal*, February 10, 1999, p. B1.
12. "Silver Lining," *Forbes*, November 21, 1994, pp. 124–125.
13. Francine S. Hall and Elizabeth L. Hall, "The ADA: Going beyond the Law," *Academy of Management Executive*, February 1994, pp. 17–26; "Able to Work," *Time*, January 25, 1999, pp. 68–72.
14. Albert S. King, "Doing the Right Thing for Employees with Disabilities," *Training & Development*, September 1993, pp. 44–48.
15. "Disabilities Act Abused?" *USA Today*, September 25, 1998, pp. 1B, 2B.
16. Michelle Neely Martinez, "FMLA—Headache or Opportunity?" *HRMagazine*, February 1994, pp. 42–45.
17. Jonathan A. Segal, "Traps to Avoid in FMLA Compliance," *HRMagazine*, February 1994, pp. 97–100; see also "Why the Law School Should Adopt More Family Leave," *Business Week*, February 1, 1999, p. 42.
18. John Montoya, "New Priorities for the '90s," *HRMagazine*, April 1997, pp. 118–122.
19. David Israel, "Check EEOC Position Statements for Accuracy," *HRMagazine*, September 1993, pp. 106–109.
20. William R. Tracey, "Auditing ADA Compliance," *HRMagazine*, October 1994, pp. 88–93.
21. David C. Ankeny and David Israel, "Completing an On-Site OFCCP Audit," *HRMagazine*, March 1993, pp. 89–94.
22. Paul R. Dorf and Ethel P. Flanders, "Classify Jobs Properly to Avoid Overtime Trap," *HRMagazine*, April 1994, pp. 29–32.
23. Robert F. Scherer, James D. Brodzinski, and Elaine A. Crable, "The Human Factor," *HRMagazine*, April 1993, pp. 92–96.
24. Neville C. Tompkins, "At the Top of OSHA's Hit List," *HRMagazine*, July 1993, pp. 54–58.
25. "Court Narrows Disability Act," *USA Today*, June 23, 1999, p. 1A.
26. Jonathan A. Segal, "Sexual Harassment: Where Are We Now? *HRMagazine*, October 1996, pp. 68–73; Gerald D. Bloch, "Avoiding Liability for Sexual Harassment," *HRMagazine*, April 1995, pp. 91–94.
27. Jonathan A. Segal, "Proceed Carefully, Objectively to Investigate Sexual Harassment Claims," *HRMagazine*, October 1993, pp. 91–95; see also "Is Sexual Harassment Getting Worse?" *Forbes*, April 19, 1999, p. 92.
28. "Justices' Ruling Further Defines Sexual Harassment," *Wall Street Journal*, March 5, 1998, p. B1.
29. "Laws, Juries Shift Protection to Terminated Employees," *USA Today*, April 2, 1998, pp. 1B, 2B.

4

The Global Environment

CHAPTER OUTLINE

The Growth of International Business

Global Issues in International Human Resource Management
International Human Resource Management Strategy
Understanding the Cultural Environment
Understanding the Political and Legal Environment

The Human Resource Function in International Business
General Human Resource Issues in International Business
Specific Human Resource Issues in International Business

Domestic Issues in International Human Resource Management
Local Recruiting and Selection Issues
Local Training Issues
Local Compensation Issues

Managing International Transfers and Assignments
Selecting Expatriates
Training Expatriates
Compensating Expatriates

International Labor Relations

CHAPTER OBJECTIVES

After studying this chapter you should be able to:

■ Describe the growth of international business.

■ Identify and discuss global issues in international human resource management.

■ Discuss the human resource management function in international business.

■ Identify and discuss domestic issues in international human resource management.

■ Describe the issues involved in managing international transfers and assignments.

■ Summarize the issues in international labor relations.

One of the most significant trends in U.S. business today is the growing practice of moving production to foreign locations to capitalize on lower labor costs. General Motors has been very successful with this practice, especially in Mexico. Almost 20 percent of the firm's North American manufacturing workforce is now based in Mexico. Indeed, GM and Delphi Automotive Systems, GM's huge parts-making subsidiary, are among the most attractive—and important—employers in Mexico.

The benefits of producing in Mexico are clear. For one thing, local wage standards are such that Mexican workers are paid about one-tenth of their counterparts in Flint, Michigan, GM's other big North American production center. Mexican workers also expect fewer benefits and the government imposes fewer regulations on employers. And the products that come out of the Mexican plants can be exported tariff-free into the United States.

For their part Mexican workers agree that they are getting a good deal. For example, although their wages may seem low by U.S. standards, most of them are actually earning far more than they would be if they were working for Mexican firms in other parts of the country. They also generally believe that they have better benefits, more job security, improved job training, and greater opportunities for advancement than if they were employed elsewhere. Indeed, some observers believe that

"It's the turn of the century all over again, now, south of the border."

(Charles Robinson, U.S.
auto industry consultant)*

the northern Mexico region today is very much like Detroit was sixty years ago in becoming a magnet for motivated but undereducated workers looking for a better way of life.

But not everything is perfect. For one thing, GM's biggest union, the United Auto Workers, or UAW, is seriously concerned about the flow of jobs to Mexico, and sees it as a major threat to the long-term job security of its own members in the United States. For another, GM's plants in Mexico experience very high turnover—as much as 50 percent a year—in large part because many of their workers leave their families behind when they come north to work and then get lonely and return home. And for another, many of the workers are poorly educated and must first be taught to read and write before true job-related training can even begin. And in the event of a long-term slowdown in the auto industry, any major job cuts by GM could seriously undermine its current reputation as a major employer of choice in Mexico. But for the present time, at least, things appear to be a true win-win situation.

"In Mexico, a GM Worker Springs into the Middle Class," *Wall Street Journal*, July 29, 1998, pp. B1, B4; Ricky W. Griffin and Michael W. Pustay, *International Business—A Managerial Perspective*, 2nd ed. (Reading, Mass.: Addison-Wesley, 1999); "The Border," *Business Week*, May 12, 1997, pp. 64–74.

I t's no secret that international business is booming these days. General Motors, like most other large firms, is always on the alert for new business opportunities anywhere in the world. Such opportunities include new markets where products and services can be sold; new locations where products and services can be created for lower costs; and areas where new information, financing, and other resources may be obtained. To effectively manage international expansion, firms need skilled and experienced managers and employees who understand both specific individual foreign markets (such as Japan or Germany) and the general international economic situation (including such issues as exchange rate fluctuations and the cost of labor). One of the fastest growing and most important concerns for human resource managers in many companies today is preparing other managers for international assignments. In reality, however, this area is only one part of international human resource management.

This chapter will explore international human resource management in detail. We begin with a general overview of the growth of international business. Global issues in international human resource management are then introduced and discussed. Next we examine the human resource function in international business. Domestic issues in international human resource management are identified and described, and then we describe the management of international transfers and assignments. We conclude by summarizing the basic issues in international labor relations.

THE GROWTH OF INTERNATIONAL BUSINESS

I nternational business is not a new phenomenon. Indeed, its origins can be traced back literally thousands of years as merchants plied their wares along ancient trade routes linking southern Europe, the Middle East, and the Orient. Silks, spices, grains, jade, ivory, and textiles were among the most popular goods forming the basis for early trade. Even in more modern times, Columbus's voyages to the so-called new world were motivated by the economic goal of discovering new trade routes to the Far East. Wars have been fought over issues arising from international commerce, and the British Empire was built around the financial and business interests of the British nobility. In more recent years, however, a number of specific trends have emerged in international business that provide a meaningful context for the study of human resource management.

The forces that shaped today's competitive international business environment began to emerge in the years following World War II. As a result of that global conflict, Japan and most of Europe were devastated. Roads were destroyed, highways were ruined, and factories were bombed. The United States was the only major industrial power that emerged from World War II with its infrastructure relatively intact. Places not devastated by the war, such as South and Central America and Africa, were not major players in the global economy even before the war, and Canada had yet to become a major global economic power.

Businesses in war-torn countries had little choice but to rebuild from scratch. They were in the unfortunate position of having to rethink every facet of their business, including technology, productions, operations, finance, and marketing. Ultimately, however, this situation actually ended up working to their advantage. During the 1950s the United States was by far the dominant economic power in the world. Its businesses controlled most major marketplaces and most major industries. At the same time, however, Japan and Germany and other countries were rebuilding their own infrastructures and developing new industrial clout.

During the 1960s this newly formed clout began to really exert itself in the world marketplace. Firms from Germany (like Siemens, Daimler-Benz, and Bayer) and Japan (like Toyota, NEC, and Mitsubishi) began to take on new industrial strength and slowly but surely began to challenge the dominance of U.S. firms in markets ranging from automobiles to electronics. In the late 1970s and on into the 1980s, businesses from other countries really emerged as major players in the world economy. At the same time, many U.S. firms began to realize that they had grown complacent, that their products and services were not of high quality, and that their manufacturing and production methods were outdated and outmoded.

Eventually, U.S. firms decided that they had little choice but to start over. Thus during the latter part of the 1980s and on into the early 1990s, many U.S. firms virtually rebuilt themselves. They shut down or renovated old factories, they developed new manufacturing techniques, and they began to focus renewed emphasis on quality. By the mid-1990s global competitiveness seemed to have become the norm, rather than the exception. The United States, Japan, and Germany remain the three leading industrial powers in the world. However, other Western European countries such as France, England, Spain, and

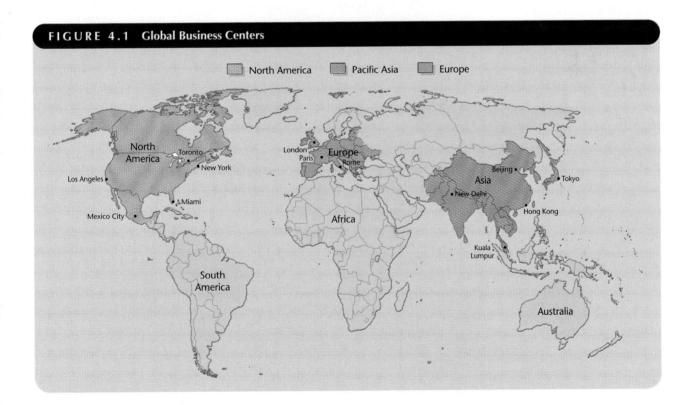

FIGURE 4.1   Global Business Centers

TABLE 4.1 The World's Largest Multinational Firms

Rank	Corporation	Home Country	Revenues $ mil.	Employees
1	General Motors	U.S.	161,315.0	594,000
2	DaimlerChrysler	Germany	154,615.0	441,502
3	Ford Motor	U.S.	144,416.0	345,175
4	Wal-Mart Stores	U.S.	139,208.0	910,000
5	Mitsui	Japan	109,372.9	32,961
6	Itochu	Japan	108,749.1	5,775
7	Mitsubishi	Japan	107,184.4	36,000
8	Exxon	U.S.	100,697.0	79,000
9	General Electric	U.S.	100,469.0	293,000
10	Toyota Motor	Japan	99,740.1	183,879
11	Royal Dutch/Shell Group	Brit./Neth.	93,692.0	102,000
12	Marubeni	Japan	93,568.6	65,000
13	Sumitomo	Japan	89,020.7	30,700
14	Intl. Business Machines	U.S.	81,667.0	291,067
15	AXA	France	78,729.3	87,896
16	Citigroup	U.S.	76,431.0	170,100
17	Volkswagen	Germany	76,306.6	297,916
18	Nippon Telegraph & Telephone	Japan	76,118.7	224,400
19	BP Amoco	Britain	68,304.0	96,650
20	Nissho Iwai	Japan	67,741.7	19,461
21	Nippon Life Insurance	Japan	66,299.6	71,015
22	Siemens	Germany	66,037.8	416,000
23	Allianz	Germany	64,874.7	105,676
24	Hitachi	Japan	62,409.9	328,351
25	U.S. Postal Service	U.S.	60,072.0	904,636
26	Matsushita Electric Industrial	Japan	59,771.4	282,153
27	Philip Morris	U.S.	57,813.0	144,000
28	ING Group	Netherlands	56,468.7	82,750
29	Boeing	U.S.	56,154.0	227,000
30	AT&T	U.S.	53,588.0	107,800
31	Sony	Japan	53,156.7	177,000
32	Metro	Germany	52,126.4	181,282
33	Nissan Motor	Japan	51,477.7	131,260
34	FIAT	Italy	50,998.9	220,549
35	Bank of America Corp.	U.S.	50,777.0	170,975
36	Nestlé	Switzerland	49,504.1	231,881
37	Credit Suisse	Switzerland	49,143.3	62,296
38	Honda Motor	Japan	48,747.7	112,200
39	Assicurazioni Generali	Italy	48,478.1	54,598
40	Mobil	U.S.	47,678.0	41,500
41	Hewlett-Packard	U.S.	47,061.0	124,600
42	Deutsche Bank	Germany	45,165.0	75,306
43	Unilever	Brit./Neth.	44,908.0	267,000
44	State Farm Insurance Cos.	U.S.	44,620.9	76,257
45	Dai-Ichi Mutual Life Insurance	Japan	44,485.6	63,427
46	VEBA Group	Germany	43,407.5	116,774
47	HSCB Holdings	Britain	43,338.3	144,521
48	Toshiba	Japan	41,470.9	198,000
49	Renault	France	41,353.3	138,321
50	Sears Roebuck	U.S.	41,322.0	324,000

Source: Fortune, August 2, 1999. Reprinted by permission of Fortune Magazine.

Belgium also were becoming increasingly important. In Asia, Taiwan, Singapore, and Malaysia were emerging as global economic powers, with China's emergence as a global power looming on the horizon. In North America, Canada and Mexico began to show promise of achieving economic preeminence in the global marketplace. Figure 4.1 illustrates the regions of the world that are especially significant in today's global economy, and Table 4.1 lists the world's largest industrial corporations.

The increasing global nature of business also provided attractive new markets for businesses to enter. The Chinese market probably has the greatest potential, while markets in Russia, India, and many regions of South America are also becoming important again. Indeed, no business can afford to ignore the global environment. Even businesses that do not sell their products and services in foreign markets are still likely to obtain at least some of their resources from foreign markets, and most must compete with businesses from foreign countries as well. As we will see, however, businesses in today's global environment can take many forms and adopt numerous strategies for competing in this environment. And human resource management is a key component in each of these forms and strategies.

THE BOTTOM LINE International business and global competitiveness have become almost commonplace for most larger organizations today, and more and more medium-size and smaller businesses are engaged in international business as well. Thus all managers, regardless of their specialization, need to be familiar with international business issues, concepts, and processes.

GLOBAL ISSUES IN INTERNATIONAL HUMAN RESOURCE MANAGEMENT

Any international firm must address a variety of global issues in international human resource management. As shown in Figure 4.2, one issue is developing an international human resource management strategy.[1] Another is developing an understanding of the cultural environment of human resource management. Yet a third is developing an understanding of the political and legal environment of international business.

International Human Resource Management Strategy

Just as the overall strategy of a business has to be logical and well conceived, so too must the effective management of a firm's international human resources be approached with a cohesive and coherent strategy. As a starting point most international businesses today develop a systematic strategy for choosing among home-country nationals, host-country nationals, and third-country nationals for various positions in their organization.[2]

Some firms adopt what is called an **ethnocentric staffing model**. Firms that use this model primarily hire home-country nationals to staff higher-level foreign positions. This strategy assumes that home-office perspectives and issues should take precedence over local perspectives and issues and that expatriate home-country nationals will be more effective in representing the views of the

■ Firms that use the **ethnocentric staffing model** primarily hire parent-country nationals to staff higher-level foreign positions.

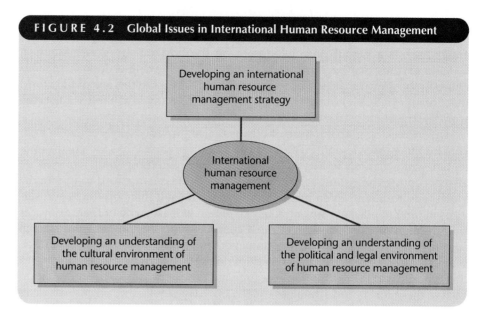

FIGURE 4.2   Global Issues in International Human Resource Management

home office in the foreign operation.[3] The corporate human resource function in organizations that adopt this mentality is primarily concerned with selecting and training managers for foreign assignments, developing appropriate compensation packages for those managers, and handling adjustment issues when managers are reassigned back home. Local human resource officials will handle staffing and related human resource issues for local employees hired to fill lower-level positions in the firm. Sony Corporation's operations in the United States follow this model. Sony Corporation of America, a wholly owned subsidiary of Sony Corporation, handles local human resource issues, but top managers at plants around the United States are Japanese, from the firm's Japanese home office.

■ The **polycentric staffing model** calls for heavy use of host-country nationals throughout the organization.

Other international businesses adopt what is called a **polycentric staffing model**. A polycentric staffing model calls for a much heavier use of host-country nationals throughout the organization, from top to bottom. Thus the use of the polycentric staffing model is based on the assumption that such individuals (that is, host-country nationals) will be better equipped to deal with local market conditions. Organizations that use this approach will usually have a fully functioning human resource department in each foreign subsidiary responsible for managing all local human resource issues for both lower-level and upper-level employees. The corporate human resource managers in such companies will focus primarily on coordinating relevant activities with their counterparts in each foreign operation. U.S. energy companies operating in Asia often adopt this model, especially since these operations are often joint ventures between the U.S. company and one or more local companies.

■ The **geocentric staffing model** puts parent-country nationals, host-country nationals, and third-country nationals in the same category, with the firm attempting to always hire the best person available for a position.

Finally, still other firms adopt what is called a **geocentric staffing model**. This staffing model puts home-country nationals, host-country nationals, and third-country nationals in the same category. The firm then attempts to always hire the best person available for a position, regardless of where that individual comes from. The geocentric staffing model is most likely to be adopted and used by fully internationalized firms such as Nestlé and Unilever.[4] In many ways the corporate human resource function in geocentric companies is the most complicated of all. Every aspect of the human resource management process—planning, recruiting, selection, compensation, and training—must be undertaken from an international perspective. Moreover, each foreign subsidiary or operation will still need its own self-contained human resource unit to handle ongoing employment issues.

Understanding the Cultural Environment

The cultural environment of international business also poses a variety of challenges and opportunities for human resource managers. A **country's culture** can be defined as the set of values, symbols, beliefs, and languages that guide behavior of people within that culture. A culture does not necessarily coincide precisely with national boundaries, but these two different constructs tend to be relatively similar in terms of geographic area and domain. All managers in an international business need to be aware of cultural nuances since, by definition human resource managers are concerned with people. Further, they must be especially cognizant of the role and importance of cultural differences and similarities in workers from different cultures.

Cultural beliefs and values are often unspoken and may even be taken for granted by those who live in a particular country. When cultures are similar, relatively few problems or difficulties may be encountered. Human resource managers can extrapolate from their own experiences to understand their function in the other culture. Thus U.S. managers often have relatively little difficulty doing business in England. Managers in both countries speak the same

> ■ A **country's culture** can be defined as the set of values, symbols, beliefs, and languages that guide behavior of people within that culture.

Managers increasingly have to address global issues as they strive to manage their firm's human resources across different countries and cultures. These issues can often result in uncertainty and complexity. For example, even though Nigeria has vast oil reserves, as a function of GDP it has the world's lowest spending on education and the second-lowest spending on health. The country has fewer than four telephones per 1,000 people and hundreds of thousands lack running water, power, and sanitation. These drivers have been waiting two days for gasoline to be delivered to this service station so they can fill their vehicles. The challenges for human resources of hiring and managing a workforce in this region are therefore clearly quite daunting. While hiring local employees will likely result in a poorly trained and low-skill workforce, many non-Nigerians would be reluctant to assume the challenges of living and working in the country.

language and have a common framework for understanding both commercial and personal relationships.

More significant issues can arise, however, when there is considerable difference between the home culture of a manager and the culture of the country in which business is to be conducted. Thus there is a higher likelihood of culturally related problems and difficulties between managers from, say, Canada and India. Differences in language, customs, and business and personal norms increase the potential for misunderstandings, miscommunication, and similar problems. In these instances human resource managers must be careful so as to not overgeneralize from their own experiences or perspectives.

Cultural differences can also have a direct impact on business practices in international situations. For example, the religion of Islam teaches that people should not make a living by exploiting the problems of others and that making interest payments is immoral. Therefore, in Saudi Arabia and the Sudan there are no outplacement consulting firms (since outplacement involves charging a fee to help terminated workers cope with their situations). Managers may encounter unexpected complexities in doing business when these sorts of cultural differences exist.

Language is another important cultural dimension that affects international human resource management practices. Most obviously, differences in specific languages such as English, Japanese, Chinese, and Spanish dramatically complicate the issues involved in dealing with international business. Unfortunately, U.S. managers who are fluent in several languages tend to be relatively rare, and when a U.S. organization does find such an employee, that individual is a very valuable asset. On the other hand, it is fairly common for Asian managers to learn English in school, and most European managers are multilingual. It is interesting to note that, a number of years ago, U.S. schools (and especially colleges of business) began dropping foreign language requirements. As it turns out, unfortunately, those decisions may result in some competitive disadvantage for managers educated in the United States.

Another cultural factor that is most directly related to human resource management practices has to do with roles that exist in different cultures. In the United States there has been considerable change over the last few decades regarding the role of women in our society. For example, women have made considerable strides in pursuing and achieving career opportunities previously closed to them. In some other parts of the world, however, the situation is quite different. In Japan, for example, women still may find it fairly difficult to launch a successful career. Similar situations exist in some European countries, as well as in virtually all the countries in the Middle East. There are also role differences related to status and hierarchy. In the United States, for example, there is relatively little psychological distance between managers and subordinates, resulting in a certain degree of familiarity and informality. But in many Asian countries, this distance is much greater, resulting in more formalized roles and less informal communication across levels in the organization.

Yet another significant cultural factor has to do with children. In the United States child labor is closely regulated, and the traditional model is for children to attend school until they become young adults. In other countries, however, this practice may be quite different. For example, in Bangladesh it is quite common for children to be a major source of income for their families. Many children do not attend school at all and begin seeking jobs at a very young age. A company doing business in this environment, therefore, faces a significant dilemma. On the one hand, local cultural factors suggest that it is all right to hire young children to work for low wages since other businesses do the same thing. On the other hand, by the standards that exist in most industrialized countries, this practice is illegal and/or unethical.

The human resource manager dealing with international issues thus faces two fundamental cultural challenges. One challenge is simply understanding and appreciating differences that exist in different cultures. The value of work, attitudes and orientation toward work, and common work-related practices vary significantly from culture to culture, and the human resource manager needs to develop an understanding of these differences to function effectively.[5]

The second challenge is more ethical in nature. On the one hand, many businesses relocate manufacturing facilities to other countries to capitalize on lower labor costs. Indeed, it is quite possible for a business from a country like Japan or the United States to set up a factory in Bangladesh, Pakistan, or some other regions of the world and have minimal labor costs there. The ethical issue, however, is the extent to which this practice becomes exploitation. Many people, for instance, would agree that it is reasonable for a company to take advantage of low prevailing wage and benefit costs to achieve low-cost production. But to the extent that a company goes too far and truly begins to exploit foreign workers, problems may subsequently arise. This issue is further illustrated in "Point/Counterpoint."

Understanding the Political and Legal Environment

It is also important for human resource managers in international businesses to understand the political and legal environment of the countries in which they do business. Figure 4.3 illustrates four fundamental aspects of the political and legal environment of international business that are of primary concern for human resource managers: government stability, potential incentives for international trade, controls on international trade, and the influence of economic communities on international trade. An additional aspect here is the very basic issue of laws that affect the management of human resources, but we will say more about that later.

Government stability can be thought of as either the ability of a given government to stay in power against opposing factions or as the permanence of government policies toward business. In general, companies prefer to do business in countries that are stable in both respects, since managers have a higher

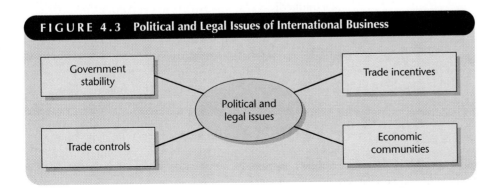

FIGURE 4.3 **Political and Legal Issues of International Business**

Government stability

Trade incentives

Political and legal issues

Trade controls

Economic communities

probability of successfully understanding how government will affect their business. Government instability in countries such as Lebanon and the Philippines has made it more difficult for international managers to fully understand how to establish and/or operate a business in those countries.

A major related human resource issue is the extent to which expatriate managers may be put at risk as a result of political instability. For example, there have been instances in which extremist groups have targeted U.S. executives for terrorist activities. Some firms have faced situations in which local govern-

---

POINT/COUNTERPOINT   Wages and Conditions in Foreign Plants

 Wages and working conditions in foreign plants are often different from those in domestic plants, even when the two are from the same organization and are performing the same functions. The press has been full of reports about the working conditions in plants in Latin America that manufacture clothing for a company owned by Kathy Lee Gifford and about working conditions in Asian plants that make the Nike shoes touted by Michael Jordan. Why do these differences exist, and should U.S. companies be forced to do something about it? Well, the differences exist because of different expectations about wages and working conditions. U.S. firms simply pay workers in a third-world country what they would otherwise earn, which is usually less than what U.S. workers doing the same thing would earn.

POINT . . . **It makes sense for organizations to allow and even encourage these differences because . . .**	COUNTERPOINT . . . **But on the other hand, this behavior is wrong, and U.S. firms should be forced to make changes because . . .**
Lower labor costs are exactly the reason the U.S. firm opens operations in these countries, and these savings allow the firm to be more competitive.	These jobs would otherwise be given to U.S. workers. The failure to do so leads to problems of unemployment and underemployment here.
Wages are lower in these countries, so paying workers there what U.S. workers make would create inequities.	U.S. companies could become a source of change, forcing other firms to raise wages and improve conditions for all workers.
Although wages are lower and conditions poorer, the cost of living is much lower in many of these countries so that workers actually live fairly well.	These employees are often required to work under appalling conditions, and their wages are often not enough to get them out of poverty.
Wages paid by U.S. firms and conditions in U.S.-owned operations are already much better than the alternatives for these foreign workers. Why should a company pay more or improve conditions more than it has to?	This is the basic issue—should U.S. firms have some social responsibility in the countries where they do business, or are these countries simply resources to be exploited?
U.S. firms are already helping these workers by providing jobs that otherwise would not be available.	This is basically true, but this system does deprive the United States of jobs.

So . . .   This issue is a complex one. When most Americans see how workers in foreign plants live and work, they are upset and call for change. Although we like to think of our country as being a source of positive change in the world, should U.S. companies be held to a higher standard than domestic firms are, especially if such a standard hurts competition? The answer is really a function of one's personal value system. How important is it to protect the rights and try to improve the lives of others? If one believes our country stands for something, perhaps this is a way to demonstrate it. On the other hand, if U.S. companies become less successful, they may not be in a position to help anyone. This issue is one we will continue to argue about. What do you think?

ment officials have closely watched and/or even harassed managers on the grounds that they are alleged illegal informants and/or spies for the U.S. government. Still another risk is the extent to which a business itself might become nationalized. The process of nationalization occurs when a government seizes the facilities of a company and declares them to be its own. Nationalization has occasionally happened in the Middle East and in certain countries in South America.

Another aspect of the political and legal environment is the incentives that are sometimes offered to attract foreign business. Occasionally, municipal governments offer foreign companies tax breaks and other incentives to build facilities in their area. Over the last few years, for example, both BMW and Mercedes have announced plans to build assembly factories in the United States. In each instance various state and local governments got into what essentially became bidding wars to see who could attract the manufacturing facilities. Incentives can include such things as reduced interest rates on loans, construction subsidies and tax incentives, and the relaxation of various controls on international trade. Some countries have also offered guaranteed labor contracts with local unions as an incentive designed to reduce the uncertainties an entering business might face in negotiating its own initial labor contract.

A third dimension of the political and legal environment of international business consists of those very controls that some countries place on international trade. A number of different controls exist. One is a **tariff**, essentially a tax that is collected on goods that are shipped across national boundaries. Tariffs may be levied by the exporting country, countries through which goods pass, and the importing country. The most common form of trade control, however, is the **quota**, a limit on the number or value of goods that can be traded. The quota amount is typically designed to ensure that domestic competitors will be able to maintain a predetermined market share. Honda Motors, for example, is allowed to import exactly 425,000 automobiles each year into the United States. Sometimes, however, companies are able to get around quotas. Honda has built assembly factories in the United States for just this purpose. Honda automobiles produced within the United States do not count toward the 425,000-unit quota.

For the international human resource manager a very important set of international controls involves the control of human resources. Some countries require that a foreign business setting up shop within its borders hire a minimum percentage of local employees. For example, a country might require that 80 percent of the production employees and 50 percent of the managers of a foreign-owned business come from the local citizenry. Less common but still a factor is the control of international travel. Some countries limit the number of trips that foreign managers can make in and out of their country in a given period of time. "Human Resources Legal Brief" discusses a variation on this issue related to child labor in other countries.

A final aspect of the political and legal environment is the growing importance of **economic communities**. Economic communities consist of sets of countries that agree to reduce or eliminate trade barriers among their member nations. One of the most commonly cited economic communities is the European Union, or EU. The EU consists of Denmark, the United Kingdom, Portugal, the Netherlands, Belgium, Spain, Ireland, Luxembourg, France, Germany, Italy, and Greece. For the past several years these countries have been systematically working toward a unified market system in which trade barriers and controls are gradually eliminated. This makes it easier for companies in any country of the union to do business in the other countries. This applies to

▨ A **tariff** is essentially a tax that is collected on goods that are shipped across national boundaries.

▨ A **quota** is simply a limit on the number or value of goods that can be traded.

▨ **Economic communities** consist of sets of countries that agree to reduce or eliminate trade barriers among their member nations.

Child Labor and International Business

For years, large juice distributors like Minute Maid, Tropicana, and Nestle have bought fruit juices from suppliers in South America. But a few years ago, reports began to surface that many of these suppliers relied heavily on child labor to harvest oranges, lemons, and other fruits. Children as young as nine were commonly taken out of school by their impoverished parents and put to work in the citrus groves. These parents often saw no problem with this action because they had also picked fruit as children.

In recent years, though, things have begun to change. For example, in 1997 the U.S. Congress amended a 1930 trade law to explicitly ban the importation of products made with child labor. Similarly, the International Brotherhood of Teamsters has also taken on a watchdog role to ensure that Brazilian exporters are held accountable for adhering to the law. Of course, critics claim that the teamsters' motivation is self-interest, but regardless of the reasons the union is having a positive effect.

> *"You can't take juice companies seriously about trying to eradicate child labor when they are promoting a system that clouds accountability in the workplace."*
>
> (Raimundo Limao de Mello, Brazilian attorney)*

And many South American countries are also trying to stamp out this practice. For example, child advocacy groups in Brazil have helped pass a new labor code. Among its provisions are bans on child labor and payments of $45 per month to any child who stays in school and maintains good attendance records—about the same sum that the child might earn picking fruit.

Although accurately tracing the activities of child fruit pickers is difficult, most experts do agree that, slowly but surely, things are improving. For example, government statistics suggest that child labor in general is down about 15 percent over the past three years. And more adults in Brazil also seem to be more aware of the importance of education and are actively discouraging fruit picking by children. But still, there is a long way to go.

References: "U.S. Child-Labor Law Sparks a Trade Debate over Brazilian Oranges," *Wall Street Journal*, September 9, 1998, pp. A1, A9 (*quote on p. A9); "Chile's Labor Law Hobbles Its Workers and Troubles the U.S.," *Wall Street Journal*, October 15, 1997, pp. A1, A14; "Sweatshop Police," *Business Week*, October 20, 1997, p. 39.

human resources as well because it dramatically increases the flexibility companies have for transferring managers across national boundaries.

A somewhat newer economic community was created by the North American Free Trade Agreement, or NAFTA. NAFTA attempts to dramatically reduce the trade barriers that exist between Canada, the United States, and Mexico. As with the EU, the goal was to make it easier for companies to do business in each of the three countries. Since immigration practices between Canada and the United States and Mexico have always been relatively lenient, NAFTA does not promise to dramatically change business practices regarding the difficulty or ease of transferring people across borders. However, to the extent that it does stimulate new international trade, NAFTA may very well increase the need for human resource managers to prepare people for international assignments.

THE BOTTOM LINE   Managers should know that the basic global issues affecting human resources include the firm's international human resource strategy, as well as the cultural and the political and legal environments. Having a clear and well-articulated international human resource strategy can be invaluable. Further, managers must understand cultural, political, and legal issues and forces from both a business and an ethical context.

THE HUMAN RESOURCE FUNCTION IN INTERNATIONAL BUSINESS

All basic international business functions—marketing, operations, finance, and human resources—play a vital role in international business. The human resource function, for example, must deal with a number of general, fundamental management challenges in international business.[6] These challenges are illustrated in Figure 4.4. In addition, the different forms of international business activity that firms can pursue have specific human resource management implications.

General Human Resource Issues in International Business

One general set of challenges relates to differences that may exist in culture, levels of economic development, and legal systems that typify the countries where the firm operates. These differences may force an international organization to customize its hiring, firing, training, and compensation programs on a country-by-country basis. A particularly difficult set of issues exists when there is conflict between the laws and/or cultures of the home country and those of the host country.

For example, as more fully described in Chapter 3, in the United States it is illegal to discriminate in an employment relationship on the basis of gender. In Saudi Arabia, on the other hand, such discrimination is not only allowed but is expected. Women are highly restricted in their career opportunities, and a firm doing business in that country has to balance its own affirmative action efforts with the legal and cultural restrictions imposed by that country. Similarly, overt discrimination is still actively practiced in many other countries as well.[7] As

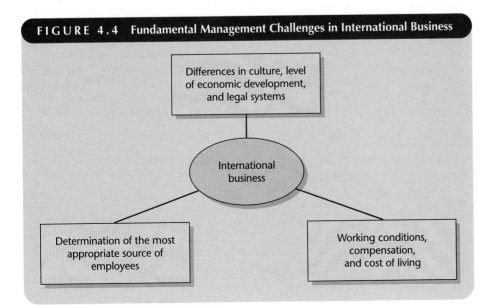

FIGURE 4.4 Fundamental Management Challenges in International Business

you may recall from Chapter 3, the Civil Rights Act of 1991 allows employees of U.S. firms but working abroad to sue their employers if they violate the Civil Rights Act. But as you may also recall, an exception exists when a country has a law that specifically contradicts the Civil Rights Act. So, for example, a woman could not sue a U.S. company operating in Saudi Arabia for sex discrimination, since some discrimination against women is actually prescribed by law. On the other hand, since Japan has no laws institutionalizing such discrimination, a woman could bring suit against a U.S. firm operating there.

A second fundamental human resource challenge in international business, as introduced earlier, is the determination of the most appropriate source of employees: the host country, the home country, or a third country. "The Lighter Side of HR" provides a humorous take on this decision. The ideal combination of employees will differ according to the location of a firm's operations, the nature of its operations, and myriad other factors. A company is more likely to hire local employees, for example, for lower-level jobs with minimal skill requirements and for which there is a reasonable local supply of labor. Again, it is also necessary to consider local laws and/or customs that may limit or constrain hiring practices. For instance, immigration laws may limit the number of work visas that a firm can grant to foreigners, or employment regulations may mandate the hiring of local citizens as a requirement for doing business in a particular country.

Third, international businesses must also deal with a variety of complex training and development challenges. At one level, for example, human resource managers need to provide cross-cultural training for corporate executives who are chosen for overseas assignments. In addition, however, training programs for production workers in host countries must be tailored to represent the education offered by local school systems. Dramatic differences in the skill and educational levels within a labor force make it necessary for an inter-

---

The Lighter Side of HR

International business has become a way of life for many managers today. Yet, some of these same managers remain woefully ignorant of many aspects of international politics, economics, customs, and cultures. A very common strategy that some businesses are using today is to move production to other countries as a way to capitalize on inexpensive labor. But as illustrated in this cartoon, any manager contemplating such an action must have a clear and thorough understanding of the country where production is being moved. Otherwise, truly embarrassing situations may arise!

national business to pay close attention to the training and development needs of all of its employees in foreign markets.[8]

Yet another important international human resource management question relates to working conditions, compensation, and the overall cost of living. A general stance adopted by most international businesses is that an employee should not suffer a loss of compensation or incur a decrement in standard of living by virtue of accepting an international assignment. Thus human resource managers must determine how to compensate executives on overseas assignments who potentially face higher costs of living, a reduction in their quality of life, and/or unhappiness or stress because of separation from family or friends.

Specific Human Resource Issues in International Business

Organizations can adopt a wide variety of strategies for competing in the international environment. Each such strategy poses a unique set of challenges for human resource managers. One common strategy is exporting. **Exporting** is the process of making a product in the firm's domestic marketplace and then selling it in another country. Exporting can involve both products and services. U.S. farmers routinely export grain to Russia, while other businesses ship gas turbines to Saudi Arabia, locomotives to Indonesia, blue jeans to Great Britain, computers to Japan, disposable diapers to Italy, and steel to Brazil.

■ **Exporting** is the process of making a product in the firm's domestic marketplace and then selling it in another country.

Such an approach to international business has many advantages. For one thing, it is usually the easiest way to enter a new market. In addition, it typically requires only a small outlay of capital. Moreover, because the products are usually sold "as is," there is no need to adapt them to local conditions. Finally, relatively little risk is involved. On the other hand, products exported to other countries are often subject to taxes, tariffs, and higher transportation expenses. In addition, because the products are seldom adapted to local conditions, they may not actually address the needs of local markets and, consequently, may not achieve their full revenue potential. The shipment of some products across national boundaries is also restricted by various government regulations. For example, textile products made in Turkey cannot be easily exported to the United States.

If the firm is functioning solely as an exporter, the human resource function faces no meaningful differences in responsibilities from those in a domestic business. An exporting company will usually have an export manager, and that manager will likely have a staff to assist in the various parts of the exporting process. Human resource managers will usually play a role in hiring people for these jobs and will oversee other aspects of their employment, such as compensation and performance appraisal. But other than perhaps some exporting-specific skills required for workers in this department, these employees will be dealt with in the same ways as employees in the operations, sales, or finance departments. Thus when a domestic firm begins to export to a foreign market, the human resource function may be extended to include another set of employees, but does not change in any other meaningful way.

Another popular form of international business strategy is called **licensing**. Under this agreement a company grants its permission to another company in a foreign country to manufacture and/or market its products in its local

■ **Licensing** involves one company granting its permission to another company in a foreign country to manufacture and/or market the first firm's products in the local market.

Direct investment is a popular form of international business, especially among large and growing businesses. For example, Dell computer recently opened a major new PC assembly factory in China. China is already the fifth-largest computer market in the world, and demand there continues to reflect strong growth. Dell reasoned that having an in-country plant is critical if it wanted to maintain its presence as a major supplier to this booming market. Moreover, the firm decided to rely primarily on local employees to establish and run its new operation.

market. For example, a clothing manufacturer might allow a manufacturer in another country to use the first firm's design, logo, and materials to manufacture clothing under the second firm's name. Under such an agreement the licensing firm typically pays a royalty or licensing fee to the original firm based on the number of units sold. Microsoft licenses software firms in other countries to produce and distribute such products as Office and Windows in their local markets.

The major advantage of this strategy is that, again, it allows the firm to enter a foreign market with relatively little risk. Licensing also enables the firm to gain some market exposure and develop some name recognition that will make it easier for that firm to enter the market more aggressively at some point in the future. On the other hand, the firm's profits are limited to its royalty payments. Likewise, the firm must also be vigilant to ensure that its quality standards are upheld.

If a firm is involved in international business activities exclusively via licensing, the human resource function is approached the same as in a pure exporting enterprise. That is, no meaningful differences in the human resource function will likely exist, but human resource managers will need to extend their existing services and responsibilities to employees associated with the licensing activities. But the human resource function itself does not really change in any meaningful way.

■ **Direct investment** occurs when a firm headquartered in one country builds or purchases operating facilities or subsidiaries in a foreign country.

A third international strategy for doing business is **direct investment**. A direct investment occurs when a firm headquartered in one country builds or purchases operating facilities or subsidiaries in a foreign country. That is, the firm actually owns physical assets in the other country. Kodak, for example, constructed a research and development laboratory in Japan. This building represents a direct investment on the part of Kodak. Other examples of direct investment include Disney's construction of Disneyland Paris, BMW's construction of a new assembly plant in South Carolina, and Ford's acquisitions of Jaguar and Volvo.

One major advantage of direct investment is that it gives the firm its own facilities in the other country and allows it to become truly integrated in a particular foreign market. There is also considerably more profit potential in direct investment, since the company itself keeps all the profits its investment earns in that country. On the other hand, this strategy involves considerable risk. Just as the investing firm can keep all its profits, so too must it absorb any and all losses and related financial setbacks. In addition, of course, the costs of direct investment are also quite high and are borne solely by the investing firm.

At this level of international business activity the human resource function changes substantively from that of a domestic firm or a business using a pure exporting or licensing strategy because in a direct investment situation employees of the firm will be working in foreign locations. Depending on the nationalities reflected in the foreign workforce (that is, whether the firm uses a polycentric, geocentric, or ethnocentric approach), the corporate human resource function will need to extend and expand its scope and operations to provide the appropriate contributions to firm performance as determined by the philosophy being used for staffing the foreign operations.

A fourth form of international strategy is a **joint venture** or **strategic alliance**. In this case two or more firms cooperate in the ownership and/or management of an operation, often on an equity basis. A joint venture is the traditional term used for such an arrangement and describes a situation that involves actual equity ownership. A strategic alliance might not involve ownership but still involves cooperation between firms. Joint ventures and strategic alliances are rapidly growing in importance in the international business environment. They represent a way for two or more firms to achieve synergy from working together, they reduce risk, and they provide mutual benefit to both partners. American Airlines and British Airways have formed a strategic alliance to make it easier for travelers to make reservations and purchase tickets on either airline.

Human resource managers in a firm that uses this strategy face a complex set of issues and challenges. If the new operation is a separate legal entity that functions as a semiautonomous enterprise, the corporate human resource staffs of each strategic partner will need to determine how to link and coordinate with their counterparts in both the new venture and their partner. If the new venture is being operated within the context of one of the existing partner's organization, the human resource function becomes more complicated still because of the disparate relationships among the human resource staff members for the new venture and their counterparts in both the partner within which they are operating and the other partner that is somewhat more distant.

■ In a **joint venture** or **strategic alliance**, two or more firms cooperate in the ownership and/or management of an operation, often on an equity basis.

THE BOTTOM LINE Human resource managers need to understand an array of both general and specific issues if their organization is involved in international business. Among the general human resource issues facing managers are those framed by the culture, economic development, and legal systems in different countries; these issues extend to determining the appropriate source of employees, addressing training and developing needs, and resolving compensation issues. Specific issues relate to business strategies for international competition, such as exporting, licensing, direct investment, and joint ventures and strategic alliances.

DOMESTIC ISSUES IN INTERNATIONAL HUMAN RESOURCE MANAGEMENT

Regardless of their level of internationalization, all firms dealing in foreign markets must confront three sets of domestic issues in the management of their human resources. These domestic issues, shown in Figure 4.5, are local recruiting and selection issues, local training issues, and local compensation issues.

Local Recruiting and Selection Issues

Nonmanagerial employees, such as blue-collar production workers and white-collar office workers, are usually host-country nationals in international business. There are basic and fundamental economic reasons for this pattern. Simply put, host-country nationals are usually less expensive to employ than are home-country nationals or third-country nationals. Host-country nationals are also frequently hired because local laws usually promote the hiring of locals.[9] Immigration visa laws, for example, may restrict jobs to citizens and legal residents of a country. Thus an international business must develop and implement a plan for recruiting and selecting its employees in a host-country market. This plan must include assessments of the firm's human resource needs, primary sources of labor in that country, labor force skills and talents, and training requirements. In addition, the plan should also account for special circumstances that exist in the local markets. Firms that hire home-country nationals for foreign assignments must obviously adhere to hiring regulations in their own countries. But when hiring host-country nationals, those firms must also be aware of the regulations, laws, and norms that govern employment relationships within the host country. Thus while the reliance on host-country nationals may be less expensive, it also adds complexity to the employment relationship.[10]

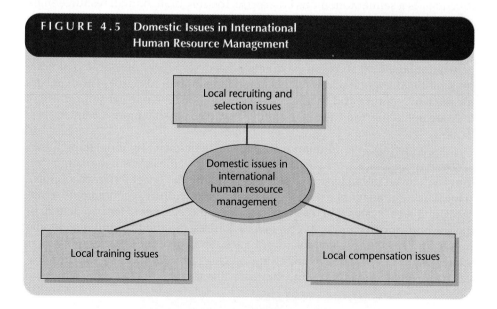

FIGURE 4.5   Domestic Issues in International Human Resource Management

Local recruiting and selection issues

Domestic issues in international human resource management

Local training issues

Local compensation issues

Local Training Issues

Human resource managers must also thoroughly understand the training and development needs of the host country's workforce to help employees perform their jobs most effectively. Training and development needs of a local workforce depend on several factors. One, of course, is the location of the foreign market. In highly industrialized markets, such as England or Japan, organizations can usually find a cadre of capable employees who may need only a small amount of firm-specific training. But in an area that is relatively underdeveloped, training and development needs will be much more extensive.

For example, when Hilton first opened hotels in Eastern Europe, it found that waiters, hotel clerks, and other customer service employees lacked the basic skills to provide high-quality service to guests. Because these employees were accustomed to working in a planned economy where there was no need to worry about customer satisfaction, they had difficulty recognizing why it was important to shift their focus. As a result, Hilton had to invest considerably more than originally planned in training employees to provide customer service. Training is also important if international business wants to take full advantage of locating production abroad. Many firms move production facilities to areas with low labor costs such as Malaysia and Mexico but then find that the productivity of the labor force is relatively low. Thus they have to invest additional training and development dollars to bring the workforce up to the necessary performance standards. Some of the methods that Toyota uses to select and train workers in the United States are described in "Human Resources Around the Globe."

Local training issues are a significant part of international human resource management. For example, consider the case of these workers learning to smile! The Korean Air Service Academy in Seoul believes that if the country's businesses are to become more competitive in international markets, their employees need to understand what it calls "international manners." Historically, people in Korea believed that business was supposed to be formal, serious, and dignified. As a result, employees often have difficulty smiling during business transactions. So, bank employees like these are sent to special seminars to help them overcome their long-held biases against smiling at work.

Toyota Wants Only the Best

When Toyota decided to open its first automobile assembly plant in the United States several years ago, the firm knew it faced real challenges in staffing the facility. In its native Japan many high school students go through special training programs funded by business to teach them various work skills. And high school graduates not heading off to college usually enroll in apprenticeship programs to further develop their skills. Because no such programs exist in the United States, Toyota realized that it would not have as large and talented a labor pool from which to hire as it has back home.

The firm initially had more than one hundred thousand applicants for twenty-seven hundred production jobs. Many applicants were initially screened out because of lack of education and/or experience. Most of those who remained under consideration underwent more than fourteen hours of testing. Finalists from this pool then participated in various work simulations under the watchful eyes of Toyota managers. And after all this, only the very best were hired. All told, Toyota esti-

"Those exercises are pretty close to what they'll experience on the assembly line."

(Mark Daugherty, Toyota assistant personnel manager)*

mated that it spent more than $13,000 hiring each worker for the factory.

Even after the plant was up and running, Toyota didn't slack off in its hiring rigor. Indeed, it still maintains the same high standards. For example, applicants who meet minimum education and experience qualifications are invited to the factory for a difficult twelve-hour assessment the company calls the "Day of Work." Throughout this day the applicants simulate work in various settings, meet with existing employees, and undergo detailed tests. The plant's managers try to make the work simulations as realistic as possible and hire only those applicants who perform at the very highest levels. Does this approach pay off? Toyota managers believe that it does and point to the fact that Toyota's product quality in the United States is comparable to what it gets at home.

References: "Toyota Devises Grueling Workout for Job Seekers," *USA Today*, August 11, 1997, p. 3B (*quote on 3B); "Toyota Takes Pains, and Time, Filling Jobs at Its Kentucky Plant," *Wall Street Journal*, December 1, 1987, pp. 1, 29.

Local Compensation Issues

Compensation must also be addressed at a local level for international businesses. Some countries, such as the United States, base compensation on individual performance. In other countries, however, such as Japan, the emphasis is more on group and less on individual performance. Dramatic differences in life styles, standards of living, and regulations also cause a wide variation in the way in which firms compensate their employees in different foreign locations.

Of course, there are also dramatic differences in benefit packages that are offered to workers in different countries. In countries with socialized medicine, such as the United Kingdom, firms do not have to worry as much about paying all or part of employee health insurance premiums (although the firms do pay higher taxes to help support the government program). In Italy most workers expect to have several hours off in the afternoon. In Germany most workers get six weeks of paid vacation time a year, and many work only thirty hours a week. German autoworkers earn $39 an hour in wages and benefits, compared to $25 in the United States and $27 in Japan.[11]

It is also important for international human resource managers to look at the total picture of compensation rather than at a simple index such as hourly wage. For example, as already noted some firms choose to move production to

Mexico to take advantage of lower labor costs. Although hourly labor costs in Mexico are lower than they are in the United States, Mexican law requires employers to pay maternity leave to their employees, provide a Christmas bonus equal to fifteen-days' pay, and provide at least three months of severance pay for workers who are terminated. Thus lower labor costs may be at least partially lost due to these expenses and higher costs for other benefits.

THE BOTTOM LINE Human resource managers need to be thoroughly familiar with several domestic issues in international business that directly relate to the human resource function. These issues include factors such as local recruiting and selection, local training, and local compensation.

MANAGING INTERNATIONAL TRANSFERS AND ASSIGNMENTS

Another extremely important part of international human resource management is the effective management of expatriate employees. **Expatriates** are employees who are sent by a firm to work in another country and may be either parent-country nationals or third-country nationals. Particularly key areas of importance here include selecting, training, and compensating expatriates.[12]

▨ **Expatriates** are employees who are sent by a firm to work in another country and may be either parent-country nationals or third-country nationals.

Selecting Expatriates

Recruiting and selecting employees for an international business requires the manager to address two sets of questions.[13] The first question is the definition of skills and abilities that are necessary to perform the work that the organization needs to have done. The second set of issues relates to defining the skills and abilities that are needed to work in a foreign location.

The first step, then, is to define the actual skills that are necessary to do the job. Plant managers must have the technical skills necessary to run a manufacturing operation, whereas marketing managers must understand advertising media distribution channels and other aspects of the marketing process. Similarly, human resource managers must understand local hiring customs and standards. Although these skills are likely to be important in determining the success or failure of an expatriate assignment, they are not likely to be critical. Instead, the skills necessary for people to be able to function in a foreign culture are likely to be the most critical determinants of success. Some of the more common skills and abilities assumed to be necessary in this regard include adaptability, language ability, overall physical and emotional health, relatively high levels of independence and self-reliance, and appropriate levels of experience and education.

The recruitment of employees for international business is an important step in the human resource management process. International businesses attempt to recruit experienced managers through a variety of channels. One common source of recruits is the firm itself. That is, a good starting place may be to seek employees already working for the firm and in the host country who might be prepared for international assignment. In some cases the firm may be selecting individuals for their first international assignment; in other cases it

Managing international transfers and assignments is an especially important issue for human resource managers in large multinational firms. For example, after Daimler-Benz and Chrysler merged to create one new international automobile company, several key executives from each firm needed to be transferred to new locations in different countries. Stefan Buchner, for example, managed Daimler's seat and steering wheel purchasing function in Germany, but Chrysler had a similar manager in Detroit who did the same job. The new DaimlerChrysler only needs one of them in this role, however. One will get the combined job, and the other will be reassigned to another purchasing area. After the final decisions are made, it's also likely that one, or both, may be transferred to the other country.

may be selecting people for their second or third international assignments. Nestlé, for example, maintains a cadre of approximately two hundred managers who are capable of and willing to accept an international assignment anywhere the firm does business.[14]

International businesses also frequently look to other organizations as a source for prospective managers. These may be home-country managers who are deemed to be qualified for an international assignment or managers already working in an international assignment for another firm. For higher-level positions in an organization, international businesses often rely on professional recruiting firms to help identify prospective managerial candidates. These recruiting firms, often called *headhunters*, actively seek qualified managers and other professionals for possible placement in positions in other organizations. Headhunting has long been an accepted practice in the United States. In both Japan and Europe, however, headhunting was considered unethical until recent times. Within the last decade or so, however, headhunting has become a more accepted practice in most industrialized countries.[15]

Increasingly, many firms are having to hire new college graduates for immediate foreign assignment. Traditionally, this practice has been relatively unpopular because organizations believed that managers needed to develop a large experience base in a firm's domestic operations before taking on an international assignment. However, because of the shortage of global managers and the recent emphasis that many colleges of business are placing on training international managers, firms are finding that they can hire younger managers and place them in foreign assignments more quickly than in the past. Potential managerial candidates with foreign language skills, international travel experience, and coursework in international business or related fields are especially attractive candidates for international assignments.[16]

After a pool of qualified applicants has been identified, the organization must then select the managers that it needs for international assignments. In general, organizations look at three sets of criteria when selecting people for international assignments: managerial competence, language training, and adaptability to new situations. Organizations must use extreme care when they select managers for international assignments. The cost of a failed international assignment is extremely high. Expatriate failure is defined as the early return of an expatriate manager to his or her home country because of an inability to perform in the overseas assignment.[17]

Experts suggest that a failed expatriate assignment for a top manager might cost the organization as much as $250,000, in addition to any salary losses. This figure includes the expatriate's original training, moving expenses, and lost managerial productivity. Failure in expatriate assignments is, unfortunately, quite high. Estimates place the expatriate failure rate in U.S. companies at between 20 and 50 percent. Japanese and European firms appear to do a somewhat better job of selecting international managers and, as a result, experience a lower expatriate failure rate.

Several factors may contribute to expatriate failure. One is the inability of the manager and/or the manager's spouse and family to adjust to a new location. As a result of this pattern, some firms are beginning to pay more attention to helping spouses and children adjust to the new environment, and many other firms are placing a greater emphasis on the nontechnical aspects of a prospective manager's suitability for a foreign assignment. For example, firms may look closely at a person's cultural adaptability, as well as the adaptability of the person's family. It is also important to consider the person's motivation for and real interest in foreign assignments. Some managers are attracted to foreign assignments because they relish the thought of living abroad or perhaps they see the experience as being useful in their career plans.[18]

Regardless of the motive, however, managers who don't have a realistic preview of what an international assignment really is become disillusioned within a few months of accepting such an assignment. Thus firms go to considerable lengths in their attempts to avoid expatriate failure. AT&T, for example, has long used personality tests and interviews as part of its selection process for choosing international managers. It also uses psychologists to help assess prospects and is investing more into learning about family considerations. General Motors spends almost $500,000 a year on cross-cultural training for 150 or so U.S. managers and their families heading to international assignments. The firm reports that less than 1 percent of its expatriate assignments fail and attributes much of its success to its training program.[19]

Training Expatriates

An international firm's human resource management function must also provide training and development for its managers. Training, as we cover more fully in Chapter 9, is instruction directed at enhancing specific job-related skills and abilities and most often focuses on operating employees and technical specialists. For example, a training program might be designed to help employees learn to use a new software package as part of an international communication network. Development, as we also cover more fully in Chapter 9, is general education devoted to preparing managers for higher-level positions and/or new assignments within the organization. For example, a development program might span several months or even years and be targeted to helping managers improve their ability to make decisions, to motivate subordinates to work harder, and to develop more effective strategies for the organization.[20]

The first step in training and development is to assess the needs of the organization. This assessment focuses on determining the difference between what managers and employees can currently do and what the organization believes they need to be able to do. For example, suppose an organization is planning to set up its first operation in Japan. The organization may determine that it needs to have at least thirty-five managers on staff who can communicate at a basic level in the Japanese language. An analysis of current employees, however, reveals that only fifteen employees are fluent in Japanese. Thus the organization will need to establish a training program to help the other twenty managers targeted for Japanese assignments learn the country's language.

After assessing training needs, human resource managers must develop training and development methods and procedures. A wide variety of alternatives exist for this set of activities. Some kinds of training are readily available in the open market at a relatively inexpensive cost; for example, in-house language-training programs and other forms of language training from cassette tapes, video tapes, and similar media are very common.[21] Prudential Insurance even markets generic packaged training programs for families of expatriates.

Some training and development is done in classroom settings; some is done at an individual's own learning pace through books, manuals, video tapes, and Web sites; and other forms of training and development take place while the individual is actually on the job. Role playing, experiential exercises, lectures, assigned readings, software-based instruction, video tapes, Web sites, and other media are becoming increasingly popular. In addition, more and more often firms are sending prospective expatriates to their ultimate foreign destination for short periods of time before their permanent move. This approach allows people to become acculturated on a gradual basis. But whatever the exact nature of the training, the goals of expatriate training are becoming clearer and more consistent. Increasingly, multinational organizations are recognizing that managers given overseas assignments must be able to communicate with people in the host country and must be able to adapt to the differences in life style and values. When we consider all the things that seem to go into expatriate success, it becomes clearer why some have suggested that a manager given an assignment in a foreign country must possess "the patience of a diplomat, the zeal of a missionary, and the language skills of a U.N. interpreter."[22]

Compensating. Expatriates

Another important issue in international human resource management is compensation. To remain competitive, an organization must provide prevailing compensation packages for its managers in a given market. Compensation packages include salary and nonsalary items and are jointly determined by labor market forces such as the supply and demand of managerial talent, professional licensing requirements, standard of living, occupational status, and government regulations.[23]

Most international businesses provide expatriate managers with differential compensation to make up for differences in currency valuation, standards of living, life-style norms, and so on. When managers are on short-term assignments at a foreign location, their salary is often tied to their domestic currency and home-country living standards. Of course, these managers are reimbursed for short-term living expenses, such as for hotel rooms, meals, and local transportation. However, if the foreign assignment is for a longer time period, compensation is usually adjusted to allow the manager to maintain her or his home-country standard of living. This adjustment is particularly important if the manager is transferred from a low-cost location to a high-cost location or from a country with a relatively high standard of living to one with a relatively low standard of living.[24]

Differential compensation usually starts with a cost-of-living allowance. This basic difference in salary is intended to offset the differences in the cost of living between the home and host countries. The logic is that if a manager accepts a foreign assignment, he or she should enjoy the same standard of living as the person would have enjoyed had he or she remained in the home country. If the cost of living in the foreign country is higher than it is at home, then the manager's existing base pay alone will result in a lower standard of living. The firm may therefore need to supplement that base pay to offset the difference. On the other hand, if the cost of living at a foreign location is lower than at home, no such allowance is needed, although few companies would actually lower the manager's salary.

Occasionally, organizations might have to provide an additional salary inducement simply to get people to accept a foreign assignment. Many employees may be relatively interested in accepting assignments to countries such as England, France, Italy, or Japan, but enticing people to accept a position in Haiti, Somalia, or Colombia may be more difficult. Thus organizations sometimes find it necessary to provide what is called a **hardship premium**, or a **foreign service premium**, to convince people to accept these kinds of assignments.

Many international businesses also must set up a tax-equalization system for their managers on foreign assignments. A tax-equalization system is designed to ensure that the expatriates aftertax income in the host country is comparable to what it would have been in the home country. Given that every country has its own unique tax laws that apply to the earnings of its citizens and/or to earnings within its borders by foreign citizens, companies must develop plans to make sure that the tax burden for individuals is equalized relative to the amount of salary they are earning.

The other part of compensation (besides salary) is benefits. In addition to providing salary adjustments, most international businesses must also provide benefit adjustments. Special benefits for managers on foreign assignments usually include housing, education, medical treatment, travel to the home country, and club membership. Housing benefits are provided as a way of helping equalize housing expenses in different areas. Since equalizing the type of housing an executive enjoys in her or his home country may be very expensive, housing is usually treated as a separate benefit for expatriate managers. If a manager is going on long-term or permanent foreign assignment, the organization may buy the manager's existing home and help the manager buy a home in the host country.

Firms also find it increasingly necessary to provide job-location assistance for the spouse of an executive being transferred abroad and to help cover the education costs for children. For example, children may need to attend private schools at the firm's expense. Medical benefits are also often adjusted for managers on international assignment. For example, some people consider medical facilities in Malaysia to be substandard, and as a result, firms that transfer employees to that country often agree to send them to Singapore for anything other than routine medical attention.

International businesses may also provide expatriates with a travel allowance for trips to the home country for personal reasons such as to visit family members or to celebrate holidays. A manager and her or his family may typically be allowed one or two trips home per year at company expense for personal reasons. If the assignment is relatively short term and a manager's family remains at home, the manager may be provided with even more trips home to compensate for the fact that the manager and her or his family are separated.

Finally, it may be necessary to provide certain kinds of club memberships. In some cultures, for example, belonging to a specific club or participating in a particular activity is a necessary part of the business world. The Japanese, for instance, often conduct business during a round of golf. At the same time, memberships in golf clubs in Japan cost thousands of dollars, and a single round of golf costs many times more there than it does in the rest of the world. As a result, managers assigned to foreign posts in Japan may be given supplemental benefits to cover the costs of golf club memberships.[25]

■ A **hardship premium** (also called a **foreign service premium**) is an additional financial incentive offered to individuals to entice them to accept a "less than attractive" international assignment.

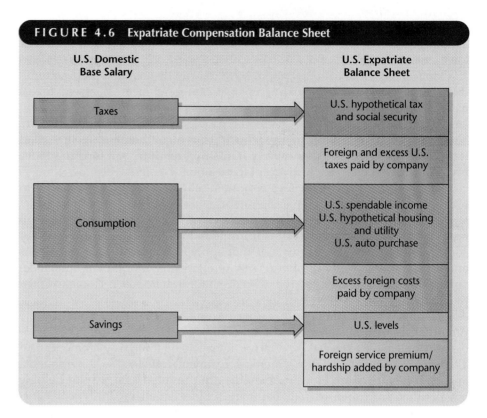

FIGURE 4.6 Expatriate Compensation Balance Sheet

Figure 4.6 illustrates how one company conceptualizes its compensation package for expatriates. The left side of its "balance sheet" summarizes what an employee is currently earning and spending in the United States, broken down into taxes, consumption, and savings. The right side breaks down these categories into greater detail, allowing the company to better provide comparable income to managers taking international assignments.

THE BOTTOM LINE   Managing international transfers and assignments is an important activity for human resource managers in international firms. Careful attention must be paid to the effective selection, training, and compensation of expatriates so as to avoid unnecessary costs and related problems.

INTERNATIONAL LABOR RELATIONS

Labor relations, as we discuss more fully in Chapter 14, is the process of dealing with employees who are organized into labor unions. Labor relations are also heavily regulated by laws, as briefly noted in Chapter 3, and the actions of management toward labor and the actions of labor toward management are heavily restricted. Different situations, however, exist in other countries. Many countries throughout the world have Labor parties, which seek to achieve the political goals of unions in those countries and are often quite powerful. Also, in many countries labor unions are much more concerned with social issues than they are in the United States, and so their political activism often extends beyond wages and conditions of employment. In any case union membership is quite large and continues to grow in many countries. In fact, more than half the world's workforce outside the United States belongs to labor unions.

In addition, different norms or expectations about the relationships between unions and management prevail in different countries. In England, labor "contracts" are not really legal contracts at all, but merely understandings that can be broken at any time by either party with no penalty. And throughout Europe, unions frequently use temporary work stoppages in a bid for public backing of their demands. In Paris, for example, one-day work stoppages among employees who work in the city's buses, subways, and railroads are frequently used for this purpose. In contrast to the situation in Europe, labor relations in Japan tend to be very cordial. Unions are created and run by the businesses themselves. Because the Japanese culture discourages confrontation and hostility, unions and management tend to work together in a very cooperative fashion. Disputes are usually resolved cordially and through mutual agreement, and a third-party mediator is rarely required. Strikes are also very unusual in Japan.

THE BOTTOM LINE Labor relations within the context of a single country are often complex, confusing, and fraught with the potential for misunderstandings and conflict. These conditions are accentuated for firms doing business in different countries. Thus international human resource managers may need to draw heavily on local expertise to help them address labor relations issues in an appropriate, effective, and legal manner.

Chapter Summary

A variety of global issues in international human resource management must be addressed by any international firm. One issue is developing an international human resource management strategy. Another is developing an understanding of the cultural environment of human resource management. Yet a third is developing an understanding of the political and legal environment of international business.

The international human resource function must deal with a number of fundamental management challenges in international business. One major set of challenges relates to differences that may exist in culture, levels of economic development, and legal systems in the countries where the firm operates. A second fundamental human resource challenge in international business is the determination of the most appropriate source of employees: the host country,

the home country, or a third country. Third, international businesses must deal with a variety of complex training and development challenges. Yet another important international human resource management question relates to working conditions, compensation, and the cost of living.

Organizations can adopt a wide variety of strategies for competing in the international environment. One strategy is exporting. Exporting is the process of making a product in the firm's domestic marketplace and then selling it in another country. In licensing, a company grants its permission to another company in a foreign country to manufacture and/or market the first firm's products in the local market. Direct investment occurs when a firm headquartered in one country builds or purchases operating facilities or subsidiaries in a foreign country. In a joint venture or strategic alliance, two or more firms cooperate in the ownership and/or management of an operation, often on an equity basis.

All firms dealing in foreign markets must also confront three sets of domestic issues in the management of their human resources. These domestic issues are local recruiting and selection issues, local training issues, and local compensation issues. International human resource management must also pay close attention to the various issues involved in the effective management of expatriate employees. Key areas of importance include selecting, training, and compensating expatriates.

Labor relations is the process of dealing with employees who are organized into labor unions. In the United States membership in labor unions has steadily declined in recent years, and labor relations are heavily regulated by laws. Different situations, however, exist in other countries.

Review and Discussion Questions

1. Summarize recent growth and trends in international business.

2. What are the basic international business strategies that firms can pursue?

3. What are the basic human resource management functions in international business?

4. What are the basic human resource management issues to be addressed by an international business?

5. What are the basic domestic issues in international human resource management?

6. What are the human resource management implications of each strategy for international business?

7. What do you see as the basic similarities and differences in the human resource function between domestic and international businesses?

8. Which do you think is more critical for international human resource management: understanding the cultural environment or understanding the political and legal environment?

9. When a basic incongruence exists between the ethical context of human resource management between the foreign-country environment and a firm's home-country environment, which do you think should take precedence?

10. Would you be interested in an international assignment as part of your employer's management development strategy? Why or why not? What factors would be most important to you in making such a decision?

Closing Case

Human Resources and International Mergers

Mergers and acquisitions, of course, are nothing new. But a new spate of megamergers between international giants in 1998 may well portend a new era in global consolidation. Two of these mergers, in particular, have the potential to reshape international competition. And each also has significant implications for international human resource practices. One megamerger involves Chrysler Corporation and Daimler-Benz. The other involves Amoco and British Petroleum.

The news about Chrysler and Daimler-Benz made headlines around the world when the deal was announced in midsummer 1998. Most experts agreed that it was a perfect match. Chrysler makes moderately priced cars and light trucks, is strong in North America but weak in Europe, and has distinctive competence in design and product development. Daimler-Benz, on the other hand, makes luxury cars and heavy trucks, is very strong in Europe, and has distinctive competence in engineering and technology. Although the transaction is billed as a merger, Daimler-Benz is actually buying Chrysler for $38 billion. The new company, to be called DaimlerChrysler AG, will remain headquartered in Germany and will be the second-largest automobile company in the world.

Although myriad strategic, technical, and operational systems must be integrated before the two firms truly become one, blending the two firms' human resources also presents a formidable challenge. Prior to merging, Chrysler and Daimler-Benz had a combined worldwide workforce of 421,000 employees. But after the merger is complete, not all of these workers will be needed. It is almost certain that job cuts will occur at the production, technical, operations, and executive levels. But the two firms must also deal with powerful unions as well, the UAW for Chrysler in the United States and IG Metall in Germany.

And then there are issues associated with employment conditions. Consider, for example, representative conditions at three plants. In Germany, Daimler-Benz auto workers have an hourly wage range of from $15 to $20 per hour, get six weeks of annual vacation, twelve sick days, and work an average of thirty-five hours a week. The Mercedes-Benz plant in Alabama, however, has substantially different conditions. Its workers earn from $14.05 to $19.20 an hour, get twelve days of vacation time, ten sick days, and work an average of forty hours per week. At Chrysler's biggest plant, in Detroit, meanwhile, workers earn between $19.37 and $23.22 an hour, get four weeks of vacation time, five sick days, and work an average of 50.5 hours per week (of which 10.5 hours is compensated at a rate of time-and-a-half). Clearly, then, integrating these disparate conditions under a single employment umbrella will be a challenge.

A second big international merger was announced later in the summer of 1998, this one between Amoco and British Petroleum, or BP. At the time of the announcement, Amoco was the fourth-largest oil producer in the United States, while BP was the third largest in the world, following only Royal Dutch/Shell and Exxon. Like the Chrysler and Daimler deal, this one is also not a true merger—BP is actually the acquirer with a 60 percent ownership stake in the new company. The firm will remain headquartered in London, but all of its U.S. operations will shift to the Amoco organization and brand name.

And again, the firms are addressing significant human resource issues as the integration of the two operations unfolds. BP's operations in the United States were based in Cleveland, while Amoco has operated out of Chicago. BP announced that it would be shutting down most of its Cleveland operation, with some employees there being transferred to Chicago. To make room, Amoco also indicated that several jobs in its own headquarters would be eliminated. All told, the firms expect to cut about six thousand of their combined ninety-nine thousand jobs. Most of these cuts will be in marketing and exploration. But no one can really say for sure exactly how many cuts will be made or when full integration will be achieved. And, of course, integrating compensation, benefits, and other human resource practices will be a complex task as well.

Case Questions

1. What are the likely advantages and disadvantages that firms in these kinds of mergers can expect?

2. What are the advantages and disadvantages for individual workers at firms that merge with international partners?

3. What are the basic human resource issues, besides those mentioned in the case, that must be addressed as a result of these mergers?

Sources: "Gentlemen, Start Your Engines," *Fortune*, June 8, 1998, pp. 138–146; James Aley and Matt Siegel, "The Fallout from Merger Mania," *Fortune*, March 2, 1998, pp. 26–56; "Labor Holds a Key to Fate of Daimler-Chrysler Merger," *Wall Street Journal*, May 7, 1998, pp. B1, B18; "Oil Companies Pump out $50 Billion Merger Deal," *USA Today*, August 12, 1998, pp. 1B, 2B.

Building Human Resource Management Skills

Purpose: The purpose of this exercise is to provide you with some critical insights into the complexities associated with international human resource management.

Step 1: Your instructor will divide your class into small groups of four to five members each. Begin by reading and discussing the following context description:

Assume you are the human resource management executive team of a large electronics firm. Your firm has several factories located throughout North and South America. The company has just decided to open its first Asian factory in Thailand. Plans call for the plant to open in two years. The plant will require a general manager, four associate managers, and ten other relatively high-level managerial positions (a purchasing manager, a warehouse manager, and so on). The plant will also require approximately thirty first-line supervisors, six hundred operating employees, and thirty maintenance and custodial workers. Finally, approximately twenty-five office and clerical workers will also be needed.

Step 2: Your boss has asked your team to develop a staffing plan for the new plant. She wants to know where each type of employee should come from, when employees should be hired, and how they should be trained. As a group spend about twenty minutes discussing this situation and outlining the basic information that you will need to adequately meet this request. That is, your task is not to actually develop the plan. Instead, your task is to decide what information you need to develop the plan and how you might obtain that information.

Ethical Dilemmas in Human Resource Management

Assume that you are a senior human resource executive for a large multinational firm. Your firm routinely buys products manufactured in factories in Asia and also operates three foreign plants itself, one in Malaysia, one in Thailand, and one in Pakistan. The company hired a new CEO a few months ago. The CEO, in turn, has a reputation for being an outspoken advocate for the rights of foreign workers. He routinely proclaims that your company's foreign workers are treated exceptionally well, that he is proud of your firm's record in this area, and that he is willing to stake his personal reputation on the ethical and humane treatment of workers who are employed both by your firm and by your firm's suppliers.

You recently returned from a fourteen-day inspection of your three international plants, plus inspections of four plants operated by two of your major suppliers. You are quite concerned about certain conditions. Although you did not see any major problems, you believe that your firm's treatment of its foreign workers is not as good as it once was. For example, the weak economy in Thailand has resulted in your plant manager there increasing work hours and withholding pay increases that had been planned. More troubling is what you saw in a supplier factory. What once was a comprehensive educational center for younger workers has been greatly reduced in scope, and you detected hints that it might be shut down altogether.

After your return, you relayed your concerns to the CEO. He seemed to be genuinely bothered by the news, but indicated that he wanted to delay taking any actions. He noted, for example, that the firm's annual shareholder meeting was coming up next month. If news of your concerns were to leak out, the firm's stock price would drop and the proposed bonuses for senior managers, including yourself, might be jeopardized. He indicated that he would prefer to keep things quiet for now but promised to take some action to improve things in the foreign plants shortly after the meeting. Meanwhile, the CEO has continued to make boastful proclamations about the company's treatment of its foreign workers.

Questions

1. What are the ethical issues in this situation?

2. What are the arguments for and against following your CEO's suggested approach?

3. What do you think most managers would do? What would you do?

Human Resource Internet Exercise

 Identify five foreign-owned companies that have large U.S. operations. For example, Toyota, a Japanese firm, has a large U.S. subsidiary that is legally incorporated as Toyota Motor Sales, U.S.A., Inc. Similarly, Nestle, a Swiss firm, owns Carnation Foods in the United States.

Search the Internet to see whether you can locate separate Web sites for both the parent company and its domestic subsidiary. Next determine the extent to which the Web site pairs contain any information regarding human resource issues. Assuming that you locate some information, see whether you can identify any parallels, extensions, or even inconsistencies between them.

Questions

1. What role might the Internet play in helping an international business coordinate its international human resources?

2. What risks does an international business run by relying on the Internet to address human resource issues?

Notes

1. Martha I. Finney, "Global Success Rides on Keeping Top Talent," *HRMagazine*, April 1996, pp. 68–74.

2. Gregory D. Chowanec and Charles N. Newstrom, "The Strategic Management of International Human Resources," *Business Quarterly*, Autumn 1991, pp. 65–70.

3. Ricky W. Griffin and Michael W. Pustay, *International Business—A Managerial Perspective*, 2nd ed. (Reading Mass.: Addison-Wesley, 1999).

4. Richard M. Steers, "The Cultural Imperative in HRM Research," in Albert Nedd (guest ed.), Gerald R. Ferris and Kendrith M. Rowland (eds.), *Research in Personnel and Human Resources Management, Supplement 1: International Human Resources Management* (Greenwich, Conn.: JAI Press, 1989), pp. 23–32.

5. Nakiye Boyacigiller, "The Role of Expatriates in the Management of Interdependence, Complexity, and Risk in Multinational Corporations," *Journal of International Business Studies*, Vol. 21 No. 3 (Third Quarter 1990), pp. 357–382.

6. Sakhawat Hossain and Herbert J. Davis, "Some Thoughts on International Personnel Management as an Emerging Field," in Albert Nedd (guest ed.), Gerald R. Ferris and Kendrith M. Rowland (eds.), *Research in Personnel and Human Resources Management, Supplement 1: International Human Resources Management* (Greenwich, Conn.: JAI Press, 1989), pp. 121–136.

7. Griffin and Pustay, *International Business*.

8. Griffin and Pustay, *International Business*.

9. "The High Cost of Expatriation," *Management Review*, July 1990, pp. 40–41.

10. Cynthia Fetterolf, "Hiring Local Managers and Employees Overseas," *International Executive*, May–June 1990, pp. 22–26.

11. Bringing back the Beetle," *Forbes*, April 7, 1997, pp. 42–44.

12. Winfred Arthur Jr. and Winston Bennett Jr. "The International Assignee: The Relative Importance of Factors Perceived to Contribute to Success," *Personnel Psychology*, Fall 1995, pp. 99–113.

13. J. Stewart Black, Hal B. Gregersen, and Mark E. Mendenhall, *Global Assignments* (San Francisco: Jossey-Bass, 1992); J. Stewart Black and Hal B. Gregersen, "The Right Way to Manage Exports," *Harvard Business Review*, March–April 1999, pp. 52–62.

14. "Global Managers Need Boundless Sensitivity, Rugged Constitutions," *Wall Street Journal*, October 13, 1998, p. B1.

15. "Firms in Europe Try to Find Executives Who Can Cross Borders in a Single Bound," *Wall Street Journal*, January 25, 1991, p. B1.

16. "Younger Managers Learn Global Skills," *Wall Street Journal*, March 31, 1992, p. B1.

17. "As Costs of Overseas Assignments Climb, Firms Select Expatriates More Carefully," *Wall Street Journal*, January 9, 1992, pp. B1, B6.

18. Margaret Shaffer and David Harrison, "Expatriates' Psychological Withdrawal from International Assignments: Work, Nonwork, and Family Influences," *Personnel Psychology*, Vol. 51, 1998, pp. 87–96; "To Smoothe a Transfer Abroad, A New Focus on Kids," *Wall Street Journal*, January 26, 1999, pp. B1, B14.

19. "Companies Use Cross-Cultural Training to Help Their Employees Adjust Abroad," *Wall Street Journal*, August 9, 1992, pp. B1, B6.

20. Paul Vanderbroeck, "Long-Term Human Resource Development in Multinational Organizations," *Sloan Management Review*, Fall 1992, pp. 95–99.

21. Kathryn Tyler, "Targeted Language Training Is Best Bargain," *HRMagazine*, January 1998, pp. 61–67.

22. Simca Ronen, "Training the International Assignee," in I. L. Goldstein and associates, *Training and Development in Organizations* (New York: Jossey-Bass, 1989), pp. 418–448.

23. Richard M. Hodgetts and Fred Luthans, "U.S. Multinationals' Compensation Strategies," *Compensation & Benefits Review*, January–February 1993, pp. 57–62.

24. Michael J. Bishko, "Compensating Your Overseas Executives, Part 1: Strategies for the 1990s," *Compensation & Benefits Review*, May–June 1990, pp. 33–43.

25. "For Executives around the Globe, Pay Packages Aren't Worlds Apart," *Wall Street Journal*, October 12, 1992, pp. B1, B5.

PART THREE

Staffing the Organization

CHAPTER 5
**Human Resource Planning
and Job Analysis**

CHAPTER 6
**Recruiting Human
Resources**

CHAPTER 7
**Selecting and Placing
Human Resources**

5

Human Resource Planning and Job Analysis

CHAPTER OUTLINE

Strategic Importance of Human Resource Planning

Job Analysis and Human Resource Planning
Purposes of Job Analysis and Human Resource Planning
Linking Job Analysis with Human Resource Planning

The Job Analysis Process
Determining Information Needs
Selecting Job Analysis Methods
Responsibilities for Job Analysis

Job Analysis Methods
Collecting Job Analysis Data
Specific Job Analysis Techniques
Job Descriptions and Job Specifications

The Human Resource Planning Process
Forecasting the Supply of Human Resources
Forecasting the Demand for Human Resources
Using the Human Resource Information System
Matching the Supply of and Demand for Human Resources

Developing Follow-up Action Plans
Planning for Growth
Planning for Stability
Planning for Reductions

Evaluating the Human Resource Planning Process

CHAPTER OBJECTIVES

After studying this chapter you should be able to:

■ Discuss the strategic importance of human resource planning.

■ Describe the job analysis process.

■ Identify and discuss common job analysis methods.

■ Describe the human resource planning process.

■ Discuss various follow-up action plans that might be developed.

■ Discuss how organizations should evaluate the human resource planning process.

It seems obvious that organizations and managers should carefully plan for their anticipated future human resource needs. If they have too few people to perform necessary work, for example, they may subsequently have to hire inefficiently and incur unnecessary expenses. But if they have too many people working, they are also incurring unnecessary labor expenses. A good case in point is Fruit of the Loom, the well-known underwear and apparel firm.

As the U.S. economy was booming a few years ago, managers at Fruit of the Loom expected that demand for their products would increase. In anticipation of this increased demand, they hired new workers and boosted production at all of their forty-one U.S. factories. Unfortunately, despite a variety of aggressive marketing promotions, the increased demand failed to materialize, and Fruit of the Loom's finished-goods inventories soared. In response, managers decided to substantially cut production. Managers decided that the firm could easily supply the projected demands for its products from existing inventory and thus believed that it was okay to reduce new production. All told, therefore, Fruit of the Loom laid off two thousand workers at its various factories, cutting production sharply and lowering labor costs substantially.

Then, unexpectedly, the demand for underwear and apparel began to increase dramatically, and Fruit of the Loom's inventories were selling much faster than ex-

"We'll be forced to leave significant dollars on the table."

(William Farley,
Fruit of the Loom CEO)*

pected. As a result, the firm was then forced to hastily recall its laid-off workers. It also hired hundreds of new workers and spent extra money to accelerate their training so that they could get right to work. Meanwhile, while the new workers were getting trained, existing workers were called on to work overtime to help meet demand.

As a result of these various efforts, Fruit of the Loom was able to partially meet the unexpected increased demand for its underwear and other apparel. But because the firm was caught short initially and then had to spend extra money on labor costs, its profits were far less than they might have otherwise been. To underscore this point, William Farley, the firm's CEO, conceded at a news conference that the firm missed opportunities to earn significant extra profits because of the errors. Indeed, some experts estimated that Fruit of the Loom lost $200 million in potential new sales during the single year in which it laid off and then rehired workers, all because the firm did not have enough workers on hand when it needed them.

"A Killing in the Caymans?" *Business Week*, May 11, 1998, pp. 50–54; "Too Much Pruning Stunts Fruit of the Loom," *Business Week*, June 6, 1994, p. 38 (*quote on p. 38); "Layoffs Continue to Hit Southern Textile, Apparel Plants; Fruit of the Loom, Uniblend Spinners Cutting Jobs," *Daily News Record*, August 20, 1997, p. 46; "The Fruits of Labor," *Time*, November 1, 1999, pp. 110U–110V.

Managers at Fruit of the Loom made a classic blunder—failing to correctly anticipate consumer demand and, as a result, earning lower profits than they could have otherwise generated. To their credit, we should note that they were not alone in their flawed planning. For example, Sara Lee Corporation, maker of Hanes underwear, also underestimated consumer demand for its products during this same period, and no one in the industry could adequately explain the sudden jump in demand. Still, Fruit of the Loom managers might have been expected to have a clearer understanding of their market and, as a result, a better grasp of their human resource needs.

With an understanding of the nature of human resource management and the human resource environment as a foundation, it is now possible to begin a more focused and detailed analysis of the specific activities and operations of the human resource management process itself. This is the first of three chapters that involve **staffing**—the process of determining the organization's current and future human resource needs and then taking steps to ensure that those needs are effectively met. This chapter addresses human resource planning and job analysis. Chapter 6 deals with the recruitment of human resources, while Chapter 7 is devoted to their selection and placement.

■ **Staffing** is the process of determining the organization's current and future human resource needs and then taking steps to ensure that those needs are effectively met.

STRATEGIC IMPORTANCE OF HUMAN RESOURCE PLANNING

Effective human resource planning is of vital strategic importance to all organizations. As we established in Chapter 2, for example, there is a clear and fundamental interdependence between effective strategic management and effective human resource management in any organization. But because human resources themselves are a fluid entity, both the number of people and the availability of people needed to get various things done in the organization change almost continuously.[1]

For example, regardless of any manager's best efforts and intentions, valuable employees will still occasionally leave the organization for better job opportunities elsewhere because of dissatisfaction with something about the organization or for personal reasons. Similarly, less-than-perfect selection decisions are also occasionally made, thereby allowing less competent employees to be hired. To complicate things further, an organization may have to launch new hiring initiatives on short notice and/or without clear-cut goals having been established. Or, at the other extreme, organizations may have to engage in layoffs or other workforce reductions with little advance notice or preparation. Thus some basic connection between human resource planning and the ongoing human resource management function of an organization is necessary to achieve an appropriate strategic balance between having too many and too few employees at any specific point in time.

An organization that makes little attempt to plan for its human resource needs must react to these changing circumstances in a piecemeal and haphazard manner. For example, its hiring may have to be undertaken with less forethought and with less systematic planning and goal setting. Likewise, terminations, layoffs, and cutbacks may similarly have to be undertaken without a clear-cut plan of action. Indeed, these human resource errors closely mirror the events and decisions at Fruit of the Loom.

On the other hand, an organization that does an effective job of human resource planning will be able to approach both hiring and workforce reductions in a much more careful and considered fashion.[2] The firm will always have a basic understanding of its current and future human resource needs and will have the information readily available to meet those needs in a logical and systematic fashion. Ford Motor Company, Wal-Mart, Royal Dutch/Shell, and Toshiba are among the companies considered to do a very effective job of recognizing the strategic importance of their human resources and planning for workforce changes in an orderly and logical fashion.

THE BOTTOM LINE   All managers should understand the strategic importance of human resource planning. The failure to plan appropriately can cause unnecessary expense and can result in ineffective hiring.

JOB ANALYSIS AND HUMAN RESOURCE PLANNING

Organizations must engage in human resource planning on a near-continuous basis. As already established, for example, people leave organizations for a variety of reasons—no organization can maintain zero turnover for any significant length of time. Likewise, the jobs the organization needs to have performed also change for a variety of reasons. New technology, shifts in labor demand, and improved work methods, for example, can each alter an organization's human resource needs. As a result, the human resource needs of an organization in six months may be quite different from its needs at present. It is through effective human resource planning that adjustments and refinements are made to transform today's workforce into what the organization expects to need in the future. Job analysis, in turn, is one of the building blocks of the human resource planning process and is a fundamental source of information for this process.

Purposes of Job Analysis and Human Resource Planning

Job analysis is the process of gathering and organizing detailed information about various jobs within the organization so that managers can better understand the processes through which they are most effectively performed.[3] Generally, then, job analysis is an effort to study and understand specific jobs in the organization so that managers can have a full sense of the nature of those jobs and the kinds of skills and abilities necessary to perform them. As already noted, job analysis is a fundamental input and building block of the planning process but, as illustrated in Figure 5.1, relates to other human resource management processes as well.

For example, as shown in the figure, job analysis affects selection, or hiring, decisions because the job analysis process indicates what tasks must be performed by the person to be hired. Job analysis results in assessments about the underlying skills and abilities needed to perform the job and leads to logical and appropriate plans to recruit individuals who are most likely to have these skills and abilities. Selection techniques, for instance, can be designed and administered to determine which of the recruited applicants have the necessary

■ **Job analysis** is the process of gathering and organizing detailed information about various jobs within the organization so that managers can better understand the processes through which those jobs are most effectively performed.

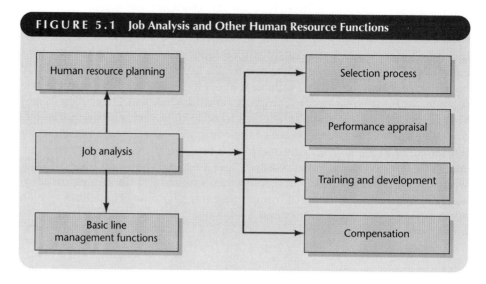

FIGURE 5.1 Job Analysis and Other Human Resource Functions

levels of these skills and abilities. These are the individuals that the organization should seek to hire.

Under the Americans with Disabilities Act (ADA), job analysis has taken on an even more important role in the selection of new employees in many companies. As we noted in Chapter 3, the ADA outlaws discrimination based on disabilities. The ADA does not require an organization to hire someone who cannot perform the job in question, of course, but it does require an organization to hire a "qualified individual with a disability." This is specified as "... an individual with a disability who, with or without a reasonable accommodation, can perform the essential functions of the employment position that such an individual holds or desires" (American with Disabilities Act, Title 1, section 101).

Consider, for example, the implications of an organization refusing to hire a disabled applicant because a manager assumes that the individual cannot perform the job. The individual might have grounds for a discrimination claim if there is ambiguity as to exactly which job elements are essential to the organization and which are less essential or optional and if the applicant can demonstrate a capacity for performing the job. Thus determining the essential functions of the jobs within the organization becomes more important than ever for managers because they must identify those parts of jobs (for example, tasks, duties) that absolutely must be carried out effectively for the person to be successful in performing the job. And this information can best be obtained through job analysis.

Figure 5.1 also indicates that job analysis relates to performance appraisal. This factor stems from the fact that it is necessary to understand what an employee should be capable of doing in a job in order to assess how well that employee is actually performing. Job analysis similarly affects training and development because it provides data and information that help managers better understand the kind of training and development programs that are necessary to enhance employee competencies and capabilities to an ideal level of performance. Job analysis information is also important for compensation (job analysis methods used for establishing compensation rates are often referred to as job evaluation) because work behaviors have traditionally been a primary basis for compensation (although, as we will see in Part V, compensation based on knowledge or competencies, rather than behaviors, is becoming more common).

In addition to its fundamental role in human resource planning and other aspects of the human resource function, job analysis is also important to line managers for a variety of general reasons. First of all, line managers must have a thorough understanding of the workflow processes that characterize their particular work units. That is, they have to understand how work flows from employee to employee, from job station to job station, and from work group to work group. To develop this understanding, of course, line managers must also have a fundamental insight into the basic mechanics, character, and nature of each job. It is job analysis that provides this insight. Also, since line managers are often involved in hiring and appraisal decisions, they must rely on the information provided by job analysis to help determine who should be hired and, eventually, how well employees are doing their jobs.

■ **Knowledge, skills, and abilities** (**KSA**) are the fundamental requirements necessary to perform a job.

■ **Job families** are groups of jobs that have similar task and KSA requirements.

Linking Job Analysis with Human Resource Planning

As already noted, human resource planners are constantly looking for the various kinds of information they need to develop the optimum workforce the organization will require both in the short-term and long-term future. Job analysis provides fundamental input to the human resource planning process by helping planners understand exactly what kinds of work must be performed. That is, job analysis helps define for managers the kinds of both general work and specific jobs that the organization will be relying on in the future.[4]

Job analysis information is important for planning in another arena as well. The focus of job analysis is typically an individual job, but in many organizations, the tasks and responsibilities of some jobs may be similar to those of other jobs. Likewise, the **knowledge, skills, and abilities** (**KSA**) requirements may be similar for a set of jobs. As a result, for planning purposes organizations often try to form **job families**—groups of jobs that have task and KSA requirements that are quite similar. These job families can be quite useful for human resource planning in several ways. First, if the jobs within a job family have similar KSA requirements, it might be possible to train employees to apply what they have learned to the entire family of jobs, making these workers a much more flexible resource for the organization. In addition, training for job families rather than for specific jobs can help employees remain useful to the organization even if their present jobs become obsolete.[5]

Well-conceived job families can also be used to help organizations in career planning. The jobs within a family represent those that have similar patterns of requirements, and assuming they occur at different levels within an organization, the jobs can represent a typical career path for an employee.

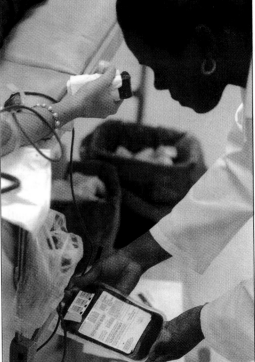

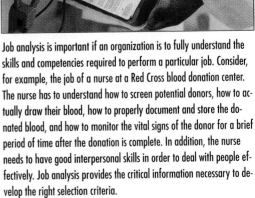

Job analysis is important if an organization is to fully understand the skills and competencies required to perform a particular job. Consider, for example, the job of a nurse at a Red Cross blood donation center. The nurse has to understand how to screen potential donors, how to actually draw their blood, how to properly document and store the donated blood, and how to monitor the vital signs of the donor for a brief period of time after the donation is complete. In addition, the nurse needs to have good interpersonal skills in order to deal with people effectively. Job analysis provides the critical information necessary to develop the right selection criteria.

Thus managers can plan where an employee might go as his or her career builds, and they might also get a good idea of where to find replacements when a job opening occurs.

Finally, job families can be used in selection decisions. We touch on this topic again in Chapter 7, but once an organization has established the selection requirements for one job within a family, managers may be able to use this information to predict requirements in other jobs within the family.[6] In fact, if there is a reasonable probability that an employee will progress through all of the jobs in a job family, the organization might well choose to select individuals based on the needs of the *highest* level job within the family, rather than on those of the specific job for which an individual is applying. For example, suppose Texas Instruments needs to hire some technicians to support engineering work teams. The human resource manager in charge of this hiring might determine that over a four-year period each technician will rotate across several groups, performing different functions for each. The astute manager might therefore set as a hiring standard for all technicians the performance requirements for all such support roles, even though some technicians may start out in less demanding roles.

THE BOTTOM LINE Job analysis is an important part of the human resource planning process. Managers should know the basic purposes of job analysis and how it relates to other important human resource and line management functions and activities.

THE JOB ANALYSIS PROCESS

The job analysis process can generally be approached in a clear and straightforward manner. As a starting point in this process, it is helpful to first understand the steps in job analysis, including who is responsible for job analysis. As illustrated in Figure 5.2, job analysis is generally a three-step process.[7]

Determining Information Needs

The first step is determining the organization's precise information needs. Indeed, a wide range of information on various jobs may be obtained during the course of job analysis. The exact type and nature of the information that is obtained, however, will depend on both the intended purposes of the job analysis information and various constraints, such as time and budget limitations, that are imposed by the organization. But regardless of constraints, the job analysis must provide enough information about what someone does on a job to allow a determination of knowledge, skills, and abilities necessary to perform the job. If the organization lacks the time and/or resources to obtain this minimum information, there is really no point in proceeding with the job analysis.

Examples of the types of job analysis information that might be gathered include general work activities (such as a description of specific tasks that are carried out, how the job interfaces with other jobs and equipment, the procedures that are used in the job, behaviors that are required on the job, and physical movements and demands of the job) and the machines, tools, equipment,

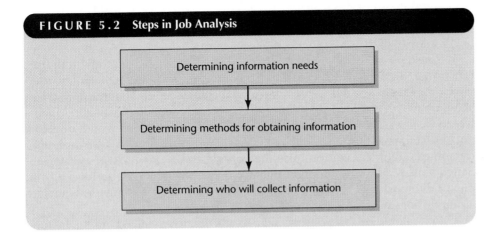

FIGURE 5.2   Steps in Job Analysis

Determining information needs

Determining methods for obtaining information

Determining who will collect information

and work aids that are used in the performance of the job. Other useful information that may be collected includes details regarding the job context (physical working conditions such as exposure to dust, heat, toxic substances; indoor environment versus outdoor environment; and so forth). Similarly, information may also be collected regarding the organizational context and social context of the job. In addition, details regarding work schedule, various financial and nonfinancial incentives, and personal requirements (job-related attributes such as specific skills, education, and training; work experience and related jobs; physical characteristics and aptitudes) are also usually desirable.[8]

Selecting Job Analysis Methods

Once human resource managers decide what types of information to collect, the next step in the job analysis process is to determine how to collect that information. A variety of methods are also used to collect job analysis information. The most common methods include the observations of task and job behaviors, interviews with job incumbents, and the use of questionnaires and check lists. For example, the individuals who actually perform the job analysis, called **job analysts**, can sometimes systematically gather the desired information on jobs simply by observing people performing those jobs. This method is especially useful for unskilled manual jobs but has less relevance for jobs involving creative thought and analytic skills. Furthermore, if job incumbents know that they are being observed, they might tend to try to do the job as it was originally specified, rather than as it is actually done, for the benefit of the observer.

In many cases it is also beneficial to actually interview individuals who are performing the jobs being analyzed.[9] These individuals are in a good position to explain both the nature of the work they are performing and the qualification and credentials that they believe necessary for the successful performance of those jobs. Of course, even though this information is both rich and relevant, there is also the possibility that it may be biased as a result of various predispositions on the part of the individuals. For example, they may be tempted to overstate the skills and qualifications needed to perform the job, and they may overstate the complexities and sophistication of the job. Although job analysis may be carried out for any number of reasons, as noted above, employees

Job analysts are individuals who actually perform job analysis in an organization.

often assume that the purpose for the job analysis is to determine compensation rates. Therefore, they might believe that by exaggerating the importance or complexity of their jobs they will receive more pay.

It is also possible to interview others who are knowledgeable about the job, rather than the actual job incumbent. So, for example, a job analyst might interview the person who supervises the incumbent, assuming that the supervisor should have a good idea of what the incumbent does and still have less incentive to exaggerate the job in any way. Although the supervisor would probably not expect to receive more pay for supervising a more complex job, some other dynamics might still compromise the honesty of the supervisor's responses. Stated simply, although it might make someone feel good to perform a complex and important job, it might feel even better to *supervise* someone who does a complex or important job.

Other people with expertise who could be interviewed might include higher-level supervisors, industrial engineers, and even human resource managers. As these individuals are further removed from the actual job, they have even less incentive to distort the job, but they are also more likely to be mistaken or misinformed about what actually takes place on the job. As a result, if critical job analysis information is collected through the interview process, it is important to interview multiple individuals who have different relationships with the actual job and then integrate or average the information collected.

Another possible way of gathering job analysis data is for the job analyst to actually perform the job for a meaningful period of time and then describe the job based on actual experience. Although this approach may be feasible in some situations, jobs requiring specialized training or jobs where errors are costly are not usually amenable to this form of job analysis. On the other hand, such cases lend themselves to alternative methods for job analysis, including such things as questionnaires and check lists. Standardized questionnaires and check lists are widely available, but sometimes organizations choose to develop their own custom measures. We discuss these methods more fully later.

Responsibilities for Job Analysis

The third step in job analysis is determining who is responsible for collecting the information—for actually conducting the job analysis. In general, the responsibility of job analysis is jointly shared by three different individuals or groups. One is the line manager who is responsible for the performance of the various jobs being analyzed. For example, the line manager is responsible for adequately conveying to the human resources function exactly what information is available, what information is needed, and the specific purpose of the job analysis. The human resource group or department is also responsible for job analysis. For example, the human resource department typically performs and/or contracts for the services necessary to perform the job analysis. Thus the human resource department may need to buy certain job analysis instruments, such as the Position Analysis Questionnaire (discussed later in the chapter), and/or subcontract with job analyst specialists to perform the job analysis.

And finally, the responsibility also partially lies with the job analyst or analysts. A job analyst, as already noted, is the individual (or individuals) who actually conducts the job analysis. Depending on the method used and the nature of the organization involved, the job analyst might be a current job incumbent (as is the case in some check-list approaches), another employee of the organization (who in a very large organization might actually be a full-time job analyst), or someone from outside the organization (such as a consultant or professional job analyst) hired to do the job analysis. In the latter instance the job analyst will probably have to rely on employees of the organization to learn enough about the job to conduct the job analysis, and the analyst might use any or several of the methods previously described to obtain this information.

Smaller firms may be more inclined to employ consultants to perform job analyses, or they may simply not bother doing job analysis at all. When they need information about jobs and their requirements, though, they may refer to a published source of this type of information, such as the Dictionary of Occupational Titles (DOT). But the DOT is being gradually replaced by a new, online source of job analysis information called O*NET.

In addition to providing a basic job description, O*NET provides information on the relative importance of 33 specific knowledge areas including administration and management, mathematics, psychology, and foreign language. O*NET also provides information about the relative importance of 46 skills including 10 "basic skills" such as reading comprehension, writing, and critical thinking; and 36 "cross-functional skills" such as: coordination, persuasion, and time management. There is also information about the importance of a large number of cognitive, psychomotor, physical, and sensory abilities. Finally, O*NET provides information about other job requirements such as legal and character requirements, and contextual factors such as work setting, job hazards, and environmental conditions.

Of course, the match between the job described in O*NET and the job that exists in the organization may not always be perfect. Nonetheless, it is clear that this is an important resource for smaller companies, or larger companies that want some type of comparison job analysis information.

> **THE BOTTOM LINE**   Since job analysis can be used for a wide array of purposes, managers should carefully determine their information needs so as to make the most efficient use of job analysis. Also embedded in this process is determining the best job analysis methods for a particular situation and making sure that responsibilities for the job analysis are well understood.

JOB ANALYSIS METHODS

As noted earlier, organizations use several methods to actually perform job analyses. In this section we discuss these methods in more detail. We also discuss two related areas, job descriptions and job specifications.

Collecting Job Analysis Data

The primary source of data for job analysis work is usually **subject matter experts** (**SMEs**). SMEs are the individuals from whom job analysts obtain data for the job analysis and may be existing job incumbents, supervisors, or other knowledgeable employees. For the job analysis to be successful, the employees selected to provide the job analysis information must be intimately familiar with the true nature of the jobs. Thus participants in job analysis tend to be

■ **Subject matter experts** (**SMEs**) are individuals presumed to be highly knowledgeable about jobs and who provide data for job analysis; they may be existing job incumbents, supervisors, or other knowledgeable employees.

Obtaining the right information is obviously a major part of effective job analysis. Current job incumbents are often among the best sources of information for job analysis. For example, Marilyn Cochrane is a well-respected trucker educator with the American Trucking Association. Her thorough and comprehensive knowledge and understanding of the job of truck driver makes her an invaluable source of information for companies and industry experts who study trucking jobs in order to hire the right people as drivers and reduce accidents on the road.

more experienced and high-performing individuals who thoroughly understand the job.[10]

The job analysis information itself takes a variety of forms. First of all, it is important to identify the major job dimensions that make up a particular job. For example, suppose a human resource manager at Exxon has been asked to conduct a job analysis of the position of administrative assistant in a particular department. Existing data already indicates the basic dimensions of the job and might include keyboarding, answering a telephone, handling routine copying, arranging appointments, greeting visitors, making certain routine administrative decisions, and handling related administrative details. When using structured questionnaires or check lists for job analysis, these dimensions are already specified in the questionnaire.

If some form of narrative about the job is to be prepared instead, the various major job dimensions must be subdivided into the specific tasks that are associated with them. For example, keyboarding, while a major job dimension, can take a variety of forms. It might include such things as typing address labels on an envelope using a conventional typewriter, keyboarding major documents into personal computers and using word processing software, operating scanning devices to input previously prepared text and graphics, and performing various other specific tasks that together constitute the job of keyboarding.

Ultimately, the job analysis must also identify the basic KSA requirements necessary to perform them. For example, the skills and abilities necessary to handle a keyboarding task may include such things as familiarity with various word processing packages, familiarity with various scanning devices, and familiarity with various computers and operating systems, as well as physical dexterity and coordination. In some cases the KSAs are developed after the job analysis is completed, by the job analyst and the SMEs. When an organization uses a standardized questionnaire, these KSAs might be identified through some computer algorithm, based on the job analysis information provided. In these cases the organization is less dependent on the decision-making skills of the job analyst.

Occasionally, job analysts go further and offer potential changes that might be forthcoming in a job. For example, if the organization is already aware of new technology that is about to be installed or is planning to implement major changes in how work is being performed, these events and circumstances may also be incorporated into the job analysis process. Some software packages today include voice-recognition dictation systems that virtually eliminate the need for physical keyboarding. To the extent that job analysts believe that this technology will become commonly used in the foreseeable future, they may need to incorporate into a job analysis the ways in which the technology might alter the job being studied.

Specific Job Analysis Techniques

Several job analysis techniques can be used by an organization. The most commonly used methods are the straight narrative, Fleishman job analysis system, task analysis inventory, Functional Job Analysis, Position Analysis Questionnaire (PAQ), and the critical incidents approach.[11]

Narrative job analysis   The most common approach to job analysis is to simply have one or more SMEs prepare a written narrative or text description of the job. These can vary in terms of length and detail. To some extent the quality of the information depends on the writing skills of the job analyst. Although it is possible to specify the format and structure of these narratives, they are typically individualistic, making it difficult to compare the tasks on one job with the tasks on another job. They are relatively inexpensive, however, and someone does not require a great deal of training to complete a narrative job analysis.

Fleishman job analysis system   Another popular method for job analysis is the **Fleishman job analysis system**.[12] This approach defines abilities as enduring attributes of individuals that account for differences in performance. The system relies on a taxonomy of fifty-two abilities that presumably represents all the dimensions relevant to work. In general, these specific abilities are presumed to reflect cognitive, psychomotor, and sensory abilities. Examples of the specific abilities included in the Fleishman system are oral comprehension, written comprehension, oral expression, written expression, fluency of ideas, night vision, depth perception, auditory attention, and speech clarity. The actual Fleishman scales consist of descriptions of each ability, followed by a behavioral benchmark example of the different levels of the ability along a seven-point scale. An organization using this job analysis technique will rely on a panel of SMEs (again, incumbent workers and/or supervisors are most commonly used). These experts indicate the point on the various scales that best represents the level of ability required for a particular job. Because of this system's complexity, job analysts require training to use this method.

■ The **Fleishman job analysis system** defines abilities as enduring attributes of individuals that account for differences in performance; it relies on the taxonomy of abilities that presumably represents all the dimensions relevant to work.

Task analysis inventory   Another method of job analysis is the **task analysis inventory**. The task analysis inventory method actually refers to a family of job analysis methods, each with unique characteristics. However, each one focuses on analyzing all the tasks performed in the focal job. Any given job may have dozens of tasks, for example. Again relying on SMEs, this method requires the

■ The **task analysis inventory** is a family of job analysis methods, each with unique characteristics; each focuses on analyzing all the tasks performed in the focal job.

generation of a list of tasks performed in a job. Once the list has been developed, a job analyst—frequently the job incumbent—evaluates each task on dimensions such as the relative amount of time spent on the task, the frequency with which the task is performed, the relative importance of the task, the relative difficulty of the task, and the time necessary to learn the task.

Task inventories require a fair amount of effort to develop. However, once they are developed they are relatively easy to use. This approach to job analysis is often used in municipal and county governments and is also the most common form of job analysis used in the U.S. military. The information generated by this approach to job analysis is often very detailed and is very useful for establishing KSA requirements and training needs. The military has used these inventories to establish career paths and job families, where the jobs clustered together have a large amount of overlap in terms of the tasks that are important.[13] Managers then use a single task inventory to analyze all the jobs in the family. Compared to other job analysis techniques, it is more difficult, though, to make comparisons across job families, which reduces the usefulness of task inventories to some degree.

Functional job analysis   One attempt to have a single job analysis instrument that could be used with a wide variety of jobs resulted in the development of Functional Job Analysis.[14] According to this approach, all jobs can be described in terms of their level of involvement with *people, data,* and *things.* For example, employees on a job at a Halliburton manufacturing site might be said to "set up" machines (things), "mentor" people, and "synthesize" data. All of these are high levels of involvement and would indicate a complex job. The exact definition of each of these terms is provided to the job analyst. The Department of Labor relies on functional job analysis for some of its classifications of jobs, but this type of analysis is not used widely in private industry. Nonetheless, this approach is important because it represents the first attempt to develop a single instrument that can describe all jobs in common terms.

Position analysis questionnaire   One of the most popular and widely used job analysis method is the **Position Analysis Questionnaire**, also known as the **PAQ**. The PAQ, developed by Ernest McCormick and his associates, is a standardized job analysis instrument consisting of 194 items. These items reflect work behavior, working conditions, or job characteristics that are assumed to be generalizable across a wide variety of jobs.[15] The PAQ items are organized into six sections. *Information inputs* include where and how a worker gets information needed to perform the job. *Mental processes* represent the reasoning, decision-making, planning, and information processing activities that are involved in performing the job. *Work output* refers to the physical activities, tools, and devices used by the worker to perform the job. *Relationships with other people* include the relationship with other people required in performing the job. *Job context* represents the physical and social context where the work is performed. Finally, *other characteristics* include the activities, conditions, and characteristics other than those previously described that pertain to the job. Figure 5.3 presents some items from the PAQ section dealing with the information inputs.

Job analysts are asked to determine whether each scale applies to the specific job being analyzed. The analyst rates the item on six scales: extent of use, amount of time, importance of the job, possibility of occurrence, applicability,

■ The **Position Analysis Questionnaire (PAQ)** is a standardized job analysis instrument consisting of 194 items reflecting work behavior, working conditions, or job characteristics that are assumed to apply to a wide variety of jobs.

FIGURE 5.3 Job Analysis Technique—Sample Items from the Position Analysis Questionnaire (PAQ)

1   INFORMATION INPUT

1.1   Sources of Job Information

Rate each of the following items in terms of the extent to which it is used by the worker as a source of information in performing his job.

Code	Extent of Use (U)
N	Does not apply
1	Nominal/very infrequent
2	Occasional
3	Moderate
4	Considerable
5	Very substantial

1.1.1 Visual Sources of Job Information

1. _U_   Written materials (books, reports, office notes, articles, job instructions, signs, etc.)
2. _U_   Quantitative materials (materials which deal with quantities or amounts, such as graphs, accounts, specifications, tables of numbers, etc.)
3. _U_   Pictorial materials (pictures or picturelike materials used as *sources* of information, for example, drawings, blueprints, diagrams, maps, tracings, photographic films, x-ray films, TV pictures, etc.)
4. _U_   Patterns/related devices (templates, stencils, patterns, etc., used as *sources* of information when *observed* during use; do *not* include here materials described in item 3 above)
5. _U_   Visual displays (dials, gauges, signal lights, radarscopes, speedometers, clocks, etc.)

37. _S_   Reasoning in problem solving (indicate, using the code below, the level of reasoning that is required of the worker in applying his knowledge, experience, and judgment to problems)

Code   Level of Reasoning in Problem Solving

1   Very limited (use of common sense to carry out simple, or relatively uninvolved instructions, for example, janitor, deliveryman, hod carrier, etc.)

2   Limited (use of some training and/or experience to select from a limited number of solutions the most appropriate action or procedure in performing the job, for example, salesclerk, postman, electrician, apprentice, keypunch operator, etc.

3   Intermediate (use of relevant principles to solve practical problems and to deal with a variety of concrete variables in situations where only limited standardization exists, for example, draftsman, carpenter, farmer, etc.)

4   Substantial (use of logic or scientific thinking to define problems, collect information, establish facts, and draw valid conclusions, for example, mechanical engineer, personnel director, manager of a "chain" store, etc.)

5   Very substantial (use of *principles* of logical or scientific thinking to solve a wide range of intellectual and practical problems, for example, research chemist, nuclear engineer, corporate president, or manage of a large branch or plant, etc.)

3.3   Activities of the Entire Body

Code	Importance to This Job (I)		
N	Does not apply	3	Average
1	Very minor	4	High
2	Low	5	Extreme

85. _I_   Highly skilled body coordination (activities involving extensive, and often highly learned coordination activities of the whole body, for example, athletics, dancing, etc.)

86. _I_   Balancing (maintaining body balance or equilibrium to prevent falling when standing, walking, running, crouching, etc., on narrow, slippery, steeply inclined, or erratically moving surfaces, for example, walking on narrow elevated beam, working on steep roof, etc.)

and special code. Special code refers to unique and special rating scales that are used with a particular item. These ratings are then submitted to PAQ services where computer software compiles a report regarding the job scores on the job dimensions.

A major advantage of the PAQ is that, like Functional Job Analysis, the PAQ dimensions are believed to underlie all jobs, which allows a wide variety of (although probably not all) jobs to be described in common terms. In the case of the PAQ, the items and dimensions describe what a worker does on the job, rather than what gets done. For example, although a baker might bake bread, whereas a pilot flies an airplane, when we examine how they get the information they need to do their jobs, we find that they both rely heavily on dials and instruments for critical information. This common factor does not suggest that the two jobs are related, just that workers perform similar functions even on very diverse jobs.

In addition, unlike Functional Job Analysis, the PAQ can provide information on 187 separate items, allowing a much richer picture of what happens on a job (there are actually 194 items in the PAQ, but the remaining items deal with methods of pay). Finally, another strength of the PAQ is that, because it has been widely used for many years, a considerable database of information attests to its validity and reliability. In general, research supports the validity and reliability of the instrument. Research also suggests that the PAQ actually measures thirty-two dimensions and thirteen overall job dimensions. A given job score on these dimensions can be very useful in job analysis.[16]

Because the instrument has been so widely used, it has also been statistically related to other measures. For example, the general aptitude test battery (GATB), a standardized ability test, is statistically related to the PAQ in a relatively well-understood manner. As a result, dimension scores from the PAQ can be used to make direct estimates of the KSA requirements to perform the job in question.[17] The fact that the PAQ allows a wide variety of jobs to be described in common terms means it is relatively easy to make direct comparisons among jobs. This further allows the PAQ to be quite useful for job evaluation—that is, for establishing compensation rates for different jobs.

Unfortunately, even though it is widely used, the PAQ also has some noteworthy shortcomings. For one thing, the PAQ instrument itself is relatively complex and an employee must have a reading level of a college graduate to be able to complete it. In addition, PAQ executives recommend that only trained experts complete the questionnaire, as opposed to using job incumbents or supervisors for this purpose. Further, although the PAQ is supposed to be applicable to most jobs, there is reason to believe that it is less useful for describing higher-level managerial jobs and white-collar jobs.[18] Despite these limitations, the PAQ remains the most popular standardized job analysis instrument available and is used by firms such as Kodak, Nestlé USA, and Delta Airlines.

■ The **critical incident approach** to job analysis focuses on those critical behaviors that distinguish between effective and ineffective performers.

Critical incidents approach   The final widely used job analysis approach we will discuss relies on **critical incidents**. Critical incidents are examples of particularly effective or ineffective performance.[19] As used for job analysis, this approach focuses on those critical behaviors that distinguish between effective and ineffective performers. Although this approach to job analysis is most widely used in connection with the development of appraisal instruments, it is generally useful as it focuses the organization's attention on aspects of the job that lead to more or less effective performance.

Although these techniques are the most commonly used in industry, we should note that, in many cases, organizations simply develop their own job analysis techniques or instruments. This is especially true for managerial jobs and when jobs are performed by teams rather than by individuals. In these cases widely accepted standardized job analysis instruments are simply not available. Regardless of which job analysis technique an organization employs, however, some type of narrative description of the job will probably be prepared. Therefore, it is important to draw a distinction between a job description and a job specification.

Job Descriptions and Job Specifications

A **job description** lists the tasks, duties, and responsibilities that a particular job entails. These are observable actions that are necessary for the effective performance of the job. The job description specifies the major job elements, provides examples of job tasks, and provides some indication of their relative importance in the effective conduct of the job.[20] A **job specification** focuses more on the individual who will perform the job. Specifically, a job specification indicates the knowledge, abilities, skills, and other characteristics that an individual must have to be able to perform the job. Factual or procedural capabilities and levels of proficiency refer more to skills. In general, enduring capabilities that an individual possesses can be thought of as abilities. Job specifications may include items such as general educational requirements, for example, having a high school or college degree, as well as the specifications of specific job-related skills, such as the ability to keyboard seventy words a minute or the requirement that an individual be fluent in Japanese or Spanish.

Taken together then, the job description and the job specification should provide a parallel and mutually consistent set of information and details that focus on the job itself and the individual most likely to be successful performing that job. This information should then inform all subsequent recruiting and selection decisions. Figure 5.4 illustrates what an actual job description and job specification for a particular kind of accountant might look like. This description and

■ A **job description** lists the tasks, duties, and responsibilities that a particular job entails and specifies the major job elements, provides examples of job tasks, and provides some indication of their relative importance in the effective conduct of the job.

■ A **job specification** focuses on the individual who will perform the job and indicates the knowledge, abilities, skills, and other characteristics that an individual must have to be able to perform the job.

FIGURE 5.4   Example Job Description and Job Specification

Job Title: Accounts Payable and Payroll Accountant, XYZ Corp.

Job Description: Business partner with Accounts Payable and Payroll Departments to develop expense forecasts and commentary; prepare Accounts Payable and Payroll shared services charge-outs to affiliates; ensure Accounts Payable and Payroll inputs are posted weekly; perform account analysis/reconciliations of Cash, Liability, and Employee Loan accounts related to Accounts Payable and Payroll; submit routine reports to Corporate; identify and implement process improvements relative to all responsibilities listed above.

Job Specification: BS degree in accounting or finance; 2+ years of accounting/finance experience; sound knowledge of Integral Accounts Payable and General Ledger Systems; working knowledge of Hyperion Software, PACT; good communication skills; able to work independently at off-site location.

specification would be created as part of a job analysis and would be used to communicate to job applicants and managers what skills and abilities are necessary to perform the job

THE BOTTOM LINE   Managers should remember that an impressive array of job analysis methods is available. The key, of course, is to determine which method best fits the needs and plans of the organization. Managers should also not underestimate the importance of well-constructed job descriptions and job specifications.

THE HUMAN RESOURCE PLANNING PROCESS

As indicated earlier, job analysis information is a major source of information that managers use in the human resource planning process.[21] The human resource planning process is of vital importance to any organization. Effective human resource planning can often make the difference between organizational success and failure. **Human resource planning**, illustrated in Figure 5.5, can be defined as the process of forecasting the supply and demand for human resources within an organization and developing action plans for aligning the two. This section examines that process in more detail.

■ **Human resource planning** is the process of forecasting the supply and demand for human resources within an organization and developing action plans for aligning the two.

Forecasting the Supply of Human Resources

An important first step in human resource planning is forecasting the future supply of human resources—predicting the availability of current and/or potential employees with the skills, abilities, and motivation to perform jobs that

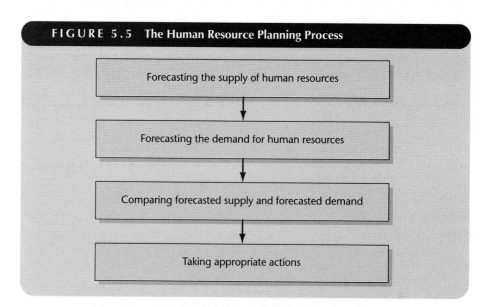

FIGURE 5.5   The Human Resource Planning Process

Forecasting the supply of human resources

Forecasting the demand for human resources

Comparing forecasted supply and forecasted demand

Taking appropriate actions

the organization expects to have available. A number of mechanisms can be used to help managers more effectively forecast the supply of human resources vis-à-vis its current employees. For one thing, by looking internally at its own records the organization is likely to be able to draw on considerable historical data about its own abilities to hire and retain employees. In addition, the organization can glean information about the extent to which people leave their jobs voluntarily or involuntarily. And all of this information, in turn, is useful in predicting the internal supply of human resources in the future.

Suppose, for example, that Atlas Industries, a regional manufacturing and supply business serving the plumbing industry, has averaged 15 percent turnover for each of the last ten years with little variation from year to year. When Atlas's human resource manager attempts to predict the future supply of existing workers, at least initially it seems reasonable to predict a relatively similar level of turnover for the forthcoming year. Thus the internal supply of its human resources at Atlas will likely decline by around 15 percent during the next year. Assuming the firm plans to maintain its current operations and will need a workforce comparable to what it has today, the organization will need to plan to recruit and hire workers to replace those individuals who will depart.

Of course, the human resources manager will also need to look carefully at impending retirements and the firm's experiences with involuntary turnover. In addition, the manager may need to consider environmental factors. For example, suppose that another plumbing equipment manufacturer is constructing a plant on a nearby site. It is likely that Atlas may see an increase in its own turnover simply because of the availability of an alternative employer needing similar kinds of workers. Thus any given employee might leave Atlas for the new firm because it's closer to their home, may pay a bit better, or may be rumored to offer great promotion opportunities.

Businesses have increasing need for employees with managerial and technical skills. The aging workforce and declining birthrate, however, have led to forecasts of a serious shortage of qualified managerial talent, especially for firms that also require technical expertise. The fact that many older workers feel unwanted in hi-tech companies makes matters even worse. But Mary Furlong, CEO of ThirdAge.com of San Francisco, is trying to plan for the future shortage by reversing some of these trends. Her company manages a web site that appeals to people in their 40s and 50s and offers training in on-line technology. More than one fourth of her employees are technologically competent *and* are over age 50. She believes these older workers are more loyal, willing to learn new technology as needed, and the key to meeting the increasing demands for experienced, technically trained employees in the future.

Because unemployment is so low in many industrial sectors, organizations today are paying especially close attention to the internal supply of workers and taking steps to retain their more valued employees. For example, even though Microsoft has a very low turnover rate—less than 7 percent—the firm nevertheless recently formed a new department within human resources focusing solely on efforts and programs to keep its more valued employees. Why is retention so important? Microsoft estimates that it spends between $10,000 and $20,000 to recruit an entry-level software engineer, not including a possible signing bonus it may have to pay.[22]

Given that a firm often expects to need new employees in the future, it is also important to forecast the supply of human resources outside the firm that will be potentially available for it to recruit and hire. Sometimes organizations can obtain valid supply information of this sort from various sources in its external environment. Most colleges and universities, for example, track their enrollment statistics and usually make that information available to the general public. If colleges and universities report a decline in the number of students who are majoring in engineering, for example, then businesses can expect a decrease in the supply of engineering graduates in a few years. Similar statistics are often available for high school graduates as well.

In addition, external data can also be used to predict the supply of labor in specific regions. Over the last several years, for example, there has been a gradual movement of population away from the north and northeastern parts of the United States and toward the south, southeast, and southwest regions. Thus the supply of labor in the North and Northeast is gradually declining while the supply of labor in the southern parts of the United States is gradually increasing. In other parts of the world, wherever immigration rules permit, workers are gradually shifting away from less developed parts of the world and more toward industrialized and economically prosperous regions. For instance, many workers in eastern regions of Europe continue to move into western areas in anticipation of better employment prospects.[23]

The basic method many organizations use to forecast future labor supplies is to develop mathematical trend models using data from the past, with appropriate adjustments for migratory trends and predictions. These models, which essentially assume that trends will continue in a linear (that is, straight line) fashion, are usually reasonably accurate. But they can be far less accurate when some unforeseen event or trend disrupts expectations. One such surprise was the unexpected increase in the labor force participation rates for women during the 1980s. Although women's participation rates had been climbing for years, statistical predictions based on simple trend lines substantially underestimated the growth rates in the 1980s. In retrospect, observers realized that new (that is, first time) entries by women into the labor force were being substantially supplemented by other women already in the labor force, but who were previously underemployed.

Aside from simply predicting the number of employees an organization will need, human resource planners frequently try to predict other characteristics of the workforce as well. For example, many experts today envision the workforce of tomorrow as being smarter, younger, and more productive than today's workforce. Moreover, they also predict greater worker mobility, more self-reliance and technical sophistication within the workforce, an increase in the number of immigrants in the workforce, and a decline in the Caucasian birthrate. And clearly, each of these trends can have an impact on an organization's supply of workers.[24]

Finally, we should also note the special forecasting situation generally known as executive succession. **Executive succession** involves systematically planning for future promotions into top management positions. To illustrate both the nature and importance of executive succession, consider first the case of organizations needing to hire new hourly workers. Suppose a retailer knows that it will need to hire an extra two thousand people to staff positions during an upcoming Christmas season. The firm doesn't really need to know very far in advance exactly who these individuals will be. Instead, it can rely on its past

■ **Executive succession** involves systematically planning for future promotions into top management positions.

history to begin recruiting through newspaper ads, perhaps during October, and then hiring the first two thousand qualified applicants. To be able to do this, the firm must know that (1) there are thousands of people who seek additional employment at this time of the year, (2) its training costs are low, and (3) the employment is temporary. And hiring a wrong person is easily remedied via routine discipline and termination procedures.

But contrast this situation with the hiring of a new senior executive. Finding just the right person may be difficult, development costs to groom this person will be very high, and the actual decision may have a major impact on the firm's future. And hiring the wrong person can be devastating to the firm. Thus many organizations try to bring as much order and logic to the process as possible. For example, senior executives usually indicate well in advance when they expect to retire—sometimes several years in advance. The firm can then draw on its cadre of up-and-coming managers for replacement candidates. Sometimes specific individuals may be moved into special high-profile jobs, with the expectation that whoever does the best job will receive the promotion when the senior person steps down. In other cases the most likely successor is moved into the number-two spot so as to eliminate all uncertainties and to allow this person to concentrate on learning as much as possible about the senior position.[25]

This latter approach has the advantage of having the new person in line should the organization need to move more quickly than anticipated. For example, in late 1998 Procter & Gamble's board of directors realized that the firm was facing substantially greater competition than in the past and that the firm's performance was beginning to slide. To accelerate a necessary change in strategy, it promoted its new number two executive to the top spot earlier than originally planned. But the reason Procter & Gamble even had this option was that it had already done an effective job of succession planning by hiring and grooming this individual.[26]

Forecasting the Demand for Human Resources

In addition to developing forecasts about supply, managers must develop forecasts about demand. That is, managers need to ascertain the numbers and types of people the organization will actually need to be employing in the future. One very important ingredient in this assessment is the organization's own expectations and plans regarding anticipated growth, stability, or decline. For example, as we described in Chapter 2, organizations often adopt corporate strategies aimed at growth, stability, or retrenchment. Clearly, if an organization intends to grow, it is likely to need to hire additional human resources in the future.[27] Likewise, if the organization expects to enter a period of stability, its human resource demand is also likely to be relatively stable.[28] And finally, of course, if a period of decline or retrenchment is anticipated, then the organization may be confronting a decreased demand for human resources.

As with supply, statistical methods provide an effective way for capturing historic trends in an organization's demand for labor and for making rather precise predictions about future demands.[29] On the other hand, many types of important events, as well as overall social and/or industrial trends, might occur in the labor market that have no historical precedence. For example, the chart in "Human Resources in the Twenty-first Century" shows how some

HUMAN RESOURCES in the Twenty-first Century

Easy Come, Easy Go!

Managers attempting to forecast the future supply of and demand for jobs and employees face numerous uncertainties. One major uncertainty for long-term planning is the extent to which any given job may become more or less popular in the future. The following graph clearly illustrates this point. The graph rank orders the thirty "top jobs" (by millions of workers) for the years 1900, 1960, and 1995. Only eight job categories among the most popular in 1900 are still on the list by 1995. Further, some jobs, like carpenters, have consistently dropped further down the list, whereas others, such as police officers and guards, have steadily risen. But most striking is simply the array of jobs on the 1995 list that did not appear previously—jobs such as computer programmers, health technicians, and lawyers and judges!

TOP 30 JOBS (millions of workers)

	1900		1960		1995	
1	Farmers and farm laborers	10.1	Retail salespersons	4.4	Retail salespersons	6.6
2	General laborers	2.6	Farmers and farm laborers	3.8	Teachers*	4.5
3	Private household workers[1]	1.6	Teachers*	1.7	Secretaries	3.4
4	Retail salespersons[2]	1.4	Truck drivers	1.7	Truck drivers	2.9
5	Secretaries[3]	0.6	Secretaries	1.5	Farmers and farm laborers	2.3
6	Carpenters	0.6	Private household workers	1.3	Janitors and cleaners	2.1
7	Railroad workers	0.6	Manufacturing laborers	1.0	Cooks	2.0
8	Miners	0.6	Bookkeepers	0.9	Nurses*	2.0
9	Truck drivers[4]	0.5	Carpenters	0.9	Engineers*	1.9
10	Teachers*	0.4	Waiters and waitresses	0.9	Freight and stock handlers	1.9
11	Launderers	0.4	Engineers*	0.9	Policemen and guards	1.8
12	Dressmakers	0.3	Vehicle mechanics and repairers	0.9	Bookkeepers	1.8
13	Iron and steel workers	0.3	Apparel and textile workers	0.8	Nursing aides, orderlies, etc.	1.8
14	Machinists	0.3	Construction workers	0.8	Vehicle mechanics and repairers	1.7
15	Painters	0.3	Assemblers	0.7	Financial salespersons*	1.7
16	Bookkeepers	0.3	Janitors and cleaners	0.6	Health technicians*	1.6
17	Cotton mill workers	0.2	Sewers and stitchers	0.6	Wholesale commodities brokers*	1.5
18	Tailors	0.2	Cooks	0.6	Accountants and auditors*	1.5
19	Blacksmiths	0.2	Typists	0.5	Waiters and waitresses	1.4
20	Firefighters	0.2	Machinists	0.5	Hotel and restaurant managers	1.3
21	Shoemakers	0.2	Mfg. checkers, examiners, etc.	0.5	Carpenters	1.3
22	Sawyers	0.2	Policemen and guards	0.5	Precision production supervisors*	1.2
23	Masons	0.2	Packers and wrappers	0.5	Math and computer scientists*	1.2
24	Printers	0.2	Cashiers	0.5	Moving equipment operators	1.1
25	Seamstresses	0.2	Accountants and auditors*	0.5	Computer programmers*	1.0
26	Physicians*	0.1	Deliverymen and routemen	0.4	Postmen, clerks, messengers	1.0
27	Tobacco factory workers	0.1	Painters	0.4	Receptionists	0.9
28	Barbers and hairdressers	0.1	Launderers[5]	0.4	Lawyers and judges*	0.9
29	Policemen and guards	0.1	Attendants (hospital, etc.)	0.4	Child care workers	0.9
30	Butchers	0.1	Welders and frame cutters	0.4	Professors*	0.8

Over the century, the structure of U.S. employment has changed enormously. Only eight top job categories have survived throughout. And many more top job categories now require substantial education.

* Requires education. [1]Servants and housekeepers in 1900. [2]Merchants and salespeople in 1900. [3]Clerks in 1900. [4]Teamsters and coachmen in 1900. [5]Launderers and dry cleaners in 1960.

Source: Forbes, May 6, 1996, p. 17; U.S. Bureau of the Census; Dallas Federal Reserve. Reprinted by permission of Forbes Magazine © Forbes, Inc.

jobs, like retail salespersons, have remained in high demand since 1900. But other jobs, like tailors, masons, tobacco factory workers, and butchers, have dropped sharply. Still others, such as nurses, hotel and restaurant managers, and moving equipment operators, have seen demand increase significantly.

As a result of these unexpected shifts, statistical methods that are based heavily on historical trends may overlook important dynamics or even be totally worthless. In these instances, as was noted in the case of predicting supply, the expert or judgmental methods would obviously be far superior. The simplest judgmental method is **unit**, or **bottom-up**, **forecasting**. Organizations that rely on this method allow specific units, branches, departments, or line managers to predict their own future needs for employees. The general approach is for operating managers to be given some general overview of what the constraints and opportunities may be for hiring new employees. These managers then use this information to develop estimates of the human resource needs in their areas of responsibility.

Another judgmental method is called **top-down forecasting**. In this approach experienced and skilled executives and top managers forecast the future supply and demand for labor. These top managers usually meet as a group to discuss trends and business plans and perhaps go through an iterative process wherein they make various forecasts. These forecasts are then refined as a result of feedback on what other individuals in the group forecast. An extension of this method is called the Delphi technique. In the Delphi technique the experts do not actually meet face to face. Rather, they use paper and pencil or, increasingly, e-mail to make predictions and forecasts. An anonymous questionnaire is developed that asks the experts for their opinion and justification for how they formed that opinion. Results from this questionnaire are compiled and returned to the experts along with a second anonymous questionnaire. In this way the various members of the Delphi panel can learn from one another and modify or elaborate their positions in the second questionnaire. This process may continue through several rounds until the experts agree on a judgment.

A more specific set of methods of forecasting the demand for human resources in an organization involves the use of various kinds of labor-related ratios. A **productivity ratio** is the average number of units produced per direct labor employee per year. A **staffing ratio** is used to calculate the number of individuals required in other jobs in the organization aside from those directly involved in the production of actual products. A **learning curve** is a sophisticated elaboration of basic forecasting methods that takes into account increases in productivity that might be expected as employees gain experience and learn more effective ways of performing their job. These ratios can serve as an indicator of future demand by accounting for anticipated improvements in productivity and efficiency. For example, if an organization does not expect any growth in demand for its products next year but does anticipate a 4 percent increase in labor productivity, it will need fewer employees.

Multiple regression is a popular statistical forecasting technique that some firms use to forecast the demand for human resources. **Multiple regression** is a complex mathematical procedure that relies on multiple correlation indices to develop predictions about another variable called the criterion. For example, an organization may know that its current sales, current profits, inflation, overall unemployment rates, and capital investment are all related to its future demand for human resources. Multiple regression helps determine how these various indices interrelate to predict the number of employees the organization needs.

■ **Unit**, or **bottom-up**, **forecasting** involves allowing individual units, branches, departments, or line managers to predict their own future needs for employees.

■ **Top-down forecasting** involves the use of experienced and skilled executives and top managers to forecast the future supply and demand for labor.

■ A **productivity ratio** is the average number of units produced per direct labor employee per year.

■ A **staffing ratio** is used to calculate the number of individuals required in other jobs in the organization aside from those directly involved in the production of actual products.

■ A **learning curve** is a sophisticated elaboration of basic forecasting methods that takes into account increases in productivity that might be expected as employees gain experience and learn more effective ways of performing their job.

■ **Multiple regression** is a complex mathematical procedure forecasting technique that relies on multiple correlation indices.

Of course, the organization must also be careful to look at demand issues within specific areas of the organization. For example, it may be the case that the total workforce of the organization is not predicted to grow dramatically. However, organizational plans and strategies may dictate a significant reallocation of employees within the firm. For example, if an organization is shifting its strategy away from manufacturing and toward a service-based operation, its total workforce may be projected to remain the same. However, the number of employees who will be dedicated to manufacturing jobs may be expected to decline significantly while the number of jobs allocated to the service end of the business may be expected to grow dramatically. In some cases an organization may be able to retrain and transfer people from one business to another, but in other cases a firm may have to terminate or lay off employees from one business sector while it adds to the workforce in the other business sector.

Using the Human Resource Information System

One increasingly important element in the human resource planning process for most organizations is the effective use of the organization's human resource information system. While we discuss the concepts associated with human resource information systems more completely in an appendix at the end of the book, it is relevant to introduce and briefly discuss them here, particularly as they pertain to human resource planning. A **human resource information system** is an integrated and, increasingly, automated system for maintaining a database regarding the employees in an organization. For example, a properly developed human resource information system should have details on every employee's date of hire, job history within the organization, education, performance ratings, compensation history, training and development profile, and various special skills and abilities.[30]

Thus if an organization is planning to open a new office or factory and needs to identify a manager to head up the new operation, a properly designed human resource information system should be capable of retrieving all potential candidates for this job in very short order. The system can also be used to track trends and patterns in job growth, job applicant growth, starting and average wages and salaries, absenteeism, turnover rates, retirement projections,

◼ A **human resource information system** is an integrated and, increasingly, automated system for maintaining a database regarding the employees in an organization.

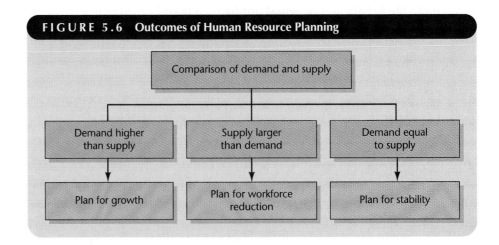

FIGURE 5.6   Outcomes of Human Resource Planning

and so forth. And each of these factors is likely to be an important consideration in human resource planning.

Matching the Supply of and Demand for Human Resources

Once the human resource planning process has been completed, managers can compare the supply of and the demand for human resources. Figure 5.6 illustrates the basic options that can result from this comparison. One possible outcome is that the firm's demand for human resources will exceed its supply. For example, it may be the case that the organization is expanding, new facilities are being opened, new operations being launched, and so forth, and the firm's current employee base and hiring patterns will simply not be sufficient to staff the various requirements of the organization in the future. Hence this organization needs to plan for growth.

On the other hand, an organization may find itself in a situation where supply exceeds demand. That is, the firm might realize that it has more employees currently on its payroll than it expects to need in the future. This situation might result from the expectation that sales are going to decline, certain operations are going to be closed or sold, new technology may eliminate jobs, or some staff functions are going to be outsourced. In this case the organization will need to plan for workforce reductions.

Of course, these simple comparisons are not necessarily reflective of the actual complexity that managers in the real world will face. For example, suppose that a firm forecasts that next year it will need one thousand employees and it currently has one thousand employees on its books. This situation would seem to be an optimal balance of supply and demand. However, there may be substantial imbalances among various job classifications in the organization. For example, among the firm's one thousand employees, there may be only fifty engineers but two hundred salespeople. The projected demand, however, may call for two hundred engineers and only one hundred salespeople. Thus although the total number of employees may be on target, the relative skill mix and skill demands may not be perfectly aligned.

THE BOTTOM LINE   Forecasting the supply of and demand for human resources is a complex and difficult, but very important, element of effective human resource management. Managers must carefully assess both supply and demand with internal and external data, augmented by the firm's human resource information system, and then develop plans for addressing discrepancies.

DEVELOPING FOLLOW-UP ACTION PLANS

Seldom will an organization have exactly the right number of employees with exactly the right skills and abilities. Thus it will usually be necessary to develop various follow-up action plans. These plans may be developed for growth, stability, or reductions.

Labor Shortage? What Labor Shortage?

 A popular lament heard in many quarters today relates to what is seen as a major labor shortage. For example, Deputy Labor Secretary Kitty Higgins recently asked, "Now, we've got the jobs—where are the workers?" Government officials and industry leaders frequently point out that thousands of jobs are going unfilled because there simply are not enough workers to go around. As a result, some firms are going to great lengths to entice new workers—lavish benefits packages, comfortable homelike work environments, and perquisites once reserved only for top executives.

The situation seems to be especially acute in high-tech quarters such as software development companies. For example, Harris Miller, president of the Information Technology Association, recently estimated that 346,000 "core" jobs in the computer industry were sitting vacant and that the number of new jobs was growing by nearly one hundred thousand a year—three times the number of computer science graduates. And Miller and other experts see no solution in sight.

But not everyone buys this story. For example, there are many reported cases of people who have spent their careers writing software, but who cannot now find even an entry-level job—James Wick, sixty-two, spent thirty years writing software for General Electric and Control

"The half-life of an engineer, software or hardware, is only a few years."

(Craig Bennett, president of Intel)*

Data; Paul Peterson, forty-six, spent fifteen years writing software for oil refineries; and Alan Ezer, forty-five, spent ten years developing expertise in Java. Each of these individuals and hundreds more like them claim to have the skills and motivation to help but argue that no one will hire them.

In general, the controversy revolves around age and education. Critics charge that many companies overtly discriminate against older workers for fear that they may demand too much salary, that their presence might disrupt their youth-centered cultures, and/or that their retraining costs are just too high. But employers themselves argue differently. They suggest that these older workers are unwilling to relocate and cannot work the long hours that characterize the industry today. They also fear that their skills are really too far out-of-date. So where does the truth lie? Like most controversial questions, probably somewhere in between the two extremes. But it remains unclear which direction may end up with the winning arguments.

References: "Too Old to Write Code?" *U.S. News and World Report,* March 16, 1998, pp. 39–45 (*quote on pp. 40–41); Douglas Powell, "Stretching Your Workforce Options," *HRMagazine,* July 1998, pp. 83–91; Anne Fisher, "What Labor Shortage?" *Fortune,* June 23, 1997, pp. 154–156.

Planning for Growth

Most managers would agree that the preferred position for an organization to be in is planning for growth. This situation would be indicative of growing sales, increasing demand, and expanding operations for the organization. And when the organization is growing and expanding, it most likely will need to hire new employees in the future. Thus the organization will need to develop plans for hiring. Indeed, it may be the case that the organization can hire employees readily without additional work. For example, if the organization is currently receiving one thousand qualified applications per year and has been hiring only fifty of those individuals, it may be able to meet its growth rate by simply increasing the number of people that it hires. Instead of fifty, for example, the firm may begin hiring seventy-five or one hundred people a year.

In other situations, however, planning for growth may be more difficult. Market conditions may be such that qualified employees are hard to find. For example, if the firm is receiving one hundred qualified applications per year and is currently already hiring as many as ninety of those individuals, then it probably will not be able to hire dramatically larger numbers of people without taking some additional actions. The organization may have to increase its recruiting efforts to attract more applicants and even perhaps begin to support apprentice or training programs. Support of various college and university programs might also be a way of increasing the supply of available labor talent in the future. "Human Resources Fad, Fashion, or Fact?" deals with some contemporary issues regarding growth plans in high-tech industries.

A related incident recently involved United Parcel Service (UPS), the giant delivery business. UPS is based in Louisville, Kentucky, and maintains a huge operation there. The firm recently wanted to launch a major expansion requiring a new distribution center but was concerned about its ability to attract enough new workers, especially those who might be interested in working the night shift. The firm threatened to build its new center in another state unless Kentucky would help. Facing the threat of losing such a big employer, the state passed major job-training legislation and funded programs to help attract and develop the type of capable workers that UPS needed.[31]

Planning for Stability

Organizations may also find themselves in the position of planning for stability. In this case the projected demand for human resources will generally be expected to match the supply of human resources. Even here, however, some specific and subtle planning nuances need to be considered. For example, the organization will naturally experience a certain amount of attrition in its employee ranks each year. As noted earlier, for example, some people will leave for better jobs, some people will retire, some people will leave because of poor performance, and other people will leave for other reasons such as career relocation on the part of a spouse or significant other. Thus even an organization that is projecting a period of stability is likely to still need to augment its human resource labor force to replace those individuals who leave the organization for various reasons. In such cases the organization could implement programs such as training to upgrade the skills of the current employees and therefore make them more "valuable" to the organization. Alternatively, the organization might implement programs designed to reduce turnover among current employees, making stability easier to maintain.

Planning for Reductions

Still another situation that an organization may find itself in is when it needs to plan for reductions. The case here would be when an organization is experiencing cutbacks such as many organizations in the United States faced in the 1980s and on into the early 1990s. Organizations such as IBM, General Motors, and Chrysler reduced their workforce by the thousands. Levi Strauss recently announced job cuts of 6,395 employees; the economic downturn that hit the United States in 1998 forced many Wall Street investment firms to lay off stockbrokers and analysts.[32]

Sometimes these reductions can be handled through normal attrition processes as described above. For example, if the organization currently has one thousand employees; knows from experience that approximately one hundred of those individuals will retire, resign, or be fired next year; and forecasts that it needs only nine hundred employees following next year, then it may need to do very little. The normal attrition processes through which these one hundred people will leave will result in the desired labor force over a twelve-month period.

More painful, however, is when the organization must proactively trim its workforce. For example, what if the organization has one thousand employees today, knows it will lose one hundred of them through normal attrition processes next year, but actually forecasts a workforce need of only seven hundred employees the following year? In this instance the organization must figure out how to eliminate the other two hundred jobs in addition to the one hundred that will "disappear" automatically. This sort of situation may call for laying off or terminating people. Neither option is pleasant, of course, and organizations try to avoid these options whenever possible because of the human costs that are involved, as well as the bad publicity that is generated.

In between these extremes, of course, are some other options that an organization might pursue. One popular plan, especially for managers, is early retirement. The idea underlying early retirement is that the organization needs to reduce its workforce by a greater number of people than will ordinarily be expected to leave through normal attrition processes. Thus the organization might make an offer to other employees to enhance their retirement benefits so that some people might consider retiring at an earlier age than they would have otherwise done. Of course, the organization may be forced to pay additional benefits to employees who accept early retirement—costs that are above and beyond what it would have ordinarily expected to pay.

Another risk of such a program is the organization might lose people that it would have preferred to keep. That is, its highest performing employees may be those who opt for early retirement. In fact, they may use this opportunity to increase their income by taking retirement benefits from their current employer while using their high performance credentials to gain new employment with another organization. On the other hand, lower performers are less likely to have this option and thus may be more likely to remain with the current organization.

THE BOTTOM LINE As a result of human resource planning, managers should have a fairly clear understanding of the extent to which they should subsequently plan for growth, for stability, or for reductions. They can then go about developing and implementing these action plans in the most efficient and effective manner possible.

EVALUATING THE HUMAN RESOURCE PLANNING PROCESS

Like other organizational functions, it is important for managers to evaluate the human resource planning process on a regular and ongoing basis. An ideal human resource planning process would enable an organization to always hire exactly the right number of people at exactly the right time. Of course, such perfection will seldom if ever be achieved. Thus a perfect planning system or cycle is not a realistic goal.

At the same time, however, the planning process can be assessed in terms of its relative accuracy and ability to provide the right mix of human resources. That is, if the organization is usually able to hire the right kinds of employees at around the time they are needed and the organization seldom has a surplus or a shortage of qualified workers, then its planning process may be deemed to be working effectively. On the other hand, if the organization is often having to scramble to hire people on short notice, if it is often hiring the wrong kinds of people, or if it ends up having too many people on the payroll, then the planning process might be flawed or defective.

Chapter Summary

Effective human resource planning is of strategic importance to all organizations. Job analysis is one of the building blocks of the human resource planning process and is a fundamental source of information for that process. Job analysis is the gathering and organizing of detailed information about various jobs within the organization so that managers can better understand the processes through which those jobs are most effectively performed. Job analysis provides input to the human resource planning process by helping planners better understand exactly what kinds of work must be performed.

Job analysis is generally a three-step process: determining and specifying what types of information are needed, determining what method or methods should be used to collect that information, and determining who should collect and provide the information for the job analysis. The responsibility of analysis is jointly shared by line managers, the human resource group or department, and the job analyst or analysts. Commonly used methods of job analysis include the narrative approach, the Fleishman job analysis system, the task analysis inventory, Functional Job Analysis, the Position Analysis Questionnaire, and critical incidents.

Effective human resource planning can often make the difference between organizational success and failure. The human resource planning process involves forecasting the supply and demand for labor and taking appropriate steps to address projected differences. One key element in the human resource planning process is the effective use of the organization's human resource information system.

An organization will seldom have exactly the right number of employees with exactly the right skills and abilities. Thus it will usually be necessary to develop various follow-up action plans. These plans may be developed for growth, stability, or reductions.

As they do for other organizational functions, managers must evaluate the human resource planning process on a regular and ongoing basis. The planning process can be assessed in terms of its relative accuracy and ability to provide the right human resources.

Review and Discussion Questions

1. Summarize the strategic importance of human resource planning.

2. Identify the basic purposes of job analysis.

3. List the steps in job analysis.

4. Compare and contrast job descriptions and job specifications.

5. Summarize the human resource planning process.

6. How do strategic management and human resource planning affect one another?

7. Compare and contrast the major techniques that organizations use for job analysis.

8. Can all jobs be analyzed? Why or why not?

9. Are there circumstances in which managers might choose to not have job descriptions and/or job specifications?

10. What are the biggest challenges managers face when they plan for growth, for stability, and for reductions?

Closing Case

One Way to Select the Next CEO

Deere & Company is the world's largest manufacturer of farm equipment and a leading producer of construction and lawn-care equipment. Its signature green tractors, harvesters, combines, and other equipment are a ubiquitous part of the rural landscape throughout the farm regions of the United States. Its chain saws, snowblowers, and lawn trimmers are common equipment in many home garages. And construction crews often rely on Deere backhoes and excavators as they go about their business. Deere also has established major international operations to complement its domestic businesses.

John Deere founded his company in 1838, and his descendants ran it until 1982 when Robert Hanson became the first nonfamily member to be named CEO. Since then, a succession of outsiders have held the top spot. But like most agriculturally based firms, Deere has struggled with the ups and downs of grain and livestock prices, famine, and recession. Indeed, the firm's financial fortunes have truly been like a roller coaster, with major highs followed by breathtaking lows. But the firm's current CEO, Hans Becherer, has put all that in the past. A thirty-year Deere veteran, Becherer has led Deere into a new era of diversification and cost cutting to better ride out economic downturns and capitalize on economic opportunities.

In late 1998, however, Becherer announced plans to retire in 2000. Deere's board of directors immediately indicated its intent to have a smooth and orderly succession, and one that would create a minimum amount of turmoil at the company. The first decision the board made was that the new CEO would come from inside. Its reasoning was based on two factors: the board strongly believed that the best person would be someone already thoroughly familiar with Deere, and the firm had a deep cadre of talented and qualified executives waiting in the wings.

But because the talent pool was so deep, there was no one obvious successor. Deere's board eventually decided to set up what could only be termed a competition among the four best and brightest choices to replace Becherer. Specifically, Deere promoted the four strongest CEO candidates to head up separate divisions for the remaining two years of Becherer's tenure. Bernard Hardiek was named president of Deere's worldwide agricultural equipment division; Ferdinand Korndorf was appointed president of the worldwide commercial and consumer equipment division; Robert Lane was promoted to senior vice president for Europe, the Middle East, and Asia; and Pierre Leroy was named president of the construction equipment division.

Deere's board of directors has essentially said that one of these four individuals will be the firm's next CEO. The board's decision as to which one will get the top job, in turn, will be largely based on the relative levels of performance and accomplishment each exhibits during the two-year competition. Thus each candidate will be clearly and strongly motivated to cut costs, boost sales, and otherwise enhance the firm as much as possible.

This strategy, of course, has both advantages and disadvantages. For one thing, the board of directors can take its time making a choice and can base that choice on its impressions of performance. That is, the process is likely to be as fair and objective as possible. On the other hand, the three talented executives who do not get selected may suffer bruised egos and may eventually elect to leave the firm. There is also the potential, of course, that during the competition they might be tempted to make decisions that boost the performance of their own division or area of responsibility but might not be in the true best interests of the firm. On balance, however, Deere's board of directors, Becherer, and the four executives all agree that this plan is the best way to pick the firm's next CEO.

Case Questions

1. What are the advantages and disadvantages of Deere's approach to executive succession?

2. What alternative approaches might the firm have used instead?

3. Under what circumstances might Deere have elected to recruit a new CEO from another firm, instead of seeking to promote an existing manager into the job?

Sources: "Bucking the Downtrend," *Forbes*, November 2, 1998, pp. 62–67; *Hoover's Handbook of American Business 1998* (Austin, Texas: Hoover's Business Press, 1998), pp. 472–473.

Building Human Resource Management Skills

Purpose: The purpose of this exercise is to provide you with insights into the processes associated with job analysis and human resource management planning.

Step 1: Your instructor will divide the class into small groups of four or five members each.

Step 2: Your group should select a job with which you have some familiarity, for example, a cook at McDonald's or a retail clerk at The Gap.

Step 3: Based on your presumed understanding of the job your group selects, outline how you would go about conducting a job analysis for that job.

Step 4: Draft a job description and a job specification that you think represent the job.

Step 5: Assume you are managers in the company you chose for analysis. Develop scenarios for the situations of planning for growth, stability, and reductions.

Ethical Dilemmas in Human Resource Management

Assume you are a manager for a large, multinational enterprise. You have just completed a detailed planning process forecasting the future supply of and demand for human resources in your firm. Your plans suggest that over the next two years you need to add approximately three thousand workers. However, beginning in about three years you expect that a workforce reduction of about four thousand workers is likely.

You see that you have two choices. One choice is to hire three thousand new workers, knowing that you will have to lay them off again in three years. Alternatively, you could go to a large temp agency and hire the workers through that source on a short-term basis. Unfortunately, your firm has had bad experiences with such agencies in the past, and you know that if you use this method, you will incur higher labor costs.

Questions

1. What are the ethical issues in this situation?

2. What are the basic arguments for each course of action?

3. What do you think most managers would do? What would you do?

Human Resource Internet Exercise

 The new O*NET system provides a remarkable amount of information about different types of jobs, with new jobs being added all the time. You have to pay to actually use O*NET, but you can get a free demonstration if you log onto the web site: www.doleta.gov/programs/onet. After you have viewed the demonstration, go to the library to look at the Dictionary of Occupational Titles.

Questions

1. How could an organization use the kinds of information that are available through O*NET?

2. What problems can you anticipate in using O*NET?

3. What do you think about the quantity and quality of the information offered by O*NET versus the DOT?

Notes

1. Charles R. Greer, *Strategy and Human Resources* (Englewood Cliffs, N.J.: Prentice-Hall, 1995).

2. Greer, *Strategy and Human Resources*.

3. Ernest J. McCormick, *Job Analysis: Methods and Applications* (New York: American Management Association, 1979).

4. Greer, *Strategy and Human Resources*.

5. Angelo S. DeNisi, "The Implications of Job Clustering for Training Programmes." *Journal of Occupational Psychology*, Vol. 49, 1976, pp. 105–113.

6. Kenneth Pearlman, "Job Families: A Review and Discussion of Their Implications for Personnel Selection." *Psychological Bulletin*, Vol. 87, 1980, pp. 1–27.

7. Ernest J. McCormick, *Job Analysis: Methods and Applications*.

8. U.S. Department of Labor, Employment, and Training Administration, *The Revised Handbook for Analyzing Jobs* (Washington, D.C.: United States Government Printing Office, 1991).

9. Frank Landy and Joseph Vasey, "Job Analysis: The Composition of SME Samples," *Personnel Psychology*, Vol. 44, No. 1, 1991, pp. 27–50.

10. Landy and Vasey, "Job Analysis: The Composition of SME Samples."

11. U.S. Department of Labor, Employment, and Training Administration, *The Revised Handbook for Analyzing Jobs*.

12. E. A. Fleishman, *Manual for the Ability Requirements Scale (MARS, Revised)* (Palo Alto, Calif.: Consulting Psychologists Press, 1991).

13. For example, see Joseph Morsh, *Job Types Identified with an Inventory Constructed by Electronics Engineers* (U.S. Air Force Personnel Research Laboratory, Lackland Air Force Base, 1966).

14. Sidney A. Fine and W. W. Wiley, *An Introduction to Functional Job Analysis* (Kalamazoo, Mich.: W. E. Upjohn Institute for Employment Research, 1971).

15. Ernest J. McCormick, P. Richard Jeanneret, and Robert C. Mecham. "A Study of Job Characteristics and Job Dimensions as Based on the Position Analysis Questionnaire (PAQ)," *Journal of Applied Psychology*, Vol. 56, 1972, pp. 347–368.

16. McCormick, *Job Analysis: Methods and Applications.*

17. Ernest J. McCormick, Angelo DeNisi, and James Shaw, "The Use of the Position Analysis Questionnaire (PAQ) for Establishing the Job Component Validity of Tests," *Journal of Applied Psychology*, Vol. 64, 1978, pp. 51–56.

18. Angelo DeNisi, Edwin Cornelius, and Alyn Blencoe, "A Further Investigation of Common Knowledge Effects on Job Analysis Ratings: On the Applicability of the PAQ for All Jobs," *Journal of Applied Psychology*, Vol. 72, 1987, pp. 262–268.

19. John Flanagan, "The Critical Incident Technique." *Psychological Bulletin*, Vol. 51, 1954, pp. 327–358.

20. Milan Moravec and Robert Tucker, "Job Descriptions for the 21st Century," *Personnel Journal*, June 1992, pp. 37–40.

21. Lee Dyer, "Human Resource Planning," in K. Rowland and G. Ferris (eds.), *Personnel Management* (Boston: Allyn & Bacon, 1982), pp. 52–77.

22. "Fleet-Footed Workers Thrive in Job-Fertile Silicon Valley," *USA Today*, August 21, 1998, pp. 1B, 2B.

23. "The Geography of Work," *Time*, June 22, 1998, pp. 98–102.

24. "Tea Leaves," *Forbes*, November 2, 1998, p. 78.

25. Carla Joinson, "Developing a Strong Bench," *HRMagazine*, January 1998, pp. 92–97.

26. "P&G Will Make Jager CEO Ahead of Schedule," *Wall Street Journal*, September 10, 1998, pp. B1, B8.

27. "Firms Plan to Keep Hiring, Spending," *USA Today*, January 26, 1995, p. B1.

28. "Firms Find Ways to Grow without Expanding Staffs," *Wall Street Journal*, March 18, 1993, pp. B1, B2.

29. Dyer, "Human Resource Planning."

30. R. G. Murdick and F. Schuster, "Computerized Information Support for the Human Resource Function," *Human Resource Planning*, Vol. 6, No. 1, 1983, pp. 25–35.

31. "When UPS Demanded Workers, Louisville Did the Delivering," *Wall Street Journal*, April 24, 1998, pp. A1, A10.

32. "Layoffs on Wall Street Will Bruise Big Apple," *USA Today*, October 15, 1998, pp. 1B; "Its Share Shrinking, Levi Strauss Lays Off 6,395," *Wall Street Journal*, November 4, 1997, pp. B1, B8.

6

Recruiting Human Resources

CHAPTER OUTLINE

Goals of Recruiting
The Organization's Goals in Recruiting
The Prospective Employee's Goals in Recruiting

Sources for Recruiting
Internal Recruiting
External Recruiting

Methods of Recruiting
Methods for Internal Recruiting
Methods for External Recruiting
Techniques for External Recruiting

Realistic Job Previews
Job Choice from the Prospective Employee's Perspective
Alternatives to Recruiting
Overtime
Temporary Workers
Employee Leasing
Part-Time Workers

Evaluating the Recruiting Process

CHAPTER OBJECTIVES

After studying this chapter you should be able to:

■ Identify the organization's and the individual's goals in recruiting.

■ Identify and discuss the basic sources for recruiting.

■ Describe various methods for recruiting and note their advantages and disadvantages.

■ Discuss realistic job previews and their role in effective recruiting.

■ Describe realistic job previews and discuss job choice from the prospective employee's perspective.

■ Discuss how organizations evaluate the recruiting process.

Although its name is not a household word, Cisco Systems is one of the hottest companies in California's fabled Silicon Valley. Founded in 1984 by two enterprising Stanford University employees, Cisco specializes in technology to link networks. By 1998 the firm's annual sales exceeded $6.5 billion, and it was selling its products in eighty countries. To maintain its phenomenal growth level, Cisco has found it necessary to continually add new employees. For example, the company recently doubled the size of its workforce in a single eighteen-month period. In some areas and in some industries, this level of growth would be relatively easy to manage. But in the Silicon Valley and in the world of high technology, finding and keeping bright and talented people is difficult even during periods of normal growth. But the pace of growth experienced by Cisco is dizzying, thus making the firm's challenges all the more daunting.

Nevertheless, Cisco has been able to identify, hire, and—most important of all—retain the best employees through the use of an exceptionally well-developed and well-executed recruiting strategy. The Cisco approach began when top managers first clearly defined the kinds of employees they wanted to hire. In particular, they set a goal of hiring only from among the top 15 percent of the people working in the industry. Next they systematically studied exactly how this caliber of person goes about looking for a job. For example, Cisco prefers to hire high-caliber employees who are relatively content with their

> *"Our philosophy is very simple—if you get the best people in the industry to fit into your culture and you motivate them properly, then you're going to be an industry leader."*
>
> (John Chambers, Cisco CEO)*

present jobs, but who are willing to consider challenging, exciting, and rewarding alternatives. As it turns out, these people often dislike actually looking for new jobs, and instead are more likely to be enticed by Web sites with interesting graphics.

And finally, the managers developed innovative hiring procedures for getting these people interested in Cisco. For example, potential recruits can actually indicate their interest in Cisco electronically. And the firm will also reply electronically and provide answers to many common questions about issues such as pay, benefits, and so forth. Cisco's Web site currently gets fifty thousand job queries a month. Of course, after the firm hires these employees, it must still work to keep them. Thus Cisco offers among the highest salaries in the industry. It also provides an exhaustive set of leading-edge benefits for its employees and maintains a casual and relaxing corporate culture in which employees like to work. As a result, it also has among the lowest turnover rates in its industry. And Cisco managers believe that these loyal and talented employees will help keep the firm on top for a long time to come.

"Cisco Embraces 'Internet Economy,'" *USA Today,* September 23, 1998, p. 3B; Andrew Kupfer, "The Real King of the Internet," *Fortune,* September 7, 1998, pp. 84–90; Patricia Nakache, "Cisco's Recruiting Edge," *Fortune,* September 29, 1997, pp. 275–276 (*quote on p. 275); "The Corporation of the Future," *Business Week,* August 31, 1998, pp. 102–106.

Managers at Cisco Systems made a significant strategic decision to recruit and retain the very best employees in the industry and then implemented this decision in a highly effective manner. And while numerous other decisions have no doubt contributed to the firm's success, the people who choose to work for Cisco clearly are playing a critical role in helping to keep the company on its growth trajectory and at the leading edge of its industry.

In one way or another, all organizations must address the problems and opportunities faced by Cisco Systems—the need to recruit new people who are both interested and capable of working for them. In this chapter we examine the recruiting process in more detail. We start by assessing the goals of recruiting. We then look at the sources and methods of recruiting. After describing the importance of realistic job previews in effective recruiting, we discuss the recruitment of part-time and temporary workers, as well as alternatives to recruiting. Finally, we briefly note how organizations evaluate the effectiveness of their recruiting efforts.

G O A L S   O F   R E C R U I T I N G

■ **Recruiting** is the process of developing a pool of qualified applicants who are interested in working for the organization and from which the organization might reasonably select the best individual or individuals to hire for employment.

Recruiting is the process of developing a pool of qualified applicants who are interested in working for the organization and from which the organization might reasonably select the best individual or individuals to hire for employment.[1] As we will see, however, and as Figure 6.1 illustrates, recruiting is a two-way street. That is, just as the organization is looking for qualified job applicants, those applicants are also likely to be looking at a variety of potential employment opportunities. Thus both organizations and individuals have recruiting goals.[2] The best hiring for organizations and employment opportunities for job seekers emerge when these different goals are consistent.

The Organization's Goals in Recruiting

The most basic and fundamental goal of an organization's recruiting efforts is to accomplish exactly what is stated in the definition—develop a pool of qualified applicants. This overriding goal, however, suggests a number of related goals that are also of importance as a part of the recruiting process.

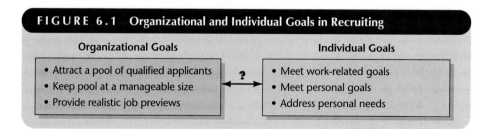

FIGURE 6.1 Organizational and Individual Goals in Recruiting

Organizational Goals		Individual Goals
• Attract a pool of qualified applicants • Keep pool at a manageable size • Provide realistic job previews	**?**	• Meet work-related goals • Meet personal goals • Address personal needs

One of these goals is to optimize the size of the pool of qualified applicants. If an organization has, say, ten openings, and somehow ends up attracting several thousand applicants for those jobs, then the organization has actually created a rather large problem for itself. Enormous amounts of time and resources will be necessary to process the large number of applicants for the positions, and if this processing is not handled effectively and efficiently, then ill will for the organization will be created as well. Thus the human resource department handling the recruiting process does not really want to attract a pool of applicants that is too large.

Of course, the human resource department should also usually have as a goal attracting a talent pool that is greater than the number of available positions. That is, the organization presumably wants to have some discretion over whom it hires. Thus a recruiting process that generates ten applicants for ten jobs is not necessarily effective. In this case the organization is not completely sure that it has the ten best people for the job, but managers may have little choice over whom they will hire. We touch again on this notion of optimizing rather than maximizing the size of the recruit pool, but in a different context, in the next chapter.

To recruit effectively, an organization must clearly understand the goals it hopes to accomplish. For example, Dan Ling, director of research for Microsoft, was recently given a mandate to double the size of the staff at the firm's research lab. This goal provided him with unambiguous insights into the priorities Microsoft had for this expansion. Coupled with his own knowledge of the lab's inner workings, Ling was thus able to formulate an effective recruiting plan for getting just the right people at just the right time.

Nor is it the goal of the recruiting process to necessarily achieve fine grades of differentiation among job applicants. That concern is really a part of the selection process that we cover in detail in Chapter 7. The goal of the recruiting process is to simply generate a reasonably large pool of qualified applicants who are interested in working for the organization and to then allow the selection process to help determine which individual applicant or which set of applicants should be hired.

A final goal of the recruiting process is to offer an honest and candid assessment to perspective applicants of what kinds of jobs and what kinds of opportunities the organization can potentially make available to them. It does no one any good to trick or to mislead job applicants into thinking that they are going to have more challenging or higher-level jobs than are actually available or that they will be earning higher salaries than the organization is actually prepared to pay. Thus the recruiting process needs to paint a realistic picture of what the potential job actually entails. We discuss this particular goal in more detail later when we discuss realistic job previews.

The Prospective Employee's Goals in Recruiting

Of course, it is also important for the organization to remember that the prospective employee in the recruiting pool also has goals that affect the process. Indeed, human resource managers must never forget that recruiting is a two-way process. Just as the organization is seeking qualified applicants who are interested in employment with the firm, so too are individuals likely to be approaching a number of organizations, trying to entice as many of them as possible to offer the individual employment.[3]

Thus just as the organization is attempting to develop a pool of qualified applicants, individuals are simultaneously attempting to create a pool of potentially interesting and attractive job opportunities from which they can select. As a result, it is important for the human resource manager to understand the prospective employee's goals as a part of the firm's recruiting process.

In many cases a prospective employee's goals are relatively straightforward. Although individuals work for various reasons and have multiple goals, the most common include financial income, job security, opportunity for promotion, benefits, and challenging work assignments. In addition, individuals can have a number of personal and idiosyncratic goals. For example, some people put extra emphasis on the location of a particular job opportunity. They may want to work close to their hometown, close to where they went to school, in a big city, in a small city, near family, near the ocean, or near recreational opportunities.[4]

Another goal that prospective employees may have is to optimize their personal situations. For example, in small cities with large universities many job applicants are students or the spouses of students, thus creating a relatively unique labor market. On the one hand an organization interested in recruiting prospective employees is likely to have a large pool from which to choose. On the other hand, because of the transient nature of students and student families, many employees recruited from such a labor pool are likely to want jobs for only a few years.

THE BOTTOM LINE   Managers must remember that the organization has a clear set of goals when it embarks on recruiting new employees and that individual job seekers have their own unique and personal goals as well.

S O U R C E S   F O R   R E C R U I T I N G

One fundamental decision that an organization must make as a part of its recruiting strategy is whether to focus recruiting efforts internally or externally. As summarized in Table 6.1 and discussed in each section below, both internal and external recruiting have unique advantages and disadvantages.

Internal Recruiting

■ **Internal recruiting** is the process of looking inside the organization for existing qualified employees who might be promoted to higher-level positions.

Internal recruiting is the process of looking inside the organization for existing qualified employees who might be promoted to higher-level positions. A major advantage of internal recruiting is motivation. Many employees want—and some expect—to advance and to move up the organizational ladder to higher-level positions. An opportunity to do just that, then, is likely to be seen as a viable reward and an important source of motivation for many people. Hence an organization that regularly and routinely promotes from within

TABLE 6.1	Advantages and Disadvantages of Internal and External Recruiting	
	Advantages	**Disadvantages**
Internal recruiting	• Increases motivation • Sustains knowledge and culture	• May foster stagnation • May cause ripple effect
External recruiting	• Brings in new ideas • Avoids ripple effect	• May hurt motivation • Costs more

through internal recruiting will usually find that it is more likely to have a committed and motivated workforce.

Another advantage of internal recruiting is that as employees are promoted to higher-level positions, they bring with them an existing familiarity and understanding of the organization, its heritage, its culture, its policies and procedures, its strategies, and its ways of doing business. As a result, their transition to higher-level positions is somewhat easier as compared to employees recruited externally, and the organization can often rely on the fact that these individuals will continue to promote and enhance the corporate culture in a positive and beneficial manner.

On the other hand, a disadvantage of internal recruiting is that it may foster stagnation and stifle creativity and new ideas. People have tended to develop a certain mindset and way of doing business, and they tend to maintain that outlook as they progress in the organization. If the corporate culture is not what managers would really like for it to be, they should recognize that promoting from within is not necessarily likely to be a positive force for change.

Another disadvantage of internal recruiting is the so-called *ripple effect*. For example, if a person is promoted from one level of the organization to a higher-level position, then the job that that individual vacates must be filled. If that job is filled from lower in the organization, it still has an open position to fill. Thus relatively few promotions sometimes can result in a large-scale set of transfers and movements from position to position within the organization.

External Recruiting

External recruiting, on the other hand, involves looking to sources outside the organization for prospective employees. Not surprisingly, external recruiting has advantages and disadvantages that are directly counter to those of internal recruiting. For example, on the plus side external recruiting has the advantage of bringing in new ideas, new perspectives, and new ways of doing things. Hence the organization can enhance its vitality, creativity, and potential ability to innovate by routinely bringing in new people from the outside. External recruiting also avoids the ripple effect. Further, in some cases there may simply not be any internal employees to fill new positions, thereby making external recruiting the only option. "Human Resources Around the Globe" illustrates an extreme example of this situation.

■ **External recruiting** is the process of looking to sources outside the organization for prospective employees.

HUMAN RESOURCES Around the Globe

To the Four Corners . . .

In a tight labor market, recruiters must often look in every nook and cranny to find new employees. But the ultra-tight labor market for high-tech workers has caused firms to seek even broader horizons in their quest for new employees. With estimates of unfilled job openings in the United States alone running close to two hundred thousand, many recruiters have added a global perspective to their search.

For example, Electronic Data Systems, a Dallas-based computer services company, recruits new programmers on three continents for its Texas operations. Andersen Consulting hires thousands of new technical employees a year to support its management consulting operations. The firm recently began recruiting at technical schools in Manila and Budapest. Texas Instruments often tries to hire technical workers who have lost their jobs in their homeland.

Indeed, this trend has opened up new career opportunities for free-lance recruiters. These individuals, often working under contract to a specific company, spend weeks or months traveling through countries such as Brazil, India, and Russia looking for skilled technical employees who might be interested in relocating to the United States. And the payoff for these people can

"This is a dream for me. Is there snow in Boston?"

(Marcio Pinheiro, Brazilian software engineer, after accepting an offer from a New England company)*

be huge. With salaries for skilled technical employees often topping out at $30,000 at their current employer, many can double or even triple their salaries by relocating.

One of the biggest challenges of hiring from abroad, however, is the immigration hurdle. Foreign workers must have a visa from the U.S. government to actually relocate to this country and accept employment. And the number and requirements for such visas are both closely regulated in ways that can cause unexpected problems. For instance, many skilled programmers in South Africa received their training at technical schools. But because a U.S. visa for technical jobs requires a college degree, these individuals, skilled though they may be, cannot come in. But savvy recruiters make it a point to both know the hurdles and how to get around them. So for the short term, at least, no hunting grounds are off limits as firms and recruiters seek more and more talent, wherever that talent may be.

References: "A U.S. Recruiter Goes Far Afield to Bring in High-Tech Workers," *Wall Street Journal*, January 8, 1998, pp. A1, A8 (*quote on p. A1); "Forget the Huddled Masses: Send Nerds," *Business Week*, July 21, 1997, pp. 110–116; "Foreigners Seeking U.S. Work Visas Often Land in Hell Instead," *Wall Street Journal*, April 23, 1998, pp. A1, A10.

A few years ago the managers and owners of a small computer software business in Iowa were frustrated because they could not seem to make the major breakthroughs necessary to fuel growth by the firm. After considerable discussion they decided that no one inside the firm had the managerial skills needed to take the company to the next stage in its growth. All current managers were professional engineers, and none really had much managerial experience. Consequently, the firm decided to hire an outsider to come in and run the business. Within a couple of years, the new CEO had increased the firm's annual sales from $750,000 to more than $11 million.[5]

On the other hand, however, external recruiting also may result in motivational problems in the organization. Current employees may believe that they have been denied opportunities and that they are more qualified than the outsiders who are brought into the organization at higher levels. External recruiting also tends to be a bit more expensive than internal recruiting because of the advertising and other search processes that must be undertaken.

Many organizations actually prefer to rely on both internal and external recruiting strategies. This flexible approach allows them to match the advantages and disadvantages of each particular recruiting effort to its own unique context. For example, during its dramatic growth period in the 1990s, Compaq Computer recruited both internally and externally. The firm wanted to ensure that current employees had ample promotion opportunity but also needed to hire people at a faster rate than could be accommodated by only looking internally. Thus each major hiring phase was carefully assessed and decisions made in advance about the sources to be used. In some instances virtually all recruiting was done internally, whereas in others only external recruiting was used. In still other cases the firm looked both inside and outside at the same time for new recruits.

THE BOTTOM LINE Recruiting can be undertaken with an internal focus, an external focus, or a combination of the two. Managers should therefore have a clear understanding of the advantages and disadvantages of each option as they plan new recruiting efforts.

External recruiting is a common and often advantageous approach for identifying prospective new employees, but sometimes it can be a challenge. For example, when Bill Pritchard decided to expand his workforce at the Wichita Tool Company, he found intense local competition for qualified employees. As a result, he developed an apprentice program whereby the firm hired less-than-qualified employees but provided them with extended on-the-job training designed to give them the skills they really needed. In addition, Pritchard has effectively recruited overseas to locate new employees.

M E T H O D S   O F   R E C R U I T I N G

Not surprisingly, internal recruiting is usually handled by using one set of recruiting methods, and external recruiting typically relies on different methods.[6] In this section we first examine methods used for internal recruiting and then look at other methods that are more likely to be used for external recruiting.

Methods for Internal Recruiting

The three most common methods used for internal recruiting are job posting, supervisory recommendations, and union halls.

Job posting Perhaps the most common method organizations use for internal recruiting is a relatively simple procedure called **job posting**. Vacancies in the organization are publicized through various media such as company newsletters, bulletin boards, internal memos, and/or the firm's intranet. Any individual who is interested in being considered for the position simply files an application with the human resource department. Some organizations that rely heavily on internal recruiting go so far as to require that jobs be posted internally before any

■ **Job posting** is a mechanism for internal recruiting in which vacancies in the organization are publicized through various media such as company newsletters, bulletin boards, internal memos, and the firm's intranet.

FIGURE 6.2 Sample Job Posting at Xerox

Job Key-Properties		
Job Number XBS-F85	**Job Grade** 4-6	**Post Date** 3/1/95
Location Non-Monroe	**Comp Type** Exempt	**Apply Before** 3/16/95

OPEN JOB POSTING

Please Attach
- OJP application (Form 58760)
- Personal history (Form 58047)
- Copy of last two (2) performance appraisals
- El Segundo OJP application (Form 58666)—IF APPLICABLE

Hiring Manager Information	
Name Al Harrington	**Mail Stop** L750
eMail Address mcart:san antonio-xbs	**Internet Number** 8*759-1781

External Number
(210) 821-6688

Open Job Information

Job Title
Production Supervisor

Organization XBS	**Job Location** *[Refers to the actual city location]* San Antonio, Texas

Job Description

Complete and thorough knowledge of Xerographic processes on Xerox equipment and production operational knowledge of Non-Xerox equipment. Practical knowledge and understanding of Offset Lithography with the ability to converse on the subject. A complete and thorough knowledge of operational processes designed to deliver key business results. Must exemplify and role model the concepts, processes, practices, and analytical tools of Leadership Through Quality (proven performance in QIP/PSP teams). Computer skills/knowledge of DocuTech and/or systems a must. On call status during off hours and weekends. May be called upon to operate various XBS equipment due to personnel absences or other lost time or in start-up situations. Management tasks include responsibility for Customer Satisfaction, Employee Satisfaction, Personnel, Inventory, and scheduling of staff.

Essential Functions

- Day to day supervision of FM personnel in a multiple account territory.
- Efficient utilization and coordination of all center resources to meet expected productivity levels.
- Provide purposeful guidance to production staff in order to facilitate achievement of center goals and objectives.
- Work toward maintaining or exceeding FM Customer Satisfaction targets.
- Employ proactive approach in addressing potential customer dissatisfiers.
- Provide management with useful analysis and recommendations for continuous improvement while using good business judgment to satisfy all objectives.
- Support all sales activities toward generating new FM business whenever possible.
- Foster good relationships with other Xerox disciplines such as sales, admin, and district partners.
- Ensure compliance to all HRM policies and procedures.

Applicant Qualification

18 months prior Xerox Supervisory/Management experience or panel interview result is "Ready Now"; Minimum Associates Degree, BS/BA Degree or equivalent

1 position available

KEY MESSAGES:
1. This job is available to ANY organization.
2. Relocation is not available for this job.
3. The entire posting cycle generally takes between 30-60 days.

Source: Xerox Corporation. Used by permission.

external recruiting may be undertaken. Note that a candidate obtained through job posting could be applying for a promotion or merely for a transfer. A sample job posting is shown in Figure 6.2.

Supervisory recommendations   Another method of internal recruiting is through supervisory recommendations. In this case, when a new position needs to be filled, a manager simply solicits nominations or recommendations for the position from supervisors in the organization. These supervisors look at the individuals for whom they are responsible, and if any of them are particularly well suited for the new job opening, then the supervisors recommend that individual to the higher-level manager. It is important, however, that supervisors give equal consideration to all potential candidates in these cases. In a landmark decision, Rowe vs. General Motors, the Supreme Court found GM guilty of discrimination because, under a system where supervisory recommendations were needed for promotions, supervisors failed to recommend qualified black candidates as frequently as they recommended white candidates. As a result, at the time of the suit there were almost no black supervisors at most GM facilities.

Union halls   Still another method of internal recruiting is through union halls. This method is particularly common in organizations that have strong and well-established unions. Indeed, the union contract itself may specify that union members be accorded the opportunity to apply for new positions on some sort of a priority basis. The mechanics of this approach may parallel those of job posting—job openings will be listed, along with application procedures, and this information is made available to union members through various channels such as newsletters and bulletin boards.

We should also point out that, given the large numbers of layoffs and workforce reductions (from downsizing) in recent years, one group of potential applicants is somewhere between internal and external candidates. Individuals who have been laid off (as opposed to terminated) are usually considered first when openings occur in the organization (and indeed this condition may be mandated by certain union contracts). These individuals may not be active employees at the time, but they would still be considered as internal candidates. On the other hand, individuals who actually lost their jobs during downsizing—that is, they were officially terminated—are technically no longer employees of the organization and so would be considered external candidates. Because they had worked for the organization previously, however, they would share more characteristics in common with internal candidates and may constitute a good source of potential applicants.

Methods for External Recruiting

Somewhat different methods are likely to be used by an organization engaged in external recruiting because the organization needs to reach potential applicants from outside the company. We first consider three sources or types of external applicants and then some techniques that a firm might use to attract these applicants.

One major source for external applicants is the **general labor pool** from which an organization draws its employees. A labor pool is reflective of the local labor market and is generally tapped through the various techniques discussed next. A **referral** is an individual who is prompted to apply for a position

■ The **general labor pool** is the local labor market from which a firm hires its employees.

■ A **referral** is an individual who is prompted to apply for a position by someone else within the organization.

by someone else within the organization. For example, an employee might tell a neighbor or friend about an impending job opening at the organization and thus encourage that individual to apply for the position.[7] In almost all instances, some portion of a company's external candidates are referrals. The job market has gotten so tight in some areas that organizations are providing incentives to their employees to seek out their friends. At the major accounting firm of PriceWaterhouseCoopers, for example, accountants can earn bonuses of up to $7,000 if they locate a new partner who accepts work and remains with the firm for six months.[8]

Direct applicants (also called *walk-ins* and *drop-ins*) are also a common source of external applicants. Direct applicants are simply individuals who apply for a position with the organization without any proactive action from the organization. In fact, the organization may not even have an opening at the time application is made. For example, sometimes when people are looking for work they simply travel from one prospective employer to another asking to fill out an application for employment. Individuals who are seeking part-time work in retailing, for instance, may go to a shopping mall and simply walk from store to store, filling out application blanks as they go. As a result, the organization really doesn't need to do anything to attract these candidates.

> ■ **Direct applicants** are individuals who apply for a position with the organization without any proactive action from the organization.

Techniques for External Recruiting

Several techniques are commonly used for external recruiting. These are summarized in the following paragraphs.

Word of mouth   Referrals come to an organization via **word-of-mouth recruiting**. In most cases the organization simply informs present employees that positions are available and encourages them to refer friends, family members, or neighbors for those jobs. From the organization's perspective word of mouth is an inexpensive way to generate a large number of applicants. In addition, if we assume that the present employees are satisfactory and that people generally associate with people who are similar to them, the organization should also have a reasonable chance of generating high-quality applicants in this way. In most organizations some portion of the applicants are always obtained through word of mouth. However, if an organization relies on this recruiting technique exclusively, there may be problems. If the present workforce is, for example, almost completely white and male, the individuals referred will most likely be primarily white males as well, and this situation might represent discrimination in recruitment.

> ■ **Word-of-mouth recruiting** is when the organization simply informs present employees that positions are available and encourages them to refer friends, family members, or neighbors for those jobs.

Advertisements   Advertisements in newspapers and related publications are also a popular method for external recruiting. Any local newspaper is likely to have help-wanted sections ranging from perhaps a few listings to as many as several pages, sometimes organized by different kinds of job openings such as sales, professional/nonprofessional, technical, and so forth. Depending on the job, these advertisements might be placed in local newspapers or national newspapers such as the *Wall Street Journal*. Figure 6.3 shows some newspaper advertisements placed by organizations for different kinds of job openings.

Some professional periodicals and publications also have similar kinds of spaces set aside for help-wanted recruiting ads. This form of advertising tends to be relatively expensive and, perhaps surprisingly, attracts somewhat fewer qualified applicants than some of the other methods of recruiting. However, it does enable the organization to cast a wide net, to publicize its affirmative action programs, and to demonstrate an effort to reach every sector of the labor market. By targeting specialized publications that might appeal primarily to members of groups that are underrepresented in the workforce, the organization might also actually advance its affirmative action goals. On the other hand, restricting advertisements to publications that are not widely available could be considered discriminatory.

Public employment agencies   Working through public employment agencies is also a common method for external recruiting. Although public employment agencies have been around for some time, their activities were formalized with the passage of the Social Security Act of 1935. This law requires that anyone who is to be paid unemployment compensation must register with a local state employment office. These state agencies work closely with the United States Employment Service. Their joint goal is to get unemployed individuals off state aid as quickly as possible and into permanent jobs. The agencies start by collecting basic employment-related information about the individuals, such as their experience, their aptitudes, and their abilities. The agencies may, for example, administer various tests to individuals to gain some insight into the abilities of a potential worker. The General Aptitude Test Battery is frequently used for this purpose.

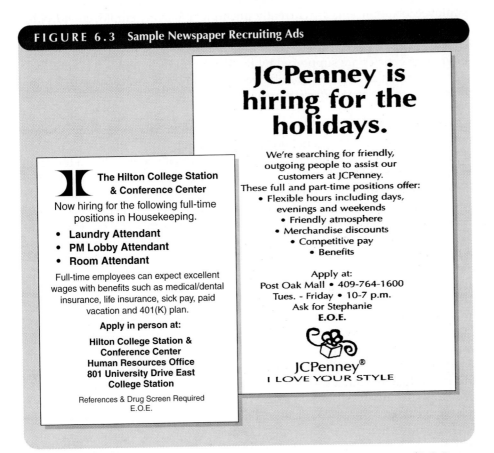

FIGURE 6.3   Sample Newspaper Recruiting Ads

The Hilton College Station & Conference Center

Now hiring for the following full-time positions in Housekeeping.

- **Laundry Attendant**
- **PM Lobby Attendant**
- **Room Attendant**

Full-time employees can expect excellent wages with benefits such as medical/dental insurance, life insurance, sick pay, paid vacation and 401(K) plan.

Apply in person at:

Hilton College Station & Conference Center Human Resources Office 801 University Drive East College Station

References & Drug Screen Required E.O.E.

JCPenney is hiring for the holidays.

We're searching for friendly, outgoing people to assist our customers at JCPenney. These full and part-time positions offer:
- Flexible hours including days, evenings and weekends
- Friendly atmosphere
- Merchandise discounts
- Competitive pay
- Benefits

Apply at:
Post Oak Mall • 409-764-1600
Tues. - Friday • 10-7 p.m.
Ask for Stephanie
E.O.E.

JCPenney®
I LOVE YOUR STYLE

Source: Bryan-College Station *Eagle* (October 28, 1998). Reprinted by permission of J. C. Penney.

Employers register their job openings with the local state employment agency. That agency, in turn, attempts to match qualified individuals for whom it has documentation to available jobs. For example, suppose a local construction firm needs to hire several unskilled or semiskilled workers for various construction projects. It might start by contacting the local state employment agency and explain the kind of workers it needs. The agency, in turn, may call various individuals it has on file who seem to fit what the organization needs. Those individuals are then referred to the firm, which processes their applications through its normal selection process, such as application blanks, interviews, and so forth (as discussed more fully in the next chapter). Two significant advantages of public employment agencies are that (1) they are free and (2) they are a particularly useful source of job applicants for minorities, handicapped individuals, and other protected classes. As state agencies, they are fully cognizant of the requirements that organizations must face and work hard to maintain an adequate labor pool of all classes of employees.

Private employment agencies   Whereas public employment agencies tend to cater primarily to blue-collar workers, private employment agencies are more likely to serve the white-collar labor market (although some serve specialized niches such as office workers). One major difference, however, is that private employment agencies charge a fee for this service. Sometimes this fee is paid by the individual and sometimes by the organization if it hires an individual that is referred to it. Unlike a public employment agency, in which all potential employee job applicants are currently unemployed, many employed individuals use the services of private employment agencies in an effort to find better jobs for themselves while maintaining their current jobs. Because private employment agencies are supported by the firms and individuals who use their services, however, they may be able to devote more resources to performing their function in a more effective manner.

Executive search firms   Using executive search firms is a common method of recruiting top level managers. Individual recruiters at executive search firms are also known as **headhunters**. An organization that wants to hire a top level manager might go to an executive search firm and explain exactly what kind of individuals it is looking for. For example, the organization might specify the kind of work experience it wants the individual to have, the degree that is necessary or years of experience, and perhaps a salary profile as well. The executive search firm then goes out and attempts to locate individuals that fit this profile for the organization. Typically, the search firm screens potential candidates and then presents the organization with a small number of candidates, all of whom are highly qualified and interested.

On the other side of the coin, some highly successful executives routinely are known to be available for other jobs. They network with members of executive search firms and are receptive to any overtures that might be made toward them. An important advantage of an executive search firm is confidentiality. The organization that is seeking a new employee may be able to pursue this individual in a quiet and discreet manner. Likewise, the individual who is being pursued may also be able to keep a relatively low profile and maintain a reasonable degree of confidentiality. Kodak hired CEO George Fisher, who had only recently taken the position of CEO at Motorola. The executive recruiter who was in charge of the search, Gerald Roche, had been an acquaintance of Fisher's for several years. His personal relationship with Fisher played an important role in his ability to convince Fisher to leave Motorola for Kodak.[9]

■ A **headhunter** is an employee of an executive search firm who seeks out qualified individuals for higher-level positions. The term is also sometimes used informally to refer to the executive search firm itself.

Job fairs are an increasingly common method for external recruiting. For example, Los Angeles Valley College sponsors an annual job fair that attracts dozens of local and regional employers. Students such as these can stop by company tables, visit with recruiters, and pick up copies of materials detailing career opportunities. These fairs are a cost-effective method for making contacts with large numbers of prospective employees. Of course, few companies rely only on job fairs; most also use more substantive, intensive, and/or focused recruiting techniques as well.

On the other hand, executive search firms tend to be among the most expensive methods for external recruiting. In addition, one caveat that applies to any type of agency relates to potential discrimination. There have been many stories in the popular press about employment agencies (both public and private) that referred individuals of one race, ethnicity, or gender for some jobs, but not for others. If an organization engages the services of an employment agency that discriminates, the organization almost certainly will be held liable for the discrimination.

College placement offices   Another source for recruiting that is particularly relevant to college students is the school's placement office. Most large organizations routinely visit college campuses every year to interview graduates for jobs within the organization. Large firms may visit many colleges and universities scattered across the country or may choose to visit only regional or local colleges and universities.

An advantage of this method for the organization is that it can specify qualifications such as major, grade-point average, and work experience. It is also a relatively inexpensive method of recruiting, since the colleges and universities typically provide the facilities, schedule the appointments, and so forth. The organization need only send the interviewer to campus and have that individual sit in the interview room and meet prospective applicants. For students this method of job search is also quite efficient. The student can visit the local placement office on a regular basis, keep apprised of which companies are coming to interview, and sign up for interviews according to whatever methods and protocols the college or university has established.

Microsoft relies heavily on college recruiting in its efforts to bring in new talent. The firm has a staff of twenty-two full-time campus recruiters who visit schools each year. These recruiters conduct half-hour interviews with thousands of prospective employees, selecting about 450 for follow-up visits to company headquarters.[10]

Recruiting with the Web

 While many pundits continue to speculate about future uses for the Internet, recruiting and job seeking have quietly become major applications almost overnight—and promise to become increasingly significant with each passing day. Indeed, experts estimate that more than 25 percent of all job seekers today use the Internet to look for jobs, and that percentage is growing rapidly.

Four basic tools on the Internet can assist job seekers: general job search sites, company sites, research sites, and online networking resources such as chat rooms. Although all of these can be of some benefit to job seekers, experts caution against relying too heavily on chat rooms because they often generate little more than idle conversation. In contrast, many experts highly recommend the job search sites especially created for job seekers. For instance, CareerMosiac generally has upward of seventy thousand jobs and fifty thousand resumes posted at any one time. Other big-time job search sites include Career Path, Hoover's Online, and Online Career Center. For the most part, job seekers can use these sites for free—it's the companies and recruiters who pay if they hire someone from the site.

In part because of the aforementioned problem with chat rooms, an even more recent innovation has been

"The Web page let me know what they were looking for. I knew what to pinpoint and how to align myself."

(Debra Stephenson, recent recruit to Medtronic in Minneapolis)*

the emergence of specialized job search sites. For example, attorneys can browse employment opportunities at **Attorneys @Work.net**. Similar sites exist for everyone from physicians to engineers to accountants. In contrast to the general sites, these specialized sites usually require users to pay a fee. But most don't complain, though, because of the enormous potential they see in this form of recruiting.

But human resource professionals caution that job seekers should not get too casual about relying on the Internet. For one thing, whereas Web sites can do some basic screening, a human touch is still required to ensure the accuracy of what a person puts on a resume. And sometimes a job seeker can make a positive impression by taking the time to drop by or call for an appointment to discuss job opportunities face to face. But regardless of the result, the Internet is clearly redefining how employers and employees attempt to find each other!

References: "For Sale Online: You," *Fortune*, July 5, 1999, pp. 67–78; "Changing Jobs? Try the Net," *Fortune*, March 2, 1998, pp. 205–208 (*quote on p. 208); "Web Spawns Specialty Sites for Job Seekers," *USA Today*, April 22, 1998, p. 1B; Stephanie Overman, "A Creative Net Will Snare the Best," *HRMagazine*, May 1998, pp. 88–94.

New methods   In recent years some companies have started experimenting with new and high-tech recruiting methods. One method is use of the Career Television Network, a regional cable television network dedicated to listing job applicants and job openings. Radio recruiting is also becoming much more common.[11] Another new recruiting method is the use of the Internet. Some firms today are routinely listing job openings on their home page on the Internet, hoping to attract the interest of qualified applicants. Of course, at present this method is useful only for jobs and positions where possible applicants might be using the Internet for their own job search activities.[12] More details about this approach are outlined in "Human Resources Tech Talk."

THE BOTTOM LINE   Managers can pick from a wide variety of recruiting methods. As a result, it's important to know the relative costs, advantages, and limitations of each. Only through such awareness can managers make informed decisions. The human resource function can serve as an especially important center of expertise for making these decisions.

R E A L I S T I C   J O B   P R E V I E W S

Many organizations today are finding that it is important to provide prospective employees with what is called a **realistic job preview**. In the past many recruiters were guilty of painting a glowing picture of what a particular job might entail. They made the job sound glamorous, exciting, fun, challenging, and rewarding. In reality, however, once employees accepted the job they often found just the opposite to be true. The job they were hired to fill proved to be boring, tedious, monotonous, and routine.

Because their expectations were set so high and the reality they faced proved to be so different, these employees were extremely unsatisfied with their work and consequently were prone to high turnover. These problems can be partly minimized, however, if recruiters paint a more realistic picture of what the job entails. If the job is relatively routine, then prospective job applicants should be told. The idea is simply to present as realistic a preview of the actual job and its working conditions as possible without sugar coating or glossing over some of the more unpleasant characteristics of the job or the working conditions surrounding that job.[13]

One relatively straightforward method for providing a realistic job preview is to provide job applicants with an opportunity to actually observe others performing the work. This might be accomplished by taking them to the job site and letting them watch people work for a while or showing a videotape of people actually performing the job. If neither of these alternatives is feasible, then, at a minimum, the recruiter should describe in as realistic terms as possible the job itself and the circumstances under which it will be performed.

Disney has found that using realistic job previews has greatly improved its recruiting and selection processes. At its vast Disney World complex, the firm has an employment office it calls its Casting Center. Before ever being interviewed or asked to complete a job application, people who visit the center seeking employment are instructed to watch a videotape. The video informs job seekers about the firm's strict appearance guidelines and the difficult and rigorous working conditions. The goal is to provide a candid and realistic introduction to what it's like to work for Disney.[14]

Considerable research has been done to document the benefits of realistic job previews. If applicants are given realistic previews before they make a decision, some potential applicants will be discouraged and withdraw from consideration.[15] But those who know what to expect and still choose to join the organization generally are more successful. This research shows that newly hired employees who have received realistic job previews have a higher rate of job survival than those who are hired without realistic previews. Employees who are hired following a realistic job preview also report higher levels of job satisfaction, higher levels of trust in the organization, and a more realistic set of expectations. The effectiveness of realistic job previews has been demonstrated with such jobs as bank teller,[16] Army recruit,[17] and prison guard![18]

■ A **realistic job preview** is an effective technique for ensuring that job seekers understand the actual nature of the jobs available to them.

THE BOTTOM LINE   Realistic job previews are a common and effective way to ensure that job seekers have an accurate understanding of the jobs that may be available to them. Although this information may discourage some applicants, it increases the chances that those who remain interested in employment have not been misled and will not become disenchanted or unhappy when they learn the true nature of the job.

JOB CHOICE FROM THE PROSPECTIVE EMPLOYEE'S PERSPECTIVE

To this point we have primarily been discussing ways in which organizations try to attract interested job seekers to apply for their jobs. Earlier in this chapter we discussed briefly the goals of the prospective employee in this process. We now return to that perspective, because it is ultimately up to the applicants to accept an offer of employment from an organization. That is, once an organization attracts a recruit and subsequently decides to offer a job to that person, the prospective employee still must decide whether or not to accept the job. The actual selection process is the subject of the next chapter, but the recruitment process has a great deal of influence over whether a person accepts a job once offered.[19] Specifically, the messages sent to a potential employee during this process will provide him or her with much of the information needed to make a decision.

From the outset the recruiter will play a large role in this decision. At the simplest level the recruiter is probably the first real contact the potential employee has with the company. If the recruiter doesn't seem competent or acts rudely, or even worse, inappropriately, the potential employee will form a negative impression of the organization as a whole and will be less likely to accept a job. Also, as we noted earlier in the chapter, many potential employees make decisions about which job to take based on beliefs about which job will best meet their needs or desires. And this information, in turn, is usually communicated during the recruitment process.

But there is reason to believe that more complex "signaling" is also taking place during the recruitment process. Although potential employees are clearly attracted to an organization because they believe it can provide valued outcomes, they are also attracted to organizations where they believe they "fit in." That is, potential employees seem to be more likely to accept jobs from organizations that applicants perceive as sharing their own values and "style." As we

The Lighter Side of HR

Job applicants and recruiters must always keep in mind that recruiting is a two-way street—both parties are trying to "sell themselves" to the other. But as illustrated in this cartoon, people occasionally come across as being arrogant, rude, or abrupt. And when they do, the chances for a successful matching of applicant and employer go down significantly.

discuss in the next chapter, organizations are increasingly relying on "fit" in making selection decisions as well, but there is considerable evidence that applicants also use the recruiting process to gain information about the company relative to fit.[20]

Thus organizations signal, through recruiting materials or recruiter behavior, that they are "family friendly," that they are concerned about the environment, or that they value competitive people. Prospective employees read these signals, which are important determinants of applicants' job choice. For example, the U.S. Marine Corps advertisements are meant to attract individuals who believe they can be one of the "few and the proud," whereas many U.S. Army advertisements are meant to attract individuals who see military service as providing work experience and money for college. By all accounts the signaling aspect of recruitment and how it influences job choices will increase in importance over the next few years.

At the same time, recruiters and organizations are forming impressions of job seekers and applicants. The manner in which a person dresses and behaves is often an important consideration for a recruiter, for example. And just as recruiters can make a bad impression if they are rude or inappropriate, so too can a job seeker be offensive or rude. "The Lighter Side of HR" clearly illustrates how this situation can occur.

THE BOTTOM LINE Managers must remember that recruiting and employment decisions are a two-way street. But so, too, must job seekers remember their role in this process. It is important that each party treat the other with respect and dignity so as to maintain the best possible relationships regardless of whether a person actually accepts a job.

A L T E R N A T I V E S   T O   R E C R U I T I N G

Thus far our discussion of the recruiting process has focused on the circumstance in which the organization needs to acquire new human resources and is engaged in activities aimed at acquiring job applicants for permanent positions. It is also the case, however, that organizations should fully explore various alternatives to recruiting whenever feasible. It does no one any good, either to the organization or the employee, for a firm to hire someone only to have to fire or lay off that person because of the downturn in work. Thus if the organization is not fully committed to a longer-term permanent employment relationship or if the organization is not sure that it can find exactly the kinds of people that it wants to hire for the long term, it might engage in various alternatives to traditional recruiting methods.

Overtime

One alternative to recruiting is overtime. **Overtime** simply means asking current workers to put in longer hours. This alternative is especially beneficial when the increased need for human resources is of a very short-term nature. For example, a manufacturing plant facing a production crunch might ask some of its production workers to work an extra half-day, perhaps on Saturday, for two or three weeks to get the work done. This method has two basic

■ **Overtime** is an alternative to recruiting in which current employees are asked to work extra hours.

The use of temporary workers is an increasingly common alternative to recruiting for many larger companies. This temporary worker, for example, is helping make eyeglasses for Sola Optical. At any one time, the firm has about 1,400 permanent employees and about another 100 temporary employees. The firm prefers this mix for two basic reasons. First, its managers cite the increased flexibility as a major advantage. And second, it allows the firm to try out prospective permanent employees before making a longer-term commitment to them.

advantages. One advantage is that it gives employees the opportunity to earn extra income. Some employees welcome this opportunity and are thankful to the organization for making it available. In addition, it keeps the organization from having to hire and train new employees. Because the existing employees already know how to do their work, the organization does not have to provide them with additional training.

On the other hand, overtime may have some negative characteristics as well. For one thing, the labor costs per hour are likely to increase. The Fair Labor Standards Act, as described earlier in Chapter 3, stipulates that employees who work more than forty hours a week must be compensated at a rate of one-and-a-half times their normal hourly rate. Thus if an employee is making $10 an hour for a normal work week, the organization may have to pay that same individual $15 an hour for the extra hours beyond forty each week. Another disadvantage of relying on overtime relates to the potential problems for conflict and/or equity considerations. For example, the organization may not really need all the members of a work group for overtime and thus may face a complicated situation in deciding who gets to work the overtime. Unionized organizations often have contracts that specify the decision rules that must be followed when offering overtime. Yet another problem is the potential for increased fatigue and anxiety on the part of employees, particularly if the overtime is not particularly welcome and if they have to work the overtime for an extended period of time.

Corning has a small ceramics plant in Blacksburg, Virginia. Because the plant is quite small, Corning is reluctant to add new workers whenever there is a temporary increase in production requirements. As a result, the firm routinely offers overtime to its employees. Although not everyone is eager to accept this offer, enough are so that the firm can function effectively. For example, one of its employees, Joe Sizemore, routinely works between sixty and seventy hours a week. He points out that the extra income has allowed him to elevate his lifestyle. Corning, meanwhile, keeps a highly productive worker happy and avoids having to hire a new employee.[21]

Temporary Workers

■ **Temporary employees** join the organization to work a specific period of time, rather than with the expectation of permanent or continued employment.

Another increasingly popular alternative to the recruitment of full-time employees is a growing reliance on **temporary employees**. The idea behind temporary employment is that an organization can hire someone for only a specific period of time. A major advantage of temporary employment to the organization is that such workers can usually be paid a lower rate and are often not subject to benefits that are provided to permanent and full-time employees. Considerable flexibility is also involved because employees themselves realize their jobs are not permanent and therefore the organization can terminate their relationship as work demands mandate.[22] On the other hand, temporary employees tend to not understand the organization's culture as well as permanent employees. In addition, temporary employees are not as likely to be as productive as are permanent full-time employees of the organization. We cover temporary employees more fully in Chapter 17.

Employee Leasing

Yet another increasingly popular alternative to the recruitment of permanent full-time workers is **employee leasing**. In this circumstance the organization pays a fee to a leasing company that provides a pool of employees to the firm. This pool of employees usually constitutes a group or crew intended to handle all or most of the organization's work needs in a particular area. For example, an organization might lease a crew of custodial and other maintenance workers from an outside firm specializing in such services. These workers appear in the organization every day at a predetermined time and perform all maintenance and custodial work. To the general public they may even appear to be employees of the firm occupying the building. In reality, however, they actually work for a leasing company.

■ **Employee leasing** is an alternative to recruiting in which the organization pays a fee to a leasing company that provides a pool of employees to the first firm.

The basic advantage to this approach to the organization is that it essentially outsources the human resource element of recruiting, hiring, training, compensating, and evaluating those employees to the leasing firm. On the other hand, because the individuals are not employees of the firm, they are likely to have less commitment and attachment to the organization. In addition, the cost of the leasing arrangement might be a bit higher than if the employees have been hired directly by the firm itself.

Part-Time Workers

A final alternative to recruiting permanent workers is to rely on part-time workers. **Part-time workers** are individuals who routinely expect to work less than forty hours a week. One major advantage of part-time employment is that these employees are usually not covered by benefits, thus lowering labor costs. In addition, part-time workers provide the organization with considerable flexibility. That is, they are routinely called upon to work different work schedules from week to week, thereby allowing the organization to cluster its labor force to meet peak demand times and have a smaller staff at hand during down times. Part-time workers are very popular and common in organizations like restaurants. Wait persons, bus persons, kitchen help, and other employees of an organization might be college students who want to work only fifteen or twenty hours a week to earn spending money. Their part-time interest provides considerable scheduling flexibility to the organization that hires them.

■ **Part-time workers** are individuals who routinely expect to work less than forty hours a week.

THE BOTTOM LINE Recruiting new employees can be an expensive process, and adding permanent employees to the workforce is an important step to take. As a result, managers should be aware of the various alternatives to recruiting that might exist and use these alternatives when appropriate.

EVALUATING THE RECRUITING PROCESS

Given that recruiting is such a vital part of the human resource management process for most organizations, it stands to reason that the organization should periodically evaluate the effectiveness of its recruiting process. Essentially, an effective recruiting process is one that results in a reasonable pool of qualified employees being available to the organization and from which the organization is able to hire people that it wants to perform various jobs. Moreover, this recruiting process needs to be executed with relatively low cost. Thus if an organization is having a difficult time attracting people to apply for its jobs or is having too many people apply for its jobs, then its recruiting efforts are probably less than ideal. Similarly, if the recruiting expenses being incurred by the organization are excessive or higher than they should be for the kinds of employees being recruited, then the organization should look carefully at its recruiting methods to see whether efficiencies or cost savings might be justified.

In addition, it is possible and often useful to assess the effectiveness of different recruiting sources. This process could involve simply calculating the yield, or the number of applicants, generated by each source. But some studies have found that applicants who learn about the organization through different sources are more likely to accept jobs and remain in those jobs than are applicants who learn about it through other sources.[23] Unfortunately, other than to suggest that learning about an organization through a combination of formal and informal methods (for example, newspaper ads and word of mouth) is best,[24] the results of these studies are inconclusive. Nonetheless, they suggest that it may be possible for an organization to target recruiting efforts at those sources that seem to yield the "best" applicants.

Chapter Summary

Recruiting is the process of developing a pool of qualified applicants who are interested in working for the organization and from which the organization might reasonably select the best individual or individuals to hire for employment. Organizational goals in recruiting are to optimize, in various ways, the size of the pool of qualified applicants and to offer an honest and candid assessment to prospective applicants of what kinds of jobs and what kinds of opportunities the organization can potentially make available to them. Individual goals in recruiting include satisfying personal work goals, meeting various idiosyncratic goals, and perhaps optimizing their personal situations.

Internal recruiting is the process of looking inside the organization for existing qualified employees who might be promoted to higher-level positions. Advantages of internal recruiting are motivation and continuity. On the other hand, disadvantages include stifling creativity and new ideas and starting the ripple effect.

External recruiting involves looking to sources outside the organization for prospective employees. Advantages of this approach include bringing in new ideas, new perspectives, and new ways of doing things and avoiding the ripple effect. On the negative side, external recruiting also may result in motivational problems in the organization and a lack of continuity.

The three most common methods used for internal recruiting are job posting, supervisory recommendations, and union halls. Job posting involves publicizing openings through various media such as company newsletters, bulletin boards, and internal memos. Supervisory recommendations involve soliciting nominations or recommendations from supervisors in the organization. Using union halls involves notifying local union officials about job openings.

Different methods are likely to be used by an organization engaged in external recruiting. Sources of prospective employees include the general labor pool, direct applicants, referrals, people who respond to advertisements, employment agencies, and colleges and universities.

Many organizations are finding that it is increasingly important to provide prospective employees with what is called a realistic job preview. Realistic job previews might involve providing job applicants with an opportunity to actually observe others performing the work.

While the organization is trying to attract applicants, those potential employees must eventually decide which jobs to accept. Although these decisions are based largely on factors such as which company pays more or meets other needs better, there is an increasing awareness that these decisions are also based on perceptions of "fit." That is, potential employees often choose organizations the applicants believe share their general values.

If the organization is not fully committed to a longer-term permanent employment relationship or is not sure that it can find exactly the kinds of people that it wants to hire for the long term, it might engage in various alternatives to traditional recruiting methods. Alternatives include overtime, temporary workers, employee leasing, and part-time workers.

Review and Discussion Questions

1. Summarize organizational and individual goals in the recruiting process.

2. Compare and contrast the advantages and disadvantages of internal versus external recruiting.

3. Identify and describe the basic methods used by organizations for external recruiting.

4. What is a realistic job preview? What function does it serve?

5. What alternatives to recruiting do organizations use?

6. What goals do you expect will play the biggest role in your own personal job search process?

7. How would you feel if you thought you deserved to be promoted, but instead the organization hired someone from outside and made that person your boss? What would you do about it?

8. Which recruiting methods would be most likely to attract your attention?

9. Do you think the Internet will become a major recruiting tool in the future? Why or why not?

10. Assume that you are talking to a high school senior who is thinking about going to your college or university. What "realistic job preview" details would you provide?

Closing Case

The Recruiter's Edge

When labor markets are tight, corporate recruiters are often put into the position of having to look for an extra edge, an edge that will cause a talented job seeker to make the decision to join the recruiter's firm instead of others. And as the turbulent decade of the 1990s drew to a close, recruiters were seeking any and every edge possible. The first step for many big recruiters is to extend traditional channels and increase their recruiting budgets.

For example, State Street Corporation, a Boston-based financial services company, has recently started promoting itself as an attractive employer at such high-profile events as the Boston Marathon. The firm has also made a pitch at working mothers by paying to put its corporate logo on baby bottles given away at the Baby Fair retail exposition. Insurer CNA recently cut its advertising budget so that it could divert funds to its corporate recruiting budget.

Sometimes recruiting efforts are undertaken not by individual companies but by state or local economic development groups. For example, the state of Michigan recently spent $47,000 on ads in East Coast and Midwestern newspapers to attract workers to the region. And one of the hottest high-tech areas today, labor-strapped Austin, even went so far as to sponsor a Boston-to-Austin Job Fair in Massachusetts, trying to lure skilled workers to Texas.

But many companies have realized that they have to do more than just increase the size of their newspaper ads to attract today's worker. Instead, they have to work hard to become seen as an attractive employer, an "employer of choice," as it were, to be truly competitive today. And because both signing bonuses and similar incentives are relatively common now, and easily duplicated or matched by competitors, firms often go the extra mile of trying to convince job seekers that their firm is an exciting, fun, and enjoyable place to be.

Southwest Airlines, for example, a firm known as both a casual and an interesting place to work, often treats job seekers to theme days. Interviewers may show up at the firm's recruiting center wearing pajamas or beach attire, for example, and job applicants may be asked to join in by selecting props such as nightcaps or sunglasses to wear during their interviews. Of course, in addition to selling Southwest as a fun place to work, the firm's savvy recruiters also get a firsthand opportunity to observe how the job seekers themselves might fit into its quirky corporate culture.

Other companies are playing this same game. At PeopleSoft, a leading human resource software company, top executives perform rock music at employee meetings. Cognex, another big software developer, sponsors Ultimate Frisbee contests, Friday afternoon socials, and free movie nights and even has a pinball and video game room for its employees. And many high-tech companies in the Silicon Valley provide jogging paths, basketball courts and gyms, and cappuccino machines for their employees. Even staid, old-line firms like IBM and State Farm Insurance are trying to get into the act—both firms recently started sponsoring job and career fair exhibits at such popular spring-break beach sites as Panama City and Daytona Beach.

Beyond fun and games, companies also find that taking more serious steps to be seen as attractive employers can pay dividends. For example, increasingly savvy job seekers are relying more and more on "best places to work" lists and rankings. These lists, in turn, take into account such things as pay, job security, benefits, promotion opportunities, flexibility, and communication. And many are now taking an even more focused look by ranking firms on the basis of their attractiveness to women, single parents, and families.

And at the extreme, some firms are investing heavily in new facilities with employee recruiting and retention as a major goal. Sprint Corporation, for example, is building a new corporate headquarters center in Overland Park, Kansas. When complete, the complex will consist of eighteen office buildings, encompassing almost four million square feet, spread across two hundred acres. But beyond offices and administrative facilities, the Sprint complex will include a 75,000-square-foot fitness center, a 44,000-square-foot child-care center with private nursing rooms for mothers, two athletic fields, an eight-acre lake, jogging paths, and work facilities designed to optimize productivity and comfort. In addition, the site will include banks, dry cleaners, restaurants, and a post office—all intended to make life easier for workers. And Sprint executives seem firmly convinced that the $700 million investment will pay huge dividends as a lure for attracting and keeping new employees.

Case Questions

1. Based on current practices, what other practices do you think aggressive recruiters might try to further increase the number of qualified applicants in the future?

2. What are the risks and potential drawbacks of these recruiting strategies?

3. What specific things might a firm offer to attract your own personal interests?

Sources: "Southwest Airlines Makes Flying Fun," *USA Today*, September 22, 1998, pp. 1E, 2E; "Labor Recruiters Get Creative," *USA Today*, July 22, 1997, p. 1B; "Recruiters Work Hard to Showcase Fun Side of Jobs," *USA Today*, December 29, 1997, p. 5B; "No Shirt, No Shows, No Problem at Spring Job Fairs," *USA Today*, March 19, 1998, p. 1A; "Those Lists Ranking Best Places to Work Are Rising in Influence," *Wall Street Journal*, August 26, 1998, p. B1; "Can Trees and Jogging Trails Lure Techies to Kansas?" *Wall Street Journal*, October 21, 1998, p. B1; Shelly Branch, "You Hired 'Em, but Can You Keep 'Em?" *Fortune*, November 9, 1998, pp. 247–250; "Small Employers Offer Health Benefits to Lure Workers to Kansas City," *Wall Street Journal*, April 15, 1999, pp. A1, A8.

Building Human Resource Management Skills

Purpose: The purpose of this exercise is to give you insights into more and less effective recruiting via advertisements.

Step 1: Obtain a section of a newspaper that contains numerous recruiting ads (no longer than one page). Working alone, identify the one ad that you think is most effective and the one ad that you think is least effective. Jot down on a piece of paper your reasoning for each choice.

Step 2: Exchange ad pages with one of your classmates. Pick the ads from the other paper that you think are most and least effective, again jotting down your rationale.

Step 3: Each of you should next reveal your own choices for most and least effective recruiting ads, along with the respective rationales for your choices.

Step 4 (optional): Your instructor may ask for a few examples of particularly effective and less-effective ads to be shared with the entire class.

Ethical Dilemmas in Human Resource Management

Assume you are a midlevel human resource manager in a major diversified corporation. For years your company has aggressively recruited on the basis of opportunities for advancement. That is, your advertising and other recruiting materials have stressed that the company promotes only from within and that highly motivated employees can expect to advance rapidly into increasingly responsible and higher-paid positions. An internal study done about 10 years ago found that the average promotion time for top performers was about 1 to 1.5 years per promotion. Your interviewers have continued to emphasize this fact to prospective employees.

Over the past few years your firm has gone through some major organizational changes that have resulted in a much flatter organization design. You have begun to suspect that the firm now has fewer opportunities for meaningful advancement. You recently submitted a proposal to the head of corporate human resources for a new study to see whether promotion cycles have slowed. You believe that they have and that the company should soften its statements about advancement.

The director's top assistant just called and left you this voice message: "Hi, Pat, this is Bill. Listen, I've read through your proposal about the promotion study and think you should just let this die. I think we all know that promotion cycles aren't what they used to be, but who wants to step forward and really prove it? It can't do anything but hurt us. And anyway, the really sharp people still move up, and maybe one day things will go back to how they used to be. My reading is that the top brass want to carry on like we always have, and taking a look at this might cause some real problems. If I don't hear from you within the next few days, I'll just put your proposal in the circular file [trash container]. But if you really want to stick your neck out, let me know."

Questions

1. What are the ethical issues in this situation?

2. What are the basic arguments for and against proceeding with your proposal?

3. What do you think most managers would do? What would you do?

Human Resource Internet Exercise

 The "Human Resources Tech Talk" box on page 182 describes several Internet sites dedicated to employment opportunities for job seekers. Use a search engine to locate the addresses for three sites of this type. Visit each site. As you move through the site, try to place yourself in the role of a job seeker looking for employment in each of the following areas:

Production manager in a manufacturing plant

Sales representative for a consumer products group

Restaurant manager

Questions

1. Are there any differences in ease of use and perceived value for job searches across the three sites?

2. Are there any differences in ease of use and perceived value for each of the three kinds of jobs being searched?

3. Identify the basic quality requirements in such a site to maximize its potential value to a job seeker.

Notes

1. James A. Breaugh, *Recruitment: Science and Practice* (Boston: PWS-Kent, 1992).

2. Robert Bretz Jr. and Timothy Judge, "The Role of Human Resource Systems in Job Applicant Decision Processes," *Journal of Management*, Vol. 20, No. 3, 1994, pp. 531–551.

3. Alison Barber, Christina Daly, Cristina Giannatonio, and Jean Phillips, "Job Search Activities: An Examination of Changes over Time," *Personnel Psychology*, Vol. 47, 1994, pp. 739–750.

4. Timothy Judge and Robert Bretz, "Effects of Work Values on Job Choice Decisions," *Journal of Applied Psychology*, Vol. 77, No. 3, pp. 261–271.

5. "'Right Here in Dubuque,'" *Forbes*, March 29, 1993, pp. 86–88.

6. Charles Williams, Chalmer Labig Jr., and Thomas Stone, "Recruitment Sources and Posthire Outcomes for Job Applicants and New Hires: A Test of Two Hypotheses," *Journal of Applied Psychology*, 1993, Vol. 78, No. 2, pp. 163–172.

7. Andy Bargerstock and Hank Engel, "Six Ways to Boost Employee Referral Programs," *HRMagazine*, December 1994, pp. 72–77.

8. "Your Buddy May Be Worth 30 Grand," *Business Week*, October 12, 1998, p. 8.

9. "Executive Recruiter Scored Major Coup by Enticing Motorola's Fisher to Kodak," *Wall Street Journal*, November 1, 1993, p. B8.

10. "Software Firm Tests College Job Hopefuls," *USA Today*, April 8, 1993, pp. B1, B2.

11. Carla Johnson, "Turn Up the Radio Recruiting," *HRMagazine*, September 1998, pp. 64–70.

12. Bill Leonard, "Looking for a Job? Then Turn on Your TV," *HRMagazine*, April 1993, pp. 58–62; Stephanie Overman, "Cruising Cyberspace for the Best Recruits," *HRMagazine*, February 1995, pp. 52–54; "Hunting CEOs on a 32-Inch Screen," *Wall Street Journal*, April 27, 1999, pp. B1, B4.

13. John P. Wanous and Adrienne Colella, "Organizational Entry Research: Current Status and Future Directions," in K. Rowland and G. Ferris (eds.), *Research in Personnel and Human Resource Management* (Greenwich, Conn.: JAI Press, 1989). See also Peter W. Hom, Rodger W. Griffeth, Leslie E. Palich, and Jeffrey S. Bracker, "Revisiting Met Expectations as a Reason Why Realistic Job Previews Work," *Personnel Psychology*, Vol. 52, 1999, pp. 97–107.

14. "Its Not Easy Making Pixie Dust," *Business Week*, September 18, 1995, p. 134.

15. Bruce M. Meglino and Angelo S. DeNisi, "Realistic Job Previews: Some Thoughts on Their More Effective Use in Managing the Flow of Human Resources," *Human Resource Planning*, Vol. 10, 1987, pp. 157–167.

16. R. A. Dean and John P. Wanous "Effects of Realistic Job Previews on Hiring Bank Tellers," *Journal of Applied Psychology*, Vol. 69, 1984, pp. 61–68.

17. Bruce M. Meglino, Angelo S. DeNisi, Stuart A. Youngblood and Kevin J. Williams, "Effects of Realistic Job Previews: A Comparison Using Enhancement and Reduction Previews," *Journal of Applied Psychology*, Vol. 73, 1988, pp. 259–266.

18. Bruce M. Meglino, Angelo S. DeNisi, and Elizabeth C. Ravlin, "The Effects of Previous Job Exposure and Subsequent Job Status on the Functioning of Realistic Job Previews," *Personnel Psychology*, Vol. 46, 1993, pp. 803–822.

19. Sara L. Rynes, Robert D. Bretz, and Barry Gerhart, "The Importance of Recruitment in Job Choice: A Different Way of Looking," *Personnel Psychology*, Vol. 44, 1991, pp. 487–521.

20. Timothy A. Judge and Robert D. Bretz, "Effects of Work Values on Job Choice Decisions" *Journal of Applied Psychology*, Vol. 77, 1992, pp. 261–271; Allison Barber and Mark Roehling, "Job Postings and the Decision to Interview: A Verbal Protocol Analysis," *Journal of Applied Psychology*, Vol. 78, 1993, pp. 845–856.

21. "Living Overtime: A Factory Workaholic," *Wall Street Journal*, October 13, 1998, p. B1.

22. Lee Phillion and John Brugger, "Encore! Retirees Give Top Performance as Temporaries," *HRMagazine*, October 1994, pp. 74–78.

23. Adam Saks, "A Psychological Process Investigation for the Effects of Recruitment Source and Organizational Information on Job Survival," *Journal of Organizational Behavior*, Vol. 15, 1994, pp. 225–244.

24. Charles R. Williams, Chamer E. Labig, and Thomas Stone, "Recruitment Sources and Posthire Outcomes for Job Applicants and New Hires," *Journal of Applied Psychology*, Vol. 78, 1993, pp. 163–172.

7

Selecting and Placing Human Resources

CHAPTER OUTLINE

The Selection Process
Steps in Selection
Responsibilities for Selection

Basic Selection Criteria
Education and Experience
Skills and Abilities
Personal Characteristics

Popular Selection Techniques
Applications and Background
  Checks
Employment Tests
Work Simulations
Personal Interviews
References and Recommendations
Physical Examinations

**Special Selection Methods for
Managers**
Assessment Centers
Networks and Contacts

**Selection Technique Reliability and
Validity**
Reliability
Validity
Single- versus Multiple-Predictor
  Approaches

The Selection Decision
Job Offer and Negotiation
Determining Initial Job Assignments

**Evaluating Selection and Placement
Activities**

CHAPTER OBJECTIVES

*After studying this chapter you should
be able to:*

- Describe the steps in and responsibilities for the selection process in organizations.

- Identify and summarize basic selection criteria that organizations use in hiring new employees.

- Discuss popular selection techniques that organizations use to hire new employees.

- Describe special methods for selecting managers.

- Discuss reliability and validity and note the importance of multiple predictors.

- Discuss the selection decision, including job offers and negotiations and initial job assignments.

Hiring the "wrong" person for a job is always a regrettable decision. Poor performance and wasted hiring and training expenses are just some of the costs incurred by the organization, while the individual suffers disappointment and lost opportunity. In some job situations, however, hiring the wrong person can be an even bigger mistake. For example, improper hiring for the job of police officer can result in, at best, increased risk for innocent citizens and other police officers. At worst, it can create situations that are recipes for disaster.

Experts agree that among the most important selection criteria for police officers is their attitude toward and beliefs about minorities. Other important criteria include aggressiveness, self-esteem, and emotional stability. Of course, these characteristics are not necessarily things that can be easily observed or measured. Consequently, many police departments use psychological tests in their attempt to assess these criteria.

Individual applicants for positions in police departments are usually asked to complete a questionnaire or test that purports to assess the individual's psychological

> *"The tests weed out undesirables, including people with the wrong attitudes."*
>
> (Jeff Nielson, deputy chief of police, Rockford, Illinois)*

profile and to measure the specific individual characteristics that the department believes are important. Sometimes these tests are standardized instruments widely used in many different contexts, whereas in other circumstances the tests are created for a specific police department, usually by trained psychologists.

Not surprisingly, these tests are somewhat controversial. Some departments, for example, swear by them. Officials in both Fort Lauderdale, Florida, and Rockford, Illinois, have reported that such psychological tests have reduced racism among their police officers by weeding out candidates with racial prejudices. In other departments, however, such as Chicago and Portland, Oregon, some critics have argued that the psychological tests used to make selection decisions are themselves biased and prejudiced against minorities.

"Bid for Diversity Lands Police Force in Tangle of Recriminations," *Wall Street Journal*, October 12, 1998, pp. A1, A11; "Psychological Tests Designed to Weed Out Rogue Cops Get a 'D,'" *Wall Street Journal*, September 11, 1995, pp. A1, A6 (*quote on p. A1).

Like all organizations, police departments want to hire individuals best suited for the work that needs to be performed. And like other organizations, police departments must confront the fact that determining what criteria best predict effective performance and then figuring out how to best measure and evaluate those criteria is an imperfect process. Still, imperfections aside, organizations can use a number of basic activities to improve the likelihood that they are hiring the best possible employees.

As we noted in Chapter 6, the recruiting process is designed to develop a pool of qualified applicants interested in employment with the organization. The premise is that the organization can then select from among the members of that pool the specific individuals that it wants to employ. Thus the **selection process** is concerned with identifying the best candidate or candidates for jobs from the pool of qualified applicants developed during the recruiting process.

This chapter is concerned with the selection process. After presenting an overview of this process, we look at basic selection criteria. Next we introduce and discuss various popular selection techniques that many organizations use, including special selection methods and techniques used for managers. Reliability and validity, important attributes of effective selection techniques, are then described. Finally, we describe the selection decision itself and the determination of initial job assignments.

■ The **selection process** is concerned with identifying the best candidate or candidates for jobs from the pool of qualified applicants developed during the recruiting process.

THE SELECTION PROCESS

Although virtually every organization has its own unique selection system, most such systems reflect some basic commonalities. An important aspect of the selection process is establishing who in the organization has the responsibility for selecting new employees.

Steps in Selection

At a general level, as shown in Figure 7.1, the selection process involves three distinct steps.[1] The first step is to gather information about the members of the pool of qualified recruits. This information is gathered through a number of methods and techniques, most of which are discussed later, but relates primarily to determining the levels of KSA requirements possessed by an applicant. Information about such things as education and experience is objective. Other information, such as the attitudes of the individuals toward work and the impressions of current managers about the individual's likelihood of succeeding

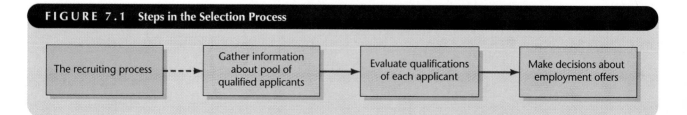

FIGURE 7.1   Steps in the Selection Process

The recruiting process ⇢ Gather information about pool of qualified applicants → Evaluate qualifications of each applicant → Make decisions about employment offers

in the organization, is much more subjective and perceptual. As we discuss later, information about the individual's specific skill levels or personality is somewhat objective but still open to subjectivity and interpretation.

The second step in the selection process is to evaluate the qualifications of each applicant from the recruit pool. This evaluation process occurs through the application of explicit or implicit standards to the information gathered in step one. For example, if the standard for hiring is that a person be able to keyboard seventy words per minute, a manager could give the applicants a keyboarding test and compare each applicant's score to the standard. Similarly, if the standard calls for a certain personality type, a manager could give personality tests and compare scores on the test to the standard. But sometimes applying standards is not so straightforward. For example, if the standard is ten years of relevant work experience, someone must make the decision as to whether or not people who exceed that standard are more qualified than individuals who simply meet it. For example, is a prospective employee with fifteen years of experience a more desirable candidate than someone who has exactly ten years of experience, or are these two candidates to be treated as equal on this

The selection process is extremely important for any organization seeking to hire new employees. In recent years the Internet has come to play an ever-growing role in the selection process for both job seekers and organizations to learn more about each other, to exchange information, and to make better-informed decisions. One of the biggest and most successful Web sites created for this purpose is Monster.com. During one recent month, for example, Monster.com attracted over 2 million unique visitors.

dimension because they each meet the standard? We discuss some important implications of decisions such as this one later in the chapter.

The third step in the selection process is making the actual decision as to which candidate or candidates will be offered employment with the organization. This decision involves careful assessment of the individual's qualifications relative to the standards of the job and the extent to which those qualifications best prepare and give an individual the requisite skills and abilities for the position. In some cases, an organization may be selecting large numbers of people to hire simultaneously. For example, a firm opening a new factory may be hiring hundreds of operating employees from a pool of thousands of applicants, or a rapidly growing restaurant chain may need to hire dozens of management trainees to take over the management of new restaurants in a year or two. In both of these cases the manager doesn't necessarily have to make fine gradations between candidate number eleven and candidate number twelve. The only decision is the extent to which a candidate is in the set of desirable people to hire or is outside that set because of job-relevant characteristics.

But if the selection decision involves hiring a specific single individual for a specific position in the organization, such as a new director of marketing or a vice president of human resources, then one individual must be selected. Moreover, it is sometimes helpful at this point to actually rank the candidates who are being considered for the job. This way, if the organization does not succeed in hiring its top choice for the job, then decisions will have already been made regarding the relative acceptability of candidates number two, three, and so on. In some cases, for example, if the recruiting process has been handled effectively, there may be more than one qualified applicant in the subject pool that the organization would like to hire. Hence it may be helpful to develop a backup plan in case the top choice cannot be employed.

Responsibilities for Selection

Who in the organization actually has the responsibility for hiring new employees? In most cases the answer is that the responsibilities for selection are jointly shared by human resource managers and operating managers. For example, following the center of expertise logic, human resource managers in an organization are responsible for designing the selection system and for gathering basic preliminary selection data, such as experience, education, and similar background information. Employees in the human resource department may then screen out individuals who do not meet those standards. Although in theory such screening should have happened during the recruiting process, sometimes people still slip through the cracks. Thus the human resource function may be responsible for providing relatively objective assessments of the various candidates in the recruiting pool.

Operating managers also play a major role in this process. For example, in most organizations today operating managers usually conduct the interviews with applicants and make decisions about the relative likelihood of a given applicant fitting into the organization's culture, the existing work group, and so forth. Thus operating managers are likely to be called on to make more subjective and personal assessments as to the relative qualifications of a given employee.

In some cases operating employees and potential colleagues of the prospective applicant may also play a role in the selection process, especially in organizations that rely heavily on teams. Because the coworkers will be working with the individual, many organizations find it appropriate and effective to solicit their input as to the relative attractiveness of various candidates being considered for the job. When hiring new managers, for example, Trammell Crow Real Estate Investors asks two or three other managers, as well as a secretary or a young leasing agent, to interview candidates. This process provides information about how the prospective manager relates to nonmanagers. Chaparral Steel Company relies heavily on work teams in its mill. Team members interview and make recommendations about various applicants for a job in their team.

In smaller organizations that lack a full-time human resource manager or self-contained human resource department, responsibilities for selection may fall on a single individual, usually the owner/manager of the organization. This person may handle the recruiting process, develop a pool of applicants, interview each one, and then make the selection as to whom she or he wants to hire. Many smaller retailing stores located in shopping malls, such as Limited Express, Eddie Bauer, and Foot Locker, operate this way.

THE BOTTOM LINE Managers need to have a basic familiarity with the steps in selection. They should also know who is responsible for which parts of the selection process in their own organization.

B A S I C   S E L E C T I O N   C R I T E R I A

On what basis does a manager or an organization go about trying to select a given individual from a pool of qualified applicants? As we discussed in Chapter 5, a major outcome of the job analysis process is the generation of job specifications, or KSAs. These are the individual characteristics that the organization believes people need to be able to perform specific jobs, for example, education and experience, specific skills and abilities, and personal characteristics.

Education and Experience

Education and experience are relatively straightforward to assess. In a selection context **education** refers to the formal classroom training an individual has received in public or private schools and college, university, and/or technical school. Some jobs require that people have a high school diploma, other jobs require a two-year associate degree from a community or junior college, and still other jobs might require a four-year college education. Sometimes the educational fields are open, whereas in other cases they must be within a specified area such as mechanical engineering or French or human resource management. Occasionally, jobs may require advanced degrees such as a master's degree or perhaps even a doctorate in a specific field of study. In some cases a technical certification may also be a good indicator of education; for example, many vocational and technical schools offer certificates when they train people for craft work such as electrical work, mechanical work, plumbing, and so forth.

In the last few years U.S. automobile manufacturers have started placing a higher premium on education when hiring new assembly workers. Managers at these firms have realized that a better-educated workforce will be more conducive to new training and learning and will better appreciate the importance of product quality. At Ford, for example, about 80 percent of the firm's total number of production workers have a high school degree. However, 97 percent of workers hired since 1991 have a high school diploma. Thus as less-educated workers retire or leave for various reasons, the overall educational level of the company's workforce will gradually increase.[2]

Although education is likely to continue to play an important role in the selection process, there is some concern that general education level—such as specifying that an individual needs a high school diploma or two years of college—might be a bit too removed from what many employers today need from a person on the job. Instead, an alternative model to focusing on education per se is to assess "competencies." Although the definitions of **competencies** vary from organization to organization, they basically refer to relatively broad capabilities that are necessary for effective job performance.

For example, a firm hiring someone to work in the accounting department might consider general bookkeeping skills as a requisite competency. An applicant might submit a list of courses and grades as evidence that he or she possesses the competency. What is important, however, is that the person can do bookkeeping, rather than just prove that he or she has taken bookkeeping courses. Thus although education may be related to competencies in many cases, the idea of a competency actually goes beyond education and deals, instead, with whether or not someone can actually do something.

■ **Education** refers to the formal classroom training an individual has received in public or private schools and college, university, and/or technical school.

■ **Competencies** vary in meaning from organization to organization but basically refer to relatively broad capabilities that are necessary for effective job performance.

Skills and abilities are important selection criteria for most jobs. But Mary Ann Elliott, president of Arrowhead Space and Telecommunications, Inc., believes that they are especially important to her business. Arrowhead is an engineering firm specializing in satellite communications and telecommunications technologies. Among the skills and abilities that Elliott looks for are specialized technical skills. Because her business relies heavily on defense contracts, the ability to network and interact with military officials is also important. Indeed, she finds that employees with previous military backgrounds make very good employees at Arrowhead.

■ **Experience** is the amount of time the individual may have spent working, either in a general capacity or in a particular field of study.

Experience refers to the amount of time the individual may have spent working, either in a general capacity or in a particular field of study. Experience is presumably an indicator of an individual's familiarity with work, his or her ability to work, and a surrogate measure of a person's competencies as an employee. In some cases it may be necessary that the individual have a predetermined level of experience in a certain field of study. For example, a large organization looking for a director of advertising is quite likely to expect applicants to have experience in the advertising field. In other cases, however, the experience requirement may be more general. Simply having a certain number of years of experience in full-time work activities might be sufficient evidence of an individual's employability. And some entry-level jobs may require no experience at all.

Skills and Abilities

■ **Skills and abilities** relate precisely to the specific qualifications and capabilities of an individual to perform a specific job.

Another common set of selection criteria is skills and abilities. **Skills and abilities** relate more precisely than do experience or education to the specific qualifications and capabilities of an individual to perform a specific job.[3] For example, even though an individual may have a college degree and a wealth of work experience, she or he may not have good skills and abilities regarding spatial relations (the ability to mentally manipulate three-dimensional objects in space). To the extent that the organization needs someone who has high levels of spatial-relations skills (which would be the case for many assembly-line jobs), an applicant who lacks that skill will not be an attractive candidate for the organization.

As organizations move more toward teamwork and team-based operating systems, many firms are also putting more emphasis on hiring individuals with the skills necessary to function effectively in a group situation.[4] Recall, for example, the earlier example of Chaparral Steel's use of existing team members to help hire new members. The rationale for this practice is that current team members are well placed to assess a given individual's ability to fit in and become an effective member of the team.

Personal Characteristics

In some jobs it is also important to an organization to assess the personal characteristics of individual job applicants. These personal characteristics are usually thought to reflect the individual's personality and may be an important factor in certain kinds of jobs. For example, a department store manager may believe that good salespeople are extroverted and have an outgoing and pleasant personality. Thus this manager, when interviewing prospective job applicants, might look closely at their friendliness, their ability to converse, and the extent to which they are comfortable dealing with a variety of circumstances. In contrast, a person who is more introverted, shy, and less willing to talk to people might not be as good an applicant for this particular kind of job.

Of course, when basing a selection decision on something such as personal characteristics, the organization must be able to clearly document a performance-related basis for this decision. For example, if the department store manager cannot demonstrate empirically that an outgoing individual will be a more productive salesperson than a shy and introverted individual will be, then that qualification may be of questionable legality. Indeed, as we will discuss later, personal characteristics are among the most complex and sensitive selection criteria to assess and to validate.

In recent years there has been a real shift in the focus of selection instruments designed to measure these personality variables. A great deal of attention has been paid to instruments that measure the **"big five" personality traits**. These traits tend to be more behavioral than cognitive or emotional, and recent research has suggested that they are likely to be more important for job performance than are more traditional personality traits.[5] The big five traits are *neuroticism* (disposition to experience things like anxiety and guilt rather than being better adjusted emotionally), *extraversion* (tendency to be outgoing, sociable, and upbeat), *openness to experience* (tendency to be imaginative and intellectually curious), *agreeableness* (tendency to be altruistic and cooperative), and *conscientiousness* (tendency to be purposeful, dependable, and attentive to detail).

An interesting controversy in selection today revolves around the issue of hiring for fit versus skill. Traditionally, human resource managers believed that they should hire the person with the best set of job-specific skills relative to the work that needed to be performed. But as detailed more fully in "Point/Counterpoint," others today are arguing that better candidates are those who best fit into the organization itself. These human resource managers believe that selection decisions should therefore be based on other factors such as personal characteristics, values, and so forth.[6]

■ The **"big five" personality traits**, which tend to be more behavioral than cognitive or emotional, are likely to be more important for job performance than are more traditional personality traits. The big five are *neuroticism, extraversion, openness to experience, agreeableness,* and *conscientiousness.*

POINT/COUNTERPOINT   Selecting for Fit versus Skills

 The basis for a selection decision has traditionally been whether or not a person could do the job. That is, organizations would identify the knowledge, skills, and abilities (KSAs) needed to do a job and then select the best-qualified candidate(s). More recently, organizations have begun basing selection decisions on whether or not a person "fits" with the organization. That is, the decision is based on whether the applicant seems to share values and personality with the organization as a whole. This is not to say that KSAs become irrelevant; they are simply of secondary importance.

POINT . . . Organizations should select people primarily upon the basis of FIT because . . .	COUNTERPOINT . . . Organizations should select people primarily upon the basis of KSAs because . . .
Even if they are "qualified," people who don't fit in the organization will probably never succeed.	No matter how well someone fits in, he or she will never perform as well as someone who is more qualified.
Strong organizational or corporate culture depends on hiring people with consistent values.	Organizations who rely on fit simply hire more of the "same" kind of people.
Teams are easier to form and are more likely to be successful when all team members share some basic values.	Lack of diversity in backgrounds and interests can result in fewer ideas, less originality, and perhaps even lead to discrimination.
People will be more attracted to and committed to organizations with which they believe they share values.	Diverse populations will be committed to organizations that value diversity.
It is easier to determine whether or not an applicant is "one of us."	Determinations of fit are always subjective, whereas determinations of KSAs can be more objective, and so, less biased.

So . . .   Organizations will always use both of these factors to some extent, but the issue is which one gets precedence. As long as all persons selected are reasonably qualified, there would seem to be no problems with selecting people on the basis of fit, and there would surely be benefits of such an approach. The biggest potential downside to a reliance on fit is that it can lead to the exclusion of people who are different (on the base of race and/or gender), which is illegal. Of course, a tolerant, diverse culture might be exactly the culture the organization is trying to foster.

THE BOTTOM LINE   Managers need to have a clear understanding of the basic selection criteria relevant for their organization. Such criteria typically include factors such as education and experience, skills and abilities, and personal characteristics, although fit with the overall organization may also be important.

P O P U L A R   S E L E C T I O N   T E C H N I Q U E S

Organizations use a variety of techniques for gathering information about an individual's education and experience, skills and abilities, and personal characteristics. Indeed, most organizations rely on a comprehensive system involving multiple selection techniques to ensure that they gather all the relevant data and that they assess this data rigorously, objectively, and in a nondiscriminatory fashion. In the sections that follow we identify and discuss some of the more popular and commonly used selection techniques. There may be some logic underlying the sequence in which organizations use these techniques, but at the same time many organizations vary the order to fit their own particular needs, circumstances, and beliefs. Figure 7.2 illustrates one selection sequence that an organization might employ.

Applications and Background Checks

One of the first steps in most selection systems is to ask applicants to complete an employment application or an application blank (see Figure 7.3 for a sample). An **employment application** asks individuals for various bits of personal information, such as a candidate's name, educational background, career goals, and experience. Of course, all information on an employment application must bear on an individual's ability to perform the job. For example, an employment application cannot ask for a person's gender, age, or marital status because these questions have no bearing on a person's ability to perform specific jobs. An organization will need answers to these questions after someone is hired, but since it is illegal to make selection decisions based on these variables, they should be avoided on application blanks.

■ An **employment application** asks individuals for various bits of personal information.

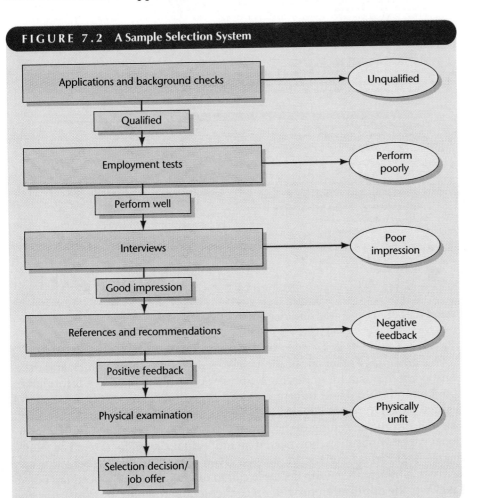

FIGURE 7.2 A Sample Selection System

Applications and background checks → Unqualified

↓ Qualified

Employment tests → Perform poorly

↓ Perform well

Interviews → Poor impression

↓ Good impression

References and recommendations → Negative feedback

↓ Positive feedback

Physical examination → Physically unfit

↓

Selection decision/ job offer

FIGURE 7.3 Sample Employment Application

SEARS
APPLICATION FOR EMPLOYMENT
PLEASE PRINT REQUESTED INFORMATION IN INK.

Date

Sears is an Equal Opportunity Employer and does not discriminate against any individual in any phase of employment in accordance with the requirements of local, state, and federal law. In addition, Sears has adopted an Affirmative Action Program with the goal of ensuring equitable representation of qualified women, minorities, Vietnam Era and disabled veterans, and other disabled individuals, at all job levels.

Applicants may be subjected to testing for illegal drugs. In addition, applicants for certain positions who receive a conditional offer of employment must pass a medical examination prior to receiving a confirmed offer of employment.

This application will be considered active for 60 days. If you have not been employed within this period and are still interested in employment at Sears, please contact the office where you applied and request that your application be reactivated.

PERSONAL INFORMATION   SEARS   SEARS   SEARS   SEARS   SEARS   SEARS   SEARS   SEARS

First Name   M.I.   Social Security Number

Last Name

Street   City   State   Zip Code   County   Telephone No.

Previous address if less than 2 years at present address.
Street   City   State   Zip Code   County

If hired, can you furnish proof of age?   If hired, can you furnish proof that you are legally entitled to work in the U.S.?
☐ Yes ☐ No   ☐ Yes ☐ No

Answer the following questions only if the position for which you are applying requires driving.
Are you licensed to drive a car?   Is license valid in this state?
☐ Yes ☐ No   ☐ Yes ☐ No

Have you ever been employed by Sears or a subsidiary of Sears?   ☐ Yes ☐ No
If Yes, note unit number and address   Termination Date   Position

Do you have any relatives employed by Sears   If Yes,
in the store or unit in which you are applying? ☐ Yes ☐ No   Name/Relationship:

In order to assure proper placement of all associates, please list any special skills, training, or experiences which qualify you for the position for which you are applying.

AVAILABILITY   SEARS   SEARS   SEARS   SEARS   SEARS   SEARS   SEARS   SEARS   SEARS

I am applying for the following position:
☐ Sales ☐ Office ☐ Merchandise Handling

☐ Other _____   Date you are available
to start work: _____

I am seeking (check only one):   I am available for:
☐ Inventory/Special Projects (6 days or less)   ☐ Part-time employment ☐ Full-time employment
☐ Seasonal employment (one season, e.g., Christmas)   Complete the Hours Available For Work Chart below.
☐ Regular employment (employ. for indefinite per. of time)

	Sun.	Mon.	Tues.	Wed.	Thur.	Fri.	Sat.
FROM							
TO							

If temporary, indicate dates available: _____
Total hours available per week: _____

10534 Rev. 10/97   27500

Source: The Sears Employment Application within this book is reprinted by arrangement with Sears, Roebuck and Co., and is protected under copyright. No duplication is permitted. Reprinted courtesy of Sears, Roebuck and Co.

One advantage of an application blank is that it provides a quick and inexpensive mechanism for gathering a number of kinds of objective information about an individual and information of a type that can be easily verified. As discussed in "Human Resources Tech Talk," some organizations today are even using electronic screening devices to review applications. Even with a traditional paper application, however, if an individual claims to have a bachelor's degree in electrical engineering from a given university, the organization can verify this information with a simple call to that university's placement office. Likewise, the application provides a convenient barometer for measuring the extent to which a person meets the basic selection criteria. For example, if the organization has appropriately determined that it must hire someone with five years of work experience and a bachelor's degree, and an applicant for the job has three years of experience and a high school diploma, the organization has reasonable cause to exclude that person from further consideration. Likewise, if the applicant specifies that she or he has a master's degree and fifteen years of experience, the organization may perhaps conclude that the individual is overqualified for the job.

In recent years, some organizations have experimented with new and more sophisticated versions of the traditional employment application. For example, one method that some organizations are experimenting with is the so-called **weighted application blank**.[7] A weighted application blank relies on the determination of numerical indices to indicate the relative importance of various personal factors for predicting a person's ability to perform a job effectively. Using information gathered from current high and low performers in the organization, a firm may be able to determine whether various specific levels of education, experience, and so forth are related to a person's ability to perform a job effectively.

As noted in the text, organizations usually rely on multiple selection techniques when they are hiring new employees. Further, as noted in Chapter 1, some firms today are outsourcing some of their human resource functions and activities. William Greenblatt has built a very successful business, Sterling Testing Systems, by contracting to screen prospective employees for other businesses. Among the other services the firm provides, Sterling checks job applicants' backgrounds for criminal records, motor-vehicle violations, and credit abuses; verifies past employment; performs certified drug tests; and administers written tests designed to assess honesty.

Another recent innovation is the biodata application blank. **Biodata applications** focus on the same type of information as found in regular applications but also go into more complex and detailed assessments about that background.[8] For example, in addition to asking about an applicant's college major, a biodata application might ask questions about which courses the applicant enjoyed most and why a particular field of study was chosen. As with weighted application blanks, responses to these questions are then studied for groups of good and poor performers. Responses to items that seem to differentiate between those who do well and those who do poorly are then used to predict the expected future performance of applicants.

Note that weighted and biodata applications focus on responses that help predict performance on the job. For example, an organization would not be interested in why individuals who once collected stamps perform better than other applicants and would certainly not suggest that collecting stamps leads to the better performance. The organization only cares that certain patterns of responses seem to be associated with high performance and so seeks applicants with these patterns while seeking other information as well.

■ A **weighted application blank** relies on the determination of numerical indices to indicate the relative importance of various personal factors for predicting a person's ability to perform a job effectively.

■ **Biodata applications** focus on the same type of information as found in regular applications but also go into more complex and detailed assessments about that background.

Employment Tests

Another popular selection technique used by many organizations is an employment test.[9] An **employment test** is a device for measuring characteristics

■ An **employment test** is a device for measuring characteristics of an individual, such as personality, intelligence, or aptitude.

Computerized Employee Screening? You Bet!

Back in the "old days," job seekers usually started exploring an employment opportunity by completing an application blank or submitting a copy of their resume to the employer's human resource department. A clerk or human resource manager reviewed the applicant's credentials and made a preliminary judgment as to whether the applicant met basic employment requirements—in which case the person advanced to richer and more thorough selection activities—or did not meet those requirements—in which case the individual was informed that the company did not have a job opening for which the applicant was qualified.

But increasingly, in today's fast-paced and high-tech world companies are using electronic screening mechanisms to make initial decisions about individuals. Among the pioneers in this area are Sony, Coca-Cola, IBM, Paine Webber, NationsBank, Avis, Microsoft, Pfizer, and Shell. The process usually starts in one of two ways: applicants are instructed to submit their application or resume electronically, or paper media are scanned into a firm's human resource database. Then the firm's human resource information system often takes over. For example, one pass might eliminate any and all applicants who do not meet the basic qualifications the firm requires of all its employees—U.S. citizenship, for example, or a high school education. The system may even generate and mail a "rejection" letter to the applicant.

For those individuals who make the preliminary "cut," the information system may take another pass through an individual's electronic records, seeking out certain key words, criteria, or qualifications. For instance, a software

> *"It's just another bit of machinery that gets in the way of the human-touch process."*
>
> (Steve Stahl, cofounder of Golden Handshakes, Virginia-based support group for unemployed managers and an outspoken critic of electronic employment screening)*

firm like Microsoft may have its system flag job seekers who indicate expertise in a specific programming language such as Java or HTML. Those individuals are then highlighted for human resource managers, who can follow up on a more personal level.

Other records are stored for later review for managers seeking new employees. For example, a manager seeking to hire a new sales representative may indicate any number of specific qualifications, such as education, experience, and type of experience; query the system for applicants who meet those qualifications; and then obtain copies of the application materials for everyone in the system who is qualified. Alternatively, the manager may also request information about a predetermined set of applicants—say, five or ten, for example—who most strongly meet the qualifications.

Of course, these kinds of systems are not without their problems and shortcomings. Some critics argue that it further depersonalizes larger employers. Other critics believe that since such systems are not perfect, they may open the door for savvy people who just know how to "work the system" while increasing the odds that a strong applicant may not get consideration because certain buzz words are not included on that person's application materials. Still, electronic screening seems like it's here to stay, so critics may just need to get used to it!

References: "Sir: Your Application for a Job Is Rejected; Sincerely, Hal 9000," *Wall Street Journal*, July 30, 1998, pp. A1, A12 (*quote on p. A1); Linda Thornburg, "Computer-Assisted Interviewing Shortens Hiring Cycle," *HRMagazine*, February 1998, pp. 73–78.

---

of an individual. These characteristics may include factors such as personality, intelligence, or aptitude. Although we usually think of employment tests as being of a paper-and-pencil variety (that is, the individual using a test booklet or an answer sheet to respond to written questions), the courts consider any device used to make an employment decision, including interviews, to be a test. In fact most employment tests are either administered on paper (and the organization may then score the employment test itself or send it to the agency from which it acquired the test for scoring) or are computer-administered tests (where the applicant sits at a computer and enters answers to questions using the keyboard or mouse). Figure 7.4 shows samples from several popular employment tests.

FIGURE 7.4 Sample Items from an Employment Test

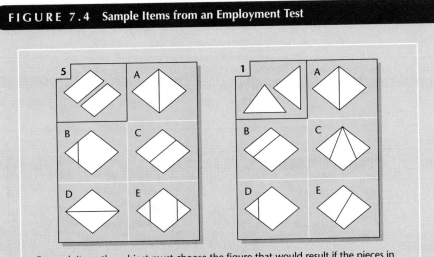

For each item, the subject must choose the figure that would result if the pieces in the first section were assembled.

Sample Items from the Revised Minnesota Paper Form Board.

When the two numbers or names in a pair are <u>exactly the same</u>, make a check mark on the line between them.

66273894	_____	66273984
527384578	_____	527384578
New York World	_____	New York World
Cargill Grain Co.	_____	Cargil Grain Co.

Sample Items from the Minnesota Clerical Test.

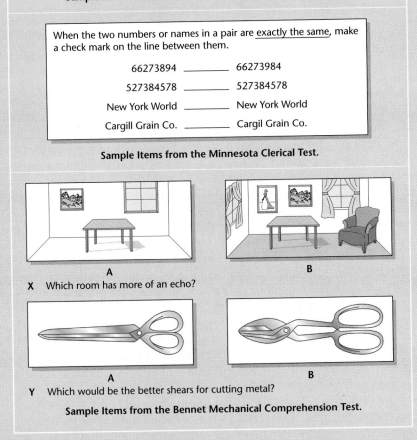

X   Which room has more of an echo?

Y   Which would be the better shears for cutting metal?

Sample Items from the Bennet Mechanical Comprehension Test.

Various types of employment tests are commonly used. Before identifying them, however, we should make the distinction between aptitude and achievement tests. These terms often refer to how the test is used rather than the nature of the test, but aptitude tests focus on predicting future performance, whereas achievement tests focus on the mastery of some set of learned skills. So, for example, keyboarding tests are usually seen as achievement tests (focusing on whether or not the applicant has basic proficiency or mastery in using a keyboard), whereas cognitive ability tests are seen as aptitude tests (focusing on the question of whether the person will be able to perform some specific task in the future). "The Lighter Side of HR" illustrates how *not* to complete an aptitude test!

Cognitive ability tests measure mental skills. The applicant is not required to do anything physical, but is required to demonstrate some type of knowledge. Therefore, knowing how a specific tool is used reflects a cognitive ability, but being able to actually use the tool is a psychomotor ability (which we discuss below). An extremely important cognitive ability is intelligence. General intelligence, or g, refers to reasoning, or problem-solving, skills but is typically measured in terms of things one learns in school. The Scholastic Aptitude Test (SAT) is a test of general intelligence. Scores on SATs can be expressed in terms of IQ, or intelligence quotient. The way these quotients are computed is beyond the scope of this discussion but reflects performance on a test relative to other people of the same age.

Two important facts make the use of intelligence tests in a selection setting quite controversial. First, IQ is related to performance on a wide variety of jobs, such that people who score better on IQ tests perform better on most jobs than do people who receive lower IQ test scores.[10] This factor makes the use of IQ tests in selection very popular and is consistent with the ideas discussed earlier about the value of a more highly educated workforce. The second fact is that black Americans tend to score lower on these tests than do white Americans. Therefore, using intelligence tests is likely to result in disparate impact (as discussed in Chapter 3). There are many explanations for why these differences

> ■ **Cognitive ability tests** measure mental skills.

might exist and what they should mean for selection.[11] Among the most common explanations are bias in test construction and fundamental cultural differences that result in different frames of reference. The key point vis-à-vis our discussion is simply that intelligence tests are potentially useful but controversial indicators of a special cognitive ability.

Other cognitive abilities include vocabulary skills and reading comprehension (verbal ability) and mathematics skills (quantitative ability), clerical ability (such as the ability to put names in alphabetical order and to recognize when two names are alike or different from each other), and spatial relations skills (which we defined earlier). These cognitive abilities are important for performance on a wide variety of jobs and are widely used in selection settings. For example, as noted earlier, auto manufacturers are seeking to improve the general intelligence level of their workers. Ford and Chrysler both now rely on cognitive ability tests to assess basic reading and mathematical abilities.

Psychomotor ability tests measure physical abilities such as strength, eye-hand coordination, and manual dexterity. These abilities can be practiced and perfected, and the tests to measure them are usually some type of performance test. For example, the *O'Connor Tweezer Dexterity test* requires an applicant to actually pick up and move small parts with a pair of tweezers (eye-finger coordination). (It is also interesting to note that a popular children's game called *Operation* requires the same essential skills as those tapped by this test.) Psychomotor tests are popular because they "look like" they measure what is important for performance on the job (human resource experts say these tests have high "face validity"). In addition, they do often measure skills that are important for jobs (for example, eye-hand coordination is important for any job requiring someone to drive a vehicle), and there is little evidence of disparate impact when they are used.

Personality tests measure traits, or tendencies to act, which are relatively unchanging. Although various tests are designed to measure a wide spectrum of personality traits or dimensions, as noted earlier, measures of the big five personality dimensions have become very popular in recent years and seem useful for predicting who will do well on jobs. The two basic ways of measuring personality are self-report inventories and projective techniques.

A **self-report inventory** is a paper-and-pencil measure in which an applicant responds to a series of statements that might or might not apply to the person. The most commonly used personality inventories include the *Minnesota Multiphasic Personality Inventory*, or *MMPI*, and the *California Psychological Inventory*, or *CPI*. Although both have been used widely in selection settings, the MMPI measures what we would consider "abnormal" personality traits such as schizophrenia, paranoia, and psychopathology. Therefore, it is more appropriate with clinical populations (persons who are being treated for psychological disorders) and is probably best used in selection settings as a means of screening out potentially dangerous job applicants. The CPI, on the other hand, was designed to measure more "normal" personality traits such as introversion-extraversion, dominance, and masculinity-femininity. Instruments designed to measure the big five personality traits are also growing in popularity.[12]

The other type of personality measure is known as a **projective technique**. This approach involves showing an individual an ambiguous stimulus, such as an inkblot or a fuzzy picture, and then asking what he or she "sees." Since there isn't really anything to see, whatever the applicant reports is presumed to be

Psychomotor ability tests measure physical abilities such as strength, eye-hand coordination, and manual dexterity.

Personality tests measure traits, or tendencies to act, which are relatively unchanging in a person.

A **self-report inventory** is a paper-and-pencil measure in which an applicant responds to a series of statements that might or might not apply to the person.

The **projective technique** involves showing an individual an ambiguous stimulus, such as an inkblot or a fuzzy picture, and then asking what he or she "sees."

reflective of his or her personality. The best-known projective technique is the *Rorschach inkblot test*, which requires trained clinicians to interpret its results. The *thematic apperception test* asks applicants to look at an ambiguous picture and then to write a story describing the people and what they are doing. This instrument can be scored relatively objectively (with a scoring key) and yields scores on personality traits such as "need for achievement" (which is a need to excel at all things).

The evidence regarding the relative effectiveness of measurement devices for the big five notwithstanding, personality tests are not without their critics.[13] Furthermore, there is some disagreement over whether cognitive ability tests (especially intelligence tests) or personality tests provide the most useful information for selection decisions.[14] Regardless of the merits of these arguments, however, both personality and cognitive ability remain popular selection techniques, as do all employment tests in general.[15] Later in the chapter we discuss issues of reliability and validity that are critical for choosing which tests to use; however, because employment tests are relatively objective and easy to interpret, they are likely to remain an important part of most organizations' selection systems.

■ **Integrity tests** attempt to assess an applicant's moral character and honesty.

Other increasingly used forms of employment tests are designed to assess an individual's honesty or integrity. **Integrity tests** attempt to assess an applicant's moral character and honesty. Most of these tests are fairly straightforward, and they include such questions as "Do you think most people would cheat if they thought they could get away with it?" and "Have you ever taken anything that didn't belong to you at work?" Other tests are less obvious and are based more on personality measures. It is interesting to note that many personality tests include items such as the second example above ("have you ever . . .") as a type of check. That is, they assume that most people *have* taken *something* that didn't belong to them at work (even if it was just a pen). Therefore, when someone replies that he or she disagrees with this item (that is, the person hasn't taken anything), it is seen as an indication that the person is not being totally honest. However, when the same item appears on an integrity test, a person agreeing with the item (he or she has taken something) is assumed to be dishonest and not to be trusted.

The use of integrity tests is growing dramatically, with an estimated several million administered annually in the United States,[16] and the likelihood is that the number will continue to rise as the cost of employee theft rises. Despite their popularity, however, the use of integrity tests in selection faces serious questions. First, evidence for their accuracy is almost entirely supplied by the publishers of the tests, and some possibility of conflict of interests exists. Second, there is evidence that although these tests may do a good job of identifying potential "thieves," many other individuals not identified by the tests steal and simply do not get caught. Finally, there is evidence that some applicants find these tests invasive and respond negatively to them.[18]

Work Simulations

■ **Work simulations** involve asking the prospective employee to perform tasks or job-related activities that simulate or represent the work for which the person is being considered.

Work simulations (sometimes referred to as **work samples**) are similar to tests, but instead of focusing on paper-and-pencil responses to printed questions, they ask the prospective employee to perform tasks or job-related activities that simulate or represent the work for which the person is being considered. For example, suppose an organization needs to hire a new secretary. Moreover, suppose the organization has determined that the secretary needs to be proficient with Windows 95 software and must be capable of keyboarding seventy-five words a minute. A relatively easy method for assessing a candidate's qualifications, then, is to seat the individual at a computer, ask him or her to perform various tasks and activities using Windows 95 software, and then to ask the applicant to keyboard a prepared letter or document to measure how quickly the person can actually do the keyboarding. Other jobs for which work simulations are appropriate are machinist jobs, where the individual can actually work on the machine under close supervision, a driving test for taxi drivers or school bus drivers, and an audition for a performing arts organization such as a musical group. **In baskets**, which consist of collections of hypothetical memos, letters, and notes that require responses, are sometimes used as part of management simulations.

Personal Interviews

Although tests are popular, the most widely used selection technique in most organizations is the employment interview. **Interviews** are face-to-face conversations between prospective job applicants and representatives of the organization.[19] Three basic types of interviews are commonly used: structured, semistructured, and unstructured interviews.

In a *structured employment interview*, the interviewer either prepares or is given by others a list of standard questions that are to be asked during the interview. All interviewers ask the same questions of each candidate so as to achieve consistency across interviewers. Also, since the questions are presumably prepared based on a careful study of the job, these are better questions than many interviewers would generate on their own. In some cases, after the questions are determined, potential answers are also devised, and these are given scores. In these instances the questions are often of a forced choice nature, where the answer might be yes or no, or a number, such as number of years or salary expectations. The interviewer then simply reads the questions in sequence, records the answer on the interview protocol, and assigns scores according to a key.

The *semistructured employment interview* involves advanced preparation of major or key questions to be asked. This type of interview provides a common frame of reference for all people who are interviewed for a job and requires that they all answer a predetermined set of specific questions. However, the interviewer is also given the prerogative to ask follow-up questions to probe specific answers that the interviewee provides. A popular strategy used in some firms today, especially high-tech firms, is to ask challenging and unusual questions designed to assess creativity and insight. For example, Microsoft interviewers often ask applicants "Why are manhole covers round?" There are then four different relatively correct answers, each of which allows the interviewer to probe more in different areas.[20]

Finally, the *unstructured employment interview* involves relatively little advanced preparation. The interviewer may have a general idea of the kinds of things that she or he wants to learn about the job applicant but has few or no advance questions that are formerly constructed and ready to be asked. Thus compared to other interview types, the unstructured interview is likely to be more spontaneous and more wide-ranging in its focus.

In general, interviewers prefer unstructured interviews because they view their role in the structured interview as a simple recorder of information. Thus they believe they lose a lot of the richness and value that is presumably associated with interviews. But this reaction is based, in part, upon interviewers'

■ **In baskets** are special forms of work simulations for prospective managers and consist of collections of hypothetical memos, letters, and notes that require responses.

■ **Interviews** are face-to-face conversations between prospective job applicants and representatives of the organization.

beliefs that they can make good employment decisions on their own and so don't require the structure. In fact, however, evidence suggests that structured interviews are much better predictors of subsequent job performance (i.e., they are more valid) than are unstructured interviews.[21] Furthermore, structured interviews that ask how a person would react in a given situation (that is, situational interviews) are the best predictors of future performance. These predictive relationships, or validities, tend to be a bit lower than those for tests, but only interviews are good at assessing KSA such as interpersonal skills. Interviews are also very good at allowing organizations to decide who "fits" best in the organization. Therefore, interviews will continue to be a popular and useful means for making selection decisions.

It is also important to recognize, however, that a number of mistakes, errors, and problems may be encountered in the use of interviews. For example, one type of error is the *first-impression error.*[22] Interviewers who make a decision very early in the interview process tend to make this mistake. For example, the candidate being interviewed might arrive a minute or two late or might have a few awkward moments at the beginning of the interview. This may cause the interviewer to make a negative decision about that individual, even though later evidence that comes out in the interview may have been more positive.

The *contrast error* occurs when the interviewer is unduly influenced by other people who have been interviewed. For example, suppose an interviewer meets with one candidate who is extremely good or extremely bad. The next person who is interviewed may suffer or benefit by contrast. That is, if the previous candidate was extremely good and the second candidate is only slightly above average, the interviewer may be prone to provide a lower evaluation for this person than would have otherwise been the case. Similarly, if the previous candidate is very, very poor and unacceptable to the interviewer, the next candidate, who again may only be about average, may appear to be even better in the eyes of the interviewer and receive a more positive evaluation than is warranted.

A *similarity error* occurs when the interviewer is unduly influenced because the interviewee is similar to the interviewer in one or more important ways. For example, consider the case of a person who has graduated from a particular college or is from a certain town and interviews someone who has graduated from the same college or who is from the same hometown. As a result of the perception of similarity, the interviewer may be more favorably disposed toward the candidate than the candidate's credentials actually warrant.

Yet another type of error that interviewers can make is that of *nonrelevancy*. In this case, the interviewer may be inappropriately influenced by an individual's posture, dress, or appearance. For example, an interviewer may rely too heavily on the extent to which an interviewee is able to maintain eye contact with him or her for an extended period of time. The interviewee may be shy or bashful or simply doesn't want to seem too aggressive, but by not maintaining eye contact with the interviewer the individual may be creating a false impression that she or he isn't assertive enough to do the job.

A final type of error that is common in interview situations has to do with the interviewer's knowledge of the job. Some organizations do not pay adquate attention to selecting appropriate interviewers and may select interviewers who know little or nothing about the particular job. Thus the interviewer may be basing her or his assessment of the individual's abilities to perform the job on incomplete or inaccurate assessments of the nature of that job.

These problems exist, to a greater or lesser extent, in all interviews. Their effects can be minimized, however, by proper training of interviewers. Experience itself is not a good substitute for training, and this training should focus on the occurrence of the problems outlined above, making the interviewer aware of the things he or she says and does. In addition, the training should provide interviewers with the means to replace behaviors that lead to errors with behaviors more likely to lead to their deciding on the best person for the job.

References and Recommendations

Another popular and widely used selection technique is the use of references and recommendations. The job applicant is usually asked to provide either letters of recommendation or the names and addresses of individuals who may be contacted to write such letters. Presumably, the organization can use this information as a basis for knowing about a person's past experiences and work history.

Unfortunately, references and recommendations are often of little real value. If a job applicant selects those who are going to provide recommendations, the individual is likely to pick people who will write positive letters of recommendation. For example, a student is more likely to ask a professor who gave him or her an A in a course for a recommendation than a professor who gave the student a D. Likewise, a former boss who gave the individual high performance evaluations is a more likely reference than is a former boss who gave the individual average or below average recommendations. Thus the organization must take with a grain of salt a file of glowing recommendation letters that a job applicant submits for consideration.

A related problem is a growing concern for legal liability in the preparation of recommendation letters. There have been some cases in which a job applicant has sued someone who wrote a negative letter of recommendation, which was, in turn, the basis for the individual subsequently not being offered employment. Likewise, there have also been instances in which organizations themselves have sued people who favorably recommended job candidates who were then found to be highly unsuitable. As a result of these legal concerns, many individuals will provide only objective information about a job candidate as a part of a reference letter. Thus they might be willing to verify dates of employment, salary history, job title, and so forth, but may be very unwilling to provide any assessment regarding the person's performance, capabilities, or likelihood for success in a new setting.[23]

Physical Examinations

A final popular selection technique is a physical examination. Few organizations require all applicants to submit to a physical examination but, instead, may ask only those finalists who are most likely to receive an offer of employment to take a physical examination. Organizations may require physical exams to determine if the person is physically healthy enough to perform a job, to determine whether or not the applicant has any serious communicable diseases, and/or to determine the extent to which the person may have appropriate levels of stamina and physical condition for performing hazardous or strenuous jobs. As we discussed in Chapter 3, the Americans with Disabilities Act prohibits the discrimination against prospective employees on the basis of physical disabilities. As a result, many organizations have stopped using physical exams prior to an offer of employment, but instead may require a physical or medical exam only after a job offer has been made.

HUMAN RESOURCES Fad, Fashion, or Fact?

The Fine Print: Hiring through Handwriting Analysis

Some employers are taking their search for letter-perfect employees literally.

They're analyzing job candidates' handwriting for personality clues. Despite skepticism, the unconventional approach is slowly gaining acceptance.

"It's almost uncanny," says Jack Parker, a certified public accountant in Dallas who asks hires to submit to the analysis. "At first, I just thought it was a nice thing to do at a party. But it's so accurate."

It's called graphology or document examination, a controversial practice long popular in parts of Europe. Employers in the USA, however, often have dismissed it as unscientific.

But not all agree. A spokeswoman for high-tech firm Cognex says all hires are asked to submit handwriting.

"We give them the handwriting analysis so we have more pieces of the picture," says Kathy Bedrosian at the Natick, Mass.-based firm. "People have generally been open to it, and occasionally they're even enthusiastic because it's something different."

Job seekers may be asked to write on a blank page. Their prose is faxed or sent to handwriting experts, who

"By the time we're done, we know everything about them except their underwear size."

(Mark Hopper, president of Handwriting Research, a Phoenix-based firm)

prepare a personality profile. Some give consultations based on their findings.

Many handwriting experts have their own analysis styles and charge from $75 to $250 per person. Some say those who cross their t's low may have low self-esteem. A line of writing that slants upward suggests optimism. Large letters hint at extraversion.

"By the time we're done, we know everything about them except their underwear size," says Mark Hopper, president of Handwriting Research, a Phoenix-based firm. "We do everything from *Fortune* 100 companies to health spas."

Not everyone is sold. Some say the practice is akin to using tarot cards to make hires. Others say firms that use it may be vulnerable to legal challenges.

"It's just not fair," says Lewis Maltby at the American Civil Liberties Union. "People are entitled to be judged by the quality of the work."

But supporters argue that's what critics once said about drug and personality tests, which are now widely used.

Source: Reprinted from *USA Today*, July 21, 1998, p. B1. Copyright 1998, *USA Today*. Reprinted with permission.

A related type of physical examination that organizations rely on is drug testing, and it is becoming increasingly common. Like other types of physical examinations, drug tests are most commonly given to people to whom the organization is prepared to make an offer of employment. Of course, as with all selection techniques, reliance on a drug test as a condition of employment requires that the organization be absolutely sure the test that is being administered is valid and reliable. That is, the organization must be prepared to demonstrate that the test is conducted under rigorous conditions and that its results are true and verifiable.

Organizations also continue to seek new and better predictors of future job performance to integrate into their selection systems. "Human Resources Fad, Fashion, or Fact?" discusses one interesting new approach. Other techniques that some organizations have tried include credit history (as an indicator of overall stability), interviews with customers, and psychological assessments by trained therapists. The owner of a tax consulting firm in Florida even inspects an applicant's car because he believes that a dirty and messy car is indicative of a disorganized person who lacks the ability to do technical accounting work.[24] Regardless of the implicit connection between these indicators and behavior on the job, however, human resource managers must be able to demonstrate how any given predictor actually forecasts future job performance.

> **THE BOTTOM LINE** Managers can select from an array of techniques to include in a selection system. However, managers must have a clear understanding of the strengths and weaknesses of each selection tool, and the tools must be logically and rationally linked and integrated.

SPECIAL SELECTION METHODS FOR MANAGERS

Although companies may use any or all of the selection methods described in the preceding section when selecting managers, special selection methods may also be appropriate. Assessment centers are commonly used, as are networks and other personal contacts.

Assessment Centers

One special method for selecting managers that is widely used in many organizations is the assessment center concept.[25] An **assessment center** is not really a place, but is instead an approach to selecting managers based on measuring and evaluating a person's ability to perform critical work behaviors. Individuals who are participating in an assessment center are likely to be either current managers who are being considered for promotion to higher levels or external recruits, such as upcoming college graduates, who are being considered for management positions.

The individuals to be assessed are brought together in a convenient location such as the company's training headquarters or perhaps a hotel conference facility. While there they undergo a series of tests, exercises, and feedback sessions. A normal assessment center schedule lasts two to three days and involves around ten to fifteen individuals at a time. During the period of the assessment center, these individuals may participate in experiential exercises, group decision-making tasks, case analyses, role-playing exercises, and other methods for assessing their potential skills and abilities and may also be given individual employment tests, such as personality inventories.

A panel of current line managers from the organization will likely be attending the assessment center as well in the role of evaluators. These individuals oversee the conduct of the assessment center and provide evaluations as to the likely suitability of each attendee for various management positions within the organization. At the conclusion of the assessment center, each evaluator provides an in-depth evaluation of each candidate. These evaluations are then screened by other managers who are responsible for making the actual selection decisions. Among the things that are looked at during an assessment center are the individual's abilities for performing a particular kind of work, the extent to which the evaluators believe the individual will be successful in the organization, the extent to which the individual will likely be a candidate for further promotion in the firm, how the individual functions in groups, and the kinds of training and development that may be necessary to help the individual develop more fully.

AT&T is one company that makes widespread use of assessment centers. Indeed, AT&T was one of the first companies in the United States to use the assessment center concept and since 1956 has run more than two hundred thousand people through various assessment centers. AT&T's evaluation of its assessment center's usage suggests that this method for selecting managers is a fairly effective technique for identifying those who are more and less likely to

■ An **assessment center** is an approach to selecting managers based on measuring and evaluating a person's ability to perform critical work behaviors.

be successful in the organization. Assessment centers do have some disadvantages, however. Among the most significant is cost. The organization typically must pay for transportation, lodging, meals, and other expenses for all candidates, and must provide the same expense coverage for the line managers who are doing the evaluation. Further, those managers are away from their workstations, and thus there is lost productivity to consider as well.[26]

Networks and Contacts

Another special method that many organizations use for the selection of managers is a heavy reliance on networks and contacts. This method is not necessarily a formal or objective selection system, but is instead more of an informal tendency to rely on familiarity and personal acquaintances in making selection decisions. For example, a discreet phone call to a colleague may yield more valuable and richer information about the prospects of a potential job candidate than will a formal request for the person to write a letter of recommendation. Sometimes something as subtle as a few moments of silence or a brief head shake or nod may convey considerable information to the astute manager who made the request. Of course, the manager who is relying on such networks and contacts must be careful to evaluate all information and would be ill advised to make the primary selection decision on the basis of one such informal contact.

As already noted, in the eyes of the courts and the EEOC, any technique used to make an employment decision is considered a "test." If the use of any such test results in disparate impact, the organization must prove that it is not using the test to discriminate by demonstrating that the test is job related (we discuss this factor in the next section). Therefore, from a legal perspective, these different selection techniques are interchangeable. From a practical perspective, though, an organization must decide which KSA it wishes to measure and then determine which selection techniques are most suitable. Therefore, in practice, organizations will typically use some combination of the techniques we discussed.

THE BOTTOM LINE   Managers should understand special approaches to selecting other managers, such as assessment centers and networks and contacts. They should also be aware, however, of the continued requirement that all selection techniques be valid predictors of performance.

SELECTION TECHNIQUE RELIABILITY AND VALIDITY

Regardless of which technique or techniques an organization uses in making selection decisions, it must ensure that those techniques are reliable and valid. Without such evidence the organization is holding itself open to the possibility of discrimination. As noted above (and in Chapter 3), when there is evidence of disparate impact, the organization must prove that it is not discriminating. Managers can do so by demonstrating that the selection technique is job related. In practice, however, they must prove that the selection technique is a valid predictor of performance on the job. As we discuss below, though, even without laws concerning discrimination, an organization is wasting its resources if it uses a selection technique that is not valid. We begin with reliability because a test that is not reliable can never be valid.

Reliability

Reliability refers to the consistency of a particular selection device. Specifically, reliability means that the selection device measures whatever it is supposed to measure, without random error. Systematic error may be present, though, so reliability is not the same as accuracy. For example, suppose you get on your bathroom scale in the morning and the scale says you weigh 137 pounds, but you actually weigh 135 pounds. The next day, suppose you still actually weigh 135 pounds, but now the scale says you weigh 134 pounds. Finally, on the third day, you still really weigh 135 pounds, and now the scale also says you weigh 135 pounds. In this case you have an unreliable scale, although not because it is usually not accurate. The scale is unreliable because the amount and direction of error are random—on the first day the error is plus-two pounds, on the second day it is minus-one pound, and on the third day the error is zero. In contrast, if your scale indicated that your weight was two pounds more than it actually was every single day, your scale would still be inaccurate, but at least it would be reliable—always off by two pounds in the same direction. In fact, you always learn your true weight by simply subtracting two pounds from the weight indicated on your scale.

All measures organizations use in selection have error, and all measures are less than perfectly reliable. In the bathroom scale example, for instance, notice that your actual weight is the biggest contributor to the weight indicated on the scale, with only a small amount due to the measurement error. We could imagine cases, though, where the error component is much larger—so large, in fact, that it wouldn't make any sense to use the scale to weigh yourself. In a selection context this condition might mean that although person A scores higher on an arithmetic test than person B does, the difference is due solely to random error, rather than to the fact that person A is actually better at arithmetic. Managers responsible for selecting new employees should always seek to know what part of a given score on a selection technique is due to error and what part is due to the underlying phenomenon they are trying to measure. Reliability, then, can be viewed as that part of a score that is not due to random error.

Reliability can be assessed in a variety of ways. One common method of assessing the reliability of a selection technique is called *test-retest reliability*. In this case the same individual or individuals are subjected to the selection technique at two points in time. If there is a high positive correlation between their scores or evaluation between the two time points, then reliability can be inferred. That is, test results seem to be consistent over time and thus may be taken as being reliable. Any random error component would change over time, resulting in inconsistencies, so the degree of consistency is an indication of how much of the score is due to what is being measured, rather than to error. Another method of establishing reliability, particularly for employment tests, is called *alternative-form reliability*. In this case the organization develops multiple forms of the same instrument, and these are administered to various individuals. To the extent that the alternative forms of the instrument yield the same score, then again reliability can be inferred, using the same logic as above. In this case, however, reliability is being demonstrated across alternative forms, as opposed to over time.

Validity

Validity refers to the extent to which a measure or indicator is, in fact, a real reflection of what it is assumed to be. For example, an organization would be ill

■ **Reliability** refers to the consistency of a particular selection device.

■ **Validity** refers to the extent to which a measure or indicator is a real reflection of what it is assumed to be.

advised to use a keyboarding test as a measure of a person's potential ability as a truck driver. The ability to keyboard would have no obvious predictive relationship with an individual's ability to be an effective truck driver, and thus the measure of keyboarding skill lacks validity relative to the job of driving a truck.

The first condition for a measure to be valid is that it be reliable, as described above. If a test is measuring pure error, it cannot be measuring what it is supposed to measure. Beyond this condition, various kinds of validity are relevant to the selection process. One type of validity is content validity. *Content validity* is the extent to which a selection technique such as a test or interview actually measures the skills, knowledge, and abilities that are necessary to perform the job. A keyboarding test would, therefore, be a content-valid test for a job of secretary. This test replicates conditions on the job and provides a true reflection of a person's capabilities for performing a particular job.

Content validity is relatively easy to demonstrate for operating jobs, for the performance measures themselves are objective and verifiable. Hence bricklaying, manufacturing work, and construction work are all jobs that can be predicted using work sample tests and other measures that have content validity vis-à-vis that particular job. When a student complains that an exam in class is not "fair" because some questions on the test were not covered in the book or in class, the student is really complaining about the content validity of the exam. In a case such as this, as opposed to the situations described above, content validity is usually assessed by expert judgment. That is, experts indicate that the items on the test are a reasonable sample of what was covered in class or what is needed on the job.

A second kind of validity is called construct validity. *Construct validity* is the extent to which a relationship exists between scores on the measure and the underlying trait the measure is supposed to tap. For example, if an organization wanted to measure the "conscientiousness" of applicants but was not happy with existing measures, it might set about to develop its own measure of this personality trait. The question would be whether the measure that was developed really assessed conscientiousness—this is the fundamental issue in construct validity.

How would an organization demonstrate that it was really measuring this trait? There are several things the organization could do, all of which would provide evidence of construct validity (construct validity is never really proven; instead, inferences can be drawn based on information suggestive of construct validity). One method would be to administer the new measure along with an established and recognized measure to a group of employees. High correlations between the two measures would constitute evidence of construct validity. The organization might also believe that people who are high in conscientiousness would be more likely to stay late at work and less likely to leave jobs unfinished. If the firm found that individuals scoring higher on the new measure did in fact also tend to stay later and did not leave jobs unfinished, this finding would provide further evidence of construct validity. Basically, then, human resource managers provide evidence for construct validity by thinking about things that should and should not be related to a measure if it were tapping what was wanted. The more these relationships are borne out, the more confident managers are that they are really measuring what they intend.

A third kind of validity that is relevant to selection decisions is criterion-related validity. Although construct validity may be the most difficult type of validity to establish, criterion-related validity is the most critical to the selection process. *Criterion-related validity* is the extent to which a particular selection technique can accurately predict one or more elements of performance. Criterion-related validity is most typically demonstrated by establishing a correlation between a test or measured performance in a simulated work environment with measures of actual on-the-job performance. In this approach the test or performance measure represents a predictor value variable, and the actual performance score itself is the criterion. A meaningful (that is, statistically significant) correlation not only suggests that a relationship exists between test scores and performance but also suggests that the test is job related.

It is also important to note that even if establishing criterion-related validity were not important in civil rights cases, organizations would still need to be sure of the relationship between scores on their selection devices and performance on the job. If this relationship is missing, the selection device will not help to select better performers. In other words, if organizations select individuals merely on the basis of chance (for example, the flip of a coin), they will produce a workforce that is as effective as that selected using the test. Since it costs time and money to administer any selection device, the company would be throwing away money on a selection system that produced no benefits in terms of performance.

Single- versus Multiple-Predictor Approaches

No selection technique is perfectly reliable and valid. Hence most organizations rely on a number of selection techniques and, in fact, may use all or most of the selection techniques discussed earlier. Hence a person who applies for a job may be (1) subjected to a preliminary screening interview to make sure that he or she meets the minimum qualifications, (2) asked to complete an application and agree to background checks, and (3) required to undergo employment tests and/or participate in work simulations. For example, virtually all of the so-called one hundred best companies to work for in America, ranging from Southwest Airlines to Worthington Industries, rely heavily on multiple predictors when making hiring decisions.[27]

An individual who is found to be qualified for employment, based on his or her performance on these various selection techniques, may be subjected to more in-depth interviews, followed by references and recommendation checks. Finally, physical examinations might be authorized for those who are about to be offered employment. For managers, assessment centers and personal contacts may be added to these other selection techniques. By using multiple approaches in this way, the organization is presumably able to counterbalance the measurement error in one selection technique against another. For example, if a particular candidate for the job scores well on all selection techniques except one, the organization may choose either to ignore the results of that one technique or to try to learn more about why the individual didn't perform better. Thus the basic reasoning behind multiple predictor approaches is to enhance the validity and reliability of the overall selection process by taking advantage of a wider variety of information.

THE BOTTOM LINE The ability to demonstrate that selection techniques are true predictors of future performance is a complex and sophisticated process. Managers need to understand and appreciate the meaning of reliability and validity and the power of multiple-predictor approaches to selection. The human resources department can play an especially important function in this regard in terms of its role as a center of expertise.

T H E   S E L E C T I O N   D E C I S I O N

After subjecting the pool of qualified applicants to the organization's selection system, it will then be necessary to make the actual selection decision. In some cases the decision may be relatively simple. If the organization is seeking to hire only one individual for a particular position, then the top-ranked candidate from the pool of applicants is the person likely to be hired. On the other hand, if the selection process is part of a large-scale program in which the organization may be hiring dozens or perhaps hundreds of employees for similar kinds of positions, then the selection decision may consist of choosing where to draw the line between those who qualify for employment and those who do not.

But the person ranked highest in the pool might not always be the person who scored highest on a particular selection device (or even on a combination of such devices). As noted earlier an organization might select a person who has "acceptable" levels of KSA, but who is a better fit with the culture and style of the organization. It is also common for organizations to cluster applicants who, although they may differ somewhat in terms of KSA, don't differ enough from each other to be critical. Thus the organization could use any decision rules it wished to select among the people in such a cluster without really sacrificing performance on the job. This procedure, known as **banding** could, for example, allow an organization to select an applicant from some underrepresented group in the organization without compromising high performance standards.

In any case the selection decision may be made by a single individual, or it may be made by a committee. Moreover, as noted earlier, sometimes the selection decision is actually sequential. For example, there might be four finalists for the job. After subjecting each to various elements of the selection process, it may be determined that two individuals do not fit the organization's needs but the other two may be attractive candidates for the job. Thus the organization may rank these candidates as number one and number two and proceed with offering number one the job. Then if that person says no or an agreement cannot be reached, the organization may turn to its number-two candidate who is also perfectly acceptable. Occasionally, none of the candidates who reach the finalist pool for the job are suitable for employment. In this case the organization may actually decide to not make an employment offer to anyone in its pool, but instead start over with a different group of applicants.

■ Banding involves creating clusters of job applicants who do not differ substantially from one another, allowing an organization to select an applicant from some underrepresented group in the organization without compromising high performance standards.

Job Offer and Negotiation

Assuming that the organization decides to hire one or more people from its applicant pool, it must communicate that fact to the individual or to those individuals. Sometimes an offer for employment comes in the form of a telephone call. In other cases it may be a letter, and in a few cases, it might actually be a face-to-face conversation as a result of the screening process. That is, the individual may pass through the recruiting process so effectively that by the end of the process, such as the interview session, the organization makes an employment offer. Microsoft uses this approach. Candidates who are invited to the company's headquarters are interviewed by six or seven managers during a one-day period. As each interview is completed, that interviewer sends his or her evaluation and comments to the next interviewer by e-mail. By the end of the day, the final interviewer will have her or his own assessment plus the as-

The culmination of the selection process occurs when the employer decides whom to hire and extends an offer of employment to that person. The two parties then discuss and negotiate terms, including compensation and benefits. An increasingly common area of negotiation today also involves stock and/or stock options. For example, when Marcia Thompson negotiated for her job with MCI WorldCom, she agreed to take a portion of her compensation in stock. And so far, at least, this has really paid off for her; the value of the stock rose 137 percent in 1998!

sessments of several managers. If the assessments are all very positive, the final manager has the authority to make a job offer on the spot.

Of course, it is also important for the organization to appropriately communicate with those individuals it has decided not to employ. Some organizations do a relatively poor job of this step. Nevertheless, to maintain good public relations and to treat people fairly and with dignity, companies must communicate with rejected applicants in a professional manner. This process is more likely to be handled in a letter but in certain circumstances may also be handled through a phone call. In general, the organization simply informs the individual that he or she will not be offered employment and wishes the person good luck. It is the policy of many organizations to provide no further details.

Another related issue is the potential for negotiation regarding the employment relationship. For some jobs, such as entry-level and operating jobs, the job offer is implicitly presented in a take-it-or-leave-it form. For example, the human resource manager may say, "We want to hire you for this particular position. The starting pay for the job is $9.00 an hour, and we would like for you to start work in two weeks." The individual who is considering the employment may have little opportunity for altering the terms of this offer. For example, the pay may very well be nonnegotiable if it is the the organization's standard starting wage. Perhaps the best the individual can do, if necessary and if circumstances warrant, is to negotiate and/or modify the start date. For example, the individual may ask for a couple of extra days to find a new place to live close to the work site, to finish outstanding tasks for the current employer, and so forth. But in general, this is the extent of negotiation that is usually allowed for entry-level employees.

On the other hand, it is very common for organizations to negotiate with managers, especially with those being hired at the senior ranks. Sometimes, for instance, complex incentive packages need to be constructed that rely heavily on base salary plus bonuses and incentives, stock options, and other considerations. Moreover, since these arrangements are frequently put in writing, it is necessary and important for both the individual and the organization to carefully understand what they are and are not agreeing to. Thus there may be considerable opportunity for negotiation on salary, start date, initial job responsibilities, and so forth.[28]

Determining Initial Job Assignments

Yet another important part of the selection process is the placement of individuals in their first job in the organization. In some cases the initial job assignment may be known in advance. For instance, if a firm is hiring a new operations manager for a factory it intends to open at a certain location, the initial job assignment is essentially predetermined. But in many cases there is some flexibility regarding initial job assignments. When a firm like Wal-Mart, for example, hires one hundred new college graduates within a one-month period to enter its management-training program, in some ways it makes no difference to the organization when these people begin their work. The idea is that they will serve as assistant managers in various Wal-Mart stores for a few years with increasing responsibility until they are ready to become manager of their own store. Thus whether a given individual is initially assigned to a store in Orlando, Houston, or Los Angeles is not significant.

In this situation the organization must take into account a number of factors. One important factor is the extent to which the current manager in a particular store is a good developer of managerial talent. Some store managers may be known to be excellent at developing brand-new assistant managers and enhancing their skill level effectively. But other managers, while they may be excellent merchandisers and managers themselves, may do a relatively poor job of developing new managerial talent. In this light the initial job assignment may be very critical.

Location is also an important factor, especially if the organization is responsible for paying people's moving expenses. For instance, if a national organization is hiring someone who currently resides in Houston and someone else who currently resides in Atlanta it may make sense to assign the new Houston employee to the firm's Texas office and the new Atlanta manager to the Georgia office. This arrangement will cut down on moving expenses and thus save the organization money. At the same time, of course, there may also be very valid reasons for assigning people to locations that are far from their current home even if it means incurring additional moving costs.

THE BOTTOM LINE Managers should remember that, after using various selection techniques to gauge the relative quality of prospective employees, they must still make the actual selection decision. In addition, they must make job offers properly and be prepared, as appropriate, to negotiate employment terms. The initial job assignment must be carefully determined as well.

EVALUATING SELECTION AND PLACEMENT ACTIVITIES

Selection is clearly one of the most important functions that human resource managers engage in. The ability to attract qualified human resources and to select the individuals who are most suitable for employment by the firm goes a long way toward determining the future vitality and effectiveness of the organization. An effective and ongoing infusion of new talent, new attitudes, and new perspectives can be a major ingredient in the success of an organization.

On the other hand, if the selection process results in inbreeding or continued process of hiring ineffective employees, then the organization and all who work for it will eventually pay the price. Thus the selection process must be periodically examined to ensure that it is being conducted effectively, appropriately, and legally. The evaluation of the selection process might be best approached from the standpoint of operating managers who rely on it to supply them with effective new employees.

To the extent that these managers report that the human resource function is indeed providing them with qualified employees, then there is implied evidence for the effectiveness of the selection process. On the other hand, if operating managers report that the human resource function is not providing them with effective employees or if managers are unhappy with the process in other ways, then there may be evidence to suggest that changes in the selection process are warranted.

Similarly, initial job placement can also be evaluated in much the same way. If people who begin their employment with the organization express satisfaction with the organization and positive feelings about their initial job experiences, then initial job placement may have been undertaken appropriately and effectively. But if many employees are grumbling and complaining that their initial job assignment isn't what they expected it to be, then in addition to the possibility that the firm is not providing realistic job previews, it may be the case that initial job placement is not being handled satisfactorily.

Chapter Summary

The selection process involves three distinct steps: gathering information about the members of the pool of qualified recruits, evaluating the qualifications of each applicant from that pool, and making the actual hiring decision. The responsibilities for selection are jointly shared by human resource managers and operating managers.

The basic selection criteria most organizations use in deciding whom to hire are education and experience, skills and abilities, and personal characteristics. The job specification determines which criteria will apply to any given situation. Firms must also decide whether to focus on fit or skills.

Organizations use a variety of techniques for gathering information about job candidates. The most common ones are employment applications and background checks, employment tests, work simulations, employment interviews, references and recommendations, and physical examinations. Each technique has unique strengths and weaknesses, but each can also play an important role in selection.

Although managers are likely to be subject to any or all of the selection methods, special selection methods may also be appropriate. Two of the most common are assessment centers and networks and contacts. But organizations using networks and contacts must be especially careful to avoid bias and discrimination.

Regardless of which technique or techniques an organization uses in making selection decisions, it must ensure that those techniques are reliable and valid. Reliability is the consistency of a particular selection device. Validity refers to the extent to which a measure or indicator is a real reflection of what it is assumed to be. Most organizations rely on a number of selection techniques and, in fact, may use all or most of the selection techniques discussed in the chapter.

After subjecting the pool of qualified applicants to the organization's selection system, the firm must make a final selection decision. The job offer must be extended, and appropriate negotiations undertaken. Those not selected must also be informed. Another important part of the selection process is the placement of an individual in his or her first job in the organization. It is also important that the organization periodically evaluate its selection and placement activities.

Review and Discussion Questions

1. What are the basic, general steps in the selection process?

2. What are the most common selection criteria that organizations use when making selection decisions?

3. Identify and describe several popular selection techniques.

4. What is an assessment center? How is it used?

5. What do reliability and validity mean with respect to selection techniques?

6. Can you identify various kinds of jobs where experience is more important than education?

Where education is more important than experience?

7. Which selection techniques would you feel most and least confident in using? Why?

8. What are the major risks in relying too heavily on networks and contacts to hire a new manager?

9. Why do you think so many organizations do a poor job of communicating decisions to individuals they have decided to not hire?

10. What steps might an organization undertake to improve the quality of its initial job assignments?

Closing Case

Hiring High-Risk Employees Can Pay Off for Business

When most people think of new employees starting to work for an organization, they most likely imagine only the brightest, most highly motivated, and most upstanding and respectable of applicants being chosen for employment. But with surprising frequency these new employees may be former drug addicts, alcohol abusers, welfare recipients, and homeless people. What could possibly prompt a business to expand its workforce from these ranks? The reasons run the gamut from absolute necessity to social conscience. But regardless of the motive, many managers report that with a little extra attention and caution, new employees chosen from what might be considered high-risk labor pools can actually pay big dividends.

One good example is Candleworks, a small candle-making company based in Iowa City, Iowa. The firm's owners, Lynette and Mike Richards, didn't start out looking to hire high-risk employees. Instead, they first tried to follow the conventional wisdom of hiring only the best and brightest. The problem was, however, that they simply couldn't find enough "qualified" workers from this pool who were interested in working long hours for relatively low wages. Unfilled jobs and high turnover eventually forced the owners to look elsewhere for employees, and in near-desperation, they took a big chance on hiring one applicant who was undergoing treatment for alcohol abuse.

As it turned out, because he had few other opportunities, he greatly valued his job and was very appreciative of the Richards' trust. He ended up eventually becoming a highly committed and valuable employee. Because of this positive experience, the Richards subsequently began to systematically and routinely recruit and hire high-risk employees, and these individuals are now the foundation of Candleworks' workforce.

Similarly, Ken Legler, owner of Houston Wire Works, a Texas-based enterprise, has also been experiencing a major labor shortage. Legler's solution has been to tap into a works program sponsored by the Texas Department of Corrections. Depending on the situation, convicts may be bused to and from a work site, or work may instead be shipped to and from a prison. Convicts receive training in how to perform the necessary work and are paid (usually at the minimum wage rate) for their work.

But not all employers use high-risk employees purely out of necessity. For example, Microboard Processing, Inc., a small New England electronics firm, makes giving troubled people a second chance a basic part of its business philosophy. Microboard Processing, or MPI, is owned and managed by Craig Hoekenga. Mr. Hoekenga has always had a strong sense of social responsibility and believes that his very best way of making a contribution to society is by offering second chances to high-risk employees.

Indeed, almost one-third of MPI's employees today might be classified as high risk and include former welfare recipients, people who never held a steady job before, convicted felons, and former drug addicts. And Hoekenga insists that at least 10 percent of the firm's new hires each year be from one of these high-risk categories. Although the firm also hires plenty of "conventional" employees— those with respectable backgrounds and solid work histories—Hoekenga considers his high-risk workers to be the backbone of the company.

For example, Ruth Tinney recently applied for employment at MPI. At the time of her application, she had not worked for several years and had spent the three previous years on welfare. Hoekenga gave her a two-week trial, and now she has a regular position as an assembly-line worker. He can also point to numerous other success stories throughout his business and can describe many former employees who were essentially rehabilitated while working at MPI but who then left for jobs elsewhere—for advancement opportunities, to relocate to another part of the country, and so forth.

But not all of his new hires succeed, of course. He estimates that two or three out of every ten he hires eventually fail. For example, one former drug addict who had worked at the firm for more than a year recently returned to drug abuse and went back to jail. Hoekenga also points out that he has to give newly hired high-risk employees a while to learn the ropes. Many, for example, have never held a steady job and do not understand or appreciate the need for regular and prompt attendance. Consequently, they may tend to come in late for work and/or not show up regularly.

Therefore, MPI allows them considerable latitude in absenteeism and tardiness during the first few weeks. Each instance of tardiness or absenteeism is followed by a conversation with Hoekenga or a supervisor who stresses the need for punctual and regular work schedules and focuses on the need for improvement. MPI's goal is to teach its high-risk employees proper work habits during the first six months of employment. After that time the firm takes a much harder line and cuts people less and less slack. But the ones who do make it feel an especially strong sense of loyalty and appreciation toward Hoekenga and his company and make enormous contributions to the firm's continuing profitability and growth.

Case Questions

1. What do you see as the major advantages and disadvantages of hiring high-risk employees?

2. What differences in employment strategies exist between firms like Candleworks and MPI?

3. The examples cited in this case are generally smaller businesses. How might a big corporation like IBM or Ford go about using high-risk employees?

Sources: "Worker Shortage Forces Small Businesses into Creative Hiring," *USA Today*, October 30, 1998, pp. 1B, 2B; "Making Risky Hires into Valued Workers," *Wall Street Journal*, June 19, 1997, pp. B1, B2.

Building Human Resource Management Skills

Purpose: The purpose of this exercise is to provide students with insights into the strengths and weaknesses of the employment interview as a selection technique.

Step 1: Your instructor will divide the class into groups of three. If there are one or two extra students, they can join an existing group.

Step 2: The three members of each group should select a job with which they all have some basic familiarity, for example, a counter person at a fast-food restaurant such as McDonald's, a retail clerk at an apparel store such as The Gap or Limited, or an attendant at a convenience store.

Step 3: Working together, discuss the basic selection criteria that the organization is most likely to employ in selecting someone to perform the job identified in step 2.

Step 4: Randomly select (tossing coins, drawing names from a cap, and so on) one person to play the role of manager, one to play the role of job applicant, and one to be the observer (if a group has four members, there will be two observers).

Step 5: The manager should conduct a brief (about ten minutes) interview with the job applicant. The manager should attempt to focus on assessing the applicant regarding the criteria identified in step 3. The applicant can provide hypothetical answers to questions but should attempt to be realistic and consistent in answering questions.

Step 6: At the end of the interview, the observer(s) should first comment on his/her perceptions of the effectiveness of the interview, noting the quality of the questions asked and the appropriateness of the answers elicited. Then the manager and applicant should comment on how they felt during the interview.

Ethical Dilemmas in Human Resource Management

Assume that after working for several years you returned to graduate school to take some advanced courses and earn a master's degree as a way of improving both your specific job skills and your overall prospects for career advancement. Although your degree program was relatively technical in nature, you did take a course in industrial psychology. One of the topics covered in this course was personality testing and measurement. As a term paper for this course, you thoroughly studied and reviewed the most popular personality tests used by companies as selection techniques.

You recently completed your degree and are now looking for a new position. Your are especially interested in working for one particular company, and this firm is also actively considering you. As part of its selection process, the firm has requested that you complete a battery of tests, including some personality measures. Because you (1) understand these tests so well and (2) have a good understanding of the type of person the firm is looking for, you know that you can answer the questions in the personality measure so as to make you a near-perfect candidate for the job. On the other hand, you also know that the personality traits the company is seeking, and on which you can score highly, are not exactly descriptive of your own personality. But you also believe that you are so highly motivated that you will excel if given the right opportunity.

Questions

1. What are the ethical issues in this situation?

2. What are the basic arguments for and against "cheating" on the personality tests?

3. What do you think most job seekers would do? What would you do?

Human Resource Internet Exercise

Assume that you are interested in seeking a new job. Identify five large companies for whom you think you might be interested in working. If you don't want to work for a big company, simply select five major companies with which you have some basic familiarity and then imagine that you are a job seeker who might be interested in them. Next write a brief description of how you seek and gain employment with each one through "traditional" methods—writing the firm, scheduling an appointment for an interview, and so on.

Next visit their Web sites and see how they deal with "employment opportunities." Do not actually submit application materials to any of the firms (unless, of course, you are genuinely interested in working there!). Go as far as you can, however, into their application/preemployment options and menus and learn as much as you can about their Internet-based recruiting and selection methods and techniques.

Questions

1. As a job seeker, which approach—traditional or Internet based—made you feel more interested in each firm?

2. As a job seeker, what are the relative advantages and disadvantages of each approach?

3. From a company's perspective, what do you see as the relative advantages and disadvantages of each approach?

Notes

1. See Neal Schmitt and Ivan Robertson, "Personnel Selection," *Annual Review of Psychology*, Vol. 41, 1990, pp. 289–319.

2. "Auto Plants, Hiring Again, Are Demanding Higher-Skilled Labor," *Wall Street Journal*, March 11, 1994, pp. A1, A4.

3. Wendy Dunn, Michael Mount, Murray Barrick, and Deniz Ones, "Relative Importance of Personality and General Mental Ability in Managers' Judgments of Applicant Qualifications," *Journal of Applied Psychology*, Vol. 80, No. 4, 1995, pp. 500–509.

4. Michael Stevens and Michael Campion, "The Knowledge, Skill, and Ability Requirements for Teamwork: Implications for Human Resource Management," *Journal of Management*, Vol. 20, No. 2, 1994, pp. 503–530.

5. Murray R. Barrick and Michael K. Mount, "The Big Five Personality Dimensions and Job Performance: A Meta-analysis," *Personnel Psychology*, Vol. 44, 1991, pp. 1–26.

6. Orlando Behling, "Employee Selection: Will Intelligence and Conscientiousness Do the Job?" *Academy of Management Executive*, February 1998, pp. 77–87.

7. John E. Hunter and R. F. Hunter, "Validity and Utility of Alternative Predictors of Job Performance," *Psychological Bulletin*, Spring 1984, pp. 72–98.

8. Craig J. Russell, J. Mattdson, S. E. Devlin, and D. Atwater, "Predictive Validity of Biodata Items Generated from Retrospective Life Experience Essays," *Journal of Applied Psychology*, Vol. 75, 1990, pp. 569–580. See also Margaret A. McManus and Mary L. Kelly, "Personality Measures and Biodata: Evidence Regarding Their Incremental Predictive Value in the Life Insurance Industry," *Personnel Psychology*, Vol. 52, 1999, pp. 137–146.

9. See "Can You Tell Applesauce from Pickles?" *Forbes*, October 9, 1995, pp. 106–108 for a variety of examples.

10. John E. Hunter, "Cognitive Ability, Cognitive Aptitudes, Job Knowledge, and Job Performance," *Journal of Vocational Behavior*, Vol. 29, 1986, pp. 340–362.

11. Arthur R. Jensen, *Bias in Mental Testing* (New York: Free Press, 1980).

12. Michael K. Mount and Murray R. Barrick, *Manual for the Personal Characteristics Inventory* (Iowa City, Iowa: Author, 1995).

13. Daniel P. O'Meara, "Personality Tests Raise Questions of Legality and Effectiveness," *HRMagazine*, January 1994, pp. 97–104.

14. See Leaetta M. Hough, "The Big Five Personality Variables-Construct Confusion: Description versus Prediction," *Human Performance*, Vol. 5, 1992, pp. 139–155 vs. J. E. Hunter and R. F. Hunter, "Validity

and Utility of Alternative Predictors of Job Performance," *Psychological Bulletin*, Vol. 96, 1984, pp. 72–98.

15. "Employers Score New Hires," *USA Today*, July 9, 1997, pp. 1B, 2B.

16. Paul R. Sackett, "Integrity Testing for Personnel Selection," *Current Directions in Psychological Science*, Vol. 3, 1994, pp. 73–76.

17. R. C. Hollinger and J. P. Clark, *Theft by Employees* (Lexington, Mass.: Lexington Books, 1983).

18. U.S. Congress, Office of Technology Assessment, *The Use of Integrity Tests for Pre-employment Screening* (Washington, D.C.: U.S. Government Printing Office, 1990); S.W. Gilliland, "Fairness from the Applicant's Perspective: Reactions to Employee Selection Procedures," *International Journal of Selection and Assessment*, Vol. 3, 1995, pp. 11–19.

19. Michael McDaniel, Deborah Whetzel, Frank Schmidt, and Steven Maurer, "The Validity of Employment Interviews: A Comprehensive Review and Meta-Analysis," *Journal of Applied Psychology*, Vol. 79, No. 4, 1994, pp. 599–616.

20. "Think Fast!" *Forbes*, March 24, 1997, pp. 146–151.

21. Michael A. McDaniel, Deborah L. Whetzel, Frank L. Schmidt, and Steven D. Maurer, "The Validity of Employment Interviews: A Comprehensive Review and Meta-analysis," *Journal of Applied Psychology*, Vol. 79, 1994, pp. 599–616.

22. See Thomas Dougherty, Daniel Turban, and John Callender, "Confirming First Impressions in the Employment Interview: A Field Study of Interviewer Behavior," *Journal of Applied Psychology*, Vol. 79, No. 5, 1994, pp. 659–665.

23. Paul Falcone, "Getting Employers to Open up on a Reference Check," *HRMagazine*, July 1995, pp. 58–63. See also "Internet Gives Boost to New Style of Reference-Checking, *USA Today*, April 1, 1999, p. 1A.

24. "Think Fast!" *Forbes*, March 24, 1997, pp. 146–151.

25. Richard Campbell and Douglas Bray, "Use of an Assessment Center as an Aid in Management Selection," *Personnel Psychology*, Autumn 1993, pp. 691–698.

26. Annette C. Spychalski, Miguel A. Quinones, Barbara B. Gaugler, and Katja Pohley, "A Survey of Assessment Center Practices in Organizations in the United States," *Personnel Psychology*, Spring 1997, pp. 71–82.

27. Justin Martin, "So, You Want to Work for the Best . . . ," *Fortune*, January 12, 1998, pp. 77–85.

28. Carla Johnson, "Talking Dollars: How to Negotiate Salaries with New Hires," *HRMagazine*, July 1998, pp. 73–80.

Enhancing Motivation and Performance

CHAPTER 8
Performance Management

CHAPTER 9
Training, Development,
and Organizational
Learning

CHAPTER 10
Career Planning and
Development

8

Performance Management

CHAPTER OUTLINE

Why Organizations Conduct Performance Appraisals
The Importance of Performance Appraisal
Goals of Performance Appraisal

The Performance Appraisal Process
The Role of the Organization
The Role of the Rater
The Role of the Ratee
Who Performs the Performance Appraisal?

Methods for Appraising Performance
Ranking Methods
Rating Methods

Understanding the Limitations of Performance Appraisal

Performance Management and Providing Feedback
The Feedback Interview
Archiving Performance Management Results

Performance Management and Follow-up Measures

Evaluating the Performance Appraisal and Management Processes

CHAPTER OBJECTIVES

After studying this chapter you should be able to:

■ Describe the purposes of performance appraisal in organizations.

■ Summarize the performance appraisal process in organizations.

■ Identify and describe the most common methods that managers use for performance appraisal.

■ Discuss the limitations of performance appraisal in organizations.

■ Describe how managers should provide performance feedback.

■ Discuss performance management and follow-up measures.

■ Identify and discuss performance appraisal follow-up measures that are often used.

W hat do AT&T, Allied Signal, Dupont, Honeywell, Boeing, Intel, Texaco, UPS, Xerox, and FedEx have in common? They were among the first adopters and are today comprehensive users of an interesting new method for evaluating the performance of managers. This approach is generally called 360-degree feedback.

Until just the last few years, in most companies an individual's performance was typically evaluated by the employee's direct supervisor. Unfortunately, adhering strictly and narrowly to this approach tended to focus only on a single perspective of performance—the perspective of the supervisor—and was approached in an autocratic and controlling manner. But several enlightened companies, including those identified above, began to recognize the shortcomings of the standard approach and started seeking better alternatives. They eventually all ended up at pretty much the same spot—an approach relying on evaluation and feedback from all sides of the employee's position in the organization: above, below, and beside—and sometimes even outside the organization.

Because this network of evaluators essentially "surrounds" the individual's position, this approach was quickly named 360-degree feedback. At first most companies that adopted this new approach made it only a secondary part of their formal performance appraisal systems. Indeed, the most common method was to continue to use traditional supervisory evaluations as the formal performance appraisal mechanism but to provide the 360-degree feedback as purely developmental information. In most cases, for example, only the individual being evaluated saw this information.

"How could having more raters than merely one's superior make the appraisal process any worse?"

(unidentified manager at a firm using 360-degree feedback)*

More recently, however, some firms have started going beyond straightforward development with their 360-degree feedback programs and now include more of an evaluative component as well. AT&T and Boeing, for example, now make 360-degree feedback a major part of their performance appraisal systems. Other firms have experimented with different approaches to incorporating 360-degree feedback into performance appraisal. One common method used today is to rely on the 360-degree process to identify those at the extremes—the very best and the very worst performers. Those in the middle are not differentiated. The traditional supervisory appraisal is then used to differentiate among these individuals.

But some firms are going still further with the 360-degree approach. At FedEx, for example, any manager who receives a total score from his or her 360-degree evaluation below a specified cutoff in two consecutive rating cycles is relieved of supervisory responsibilities. Although this approach might strike many managers as a bit extreme, it nevertheless clearly illustrates the variety of philosophies that companies use when trying to find better ways to assess the performance of their employees and managers.

Leanne Atwater and David Waldman, "Accountability in 360-Degree Feedback," *HRMagazine*, May 1998, pp. 96–104 (*quote on p. 104); David Waldman, Leanne Atwater, and David Antonioni, "Has 360-Degree Feedback Gone Amok?" *Academy of Management Executive*, Vol. 12, No. 2, 1998, pp. 86–94.

T he fact that so many major corporations—indeed, a veritable Who's Who of corporate America, including an estimated 90 percent of *Fortune* 1,000 corporations—seem so enamored with 360-degree feedback clearly underscores the importance of feedback in general and performance feedback in particular. This feedback serves a variety of purposes and makes potentially significant contributions to companies and individual employees alike. Indeed, we can almost think of performance-related feedback as being like a ship's navigational system. Without such a system, the ship's captain would have no way of knowing where the ship was, where it had come from, and where it was heading. Similarly, without an effective performance management system, organization's and individual employees would have no way of knowing how well they were doing or where improvements might be needed. This chapter is about performance management systems in general and its key component, performance appraisal, in particular.

Performance appraisal is the specific and formal evaluation of an employee in order to determine the degree to which the employee is performing his or her job effectively. Some organizations actually use the term *performance appraisal* for this process, whereas others prefer to use terms such as *performance evaluation, performance review, annual review, employee appraisal,* or *employee evaluation.* **Performance management** refers to the more general set of activities carried out by the organization to change (improve) employee performance. Although performance management typically relies heavily upon performance appraisals, performance management is a broader and more encompassing process and is the ultimate goal of performance appraisal activities.

■ **Performance appraisal** is the specific and formal evaluation of an employee in order to determine the degree to which the employee is performing his or her job effectively.

■ **Performance management** is the general set of activities carried out by the organization to change (improve) employee performance.

WHY ORGANIZATIONS CONDUCT PERFORMANCE APPRAISALS

P erhaps surprisingly, most people actually involved in performance appraisals are to varying degrees dissatisfied with them. This is true for both the person being rated and the person doing the rating. We discuss some of the major reasons for this dissatisfaction in this chapter. But the fact that performance appraisals are so widely used in spite of this dissatisfaction is a strong indicator that managers believe that the appraisals are important and that they play a meaningful role in organizations. In fact, managers conduct performance appraisals for various reasons. There are also a number of goals that organizations hope to achieve with performance appraisals.[1]

The Importance of Performance Appraisal

As just noted, although most managers may be unhappy with various facets of the performance appraisal process, they agree that such appraisals are nevertheless very important. One reason that appraisals are so important is that they provide a benchmark so that organizations can better assess the quality of their recruiting and selection processes. That is, recall from earlier chapters that the organization endeavors to recruit and select high-quality employees who are capable of working effectively toward accomplishing the organization's goals. Performance appraisal helps managers assess the extent to which they are indeed recruiting and selecting the most appropriate employees.

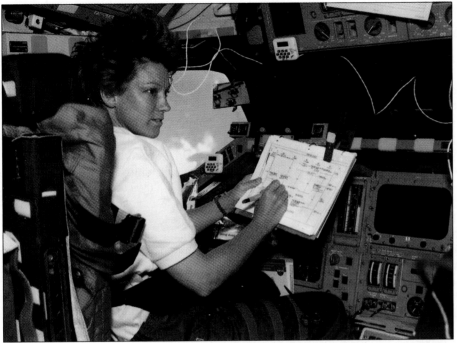

While organizations conduct performance appraisals for a variety of reasons, most experts agree on their importance of helping an organization identify those individuals most deserving of advancement and promotion. For example, consider the case of Eileen Collins, the first woman commander of a U.S. space shuttle mission. While the actual mission itself made international headlines, Collins could only have gotten to that position as a result of a long career of successful advancement from, for example, test pilot to admission to the astronaut training program to selection as a copilot. A long-standing record of very positive performance appraisals, no doubt, facilitated Collins's advancement.

In addition, as discussed in Chapter 9, performance appraisal plays an important role in training. Organizations frequently find it necessary and/or beneficial to invest in their employees by providing them with additional training and development activities and opportunities. This training and development is intended to help employees improve their performance. Performance appraisal is therefore needed to first assess the current level of performance exhibited by employees and, second, to subsequently determine the extent to which this level of performance improves or increases as a result of the training and development. That is, if training and development are presumed to improve the performance of those employees who participate, information from performance appraisals is helpful in verifying whether—and by how much—performance does indeed improve as a result.

Performance appraisal is also important because it is—or at least should be—fundamentally linked to an organization's compensation system. In theory, organizations usually prefer to provide greater rewards to higher performing employees and lesser rewards to lower performing employees. In order to provide this compensation on a fair and equitable basis, however, the organization needs to really be able to differentiate between its higher and its lower performing employees. Managers want to know that they are giving the appropriate rewards to employees for appropriate reasons. Performance appraisal plays a big role in this process.

In addition, performance appraisal is important for legal reasons. Organizations must be able to demonstrate that their promotions, transfers, discharges, and reward allocations are based on merit, as opposed to some discriminatory factor such as gender or race. Performance appraisal, therefore, is the mechanism by which the organization can provide this documentation. Managers must be able to rely on performance appraisal information to demonstrate that all of their important employment-related decisions have been based on the actual performance of those affected by the decisions. Without proper

HUMAN RESOURCES Legal Brief

An End to Age Discrimination Lawsuits?

 The Age Discrimination and Employment Act (ADEA) prohibits age discrimination against people over the age of forty. As noted in Chapter 3, age discrimination claims are declining, in part perhaps because organizations simply need everyone they can employ and perhaps in part because organizations are becoming more aware of this law and ethical issues associated with employment relationships with older workers. One additional contributing factor is that the courts are dismissing more claims on the premise that an employment action does not necessarily violate this law just because older workers are disproportionately affected.

The most frequent basis for dismissing claims to date relates to skills. Suppose, for example, that a firm decides to reduce the size of its workforce by 10 percent. Further suppose that the firm makes decisions about who will be retained and who will lose their jobs on the basis of who has the most up-to-date skill levels. If it turns out that on objective bases older workers tend to have weaker and/or fewer skills, that group will thus be adversely affected by layoff decisions. But the courts seem increasingly inclined to rule that that's okay as long as the firm is truly using job-related criteria. Organizations, meanwhile, can then rely on well-developed performance appraisal and

"Decisions based on criteria which merely tend to affect workers over the age of 40 more adversely than workers under 40 are not prohibited."

(a federal appeals court judge)*

performance management techniques and systems to demonstrate that their actions are indeed job related.

For example, two applicants for flight attendant jobs with United Airlines were rejected on the basis of their weight. They sued United under the ADEA, charging that weight limits adversely affect older workers. But the courts rejected this claim on the basis that weight was a valid criteria for the job of flight attendant, with age an incidental by-product. Similar cases have come up regarding engineering and technical skills. It stands to reason that, all else being equal, younger workers who more recently were in school may have skills that are more current than those of older workers who may not have kept up with recent developments in the field.

Basically, the courts have concluded that individuals who bring age discrimination suits against employers must do more than just demonstrate disparate impact. Instead, these individuals must show that their employer intentionally discriminated against them because of their age, not because of some job-related criterion that happened to correlate with age.

References: "Age-Bias Suits May Become Harder to Prove," *Wall Street Journal*, February 20, 1997, pp. B1, B10 (*quote on p. B1); "As Workers Grow Old, Age-Bias Lawsuits Decline," *USA Today*, June 26, 1998, p. B1.

performance appraisal, an organization is subject to concerns or charges that there is at the least the impression that promotions and other rewards may be based on some factor or factors other than actual performance. "Human Resources Legal Brief" provides more insight into some emerging legal perspectives on these issues.

Further, performance appraisal plays an important role in employee motivation and development. Most people want to know how well they are doing something so that they can correct their deficiencies, capitalize on their strengths, and improve their overall contributions to their job. And again, it is performance appraisal that provides this information to employees. An individual who is told that he or she is doing very well on three dimensions of job performance but needs to improve a fourth dimension recognizes how managers see her or him and knows where to allocate additional developmental work and effort in the future.[2]

Finally, performance appraisal provides valuable and useful information to the organization's human resource planning process. Recall from our discussion in Chapter 5 that assessing the current supply of human resources is an important element in human resource planning. The supply of human resources, however, is most effectively conceptualized from the standpoint of the quality of those human resources. For example, from the standpoint of the actual number of employees needed, an organization may have enough people on its payroll to satisfy its staffing needs. But if many of those individuals are doing a poor job, the organization may need to take a much different approach to its future recruiting and selection activities than if all employees are doing an excellent job. Likewise, knowing the distribution of qualified employees within the organizational system is an important factor for managers to be aware of. And it is performance appraisal that helps provide this information for managers.

Goals of Performance Appraisal

Given the importance of performance appraisal, as documented in the preceding section, the goals of performance appraisal are almost self-evident. For example, a basic goal of any appraisal system is to provide a valid and reliable measure of employee performance along all relevant dimensions. That is, the appraisal results should reflect the true picture of who is performing well and who is not, as well as indicate the areas of specific strengths and weakness for each person being rated. We should note, though, that it is extremely difficult to really assess the extent to which an appraisal system accomplishes this goal. Furthermore, and more critically, it is probably most important that employees have confidence that the appraisals are reliable and accurate. In other words, since managers cannot be absolutely sure that appraisals really reflect true levels of performance, organizations should not forget the importance of perceptions of accuracy and fairness. We would assume that if appraisals are accurate and meaningful, they will be perceived as such, but it is the perceptions that probably matter the most![3]

Another goal of appraisals is to provide information in a form that is useful and appropriate for the organization with regard to human resource planning, recruiting and selection, compensation, training, and the legal context. This information can help the organization ensure that it is not guilty of discriminating against employees on the basis of some nonrelevant factor such as gender, age, or ethnicity. Therefore, this goal of performance appraisal specifically and most directly relates to the organization's ability to document any employment-related decisions based on supposed or presumed performance.

But the ultimate goal for any organization using performance appraisals is to be able to improve performance on the job. This goal, moreover, actually has two parts. First, the organization needs to be able to use performance appraisals for decision making. The relevant decisions might include deciding who gets fired, who gets promoted, and how much money employees are paid. The second part of this goal relates to motivation. That is, the appraisal should provide employees with information about their strengths and weaknesses so that they can work to become more effective on the job. These two considerations serve the larger goal of improving performance by affecting motivation. Managers can generally assume that when employees get feedback about areas that need improvement, they will be motivated to make these improvements if they recognize that improving their performance will improve their chances to get promoted, to get a pay increase, or to achieve some other important outcome or benefit. At the same time, employees should also gain a clear understanding of where they stand relative to the organization's expectations of them vis-à-vis their performance.

> **THE BOTTOM LINE** All managers need to understand and appreciate both the importance of performance appraisal as well as the various goals associated with effective performance appraisal. Moreover, human resource managers can best serve their role as a center of expertise by ensuring that everyone in the organization has confidence in the performance appraisal systems used and that performance appraisals fulfill their goals.

THE PERFORMANCE APPRAISAL PROCESS

A number of things must happen for the performance appraisal process to be successful. Some of these things should be done by the organization, some by the rater(s) (the individual[s] who will be conducting the performance appraisal), and in many organizations, some by the ratee (the individual whose performance is actually being evaluated). In addition, there should be follow-up and discussion associated with the process. Although some of this follow-up and discussion may be more accurately considered performance management rather than performance appraisal, it is still an integral part of how organizations manage the entire process. Figure 8.1 illustrates the actual performance management system of one major corporation. Although some firms might make minor modifications to better reflect their philosophies, most organizations follow these general steps. The *performance appraisal* part of this overall process is highlighted and serves as the framework for much of the discussion that follows. In later sections of this chapter we address and discuss the remaining parts of the process.

The Role of the Organization

The organization, primarily through the work of its human resource function, develops the general performance appraisal process for its managers and employees to use. One of the first considerations is how to use the information gained from performance appraisals. Will it be used for developmental feedback only, for example, or will decisions about merit pay and/or other outcomes be based on these ratings as well? It is obviously important that everyone understand exactly what the ratings are to be used for and exactly how they will be used. The organization also generally determines the timing of the performance appraisals. Most organizations conduct formal appraisals only once a year, although some organizations conduct appraisals twice a year or even more frequently for new employees. However frequent the appraisals, the organization and its human resource managers must decide when appraisals will be conducted. The most common alternatives are for appraisals to either be done on the anniversary date of an employee's hiring or for all appraisals throughout the organization to be conducted during a specified time each year.

Conducting appraisals on anniversary dates means spreading out the appraisals over the entire year. Under this system supervisors are not necessarily ever required to complete an excessive number of appraisals at any one time. On the other hand, spreading out the appraisals over the year may make it more difficult to make comparisons among employees. Further, unless managers carefully budget their salary dollars over the entire year, those employees

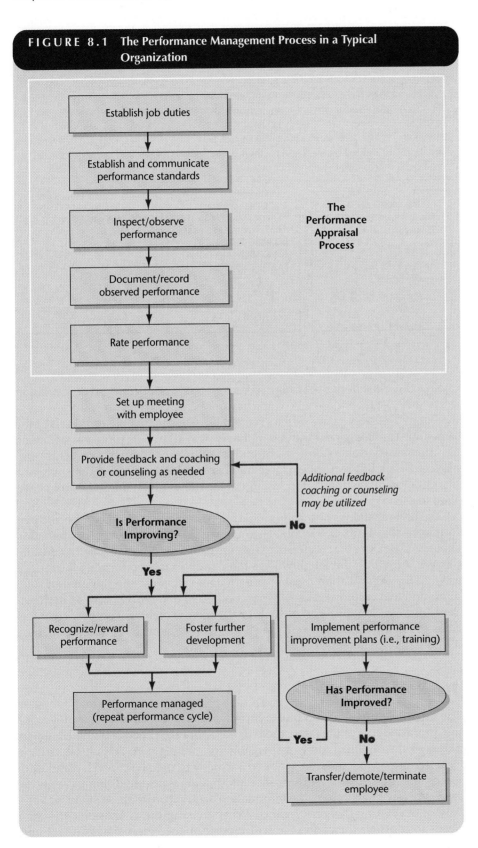

FIGURE 8.1 The Performance Management Process in a Typical Organization

The Lighter Side of HR

A major drawback of annual performance reviews is that some managers tend to be biased by recent behaviors. That is, these managers more clearly remember recent events and may have fuzzier memories of employee behaviors that are several months old. Consequently, in doing performance appraisals of subordinates, these managers may rely more heavily on recent behaviors than older ones. Although few managers will be as blatant as the one shown here, they should recognize that this situation can indeed happen and try their best to take a longer and more complete time perspective into the appraisal process.

reviewed earlier in the year may have a greater opportunity to earn a larger salary increase than those who come toward the end of the year simply because there may be fewer salary dollars remaining. Conducting all appraisals at the same time (probably near the end of the fiscal year) avoids problems of having to ration salary dollars quite as carefully and makes comparisons across employees easier. But requiring a large number of appraisals at one time may also make it more likely that a rater could not devote as much time as might be desired to each appraisal.

The organization is also responsible for ensuring that clear and specific performance standards are available to managers. Moreover, the organization should also ensure that these standards are carefully communicated to the employees. Although this step involves those individuals performing the ratings as well, the organization must ensure that all raters use the same set of standards and that employees know what is expected of them. Otherwise, performance appraisal cannot accomplish its goals, and the organization may create serious problems for itself by creating a disgruntled workforce and/or opening itself up to legal liabilities.

The Role of the Rater

The rater (traditionally and most typically the supervisor of the employee being appraised) plays the largest role in the appraisal process. As noted above, although the organization is responsible for making sure that all raters have clear performance standards, raters will actually have to help develop and learn those standards. Also, as performance information is acquired about a ratee, the rater will have to compare the information acquired with these standards as a way of evaluating the performance. When making these decisions, the rater needs to consider the context in which performance can be factored into the rating so that any extenuating conditions can be taken into consideration. In addition, each ratee will know how he or she is expected to perform the job.

But the rater has a more critical role to play as well. On a day-to-day basis, an employee behaves, or performs, on the job and exhibits many behaviors that might be relevant to performance on that job. The rater's task is to collect information about those behaviors and translate that information into the ratings. Therefore, the rater truly becomes a decision maker who must observe ratee performance and process the information gleaned from that observation. But since most formal appraisals are conducted only once a year, the rater must also somehow store this information in memory and, at the appropriate time, recall what has been stored and use the information to provide a set of ratings. This process is a potentially difficult and time-demanding task.[4] Indeed, as shown in "The Lighter Side of HR," managers may very well distort their appraisals on the basis of the most recent observations of performance rather than a longer-term perspective.

Once ratings have been completed, it is also usually the rater who must then communicate the results and consequences of the appraisal to the ratee. When the results are somewhat negative, conveying the news may be an uncomfortable task and is often stressful for managers. However, an adequate communication process will also include goals for the future and a performance plan for helping the employee improve, thus adding a positive element. This set of activities, of course, is really part of the *performance management* process. Finally, it is the rater who is ultimately responsible for preparing the employee to perform at desired levels. That is, the supervisor must be sure that the employee knows what is required on the job, has the needed skills, and is motivated to perform at the level desired.

The Role of the Ratee

Although attempts to improve appraisals often focus on the organization or the rater, the ratee also has responsibilities in the appraisal process. First, for performance appraisals to work most effectively a ratee should have a clear and unbiased view of his or her own performance. Problems can occur during the appraisal process if disagreement develops between rater and ratee, so both parties must have all the information they can collect about the ratee's performance. This step requires the ratee to gain an understanding about how his or her behavior affects performance and may require the ratee to acquire information about the performance of coworkers. This information should also allow the ratee to be more receptive to feedback from the rater (especially if it is somewhat negative), which also makes it more likely that the ratee would change behavior in response to that feedback.

Who Performs the Performance Appraisal?

Another important aspect of performance appraisal is the determination of who will actually perform it and what information will be used. The most common appraisers are illustrated in Figure 8.2.

As noted earlier, the individual's supervisor is the most likely rater. Supervisors are perhaps the most frequently used source of information in performance appraisal. The assumption that underlies this pattern is that supervisors

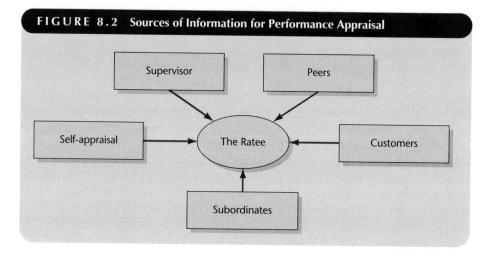

FIGURE 8.2   Sources of Information for Performance Appraisal

usually have the most knowledge of the job requirements and have had the most opportunity to observe employees performing their jobs. In addition, supervisors are usually in a position of being responsible for the performance of their subordinates. Thus the individual supervisor is both responsible for employees' high performance and accountable, perhaps, for their low performance.[5]

At the same time, it should also be recognized that supervisors are not necessarily a perfect source of information. For one thing, a supervisor may not have in-depth job knowledge to the extent that might be expected. For example, if the job has changed dramatically over the last few years owing to new technology or other factors, the supervisor might not be as familiar with the job as might have been the case in the past. Likewise, a supervisor may have been promoted from another part of the organization and may thus have actually never performed the jobs that she or he is supervising. In addition, in some job settings the supervisor may not really have an adequate opportunity to observe the employee performing his or her work. This situation is especially true in outside sales where sales representatives spend much of their time working alone with customers out of the supervisor's view.

But these limitations all relate to the supervisor's *ability* to provide a meaningful appraisal. In addition, we must also consider the question of the supervisor's *motivation* to provide such ratings. Motivational issues are actually involved regardless of who does the appraisal, but it is especially important to realize that supervisors are not always motivated to give the most accurate ratings they can give. For example, the supervisor may be biased (either for or against) the person being rated. Perhaps surprisingly, there is only mixed evidence of systematic bias against members of identifiable groups based on race,[6] age,[7] gender,[8] and disability.[9] Nonetheless, a real possibility exists that a supervisor may be negatively or positively biased toward various workers because of personal liking, attitudes, relationships, and so forth, and as a result, favoritism and/or negative bias may be present.

Before turning to other issues related to rater motivation, one additional perspective on "bias" should be discussed here. Recently, there has been a great deal of interest in what has been termed *contextual performance* and the role it plays in performance appraisals.[10] **Contextual performance** refers to things an employee does on the job that are not required as part of the job but that never-

■ **Contextual performance** refers to things an employee does on the job that are not required as part of the job but still benefit the organization in some way.

theless benefit the organization in some way. These behaviors might include staying late at work, helping coworkers get their work done, or any of the behaviors that benefit the general good of the organization often referred to as *organizational citizenship behaviors*.[11] Since these behaviors are never stated as formal requirements of the job, employees are never formally told that they are expected to do these things. They might be told informally, however, that such behaviors are valued by the organization in general and/or the manager in particular. And, in any event, they *do* benefit the organization and raters *do* consider them as part of their evaluations.[12] Whether these behaviors should be considered a source of bias or not, then, is open to interpretation.

Supervisors might also choose to be inaccurate in their ratings because they feel threatened by a particular subordinate and want to prevent him or her from getting ahead or because the supervisor wants to "get rid" of a problem subordinate and tries to do so by getting that person "promoted" into a different department. In addition, supervisors may be concerned about team member relations and decide to rate all team members the same, regardless of what they deserve, to avoid jealousies or conflict. These and other motivational factors that affect supervisory ratings are discussed by Murphy and Cleveland,[13] but the main point here is to appreciate that supervisors may choose to be inaccurate in their ratings for a wide range of reasons.

Other important potential sources of information for many performance appraisal systems are peers, colleagues, and coworkers. An advantage of using peers in a performance appraisal process is that, by definition, they do have expert knowledge of job content, and they may have more of an opportunity than does the supervisor to observe the performance of a given worker on a day-to-day basis. Peers also have a different perspective on the performance of their work in that they really understand their own opportunities and limitations regarding performance. Both Merck and 3M Corporation use peer evaluations as a major component of their performance appraisal process.

Of course, there is also the possibility that friendship, group norms, and other personal factors may intervene in this situation. And individuals may see their own performance as being significantly different than others perceive it in the group.[14] Also, in some situations coworkers might be competing with each other for a promotion (or some other reward), which may affect their motivation to be accurate in their evaluations. Furthermore, since peers or coworkers remain in a relationship with each other, someone who received poor ratings from his or her coworkers may try to retaliate and rate those coworkers poorly during subsequent evaluations.[15] Nevertheless, peer evaluation is particularly useful in professional organizations such as

One key part of the performance appraisal process is determining who will actually conduct the appraisal. Traditionally, the most common choice for this has been the individual's supervisor. As illustrated here, this approach to performance appraisal generally includes a meeting between the individual being rated and her or his supervisor. Another meeting is also commonly scheduled later to provide feedback to the employee after the performance appraisal is completed.

law firms, architectural firms, and academic departments. In addition, as more and more organizations begin to use work teams for actual production work, peer evaluations are becoming more widely used in those contexts as well.

A third source of information in the performance appraisal process is subordinates of the individual being appraised. Subordinates are an especially important source of information when their own manager's performance is being evaluated, and their opinions are perhaps most useful when the performance appraisal is focused on the manager's leadership potential. That is, if top level managers in an organization are appraising the performance of a certain middle manager on the basis of his or her leadership potential, then the subordinates whom that manager is currently leading are perhaps the best source of information for evaluating that person's performance. Of course, a major problem with using subordinates as input to the performance appraisal process is that doing so may influence the manager's behavior in the sense that she or he may be more focused on making workers happy and satisfied than on encouraging them to perform at a high level.[16]

Yet another source of information in a performance appraisal process is self-evaluation. In many professional and managerial situations, individuals may frequently be asked to evaluate their own performance. The rationale is that, more than any other single person in the organization, an individual is in the best position to understand his or her own strengths and weaknesses and the extent to which he or she has been performing at an appropriate level. Of course, the biggest negative aspect of using self-ratings is that there is a tendency on the part of many people to inflate their own performance.

A final source of information in the performance appraisal system is customers. The dramatic increase in the service sector of the U.S. economy in recent years has resulted in a major push toward the use of customers as a source of information in performance appraisal. The inclusion of customers might be accomplished through such things as having customers fill out feedback forms or respond to mail surveys whenever they receive the services of an organization. Some restaurants, like Red Lobster and Chili's, for example, insert brief feedback forms in their meal-check folders and ask customers to rate the server, the cook, and other restaurant personnel on various characteristics relevant to the meal. The advantage of this method is that customers are the lifeblood of an organization, and it is very helpful to managers to know the extent to which customers feel that employees are doing a good job. On the other hand, this method may be expensive to develop and reproduce and may ignore aspects of the job the customer doesn't see (e.g., cooperation with other employees).

One important thing for any manager to recognize is that each source of performance appraisal information is subject to various weaknesses and shortcomings. Consequently, many organizations find it appropriate and effective to rely on a variety of information sources in the conduct of a performance appraisal. That is, firms may gather information from both supervisors and peers. Indeed, some organizations gather information from all the sources described in this section. This approach, the basis for the opening case, has even gained a new term in the management literature: **360-degree feedback**.

The idea is that organizations that use 360-degree feedback gather performance-rating information from people on all sides of the manager—above, beside, below, and even from outside. By focusing on 360-degree feedback, firms obtain information on each ratee's performance from the perspective

■ **360-degree feedback** is an approach to performance appraisal that involves gathering performance information from people on all sides of the manager—above, beside, below, and even from outside the organization.

POINT/COUNTERPOINT 360-Degree Feedback

A system of evaluation and feedback in which different groups of people evaluate a target employee is called **360-degree feedback**. Typically, an employee might receive ratings and feedback from peers, supervisors, subordinates, and customers or clients. Organizations differ in how they summarize and/or present these data to the employee, and they also differ on whether the ratings are used for feedback only (to be seen only by the employee for his or her own personal development) or whether they are used for decision making as well. In either case the logic is that the employee can learn more about how he or she is viewed by a wider range of people, providing a more complete picture.

POINT . . . Evaluation systems based on 360-degree feedback are useful because . . .	COUNTERPOINT . . . But such systems cause problems because . . .
They provide ratees with information about how they are viewed by other employees.	The ratee then has to determine how to deal with all of this information.
They provide more information for development—working toward improvement by or addressing weaknesses—than any other tool.	They are useful in this respect, but the amount of information transmitted can be overwhelming.
They recognize that different groups of employees are likely to have different perspectives and thus have different views.	These differences must then be reconciled somehow. Whose view does the ratee rely on primarily if the recommendations are in conflict? This situation is especially problematic if the appraisals are to be used for decision making.
Ratings and feedback from different groups can be obtained in areas where each group has special insights (e.g., asking customers about dealing with customers).	Most organizations ask all raters to rate the ratee in all areas.
Ratees tend to view the appraisals as useful and helpful.	They probably need help and guidance (e.g., a coach) in figuring out what to do with the potentially conflicting information.
Important organizational decisions can be based on input from multiple sources.	The original proponents recommended that the ratings be used for feedback only, and we have little data on how effective they are when used for decision making. If evaluations conflict, whose recommendations does the organization rely on for making the decisions?

So . . . Appraisal systems that are based on 360-degree feedback are potentially useful, especially when they are used for feedback purposes only. Almost inevitably when organizations first implement these systems, they are meant to be used for feedback only. However, as time goes by and important decisions must be made, many organizations begin to use these appraisals for decision making as well. In any case the different perspectives are likely to result in different evaluations, and so 360-degree systems are most likely to be effective when the employee has a coach to help interpret and sort out the evaluations. We should note, however, that although these systems are becoming extremely popular, their effectiveness is still not known.

of each source of information. This approach allows organizations to match strengths and weaknesses as well as benefits and shortcomings of each informa- tion and thus gain a more realistic overall view of a person's true performance.[17] It is important to recognize, however, that the feedback from the different sources *should* be inconsistent. Otherwise, there would be no value in obtaining evaluations from different sources. Thus the manager will have to reconcile dif- ferent viewpoints, and the organization probably needs to use these ratings for feedback and development purposes only. If decisions are to be based on these evaluations, the organization will have to decide how to weight the ratings from the different sources.[18] "Point/Counterpoint" provides more details about the strengths and weaknesses of this approach to performance appraisal.

THE BOTTOM LINE Managers need to have a clear understanding of how performance appraisal fits into their organization's overall performance management system. Moreover, managers should also know how the organization, raters, and ratees contribute to the performance appraisal process and the issues involved in determining who should actually conduct performance appraisals.

METHODS FOR APPRAISING PERFORMANCE

A variety of performance appraisal methods and techniques are used in organizations. By their very nature, most appraisals are subjective. That is, we must rely on a rater's judgment of an employee's performance. Subjective evaluations are also prone to problems of bias (some of which are discussed above) and rating errors (which are discussed later in this chapter). Furthermore, raters tend to be uncomfortable passing judgment on employees, and employees generally don't care to be judged in this way. The question, then, is why do we rely on these subjective evaluations. Why not, instead, rely on objective performance information?

Subjective evaluations are far more common than objective performance measures are for several reasons. The biggest reason, however, is relatively simple—for most jobs, and for *all* managerial jobs, there are no straightforward objective measures of performance. For example, it might seem easy to evalu- ate the performance of a bookstore manager, whose performance, it would seem, could be measured by calculating total sales or sales per square foot. But a bookstore in an upscale shopping center is more likely to sell a lot of higher- priced hardcover books than is a bookstore in a rural or economically de- pressed area. If the manager of either store had played a role in choosing the location, this factor might even be relevant. But for large chains such as Barnes & Noble or B. Dalton, the corporation chooses the location. As a result, a major determinant of sales volume is really not under the manager's control, and so sales figures alone do not provide a good source of information about his or her performance. A careful evaluation will almost always result in the ac- knowledgment that many so-called objective measures of performance are based on factors not under the control of the person being evaluated and so are not really good measures of individual performance.

There are, of course, a few instances for which objective data are available and they do reflect factors under the control of the individual employee, such as sales figures for outside sales employees. But in most other cases, organizations have no choice but to rely on judgments and ratings. A great deal of effort has therefore been spent in trying to make these subjective evaluations as meaningful and as useful as they can be. Some of the methods that have been proposed are based on relative rankings, whereas others rely more on absolute ratings.

Ranking Methods

One method of performance appraisal is the simple ranking method. The **simple ranking method** involves having the manager simply rank from top to bottom or best to worst each member of a particular work group or department. The individual ranked first is presumed to be the top performer, the individual ranked second is presumed to be the second best performer, and so forth. The basis for the ranking is generally global or overall performance.

> ■ The **simple ranking method** involves having the manager simply rank from top to bottom or best to worst each member of a particular work group or department.

Advantages of the ranking method are that it is relatively simple and it provides specific performance-rating information for employees. That is, an individual who is ranked second out of five knows exactly where she or he stands relative to the other four members in his or her work group. On the other hand, the ranking method also suffers from some difficulties. One problem is that it is difficult to use for a large number of employees. Another shortcoming of the ranking method is that the basis for the ranking is often subjective and difficult to define. That is, since the rank is actually some overall and general measure of global performance, it does not generally make any allowances for specific attributes or characteristics of performance. As a result, ranking methods are acceptable for making decisions, but they do not provide very useful feedback to employees.

A variation on the ranking method is the paired-comparison method. The **paired-comparison method** of performance appraisal involves comparing each employee with every other employee, one at a time. The individual in each pair that is presumed to be the higher performer is given a one for that particular paired comparison, and the other employee is given a zero. When all possible comparisons have been made, the manager counts the points that have been allotted to each individual. The individual with the most points is deemed to be the top performer in the group; the individual with the next most points is the second-best performer, and so forth. One advantage of this method is that it allows the manager to systematically compare people in a simple and straightforward manner, that is, one person against another. On the other hand, if many people are being evaluated, the number of comparisons that are necessary increases rapidly.

> ■ The **paired-comparison method** of performance appraisal involves comparing each employee with every other employee, one at a time.

Another type of performance appraisal technique is forced distribution, a method that has been in use for many years.[19] The **forced-distribution method** involves grouping employees into predefined frequencies of performance ratings. Those frequencies are determined by the organization in advance and are imposed on the rater. For example, executives might decide that 10 percent of the employees in a work group should be grouped as outstanding; 20 percent as very good; 40 percent as average; 20 percent as below average; and the remaining 10 percent as poor. The manager then classifies each employee into one of these five performance classifications based on the percentage allowable. For example, if the manager has twenty employees, then two of those employees can be put in the top and two in the bottom category; four employees can be put in the second from the top and four in the second

> ■ The **forced-distribution method** involves grouping employees into predefined frequencies of performance ratings.

from the bottom category; and all the rest will fit into the middle category. The forced-distribution method is familiar to many students because it is the basis used by professors who grade on a so-called bell or normal curve.

An advantage of this system is that it results in a normal distribution of performance ratings, which many people see as inherently fair. Also, from the organization's perspective, if employees are to receive merit pay increases, a forced distribution ensures control over how much money is spent on merit pay. On the other hand, the distribution that is being imposed may have no relationship to the "true" distribution of performance in the work group. For example, many more than 10 percent of the employees may be "outstanding," and so the forced distribution may result in perceptions of unfairness and may even result in employees becoming demotivated. Finally, if *all* employees are performing at acceptable levels, the forced-distribution method, as well as the other ranking methods, force the rater to make distinctions that might not really be meaningful. As a result, most organizations rely instead upon some type of absolute judgments and employ a system of performance ratings rather than rankings.

Rating Methods

■ A **graphic rating scale** consists of a statement or question about some aspect of an individual's job performance.

One of the most popular and widely used performance appraisal methods is the graphic rating scale. A **graphic rating scale** simply consists of a statement or question about some aspect of an individual's job performance. Following that statement or question is a series of answers or possible responses from which the rater must select the one that best fits. For example, one common set of responses to a graphic rating scale with five possible alternatives is *strongly*

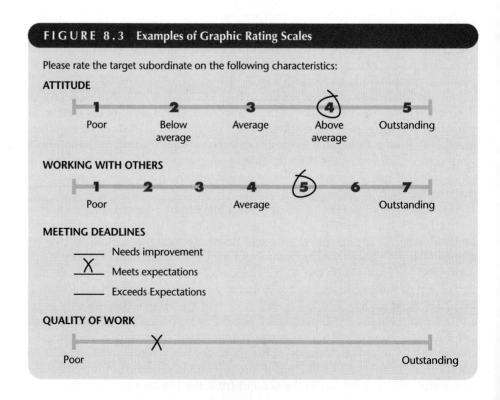

FIGURE 8.3   Examples of Graphic Rating Scales

Please rate the target subordinate on the following characteristics:

ATTITUDE

1	2	3	4	5
Poor	Below average	Average	Above average	Outstanding

WORKING WITH OTHERS

1	2	3	4	5	6	7
Poor			Average			Outstanding

MEETING DEADLINES

_____ Needs improvement
__X__ Meets expectations
_____ Exceeds Expectations

QUALITY OF WORK

Poor   Outstanding

agree, *agree*, *neither agree nor disagree*, *disagree*, and *strongly disagree*. These descriptors or possible responses are usually arrayed along a bar, line, or similar visual representation, and this representation is marked with numbers or letters that correspond to each descriptor.

Figure 8.3 illustrates a few graphic rating scales. One of the appealing features of graphic rating scales is that they are relatively easy to develop. A manager simply needs to brainstorm or otherwise develop a list of statements or questions that are presumably related to indicators of performance that are relevant to the organization. Moreover, a wide array of performance dimensions can be tapped with various rating scales on the same form. Each descriptor on the rating form is accompanied by, as noted, a number or a letter for responses. Most graphic rating scales have a range of one to five or one to seven, although occasionally a scale may use only three or perhaps as many as nine alternatives.

To develop a performance measure, the manager simply adds up the "points" for a particular employee's graphic scale items to obtain an overall index of performance (which is why these are sometimes referred to as "summated ratings"). For example, if an appraisal instrument contains five graphic rating scales and each has a possible range of one to five, then the potential performance scores for an individual can range from a minimum of five (when the individual receives an evaluation of one on each item) to a maximum of twenty-five (when the individual receives a five on each dimension). The specific dimensions measured by graphic rating scales should be based on job analysis, but this discipline is rarely observed. Instead, in order to have a single instrument that can be used with all (or most) employees in an organization, graphic rating scales typically measure performance relative to traits or behaviors such as initiative or problem-solving capabilities, or even attitudes. Also, in some cases the organization might have an overall performance scale in addition to scales for the specific dimensions.

Although they are very popular, graphic rating scales are not without problems. For one thing, managers may tend to simply go down the list of items and circle all the points at one or the other end of the scale. As we will see later, this pattern results in errors of what is called leniency or severity. On the other hand, some managers tend to circle primarily midpoints on the scale. This pattern results in what is called central tendency. In all of these cases, the real problem is a range-restriction limitation. Researchers have also suggested that graphic rating scales are particularly prone to a problem where an evaluation in one area or a general impression about the ratee influences ratings on all scales. This problem, which is also discussed later in the chapter, is usually called halo error. Another shortcoming of the graphic rating scale is that managers tend to perhaps attribute too much precision and objectivity to the results. That is, because numbers can be mathematically added and divided, a person may end up with a score such as 4.25 or 3.65. Thus people may believe that the results are more objective and precise than they actually are.

A somewhat different type of rating instrument involves the use of the **critical-incident method**. A critical incident is simply an example or instance of especially good or poor performance on the part of the employee.[20] Organizations that rely on this method often require raters to recall such instances on the job and then describe what the employee did (or did not do) that led to success or failure. In other cases the managers are asked to keep a log or diary in which they record examples or critical incidents that they believe reflect good and bad performance on the part of specific employees.[21] This technique not

■ The **critical-incident method** relies on instances of especially good or poor performance on the part of the employee.

only provides rich information for feedback to the employee but also defines performance in fairly clear, behavioral terms.

For example, a critical incident for illustrating good performance by a gasoline station attendant might be as follows: "On Monday, January 15, you were observed to have fully restocked certain merchandise counters in the store without being instructed to do so. And you also illustrated very pleasant and service-oriented behavior when dealing with three customers. You handled each customer quickly and efficiently and provided prompt and courteous attention." On the other hand, a critical incident to illustrate less-effective performance for the same job might read: "On Thursday, February 15, you were observed to be sitting behind the counter reading a newspaper when there was merchandise inventory stocking that could have been done. You were also observed to be curt and blunt with several customers. You processed their purchases quickly, but did not really provide any personal attention."

An advantage of the critical-incident method is that it allows managers to provide individual employees with precise examples of behaviors that are thought to be effective and less effective. On the other hand, the critical-incident method requires considerable time and effort on the part of managers to maintain a log or diary of these incidents and may make it difficult to compare one person with another. That is, the sample of behaviors developed from one employee may not be comparable to samples of behavior acquired for another. Nevertheless, there is some reason to believe that maintaining such diaries or logs can help raters in making evaluations and in providing clear feedback regardless of how they use the information from the diaries.[22]

■ **Behaviorally Anchored Rating Scales,** or **BARS**, appraisal systems represent a combination of the graphic rating scale and the critical-incident method.

Another method for appraising performance involves the use of **Behaviorally Anchored Rating Scales,** or **BARS.**[23] BARS appraisal systems (also known at times as "behavioral expectation scales") represent a combination of the graphic rating scale and the critical-incident method. They specify performance dimensions based on behavioral anchors associated with different levels of performance. As shown in the sample BARS in Figure 8.4, the performance dimension has various behavioral examples that specify different levels of performance along the scale.

Developing BARS is a complicated and often expensive process. In general, the managers who will eventually use these scales also develop them. First, the managers must develop a pool of critical incidents that represent various effective and ineffective behaviors on the job. These incidents are then classified into performance dimensions, and the ones that the managers believe represent a particular level of performance are used as behavioral examples, or anchors, to guide the raters when the scales are used. At each step an incident is discarded unless the majority of managers agree on where it belongs or what level of performance the incident illustrates.[24] The manager who then uses the scale has to evaluate an employee's performance on each dimension and determine where on the dimension the employee's performance best fits. The behavioral anchors serve as guides and benchmarks in helping to make this determination.

A significant advantage of BARS is that they dramatically increase reliability by providing specific behavioral examples to reflect effective and less-effective behaviors. Also, managers who develop the scales tend to be committed to using them effectively, and the process of developing the scales actually helps raters develop clearer ideas about what constitutes good performance on the job. On the other hand, a manager might select a point on the scale because one behavior sample reflected by a critical incident happens to closely mirror a specific behavior observed on the part of the employee. Furthermore, the process of developing truly effective BARS is extremely expensive and time-consuming, and so they are rarely used in their pure form. Instead, organizations often adopt some modified BARS procedures in an attempt to reap some of the benefits without incurring the costs.

A related measure of performance is the **Behavioral Observation Scale**, or **BOS**.[25] Like BARS, a BOS is developed from critical incidents. However, rather than only use a sample of behaviors that reflect effective or ineffective behavior, a BOS uses substantially more behaviors to specifically define all the measures that are necessary for effective performance. A second difference between a BOS and BARS is that rather than assessing which behavior best describes an individual's performance, a BOS allows managers to rate the frequency with which the individual employee has exhibited each behavior during the rating period. The manager then averages these ratings to calculate an overall performance rating for the individual. Although the BOS approach avoids the limitations of the BARS approach, the BOS takes even more time and can be even more expensive to develop.

Yet another method of appraising performance organizations is through a **goal-based** or **management by objectives** system.[26] Management by objectives, or MBO, is the most popular term used for this approach, although many companies that use it develop their own label to describe the system in their organization. In an MBO system a subordinate meets with his or her manager, and they collectively set goals for the subordinate for a coming period of time,

■ **A Behavioral Observation Scale, or BOS,** is developed from critical incidents, like BARS, but uses substantially more critical incidents to specifically define all the measures that are necessary for effective performance.

■ A **goal-based** or **management by objectives** system is based largely on the extent to which individuals meet their personal performance objectives.

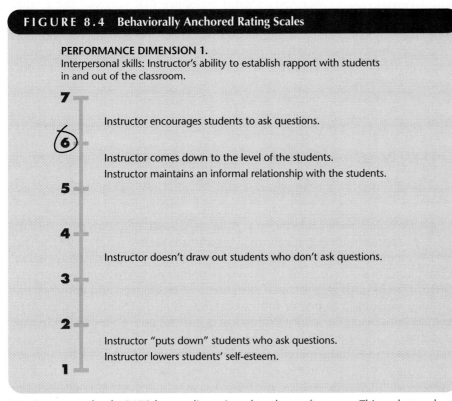

FIGURE 8.4 Behaviorally Anchored Rating Scales

PERFORMANCE DIMENSION 1.
Interpersonal skills: Instructor's ability to establish rapport with students in and out of the classroom.

7 —

(6) — Instructor encourages students to ask questions.

Instructor comes down to the level of the students.
Instructor maintains an informal relationship with the students.

5 —

4 —

Instructor doesn't draw out students who don't ask questions.

3 —

2 —

Instructor "puts down" students who ask questions.
Instructor lowers students' self-esteem.

1 —

Here is an example of a BARS for one dimension of teacher performance. This scale was developed by one of the authors with the students in his class.

usually one year. These goals are usually quantifiable, they are objective, and they are almost always written. During the year the manager and the subordinate periodically meet to review the subordinate's performance relative to attaining the goals. At the end of the year, a more formal meeting is scheduled in which the manager and employee assess the actual degree of goal attainment. The degree of goal attainment then becomes the individual's performance appraisal. That is, if an individual has attained all of his or her goals, then the person's performance is deemed to be very good. Otherwise, the individual is directly responsible for his or her performance deficiency, and the person's performance is judged to be less than adequate or acceptable.

Goal-based systems are often seen as the best alternative for rating performance, but care must be taken when these systems are used. Specifically, the kinds of behaviors that are specified in the goal-setting process are exactly what the employee will tend to focus on. It is therefore critical that these *are* the behaviors the organization really wants to encourage. For example, if a sales representative's goals are stated in terms of dollar volume of sales, he or she might exert a lot of pressure on customers to increase the dollar volume of merchandise they're ordering in a coming period in order to boost his or her performance measures. At the same time, however, the sales representative may hurt the firm's relationship with the customer by applying too much pressure or by encouraging the customer to order more merchandise than is really needed. Thus an important long-term goal may be sacrificed for the achievement of a short-term goal. The only solution to this type of potential problem is to emphasize the need for care in setting goals.

THE BOTTOM LINE   Managers should recognize that they can use a wide array of performance appraisal techniques. Managers should also understand the strengths and weaknesses of each technique so as to make the best choices for their particular situation. Human resource managers will likely play a major role in creating these techniques and then modifying them over time.

U N D E R S T A N D I N G   T H E   L I M I T A T I O N S
O F   P E R F O R M A N C E   A P P R A I S A L

We noted earlier that many people are dissatisfied with performance appraisals in organizations. This attitude stems in part from the various limitations that exist in virtually all performance appraisal techniques. Thus it is important to recognize that no performance appraisal system is perfect. All performance measurement techniques and appraisal approaches are subject to one or more weaknesses or deficiencies.[27] One deficiency is known as projection. **Projection** occurs when we tend to see in others characteristics that we have, which we think contribute to effectiveness. That is, we tend to judge people more like ourselves to be higher performers than we do people who are less like ourselves. The basis for similarity may be demographic characteristics, such as race, sex, or age, or other characteristics, such as the college the individual attended, their personal appearance, or their life style.

■ **Projection** occurs when we tend to see in others characteristics that we have, which we think contribute to effectiveness.

Another performance deficiency that can occur is contrast error. **Contrast error** occurs when we compare people against one another instead of against an objective standard. For example, suppose that a particular employee is in reality a good performer, but not an outstanding one. But if everyone else in that individual's work group is a relatively weak performer, the "average" individual may appear to be a better performer than he or she really is. Likewise, if the same person works in a group of exceptionally strong performers, the person may be seen as a poorer performer than might otherwise be the case.

Managers who conduct performance appraisals are also prone to make what is called distributional errors. A **distributional error** occurs when the rater tends to use only one part of the rating scale. Sometimes the distributional error may be *severity*, which occurs when the manager gives low ratings to all employees by holding them to an unreasonably high standard. The opposite error is *leniency*, which occurs when a manager assigns relatively high or lenient ratings to all employees.[28] Finally, a *central tendency* distributional error occurs when the manager tends to rate all employees as average, using only the middle part of a rating scale.

A final type of rating error is called the halo error and its opposite, the horns error. A **halo error** occurs when one positive performance characteristic causes the manager to rate all other aspects of performance positively. For example, suppose a given employee always comes to work early and is always full of energy and enthusiasm at the beginning of the workday. The manager may so appreciate this behavior that he or she ends up giving the employee a high performance rating on all other aspects of performance, even when those other aspects may really be only average or merely adequate.[29] The opposite of a halo error is the **horns error**. In this instance the manager tends to downgrade other aspects of an employee's performance because of a single performance dimension. For example, the manager who believes that a given employee does not dress appropriately may view that as a negative characteristic of the individual's performance. As a result, the manager may also give the individual low performance ratings on other performance dimensions when higher ratings might be justified.

Given these limitations, organizations might be advised to take reasonable and appropriate steps to reduce rating error. One method for doing so is to train managers to overcome these weaknesses. For example, sometimes simply pointing out to managers their tendency to commit distributional errors or contrast errors may be sufficient to enable those managers to do a better job. A related method for improving the accuracy of performance evaluations is so-called rater-accuracy training. This approach, which is also called frame-of-reference training, attempts to emphasize for managers the fact that performance is multidimensional and to train those managers with the actual content of various performance dimensions.[30]

Finally, as noted earlier in the chapter, even if raters can be trained to avoid errors and to provide accurate ratings, they may simply choose to be inaccurate in the ratings they give. Therefore, organizations must do whatever they can to reward raters for doing a good job in performance appraisal and to reinforce the fact that these appraisals are important. Organizations may also have to punish raters who do not take the task seriously. Nevertheless, regardless of the systems an organization puts in place, a rater who really wants to be inaccurate or unfair can probably find a way to do so. Thus the organization needs to do whatever it can to convince raters that doing the best job they can in appraising performance is in their own best interests.

> ■ **Contrast error** occurs when we compare people against one another instead of against an objective standard.

> ■ A **distributional error** occurs when the rater tends to use only one part of the rating scale.

> ■ A **halo error** occurs when one positive performance characteristic causes the manager to rate all other aspects of performance positively.

> ■ A **horns error** occurs when the manager downgrades other aspects of an employee's performance because of a single performance dimension.

THE BOTTOM LINE   Managers should be aware of the various limitations and errors that are associated with each common performance appraisal technique. The organization should also take appropriate steps to address these limitations and errors. The human resource function, in its role as a center of expertise, can help educate managers about these issues and help minimize the impact of the limitations and errors on people in the organization.

PERFORMANCE MANAGEMENT AND PROVIDING FEEDBACK

As noted at the beginning of this chapter, performance appraisal is a part of a broader process called performance management. As illustrated in Figure 8.1, after performance appraisal is completed, the next major activity is the provision of feedback, coaching, and counseling. Many managers do a poor job in this area, in part because they don't understand how to do it properly and in part because they don't enjoy it. Almost by definition performance appraisal in many organizations tends to focus on negatives, and as a result, managers may have a tendency to avoid giving feedback because they know an employee who gets negative feedback may be angry, hurt, discouraged, or argumentative. But clearly, if employees are not told about their shortcomings, they have no reason to try to improve and have no guidance concerning how to improve. Therefore, a rater must follow up on the appraisal by providing feedback to the employee. Moreover, there are techniques managers can use that can be done to improve the performance feedback process.

The Feedback Interview

One method of improving performance feedback is to provide feedback on a regular basis via feedback interviews. Instead of just providing feedback annually in concert with the performance appraisal interview, it might be more appropriate for managers to remember to provide feedback on an ongoing basis. Feedback might be provided on a daily or weekly basis, depending on the nature of the job, and should focus on various characteristics of performance, including both effective and less-effective performance.[31] In fact, if managers remember that the goal of performance management is to change behavior, they should also recognize the fact that they are clearly more likely to effect change with more frequent feedback.

Another useful method for improving performance feedback is to have the individual appraise his or her own performance in advance of an appraisal interview. This approach involves having employees think about their own performance over the rating period; it helps sensitize them to areas where they have done both a good job and a less-effective job. This technique also lends efficiency to the process because the manager and the subordinate may be able to focus most of their time and efforts in a performance appraisal interview on those areas of performance assessment where there is disagreement. That is, if the manager and the subordinate both agree that certain elements of the subordinate's performance are very good and that certain other elements need improvement, it may be possible to spend little time discussing those and to focus more energy on the performance areas that are in disagreement.

It is also important during a performance feedback interview to encourage participation and two-way communication. Some managers are prone to bring a subordinate in and, in effect, to lecture the subordinate on the outcome of the performance appraisal interview. The basic nature of the meeting, then, involves the manager telling the subordinate how he or she has been evaluated and then concluding the interview. As a result, the subordinate may feel threatened and may feel that she or he had no voice in the process. Participation and two-way dialogue, however, would have allowed the individual to express his or her own feelings and opinions about personal performance levels and to provide other kinds of feedback as appropriate.[32]

In providing performance feedback, it is also important for the manager to try to balance positive and negative feedback. As already noted, many managers tend to focus on the negative. In reality, however, employees are also likely to have many positive characteristics related to performance. Thus although the manager must clearly address the negative performance characteristics noted in the appraisal, these negative attributes should be balanced against praise and recognition of the positive aspects of the employee's performance.

Also, throughout the interview and the performance management process, the manager needs to take a developmental and problem-solving orientation to the process. That is, the manager should not focus on the individual as a person by saying things like "you are a bad employee." Instead the focus should be on providing developmental feedback targeted at behavior performance. A simple distinction between saying things like "you are a poor performer" versus "your performance is not acceptable" can help mediate this process. Thus the focus should be on behavior as opposed to the individual.

Finally, the performance appraisal interview should conclude with a future-oriented discussion of what will happen next. This phase often includes such things as setting goals for correcting performance deficiencies and discussing the possibility of pay raises, promotions, and similar kinds of awards. Of course, if performance is judged to be deficient, the feedback interview may focus on such issues as establishing a probationary period, after which time employment may be terminated, developing a training strategy for improving performance, and so forth. But regardless of the level of present performance, this interview setting should provide a time where the rater and the employee discuss the employee's future performance goals. If the organization is using a goal-based appraisal system, this discussion may be automatic, but even if a different type of appraisal model is used, it is helpful for the employee to have clear and specific goals for improving his or her performance. These goals, along with continued and regular feedback, should constitute the critical part of any performance management program.

Archiving Performance Appraisal and Management Results

It is also important that the organization develop a system for archiving performance appraisal results. That is, the results of the performance appraisal should be stored for easy retrieval. For example, if the individual is being put on probation and told that if her or his performance doesn't improve over the

FIGURE 8.5   Form for Archiving Performance Appraisal Information

Lansdale

hrly EMPLOYEE PERFORMANCE APPRAISAL   _____ 90-DAY   _____ ANNUAL   _____ PROB.

Employee Information

Name:	Reviewer:
Position:	Current Review Period:
Department:	Next Review Date:

Rate the individual in each category below from one to four with four being the highest. Provide supporting comments for all categories.

Category	Rating	Supporting Comments
Quality of Work The extent to which work produced is accurate, thorough and effective	1 2 3 4 ☐ ☐ ☐ ☐	
Job Knowledge The level of understanding of assignments and requirements in order to perform the job duties.	1 2 3 4 ☐ ☐ ☐ ☐	
Team Work The level of cooperation and contribution to a team effort within the department or with other departments. The extent to which the employee makes an extra effort in a rush operation.	1 2 3 4 ☐ ☐ ☐ ☐	
Productivity The volume of work regularly produced. Speed and consistency of output.		
Initiative The degree to which the employee seeks new tasks, makes improvements or suggestions, accepts new responsibilities and strives for self-improvement.		
Safety Adherence to safety procedures, suggestions for safety improvements, helps to minimize risk to self and others and any downtime due to failure to follow procedures.		
Attendance and Availability Available for overtime; reliable attendance record. _____ Days absent _____ Days tardy _____ Days left early		

Overall Rating = _____   (Add score total and divide by 8)

List General Areas of Strength:

Identify Areas to Target for Improvement:

List Goals and Areas to Focus On:

Supervisor's Additional Comments/Summary:

Employee Comments:

This form has been reviewed and discussed with me by my supervisor. My signature acknowledges that I read it and noted any exceptions and additional comments above.

Employee Signature: _____   Date: _____

APPROVALS
Reviewer/Supervisor: _____   Date: _____

Source: Courtesy of Lansdale, Inc.

next six months she or he will be terminated, the manager needs to have access to that information when the next performance appraisal is completed. Ready access to appraisal records is especially important given that subsequent performance appraisals may be conducted by other individuals.

Archiving of performance appraisal results is also important in terms of equal employment opportunity issues. An organization must be able to demonstrate, beyond reasonable doubt, that a given individual employee was sanctioned, rewarded, punished, terminated, or remanded for training on a basis of performance-related reasons rather than nonperformance-related factors such as sex or race. Figure 8.5 shows one method used to archive performance appraisal results. The document includes not only the performance appraisal scales but also various other forms of information, including the action plan for performance improvement. At the end of each appraisal cycle, this form is simply added to the individual employee's file. Thus in the future managers can refer to previous evaluations and have a more complete perspective of the employee's performance history.

THE BOTTOM LINE   Managers must be careful not to neglect a critical part of performance management: providing feedback, coaching, and counseling. Although this process may not always be pleasant, managers can use certain techniques to make it less onerous. The human resource function can not only help managers perform this task more effectively but also help them in archiving the results of performance appraisals for future reference.

PERFORMANCE MANAGEMENT AND FOLLOW-UP MEASURES

A typical outcome of the performance feedback interview is the development of a "plan of action" for the future. If the employee's performance has been good, average, or some similar categorization, the plan typically addresses how the employee can maintain that level in the future while identifying areas where improvements might be made. It is also likely that some sort of reward, usually a pay increase, commensurate with acceptable performance will be given at this time. If the person's performance has been outstanding, exemplary, or some similar categorization, the plan may focus more on development opportunities that might lead to promotion and advancement. And in this case the employee will likely be awarded a larger pay increase and may, in addition, receive other one-time rewards such as a bonus and/or award.

In many cases, however, the employee's performance will be deficient in one or more areas, and actions will be outlined for correcting those problems. Training and development efforts are among the most common. Sometimes the development efforts may be self-imposed. For example, if a sales representative is deemed to be deficient in one aspect of his performance, simply alerting him to that fact and suggesting that he work on doing a better job may be perfectly adequate. If the problem relates to being late for too many sales calls, for instance, he might on his own initiative start being more efficient in setting appointments and making a greater effort to be on time. In other situations, however, the deficiency may be associated with job-related skills and abilities. For example, suppose a recently promoted engineering supervisor is seen by some of the engineers in her group as being too controlling. If her previous technical education and training did not include any management courses, she might be sent to a management seminar dealing with delegation and participative management techniques.

If the individual's performance is judged to be significantly lower than desired, however, more extreme measures might be required. For example, the individual may be told that he or she is being placed on probation and will be terminated at some point in the future if performance does not improve. Of course, this disciplinary follow-up action may be also associated with such nonperformance-related factors as attendance, attitude, and so forth. Regardless of the cause, the manager should very clearly and precisely specify the organization's expectations for the employee, specify a time frame during which these expectations must be met, and outline the consequences that will result if expectations are not met.

Failure to follow such a precise process can result in problems for the organization. For example, if the manager does not closely follow the prescribed steps and/or does not clearly communicate expectations but then decides that the employee should be terminated, the employee may be in a good position to file a wrongful-termination suit. If the employee wins that suit, he or she will get the job back and perhaps even collect financial damages.

Suppose, for example, an employee has been having attendance problems. The follow-up plan might require that the individual not miss more than one day of work over the next six months. The associated characteristics of this process might be a warning that if the employee misses more than one day in the next six months, then he or she is subject to immediate dismissal. At the same time, it would also be clear that if the individual abides by this probationary period for the six-month time frame and does not miss any work, then the threat of possible sanctions is removed, at least for the time being.

EVALUATING THE PERFORMANCE APPRAISAL AND MANAGEMENT PROCESSES

At the beginning of this chapter, we noted the strategic importance of the performance appraisal system. Clearly, the organization must monitor the extent to which it is conducting its performance appraisals effectively, adequately, and appropriately. As with selection, performance appraisal must be free from bias and discrimination.

Beyond this, however, the performance appraisal system must also be doing an effective job of helping the organization identify its strongest performers so that they can be appropriately rewarded and efforts made to retain their employment within the organization. The system should also be identifying low performers so that their deficiencies can be remedied through training or other measures. Periodic audits of the performance appraisal system by trained professionals can be an effective method for assessing the effectiveness and appropriateness of the organization's performance appraisal process.

As part of the performance feedback process, organizations generally try to follow up by providing their top performers with meaningful rewards. While pay raises and bonuses are common rewards, other forms of recognition are also used. For example, the Long Beach Convention & Entertainment Center recognizes its best employees by displaying their names in lights. This very public form of recognition clearly communicates to employees how much the organization values their contributions.

But since performance appraisal feeds into the performance management process and the ultimate goal of this process is to improve performance on the job, if the process is working, managers should be able to see real improvements in organizational performance. This improvement may take the form of fewer errors in production, fewer returns in sales, higher appraisals, or lower levels of absenteeism or turnover. In the long run, however, these outcomes are not critical to the organization unless they translate into some improvement in the firm's performance. That is, if performance appraisal and performance management systems are doing what they were designed to do, the organization as a whole should perform better.

Chapter Summary

Performance appraisal is the specific and formal evaluation of an employee in order to determine the degree to which the employee is performing his or her job effectively. Performance management refers to the more general set of activities carried out by the organization to change (improve) employee performance.

Performance appraisals are important because they help ensure that the recruiting and selection processes are adequate, they play an important role in training, they can help effectively link performance with rewards, they demonstrate that important employment-related decisions have been based on performance, and they can promote employee motivation and development. Performance appraisals also provide valuable and useful information to the organization's human resource planning process. The ultimate goal for any organization using performance appraisals is to be able to improve performance on the job.

The organization, primarily through the work of its human resource function, develops the general performance appraisal process for its managers and employees to use, including issues of timing. The organization is also responsible for ensuring that clear and specific performance standards are available to managers and employees. Both the rater and the ratee have specific responsibilities as well. Raters can include the supervisor, peers, colleagues, coworkers, and subordinates of the individual being appraised;

the individual him- or herself; and customers and clients. When all of these raters are used, the appraisal is called 360-degree feedback.

Several methods can be used to assess performance. Ranking techniques include the simple ranking method, the paired-comparison method, and the forced-distribution method. Rating techniques include graphic rating scales; the critical-incident method; Behaviorally Anchored Rating Scales, or BARS; Behavioral Observation Scales, or BOS; and goal-based or management by objectives systems.

All performance measurement techniques and appraisal approaches are subject to one or more weaknesses or deficiencies. The most common problems include projection, contrast errors, distributional errors, and halos or horns errors. Organizations can take steps that include training and awareness to reduce rating error.

After the performance appraisal, the next major activity is the provision of feedback, coaching, and counseling. One method of improving performance feedback is to provide feedback on a regular basis via feedback interviews. Another useful method for improving performance feedback is to have the individual appraise his or her own performance in advance of an appraisal interview. It is also important during a performance feedback interview to encourage participation and two-way communication and to try to balance positive and negative feedback. Results of appraisals should be stored for future reference.

A typical outcome of the performance feedback interview is the development of a plan of action. This plan should specify what the organization expects the employee to do in the future regarding performance and how the organization is likely to respond. The organization must monitor the extent to which it is conducting its performance appraisals effectively, adequately, and appropriately. As with selection, performance appraisal must be free from bias and discrimination.

Review and Discussion Questions

1. Distinguish between performance appraisal and performance management.

2. Identify and briefly describe the basic steps in performance appraisal.

3. What are the basic goals of performance appraisal?

4. Summarize the roles of the organization, the rater, and the ratee in performance appraisal.

5. Who are the most common raters in the performance appraisal process?

6. Identify and critique the basic methods for performance appraisal.

7. What are the basic limitations and weaknesses of performance appraisal? Relate each to the specific technique(s) it is most likely to affect.

8. From the standpoint of the rater, what specific things might you do to ensure effective performance appraisals?

9. From the standpoint of the ratee, what specific things might you do to increase the chances of a more effective performance appraisal for yourself?

10. How might feedback interviews and meetings be most effectively conducted?

Closing Case

Accelerated Performance Reviews May Improve Retention

Most organizations have traditionally conducted performance appraisals for everyone on a routine schedule of once a year, either the anniversary of their hiring date or one common period during which everyone is evaluated. Having an appraisal at a set time was especially true for new employees, who were told when they started working when their first review would be. Part of the logic underlying this system was that newcomers may be considered to be on "probation" until their first review. In addition, organizations felt that new employees might need an extended period of time to learn the ropes and to have a reasonable time in which to establish their capabilities.

Newcomers often saw value in knowing that they had ample time to learn their jobs before they would be evaluated. But they also knew that because increased compensation and/or promotions were usually tied to performance appraisals, there would be little or no opportunity for them to seek a pay raise or to be given greater job responsibilities until after that first review. Thus the standard review cycle had both pluses and minuses for new employees.

In recent years, though, this cycle has been gradually altered in some firms. And this change has come about in large part because of the tight labor market in certain areas, especially in rapidly growing high-tech firms. Because the highly skilled workers these firms need are well aware of their value to prospective employers, some of the more enterprising and self-assured workers have started requesting—or in some cases demanding—promises of earlier reviews so as to have an opportunity to ratchet up their salaries more quickly. In addition, the practice of early reviews has also started spreading outside the high-tech environment to include areas such as banks, accounting firms, and insurers.

These firms are finding that they have a better chance of landing the very top prospects by offering earlier reviews. Moreover, a guaranteed review after six months is rapidly become almost an expectation in the eyes of some of the most promising recruits. For example, one recent survey of executive search firms found that more than 27 percent of new management positions currently being filled come with the assurance of an initial six-month review. But one thing that is often overlooked in this trend is that the recruit still has to ask. If not, the company is likely to stick with its normal one-year cycle.

So, can it get any faster? Absolutely. For example, consider the case of software programmer David Parvin, a recent college graduate being courted by Cougar Mountain Software, a Boise, Idaho, company. Parvin learned that Cougar Mountain was providing reviews of its new hires after thirty days. But Parvin wanted it even faster, so he demanded a two-week review! And sure enough, during his first two weeks on the job he so impressed his bosses that they gave him a 7.1 percent pay raise. During his first eighteen months on the job, he continued to request frequent reviews, earning a total of six raises and one major promotion.

Although this cycle may seem extreme, one reason it has worked is that Cougar Mountain has a history of rapid reviews. Indeed, about 10 percent of its new hires get a raise after thirty days, and almost all get a raise within three months. The firm's managers also believe that this practice helps Cougar Mountain retain its most valuable employees. In an industry with extremely high turnover, Cougar Mountain's turnover among all employees is only around 10 percent, and among its very best employees is an incredible 1 percent.

Of course, this approach can also create some problems. In addition to the extra administrative time and expense needed to manage a flexible performance appraisal and salary adjustment system, there are also potential morale problems with other employees. To address this concern, some companies require those who will be getting rapid reviews to keep their arrangement a secret. But word is still likely to get out, especially if more than just a few new employees are receiving this special attention.

As for the future, there seems to be a difference of opinion as to whether this practice will continue. Some experts, for example, predict that as soon as the tight labor market begins to loosen (for example, when firms stop adding jobs) that firms will quickly move to drop the rapid review process. Others, however, believe that just the opposite will occur and that firms may well come to value the flexibility that this system affords. That is, firms that review and reward their more highly valued workers on an accelerated schedule may also be able to slow the process for less-valued workers. Thus a well-established worker with a history of being judged as adequate may get evaluated even less frequently—and get fewer raises—than is the case today.

Case Questions

1. What do you see as the advantages and disadvantages of rapid performance appraisals?

2. Under what circumstances would you envision wanting a fast review? Under what circumstances would you prefer just the opposite?

3. What is your prediction about the future of rapid performance appraisal cycles?

Sources: "New Hires Win Fast Raises in Accelerated Job Reviews," *Wall Street Journal*, October 6, 1998, pp. B1, B16; "Your Year-End Review Doesn't Have to Be Quite That Horrible," *Wall Street Journal*, December 23, 1997, p. B1.

Building Human Resource Management Skills

Purpose: The purpose of this exercise is to help you develop insights into the process of developing performance appraisal methods and systems. As background, conceptualize how performance appraisal works in a typical classroom such as this course: the instructor is the rater and students are the ratees. Instructors generally use some combination of exams, tests, papers, cases, and/or class participation as the basis for evaluation and then provide the "formal" appraisal in the form of a letter grade.

Step 1: Your instructor will divide the class into small groups of four to five members.

Step 2: Working with your group, develop three methods that an instructor might use to evaluate your performance. To the extent possible, try to make your methods parallel to those discussed in this chapter.

Step 3: Evaluate each method you developed in terms of its potential usefulness. Specifically identify the strengths and weaknesses of each method relative to the traditional system.

Step 4: Discuss and respond to the following questions:

1. What barriers might exist to the adoption of one of the new methods you developed?

2. What limitations characterize the traditional system? Do any of your methods overcome these limitations?

3. At your school, do students evaluate instructors? If so, how might the current method be improved?

4. Does 360-degree feedback have any relevance in the classroom?

Ethical Dilemmas in Human Resource Management

Assume that you are a marketing executive in a major corporation. You need to hire a new staff member to fill a position that has just been created. The members of your current staff are either not interested in the position, do not have the requisite skills for the position, or else already have comparable or better positions. Thus the person you select will come from outside your group.

You have asked the human resource department to help identify three possible candidates from inside the organization. You have met with each of these people and thoroughly reviewed their educational backgrounds, experience, performance appraisals, and other qualifications. You have eliminated one person because of lack of fit, but you now face a complicated decision between the other two. Specifically, you see them as relatively equal in terms of potential. The real problem, however, is one of diversity and equal opportunity.

One candidate is a black female. You are personally committed to equal opportunity for minorities and have a reputation for helping members of protected classes whenever appropriate. You are very familiar with this candidate's current boss. You see that she has consistently received performance appraisals in the range of 3.8 to 4.2 on your firm's five-point rating scales. But because of your knowledge of her boss, you know that these numbers really mean that her performance has been in the range of 4.2 to 4.6 (because her boss rates everyone on the low side—in your opinion, about .4 below where others would rate them).

The other candidate is a white male. This individual's performance appraisal ratings have been in the range of 4.0 to 4.4. You also know this person's boss very well and believe that these scores are pretty accurate because that manager's performance appraisals are always fair, objective, and equitable. So your dilemma is whether to select the white male on the basis of the numbers or to select the black female on the basis of what you think the numbers really mean. Although you have the authority to make this decision yourself, you also want to make sure that you can defend it if the individual not selected questions how and why you chose the other individual for the position.

Questions

1. What are the ethical issues in this situation?

2. What are the basic arguments for and against selecting each candidate?

3. What do you think most managers would do? What would you do?

Human Resource Internet Exercise

Many human resource consulting firms offer services in the area of performance appraisal, including advice on how to install systems, how to use 360-degree feedback, and which forms to use. Assume that you have just taken the position of senior human resource executive for a large manufacturing business and believe that its current performance appraisal system is totally inadequate. Your plan is to scrap the current system and replace it with a new one. Because you are both quite busy with other problems and also have little direct experience with performance appraisal, you are interested in engaging the services of a consulting firm.

Using a search engine, do a Web search of the key terms "performance appraisal," "performance assessment," "performance management," and any other version of the term that you think is appropriate. Locate several consulting firms that look like they might offer the services you need. Review each site thoroughly and then narrow your list down to the three firms that look the most promising. Finally, list the additional information you would want to have before selecting one.

Questions

1. What role does the Internet play best when selecting a consulting firm for a job such as this one?

2. How realistic do you think the information on the Web truly is for reviewing and selecting a service provider for a purpose such as this one?

3. Compare notes with your classmates and see whether any of you chose some of the same firms. Compare your evaluations.

Notes

1. See Charles R. Greer, *Strategy and Human Resources* (Englewood Cliffs, N.J.: Prentice-Hall, 1995), Chapter 8, for a review of the strategic importance of performance management in organizations.

2. W. Timothy Weaver, "Linking Performance Reviews to Productivity and Quality," *HRMagazine*, November 1996, pp. 93–98.

3. Angelo S. DeNisi, *Cognitive Approach to Performance Appraisal: A Program of Research* (London: Routledge Publishers Ltd., 1996).

4. Several excellent reviews of these "cognitive" decision-making processes on the part of the rater are available. These include Angelo S. DeNisi, Thomas P. Cafferty, and Bruce Meglino, "A Cognitive Model of the Performance Appraisal Process," *Organizational Behavior and Human Decision Processes*, Vol. 33, 1984, pp. 360–396 and Daniel R. Ilgen and Jack M. Feldman, "Performance Appraisal: A Process Focus," in Barry Staw and Larry Cummings (eds.), *Research in Organizational Behavior* (Vol. 5) (Greenwich, Conn.: JAI Press, 1983).

5. Arup Varma, Angelo S. DeNisi, and Lawrence H. Peters, "Interpersonal Affect and Performance Appraisal: A Field Study," *Personnel Psychology*, Summer 1996, pp. 341–360.

6. Kurt Kraiger and Kevin Ford, "A Meta-Analysis of Ratee Race Effects in Performance Rating," *Journal of Applied Psychology*, Vol. 70, 1985, pp. 56–65.

7. See, for example, Jeanette N. Cleveland, R. M. Festa, and L. Montgomery, Applicant Pool Composition and Job Perceptions: Impact on Decisions Regarding an Older Applicant," *Journal of Vocational Behavior*, Vol. 32, 1988, pp. 112–125.

8. For example, see review by V. F. Nieva and Barbara Gutek, "Sex Effects in Evaluations," *Academy of Management Review*, Vol. 5, 1980, pp. 267–276.

9. Adrienne Colella, Angelo S. DeNisi, and Arup Varma, "A Model of the Impact of Disability on Performance Evaluations," *Human Resource Management Review*, Vol. 7, 1997, pp. 27–53.

10. Walter C. Borman, "Job Behavior, Performance, and Effectiveness," in Marvin D. Dunnette and Leaetta Hough (eds.), *Handbook of Industrial and Organizational Psychology*, 2nd ed. (Vol. 2) (Palo Alto, Calif.: Consulting Psychologists Press, 1991); Walter C. Borman and S. J. Motowidlo, "Expanding the Criterion Domain to Include Elements of Contextual Performance," in Neal Schmitt and Walter Borman (eds.), *Personnel Selection in Organizations* (San Francisco: Jossey-Bass, 1993).

11. Dennis W. Organ and K. Ryan, "A Meta-Analytic Review of Attitudinal and Dispositional Predictors of Organizational Citizenship Behavior," *Personnel Psychology*, Vol. 48, 1995, pp. 775–802.

12. Jon M. Werner, "Dimensions That Make a Difference: Examining the Impact of Inrole and Extrarole Behaviors on Supervisory Ratings," *Journal of Applied Psychology*, Vol. 79, 1994, pp. 98–107.

13. Kevin R. Murphy and Jeanette N. Cleveland, *Understanding Performance Appraisal: Social, Organizational,*

and Goal-Based Perspectives (Thousand Oaks, Calif.: Sage Publications, 1995).

14. Forest J. Jourden and Chip Heath, "The Evaluation Gap in Performance Perceptions: Illusory Perceptions of Groups and Individuals," *Journal of Applied Psychology*, Vol. 81, No. 4, 1996, pp. 369–379.

15. Angelo S. DeNisi, W. Alan Randolph, and Allyn G. Blencoe, "Potential Problems with Peer Ratings," *Academy of Management Journal*, Vol. 26, 1983, pp. 457–467.

16. Leanne Atwater, Paul Roush, and Allison Fischtal, "The Influence of Upward Feedback on Self- and Follower Ratings of Leadership," *Personnel Psychology*, Spring 1995, pp. 35–59.

17. James M. Conway, "Analysis and Design of Multitrait-Multirater Performance Appraisal Studies," *Journal of Management*, 1996, Vol. 22, No. 1, pp. 139–162.

18. Susan Haworth, "The Dark Side of Multi-Rater Assessments," *HRMagazine*, May 1998, pp. 106–112.

19. E. D. Sisson, "Forced Choice: The New Army Rating," *Personnel Psychology*, Vol. 1, 1948, pp. 365–381.

20. John C. Flanagan, "The Critical Incident Technique," *Psychological Bulletin*, Vol. 51, 1954, pp. 327–358.

21. John C. Flanagan and R. K. Burns, "The Employee Performance Record: A New Appraisal and Development Tool," *Harvard Business Review*, September–October, 1955, 95–102.

22. H. John Bernardin and C. S. Walter, "The Effects of Rater Training and Diary Keeping on Psychometric Errors in Ratings," *Journal of Applied Psychology*, Vol. 62, 1977, pp. 64–69; Angelo S. DeNisi, Tina Robbins, and Thomas P. Cafferty, "The Organization of Information Used for Performance Appraisals: The Role of Diary Keeping," *Journal of Applied Psychology*, Vol. 74, 1989, pp. 124–129.

23. Patricia C. Smith and L. M. Kendall, "Retranslation of Expectations: An Approach to the Construction of Un-ambiguous Anchors for Rating Scales," *Journal of Applied Psychology*, Vol. 47, 1963, pp. 149–155.

24. H. John Bernardin, M. B. LaShells, Patricia C. Smith, and Kenneth M. Alvares, "Behavioral Expectation Scales: Effects of Development Procedures and Formats," *Journal of Applied Psychology*, Vol. 61, 1976, pp. 75–79.

25. Gary P. Latham, Charles H. Fay, and Lisa M. Saari, "The Development of Behavioral Observation Scales for Appraising the Performance of Foremen," *Personnel Psychology*, Vol. 33, 1979, pp. 815–821.

26. For an excellent review of the variations on these methods, see, H. John Bernardin and Richard W. Beatty, *Performance Appraisal: Assessing Human Behavior at Work* (Boston: PWS Kent, 1984), Chapter 4.

27. Neal P. Mero and Stephan J. Motowidlo, "Effects of Rater Accountability on the Accuracy and the Favorability of Performance Ratings," *Journal of Applied Psychology*, Vol. 80, No. 4, 1995, pp. 517–524.

28. Jeffrey S. Kane, H. John Bernardin, Peter Villanova, and Joseph Peyrefitte, "Stability of Rater Leniency: Three Studies," *Academy of Management Journal*, Vol. 38, No. 4, 1995, pp. 1036–1051.

29. Walter C. Borman, Leonard A. White, and David W. Dorsey, "Effects of Ratee Task Performance and Interpersonal Factors on Supervisor and Peer Performance Ratings," *Journal of Applied Psychology*, Vol. 80, No. 1, 1995, pp. 168–177.

30. Juan I. Sanchez and Phillip De La Torre, "A Second Look at the Relationship between Rating and Behavioral Accuracy in Performance Appraisal," *Journal of Applied Psychology*, Vol. 81, No. 1, 1996, pp. 3–10.

31. Kate Ludeman, "To Fill the Feedback Void," *Training & Development*, August 1995, pp. 38–43.

32. Allan H. Church, "First-Rate Multirater Feedback," *Training & Development*, August 1995, pp. 42–44.

9

Training, Development, and Organizational Learning

CHAPTER OUTLINE

Purposes of Training and Development
The Nature of Training
The Nature of Development
Learning Theory and Employee
Training

New-Employee Orientation
Goals of Orientation
Basic Issues in Orientation

Assessing Training and Development Needs
Needs Analysis
Setting Training and Development
Goals
In-House Programs versus
Outsourced Programs

Designing Training and Development Programs
Outlining and Defining Training and
Development Program Content
Selecting Training and Development
Instructors

Training and Development Techniques and Methods
Work-Based Programs
Instructional-Based Programs
Training Technology

Management Development
Special Needs for Management
Development
Special Techniques for Management
Development
Organization Development

Evaluating Training and Development

CHAPTER OBJECTIVES

After studying this chapter you should be able to:

■ Identify and describe the purposes of training and development.

■ Discuss new-employee orientation.

■ Describe how training and development needs are assessed.

■ Describe how the content of training and development programs is determined and how instructors are selected.

■ Discuss common training and development techniques and methods.

■ Discuss the unique considerations in management development.

■ Describe how organizations can evaluate the effectiveness of their training and development programs.

When Joe Liemandt dropped out of Stanford in 1990 to start a software company in Austin, Texas, he was well aware of the formidable competition he would face. As part of his strategy, he decided to strive to develop and maintain a workforce composed of creative people who work well in teams, who adapt to rapid change, and who are comfortable in taking risks. And today, people with these qualities have helped build Liemandt's company, Trilogy Software, Inc., into a rapidly growing enterprise. Trilogy, which employs almost one thousand people, makes industry-leading software that helps companies manage product pricing, sales plans, and commissions.

When Trilogy hires a new group of employees, Liemandt himself oversees their training. This training takes several weeks, starting with a series of classes devoted to technical aspects of Trilogy products and its methods for software development. But after this technical phase is completed, recruits move into training and development activities designed to enhance their risk-taking skills, areas in which Trilogy really believes its employees make a difference.

Recruits are formed into teams, and each team is given three weeks to complete various projects ranging from creating new products to developing marketing

"We are known as risk takers, an important attribute in the high-tech world."

(Lauren Arbittier, new Trilogy recruit)*

campaigns for existing Trilogy products. The teams actually compete with one another, and they are scored on the basis of risk and innovation, goal setting, and goal accomplishment. Evaluations are completed by existing Trilogy managers and some of the firm's venture capital backers. The winners get a free trip to Las Vegas, but the losers get sent straight to work.

But the training isn't over, even for those who go to Las Vegas— Liemandt challenges everyone to place a $2,000 bet at the roulette wheel. He argues that $2,000 is a meaningful sum, and one that can cause real pain, but not so large an amount as to cause true financial disaster for anyone. Trilogy will actually put up the money, but losers pay it back from payroll deductions of $400 for five months. Not everyone decides to join in, of course, but enough do that the message remains clear: Trilogy aims to succeed by taking chances, and it expects its employees to share the risks. And the ones who do may earn a big return for their investment.

"How Trilogy Software Trains Its Raw Recruits to Be Risk Takers," *Wall Street Journal*, September 21, 1998, pp. A1, A10 (*quote on p. A10); "Insanity, Inc.," *Fast Company*, January 1999, pp. 100–108; Gary Hamel and Jeff Sampler, "The E-Corporation," *Fortune*, December 7, 1998, pp. 80–92.

Joe Liemandt and Trilogy Software, Inc., are doing extremely well in a very competitive industry. One key to the firm's success is its overall business strategy and the nature and quality of its products. Another is the kind of people the firm attracts. But just attracting good people usually isn't enough. Companies have to invest in those people to help them develop their skills and abilities in ways that better promote the firm's goals and objectives. For a firm its size, for example, Trilogy spends a great deal of money to train and develop its employees—$9 million for its most recent three hundred new hires alone.

Training and development together represent yet another major human resource function that managers need to address. Specifically, training and development represent a fundamental investment in the employees who work for an organization, with the overall goal of improving their ability to make contributions to the firm's effectiveness. This chapter covers a variety of perspectives on employee training and development. We first outline more specifically the purposes of training and development. We next discuss a special form of employee training and development, new-employee orientation. Next we examine how organizations go about assessing their training and development needs. Then we discuss the actual development of training and development programs. Training and development techniques and methods are then introduced and discussed. Finally, we look more closely at the challenge of management development.

PURPOSES OF TRAINING AND DEVELOPMENT

Employee training can be defined as a planned attempt by an organization to facilitate employee learning of job-related knowledge, skills, and behaviors. **Development**, on the other hand, usually refers to teaching managers and professionals the skills needed for both present and future jobs. Thus each has a slightly different orientation.[1] These differences are discussed below.

The Nature of Training

■ **Employee training** is a planned attempt by an organization to facilitate employee learning of job-related knowledge, skills, and behaviors.

■ **Development** refers to teaching managers and professionals the skills needed for both present and future jobs.

Training usually involves teaching operational or technical employees how to do their jobs more effectively and/or more efficiently. Teaching telephone operators to help customers more efficiently, showing machinists the proper way to handle certain kinds of tools, and demonstrating for short-order cooks how to prepare food orders systematically are all part of training. Responsibilities for training are generally assigned to the human resource function of an organization, although many larger firms actually create separate training departments or units within human resources. But in keeping with the spirit of the human resource function as a center of expertise, human resource managers in general and training managers in particular must fully integrate their activities with operating managers and units throughout the organization.

In general, training is intended to help the organization function more effectively. For example, suppose that a small manufacturing company has a workforce of machinists and other operating employees who are currently capable of working at 85 percent of plant capacity. That is, the space, equipment, and technology in the plant may be potentially capable of producing, say, one hundred thousand units of output per day; the existing workforce, however, can turn out only eighty-five thousand units per day. Because of anticipated growth in product demand, managers want to be prepared to meet this demand when it occurs by boosting the plant's level of potential performance. That is, they want their workforce to be able to produce more without having to hire new employees or invest in new equipment or technology. As a first step the organization might want to work toward achieving 95 percent of capacity—or ninety-five thousand units per day—using existing employees and facilities. Thus these existing employees will need to be trained in more efficient work methods with the goal of making the workers more productive.

Of course, for this approach to be effective, two conditions must exist. First, managers must be relatively sure that employees cannot *already* work at 95 percent of capacity. That is, in some situations employees may already have the requisite skills to increase their productivity, but simply do not see any reason to increase their effort enough to do so. In that case the problem is one of motivation, and a training program would probably not help. But if managers assume that employees are working as hard as they (reasonably) can and that they would be motivated to produce more if they knew how, training aimed at improving employee productivity would be a reasonable undertaking. The second condition is that managers should have reason to believe that productivity gains are actually possible with existing resources. That is, if a plant is already working at maximum efficiency—as constrained by its technology, equipment, work flow, or similar considerations—training is not likely to improve productivity.

Some training is focused on existing conditions and circumstances, as illustrated in the preceding example. That is, the training focuses on changing the behaviors of current employees as they perform their current jobs. Other training deals more specifically with accommodating changes in the work environment. For example, when new machines are placed in an organization, when new software is added to computer networks, when new production methods become available, and/or when new organizational procedures and systems are implemented, employees must be trained in the proper use of those procedures and systems.

The Nature of Development

Rather than focusing on specific job-related skills, such as using new software or performing certain specific task and job functions, development is more generally aimed at helping managers better understand and solve problems, make decisions, and capitalize on opportunities.[2] For example, managers need to understand how to manage their time effectively. Thus some management development programs have a component that deals with time management. Other management development programs may help managers better understand how to motivate employees (for example, to get the employees discussed above to exert extra effort). Thus managers do not necessarily return from such development programs with a specific new operational method for doing their job more effectively. Instead, they may return with new skills that may be of relevance to them in a general sense at some point in the future. That is, managers may have a better understanding of how to work more effectively, how to motivate their employees better, and how to make better decisions and a more complete understanding of how the overall organization functions and their role within it. Development is also usually considered a human resource function in most organizations, but because of its strategic nature and importance, one or more senior executives usually have the specific responsibility of ensuring that management development is approached in a systematic and comprehensive fashion.

Learning Theory and Employee Training

Even though there are obvious differences between training and development, they nevertheless share a common underlying foundation—learning. **Learning** is a relatively permanent change in behavior or behavioral potential that results from direct or indirect experience. The intention of training and development is for employees to learn behaviors that are more effective. Thus managers interested in training and development must understand the basic fundamentals of learning theory as they apply to training and development. In addition, some organizations in the last few years have begun to pay particular attention to the importance of learning and have even gone so far as to attempt to redefine their organizations as learning organizations. A **learning organization** is one whose employees continuously attempt to learn new things and to use what they learn to improve product or service quality. That is, such an organization and its employees see learning not as a discrete activity that starts and stops with the conduct of a specific training program, but rather as an ongoing and fundamental and continuous part of the organization and employee work relationship.[3]

Beyond this general and fundamental strategic approach to learning, however, a number of more specific learning techniques and principles also relate to employee training and development. These are illustrated in Figure 9.1. One basic learning principle has to do with motivation. Specifically, people will not learn unless they are motivated to learn. That is, the individual has to want to acquire the knowledge that the trainer or developer is attempting to impart.

Second, the learning that occurs during training and development must be reinforced in the organization. Suppose an employee learns how to do a new job in a way that takes a bit more effort but that provides a dramatic improvement in output. When the employee takes this behavior back to the workplace and attempts to put it into practice, it is helpful if the manager responsible for the employee recognizes the new behavior and provides some sort of reinforcement or reward, such as praise and positive comments. To the extent that the manager ignores the new behavior, or, even worse, questions or challenges it, then it will not have been reinforced and will likely not be repeated in the future.[4]

Another important learning principle that is related to employee training and development is the notion of practice and activity. It takes time for people to fully internalize that which they have learned in training and development. They need time to practice it, to actually use it, and to see how it really affects their work performance. As a new behavior continues to be practiced, experts say that it has been *overlearned*. Practicing something until overlearning is a good way of ensuring that it will not be forgotten in the future. This concept helps explain the traditional wisdom that once people learn to ride a bicycle or to swim, they never forget how to do so.

In addition, the behaviors that the individual is attempting to learn must be meaningful. That is, the individual who is undergoing the training and devel-

■ **Learning** is a relatively permanent change in behavior or behavioral potential that results from direct or indirect experience.

■ A **learning organization** is one whose employees continuously attempt to learn new things and to use what they learn to improve product or service quality.

opment must recognize the behavior and its associated information as being important and relevant to the job situation that he or she faces. Further, even if the material *is* meaningful and important, if this message is not communicated effectively to the trainee, he or she will not work hard to master the material, which will presumably cause problems later. Many graduate students in business administration, for example, learn too late that there really was a reason to master the calculus they were taught as undergraduates.

In addition, the training materials must be effectively communicated. That is, the individual must be able to effectively receive the information being imparted and must respond favorably to that material. To a large extent, effective communication depends on matching the training technique (discussed later) with the material to be transmitted. For some types of information, lectures may be quite acceptable, but others may require some active or experiential learning to be part of the training. Failure to recognize such differences, along with the inability to effectively use the training technique in question, results in major obstructions to the communication of information.

Finally, the material that is being taught must be transferable to the job setting of the individual employee. Mastering material in a training setting is rather pointless unless the trainee can then apply that material on the job. Two important considerations can facilitate this *transfer of training*. First, the training setting, or at least the setting in which the new behavior or skill is practiced, should resemble the actual job setting as closely as possible. Learning to assemble a piece of oil-drilling equipment machine in a warm, well-lit environment may not help the employee who is then asked to assemble the equipment in an Alaskan oil field during the winter. Of course, managers cannot always

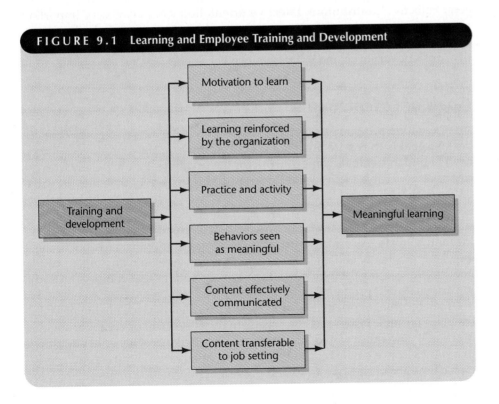

FIGURE 9.1   Learning and Employee Training and Development

Training and development → Motivation to learn / Learning reinforced by the organization / Practice and activity / Behaviors seen as meaningful / Content effectively communicated / Content transferable to job setting → Meaningful learning

know all the settings in which the material will be applied, but it is nonetheless important to try to anticipate the actual conditions on the job and replicate them in training.

Training is also facilitated if the behaviors learned in training are close to those that will be required on the job. That is, it would be pointless to teach employees to do a job on one machine if they will be using a different machine that requires different procedures when they actually return to the job setting. In fact, such training would result in *negative transfer*, which would interfere with performance on the job. But, over time, machines change and so procedures learned for one machine might no longer apply when new equipment is introduced. In this situation it is important to retrain the employees to avoid problems of negative transfer.

THE BOTTOM LINE All managers should understand the basic purposes and processes involved in both training and development. Moreover, managers should also recognize the fundamental role of learning theory in employee training and development and be familiar with how different aspects of learning relate to different areas of training and development.

NEW-EMPLOYEE ORIENTATION

■ **Orientation** is the process of introducing new employees to the organization so that they can quickly become effective contributors.

One important part of an organization's training and development program is new-employee orientation. **Orientation** is the process of introducing new employees to the organization so that they can quickly become effective contributors. Effective orientation can play a very important role in employee job satisfaction, performance, retention, and similar areas.[5] On the other hand, poor orientation can result in disenchantment, dissatisfaction, anxiety, turnover, and other employee problems.

Goals of Orientation

An orientation program generally has a clear and specific set of goals. One important goal is to reduce anxiety and uncertainty for new employees. When newly hired individuals come to work for the first time, they are likely to experience considerable anxiety and uncertainty. For example, they may be unfamiliar with such basic issues as how often they get paid, where the human resource department office is, where the company cafeteria is, where they are supposed to park, normal work hours, who will provide their job-related training, and so forth. An effective orientation program provides answers to these questions efficiently and effectively for new employees. In many organizations new employees are also briefed on their benefit options and choices and enroll in various benefit programs during orientation.

A related goal of orientation is to ease the burden that socializing newcomers place on supervisors and coworkers. In the absence of orientation, an organizational newcomer would have little choice but to direct his or her questions to a supervisor or coworkers, and those individuals would thus spend considerable time answering questions and providing information to new employees.

Some informal indoctrination is inevitable, of course, and may serve the beneficial purposes of helping new people get better acquainted and integrated into their work group. But if informal indoctrination is the only vehicle for orientation, supervisors and coworkers would have to spend a disproportionate amount of time answering questions. Moreover, newcomers might not always get complete or accurate answers to their questions, simply because other employees are not likely to be completely up-to-date on every detail of the employment relationship with the organization.

Another goal of orientation is to provide favorable initial job experiences for new employees. In Chapter 6 we describe the importance of realistic job previews as a way to avoid problems of disenchantment and disappointment when people encounter jobs that are different from what they expected. In similar fashion an effective orientation program can complement and reinforce this process by making sure that a new employee's initial job experiences are positive and effective. The orientation program, for example, will help newcomers feel like part of a team; allow them to quickly meet their coworkers, their supervisor, and other new employees; and in a variety of other ways ease the transition from being an outsider to being an insider.

Basic Issues in Orientation

In planning an orientation for new employees, human resource managers must deal with a variety of basic issues. These issues include the content of the orientation, the length of the orientation, and the decision of whom will actually conduct the orientation. A sample orientation agenda showing how one company approaches these issues is depicted in Figure 9.2. The content of the orientation is of obvious importance. Most organizations try to provide their employees with a set of basic understandings of organizational policies and

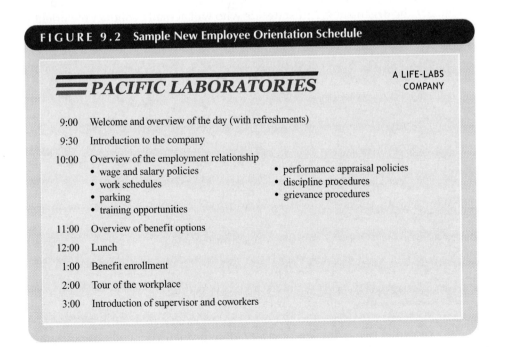

FIGURE 9.2 Sample New Employee Orientation Schedule

PACIFIC LABORATORIES

A LIFE-LABS COMPANY

9:00	Welcome and overview of the day (with refreshments)	
9:30	Introduction to the company	
10:00	Overview of the employment relationship	
	• wage and salary policies	• performance appraisal policies
	• work schedules	• discipline procedures
	• parking	• grievance procedures
	• training opportunities	
11:00	Overview of benefit options	
12:00	Lunch	
1:00	Benefit enrollment	
2:00	Tour of the workplace	
3:00	Introduction of supervisor and coworkers	

procedures that are relevant to that particular employee. For example, hourly workers who are expected to punch a time clock or sign a time card must be educated in the mechanics of where those things are located, how they are handled, how to fill them out, and so forth.

Similarly, the orientation should provide information about issues such as hours of work, compensation, and schedules and direct the individual to the appropriate offices and managers to answer various questions. For example, an orientation program might tell new employees to direct any questions or concerns regarding potential discrimination to the firm's EEOC officer.

Some organizations also find it appropriate to include as a part of their orientation a general overview and introduction to the business itself. This introduction would include such things as information about the firm's history, its evolution, its successes, and perhaps even some of its failures. Organizations that have a strong corporate culture are especially likely to include this type of information as a part of the orientation process. This approach enables newly hired employees to understand that culture and to know how to function within it. At Southwest Airlines, for example, newcomers watch a video featuring the firm's CEO, Herb Kelleher, welcoming them to the team and explaining the firm's approach to doing business. But the real message is perhaps best conveyed by the format of the video—Kelleher delivers his "speech" in the form of rap music, backed up by a team of other Southwest employees!

In many cases the duration or length of an orientation program is a function of what the organization intends to impart during that orientation. Obviously, the more material that it wants to convey to new employees, the longer the orientation will need to last. In some cases a firm may attempt to handle orientation in only an hour or two. More typically, however, orientation is likely to take a half day or perhaps even a full day. And occasionally, firms may provide an initial orientation and then have a brief follow-up session a few days or weeks later to answer questions or deal with issues that have arisen after employees have had a brief opportunity to experience life in the organization.

Finally, the organization must decide who will actually conduct the orientation session. In many situations a number of individuals are a part of the orientation process. For example, one or more human resource managers are likely to be involved in new-employee orientation. In some cases operating managers are also actively involved. Union officials occasionally involve themselves in orientation when a company's workers are represented by a strong labor union. Sometimes organizations use current operating employees to facilitate the orientation program as well.

An interesting trend that some organizations are experimenting with involves having retired employees perform the orientation. For example, Hewlett-Packard invites retired employees to coordinate and run the orientation process in a number of its manufacturing plants around the United States. The company has found this strategy to be particularly effective because it helps convey the idea to new employees that the organization must clearly be a good place to work if retirees are willing to come back and help orient newcomers.

THE BOTTOM LINE All managers need to understand the important role that orientation plays in helping newcomers to an organization learn the ropes and get off to a good start. In addition, managers should know the relevant goals of orientation for their particular organization and be willing and able to make appropriate contributions to the orientation process, especially as it affects new employees in their own area.

ASSESSING TRAINING AND DEVELOPMENT NEEDS

Orientation is generally a one-shot activity for employees. That is, they undergo orientation when they first join the organization, but then that process is complete. Beyond orientation, however, most organizations find it appropriate and effective to continue training and development on a regular basis. That is, employees must be continually trained and developed to enhance and otherwise improve the quality of the contributions they are making to the organization. The starting point is to assess training and development needs. As Figure 9.3 shows, this process generally involves consideration of three things: needs analysis, the establishment of training and development goals, and decisions regarding in-house training versus outsourced training.

Needs Analysis

The starting point in assessing training and development needs is to actually conduct a **needs analysis**. That is, human resource managers responsible for training and development must determine the organization's true needs vis-à-vis training. This analysis generally focuses on two things: the organization's job-related needs and the capabilities of the current workforce. The organization's needs are determined by the nature of the work that must be performed. That is, what knowledge, skills, and abilities does the organization's workforce need to perform the organization's work most effectively.

As a part of this analysis, the manager must carefully assess the company's strategy, the resources it has available for training, and its general philosophy regarding employee training and development. By philosophy, we mean the extent to which the organization views training as a true investment in human resources or simply as a necessity to alter or change a specific outcome or criterion measure. Workforce analysis involves a careful assessment of the capabilities, strengths, and weaknesses characterizing the organization's current workforce. That is, it is important to understand the extent to which the organization's workforce is skilled or unskilled, motivated or unmotivated, committed or not committed to the organization, and so forth.

The information for this analysis can be gathered from a variety of sources. For example, managers may learn a great deal by observing current employees to see how they appear to be working. In addition, managers may also ask employees directly what they view as their own strengths and weaknesses and in what areas they believe that further improvement is necessary. Third, managers may ask supervisors of current employees to provide information about

■ A **needs analysis** is the assessment of the organization's job-related needs and the capabilities of the current workforce.

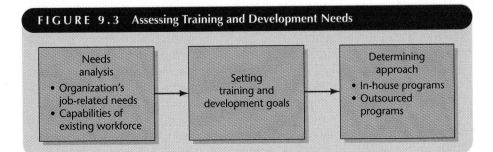

FIGURE 9.3 Assessing Training and Development Needs

If organizations are to train and develop their employees most effectively, it is critical that they truly understand their needs and set appropriate training and development goals. For example, when Paul Holt decided to transform his firm from a traditional retailer to an Internet retailer, he knew that his workers did not have the skills and abilities to function in this new medium. But rather than laying them off and hiring new workers, Holt instead hired a consultant to train all of his current workers. Because of his logical and systematic approach, virtually every employee successfully made the transition from paper-based to electronic work methods.

what training the employees should have. Fourth, managers might also evaluate the kinds of problems and difficulties that employees have been encountering. For example, if the firm seems to be experiencing a lot of work-related accidents, training aimed at improving safety might be an important activity. Finally, the organization may also ask its customers to provide input regarding the kinds of training its employees need.

Setting Training and Development Goals

One of the most important steps in any program is the establishment of training and development goals. For the organization to manage its investment properly, the organization should know in advance (that is, prior to training) what it expects of its employees. For example, consider the implications if employees are producing at a level of 80 percent of capacity before training and are still producing at a level of 80 percent after undergoing training designed to boost productivity. An appropriate question that arises is the extent to which the training was effective. It is surprisingly difficult to evaluate the effectiveness of training, however, if the organization had no predetermined goals. Thus the human resource manager responsible for planning training must look at the current state of affairs, decide what changes are necessary, and then formulate these changes in the form of specific training goals.

For example, consider the case of an insurance claims office. Assume that claims adjusters are currently processing insurance claims at an average rate of six business days per claim. Responses and feedback from customers suggest that some customers are becoming unhappy because they would like to have their claims processed more quickly. Using this information and other relevant data, the human resource manager—working with operating managers—might decide that an appropriate and reasonable goal is to cut the average processing time from six days to four days. Thus a "four-day processing average" becomes the goal of this particular training endeavor.

The human resource manager should make every reasonable effort to ensure that the training program's goals are objective, verifiable, and specific. For example, a vague and general goal such as "improving employee performance" or "enhancing employee attitudes" is very difficult to evaluate. On the other hand, specific objective and verifiable goals such as increasing performance by 10 percent, cutting turnover by 5 percent, cutting customer complaints by 3 percent, and improving accuracy or quality by 8 percent are likely to be effective goals for a training and development program, at least in terms of the manager's abilities to evaluate the effectiveness of the training.

In-House Programs versus Outsourced Programs

Another initial decision that human resource managers must make in designing training and development programs is the extent to which the training and development should be conducted in house or outsourced. An **in-house training** or **development program** is conducted on the premises of the organization primarily by the organization's own employees. Many larger organizations, such as Texas Instruments and Exxon, have large training staffs. These training staffs consist of individuals who are familiar with the company, its jobs, and its employees. Moreover, these individuals are also experts in designing and conducting training programs. Thus the organization itself assumes the responsibility for training and developing its employees.

There are several obvious advantages to in-house training and development. The major advantage is that the organization can be assured that the content of its training and development efforts are precisely and specifically tailored to fit the organization's needs. That is, by definition there will be a close working relationship between line managers and the training and development staff as the various training and development programs are planned and conducted for current employees. Another advantage is flexibility, particularly regarding scheduling, because the training and development programs can be taught at times that are most convenient for the employees. For example, an employee can usually reschedule a training and development activity with relatively little difficulty.

The alternative approach of training and development is to use an outsourcing strategy. An **outsourced training** or **development program** involves having people from outside the organization perform the training. This approach might involve sending employees to training and development programs at colleges and universities, a consulting firm's headquarters, or similar locations. The primary advantage of outsourced programs is cost. Because the organization does not have to maintain its own training and development staff, or even its own training and development facilities, the cost is typically lower than would be possible with an in-house training and development program.

Another advantage is quality assurance. Although an organization has reasonable control over its own training and development staff, the individuals who are assigned the responsibility of doing the training and development might not be particularly skilled trainers or educators. Thus the effectiveness of the training and development effort might be compromised. Professional trainers, however, are almost always highly trained themselves and are also skilled educators. On the other hand, outsourced programs may be more likely to be a bit general and even generic and thus have less applicability and direct relevance to the organization.

Most smaller to midsized firms rely strictly on either in-house or outsourced training. Most larger organizations, however, are likely to rely on a combination of in-house and outsourced training. For example, even firms like Exxon that have a large training and development operation internally are still likely to occasionally use outside trainers and developers to assist in specialized areas. And some firms are even experimenting with outsourced training provided solely in house. That is, an independent contractor, usually a consulting firm, may take over a company's training and development function, but continue to operate and conduct the training inside the company.

Finally, a special form of outsourced training and development involves partnerships between business and education. Many leading business schools

■ An **in-house training** or **development program** is conducted on the premises of the organization primarily by the organization's own employees.

■ An **outsourced training** or **development program** involves having people from outside the organization perform the training.

such as Harvard, Northwestern, and the University of Michigan run highly regarded management development programs that attract participants from major corporations from around the world. These programs may be generic, customized by industry or firm size, or even created for a single company. Many other major public and private universities also offer various programs of this type for business. And even regional schools and community colleges are moving into this area by providing basic training and development for first-line supervisors and entry-level technical employees.[6]

THE BOTTOM LINE Human resource managers should conduct a thorough and comprehensive needs analysis prior to undertaking any training and development activities. Working with operating managers, human resource managers should next set specific goals that training and development activities will be expected to achieve. Finally, human resource managers should also understand the relative advantages and disadvantages of in-house versus outsourced training and development strategies.

DESIGNING TRAINING AND DEVELOPMENT PROGRAMS

The actual design of programs, of course, is the foundation to effective training and development. Without solid and relevant content, training and development efforts are pointless. The usual approach to content development starts with outlining program content, and then expanding that outline into fully formed programs. Selecting the most appropriate instructors completes the process.

Outlining and Defining Training and Development Program Content

The first step in developing training and development programs is to create a detailed outline of the intended program.[7] This outline should include items such as a recapitulation of the training objectives, a specification of the intended audience for the training, a specification of the proposed content of the training, and estimates of the amount of time necessary to conduct the training. In addition, the outline should also specify factors such as evaluation criteria, cost estimates, and the extent to which the training can be conducted in house or whether it should be outsourced.

Once the training and development program has been outlined, the next step in the development of the program is to define its content. At a superficial level the definition of content would seem to be a relatively straightforward undertaking. In reality, however, defining the content of a training and development program is both extremely important and quite difficult. Simply stated, the content of a training and development program specifies the material that is intended to be taught. An example of how training and development programs are outlined and content specified for managers heading for international assignments is described in "Human Resources Around the Globe."

Teaching Language Skills for a Global Workforce

Defining content is a critical part of training and development. One of the fastest-growing areas of training and development involves language skills. Because of the burgeoning global marketplace and the blurring of national boundaries, more and more companies are finding it necessary to provide language training for managers being assigned to posts in foreign countries. If a U.S. company is sending a manager to work in Canada, Australia, or South Africa, language is generally not a problem. But if the manager is being sent to China, Brazil, or France, language suddenly becomes a major issue.

In the case of language training, of course, defining content is relatively straightforward—the content of the training consists of skills in the language that needs to be learned. Thus the content of the language training for a manager being sent to Germany is the German language itself. Not surprisingly, however, it is generally useful to establish more specific content guidelines than simply the language itself. For example, it is almost always easier to teach reading and writing language skills than to teach verbal skills. Consequently, depending on the nature of the work assignment, training content may be further specified as including reading, writing, and/or verbal language skills.

It is also important to consider situational factors when designing the program. For example, if a manager is being sent for a short-term assignment to a foreign operation

"We're confident you'll be able to master Chinese in the six months before you leave."

(unidentified vice president of a Midwest industrial company, speaking to a plant manager)*

that is already well established and well staffed by local managers, language skills may be less important than if the manager is being sent for a long-term assignment to launch a new operation that requires him or her to interact with local government and labor officials. Similarly, human resource managers defining training content for managers being sent abroad will likely need to look beyond language and also provide training about local customs and related life-style issues, and may also need to include the manager's family in the training program.

Human resource managers must also avoid taking an overly simplistic approach to defining content for language training. For example, simply defining training content as Chinese isn't nearly precise enough, since dozens of dialects are spoken within mainland China. It is quite important, therefore, to know exactly where in China a manager is being sent. And even languages such as English may not be as straightforward as one might think. For example, while managers in the United States take "elevators" to higher floors in their buildings, ship their products on "trucks," check the oil in their cars by looking under the "hood," and snack on "potato chips," their British counterparts use "lifts," ship products on "lorries," look under the "bonnet," and munch on "crisps."

Reference: John Freivalds, "Self-Study Programs Aid Language Training," *HRMagazine*, January 1997, pp. 57–60 (*quote on p. 57).

Another way to approach this task is to focus on what is to be learned. For example, consider a training and development program designed to prepare employees to use a certain word processing package. The content specification would need to fully describe those parts of the word processing package that are intended to be taught. Thus the definition should specify all the parameters of the program including kinds of machines that are appropriate, intended uses of the software, and indicators of how well the material has been mastered.

From the perspective of what is to be learned, however, we get a much different picture. Before discussing the word processing example from this viewpoint, it is helpful to consider a model of instructional content that was originally proposed several years ago.[8] The learning categories proposed by Gagne are presented in Table 9.1.

Using this framework, the learning goals of the training program for word processing would include the intellectual skills needed to understand how the software is to be used, the cognitive strategies needed to know how to apply the knowledge about the programs, and the motor skills needed to operate the machines. Therefore, it is useful to approach the designing training programs, both from the perspective of what is to be taught as well as from the perspective of what is to be learned.

Of course, more complex training and development programs require a more complex definition of content and of learning goals. For example, a program aimed at enhancing the decision-making capabilities of managers would need to fully specify the range of decisions that the managers must make, the circumstances under which those decisions are most likely to be made, and various other factors associated with the decision-making process. Given that decision making is an inherently more complex undertaking than using a particular piece of software, it would follow that the content of a decision-making program would need to be more abstract and tap into a higher level of cognitive ability than the content of a program to teach the use of a piece of software.

Selecting Training and Development Instructors

Another important aspect of developing training and development programs is the selection of instructors to deliver the material. Effective instruction is an important ingredient in the success of any training and development program. Effective instructors are those individuals who deliver the content of a training or development program so as to facilitate learning; ineffective instructors, in contrast, serve as barriers or impediments to learning.

The most common choices regarding instructors are whether to use full-time professional trainers that might either be hired from an external firm or available on an in-house training staff or to use operating managers. The primary advantage to using operating managers or related employees is expertise. These individuals presumably understand the organization and the task to be performed and are thus extremely qualified to present instructional material aimed at those skills and requirements. On the other hand, such individuals, although they may be experts on the task to be taught, may also be poorly trained as instructors. Thus they may do a poor job of developing training materials, may not be able to deliver those materials effectively, and may otherwise do an inadequate job of classroom instruction.

The other choice is to use a professional trainer. The primary advantage of this approach is that professional trainers are likely to be very qualified

Selecting the appropriate instructors is an important part of training and development. Robert Harding decided to install a computer network in the nursing home he owns in Waterville, New York. Harding knew that he needed help in both installing the system and in training his staff to use it for maximum effectiveness, but he lacked the resources to hire a full-time expert. His solution was to contract with Express Delta Products to provide the basic training for his employees. This allowed him to rely on the vendor for installation. As a result, Harding got his system installed and his employees trained for less expense than he had expected.

> **TABLE 9.1** **Gagne's Learning Categories**
>
> 1. *Intellectual skills* include concepts, rules, and procedures and are often referred to as *procedural knowledge.*
>
> 2. *Verbal information* enables the individual to state something about a subject and is also referred to as *declarative information.*
>
> 3. *Cognitive strategies* enable a learner to know when and how to use intellectual skills and verbal information.
>
> 4. *Motor skills* include basic human physical activities such as writing, lifting, and using tools.
>
> 5. *Attitudes* are learned preferences for different activities.
>
> *Source:* Robert M. Gagne, "Learning Outcomes and Their Effects: Useful Categories of Human Performance," *American Psychologist*, Vol. 39, 1984, pp. 377–385.

instructors. They understand the importance of instructional goals, are able to deliver the material in an effective and interesting manner, and are otherwise capable of facilitating the learning process. On the other hand, these individuals may lack the technical expertise that is associated with the task being taught. Thus, although they might be able to deliver the material in a straightforward and perhaps superficial manner, they may be inadequately prepared to answer questions or to deal with unexpected issues that might arise during the training program.

THE BOTTOM LINE Managers should know that training and development programs start with the creation of a detailed outline, followed by a more comprehensive description of program content. They should also know the advantages and disadvantages of using different kinds of instructors.

TRAINING AND DEVELOPMENT TECHNIQUES AND METHODS

Depending on both the content of the program and the instructor(s) selected to present it, a number of techniques and methods can be used for the actual delivery of information. We examine some of the more popular techniques and methods in this section.

Work-Based Programs

One major family of training and development techniques and methods consists of various work-based programs. **Work-based programs** tie the training and development activities directly to performance of the task. The most

■ **Work-based programs** tie the training and development activities directly to performance of the task.

commonly used method of work-based training is **on-the-job training**. Some experts suggest that as much as 60 percent of training in the United States occurs on the job. In this situation the employee works in the actual work situation and is shown how to perform the task more effectively by the supervisor or a current experienced employee.

The primary advantage of on-the-job training is that the organization begins to achieve some return on the labor cost of the employee almost immediately, assuming that the individual is capable of achieving at least some minimal level of competency. Likewise, the employee is actually learning the task itself and so, with practice, should presumably become increasingly proficient and avoid problems of learning transfer. Finally, direct training costs may be relatively low, because the organization may not need to hire dedicated trainers or to send employees to training programs.[9]

On-the-job training also has some disadvantages, however. One significant disadvantage is that the employee may only learn a relatively narrow approach to performing the task. That is, she or he may be able to master task performance precisely as it is being taught by the other employee, but may be unable to generalize or to extend performance to other tasks or to other job settings in the organization. Some of these problems, though, can be addressed if the training is combined with some type of rotation plan, discussed below.

In a related vein the individual being trained is also likely to pick up the bad habits and less-effective performance techniques that might be inherent in the performance of the employee or supervisor doing the training. Yet another disadvantage of on-the-job training is the potential cost to the organization of having work performed by an inexperienced employee. For example, in a restaurant an inexperienced waitperson that is being trained through on-the-job methods may potentially deliver poor-quality service to customers and consequently hurt the restaurant's reputation.

Organizations can use a variety of techniques for training employees. For example, Texas A&M University at Corpus Christi provides training in dealing with hazardous chemicals for the many refineries in the area. This training involves a combination of both work-based and instruction-based programs. These refinery workers, for example, listened to a classroom presentation about chemical disposal; now they are donning gear and equipment to actually practice what was described to them by an instructor.

■ **On-the-job training**, the most commonly used method of work-based training, involves having employees learn their job while they are actually performing it.

■ **Apprenticeship** combines on-the-job and classroom instruction.

Another work-based program for training is **apprenticeship training**, which combines on-the-job and classroom instruction. In most cases formal apprenticeship programs involve a coordinated effort by the employing organization, trainers in the workplace, one or more government agencies, and a skilled trade union. The government closely regulates most normal apprenticeship programs. In general, an apprentice entering a particular occupation must agree to a period of training and learning that may take as little as two years or as many as ten years.

For example, the job of an electrician is usually learned through a period of four to five years of apprenticeship. During this time the individual works under the tutelage of a licensed or "master" worker. The licensed or master worker earns a predetermined level of compensation, and the apprentice earns a lower wage. At the end of the formally defined apprenticeship program, the apprentice takes a test or must demonstrate other qualifications in some other way to attain his or her own license or certificate of mastery.

Another work-based program for training and development is vestibule training. **Vestibule training** involves performing a job under conditions that closely simulate the actual work environment. For example, a recent American Airlines television commercial portrays airline pilots regularly reporting to a flight simulator for updating and assessment. In this form of vestibule training, the flight simulator is designed to resemble as closely as possible the actual cockpit of a jetliner. Similarly, machine operators might be trained by using simulated equipment that is comparable to equipment they would use in the actual job setting.

■ **Vestibule training** involves performing a job under conditions that closely simulate the actual work environment.

Another method of work-based training program is **systematic job rotations and transfers**. This method is most likely to be used for lower-level managers or for operating employees being groomed for promotion to a supervisory management position. As the term suggests, the employee is systematically rotated or transferred from one job to another. The idea is to enable the employee to learn a wider array of tasks and skills and to develop a broader perspective on the overall task or work of the organization or the particular subunit.

■ **Systematic job rotations and transfers** involve employees being systematically rotated or transferred from one job to another.

Instructional-Based Programs

The second major family of training and development techniques and methods involves various **instructional-based programs**. The most commonly used instructional-based program is the **lecture or discussion approach** in which a trainer presents the material in a descriptive fashion. Just as a professor in college presents lectures to her or his students, a trainer in the organization lectures and presents the material to the trainees. Depending on the situation and the size of the training class, this approach may also include classroom discussions. Sometimes the lectures may be video or audio taped, allowing various individuals in the organization to receive the same training at different times and/or locations. One recent study found that 78 percent of the companies surveyed used lectures in 1997 but that only 61 percent expected to be using lectures by the year 2000. These firms expected to replace lecture-based training with nonclassroom training, primarily using electronic technologies.[10]

■ **Instructional-based programs** approach training and development from a teaching and learning perspective.

■ The **lecture or discussion approach** involves a trainer presenting the material in a descriptive fashion.

Southwest Airlines is using lecture and discussion training programs to help its reservations specialists cope with new federal guidelines regarding food allergies and airlines. The U.S. Department of Transportation has been pressuring airlines to better accommodate passengers with certain food-related allergies, especially allergies to peanuts and peanut products. Although such allergies are rare, they are also very dangerous. Southwest decided to use lecture and discussion training programs because they seemed to be the most cost-effective tools.[11]

Another instructional-based program for training and development is **computer-assisted instruction**. In this situation a trainee sits at a personal computer and operates special training software, using the keyboard or mouse to interface with the computer. The actual training materials are stored on the

■ In **computer-assisted instruction** a trainee sits at a personal computer and operates special training software.

computer's hard drive, a CD-ROM, or a Web site. Major advantages of this method are that it allows self-paced learning, and the trainee can receive immediate feedback.[12] "Human Resources in the Twenty-first Century" provides an interesting example of how one firm is using this approach. Moreover, a recent survey predicts that the percentage of firms using computer-assisted instruction will grow from only 9 percent in 1997 to as many as 23 percent by the year 2000.[13]

■ In **programmed instruction** the training material is bound into a manual or booklet, which the individual studies at his or her own pace.

Another method that involves basic instruction as a training device is **programmed instruction**. In this instance the training material is bound into a manual or booklet, which the individual studies at his or her own pace. Self-assessment activities generally follow each section or chapter, and the individual can then test her or his learning. Of course, a more formalized testing or assessment system is usually used at the completion of the training. (We should also note that programmed instruction is increasingly being computerized.

HUMAN RESOURCES in the **Twenty-first Century**

Training for the MTV Generation

 Marc Prensky, vice president of human resources for Bankers Trust, had a problem. For as long as anyone could remember, the training program for the firm's derivative traders consisted of their studying two-inch-thick manuals and sitting through endless dry lectures and videos. But the firm's newest and youngest traders were balking at this approach, using any excuse to skip training sessions or leaving halfway through. Finally, Prensky hit upon the answer—since the firm's young traders had grown up as part of the MTV and video-game generation, why not use a new approach to training that would be more exciting to the traders?

After getting enthusiastic approval from top management, Prensky assembled a team and went to work. Soon they had totally replaced Bankers Trust's traditional training materials and methods with a new set of materials, including board games and on-line quizzes using contemporary, and sometimes even irreverent, language and graphics. But the centerpiece of the new training model is a computer game called *Straight Shooter!*, patterned after the enormously popular video game *Doom*.

In playing *Straight Shooter!*, participants travel in cyberspace from New York to London to Hong Kong, navigating around an electronic world filled with menacing characters (bulls and bears in New York, werewolves in London, tigers in Hong Kong) representing problems and uncertainties. The traders destroy the problems, resolve

"In effect, we gave them depressants and then we wondered why they were bored."

(Marc Prensky, vice president of human resources at Bankers Trust)*

the uncertainties, and earn points by shooting dartlike "ideas" from their cell phones.

After players earn enough points, they encounter prospective investors who ask questions and pose investment problems. If players can answer the questions and solve the problems correctly—and use the firm's preferred methods to do so—the investor becomes a client and the trader earns more points. But when traders make mistakes, they may get fined or be told by the investor "Go back to business school" or "Don't call me, I'll call you." As traders earn certification, they begin competing with their colleagues around the world in an even more advanced version of the game.

Prensky says that the new training methods have been enormously successful. The derivative traders who have participated rave about both the fun and the value of the training, for example. In addition, Bankers Trust is finding that this training method is faster and cheaper than the previous approach. Indeed, Prensky's only real questions are why the firm didn't think of this approach sooner and why more companies aren't doing the same thing.

References: Jeffrey Rothfeder, "Training the 'Twitch' Generation," *Executive Edge*, September 1998, pp. 30–36; Mark Bernstein, "The Virtual Classroom: A Promising Solution for Teaching Technology," *HRMagazine*, May 1998, pp. 30–36; "Training Takes a Front Seat at Offices," *USA Today*, January 19, 1999, p. 6B; "Business Takes Up the Challenge of Training Its Rawest Recruits," *Business Week*, April 26, 1999, pp. 30–32.

However, it remains distinguished from computer-assisted instruction in both complexity and sophistication.)

Training Technology

In recent years the technology used for training has changed dramatically. Up until just a few years ago, virtually all training involved paper and pencil, individual instruction, and mechanical reproduction of tasks. In recent years, however, new technology has reshaped the way many companies deliver training to their employees. As already noted, for example, computer-assisted instruction has become more popular in recent years with the widespread adoption of personal computers.

Video teleconferencing is also increasingly useful to companies. They find that a trainer in a centralized location can effectively deliver material live via satellite hookup to multiple remote sites, thereby eliminating the travel costs necessary to transport people to a common training site. In the early days of video teleconferencing, communication tended to be one way. That is, the trainer presented the material, and attendees simply saw the material on a monitor. Now, however, there is considerably more interaction between trainers and trainees. The trainees usually have the capability of verbal interaction or electronic interaction by a keypad.

Yet another new method of training technology is interactive video. Interactive video is essentially a combination of standard video and computer-based instruction. The material is presented via video technology on a monitor from a central serving mechanism, a video disk, CD-ROM, or Web site. The trainee interacts with the system by a mouse or keyboard. Feedback can be provided when inadequate responses or improper answers are given, and the trainee can also skip familiar material.

Various team-building and group-based methods of training are also becoming increasingly popular. Given that more and more organizations are using teams as a basis for getting work done, many of these companies are finding it effective to develop training programs specifically designed to facilitate group cooperation. One popular method uses outdoor training exercises, such as a group going through a physical obstacle course involving rope climbing, crawling, and other physical activities. Outward Bound and several other independent companies specialize in these kinds of programs, and their clients include firms such as General Foods, Xerox, and Burger King.[14]

A recent extension of this model involves other team-based activities such as cooking classes.[15] Wells Fargo Bank and Genentech are among the firms using this approach. Regardless of the actual task or setting, these activities are structured so that each person can be more effective with the aid of the other members of the group. The idea is to teach group members to trust one another and to perform more effectively together.[16] Of course, as shown in "The Lighter Side of HR," not all employees see the value of these approaches!

THE BOTTOM LINE   Managers should recognize the fact that many types of training and development programs are available. The key, therefore, is to understand the strengths and weaknesses of each and to be able to balance these with costs and effectiveness to select the training and development techniques and methods best suited to the organization.

M A N A G E M E N T   D E V E L O P M E N T

Although training and management development have the same basic goal of learning, there are also significant differences between them. In this section we focus more specifically on management development needs and techniques.

Special Needs for Management Development

Many of the training and development issues and topics covered to this point are applicable to both standard training and development programs. There are also, however, specialized needs of management development. Recall from our earlier discussion that management development involves more generalized training for future roles and positions in the organization, as opposed to training for specific and immediately relevant tasks. Thus rather than attending a single training program, managers may need to participate in a variety of programs over a long period of time.

In general, management development may also be subject to somewhat different opportunities and limitations regarding material, training methods, and modes of instruction. For example, although the lecture method might be effective for certain kinds of learning and training activities, it is much less likely to be effective in teaching managers how to make decisions more effectively. Thus the learner needs to be a more active participant in a development program than is the case for many training programs.[17]

Special Techniques for Management Development

A number of specialized techniques are widely used for management development. One method or technique for management development is the so-called *in-basket exercise*. In an in-basket exercise, the individual is confronted with a hypothetical in basket of letters, memos, reports, phone messages, and e-mail messages that are associated with a particular manager. The trainee must then play the role of that manager by reading and evaluating all the items, jotting down how they should be handled, and prioritizing them. Useful feedback can then be given to help the trainee better understand correct and less correct prioritization and time management efforts.

Another popular management development technique is the *leaderless group exercise*. In this situation trainees are placed in a group setting and told to make a decision or to solve a problem. No individual in the group, however, is appointed as the chair or group leader. It is up to the group itself to realize that a leader must be appointed, and then it is up to that individual to initiate the leadership actions appropriate for helping the group effectively accomplish its goal.

Organization Development

A special form of management training that some organizations use very extensively is organization development. Organization development is generally

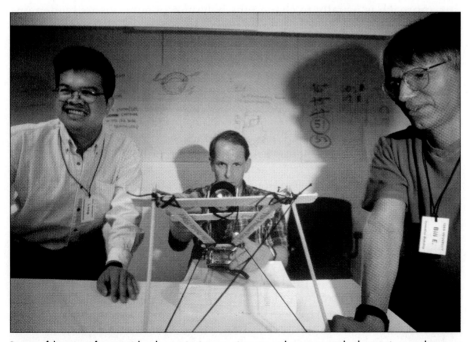

Because of the nature of managerial work, organizations sometimes approach management development in unusual ways. Moreover, they sometimes outsource some parts of their management development process to other firms. For example, Ideo U. is a specialized training firm that helps develop creativity. These employees, for example have been given 90 minutes to build a cannonball launcher. Structured exercises like this, accompanied by detailed feedback, help people better focus their creative ideas in ways that may be of more benefit to their employer. Among the firms that use Ideo are Cisco Systems, Apple Computer, Procter & Gamble, 3Com, Kodak, and Steelcase.

■ **Organization development** is a planned systemwide effort that is managed from the top of the organization to increase the organization's overall performance through interventions that rely heavily on behavioral science technology.

targeted at changing attitudes, perceptions, behaviors, and expectations. **Organization development** is a planned systemwide effort that is managed from the top of the organization to increase the organization's overall performance through interventions that rely heavily on behavioral science technology.

Organization development, or OD, as it is popularly called, assumes that employees have a desire to grow and to develop, that they have a strong need to be accepted by others in the organization, and that the organization itself and the way it is designed will influence the way individuals and groups within the organization behave. As a result, collaboration between managers and employees is necessary to take advantage of the skills and abilities of the employees and to eliminate aspects of the organization that limit employee growth, development, and group acceptance. OD is a very personal experience, and so, as a result, large organizations that want to use OD generally have one or more full-time OD consultants to implement and manage their OD programs.

A number of OD techniques are widely used. *Diagnostic OD* activities use questionnaires, opinion or attitude surveys, interviews, and meetings to analyze current conditions in an organization. The results of this diagnosis generate a profile of the organization, which is then used to identify areas in need of correction.

Survey feedback OD involves having employees respond to questionnaires that measure such perceptions and attitudes as job satisfaction and assessments of supervisory style. Everyone involved in the survey, including the supervisor, then receives the results of the survey. The purpose of this approach is usually to change the behavior of supervisors by demonstrating how their subordinates view them. After the feedback has been provided, it is common to conduct workshops to help evaluate results and to suggest constructive changes.

Sometimes OD is undertaken to solve specific problems, such as interpersonal conflict that may currently exist in the organization. *Third-party peacemaking*, for example, is a common OD technique with this goal. A third party, often an external OD consultant, comes into the organization, listens to both sides of the issues, and helps the parties arrive at a mutually satisfactory solution or agreement. Various mediation or negotiation techniques are frequently used.

Another common OD technique is called process consultation. In process consultation the OD consultant observes managers in the organization to develop an understanding of their communication patterns, decision-making and leadership processes, and methods of cooperation and conflict resolution. The consultant then provides feedback to the involved parties about the processes she or he has observed. The goal of this approach is to improve the observed processes, but this goal has, at times, led to criticism of this type of training. The issue is whether or not improved communication processes are a worthwhile goal in their own right. We touch upon this issue again in the next section, but it is worth noting here as well. In any event, for quite a few years some critics have argued that, although these programs are often successful at changing communication patterns, process consultation rarely leads to any improvement in organizational effectiveness.[18]

THE BOTTOM LINE Managers should remember that although many of the concepts associated with training are applicable to management development, development activities have special needs as well. Moreover, managers should also be familiar with special techniques for management development and should understand the uses and limitations of organization development.

EVALUATING TRAINING AND DEVELOPMENT

Although it is common to evaluate all elements of human resource management, the evaluation of training and development has perhaps the longest history and is among one of the aspects of human resources that is most important to evaluate. The reason is that, unlike many other as Aspects of human resource management, the evaluation of training and development is something that can be readily undertaken. That is, given that the purpose of training and development is to enact a fundamental change in performance behavior or other outcome variable, the outcome of the training and development program should be amenable to a clear assessment and evaluation.[19] "Human Resources Fad, Fashion, or Fact?" presents some additional sobering information that reinforces the importance of evaluating training and development activities.

For example, consider the case of a routine training program. Suppose that an organization has recently bought new copy machines for its administrative facilities. The training program might be conducted to teach employees how the copy equipment works. For example, it would be useful to know how to change paper, how to change toner cartridges, how to set the machine for various jobs, and how to do routine problem solving and trouble shooting in the case of a mild malfunction. Assuming that the training program has been properly designed, that is, instructional goals and content have been clearly specified, then it should be a relatively straightforward undertaking to determine whether or not the training has actually worked. Thus when the training program has been completed, all target employees should be able to demonstrate that they are capable of changing paper, changing toner cartridges, and so forth. Simply having individuals perform this task under the supervision of the trainer should provide a clear indication of the success or lack thereof of the training program.

Several issues must be understood, however. The most fundamental issue has to do with being able to really assess change. Thus it is important to understand a priori which behaviors and skills currently exist so that the evaluator will be able to subsequently determine whether or not changes have actually occurred. For example, if the evaluator wants to know whether training has enhanced an employee's ability to operate a particular piece of equipment at a faster pace, it is necessary to have some basis for understanding what the pre-training level of performance actually was. Thus some measures of performance should be taken before the training program begins. Then, after the training, the same variables are measured again. Statistically significant positive changes usually indicate that the training program has resulted in the appropriate outcome.

HUMAN RESOURCES Fad, Fashion, or Fact?

Training—Valuable Investment or a Waste of Money?

 Faced with crippling skill shortages, employers are spending skyrocketing amounts of money training workers.

The problem? Many programs just don't work.

Billions of dollars are spent on wasteful training courses, experts say. But new studies show most on-the-job learning happens outside the classroom.

"Companies would rather throw money at a problem than solve it, so people just pursue the program du jour," says Alan Weiss, author of *Our Emperors Have No Clothes*, on how bad management led to layoffs. "It's the white elephant no one talks about."

About $5.6 billion to $16.8 billion is wasted annually on ineffective traing programs that focus on so-called soft skills, based on estimates from a Rutgers University study. That estimate, derived from a mathematical formula, varied according to assumptions used by researchers.

The issue is getting mounting attention as training programs grow in popularity.

The Conference Board, a nonprofit research and business group, will host a gathering today in New York that will look at new training strategies.

Training problems:

• **Employees aren't motivated.** Workers who see training as a career boost will learn and feel loyal to a company, experts say.

"American industry is spending billions and billions on training programs and doing no evaluation of their effectiveness. You have to measure."

(Cary Cherniss, professor at Rutgers University)*

"You have to want to do it because it's going to take effort and it's going to take time," says Daniel Goleman, author of *Working with Emotional Intelligence*.

• **Programs are poorly designed.** Companies may unwittingly support unimaginative or dull programs that employees find deter learning.

• **Trainers lack expertise.** Those providing training may not know their audience, or they lack teaching skills.

Hoping to pique interest, some firms are turning to eclectic training approaches.

Spring Paranet in Houston requires technical analysts to take two weeks of training a year. There is also a week-long retreat for some new hires.

Bankers trust has married training with 3-D video-games. In one game, employees try to land clients by reacting to simulated problems.

Others turn to wilderness adventures, computer-based learning or mountain retreats.

But experts say businesses should check for results to separate effective programs from costly gimmicks.

"American industry is spending billions and billions on training programs and doing no evaluation of their effectiveness," says Cary Cherniss, a professor at Rutgers. "You have to measure it."

Source: "Big Lesson: Billions Wasted on Job-Skills Training," *USA Today*, October 7, 1998, p. B1 (*quote from same source), Copyright 1998, *USA Today*. Reprinted with permission.

Evaluating management development programs is also important but is a bit more complex. Given that the development program is intended to help prepare managers for future jobs, the payoff or outcome of specific development programs may not be apparent for some time. Furthermore, management development programs tend to have more complex goals in terms of what is to be learned than do more basic types of training programs. Nevertheless, the organization should not let this difficulty keep it from attempting to evaluate development programs.

Organizations often take a number of approaches in trying to evaluate these programs. Oftentimes, organizations rely on evaluations completed by the trainees after a particular training program. This practice is common even when other evaluation techniques are used, since it is potentially always useful to know how participants reacted to the training. Therefore, an organization might have the trainees in a management development program complete an evaluation form by indicating the extent to which they found the program to be useful, relevant, interesting, appropriate, and so forth.

A confound in this method, however, is that it is subject to bias based in part on the nature of the experience the trainees received as opposed to the content of the experience itself. For example, if the trainer was amusing, humorous, well organized, and made the session interesting, there may be positive bias in the evaluation, even though the content of the training program may not have been adequate. On the other hand, an individual may have delivered a very effective training program but received less positive evaluations because she or he was less interesting or didn't have as much pizzazz in the program.

Even if this potential bias does not affect the responses of trainees, there is an additional, and perhaps more serious, limitation to this approach to evaluation. Whether or not the participants believe that the content of the training program is adequate may have little impact on whether they actually change the way they behave on the job. Thus trainees might be extremely pleased with the training program and how it was delivered, but because of problems with design or other conditions on the job, the training may still have no detectable impact on their behavior. Furthermore, even if behavior does change in an area such as communication patterns with subordinates, this outcome may still not address the longer-term needs of the organization and the reason(s) that it instituted the management development program.

Ultimately, the evaluation of management development needs to focus on overall organizational effectiveness. If an organization institutes a management development program that focuses on communication skills, it would be beneficial if the participants reported that the training was useful. It would be even more beneficial if fewer arguments were observed and fewer subordinates filed grievances based on interactions with managers. But the ultimate test of the effectiveness of the program would be if these changes resulted in lower turnover among employees who were now more satisfied with their supervisors and, perhaps, more willing to exert effort on the job for those supervisors.

This discussion leads to one final consideration in the evaluation (and to some extent, in the design) of training programs. All training content can be characterized as being either specific or general in content. **General training** provides trainees with skills and abilities that can be applied in any organization. For example, sending a management employee to a program designed to improve writing skills provides that manager with a skill or with some information that he or she can carry to any other organization. In fact, the manager is now "worth" more to other organizations because of this training. As a result, turnover rates often rise when organizations provide general training. Therefore, although the development program may be accomplishing the goals set out by the organization (that is, improving communication patterns), such a program might actually *hurt* longer-term effectiveness by resulting in other firms hiring valued employees from the organization.

Specific training makes it less likely the employee has anything he or she can bring to a different organization. In these cases the organization provides the manager (or other employee) with skills or information that is of use *only* to that organization. For example, training a manager to use the new accounting procedure introduced in the organization will not do much to make that manager more attractive to a competing firm. In Chapter 11 we discuss recent trends towards skill- and knowledge-based pay in organizations. An organization that is embarking on and designing training to support such a program must consider the potential costs associated with providing general training as opposed to the costs of designing specific training programs and rewarding employees for acquiring specific skills that might be less critical in the future.

■ **General training** provides trainees with skills and abilities that can be applied in any organization.

■ **Specific training** provides the trainee with skills or information that are of use *only* to the present organization.

This discussion leads us to consider the fact that some organizations actually rely indirectly on other firms to do their management development for them. That is, some firms, such as General Electric, Arthur Andersen, and Motorola, are known in their respective industries to be outstanding developers of management talent. Thus other organizations may look to these firms as a source of professionally groomed and developed managers. So instead of doing its own management development work, an organization might allow other firms to do this work and then hire managers away once they have reached a certain point in the organization. Thus the "training" organization bears the costs of training and some of the benefits, whereas the "other" organization may have to pay more to lure away the needed management talent but is able to reap many of the benefits without incurring any of the direct costs of the training.

Chapter Summary

Training usually involves teaching operational or technical employees how to do their jobs more effectively and/or more efficiently. Development is more generally aimed at helping managers better understand and solve problems, make decisions, and capitalize on opportunities. Learning is fundamental to both, however, and must always be considered when planning, conducting, and evaluating training and development programs and activities.

One important part of an organization's training and development program is new-employee orientation. An orientation program generally has a clear and specific set of goals. In planning an orientation for new employees, human resource managers must deal with a variety of basic issues. These issues include the content of the orientation, the length of the orientation, and the decision of who will actually conduct the orientation.

The starting point in employee training is to assess training and development needs. This process generally involves consideration of three things: needs analysis, the establishment of training and development goals, and decisions regarding in-house training versus outsourced training and development.

The actual design of programs is the foundation to effective training and development. The first step in constructing training and development programs is to create a detailed outline of the intended program. The next step in the development of the program is to define its content, focusing on what is to be learned. Finally, the organization must select instructors to deliver the material.

A number of techniques and methods can be used for the actual delivery of information. Work-based programs tie the training and development activities directly to performance of the task. The second major family of training and development techniques and methods involves various instructional-based programs. New technology also plays a key role in training and development today.

The area of management development has its own specialized needs. In general, management development may also be subject to somewhat different opportunities and limitations regarding material, training methods, and modes of instruction. A number of specialized techniques are also widely used for management development. A special form of management training that some organizations use very extensively is organization development.

Organizations need to do a good job of evaluating the effectiveness of their training and development activities. Because the costs of such activities are quite high and because their effectiveness is often easy to measure, there is little reason to neglect this important activity.

Review and Discussion Questions

1. What are the basic differences between training and development?

2. How does learning theory relate to training?

3. What are the basic goals of orientation?

4. In what ways are training and orientation similar, and in what ways are they different?

5. Discuss the role and importance of needs analysis as a part of employee training.

6. What are the advantages and disadvantages of in-house training versus outsourced training?

7. Describe the basic steps and processes through which training and development programs are developed.

8. Identify and discuss the basic training and development techniques and methods discussed in the chapter.

9. What are the special techniques often used for management development?

10. What is organization development? What are the basic methods for organization development that many organizations use?

Closing Case

Boeing Trains for the Future

IntraGlobal Airlines is a company going nowhere: its sales are flat, its passengers are complaining about dirty airplanes, and the company is increasingly having to cancel flights because its old Boeing 747s are breaking down so often. Managers responsible for fixing the ailing airline face an array of tough decisions. For example, they know they need to buy new planes, but don't know which models to buy or how to pay for them. They also know they need to change their route structure, but abandoning a city that's been loyal to the company will no doubt prove to be bad public relations. And the firm's image is so bad that managers believe they may even need to come up with a new name for the carrier, along with a new logo and color scheme for its planes.

But what makes IntraGlobal especially interesting as a business is that it really doesn't even exist! Indeed, it is simply the product of some fertile minds at Boeing, the largest aircraft manufacturer in the world. IntraGlobal is a case study that serves as the centerpiece of an intense two-week management development seminar that Boeing runs quarterly for airline executives from around the world. To date, around one thousand airline employees have taken part in the program, and it is booked for at least the next year.

IntraGlobal was developed to mirror as closely as possible the very real problems that once existed at airlines such as Pan American and National, before they ceased operations, and Continental, before its recent dramatic turnaround. But because the simulation isn't based on any single airline's problems and experiences, executives attending the seminar can't simply mimic what others managers did in the past. Instead, attendees have to closely study IntraGlobal's fictitious management structure, balance sheets and other financial indicators, route map and structure, and internal memoranda that are provided by the seminar's instructor.

Many senior managers from U.S. airlines such as American, Delta, and Continental and international airlines like Lufthansa and JAI have already completed Boeing's seminar. Today the audience is primarily managers from small and medium-sized airlines in Latin America and Eastern Europe. Most of those who come are already specialists in one or more aspects of airline management, such as route management or finance. They come to Boeing to deepen their knowledge and to learn about other functions involved in effective airline operations.

And virtually everyone who attends the seminar walks away having learned new things. For example, in one recent session most attendees were surprised to learn that engineers can change the maximum power capabilities of an airplane engine. Others were surprised to hear that filling up all the seats on planes is not always a good thing—full planes mean uncomfortable and disgruntled passengers and often drive customers to competitors. And still other participants learned to appreciate for the very first time the importance of mission statements and the appearance of an airplane.

So how much does Boeing charge airlines for running this program for their executives? Nothing! The only constraints imposed by Boeing are that no single airline can send more than two individuals to any given training session and that those who are sent are indeed senior managers. Boeing argues that it runs the training to provide a service for the industry. In addition, Boeing managers claim that by interacting with a variety of airline executives and hearing about what does and does not work for them, the firm learns how to build better airplanes. There is also the possibility, of course, that executives who go through the training program may be more inclined to favor Boeing the next time their airline needs to order new jets.

Case Questions

1. What are the benefits and weaknesses of Boeing's training program from the standpoint of the airlines who send their executives to attend?

2. What are the pros and cons of the training from Boeing's point of view?

3. What other companies in different industries might consider providing training of the sort offered by Boeing?

Sources: "'Boeing U': Flying by the Book," *USA Today*, October 6, 1997, pp. 1B, 2B; "Behind Boeing's Woes: Clunky Assembly Line, Price War with Airbus," *Wall Street Journal*, April 4, 1998, pp. A1, A16; "Can a New Crew Buoy Boeing?" *Business Week*, September 14, 1998, p. 53.

Building Human Resource Management Skills

Purpose: The purpose of this exercise is to give you more insights into the processes associated with effective training and development activities.

Step 1: Select a job with which you have some familiarity. This might be one you are currently performing or have performed in the past. Alternatively, it might be a job that you have had ample opportunity to observe—service station attendant, fast-food employee, hair stylist, and so on.

Step 2: Assume that you are responsible for developing a training program to improve the job skills and performance of people currently doing the target job. Outline each step you would take, being as specific as possible for the actual job itself. Pay special attention to the steps of setting goals, selecting training methods, and evaluation.

Step 3: If you used a job that you actually perform or have performed in the past, compare your training program with whatever training the organization uses. Alternatively, interview a manager in the organization you used for the target job and learn how the organization actually does training. Ask the manager to critique your plan.

1. How easy or difficult did you find this activity?

2. Was there something about the job that made the exercise easier or harder than you might otherwise have expected?

3. How important do you think it is for a trainer to have personal experience in performing a job before trying to teach others how to do it?

Ethical Dilemmas in Human Resource Management

Assume that you are a senior manager for a medium-sized company. Your firm recently merged with two others companies to create a much larger firm. The integration of the three firms is almost complete. Your functional area will now be led by a team of nine managers, three each from the three original firms. You are the senior manager in the team. The new company is now trying to figure out how to best go about completing the integration, especially with regard to creating trust and a spirit of cooperation among the various sets of people who have little or no experience working together.

One team member has suggested that you all go through an outdoor adventure program together. She has already done some homework and suggested a company that conducts one-week survival-type, team-building programs involving white-water rafting, rope climbing, and other similar activities. You know that she has already discussed her idea with her two colleagues from her former company and that they are also very enthusiastic about the idea.

You are very concerned about one thing, however: one of your team members (let's call him Joe) from the other firm is confined to a wheelchair and also needs supplemental oxygen periodically. Although the outdoor adventure company claims to be able to accommodate participants with disabilities, you have serious doubts. Moreover, Joe has heard the rumors about the trip and has already spoken to you. He has urged you to go ahead with the idea but believes that he should not participate. He isn't sure whether he is physically up to it, and he doesn't really want to go, but you sense you can talk him into going if you try.

You are really unsure how to proceed. On the one hand, rejecting the suggestion made by your new team member might alienate her and her two colleagues. On the other hand, going ahead with her idea might cause Joe to be less integrated into the team than you would like and might cause him to feel left out. In addition, although you haven't consulted them, you worry that Joe's colleagues might resent the team doing something from which he is being excluded. Thus you see these options: (1) going on the one-week outdoor-survival program with everyone except Joe, (2) going on the survival program and convincing Joe to come along, (3) eliminating the survival program as an option and seeking another, more inclusive activity with you making the decision, (4) eliminating the survival program as an option but allowing the group to find an alternative, or (5) not doing anything but assuming that team building will occur naturally as the new group members begin to really work together.

Questions

1. What are the ethical issues in this situation?

2. What are the basic arguments for and against the different options available to you?

3. What do you think most managers would do? What would you do?

Human Resource Internet Exercise

 As noted in the chapter, computer-assisted training is becoming more and more popular. And increasingly, this training is being provided via the Internet. As a first step, search the Web to see what information you can find about Internet-based training. For example, see what you can find in terms of actual Internet-based training programs, consulting support for managers interested in Internet-based training, and so forth. Next respond to the questions below.

Questions

1. What do you see as the primary advantages and disadvantages of Internet-based training and development?

2. Are there certain kinds of jobs that would seem to be more and less amenable to Internet-based training? On what do you base your answer?

3. Do you think Internet-based training might someday replace all or most other forms of training? Why or why not?

4. If you were interested in a career as a trainer for a major corporation, what Internet skills do you think would be most beneficial to you personally? How might you most effectively learn these skills?

Notes

1. See Charles R. Greer, *Strategy and Human Resources* (Englewood Cliffs, N.J.: Prentice-Hall, 1995), Chapter 1 for an overview of the importance of training and development; see also "Teach a Man to Fish," *Forbes*, April 19, 1999, pp. 94–104.
2. Paul Chaddock, "Building Value with Training," *Training & Development*, July 1995, pp. 22–26.
3. Marcia Atkinson, "Build Learning into Work," *HRMagazine*, September 1994, pp. 60–64.
4. J. Bruce Tracey, Scott I. Tannenbaum, and Michael J. Kavanagh, "Applying Trained Skills on the Job: The Importance of the Work Environment," *Journal of Applied Psychology*, Vol. 80, No. 2, 1995, pp. 239–252.
5. Kathryn Tyler, "Take New Employee Orientation off the Back Burner," *HRMagazine*, May 1998, pp. 49–54.
6. "Corporate America Goes to School," *Business Week*, October 20, 1997, pp. 66–72; see also Ed Brown, "A Day at Innovation U.," *Fortune*, April 12, 1999, pp. 163–165.

7. Teresa L. Smith, "The Basics of Basic Skills Training," *Training & Development*, April 1995, pp. 44–49.

8. Robert M. Gagne, "Learning Outcomes and Their Effects: Useful Categories of Human Performance," *American Psychologist*, Vol. 39, 1984, pp. 377–385.

9. Jack Stack, "The Training Myth," *Inc.*, August 1998, pp. 41–42.

10. "Training Takes Front Seat at Offices," *USA Today*, January 19, 1999, p. 6B.

11. "U.S. Tells Airlines They Should Offer Peanut-Free Rows," *Wall Street Journal*, September 2, 1998, pp. A1, A8.

12. Jane Webster and Joseph J. Martocchio, "The Differential Effects of Software Training Previews on Training Outcomes," *Journal of Management*, Vol. 21, No. 4, 1995, pp. 757–787.

13. "Training Takes Front Seat at Offices," *USA Today*, January 19, 1999, p. 6B.

14. "Leader of the Pack in Wilderness Training Is Pushed to the Wall," *Wall Street Journal*, July 24, 1997, pp. A1, A6.

15. "Work Week," *Wall Street Journal*, November 24, 1998, p. A1.

16. Christine Clements, Richard J. Wagner, and Christopher C. Roland, "The Ins and Outs of Experiential Training," *Training & Development*, February 1995, pp. 52–54.

17. Kathryn Tyler, "Simon Says, 'Make Learning Fun,'" *HRMagazine*, June 1996, pp. 162–166.

18. Marvin D. Dunnette and John P. Campbell, "Laboratory Education: Impact on People and Organizations," *Industrial Relations*, Vol. 8, 1968, pp. 1–27, 41–44.

19. Hyuckseung Yang, Paul R. Sackett, and Richard D. Arvey, "Statistical Power and Cost in Training Evaluation: Some New Considerations," *Personnel Psychology*, Autumn 1996, pp. 651–668.

10

Career Planning and Development

CHAPTER OUTLINE

The Nature of Careers
The Meaning of Career
Traditional Career Stages
Emerging Career Stages

Human Resource Management and Career Management
Organizational Perspectives on Careers
Individual Perspectives on Careers

Career Planning and Career Management
The Importance of Career Planning
The Consequences of Career Planning
Limitations and Pitfalls in Career Planning

Career Management for New Entrants
Early-Career Issues
Coping with Early-Career Problems

Career Management for Midcareer Employees
Midcareer Issues
Coping with Midcareer Problems

Career Management for Late-Career Employees
Late-Career Issues
Coping with Late-Career Problems

Career Development Issues and Challenges
Career-Counseling Programs
Dual-Career and Work-Family Issues

Evaluating Career Management Activities

CHAPTER OBJECTIVES

After studying this chapter you should be able to:

- Describe the nature of careers.

- Relate human resource management to career development.

- Discuss career planning and career management for new entrants, mid-career employees, and late-career employees.

- Identify and describe related contemporary career development issues and challenges.

For decades the career path to the executive suite was the near-exclusive domain of white males. But in recent years things have begun to change, and more and more women and minorities are entering executive management positions. A few are even making it to the very top, and many more seem destined to make it in the next few years. One of the most recent to achieve the senior management position in a major corporation is Jill Barad, chairman and chief executive officer of toy giant Mattel Inc.

Ms. Barad started her education by majoring in English and drama at Queens College. She dropped out after three years and took an $18,000-a-year job selling makeup for Love Cosmetics. But a year later she quit this job, returned to school and earned her degree. After graduation in 1974 she went to work for Coty Cosmetics as a traveling cosmetician-trainer. While selling Coty cosmetics, she began to develop a knack for understanding what both customers and sales people really wanted and to develop new packaging and display ideas that better suited both audiences.

A few years later she followed what was then the normal path for most women—she got married, quit work, and had a baby. But Barad quickly realized that being a stay-at-home wife and mom was not for her. She returned to work at a relatively low-level job in the novelty-development unit of Mattel. She immediately impressed top management with her knowledge of the business and her aggressiveness. Almost immediately she started demanding better assignments and got them.

"My mother gave me a bumblebee pin when I started work. She said: 'Aerodynamically, bees shouldn't be able to fly. But they do.' Remember that. I can say that for you girls, anything is possible."

(Jill Barad, chairman and CEO, Mattel Inc.)*

And after only two years with the company, Barad was made a product manager on the Barbie team.

Although Barbie had always been a Mattel mainstay, at the time of her promotion sales of the venerable doll had been stalling. Barad began segmenting the Barbie market, introduced products such as the Day to Night Barbie, and in the process, boosted annual Barbie sales from $200 million to $1.9 billion. Barad's career began to take off, and she was eventually appointed to the position of vice president. In 1992 she became co-president and was appointed chairman and CEO in 1997.

Barad admits that her career has cost her time with her family, and she credits her husband's willingness to do a major share of the parenting as enabling her to pursue her career. She is often held up as a role model for women in management but shies away from this label. She does not see herself as a model for anyone, but as someone who has worked hard and made it. Furthermore, she has made it on her own terms. She is not particularly nurturing (although she is *very* supportive of women in business), she has high standards, and she has been described as abrasive and rude. She is also known as an exemplary manager and an outstanding executive—and one that just happens to be female.

"The Rise of Jill Barad," *Business Week,* May 25, 1998, pp. 112–119 (*quote on p. 112); *Hoover's Handbook of American Business 1999* (Austin, Texas: Hoover's Business Press, 1999), pp. 914–915.

Jill Barad's adult life has followed an interesting series of twists and turns—education, work, more education, more work, stopping work for husband and family, return to work, advancement in the organization, and finally, reaching the organization's pinnacle, the position of chairman and CEO. No other top executive has followed this exact path to his or her job—each has had a unique series of events that brought him or her there. Some of these events are determined by the individual, some by the organization, some by circumstance, and some by luck. But regardless of the exact set of events or their sequence, each makes up a successful career that has shaped not only the life of the specific executive but also the fortunes of thousands of others.

Performance appraisal and management (the topics of Chapter 8) and training, development, and organizational learning (covered in Chapter 9) are obviously important components of how organizations go about enhancing the motivation and performance of their employees. An equally important element of the enhancement of motivation and performance is the set of activities and processes that constitute career planning and development. This chapter explores the concepts of career planning and development in detail. We first establish the nature of careers and then relate human resource management and career management more explicitly. After discussing career planning and career management issues, we turn to career management for new entrants to an organization. Subsequent sections examine career management for midcareer and for late-career employees. After examining of career development issues and challenges, we conclude by discussing how organizations can evaluate career management activities.

T H E   N A T U R E   O F   C A R E E R S

Most people have a general idea of the meaning of career. For instance, people generally agree that careers have something to do with the work a person does in an organization but also recognize that a career is a broader and more general concept than a single job or task in an organization.

The Meaning of Career

■ A **career** is the set of work-related experiences and activities that people engage in related to their job and livelihood over the course of their working life.

We will define a **career** as the set of work-related experiences and activities that people engage in related to their job and livelihood over the course of their working life. This definition, then, suggests that a career includes the various specific jobs that a person performs, the kinds of responsibilities and activities that make up those jobs, movements and transitions between jobs, and an individual's overall assessment of and feelings of satisfaction with these various components of her or his career.

According to the traditional viewpoint, the various components of a person's career generally have some degree of interrelationship. This belief stems from the fact that, in the past at least, people generally wanted to work for a single organization and spent most of their work life within that single organization. For example, Jacques Nasser, the new president and CEO of Ford Motor

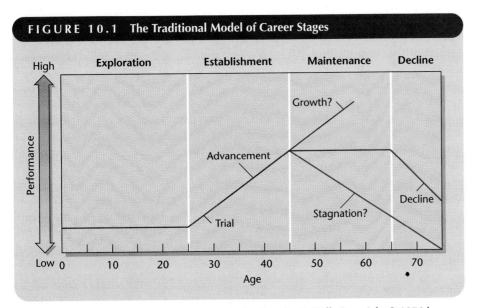

FIGURE 10.1 **The Traditional Model of Career Stages**

Source: Adapted from *Careers in Organizations,* by Douglas T. Hall. Copyright © 1976 by Scott, Foresman and Co. Reprinted by permission of Douglas T. Hall and Lyman Porter.

Company, has worked for more than thirty years with that same company. Presumably, if people performed effectively and were successful at their work, they advanced up the organizational hierarchy. And even when people changed jobs, they tended to go to work for other organizations in the same industry. For example, although Lee Iacocca is perhaps best known for saving Chrysler a few years ago, at earlier times in his career he worked for both General Motors and Ford.

But in recent times conceptualizations of careers have become considerably more general. Because of organizational downsizing efforts and innovations such as outsourcing and shared services, the work patterns of individuals are considerably more varied than they were in the past.[1] Increasingly, for instance, people are likely to leave an organization in one industry and go to work for an organization in a totally different industry; they may also spend some time between jobs and organizations consulting or working in otherwise independent contractor–type positions. Louis Gerstner, chairman and CEO at IBM, was hired away from RJR Nabisco, a major food-processing company.

And more and more frequently, people are also taking breaks from their work. These include sabbaticals, discretionary periods of unemployment, and similar activities that may make a positive contribution to a person's overall work life, but do not involve formal employment by an organization. Recall, for example, that Jill Barad took a break from work before joining Mattel. And people who return to school to enhance their education are likely to consider that period of their life as a part of their career.

Traditional Career Stages

There has long been a generally accepted view of the career stages that a typical individual progresses through. As shown in Figure 10.1, the first stage is called **exploration.** This period typically starts in a person's mid- to late teens

■ **Exploration** is the first traditional career stage and involves identifying interests and opportunities.

and lasts through the mid- to late twenties. It generally encompasses the time when people really try to assess their interests, values, preferences, and career opportunities and to relate them to a feasible career option. Coursework in school and first jobs play an important role in the exploration stage of career development.

For example, it is not uncommon for students to change majors once they begin taking courses in an area. Similarly, sometimes people take their first job in a particular field, discover it's not what they expected, and then begin to look for alternative options. But of course, sometimes people are perfectly happy with the outcomes of the exploration stage. They find that the coursework of their field is indeed of high interest to them, and their first job assignment is exciting, challenging, and just what they expected it to be.

■ The **establishment** stage of the traditional career model involves creating a meaningful and relevant role in the organization.

The second stage of a typical career is called the **establishment** stage. During this period individuals begin to create meaningful and relevant roles for themselves within the organization. Someone may, for example, become a valuable member of a work team, achieve success and recognition by superiors, and be acknowledged by the organization as someone that the company values and wants to retain. Although there is, of course, considerable range in terms of age and time in this stage, it generally encompasses the late twenties through the mid- to late thirties.

■ The **maintenance** stage involves optimizing talents or capabilities.

The **maintenance** stage is the next stage in a typical career. During this period individuals begin to reach a level in the organization that optimizes their talents or capabilities. Clearly, for example, not everyone can become a CEO, and only a few employees in any organization ever attain top executive status. Many very successful managers, especially in larger companies, never progress beyond the ranks of middle management but nevertheless enjoy highly productive and worthwhile careers. Individuals in the maintenance stage of their career must often devote extra effort to learning new job skills and remaining current in their professional skills and abilities. Similarly, they are also frequently called upon to play mentoring roles in which they help newcomers to the organization get their feet on the ground and launch their own careers.[2]

■ In the fourth traditional career stage, **disengagement,** the individual gradually begins to pull away from work in the organization, priorities change, and work may become less important.

Finally, the fourth stage of a typical career is the **disengagement** stage. During this period individuals gradually begin to pull away from work in the organization, their priorities change, and work may become less important. Consequently, they begin thinking more and more about leaving the organization and finding other sources for fulfilling personal needs and goals. Some may evolve toward part-time work status, some may retire from the organization, and some may simply reduce their activities and responsibilities.

Emerging Career Stages

Of course, in the contemporary era of downsizing and layoffs, sometimes people go through these four stages of career development in a relatively short period of time. Indeed a person may find her- or himself disengaging from the organization at a relatively young age and may also anticipate beginning the entire process again by seeking new opportunities, new challenges, and new interests.[3] Indeed, many experts agree that while the traditional model of careers summarized above still has conceptual value, a new perspective such as the one shown in Figure 10.2 is a more accurate representation of career stages now and in the future.

HUMAN RESOURCES **Fad, Fashion, or Fact?**

The New Career Model . . . or a Model for Failure?

Many people are familiar with what has been called the "traditional" career model. Under this model employees went to work for an organization and remained there for most, if not all, of their careers. Changing organizations was rare and was usually precipitated by unusual problems or opportunities. More recently, some experts are arguing that this traditional model is disappearing and that, in today's world, the only way to manage one's career is to move around (and up) as often as possible. In fact, many organizations have introduced programs to try to induce employees to remain in one place, presumably because so many employees have come to see job changing as a positive career move.

And indeed, there is considerable evidence to suggest that managers are switching jobs at an unprecedented rate. And according to a New York–based search firm, many firms are increasingly looking outside when they have a managerial position to fill, further feeding the tendency to switch jobs. But is job switching, in fact, a good career strategy? Recent information raises some serious questions.

Two recent studies, for example, report that about 40 percent of new managers fail within the first eighteen months, and their performance was judged "significantly below expectations." With those kinds of numbers, perhaps switching jobs is not the best way to manage a career. Whether or not this is the case, though, depends largely on the reasons why organizations are experiencing such high rates of failure. The most frequent reason given for failure is that the new managers failed to build good relationships with peers and subordinates. This was followed by (in order) confusion or uncertainty about what top management expected, a lack of internal political skills, and an inability to achieve the two or three

"When the job market is booming like this, traditional search firms can't do quality work. Some of these people are handling seventeen searches at a time. How can you do a really good job at any of them?"

(Bill Morin, search firm and career-coaching expert)*

most important objectives of the new job. These reasons raise suspicions about a more significant underlying concern.

With all the job switching activity that is going on and all the pressures on search firms to identify suitable candidates, there is a good chance that no one is paying enough attention to the importance of fit between the new manager and the new company. Search firms conducting multiple searches simultaneously, for example, may not have the time or the resources to really understand the needs of the job and how well the candidate fits those needs. The managers themselves, thrilled with the myriad of new possibilities and the impression that job switching is a good career move, may not be assessing their fit very well, either. Perhaps as important, from the manager's point of view, these pressures may cause the new manager to fail to identify those critical expectations held by the new organization.

Is job switching a good career move, then? Perhaps not always. It is becoming clear that failure rates are rising, and if you switch jobs *too* often, you may face other obstacles later in your career. We have clearly moved away from the model where a manager remains with the same organization throughout a career, but perhaps managers who are contemplating switching organizations as a career move should be more cautious about the choices they make. More time spent in ensuring that the manager is a good fit with the new company and in discussing expectations and timetables may be the critical factors in determining whether switching really is a wise career move or just an invitation to failure.

References: Anne Fisher, "Don't Blow Your New Job," *Fortune,* June 22, 1998, pp. 159–162 (*quote on p. 160); Bill Breen, "Interview with a Headhunter," *Fast Company,* January 1999, pp. 154–161.

This model also suggests a progression of career stages. But it focuses more on "career age" (that is, how long a person has been in a particular job), rather than chronological age, and directly incorporates the premise of multiple career states. The model describes career stages of exploration, trial, and establishment, followed by another period of exploration. This second level of exploration, in turn, is likely to take the person away from the current career and

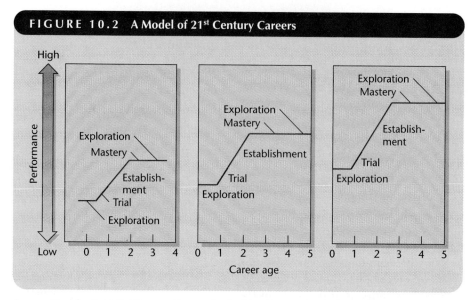

FIGURE 10.2   A Model of 21st Century Careers

into a new one where the process begins again. "Human Resources Fad, Fashion, or Fact?" on page 301 discusses some related issues associated with job switching.

THE BOTTOM LINE   Managers need to understand the basic conceptual model of traditional career stages for situations in which it may still be applicable but also need to be aware of newer and emerging perspectives on careers. The most important issue, however, is that careers have stages, and managers need to understand how they got to where they are now and where they are likely to go next.

HUMAN RESOURCE MANAGEMENT AND CAREER MANAGEMENT

Most successful organizations and managers today recognize that careers aren't something that simply happen. Indeed, successful careers must be planned and managed. Part of this responsibility resides with the organization, but the individual must also play an important role.[4] This section examines the organizational and individual perspectives on careers shown in Figure 10.3.

Organizational Perspectives on Careers

Organizations are generally responsible for determining the jobs that people will perform for the organization, the pattern of interrelationships between jobs in an organization, the kinds of people that will be hired for those jobs, the development of those individuals to prepare them for more meaningful jobs, and the decisions regarding the movement of people from one job to another. Clearly, then, it is in the organization's best interest to take an active role in career management for its people.[5]

From the outset organizations can facilitate career management. For example, in Chapter 7 we discussed the idea of selecting individuals not because of their match with the requirements of a specific job, but because of their "fit" with the organization. Despite any other problems associated with this selection strategy, it should be helpful for career management, since the organization would presumably be hiring individuals who would fit a variety of jobs. In fact, even when organizations select individuals for a specific job, it is still possible to do so with subsequent career moves in mind. That is, if an entry-level position is not particularly demanding, an organization may hire people whose skills and abilities match a higher-level job that they might be expected to move into later. This practice is defensible as long as there is a "high" probability that the employee will, in fact, move up the ladder eventually.

If an organization does indeed help its employees to more effectively plan and manage their careers, it can expect to achieve a number of benefits. For one thing it will find itself with a larger and deeper pool of talented individuals. In addition, this workforce will generally be more satisfied and motivated because it is likely to recognize the opportunities the organization has provided and the care with which job assignments are managed. And when an organization finds that it must reduce the size of its workforce, it will have a better understanding of which individuals are more (and less) valuable to the success and effectiveness of the organization itself.

On the other hand, if the organization does a poor job with the careers of its people, it will face a number of difficulties. For one thing the quality of its talent pool might vary in inefficient and erratic ways. That is, it might have an abundance or surplus of highly talented and qualified employees in some areas and at some levels but face a shortage of talented and capable people elsewhere in the organization. In addition, the workforce of such an organization might be more dissatisfied and unmotivated because people are not being given appropriate promotion opportunities and/or are not properly placed in appropriate positions. And when the organization needs to transfer or lay off people, it may not have enough information to make the appropriate decisions.

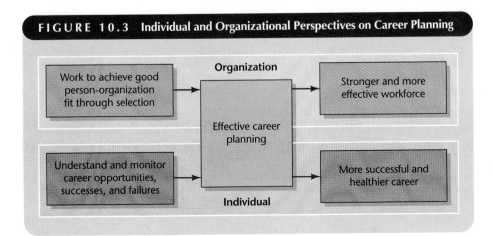

FIGURE 10.3 Individual and Organizational Perspectives on Career Planning

Organization

Work to achieve good person-organization fit through selection → Effective career planning → Stronger and more effective workforce

Understand and monitor career opportunities, successes, and failures → Effective career planning → More successful and healthier career

Individual

Individual Perspectives on Careers

Individuals obviously have an important stake in their own careers. They are the ones who most directly experience the benefits and rewards of successful careers and who incur the cost and frustrations of less successful careers. Further, a person's perceived and experienced career success or failure is also likely to have a major impact on his or her self-esteem and similar indications of self-worth.

People who carefully understand and monitor their careers are likely to understand the reasons behind their successes and failures. That is, these individuals will know why they were or were not promoted and will have a good assessment of their future promotion prospects and possibilities. In addition, an individual who accepts responsibility for managing her or his own career will also be better prepared to deal with an unanticipated career setback such as job loss or demotion.

But many people are surprisingly uninformed and uninvolved in their own careers. They accept jobs and go to work but pay relatively little attention to their role in the organization beyond the scope of a specific job. Thus they may have little understanding as to how they came to be in a particular position, what their next position is likely to be, and how they might better prepare to handle that position when they are placed in it.

THE BOTTOM LINE Managers need to understand that career development and effective human resource management are closely related. Both organizations and individuals play an important role in individual career development. And both also gain or suffer when career development is handled effectively or ineffectively.

CAREER PLANNING AND CAREER MANAGEMENT

Career planning is clearly important to both organizations and to individuals. Most organizations that are genuinely interested in the careers of their employees develop sophisticated career management systems. These systems, in turn, are based on career planning.

The Importance of Career Planning

Career planning requires careful coordination between individual employees and the organization. It is usually human resource managers who represent the

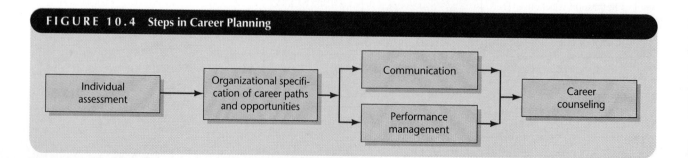

FIGURE 10.4   Steps in Career Planning

Individual assessment → Organizational specification of career paths and opportunities → Communication / Performance management → Career counseling

organization in the career planning process. General Electric and Shell Oil are known to be especially effective in the area of career planning and development for their managers. In general, most career planning systems involve the steps shown in Figure 10.4.

The first step is generally called the **individual assessment phase**. As the term suggests, individual assessment requires individuals to carefully analyze what they perceive to be their own abilities, competencies, skills, and goals. Many organizations provide employees with forms or questionnaires that are used to develop this information. These may take the form of a test or personality inventory, or they may simply be open-ended questions.

The organization also plays an important role in career planning. From the organization's standpoint human resource managers should develop specifications regarding typical career paths. That is, a determination might be made that a person in a particular job category is likely to be promoted to one of two or three other job categories. Thus the organization is specifying potential career paths that an individual might take up the organizational hierarchy.[6] Shell's career-path model, for example, is available to managers on the firm's corporate intranet. And "Human Resources Around the Globe" highlights the growing importance of international assignments as part of career management.

The organization must also integrate its performance management system with its career management system. That is, a person should not automatically expect to progress from one job to another along a certain path, but instead recognize that this movement is going to be determined in part by his or her own performance effectiveness. That is, just because occupying a certain job for a few years may potentially lead to a particular promotion doesn't make such a progression automatic. If an individual performs poorly in the first job, for example, the person may be demoted, terminated, or transferred laterally into another job without a promotion.

A career is the work-related experiences and activities that people engage in related to their job and livelihood over the course of their working life. Consider, for example, the career of Lloyd Ward, recently appointed as CEO of Maytag, the big appliance business. Ward embarked on his career by first getting a degree in engineering from Michigan State University and then landing a position at Procter & Gamble. After several different assignments and promotions, he thought his prospects for further advancement had stalled, so he left P&G and took a job at Ford. A year later he was lured back to P&G and spent several years moving up the firm's hierarchy and working in a variety of different areas. Ward eventually left again, this time to run PepsiCo's Frito-Lay business. Finally, he was lured to a senior position at Maytag and promoted to the top spot in August 1999.

Communication is also an important part of this process. For example, the organization may know the paths that are most likely to be followed from one position to another and may be able to gauge the probability or likelihood that a specific individual or person will follow this path at a prescribed pace. But if this information isn't communicated to the individual employee, then it will be of little or no value to anyone.

The final step in effective career planning is career counseling. And as the term suggests, **career counseling** involves interaction between an individual employee or manager in the organization and either a line manager or a human resource manager. This counseling session typically involves some form of frank and open dialogue with the goal of making sure that the individual's assessment and the organization's assessment of the individual's role and prospects in the organization are congruent with one another. We discuss career counseling programs in more detail later in this chapter.

■ The **individual assessment phase** of career planning requires individuals to carefully analyze what they perceive to be their own abilities, competencies, skills, and goals.

■ **Career counseling** involves interaction between an individual employee or manager in the organization and either a line manager or a human resource manager.

HUMAN RESOURCES **Around the Globe**

International Assignments and Career Development

The importance of global thinking in business is becoming more obvious each day. If firms are to be truly competitive in the future, they will need to think strategically on a global level. Jack Welch, CEO of General Electric, is among the many leading business leaders who believe that global thinking is a key to future business success. He also believes international assignments are the single best means to help managers learn to think globally. As a result, it may become increasingly important for anyone who hopes to rise through the levels of management to have as many international assignments as possible.

But before you volunteer for the next international assignment that becomes available, you must be sure that your company has a strategic view of international assignments and globalization. Otherwise, you might want to think twice about that six-month assignment in Europe, or think about finding a job with a company that does consider the broader role of international assignments.

Many managers were traditionally somewhat reluctant to accept international assignments because not only

"The next head of General Electric will be someone who spent time in Bombay, in Hong Kong. . . . We have to send our best and brightest overseas and make sure they have the training that will allow them to be the global leaders who will make GE flourish in the future."

(Jack Welch, CEO of
General Electric)*

were these jobs not seen as the key to the future, but they were, in fact, often seen as risky from a career management perspective. Many managers were especially concerned about what they would face when they returned from the international assignment. Many feared they would not be able to return to their old job (or a similar job) and that they would actually be demoted upon return. In addition, they may have missed out on different performance incentives while they were away, and they would clearly be out of sight (and out of mind?) of senior management. Further, there were always the shocks associated with repatriation, including the loss of status and the higher cost of living when perks such as rent subsidies, domestic help, chauffeur, or club memberships disappeared.

It is also typical for companies to lose about 20 percent of their returning expatriate managers within a year of repatriation, and many more returning managers report that they have seriously thought about leaving their organization. Much of this turnover is due to failures on the part of the organization to effectively manage the repatriation process and the problems outlined above, but some

---

The Consequences of Career Planning

When an organization does an effective job of career planning, both it and its employees can expect to achieve numerous benefits. As noted in the earlier section, for example, effective career development and management can result in a more effective workforce and in employees who are more motivated and satisfied with the organization.

But the organization that engages in effective career management should also expect to achieve cost savings. This stems from the fact that a higher level of person-job fit should be achieved, with the resulting benefits of lower absenteeism, lower turnover, and a more satisfied and productive workforce. Moreover, the costs of identifying managers for promotion should be lowered because that task should be part of the firm's regular and ongoing career development processes.

Individuals in organizations that handle career planning effectively should also achieve numerous benefits. They should have a realistic understanding of their place in the organization and an accurate assessment of their career opof it is due to a simple failure to effectively communicate the importance placed on international experience. The problem is quite serious in any case. Unless the organization can do something to reduce this turnover, it will not reap the benefits of an international assignment (in terms of increasing global thinking) and will actually be paying for its competitors to gain such an advantage.

But many of these problems stem from a narrow view, on the company's part, of the role of international assignments. Many companies make such assignments only when no host-country has a specific set of skills. The realization that organizations must compete globally in the future, however, has also begun to change thinking about international assignments.

More organizations are beginning to see these assignments as a developmental activity rather than a response to a specific need. It is becoming clearer that successful leaders in the future will be those who can understand and appreciate cultural differences and understand how to integrate needed company practices with these cultural differences and the expectations associated with them. In an attempt to ensure that future managers have this understanding, multinational organizations are increasingly viewing an international assignment as a prerequisite to upper-management assignments.

This recognition also means that the organization must manage the international assignment properly and not lose its repatriated managers. It is clearly important, then, to select the right people for international assignment, provide them with the training they need, support them

(financially and psychologically) while they are abroad, and successfully repatriate them upon return.

Organizations are also becoming more creative and thoughtful about the exact nature of international assignments. For example, an organization such as Exxon would traditionally send domestic managers to Saudi Arabia or would have Saudi managers come to the United States. But more strategic thinking about international assignments might well have Exxon sending Saudi managers to Indonesia to familiarize them with the Indonesian culture. Once international assignments are viewed in this new way, the key is to expose the manager to a range of cultures and countries to prepare him or her for the future.

The implications of this new thinking for how people manage their career should be obvious. There are surely still some risks associated with an international assignment, especially if the organization is not sensitive to the problems of repatriation. But in the global firm of the future, it will be impossible to advance up the management career ladder without some international experience. Thus the successful career of the future is sure to include one or more international assignments.

References: James S. Black, Hal B. Gregersen, Mark E. Mendenhall, and Linda K. Stroh, *Globalizing People through International Assignments* (Reading, Mass.: Addison-Wesley, 1999) (*quote on p. 1); "An American Expatriate Finds Hong Kong Post a Fast Boat to Nowhere," *Wall Street Journal,* January 21, 1999, pp. A1, A8.

---

portunities within that organization. In addition, they can make better informed decisions about alternative career options, educational opportunities, and so forth.

Limitations and Pitfalls in Career Planning

Even though career planning is very important to both organizations and to individuals, and effective career planning benefits both, everyone should also recognize that career planning has limitations and potential pitfalls. For example, no amount of sophisticated forecasting can predict with absolute certainty the level of talent, expertise, motivation, or interest a given individual is going to have at some point in the future. People experience changes in interests, for example, and may redefine their priorities. Even though the organization and the individual may expect a person to be capable of performing a certain job in the future, both parties may well turn out to be wrong, and so career plans may need to change.

The organization's future human resource needs can also change. For example, it may become more successful or less successful than envisioned, or it may decide on new strategies to pursue. Or new managers may come in and want things done differently than in the past. And new opportunities may present themselves to both the individual and the organization. For instance, an organization may have a certain current member of its workforce tapped to assume an important position in a couple of years. But a substantially stronger individual for that same position may unexpectedly emerge. In this case the organization may have to alter its original strategy, even at the risk of alienating the individual originally tapped for the job.

Similarly, individuals sometimes find new opportunities at unexpected times. Both an individual and the organization, for instance, may expect a person to take a certain job at some time in the future. But another organization may appear on the scene to lure the individual away, perhaps at a substantially higher salary. In this instance the individual is likely to be happy with the turn of events, of course, because he or she will have a new position and a higher salary. The organization, on the other hand, may face disruption and may have to alter its existing plans.

In a related vein unanticipated mergers and acquisitions can also result in changes in career opportunities. For example, when Amoco was acquired by British Petroleum in 1998, the new organization found itself with a surplus of qualified managers and had to offer early retirement incentives to some of them. Others were presented with unanticipated opportunities for new assignments that were substantially different from the ones they might have expected. For example, a senior Amoco manager based in Houston had been on a career path that did not include the possibility of an international assignment. But shortly after the integration of the firms, this manager was offered a promotion to a new job in London.

THE BOTTOM LINE Managers should recognize that like all planning activities, career planning should be seen only as an approximation of what the individual and the organization should expect to happen. Although plans should be developed with reasonable expectations that they will, in fact, materialize as formulated, both individuals and organizations should recognize that no plan is perfect and every plan is subject to change.

CAREER MANAGEMENT FOR NEW ENTRANTS

In many ways the early-career stages faced by an individual are the most tumultuous. Regardless of whether they are taking their first jobs or moving into a new job after a long period of employment elsewhere, new entrants into an organization always feel a certain degree of uncertainty and apprehension about their new employer. Thus an important starting point for human resource managers interested in more effectively managing the careers of their employees is understanding some of the early-career problems that such employees often encounter.

Early-Career Issues

When people first enter an organization, they encounter a number of potential problems. One of the most common problems new entrants into an organization face is the initial job and its accompanying challenges. When people are in college preparing for a career in a particular field, they often envision themselves performing high-profile, challenging, exciting functions in glamorous settings. But in reality, most people start at the bottom of an organization, and they may be performing a job that is relatively tedious, menial, and far below what they perceive to be their level of competence and capability.

Disappointment with initial job assignments frequently spills over into their attitudes and job satisfaction. More specifically, people at lower levels of the organization with relatively short tenure often express low levels of job satisfaction. These low levels of satisfaction, in turn, are a function of unmet expectations regarding the kind of work the individuals might be performing.

Yet another common early-career problem has to do with initial job performance appraisals. As we discussed in Chapter 8, organizations routinely evaluate the performance of their employees. Moreover, this evaluation is an important and ongoing process that plays a number of vital roles. But just as many people frequently are surprised at the nature of their initial job assignment, many are also surprised and disappointed as a result of their initial performance appraisals.

Even though they may be anxious about the nature of their initial work assignments, many people nevertheless believe that they are doing an exemplary job. But many managers make a point of focusing a lot of their initial performance appraisals on those areas most in need of correction. In short, these managers focus primarily on examples and illustrations of poor performance. As a result, then, the individual's first performance appraisals may tend to be somewhat more negative than originally envisioned.

The early stages of a person's career are often tumultuous and are frequently characterized by any number of problems and disappointments. For example, David Geffen's first job was as a receptionist for CBS. He was quickly fired after offering some unsolicited advice to a television producer about a script. As he was gathering his belongings to leave, someone joked that he might try working as a theatrical agent. Geffen didn't realize the person wasn't serious, so he applied for a job with the William Morris Agency, the top firm in the industry. And he was hired—to work in the mailroom! But he was able to use that job as a springboard, managing numerous performers and founding Geffen Records. He eventually sold the music business and co-founded DreamWorks with Steven Spielberg and Jeffrey Katzenberg.

Coping with Early-Career Problems

Organizations and managers interested in trying to head off some of these problems can rely on a number of techniques to make the early-career experiences of people more positive. One of the key aspects here is a realistic job preview, or an RJP. As discussed in Chapter 6, some managers tend to paint an initial picture of a job as being particularly exciting and engaging—perhaps in an effort to attract the most qualified applicants for the job. But when expectations for that job are not met, initial disappointments might be magnified. Thus RJPs help set more realistic expectations on the part of new entrants.

Another important strategy that can be used for dealing with early-career problems is to make an individual's first job assignment a challenging one. For example, rather than assuming that the incoming employee is incapable of performing a challenging and fulfilling task, perhaps a different assumption might be made and the individual given a more exciting job to perform. Fastenal, for example, is a growing supplier of commercial fastening and packaging supplies and materials. The firm hires new college graduates, gives them a short orientation and training experience, and then almost immediately assigns them their own store to manage. Although some new managers find this job a bit overwhelming, most report that they enjoy the challenge and responsibility.

A final strategy that many human resource managers recommend for dealing with early-career problems is to assign new employees to managers who have demonstrated an ability to mentor and to challenge new employees. For various reasons some managers are more astute than others at understanding the needs, motives, and aspirations of employees and at taking a stronger and more beneficial interest in their careers contributions to the firm. Such managers are obviously more likely to help address some of the early-career problems of individuals than are managers who are less interested in the personal development of subordinates.

THE BOTTOM LINE   Both individuals and organizations should be aware of the issues facing people during their early-career period and take whatever steps feasible to minimize the problems that might arise during this period.

CAREER MANAGEMENT FOR MIDCAREER EMPLOYEES

After an individual progresses successfully through the first few years of a job, many of the problems alluded to above may have been addressed. For example, the individual will presumably have progressed into a more fulfilling job that is perhaps more in line with his or her training and expectations. Likewise, job satisfaction will have adjusted, and the individual will have attained more positive performance reviews. Alternatively, under the new career model an individual may have left behind one (or more) careers and be starting on another. But problems still loom on the horizon for these individuals once they reach the midcareer stage.

Midcareer Issues

The most common midcareer problem most individuals in corporations face today is the **midcareer plateau.** Most people, after progressing through two or three levels of the organization and receiving commensurate promotions are likely to encounter a plateau in their career when further advancement is less likely and when promotions and more challenging job assignments are less frequent. That is, if we think about a person's movement in the organization as being a series of steps upward, like part (a) of Figure 10.5, then unless the individual reaches the executive ranks, his or her level of advancement in the organization is going to level off. That is, the individual reaches a plateau, as illustrated in part (b) of Figure 10.5.

▓ A **midcareer plateau** means that an employee is no longer receiving promotions or advancement opportunities in the organization.

Unfortunately, some people who reach a midcareer plateau react quite negatively. They may become bitter and resentful toward the organization, blaming it for their lack of career advancement. They may also enter a period of stagnation in which they simply go through the motions without really making substantive contributions to the organization and may lose interest, not only in work, but in various life experiences in general.

An increasingly common midcareer problem is job loss. Indeed, people at midcareer levels are often among the first to go in an organization. Organizations that are undergoing downsizing may be reluctant to let new entrants leave in part because these individuals may be working at lower salaries and in part because these individuals represent the newest and freshest ideas that might be available within the organization. Similarly, more senior employees may also be more difficult to consider eliminating because they are perhaps the ones with the most experience and are guiding and directing the overall fortunes of the organization.

Moreover, some organizations might be especially reluctant to terminate more senior employees because they are more likely to be older and the organization may fear the threat of age-discrimination lawsuits. But midcareer employees, especially those who have reached a plateau, might be perceived as the more likely candidates for elimination. Thus job loss as a result of downsizing and similar factors represents an important midcareer problem.

Coping with Midcareer Problems

Midcareer problems are perhaps among the most difficult for managers in an organization to help address. If an individual is experiencing problems associated with a midcareer plateau, and such a plateau has been reached for understandable reasons, then clearly the organization doesn't want to solve this problem by reversing its course and providing a promotion after all.

But there are some actions that an organization can take.[7] One is to provide specially designed career counseling services for people at midcareer positions. These counseling efforts are intended to help individuals better understand their importance to the organization and to perhaps understand more ways to

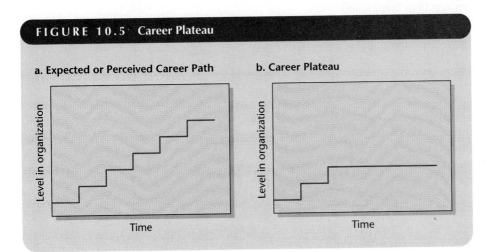

> **FIGURE 10.5** **Career Plateau**
>
> **a. Expected or Perceived Career Path**
>
> Level in organization
>
> Time
>
> **b. Career Plateau**
>
> Level in organization
>
> Time

Transforming the Technician

Organizations will probably always have a need for employees with specialized technical skills. Computer experts, finance experts, and engineers continue to be in demand, of course, but a new trend has been influencing how these employees build their careers. In many organizations, for example, if employees enter as engineers, their long-term career opportunities are limited. They can eventually supervise other engineers, but at some point, unless an individual moves to a general management track, career opportunities are limited.

In the last few years, however, technical employees have been transforming themselves into internal consultants. This approach allows the entire organization to derive some benefit from the employee's technical knowledge and affords the employee an alternative career path. Unfortunately, the technical skills that such an employee has available are often not really sufficient for them to become successful internal consultants. Instead, they need to develop an additional set of tools or skills to allow them to become effective as consultants. Generally, we think of six such tools or skills that are helpful. These are credibility, a strong customer orientation, clear agreements about boundaries and expectations, leadership skills, diagnostic skills, and versatility.

One important skill for any successful internal consultant is credibility. Fortunately, technical employees usually have already established credibility in their own areas of expertise, and some attention paid to learning more about the larger business issues can help them gain wider credibility as a consultant as well. Internal consultants also need to have a clear customer orientation,

"Learning the five essential qualities of a consultant helps technical employees fulfill new roles as leaders and change agents."

(Marilyn Condon, human resource consultant)*

which often involves recognizing limitations and bringing in additional experts where needed. The goal must be to meet the customer's needs rather than to demonstrate the consultant's own skills and expertise. It is also useful to have informal letters of agreement to define the boundaries of any consulting project and to clarify expectations. At the same time, though, successful internal consultants need to demonstrate some leadership skills. Technical employees can best demonstrate leadership skills when they use their technical expertise to help a customer solve a business problem and demonstrates flexibility in dealing with those problems.

Finally, successful internal consultants need diagnostic skills, to help analyze problems, and versatility. Technical training often involves problem solving and problem analysis, and so technical employees are often well suited to diagnose problems. Versatility, on the other hand, often involves the need to work as part of a team on some projects, and this skill is often *not* a part of technical training. The key, then, is for technical employees to take stock of which skills or capabilities they presently possess relative to these five key factors. They should then seek work opportunities that might help them develop the skills in which they are deficient. If they can manage this process successfully, they will usually find new career opportunities, new roads toward advancement, and greater job security as they become more valuable resources for their organizations.

References: Marilyn Condon, "Turn Technical Specialists into Consultants," *HRMagazine,* January 1998, pp. 106–110 (*quote on p. 106).

---

derive various rewards and sources of satisfaction from their present position. Individuals should also assume some responsibility in this area by seeking out information and insights into why they might have been passed over for promotion and if they can do anything (such as getting more education) to improve their promotion prospects.

Some organizations also do an excellent job of incorporating special career-path options for their employees at the midcareer level. For example, one very popular career-path option for such individuals relies heavily on lateral transfers. Thus rather than the individual moving up the organization in terms of promotions to higher levels, the individual may be transferred to other areas of the organization while remaining at the same hierarchical level. Although increases in salary or responsibility are not likely to accompany such transfers, they nevertheless may be a source of increased stimulation and interest for the employee as he or she gets the opportunity to perform new kinds of work and to experience new challenges and responsibilities. Wal-Mart, for example, may transfer store managers to new stores, larger stores, and/or stores in different parts of the country not so much to offer a promotion but to provide a different kind of work experience. "Human Resources Tech Talk" discusses the related practice of retraining people and/or redefining their roles to better meet the organization's needs.

And occasionally, organizations find that transferring people to a lower-level position in the organization can also be an effective strategy for dealing with midcareer plateaus. Although many individuals think of downward transfers as being a demotion and therefore undesirable, they may still be a viable option for people in certain circumstances. For example, a midcareer employee with no prospects for substantial promotions might accept a downward transfer to a site within the organization at a more attractive place to live.[8]

In terms of helping people deal with job loss, assuming the organization has made a carefully calculated and appropriate decision that the downsizing effort is necessary, it can still do certain things and provide certain services to perhaps make this experience less painful for employees. For instance, many organizations that are downsizing provide counseling services for employees who are losing their jobs. Although not strictly a career counseling option, it is nevertheless a humane way for helping members who have made valuable contributions to the firm.

THE BOTTOM LINE Midcareer employees may face a difficult time coping with problems such as plateaus. Both organizations and individuals need to be aware of such problems and do whatever is possible to help people cope with them.

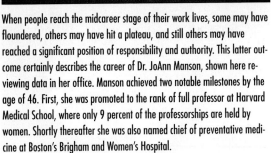

When people reach the midcareer stage of their work lives, some may have floundered, others may have hit a plateau, and still others may have reached a significant position of responsibility and authority. This latter outcome certainly describes the career of Dr. JoAnn Manson, shown here reviewing data in her office. Manson achieved two notable milestones by the age of 46. First, she was promoted to the rank of full professor at Harvard Medical School, where only 9 percent of the professorships are held by women. Shortly thereafter she was also named chief of preventative medicine at Boston's Brigham and Women's Hospital.

CAREER MANAGEMENT FOR LATE-CAREER EMPLOYEES

In the later stages of a person's career, it is perhaps even more important for the organization to provide career management services. Many of these center around problems that people in their late-career years experience.

Late-Career Issues

Many of the problems people experience in the later career years revolve around issues associated with retirement. Some people think about retirement prospects in glowing and happy terms. For example, they may view retirement as throwing off the shackles of employment and leading a grand and glorious life style lying on the beach or hiking in the mountains. But in reality, many people facing retirement prospects are quite anxious and nervous.[9]

For example, they may wonder about what their lives will be like without having a job or an office to go to every day. They may also wonder about financial pressures such as whether or not they will have sufficient income to live the kind of life style they would like to have. They also begin to realize that what may be very rewarding social relationships with their colleagues at work are going to be changing fundamentally.

And from the organization's perspective, a related question is the extent to which the individual's retirement will be abrupt or gradual. In many cases the new retiree simply doesn't come to work any longer. However, retirement may be much more palatable if it is handled gradually. This approach might include a period of reduced working hours and/or a gradual reduction in responsibilities. A university professor, for example, might move from teaching full-time all year long to teaching half-time all year long to teaching part-time only a portion of the year.

In recent times, with a spate of corporate restructuring and downsizing, the problems of early retirement are becoming more important as well. Senior employees were always free to retire early (typically with reduced benefits), and this practice was unusual, but certainly not unheard of, especially in cases where the employee became ill. But now, as organizations face the need to reduce staff, a popular tactic is to offer early-retirement packages to employees. The point here is quite simple—if enough senior employees can be persuaded to retire early, there may be less need to lay off younger workers. One potential problem with this tactic is that some of the more valuable senior employees may take advantage of the opportunity and the organization would lose important resources. In any event these plans are now seen as another part of the career management process.

Early-retirement plans typically include a package of financial incentives and a defined window of opportunity, after which the special incentives are no longer available. These incentives might include additional "credit" for years of service used in computing retirement benefits or a cash bonus. But as more or-

As people enter the later stages of their careers, both they and their employers are likely to focus more attention on issues related to retirement. For example, Madeline Etzold has spent most of her career working as a secretary for Merck, a big pharmaceuticals company. Merck offers all its employees stock option plans, and Etzold has taken full advantage of these opportunities. As a result, she will be fully prepared to retire when she turns sixty. Alternatively, she can continue to work for several more years, adding to her financial security for later in life.

ganizations adopt this tactic, the size of the incentives has slowly been shrinking.[10] In any case the hope is that the employee will see these incentives as sufficient motivation to retire early, which will subsequently reduce the size of the present workforce. Of course, the organization can help this final stage of career management as well. Programs that help in estate planning, introduced early in an employee's career, help those employees accept early-retirement packages later.[11]

Finally, though, we must note that early-retirement packages are typically offered in connection with anticipated reductions in the workforce. Therefore, although more-senior employees may not see the early-retirement packages as being extremely attractive, their benefits must often be weighed against the fact that the employee might well lose his or her job anyway as part of the downsizing and receive no special considerations.

Coping with Late-Career Problems

Counseling is again one of the most effective strategies for helping people in their late-career years deal with impending retirement. Typical preretirement counseling programs have a number of components, including financial planning. Other common ingredients are helping people prepare for the time when work will play a reduced role in their lives and their daily routines will become less structured.

THE BOTTOM LINE   Late-careers problems are often among the most traumatic because the person may be facing loss of work, rather than a change in work. Both organizations and individuals, therefore, should be especially sensitive when coping with late-career issues, especially those related to retirement.

CAREER DEVELOPMENT ISSUES AND CHALLENGES

Regardless of career stage, many organizations that are sincerely interested in effective career management for their employees deal with and address a variety of issues and challenges. In this section we introduce and describe some of these issues and challenges in more detail.

Career-Counseling Programs

As already noted, career counseling programs are very important to an organization and its employees. Such programs usually address a wide variety of career-related issues and are readily accessible to people in the organization. Moreover, some are very formal, whereas others are considerably more informal.

Formal career counseling programs usually take the form of workshops, conferences, and career development centers. In some cases the organization will establish "general purpose" career counseling programs that are available to all employees. Organizations may also create special counseling programs targeted at certain categories of employees such as fast-track managers, women managers, and minority managers. These programs serve various purposes, including addressing specific needs of certain categories of employees, helping to better integrate those employees into the organization, and creating important networking opportunities for them.

Organizations commonly offer counseling of an informal nature as well. Much of this counseling takes the form of one-on-one interactions between an employee and the employee's supervisor and typically occurs during the performance appraisal period. For example, when supervisors appraise and evaluate the performance of a subordinate and then provide performance feedback to that individual, a part of the conversation often deals with such issues as promotion prospects, skill development issues, and so forth. In addition, employees may simply drop by the human resource department to discuss some career-related questions and issues. In this case the human resource department needs to fulfill its center of expertise role so as to provide useful and accurate information.

Dual-Career and Work-Family Issues

Back in the 1950s and on into the 1960s, most married couples in the United States were characterized by roles that gave the male partner's career precedence over the female partner's career. That is, the family tended to live where the husband needed to live. When the husband was given a transfer, there was little or no question as to whether or not he would take it. And if the wife happened to be employed outside the home, it was assumed and expected that she would resign from her job and the family would move.

But as more and more women entered the workforce, primarily beginning in the mid- to late 1960s, this pattern changed substantially. Now for many married couples, the wife's career is on an equal footing with, or perhaps may be given precedence over, that of the husband. Thus when organizations offer a transfer to someone, they must be prepared to deal with the complexities associated with two careers. Furthermore, the entire process of career planning must take into consideration the fact that often two careers must be managed simultaneously.

Perhaps related to this trend is the growing concern over balancing family needs with the demands of work. As dual-career and single-parent employment increases, these concerns pose yet another interesting challenge to career management.[12] First, concerns over "family friendly" work practices (such as childcare, elder care, and flexible work schedules) have an influence over the choices employees make concerning where to work. In fact, many organizations are now advertising their family-friendly practices as a means of competing for employees.[13] Also, it is increasingly clear that concerns at home and with the family affect an employee's behavior at work, and so stress over how to arrange for childcare or who will care for an ailing parent will cause the employee problems at work. Relieving these pressures, then, will allow the employee to concentrate more on the job and so more fully realize his or her career potential.[14]

Finally, there is also evidence that work stressors influence family stress, which in turn is related to long-term health.[15] Thus as the workforce becomes more diverse, organizations will have to recognize that both dual-career issues and concerns over work-family balance will become increasingly important factors for determining career success and must be considered as part of career management.

THE BOTTOM LINE   Organizations should take a proactive role in helping to facilitate career development for their employees. Formal and well-developed career counseling programs and sensitivity to dual-career and work-family issues are becoming increasingly important.

EVALUATING CAREER MANAGEMENT ACTIVITIES

The ultimate goal of career management is to have employees that have reached their full potential at work, enjoy productive and satisfying work careers, and then successfully move into retirement. As such, full appreciation of career management activities may not come until after retirement. But as employees are increasingly unlikely to spend their entire careers in a single organization, success in retirement is much more likely to be a function of the individual's own career management efforts, as well as the good fortune to remain healthy through retirement years. Furthermore, for many employees (especially those in higher status jobs or those for whom work is an important part of self-image) leaving one's career does not mean the end of work. For these employees managing the transition to what have been called "bridge" jobs (and eventually on to full retirement) is most important for their continued satisfaction.[16]

Therefore, the success of career management activities can be judged only at one point in time. If an employee is satisfied with his or her career at this point, then career management must be judged successful *up to that point*. We have focused primarily on actions the organization can take to manage this process, but clearly, a great deal depends on the employee's efforts at career management as well. Employees who go into careers for which they are not well suited (either in terms of abilities or temperament) will obviously be more likely to suffer dissatisfaction with their careers than will those who have made more appropriate career choices. Therefore, although organizational career management efforts are important, the successful management of one's career depends heavily on the employee's efforts to accurately assess his or her own abilities and interests and to formulate a plan for what a successful career should look like.

Chapter Summary

A career is the set of work-related experiences and activities that people engage in related to their job and livelihood over the course of their working life. People generally think of the various components that make up a person's career as having some degree of interrelationship. In this view a typical individual progresses through four career stages: exploration, establishment, maintenance, and disengagement. A more recent perspective refocuses career stages on career age and acknowledges the likelihood of multiple careers.

Most successful organizations and managers today recognize that careers don't simply happen. Indeed, successful careers must be planned and managed. Part of this responsibility resides with the organization, but the individual must also play an important role.

Career planning is clearly important to both organizations and to individuals. Most organizations that are genuinely interested in the careers of their employees develop sophisticated career management systems. These systems, in turn, are based on career planning. Career planning requires careful coordination between individual employees and the organization. But even though career planning is very important to both organizations and to individuals and effective career planning benefits both, everyone should also recognize that career planning has limitations and potential pitfalls.

In many ways the early-career stages are the most tumultuous. Regardless of whether people are taking their first jobs or are moving into a new job after a long period of employment elsewhere, new entrants into an organization always feel a certain degree of uncertainty and apprehension. Thus an important starting point for human resource managers interested in more effectively managing the careers of their employees is understanding some of the early-career problems that such employees often encounter.

After an individual progresses successfully through the first few years of a job, many of the early-career problems may have been addressed. But problems still loom on the horizon for these individuals when they reach the midcareer stage. The most common midcareer problem most individuals face in corporations today is the midcareer plateau.

In the later stages of a person's career, it is perhaps even more important for the organization to provide career management services. Many of the problems that people face in their late-career years revolve around retirement issues.

Regardless of career stage, organizations that are sincerely interested in effective career management for their employees deal with and address a variety of issues and challenges. Career counseling programs are very important to an organization interested in career development for its employees. Such programs usually address a wide variety of career-related issues and are readily accessible to people in the organization. Dual-career and work-family issues are also an important part of today's career management activities and concerns.

The success of career management activities must be judged at a particular point in time. If an employee is satisfied with his or her career at that moment, then career management must be judged successful up to that point.

Review and Discussion Questions

1. What is a career?

2. Compare and contrast the traditional and emerging models of careers.

3. Which model are you most comfortable with? Why?

4. Describe the importance and limitations of career planning.

5. To the extent that you see yourself as soon beginning a career, what issues most concern you? How might an employer help you deal with these?

6. Do you anticipate ever hitting a career plateau? Why or why not?

7. From the standpoint of an individual, under what circumstances might a career plateau actually be a good thing?

8. Would you like to have an international assignment as an anticipated part of your career? What issues and concerns might you have about such a possibility?

9. What sort of retirement do you envision for yourself? How likely do you think this is to change?

10. Can you foresee any new career development issues and challenges that may emerge in the near future?

=== **Closing Case**

Retaining Valued Employees through Multiple Career Paths

When bright employees find that they have "outgrown" their job, they will probably feel they are ready for a promotion. In fact, organizations have traditionally retained these valued employees by promoting them into the ranks of management. But employees in increasing numbers are not interested in careers in management. They may believe that management jobs are too stressful or too time demanding, but whatever the reason, some employees are simply not interested in becoming managers. At the same time, as organizations grow flatter and leaner, fewer managerial jobs are actually available to rising stars. Thus, for various reasons, the traditional model of rewarding bright employees by making them managers is not as viable as it once was. But if promoting people to management is not the way to retain bright employees, how does an organization retain these valued resources?

One increasingly popular strategy that some human resource management experts advocate assumes that organizations can retain and reward their highly valued employees by creating new and imaginative career paths. What do these new career paths look like? It depends on the organization involved, of course, but a number of companies have been developing new kinds of career paths as a method of employee retention.

For example, Southwest Airlines recognizes that many of its technical employees (such as mechanics and maintenance workers) actually enjoy the hands-on nature of their jobs and do not want to move into management. Thus Southwest has initiated a policy that guarantees challenge, as well as opportunities for pay increases, to any employee who wants to stay at his or her job. Similarly, Microsoft actually publishes a document called "Career Ladders," which lays out the various career paths within the company, and explains to all employees how they can move from any one career ladder to any other.

In a much different setting, South Texas Veterans' Health Systems has developed a series of clinical career tracks that offer the same prestige and pay as management positions. As a result, employees such as clinical nurses can remain in a clinical setting and still advance their careers. In fact, for many of these clinical tracks the educational requirements are often more demanding than for management tracks. Finally, Electronic Data Systems (EDS) has a program where employees can utilize the resources in a Career Resource Library to develop more specialized skills in their area of expertise. Thus, programmers as well as salespersons can work at their own pace and move up to the level of EDS Fellow—a recognized industry expert with the earnings potential of an executive.

In each of the cases described here, the company has responded to its inability to promote all deserving employees and/or the employees' unwillingness to move into management by developing alternative career models. Although each plan is unique, human resource managers at these organizations agree that several key factors must be considered for these plans to work.

One critical component is a clear definition of job families and career paths. That is, the organization must decide exactly which jobs constitute these alternative career paths, and this information must be clearly communicated to employees. It is also important, when designing an alternative career path, to include jobs that are comparable to managerial jobs—not necessarily in terms of responsibility and requirements, but in terms of the value to the organization.

It is also necessary to have the proper infrastructure to make sure that the plan works. Such an infrastructure should include being able to specify skill sets required for different career paths and the ability to recruit employees internally for these different paths. Not surprising, the compensation aspect of the program is also important. It is difficult for a program to succeed if the firm decides that a high-level technical specialist can never be paid as much as a manager. The whole idea behind alternative career paths is to provide key employees with rewards and challenges without moving them into management. If employees are penalized in terms of their compensation for choosing such a path, the alternative paths will not be attractive and cannot accomplish their basic goals.

Good career counseling must also be available. Employees must understand all the opportunities, as well as the true drawbacks, of choosing an alternative career path. Furthermore, there must be some means for dealing with employees for whom management positions are not suitable or attractive. The driving force behind alternative career paths is to allow organizations to retain valuable employees who cannot or who do not wish to move into management positions. As the retention of "knowledge workers" becomes even more important in the future, plans such as alternative career paths can become an important part of any retention program.

Case Questions

1. Compare and contrast the alternative career path models at the companies noted in this case.

2. Which model would have the most personal appeal to you? Which would have the least? Why?

3. Do you think alternative models such as these will become more or less common in the future? Why?

Sources: Carla Johnson, "Multiple Career Paths Help Retain Talent," *HRMagazine,* October 1997, pp. 59–64.

Building Human Resource Management Skills

Purpose: The purpose of this exercise is to help you better appreciate the similarities and differences in career management from the standpoint of individuals and of organizations.

Step 1: Outline an "ideal" career management plan from a personal standpoint. Start by selecting an entry-level job in an organization that you might have an interest in working for. Then outline the various jobs you would be interested in moving into, the time you would like to spend in each, the salary you might expect to receive, and similar considerations, on up to the position of CEO. Be realistic but also design the plan with your personal interests in mind.

Step 2: Now assume that you are the senior human resource executive in that firm and look "down" to the entry-level position you used as a starting point. Outline a career development plan for someone starting out in that position.

As above, outline the steps and expectations for a person progressing all the way through the hierarchy to the very top, noting time and salary at each step along the way. Be fair to the individual but keep the best interests of the organization first and foremost at all times.

Step 3: Compare and contrast the two career management plans you developed. Identify particular areas where the plans are similar and where they are different. Note the reasons for these similarities and differences.

1. Is it possible for a career management plan to be perfectly fair and equitable for both the individual and the organization? Why or why not?

2. Do you think it would be a good idea for an organization to have its employees develop their own career management plans, as in step 1, and then compare them with organizational plans? Why or why not?

3. Which type of plan—the individual plan or the organization plan—is likely to be the most flexible? Why?

Ethical Dilemmas in Human Resource Management

 Assume that you have recently been recruited to join a company in an executive position. As part of the recruiting process, the firm's top managers repeatedly stressed the importance of stability—the firm has been "raided" a lot in recent months, and several key executives mentioned that they were looking for someone committed to staying with the firm for the long term. At each juncture you affirmed your own interest in stability. You have only worked for two other firms, for about eight years each, and you had no plans to resign from your "new" job any time soon.

But things have now changed. A headhunting firm is inquiring about your interest in another senior executive position. In almost any case you would have said no. But this opportunity is unique in that it is near your hometown (where your elderly parents still live); the city has an extremely well-regarded quality of life; you would be given a great deal of responsibility, authority, and an opportunity to really show what you can do; and your salary would be nearly double what you now make. All in all, it seems like an opportunity that is just too good to pass up.

Unfortunately, you also feel that if you even look at this opportunity, you are violating the implicit agreement you made with your current employer about stability. So, on the one hand, you might elect to say no to the headhunter and remain in the job you just started. Alternatively, you can take a look at this new job prospect on a confidential basis and hope that your current employer doesn't learn about your interest until and unless you decide to take the job. Finally, you can tell your boss about the position and explain why it might be too good to pass up.

Questions

1. What are the ethical issues in this situation?

2. What are the basic arguments for and against each of your options?

3. What do you think most managers would do? What would you do?

Human Resource Internet Exercise

 Many companies today are putting information about career opportunities on their Web sites. Identify several companies that you are interested in knowing more about. Visit enough Web sites from this list until you locate five that purport to have career information available. Review that information and assess its value to you as a prospective employee.

Questions

1. Is the information provided on the Web sites you visited really relevant to careers, or does it simply summarize job opportunities?

2. Rank the five Web sites in order of best to worst as they relate to career information. What differences account for the rankings?

3. Do you think the organizations have "different" career information available for people who already work for them? Why or why not?

Notes

1. Manuel London, "Redeployment and Continuous Learning in the 21st Century: Hard Lessons and Positive Examples from the Downsizing Era," *Academy of Management Executive,* November 1996, pp. 67–79.

2. Adrianne H. Geiger-DuMond and Susan K. Boyle, "Mentoring: A Practitioner's Guide," *Training & Development,* March 1995, pp. 51–55.

3. Douglas T. Hall, "Protean Careers of the 21st Century," *Academy of Management Executive,* November 1996, pp. 8–16.

4. Gregory K. Stephens, "Crossing Internal Career Boundaries: The State of Research on Subjective Career Transitions," *Journal of Management,* Vol. 20, No. 2, 1994, pp. 479–501.

5. Suzyn Ornstein and Lynn A. Isabella, "Making Sense of Careers: A Review 1989–1992," *Journal of Management,* Vol. 19, No. 2, 1993, pp. 243–267.

6. Kenneth R. Brousseau, Michael J. Driver, Kristina Eneroth, and Rikard Larsson, "Career Pandemonium: Realigning Organizations and Individuals," *Academy of Management Executive,* November 1996, pp. 52–66.

7. Edgar H. Schein, "Career Anchors Revisited: Implications for Career Development in the 21st Century," *Academy of Management Executive,* November 1996, pp. 80–88.

8. "How One Man Handled Going from Success to Losing a Promotion," *Wall Street Journal,* November 24, 1998, p. B1.

9. Daniel C. Feldman, "The Decision to Retire Early: A Review and Reconceptualization," *Academy of Management Review,* Vol. 19, No. 2, 1994, pp. 285–311.

10. "Out in the Cold: Many Early Retirees Find the Good Deals Not So Good at All," *Wall Street Journal,* October 25, 1993, B1.

11. Daniel Feldman "The Decision to Retire Early: A Review and Conceptualization," *Academy of Management Review,* Vol. 19, 1994, pp. 285–311.

12. M. Ferber, B. O'Farrell, and L. Allen, Work and Family: *Policies for a Changing Workforce* (Washington, D.C.: National Academy Press, 1994).

13. H. Morgan and K. Tucker, *Companies That Care: The Most Family-Friendly Companies in America, What They Offer, and How They Got That Way* (New York: Simon and Schuster, 1991).

14. Sheldon Zedeck and K. L. Mosier, "Work in Family and Employing Organizations," *American Psychologist,* Vol. 45, 1990, pp. 240–251.

15. V. J. Doby and R. D. Caplan, "Organizational Stress as Threat to Reputation: Effects on Anxiety at Work and at Home," *Academy of Management Journal,* Vol. 38, 1995, pp. 1105–1123.

16. Peter B. Doeringer, "Economic Security, Labor Market Flexibility, and Bridges to Retirement," in P. B. Doeringer (ed.), *Bridges to Retirement* (Ithaca, N.Y.: Cornell University ILR Press, 1990), pp. 3–22.

PART FIVE

Compensating and Rewarding the Workforce

CHAPTER **11**
Basic Compensation

CHAPTER **12**
Incentives and
Performance-Based
Rewards

CHAPTER **13**
Employee Benefits
and Services

11

Basic Compensation

CHAPTER OUTLINE

Developing a Compensation Strategy
Basic Purposes of Compensation
Wages versus Salary
Strategic Options for Compensation
Determinants of Compensation
Strategy
Pay Surveys and Compensation

Determining a Wage and Salary Structure
Job Evaluation and Job Worth
Establishing Job Classes
Establishing a Pay Structure
Pay for Knowledge and Skill-Based
Pay

Wage and Salary Administration
Managing Compensation
Determining Individual Wages
Pay Secrecy
Pay Compression

Evaluating Compensation Policies

CHAPTER OBJECTIVES

After studying this chapter you should be able to:

■ Describe the basic issues involved in developing a compensation strategy.

■ Discuss how organizations develop a wage and salary structure.

■ Identify and describe the basic issues involved in wage and salary administration.

■ Note variable employee benefits and how organizations can evaluate their compensation and benefits practices.

Back in 1938 the U.S. Congress passed the Fair Labor Standards Act (FLSA). Among its other provisions the FLSA mandated that hourly employees working in excess of forty hours a week must be paid a premium wage of 1.5 times their normal hourly rate for those additional hours. The FLSA also specified that, because of the nature of their work, managerial and professional employees were exempt from this regulation. That is, because these individuals are paid salaries rather than hourly wages, they receive the same pay regardless of the number of hours they work during any given period.

Although it is up to the organization to determine which jobs are exempt and which are not, a number of legal standards have traditionally been used in making these distinctions. Recently, however, the distinctions have become blurred in some organizations. For example, some experts have suggested that businesses occasionally reclassify a number of their wage-based, lower-level jobs as managerial positions and then refuse to pay overtime to individuals holding those jobs. Even more extreme are charges that some organizations today are pressuring hourly employees to work "off the clock"—to work when they are not being paid at all! Sometimes such work is legal, but other times it's not.

Because of corporate downsizing programs in the 1990s, some firms believe that the remaining employees need to carry a greater workload, which means working harder and being more productive. It may also mean working longer hours. In some cases work spills over into what used to be free time. At AT&T, for example, workers are encouraged to participate in the firm's Ambassador Program by selling AT&T products to their friends, relatives, and neighbors during nonwork hours. Employees can win prizes for their efforts but earn no additional income.

> "Many companies have explicit policies that limit overtime. But they have management systems that absolutely dictate too many tasks for the amount of time allotted."
>
> (John Frazier, U.S. Department of Labor)*

But other cases are more troubling. In the state of Washington, for example, a jury ruled that Taco Bell was guilty of pressuring its employees to do paperwork such as timesheets and schedules at home. And workers were sometimes asked to do some food preparation work after arriving at work but before "clocking in." Mervyn's, a chain of discount stores, was sued by a group of its lower-level managers called team coordinators. These managers charged that they were routinely ordered to work through lunch and to take paperwork home. And Albertson's, the nation's fourth-largest grocery chain, has been charged with pushing employees to work past their assigned quitting time without receiving additional wages.

Sometimes, of course, individual employees might simply be misinterpreting events and suggestions from their boss. In other situations companies charge that unions are distorting things. And even in cases where the law is being broken, the actions might be the isolated tactics of only one or a few managers working outside formal organizational policies to get a bit more productivity out of their employees. But regardless of the circumstances, it does seem like some organizations today are seeking ways to get more and more work out of fewer and fewer people. And although there may be a variety of legitimate ways to do so, some managers may be crossing the line in how they are seeking to get more from their employees—without having to give anything in return.

"Pay? How about a Pizza?" *Newsweek*, April 20, 1998, pp. 42–43 (*quote on p. 43); "'Off-the-Clock' Time: More Work for No Pay," *USA Today*, April 24, 1997, p. 1B.

The basic issue in the cases at Taco Bell, Mervyn's, and Albertson's involves payment to employees in relation to their time spent working for the respective company. Organizations clearly have the right to expect that their employees will perform their jobs to the best of their abilities and to be as productive as possible during the time they are being paid to work. But individual workers also have the right to be fairly, legally, and appropriately compensated for their work. Ensuring that the financial arrangements between the organization and its employees are legal, ethical, fair, and appropriate is generally the responsibility of the organization's human resource function.

■ **Compensation** is the set of rewards that organizations provide to individuals in return for their willingness to perform various jobs and tasks within the organization.

Compensation is the set of rewards that organizations provide to individuals in return for their willingness to perform various jobs and tasks within the organization. As we will see, compensation includes various elements such as base salary, incentives, bonuses, benefits, and other rewards. In this chapter we cover basic compensation. We start by examining how compensation strategies are developed. Next we look at how wage and salary structures are created. Issues associated with wage and salary administration are then introduced and discussed. Finally, we conclude by noting how organizations evaluate their compensation and benefits policies. Chapter 12 covers compensation that is linked to performance, and employee benefits, another important element in compensation, is the subject of Chapter 13.

DEVELOPING A COMPENSATION STRATEGY

Compensation should never be a random decision but, instead, the result of a careful and systematic strategic process.[1] Embedded in the process is an understanding of the basic purposes of compensation, an assessment of strategic options for compensation, knowledge of the determinants of compensation strategy, and the use of pay surveys.

Basic Purposes of Compensation

Compensation has a number of fundamental purposes and objectives. For one thing, the organization needs to provide appropriate and equitable rewards to employees. Individuals who work for organizations want to feel valued and want to be rewarded at a level that is commensurate with their skills, abilities, and contributions to the organization. In this regard, an organization must make two types of equity considerations. These relate to two different comparison groups an employee might refer to in deciding whether he or she is paid equitably.

■ **Internal equity** in compensation refers to comparisons employees make to other employees within the same organization.

Internal equity in compensation refers to comparisons employees make to other employees within the same organization. In making these comparisons the employee questions whether he is being equitably paid for his contributions to the organization relative the way other employees in the firm are paid. For example, suppose a department manager learns that all the other department managers in the firm are paid more than he is. He subsequently looks more closely at the situation and finds that his experience and responsibilities are similar to theirs. As a result, he would become unhappy with his compensation and would be likely to request a salary increase. Alternatively, he might actually discover that he has much less work experience and fewer responsibilities than the other managers and thus conclude that there is really no equity problem. Problems with internal equity can result in conflict among employees, feelings of mistrust, low morale, anger, and perhaps even legal actions if the basis for inequity is perceived to result from illegal discrimination.

External equity in compensation refers to comparisons employees make with similar employees performing similar jobs at other firms. For example, an engineer may experience internal equity relative to her other engineering colleagues in her work group because she knows they are all paid the same salary. But if she finds out that another major employer in the same community is paying its engineers higher salaries for comparable work, she begins to be concerned about external equity. Problems with external equity may result in higher turnover as employees leave for better opportunities elsewhere, generally dissatisfied and unhappy workers, and difficulties in attracting new employees

Both types of equity are clearly important, but there is one further consideration concerning internal equity. The Equal Pay Act of 1963 stipulates that men and women who perform essentially the same job must be paid the same. Generally speaking, internal equity problems occur when employees on one job believe that they are being undercompensated relative to employees on some other job or jobs within the organization. However, it is illegal to pay a woman less than a man (or vice versa) for performing the same job when there is no objective basis for such a differential. If the organization can prove that such differences are based on differences in performance and/or seniority (see below), the organization will probably avoid litigation, but even the *perception* by a woman that she is being paid less than a man doing the same job is likely to lead to problems. Also, if some jobs in the organization are performed mostly by men and others mostly by women, differences in pay between the two jobs (real or perceived) must be attributable to differences in job demands or, again, the organization might face legal problems.

Compensation also serves a motivational purpose. That is, individuals should perceive that their efforts and contributions to the organization are recognized and rewarded. Individuals who work hard and who perform at a high level should likely be compensated at a level higher than should individuals who do just enough to get by and who perform at only an average or below-average rate.[2] Employees who perceive that everyone is compensated appropriately will believe that the reward system is just and that internal equity exists. In general, employees in this organization will probably be motivated to perform at their highest level.

Organizations must adequately and effectively manage compensation because employee compensation is one of their major expenses. Although employees must be appropriately and equitably rewarded, organizations must also control their compensation costs. For example, organizations should be careful to neither overpay individuals for the value of their contributions (which could lead to problems with internal equity) nor provide excess, superfluous, or unnecessarily extravagant benefits or rewards.[3] Thus the ideal compensation system reflects an appropriate balance of organizational constraints, costs, budgets, income, and cash flow relative to employee needs, expectations, and demands.

The fundamental purpose of compensation, then, is to provide an adequate and appropriate reward system for employees such that they feel valued and worthwhile as organizational members and representatives. Compensation

■ **External equity** in compensation refers to comparisons employees make to others performing similar jobs in different organizations.

represents more than simply the number of dollars a person takes home in her or his pay envelope on Friday or that is deposited directly into their checking account every month. Instead, it provides a measure of their value to the organization and, indirectly, is an indicator of their self–worth.[4]

Wages versus Salaries

■ **Wages** generally refer to hourly compensation paid to operating employees; the basis for wages is time.

Fundamental to understanding compensation is understanding the distinction between wages and salaries. **Wages** generally refer to hourly compensation paid to operating employees; the basis for wages is time. That is, the organization is paying individuals for specific blocks of their time. The current minimum wage is $5.15 dollars an hour. Most organizations calculate wages on an hourly basis. If an individual works eight hours, he or she earns eight hours times the hourly wage rate. But if an individual works only four and a half hours, then she or he make 4.5 times the hourly wage rate. Individuals who are paid on an hourly basis typically receive their income on a weekly or biweekly basis. Most of the jobs that are paid on an hourly wage basis are lower-level and/or operating-level jobs within the organization.

Rather than expressing compensation on an hourly basis, the organization may instead describe compensation on an annual or monthly basis. For example, many college graduates compare job offers on the basis of annual salary, such as $36,000 versus $38,000 a year. Sometimes salaries are quoted on the basis of a monthly rate. In general, salaries are paid to professional and managerial employees within an organization. Plant managers, product managers, and professional managers in areas such as marketing, finance, and accounting, for example, are likely to be paid on this basis. A **salary** compensates an individual not for how much time he spends in the organization, but for his overall contributions to the organization's performance. On a given day if a manager leaves work a couple of hours early or works a couple of hours late, that time has no bearing on the individual's compensation. She does not get docked for leaving early and does not get overtime pay for working extra.

■ **Salary** is income that is paid to an individual not on the basis of time, but on the basis of performance.

Strategic Options for Compensation

Most organizations establish a formal compensation strategy that dictates how they will pay individuals, and several decisions are embedded within this strategy. The first decision relates to the basis for pay. Traditionally, most organizations have based pay on the functions performed on the job. But, more recently, there has been increased reliance on skill-based pay and pay-for-knowledge programs.

A second decision in developing a compensation strategy focuses on the bases for differential pay within a specific job. In some organizations, especially those that have a strong union presence, differences in actual pay rates are based on seniority. That is, with each year of service in a particular job, wages go up by a specified amount. Therefore, the longer one works on the job, the more that person makes, regardless of the level of performance on the job. Most public school systems use a seniority system to pay teachers—they get a base salary increase for each year of service they accumulate. And as already noted, unions have historically preferred to base pay at least in part on seniority.

When developing a compensation strategy, managers need to decide whether to pay above, below, or at market levels. When Sean Suhl, shown in the center of this group, set out to attract talent to Lemonpop.com, an online network for Generation Y, he knew that he would have to pay top-dollar. That is, he knew that he needed to hire the best and brightest people who are skilled and knowledgeable in all ways of the Internet. Suhl also knew that to get such people Lemonpop.com would have to pay salaries well above market averages, plus toss in numerous additional benefits and incentives ranging from stock options to free cell phones.

Sometimes the relationship between seniority and pay is expressed as something called a maturity curve. A **maturity curve** is simply a schedule specifying the amount of annual increase a person will receive and is usually used when the annual increase depends on the actual number of years of service the person has accumulated. Organizations that use maturity curves might, for example, argue that newer workers need to learn more, in part just because there is more to learn, than more experienced employees and thus may deserve a larger increase. More senior people, meanwhile, may already be earning considerably higher income anyway and also have fewer new things to learn. In any event the assumption under a seniority-based pay system is that employees with more experience can make a more valuable contribution to the organization and should be rewarded for that. These systems also encourage employees to remain with the organization.

Other organizations base differences in pay on differences in performance, regardless of time on the job. These systems are generally seen as rewarding employees who are good performers rather than those who simply remain with the organization. For such systems to work effectively, however, the organization has to be certain that it has a good system for measuring performance. Most major companies base at least a portion of individual pay on performance, especially for managerial and professional employees. Performance-based incentives are discussed in more detail in Chapter 12.

A third decision in developing a compensation strategy deals with the organization's pay rates relative to "going rates" in the market. As shown in Figure 11.1, the three basic strategic options are to pay above-market compensation rates, market compensation rates, or below-market compensation rates.[5] This decision is very important because of the costs it represents to the organization.[6]

A firm that chooses to pay above-market compensation, for example, will incur additional costs as a result of this decision. This strategic option essentially indicates that the organization will pay its employees a level of compensation that is higher than that paid by other employers competing for the same kind of employees. Of course, it also anticipates achieving various benefits as

■ A **maturity curve** is a schedule specifying the amount of annual increase a person will receive.

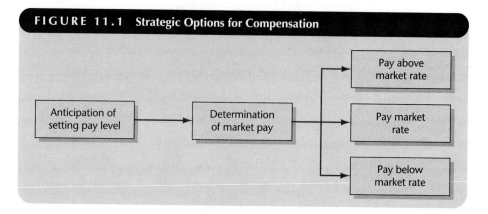

FIGURE 11.1   Strategic Options for Compensation

well. Some organizations believe that they attract better employees if they pay wages and salaries that are higher than those that are paid by other organizations. That is, they view compensation as a competitive issue. They recognize that high-quality employees may be selecting from among several potential employers and that companies willing to pay an above-market rate have a better chance of attracting the best employees. Above-market pay policies are most likely to be used in larger companies, particularly those that have been performing well.

In addition to attracting high-quality employees, an above-market strategy has some other benefits as well. For one thing, paying above-market rates tends to minimize voluntary turnover among employees because, by definition, an employee who leaves a company that is paying above-market wages may have to take a pay cut to find employment elsewhere. Another reason that paying above-market rates might be a good idea is that it can create and foster a culture of elitism and competitive superiority.

For example, at Wal-Mart no one earns the minimum wage. The reason for this policy is that the company doesn't want employees to feel that they are only worth the minimum amount the company could get away with paying. Thus it pays a bit more for entry-level positions than do certain competitors such as Kmart, which is more likely to pay the minimum wage. Cisco Systems, a Silicon Valley computer company, also pays higher-than-average salaries specifically as a way of retaining its valued employees in an industry where turnover and mobility are very high.

The downside to above-market compensation levels, of course, is cost. The organization simply has higher labor costs because of its decision to pay higher salaries to its employees. Moreover, once these higher labor costs become institutionalized, employees may begin to adopt a sense of entitlement, becoming to believe that they deserve the higher compensation and making it very difficult for the organization to ever be able to adjust its compensation levels down to lower levels. The "Human Resources Fad, Fashion, or Fact" box highlights some of the issues associated with minimum wage compensation when state or local governments impose minimums that are higher than federal minimums. This situation reflects people being paid higher wages and knowing that their wages are better than those of people of many other states.

Another strategic option is to pay below-market rates. The organization that adopts this strategy is essentially deciding to pay workers less than the compensation levels offered by other organizations competing for the same kinds of employees. Thus it is gambling that the lower-quality employees it is able to attract will be more than offset by the labor savings it achieves. Organizations that are most likely to pursue a below-market rate would be those in areas where is high unemployment. If lots of people are seeking employment and relatively few jobs are available, then many people would be willing to work for lower wages. Thus the organization may be able to pay below-market rates and still attract reasonable and qualified employees. Again the benefit to this strategy is lower labor costs for the organization.

On the other hand, the organization will also have to face a number of negative side effects. For one thing, morale and job satisfaction might not be as high as the organization would otherwise prefer. Individuals are virtually certain to recognize that they are being relatively underpaid, and this factor will result in feelings of job dissatisfaction and potential resentment against the organization. In addition, turnover may also be higher as employees will be continually looking for better-paying jobs and, when those jobs become available, leave the organization in order to take them. And compounding the problem is the fact that the higher-performing employees will be among the most likely to leave and the lowest-performing employees will be among the most likely to stay.

Finally, a third strategic option for compensation is to pay market rates for employees. That is, the organization may elect to pay salaries and wages that are comparable to those that are available in other organizations, no more and

---

HUMAN RESOURCES **Fad, Fashion, or Fact?**

Minimum Wage . . . But Which One?

 Most people are aware of the federally mandated minimum hourly wage in the United States, currently set at $5.15. But fewer people know that several states actually set a higher hourly minimum wage for their in-state workers. The current highest hourly minimum is Oregon's $6.50 an hour. Other states that have a higher minimum wage include California, Washington, Alaska, Connecticut, Hawaii, Massachusetts, and Vermont, as well as the District of Columbia. Oregon's latest jump went into effect January 1, 1999, and was the third of three such increases phased in starting in 1996. The goal of Oregon's initiative was to help workers catch up with cost-of-living increases during the 1970s and 1980s when wages failed to keep pace with inflation.

In another recent development some cities and counties, especially in high-cost urban areas, have started imposing their own minimum wages, at least for certain kinds of jobs. For example, the city of San Jose, California, mandates that construction workers be paid either

"The idea was to catch up with the cost-of-living increases in the 1970s and 80s."

(Diane Rosenbaum, Oregon state representative)*

$9.50 an hour plus health benefits or $10.75 without health benefits. Although this trend is just starting to attract national attention, experts are divided as to whether it will grow in popularity or fall by the wayside.

Thus whether these kinds of practices become "business as usual" or eventually fall from favor and are replaced by some other approach remains to be seen. For example, although the states with higher minimum wages seem basically satisfied with their arrangements, few other states seem particularly interested in moving to the higher rate. And although some cities are committed to the concept of a higher "livable wage" for their citizens, other cities are more cautious. In addition, some that try it abandon the idea if businesses start moving to other nearby locations or suburbs to avoid the higher wage levels.

References: "Minimum-Wage Increases Debated Anew," *USA Today,* January 6, 1999, p. 3A (*quote on p. 3A); "How the Federal Minimum Wage Has Grown," *Nation's Business,* May 1999, p. 12.

no less. Clearly, the organization that adopts this strategy is taking a midrange perspective. The organization not only is assuming that it will get higher-quality human resources than will a firm that takes a below-market strategy but also is willing to forego the ability to attract as many high-quality employees as an organization that takes an above-market-rate strategy.

The advantages and disadvantages of this strategy are also likely to reflect midrange comparisons with the other strategies. That is, the organization will have higher turnover than will a firm that pays above-market rates but lower turnover than an organization that is paying below-market rates. An organization that adopts a market-rate strategy is likely to believe that it provides other intangible or more subjective benefits to employees in return for their accepting a rate that is perhaps lower than they might otherwise be able to get. For example, job security is one important subjective benefit that some organizations provide.

Employees who perceive that they are being offered an unusually high level of job security may therefore be willing to take a somewhat lower wage rate and accept employment at a market rate. Universities also frequently adopt this strategy because they believe that people who work for such organizations do not necessarily expect higher salaries or higher wages. Microsoft also uses this approach. It offsets average wages with lucrative stock options and an exceptionally nice physical work environment.

Determinants of Compensation Strategy

A number of factors contribute to the compensation strategy that a firm develops. One general set of factors has to do with the overall strategy of the organization. As detailed in Chapter 2, a clear and carefully developed relationship should exist between a firm's corporate and business strategies and its human resource strategy.[7] This connection, in turn, should also tie into the firm's compensation strategy. Thus a firm that is in a high-growth mode will be constantly striving to attract new employees and may find itself in a position of having to pay above-market rates to attract them. On the other hand, a firm that is stable may be more likely to pay market rates, given the relatively predictable and stable nature of its operations. And finally, an organization that is in a retrenchment or a decline mode may decide to pay below-market rates given that it wants to reduce the size of its workforce anyway.[8]

In addition to these general strategic considerations, a number of very specific other factors also determine an individual's compensation strategy. One obvious factor is simply the organization's ability to pay. An organization that has a healthy cash flow and/or substantial cash reserves is more likely to be able to pay above-market wages and salaries. On the other hand, however, if the organization is suffering from a cash-flow crunch, has few cash reserves, and is operating on a very tight budget, it may be necessary to adopt a below-market-wage strategy. Thus the organization's ability to pay is an important consideration.

The overall ability of the organization to attract and retain employees is also a critical factor. For example, if the organization is located in a very attractive area; has a number of noncompensation amenities; and provides a comfortable, pleasant, and secure work environment, then it might be able to pay somewhat lower wages. But if the organization is located in, for example, a high-crime area or a relatively unattractive city or region, and provides few noncompensa-

Labor unions can be an important determinant of a business's compensation strategy. The United Auto Workers, for example, has long been the dominant union in the automobile industry. Today the UAW is embarking on a major organizing campaign to unionize more people who work for the major suppliers to firms like Ford and General Motors. Moreover, the UAW is pressuring the auto makers themselves to help it meet its organizing goals. In return, the union has agreed to relax its opposition to them transferring more of their own production to those suppliers. Thus, the UAW's efforts might lead to lower wages in the auto companies, but higher wages for their suppliers.

tion amenities to its employees, it may be necessary to pay higher wages simply as a way of attracting and retaining employees.

Yet another important determinant of a firm's compensation strategy is its legal context. As we discussed in Chapter 3, laws and other government regulations affect what an organization can pay its employees and how various benefits must be structured. For example, the FLSA of 1938 establishes a minimum wage; thus organizations must pay at least that wage to hourly employees (as of September 1, 1997, the minimum wage is $5.15 an hour). The same act also defines exempt versus non-exempt employees, which has implications for overtime compensation for employees as well.

Another important determinant of an organization's compensation strategy is union influences. If an organization competes in an environment that is heavily unionized, such as the automobile industry, then the strength and bargaining capabilities of the union will influence what the organization pays its employees. On the other hand, if few or no unions are representing the employee or the strength of a particular union is relatively low, then the organization may be able to pay somewhat lower wages and the union influence will be minimal or nonexistent.

Pay Surveys and Compensation

The critical source of information that many organizations use in developing compensation strategies is pay surveys. **Pay surveys** are surveys of

■ **Pay surveys** are surveys of compensation paid to employees by other employers in a particular geographic area, an industry, or an occupational group.

compensation paid to employees by other employers in a particular geographic area, an industry, or an occupational group. As such, pay surveys provide the information an organization needs to avoid problems of external equity. Some wage surveys are conducted by professional associations, especially for managerial and professional jobs. For example, the Society for Human Resource Management conducts salary surveys for human resource executives every other year. This information is then made available to all members of the society. They and the organizations they represent can then use the information in making wage and salary decisions within the human resource area. Moreover, organizations should keep in mind that their employees also look for information about external wages and salaries. Indeed, as discussed more fully in "Human Resources Tech Talk," the Internet is making this practice increasingly common.

Other organizations also conduct wage surveys. Business publications such as *Business Week, Fortune,* and *Nations Business* routinely publish compensation levels for various kinds of professional and executive positions. In addition, the Bureau of National Affairs and other government agencies also routinely conduct wage surveys within certain occupational groups, certain regions, and so forth. The Bureau of Labor Statistics is also an important source of government-controlled wage and salary information.

HUMAN RESOURCES Tech Talk

Negotiating Salaries on the Web

Back in the "old days" wages and salaries were typically negotiated in a meeting between the employee and his or her manager. This approach was used both for individuals who were being offered their first job with the company and for existing employees who felt they deserved a raise. But in both cases the manager and the organization usually had the upper hand because prospective and current employees generally had relatively little information about prevailing wage and salary levels. Workers rarely knew what others in the firm were being paid, for example, or what similar companies were paying for similar jobs in different parts of the region or country.

But the Internet is rapidly changing all that. For one thing, several large Web sites now provide salary information for anyone interested. These sites include salary-survey data, job listings with specified pay levels, and even customized compensation analyses. And armed with such detailed information, more and more people today are negotiating better deals for themselves with their employers.

"The Internet has become the big level playing field for everyone" by exposing businesses that "are way below everyone else as far as pay is concerned."

(Brian Krueger, consultant)*

And sometimes, especially for crafty negotiators, the Web can provide even more insights. For example, some people have been known to use Internet bulletin boards to track down other individuals who have recently been offered employment with a particular firm, find out how much they were offered, and then use that information as leverage in their own negotiations.

In another unforeseen development the big-time recruiting firm of Korn/Ferry recently set up its own salary site called Futurestep. But the firm faced some negotiations of its own when some of its employees used the site to determine that they were being underpaid! On balance, then, it seems that the Internet will be playing a major role from now on in the kinds of wages and salaries that employees expect and that companies pay.

References: "Web Transforms Art of Negotiating Raises," *Wall Street Journal,* September 22, 1998, pp. B1, B16 (*quote on p. B16); "Pushing the Pay Envelope," *Business Week,* March 8, 1999, pp. 93–94.

FIGURE 11.2 **Example of a Pay Survey**

Organization: ABC Trucking
Location: Dallas, TX

Benchmark Jobs	No. of workers (this title)	No. of workers (total)	Average weekly hours	Base Pay			Median total compensation (base pay + benefits)	Industry			
				25th %-tile	50th %-tile	75th %-tile		Mfg.	Trans.	Utilities	Trade
File clerk	10	300	40	$15,000	$20,000	$25,000	$28,000		✓		
Order clerk											
Accounting clerk											

A survey such as this would be sent to other organizations in a given region. In this case, the survey would go to organizations in a variety of industries, but other surveys might be targeted to a specific industry. The jobs that are the focus of the survey should be benchmark jobs, where everyone understands the nature of the job, the content is fairly stable, and the job is likely to be found in a wide variety or organizations. In some surveys, specific benchmark jobs are coded to further ensure that everyone is reacting to the same job. Also, some surveys ask more specific questions about other areas of compensation. Data from surveys such as this are then summarized for each job.

In general, the idea behind a wage and salary survey is simply to ask other organizations what they pay people to perform various jobs. For example, eight large electronic companies in the United States routinely survey one another to determine what they pay new engineers and other professional employees who are hired directly out of college. They alternate the responsibility for conducting the surveys from year to year, and then each organization shares its results with the other members of the consortium. Similar arrangements exist in the petroleum industry and in certain segments of the construction industry.

Designing a wage and salary survey is actually a much more complex process than might originally be thought, however. For example, it is necessary to identify and name various jobs and job families such that anyone who reads the survey and responds to it will have the same frame of reference and the same understanding regarding what is being asked. For this reason, organizations frequently rely on consulting firms and other outside groups to actually plan and conduct wage and salary surveys on their behalf. This approach allows firms to take advantage of the expertise available in such sources and to minimize the risk of making a significant error or mistake in the conduct of the survey.[9] Figure 11.2 presents a sample section from a pay survey questionnaire.

THE BOTTOM LINE All managers need to understand the various purposes played by compensation in organizations. Further, all managers, but most especially human resource managers, should clearly understand the importance of a well-formulated compensation strategy. Managers involved with the human resource function in an organization can help fulfill its role as a center of expertise by taking the lead in managing pay survey information and relating it to compensation.

DETERMINING A WAGE AND SALARY STRUCTURE

After human resource managers have developed their compensation strategy, they are prepared to establish a wage and salary structure for their organization. The starting point in this effort has traditionally been job evaluation. We first describe this more traditional method and then introduce a relatively new but increasingly popular approach to creating wage and salary structures.

Job Evaluation and Job Worth

One of the basic building blocks of an effective compensation system is job evaluation. Job evaluation should not be confused with job analysis, as discussed in Chapter 5. Recall that job analysis attempts to help managers better understand the requirements and nature of the job and its performance so that appropriate individuals can be recruited and selected for that particular job. **Job evaluation** is a method for determining the relative value or worth of a job to the organization so that individuals who perform that job can be adequately and appropriately compensated. That is, job evaluation is mostly concerned

◼ **Job evaluation** is a method for determining the relative value or worth of a job to the organization so that individuals who perform that job can be adequately and appropriately compensated.

As noted in the text, organizations sometimes choose to differentiate among workers performing jobs within a given job class. While any such differentiation in the United States must be based on job-related factors such as performance or seniority, employers in Japan have long been able to differentiate on the basis of gender. For example, male assembly workers in this Mazda factory are able to earn up to 30 percent more than their regular pay by working night shifts. But Japanese laws have forbidden women like Madoka Matsumae from working after 10 P.M. and from putting in more than six hours of overtime per week, regardless of work hours. A recently passed new law, however, will gradually phase out this practice and eventually enable female workers like Matsumae to earn as much as their male counterparts.

with establishing internal pay equity. A number of well-established job evaluation techniques and methods have been established.[10] Among the most commonly used are job ranking, factor comparison, classification, a point system, and a regression-based system. We discuss each of these methods for job evaluation in more detail in the sections that follow.

Job ranking   One of the most basic job evaluation systems is **job ranking.**[11] Job ranking is most likely to be used in relatively small and simple organizations in which a relatively small number of different jobs are being performed. In using the job ranking method, the manager will essentially rank jobs based on their relative importance to the organization from most important to least important. The premise then is that the most important job will be compensated at the highest level, the next most important job will be compensated somewhat below this level, and so forth down to the least important job, which is accorded the lowest level of compensation in the organization.

> ■ **Job ranking** is a job evaluation method requiring the manager to rank jobs based on their relative importance to the organization from most important to least important.

Job ranking will not work very effectively, however, in an organization with many different jobs. For one thing, it becomes difficult to differentiate among large numbers of jobs. Another shortcoming of the job ranking method is that how much differential to allow between jobs that are ranked at different levels is not always clear. For example, the most important job and the second most important job might be differentially compensated at an amount of, say, $5,000. However, the differential between the second and the third most important job might theoretically need to be substantially greater or substantially lesser. The ranking system alone does not really provide adequate information to make these decisions.

Classification system   Another popular method of job evaluation is the **classification system.**[12] An organization that uses a classification system attempts to group sets of jobs together into classifications. These classifications are often called *grades.* Each set of jobs is then ranked at a level of importance to the organization. Importance, in turn, may be defined in terms of relative difficulty, sophistication, or skills and abilities necessary to perform that job. A third step is to determine the number of job categories or classifications. The most common number is between eight and ten, although some organizations use the system with as few as four grades and some with as many as eighteen. The U.S. Postal Service (USPS) is a good example of an organization that uses this system. The USPS has sixteen job grades with nine pay steps within each grade. Once the grades have been determined, the job evaluator must write definitions and descriptions of each job class. These definitions and descriptions serve as the standard around which the compensation system will be built. That is, once the classes of jobs are defined and described, jobs that are being evaluated can be compared with the definitions and descriptions and placed into the appropriate classification.

> ■ The **classification system** for job evaluation attempts to group sets of jobs together into clusters, often called grades.

A major advantage of the job classification system is that it can be constructed relatively simply and quickly. It is easy to understand and easy to communicate to employees. It also provides specific standards for compensation and can easily accommodate changes in the value of various individual jobs in the organization. On the other hand, the job classification system is more complicated than simple ranking. The former is based on the assumption that a constant and inflexible relationship exists between the job factors and their value to the organization. Because of this shortcoming, some organizations

FIGURE 11.3 Job Classification System

Grade GS–1

Grade GS–1 includes those classes of positions the duties of which are to perform, under immediate supervision, with little or no latitude for the exercise of independent judgment:

    A. the simplest routine work in office, business, or fiscal operations; or

    B. elementary work of a subordinate technical character in a professional, scientific, or technical field.

Grade GS–6

Grade GS–6 includes those classes of positions the duties of which are:

    A. to perform, under general supervision, difficult and responsible work in office, business, or fiscal administration, or comparable subordinate technical work in a professional, scientific, or technical field, requiring in either case–
        1. considerable training and supervisory or other experience;
        2. broad working knowledge of a special and complex subject matter, procedure, or practice, or of the principles of the profession, art, or science involved; and
        3. to a considerable extent the exercise of independent judgment; or

    B. to perform other work of equal importance, difficulty, and responsibility, and requiring comparable qualifications.

Grade GS–10

Grade GS–10 includes those classes of positions the duties of which are:

    A. to perform, under general supervision, highly difficult and responsible work along special technical, supervisory, or adminstrative lines in office, business, or fiscal administration, requiring–
        1. somewhat extended specialized, supervisory, or administrative training and experience which has demonstrated capacity for sound independent work;
        2. thorough and fundamental knowledge of a specialized and complex subject matter, or of the profession, art, or science involved; and
        3. considerable latitude for the exercise of independent judgment; or

    B. to perform other work of equal importance, difficulty, and responsibility, and requiring comparable qualifications.

Source: U.S. Office of Personnel Management

Job classification systems require clear definitions of classes and benchmark jobs for each class. The most widely known example of a job classification system is the General Schedule (GS) system used by the federal government. In this system, there are eighteen "grades" (or classes). Most federal employees fall into one of fifteen grades, while the top three grades have been combined into a single "supergrade" that covers senior executives.

The information above outlines the descriptions of three grades from the GS system. An example of a job classified as a GS-1 would be a janitor; an example of a GS-6 job would be a light truck driver; and an example of a GS-10 job would be an auto mechanic. Within each grade, there are ten pay "steps" based on seniority, so that the range of salaries for a GS-6 starts at just under $20,000 a year and goes up to over $25,000 a year.

■ The **point system** for job evaluation requires managers to quantify in objective terms the value of the various elements of specific jobs.

find it necessary to group together jobs that do not necessarily fit together very well. Figure 11.3 presents an example of a job classification system.

Point system   The most commonly used method of job evaluation is the **point system.**[13] The point system is more sophisticated than either the ranking or the classification system and is also relatively easy to use. The point system requires managers to quantify in objective terms the value of the various elements of specific jobs. Using job descriptions as a starting point, managers assign points to various compensable factors that are required to perform that job. **Compensable factors** include any aspect of a job for which an organization is willing to provide compensation. For instance, managers might assign points based on the amount of skill that is required to perform a particular job, the amount of physical effort that is needed, the nature of the working conditions involved, and/or the responsibility and authority that are involved in the performance of the job. Job evaluation simply represents the sum of the points that are allocated to each compensable factor for each job.

Point systems typically evaluate eight to ten compensable factors for each job. The factors chosen should not overlap with one another, but should be able to immediately distinguish between substantive characteristics of the jobs, be objective and verifiable in nature, and be well understood and accepted by both managers and employees. Given that not all aspects of a particular job may be of equal importance, managers can allocate different weights to reflect the relative importance of these aspects to a job. These weights are usually determined by summing the judgments of a variety of independent but informed evaluators. Thus an administrative job within an organization might result in weightings of required education 40 percent, required experience 30 percent, predictability and complexity of the job 15 percent, responsibility and authority for making decisions 10 percent, and working conditions and physical requirements for the job 5 percent.

As the point system is used to evaluate jobs, most organizations also develop a **point manual.** The point manual carefully and specifically defines the degrees of points from first to fifth. For example, education might be defined as follows: (1) First degree, up to and including a high school diploma, 25 points; (2) second degree, high school diploma and one year of college education, 50 points; (3) third degree, high school diploma and two years of college, 75 points; (4) fourth degree, high school education and three years of college, 100 points; and (5) fifth degree, a college degree, 125 points. These point manuals would then be used for all subsequent job evaluations.

Factor comparison method   A fourth method of job evaluation is the factor comparison method. Like the point system, the **factor comparison method** allows the job evaluator to assess jobs on a factor-by-factor basis. At the same time, however, this method differs from the point system in that jobs are evaluated or compared against a standard of key points. That is, instead of using points, a factor comparison scale is used as a benchmark. Although an organization can choose to identify any number of compensable factors, commonly used systems include five job factors to compare jobs; these factors are responsibilities, skills, physical effort, mental effort, and working conditions.

Managers performing a job evaluation using a factor comparison system are typically advised to follow six specific steps. First, the comparison factors to be used are selected and defined. The five universal factors are used as a starting point, but any given organization may need to add factors to this set. Second, benchmark or key jobs in the organization are identified. These are typically representative and common jobs that are found in the labor market of a particular firm. Usually, ten to twenty benchmark jobs are selected. The third step is to rank the benchmark jobs on each compensation factor. The ranking itself is usually based on job descriptions and job specifications, derived from a job analysis.

■ **Compensable factors** include any aspect of a job for which an organization is willing to provide compensation.

■ The **point manual,** used to implement the point system of job evaluation, carefully and specifically defines the degrees of points from first to fifth.

■ The **factor comparison method** for job evaluation assesses jobs on a factor-by-factor basis, using a factor comparison scale as a benchmark.

The fourth step is to allocate a part of each benchmark's job wage rate to each job factor. This allocation is based on the relative importance of that factor. In this step each manager participating in the job evaluation might first be asked to make an independent allocation. Then the managers meet as a group to develop a consensus about the assignment of monetary values to the various factors. The fifth step in using the factor comparison system is to prepare the two sets of ratings based on the ranking and the assigned wages to determine the consistency demonstrated by the evaluators. Sixth, a job comparison chart is developed to display the benchmark jobs and the monetary values that each job receives for each factor. This chart can then be used to rate other jobs in the organization as compared to the benchmark jobs.

A major advantage of the factor comparison system is that it is a detailed and meticulous method for formally evaluating the jobs. Thus it provides a reasonably rigorous assessment of the true value of various jobs. It also allows managers to fully recognize how the differences in factor rankings affect the dollars that it allocates to compensation for various jobs. On the other hand, the factor comparison method is also extremely complex and difficult to use. Therefore, it is time-consuming and expensive for an organization that chooses to adopt it. In addition, a fair amount of subjectivity is involved, and people whose jobs are evaluated with this system may feel that inequities have crept into the system either through managerial error or politically motivated oversight. Hay and Associates, a well-known compensation consulting firm that often does job evaluation for large organizations, uses a factor comparison system based on three factors: know-how, problem solving, and accountability.

■ A **regression-based system** for job evaluation uses a statistical technique called multiple regression to develop an equation that establishes the relationship between different dimensions of the job and compensation.

Regression-based system   A **regression-based system** uses a statistical technique called multiple regression to develop an equation that establishes the relationship between different dimensions of the job and compensation. Although any job analysis technique that allows direct comparisons across jobs could be used in such a system, the Position Analysis Questionnaire (or PAQ, as discussed in Chapter 5) is frequently used as the basis for such a system. To develop the job evaluation system, it is necessary to collect job analysis data for a wide variety of jobs. These data should be in the form of scores on some common metric, and the job dimensions underlying the PAQ are perfectly suited for this task. Next, for each job in the sample, managers obtain data on the current rate of compensation. The multiple-regression technique then allows the organization to model how the presence or absence of different job dimensions, in different amounts, is related to compensation.

Notice that the resulting equation simply tells us that jobs with certain characteristics tend to be paid a certain amount. This information is not a recommendation, but simply a report of current conditions. Therefore, the purpose of this approach to job evaluation is to capture and retain the present compensation system, rather than to present an ideal system. Once the equation is developed, managers can determine what any new job should be paid based on this compensation system by simply conducting a job analysis, plugging the scores for the new job into the equation, and then letting the equation indicate what the job should be paid. Although the equation could be adjusted for market factors, this approach to job evaluation is more concerned with internal equity issues and, as noted above, assumes that the jobs in the sample are being compensated fairly.

Establishing Job Classes

Once the job evaluation has been completed, the next step in the development of a wage and salary structure is the establishment of job classes. Job classes represent gradations of responsibility and competence that exist regarding the performance of a specific job. For example, in an assembly factory one job that may be crucial to the conduct of the firm's business is that of a mechanic. A mechanic might be the individual responsible for maintaining and repairing various pieces of equipment and technology.

Obviously, however, different mechanics can have different levels of competence. For example, one mechanic might be relatively inexperienced and, although technically proficient at his or her job, only be capable of repairing a small percentage of the total number of machines or pieces of equipment in the factory. In contrast, other mechanics might be capable of maintaining and repairing all of the equipment within the factory.

It would seem reasonable, then, that the organization might want to differentiate between people with these different competencies. As a result, the organization might create a series of job grades for this class of job. For example, mechanic I might be the entry-level position for an individual with relatively little experience and limited capabilities. At the other extreme mechanic V might be for an individual who is capable of performing a variety of mechanical tasks and of repairing all machines within a particular factory. In between, of course, would be mechanic grades II, III, and IV.

Recall from our discussion of job evaluation methods in the previous section that the job classification or grading system actually results in groups of jobs being identified. As a result, organizations that use this method of job evaluation essentially establish their job classes as a part of the job evaluation process itself. But organizations that use job rankings, the point system, or the factor comparison system are still likely to take this additional step once those job evaluations are complete and create job classes as described above.

Establishing a Pay Structure

The final traditional step in the development of a wage and salary structure is the establishment of a pay structure. A pay structure actually needs to do two things. First, it has to specify the level of pay the organization is going to provide to each job class as described in the preceding section. Second, it must also identify the pay differentials to be paid to individuals within each job class. A sample pay structure is shown in Figure 11.4.

The determination of compensation for different job classes is based on the organization's assessment of the relative value of each of those job classes to the organization itself. Thus there should be a logical ordering of compensation levels from the most to the least valuable job class throughout the organization. Of course, the organization may also find it appropriate and necessary to group some job classes together. That is, two or more classes of jobs may be of relatively equal value to the organization and thus should be compensated at approximately the same level. For example, using the five grades of mechanic discussed earlier, the organization might see little difference between mechanic II and mechanic III and thus might pay very little additional when a person progresses from the lower grade to the higher one.

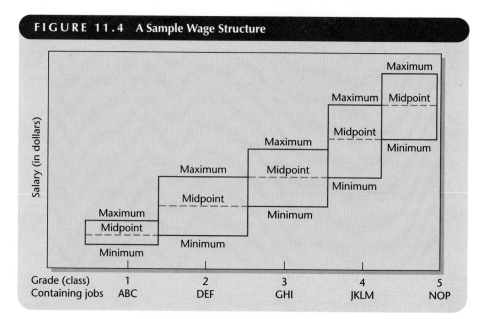

FIGURE 11.4   A Sample Wage Structure

Jobs are grouped into classes or grades, based on similar responsibilities or similar scores from a job evaluation technique. All jobs within a grade should be paid the same. As illustrated above, there is a range of pay within each class or grade and there is also overlap among grades such that the highest-paid person in any grade is paid more than the lowest-paid person in the next highest grade. This overlap allows for easier pay adjustments when someone is promoted, but the exact degree of overlap can vary from organization to organization.

A related issue is the determination of the differential in pay to be accorded to different job classes. For example, two job classes that are relatively close in a ranking sense may still be so fundamentally different in terms of their importance to the organization that the differential in compensation is substantial. On the other hand, some job classes may be relatively close to one another in both importance and ranking, and as a result, the pay differential may be modest. Second, as noted, it is also important to establish pay ranges to be applied to different jobs within a particular job class. Recall, for example, our earlier instance of the mechanic I through V job classification system. The organization has to decide both the minimum and the maximum pay that it will provide to an individual within each pay category.

Pay for Knowledge and Skill-Based Pay

The steps, decisions, and processes outlined above still apply to most jobs in most organizations, but some recent proposals suggest a whole different approach to compensation. This approach suggests that employees should be rewarded for what they know, rather than what they are specifically required to do on the job. The relative advantages and disadvantages of these two philosophies are summarized in "Point/Counterpoint."

■ **Pay for knowledge** involves compensating employees for learning specific material.

Pay for knowledge involves compensating employees (usually managerial, service, or professional employees) for learning specific material. For example, this approach might include paying programmers for learning a new programming language or rewarding managers who master some new manufacturing system. These systems could also be designed to pay for learning supervisory skills or for developing more in-depth knowledge about some organizationally relevant topic. Pay-for-knowledge systems reward employees for mastering material that will allow them to be more "useful" to the organization and are based around mastering new technology or mastering information that relates to global issues. These systems tend to be fairly expensive to start up, since the organization needs to develop methods for testing whether the employee has actually mastered the information in question. However, after the systems are in place, the costs are usually not excessive. In addition, these plans have the potential to clash with more traditional incentive systems (see Chapter 12) in

---

POINT/COUNTERPOINT   What Should Be the Basis for Compensation?

 The basis for compensation in most organizations is some function of the job requirements. That is, employees who are expected to perform more complex, difficult, dangerous, or even numerous tasks are generally paid more than other employees. Thus the basis for compensation is the set of tasks that are required, and these are usually spelled out in a job description. It has been argued, however, that this set of tasks is not the best basis for compensation. Instead, critics say that we should pay for knowledge, skill, or competency. In other words, we should not pay a person for what he or she does, but rather for what he or she knows. Under these systems an organization specifies the knowledge bases or skills it is willing to pay for, and as employees acquire this information and can demonstrate mastery, their compensation increases. We refer to this alternative as **knowledge-based pay.**

POINT . . . **We should base compensation on what a person is required to do on his or her job because . . .**	COUNTERPOINT . . . **We should base compensation on what a person knows because . . .**
Assessing what a person does (or should do) is easier than assessing what she or he knows.	Developing a system to certify whether employees have mastered some skill or knowledge base is relatively easy.
Most employees see this is a fair way to compensate, and they can easily see the basis for compensation differences.	The organization pays people for what they can contribute in terms of special knowledge or expertise—employees are paid for what they are worth to the company.
All employees know what is expected of them and how they will be rewarded.	All employees focus on growth and the accumulation of new knowledge or skills as the means to rewards.
Paying people for what they actually do makes sense.	Paying people for what they bring to the job that is useful to the organization makes sense.
What do we do when everyone has mastered all the knowledge bases or skills specified?	Under such a system employees will strive to improve themselves, and the organization with gain flexibility as well as a more knowledgeable workforce.

So . . .   Knowledge-based systems reward people who learn more and acquire more skills that are relevant to the job. In the long run this plan is likely to benefit the company as it tries to grow and react to changes in the environment. However, there is actually very little data to either support or refute this position. In addition, many bureaucratic systems must be in place to determine requisite skills and to certify mastery of those skills and knowledge bases. Furthermore, it is possible for an employee to master all the specified skills or knowledge bases and, at that point, have the compensation decision become complicated. Nonetheless, if knowledge-based systems can be implemented, they do seem to have the potential for aiding long-run competitiveness.

■ **Skill-based pay** rewards employees for acquiring new skills.

that employees might choose to perfect and apply knowledge they already have, rather than learn new material.[14]

Skill-based pay operates in much the same way as pay for knowledge but is more likely to be associated with hourly workers. Here, instead of rewarding employees who master new material, employees are rewarded for acquiring new skills. So, for example, under such a plan a secretary would be paid for learning how to use a new word processing program. The skills involved can either be for the same job (or in the same job family) or be relevant for other jobs in the organization. For example, manufacturing plants often cross train employees so that they have the skills to do a number of different jobs in the plant. This approach affords management a great deal of flexibility in scheduling, and benefits employees as well because they can rotate through different jobs (providing some variety) and acquire skills that may increase their market value if they choose to seek another job.

THE BOTTOM LINE Managers should know the basic elements in the traditional methods for developing wage and salary structures but should also keep abreast of new and emerging alternative methods. Human resource managers play an especially important role in helping determine the best approach for any given organization.

WAGE AND SALARY ADMINISTRATION

Once a wage and salary structure has been developed through the job evaluation process and the establishment of job classes and pay structure, that wage and salary structure must still be administered on an ongoing basis. Most organizations call this process **wage and salary administration,** or compensation administration.

■ **Wage and salary administration** is the ongoing process of managing a wage and salary structure.

Managing Compensation

As we noted at the beginning of this chapter, compensation and benefits expenses are among the largest cost that any organization will incur. Thus all managers must be sensitive to these costs and must be vigilant about their proper management. If an organization is paying excess wages and salaries, it is incurring unnecessary expenses. On the other hand, if the organization is not paying sufficient wages and salaries to its employees, then it will likely experience turnover and other dysfunctional consequences.

The ongoing management of compensation and benefits is a critical part of effective wage and salary administration. In addition to monitoring costs, however, the organization needs to also maintain an ongoing assessment of how well it is managing the compensation and benefits system. For example, organizations may occasionally need to change their compensation strategies. As described earlier, some organizations pay above-market rates, whereas other organizations pay at or below-market rates. But as organizational circumstances and needs change, it may also be necessary for the organization to change or modify its compensation strategy. Likewise, job evaluation is not a

Robert and Benjamin Bynum are credited with playing major roles in the revitalization of downtown Philadelphia by opening a variety of innovative restaurants and nightspots. Places such as Warmdaddy's, Brave New World, and Willemina's have attracted new customers to the area and turned the Bynums' business interests into a burgeoning regional empire. Because many of their employees live partially on tips, the Bynums have always taken an interest in helping employees better manage their finances and achieve financial security. For example, as part of their ongoing wage and salary administration programs, the Bynums have set up an employee investment club and routinely offer credit and financial planning seminars for their employees.

one-time operation. Although job evaluations need not be conducted monthly or even yearly, it is still worthwhile for the organization to periodically reevaluate its jobs to ensure that it has an appropriate worth attached to each job, that job classes are valid, and that the pay structure of the organization is fulfilling its purpose.

Determining Individual Wages

Organizations must also develop a stance toward the determination of individual wages. Regardless of the job evaluation results, most firms find it necessary and appropriate to provide opportunities for differential compensation for individuals performing the same job. It is important for both ethical and legal reasons that the basis for differential pay not be some non-job-related factor such as gender or race. However, it is perfectly appropriate, and indeed very desirable, for the organization to reward people with differential compensation based on job-related qualifications.

As noted earlier, for instance, the organization might want to reward seniority by paying long-time employees a higher wage or salary than it pays to relative newcomers. Likewise, the organization may want to reward people on the

The Lighter Side of HR

Pay secrecy is a long-standing practice in many companies today. But there seems to be a gradual willingness in some companies to consider open-pay systems. At the same time, however, organizations that are interested in open-pay systems should be prepared for cries of favoritism, politics, and worse! As shown here, for example, workers who are paid less than they think they deserve will likely find reasons to criticize the pay of others, especially upper-level managers whose salaries are likely to be relatively high.

basis of performance. Thus high performers may be paid more than average or low performers, even though they are all assigned to the same job. Such an arrangement provides an effective motivational framework for the organization, but again, the basis for differential pay should always be based on true job-related factors, such as performance or seniority, as opposed to non-job-related factors.

Pay Secrecy

■ **Pay secrecy** refers to the extent to which an individual's compensation in an organization is secret.

Another important aspect of wage and salary administration is pay secrecy. **Pay secrecy** refers to the extent to which an individual's compensation in an organization is secret. Those who advocate pay secrecy suggest that what an individual is paid is his or her own business and not for public knowledge. They also argue that if pay levels are made known to everybody else, then jealousy and/or resentment may result. Indeed, most businesses practice pay secrecy, sometimes even to the point of formally forbidding managers from discussing their pay with other people.

On the other hand, some organizations adopt more of an open-pay system where everyone knows what everyone else makes. The logic behind this strategy is that it promotes equity and motivation. To the extent that high performers are known to be making more money than low performers, then it follows logically that people throughout the organization will be motivated to work harder under the assumption that they too will be recognized and rewarded for their contributions. Many publicly funded organizations such as state universities and public schools have open pay systems whereby any interested individual can look at budgets or other information to determine how much any given individual is being paid. This issue is illustrated in an amusing way in "The Lighter Side of HR."

Pay Compression

A problem that some organizations occasionally have to confront during wage and salary administration is pay compression. **Pay compression** is a circumstance in which individuals with substantially different levels of experience and/or performance abilities are being paid wages or salaries that are relatively close together. Pay compression is most likely to develop when the market rate for starting salaries increases at a rate faster than an organization's internal ability to raise pay for individuals who are already on the payroll.

For example, suppose that an organization hires a new engineer one year at a starting salary of $35,000 a year. Further suppose that the next year the organization wants to hire another engineer in the same field. Overall market conditions suggest that such engineers are now worth $37,000 a year, and the organization has to pay that rate in order to attract a new engineer. Presumably, the first engineer hired now has a year of experience and is performing at a reasonable level in the organization and ought to be paid more than someone who is just starting out. The organization is likely to avoid any major problems to the extent that it has the resources to adjust the existing employee's salary beyond the $37,000 level. On the other hand, if internal budget constraints and other considerations limit the organization's ability to adjust the compensation of its existing employees, then pay compression may result.

Indeed, it may even be possible for a newcomer just starting out in an organization to be paid a higher salary than an individual who has been working for the organization for a year or two. To the extent that this knowledge is known among employees, then, again, the possibility for resentment and disappointment is likely to increase. Organizations sometimes have little remedy in the event of pay compression. On the one hand they have to respond to market shifts to continue to hire at a competitive level. At the same time, internal resources may be such that organizations can't maintain pay increases at the same rate that the market rate is increasing. This situation may require organizations to provide other kinds of rewards, such as intangible benefits like recognition, or simply face the consequences of disgruntled employees leaving because they feel that they are being underpaid relative to newcomers in the organization.

> ■ **Pay compression** is a circumstance in which individuals with substantially different levels of experience and/or performance abilities are being paid wages or salaries that are relatively close together.

THE BOTTOM LINE All managers should understand the basic issues involved in wage and salary administration. They should especially be sensitive to issues associated with individual wages, pay secrecy, and pay compression in their organization.

E V A L U A T I N G   C O M P E N S A T I O N   P O L I C I E S

Given the enormous cost to an organization of compensation packages, it is clearly important that managers carefully assess the benefit that accrues to the organization because of those packages. On the one hand, the organization must provide reasonable compensation and appropriate benefits to its employees. At the same time, it is in the best interest of the stockholders and other constituents of the organization that the firm manage its resources wisely. Thus it is important to periodically assess the extent to which costs are in line.

One way of evaluating compensation policies is through the use of the wage surveys, as noted earlier in this chapter. Similar comparisons can also be made for wage structures, benefit packages, and so forth. Any organization, for example, can learn the average insurance premium costs that other organizations are paying. Although that organization may not be able to match these premiums, particularly if it has a history of high accident rates, illnesses, and so forth, it can nevertheless get a better feel for how close its costs are to those of other firms.

Likewise, an organization may need to audit its overall compensation program to determine whether or not the program is competitive. As a part of the recruiting process, it is necessary, of course, for the organization to be seen as an attractive employer in order to hire high-quality human resources. Of course, the attractiveness of a firm as an employer is a function, in part, of the total compensation package, which includes employee benefits, a topic we discuss in Chapter 13.

THE BOTTOM LINE For a variety of reasons, managers should appreciate the importance of regular evaluations of an organization's compensation policies. Paying employees either too much or too little can have serious consequences for a business. Hence, it's important to all managers that they have a clear strategy of where they want compensation to be relative to market and to take regular steps to ensure that they are, in fact, maintaining that desired position.

Chapter Summary

Compensation has a number of purposes and objectives. However, the fundamental purpose is to provide an adequate and appropriate reward system for employees such that they feel valued and worthwhile as organizational members and representatives. The three basic strategic options are to pay above-market compensation rates, market compensation rates, or below-market compensation rates. Various factors contribute to the compensation strategy that a firm develops. The critical source of information that many organizations use in developing compensation strategies is pay surveys.

After human resource managers have developed their compensation strategy, they are then prepared to establish a wage and salary structure for their organization. The starting point in this effort is job evaluation, a method for determining the relative value or worth of a job to the organization so that individuals who perform that job can be adequately

and appropriately compensated. A number of well-established job evaluation techniques and methods are available. Once the job evaluation has been completed, the next step in the development of a wage and salary structure is the establishment of job classes. The final step is the establishment of a pay structure. Increasingly popular alternative approaches to compensation include pay-for-knowledge plans and skill-based pay.

Once a wage and salary structure has been developed through the job evaluation process and the establishment of job classes and pay structure, then that wage and salary structure must still be administered on an ongoing basis. The ongoing management of compensation and benefits is a critical part of effective wage and salary administration. Organizations must also develop a stance toward the determination of individual wages. Another important aspect of wage and salary administration is pay secrecy. A problem that some organizations occasionally have to confront during wage and salary administration is pay compression.

Given the enormous cost to an organization of its compensation packages, managers must carefully assess the effectiveness of the firm's compensation structure to ensure that organizational and employee interests are being optimized.

Review and Discussion Questions

1. What is compensation?

2. What are the basic differences between wages and salaries?

3. What are the basic strategic options an organization has for its compensation policies?

4. What role do pay surveys play in compensation?

5. Identify and summarize the basic methods of job evaluation.

6. Why are job classes needed? How are they developed?

7. How does an organization create a pay structure?

8. What are the basic issues involved in determining individual wages?

9. What are the advantages and disadvantages of open versus secret pay information?

10. How does pay compression develop? Why is it a problem?

Closing Case

Working by the Hour at General Motors and Wal-Mart

Hourly workers—people who are paid a set dollar amount for each hour or fraction of an hour they work—have long been the backbone of the U.S. economy. But times are changing and so is the lot of the hourly worker. Like all things, of course, some of this change is for the better, but some of it is clearly for the worse, at least from the workers' standpoint. And nowhere are these differences more apparent than the contrasting conditions for hourly workers at General Motors and Wal-Mart.

General Motors, of course, is an old, traditional industrial company that up until recently was the nation's largest employer. And for decades its hourly workers have been protected by strong labor unions like the United Auto Workers, or UAW. These unions, in turn, have forged contracts and working conditions that almost seem archaic in today's economy. Consider, for example, the employment conditions of Tim Philbrick, a forty-two-year-old plant worker and union member at the firm's Fairfax plant near Kansas City who has worked for GM for twenty-three years.

Mr. Philbrick makes almost $20 an hour in base pay. With a little overtime, his annual earnings top $60,000. But even then he is far from the highest-paid factory worker at GM. Skilled-trade workers like electricians and toolmakers make $2 to $2.50 an hour more and with greater overtime opportunities often make $100,000 or more per year. Mr. Philbrick also gets a no-deductible health insurance policy that allows him to see any doctor he wants. He also gets four weeks of vacation per year, plus two weeks at Christmas and at least another week in July when the plant is closed. In addition, he gets two paid twenty-three-minute breaks and a paid thirty-minute lunch break per day. He also has the option of retiring after thirty years with full benefits.

GM estimates that, with benefits, its average worker makes more than $43 an hour. Perhaps not surprisingly, then, the firm is always looking for opportunities to reduce its workforce through attrition and cutbacks, with the goal of replacing production capacity with lower-cost labor abroad. The UAW, of course, is staunchly opposed to further workforce reductions and cutbacks. And long-standing work rules strictly dictate who gets overtime, who can be laid off and who can't, and myriad other employment conditions for Mr. Philbrick and his peers.

But the situation at GM is quite different—in a lot of ways—from conditions at Wal-Mart. Along many dimensions Wal-Mart is slowly but surely supplanting GM as the quintessential U.S. corporation. For example, Wal-Mart is growing rapidly, is becoming more and more ingrained in the American life style, and now employs more people than GM did in its heyday. But hourly workers at Wal-Mart have a much different experience from those at GM.

For example, consider Ms. Nancy Handley, a twenty-seven-year-old Wal-Mart employee who oversees the men's department at a big store in St. Louis. Jobs like Ms. Handley's are paid between $9 and $11 an hour, or about $20,000 a year. About $100 a month is deducted from her paycheck to help cover the costs of benefits. Her health insurance has a $250 deductible; she then pays 20 percent of her health care costs as long as she uses a set of approved physicians. Her prescriptions cost between $5 and $10 each. She also has dental coverage; after her $50 deductible, she pays 20 percent of these costs as well. During her typical workday, Ms. Handley gets two 15-minute breaks and an hour for lunch, but she has to punch out at the time clock and doesn't get paid during these times.

But Ms. Handley doesn't feel mistreated by Wal-Mart. In fact, she says she is appropriately compensated for what she does. She has received three merit raises in the last seven years, for example, and has considerable job security. Moreover, if she decides to try for advancement, Wal-Mart seems to offer considerable potential. For example, several thousand hourly workers a year are promoted to the ranks of management. Although the length of their work week increases, so too does their pay. And Ms. Handley is clearly not unique in her views—Wal-Mart employees routinely reject any and all overtures from labor unions and are among the most loyal and committed in the United States today.

Case Questions

1. Compare and contrast hourly working conditions at General Motors and Wal-Mart.

2. Describe the (apparent) wage structures at GM and Wal-Mart.

3. Summarize the basic issues in wage and salary administration that managers at GM and Wal-Mart are most likely to face.

Sources: Hoover's Handbook of American Business 1999 (Austin, Texas: Hoover's Business Press, 1999); "'I'm Proud of What I've Made Myself Into—What I've Created,'" *Wall Street Journal,* August 28, 1997, pp. B1, B5; "'That's Why I Like My Job . . . I Have an Impact on Quality,'" *Wall Street Journal,* August 28, 1997, pp. B1, B8.

Building Human Resource Management Skills

Purpose: The purpose of this exercise is to help you better understand the impact of hourly wages on operating costs and profit margins.

Step 1: Working alone or with a group (your instructor will specify which) identify a local small business that likely depends heavily on hourly employees and whose owner or manager would be willing to help students with a class project. Good examples might be a fast-food restaurant like McDonald's or Taco Bell, a dry-cleaning establishment, or a specialty retailer.

Step 2: Interview the owner or manager of the business and obtain as much of the following information as possible:

- Total number of hourly employees
- Total number of labor hours needed per week
- Average hourly wage currently being paid
- Approximate annual revenues
- Approximate profit margin

[Note: If the owner or manager will not or cannot provide some of this information, ask for general or approximate figures or ranges that might characterize a similar business.]

Step 3: Assume that because of an increase in the minimum wage, increased competition or demand for hourly workers, mandated increases from the "home office," or some similar factor that hourly wages have to be increased. Assuming wage increases of 10, 25, and 50 cents an hour, calculate the following:

- Total annual labor cost increases for each level of hourly wage increase
- The effect of each increase on current profit margins
- The necessary increase in annual revenues needed to maintain current profit margins for each level of wage increases

Step 4: Respond to the following questions:

1. What other costs and profit factors do wage increases affect?

2. How would you incorporate salaries into a problem such as this?

3. In larger firms union contracts might be the catalyst for increased wages. How similar or different would this sort of analysis be for a much bigger company?

Ethical Dilemmas in Human Resource Management

Assume you are the manager of a company-owned fast-food restaurant. Although you have a few permanent full-time employees, your workforce consists primarily of older retired people working to supplement their social security benefits and college students working to help cover their educational expenses. Altogether, you employ ten older workers and twenty-five students. Each individual works an average of fifteen hours per week and earns the minimum wage.

A recent mandated increase in the minimum wage, however, has cut into your profit margins, and the home office has dictated that you must lower labor costs. While you know that everyone will have to work harder, you do recognize that you can still manage the business effectively with fewer labor hours per week.

Your analysis has indicated that any one of four options will work. One option is to terminate four of your older workers. A second option is to terminate four college students. A third option is to terminate two older workers and two college students. The final option is to retain all of your current workers but to reduce their average hours from fifteen to twelve per week.

Questions

1. What are the ethical issues in this situation?

2. What are the basic arguments for and against each option?

3. What do you think most managers would do? What would you do?

Human Resource Internet Exercise

Search the Internet for sites devoted to wages and/or salaries. Visit at least three such sites. Two especially good ones are **http://jobs-mart.org/tools/salary** and **http://www.experienceondemand.com /features/salary.html**.
Learn as much as possible about each site.

Questions

1. How might you most effectively use these kinds of Web sites as a job seeker to ensure that you are paid an equitable wage or salary?

2. How might you most effectively use these kinds of Web sites as a human resource manager to ensure that your firm is paying an appropriate wage or salary?

3. What information seems to be common to all of the sites you visited?

4. Is there information you expected to find or would like to have found that did not appear to be on the site?

Notes

1. Kathryn Tyler, "Compensation Strategies Can Foster Lateral Moves and Growing in Place," *HRMagazine,* April 1998, pp. 64–69.
2. J. Stacey Adams, "Inequity in Social Exchange," in L. Berkowitz (ed.), *Advances in Experimental Social Psychology* (New York: Academic Press, 1965), pp. 267–299.
3. Jeffrey Pfeffer, "Six Dangerous Myths about Pay," *Harvard Business Review,* May–June 1998, pp. 109–119. See also Matt Bloom, "The Performance Effects of Pay Dispersion on Individuals and Organizations," *Academy of Management Journal,* Vol. 42, No. 1, 1999, pp. 25–40.
4. See "Is Minimum Wage Minimum Life?" *Associated*

Press News Story, January 23, 1995.

5. Brian S. Klaas and John A. McClendon, "To Lead, Lag, or Match: Estimating the Financial Impact of Pay Level Policies," *Personnel Psychology,* 1996, pp. 88–98.

6. Edward E. Lawler III, "The New Pay: A Strategic Approach," *Compensation & Benefits Review,* July–August 1995, pp. 145–154.

7. Sandra O'Neil, "Aligning Pay with Business Strategy," *HRMagazine,* August 1993, pp. 76–80.

8. Charles Greer, *Strategy and Human Resources* (Englewood Cliffs, N.J.: Prentice-Hall, 1995).

9. Emily Pavlovic, "Choosing the Best Salary Surveys," *HRMagazine,* April 1994, pp. 44–48.

10. Judith Collins and Paul Muchinsky, "An Assessment of the Construct Validity of Three Job Evaluation Methods: A Field Experiment," *Academy of Management Journal,* Vol. 36, No. 4, 1993, pp. 895–904.

11. George Milkovich and Jerry Newman, *Compensation* (Homewood, Ill.: Irwin/BPI, 1990).

12. Milkovich and Newman, *Compensation.*

13. Milkovich and Newman, *Compensation.*

14. G. Douglas Jenkins and Nina Gupta, "The Payoffs of Paying for Knowledge," *National Productivity Review,* Vol. 4, 1985, pp. 121–130.

12

Incentives and Performance-Based Rewards

CHAPTER OUTLINE

Purposes of Performance-Based Rewards
Rewards and Motivation
Rewards and Performance
Rewards and Other Employee Behaviors

Merit Compensation Systems
Merit Pay Plans
Limitations of Merit Compensation Systems
Skill- and Knowledge-Based Pay Systems and Merit

Incentive Compensation Systems
Incentive Pay Plans
Other Forms of Incentives
Limitations of Incentive Compensation Systems

Team and Group Incentive Reward Systems
Team and Group Pay Systems
Other Types of Team and Group Rewards
Limitations of Team and Group Reward Systems

Executive Compensation
Standard Forms of Executive Compensation
Special Forms of Executive Compensation
Criticisms of Executive Compensation

New Approaches to Performance-Based Rewards

CHAPTER OBJECTIVES

After studying this chapter you should be able to:

■ Summarize the purposes of performance-based rewards.

■ Discuss merit compensation systems and their limitations.

■ Identify and discuss forms and limitations of incentive compensation systems.

■ Identify and describe forms and limitations of team and group incentive reward systems.

■ Discuss both standard and special forms of executive compensation and summarize criticisms of recent trends in executive compensation.

■ Summarize new approaches to performance-based rewards in organizations.

Organizations often attempt to reward employees for exceptional performance or for their loyalty when they remain with the firm for many years. These rewards have traditionally been in the form of cash payments such as bonuses or symbolic gifts like service pins or watches. In recent years, however, organizations have started to search for more creative ways to reward their top performing and/or dedicated employees, and the trend would suggest that even more innovative ideas are on the horizon.

For example, Fighter Pilots USA is an Illinois-based entertainment company that offers customers a flight with an instructor in a fighter-trainer, complete with a simulated dogfight! Some major corporations have started offering the Fighter Pilots program as a reward for their best employees. For example, Lucent Technologies offers Fighter Pilots prizes to its best performers. And Ford Motor Company offers the prizes to its best and most loyal auto dealers.

In fact, the trend toward more creative incentives has sparked growth in a related industry devoted to provide them. The Incentive Federation, which represents companies in the industry, is optimistic about the future. One such Atlanta-based firm, Fennell Promotions, for example, has reported strong revenue growth over the last several years. Firms like Fennell put together incentive packages and sell them to other businesses. These businesses, in turn, use them to reward their best employees, customers, or clients.

> *"The economy is doing well and unemployment is so low, employers are looking for ways to keep employees. Money doesn't do it anymore."*
>
> (Frank Fennell, CEO of Fennell Promotions)*

Some of the packages that have become popular include fly-fishing trips to ranches in the western United States, kayaking trips to the mountains, whitewater rafting trips, and race-car driving schools. In addition, many companies continue to use traditional incentives such as dinners, cruises, and even preferred parking privileges to reward employees who meet certain targets or performance goals. Furthermore, although incentives have long been used for employees in sales, organizations are now expanding the programs to include almost any employee who can help the firm meet its goals.

These incentive programs are used both to reward performance and to help retain valued employees. Typically, employees must have been with an organization for a given period of time to be eligible to participate in these programs, thereby providing some incentive for remaining for at least that long. In addition, organizations are becoming rather competitive and secretive about these new incentive plans. The logic is that although competitors may offer more money, unless they also offer Caribbean cruises or weekend trips to a resort, an employee might view the total compensation package as less attractive and so be less tempted to change jobs.

"Employers Give Creative Gifts to Reward Workers," *USA Today*, March 26, 1998, p. 1B.

As we explain in detail in Chapter 11, organizations must provide basic compensation to all their employees. This basic compensation is intended to satisfy fundamental human needs and to fulfill the organization's component of the psychological contract regarding pay. Specifically, the basic compensation strategies discussed in Chapter 11 focus on the simple and straightforward compensation that people receive for performing their jobs at a minimally satisfactory level. But many organizations find it very useful to go even further with the compensation they provide and to tie at least some of the rewards that individuals receive to performance of the individual or to the group to which the individual belongs. Indeed, rewarding employees for their performance is clearly not a new idea. As long ago as the days of Frederick Taylor and scientific management, experts were advising managers to use "piece rate" pay systems to compensate employees in proportion to their productivity. But as indicated in the opening vignette, companies today are still striving to find the best kinds of incentives and rewards to offer to their most valued employees.

This chapter explores the role of incentives and performance-based rewards in organizations. First, we examine the various purposes of performance-based rewards. Then we describe merit compensation systems, incentive compensation systems, group incentive reward systems, and executive compensation. We conclude this chapter with a discussion of new approaches to performance-based rewards.

PURPOSES OF PERFORMANCE-BASED REWARDS

Performance-based rewards play a number of roles and address a variety of purposes in organizations. The major purposes involve the relationship of rewards to motivation and to performance. Specifically, organizations want employees to perform at relatively high levels and need to make it worth their efforts to do so. When rewards are associated with higher levels of performance, employees will presumably be motivated to work harder to achieve those awards. At that point their own self-interests coincide with the organization's interests. Performance-based rewards are relevant to other employee behaviors as well.

Rewards and Motivation

Back in Chapter 2 we introduced and briefly described some of the more basic frameworks for understanding individual motivation in the workplace. As illustrated in Figure 12.1, rewards play a fundamental role in how motivation occurs in organizations.[1] For example, one of the most important theories of motivation is the expectancy theory. Expectancy theory essentially suggests that people are motivated to engage in behaviors if they perceive that those behaviors are likely to lead to outcomes that they value. Thus to the extent that pay and other performance-based rewards might be of value to individual employees, it follows logically that employees who believe that their hard work will lead to the attainment of those rewards will be more likely to actually engage in behavior directed at hard work.

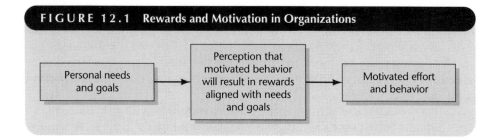

FIGURE 12.1   Rewards and Motivation in Organizations

Notice, though, that this theory also illustrates what can go wrong with performance-based pay systems. Rewards are typically based on performance, not on hard work or effort. Therefore, if employees feel that their hard work will *not* result in increased performance (perhaps because the job is too difficult or they believe they are not properly trained), then there would be no reason to increase effort, even though the employees can see that increased performance will be rewarded. Clearly, if employees don't see that rewards are tied to increased performance (for example, when all pay raises are across-the-board) or when there are also (or only) outcomes associated with increased performance that are *not* attractive (for example, the expectation of higher-level performance in the future), there will also be little reason to work harder.

Another important viewpoint on individual motivation in organizations is reinforcement theory. Reinforcement theory is based on the assumption that behavior is a function of its consequences. That is, employees who choose to engage in behaviors that result in a pleasurable outcome are more likely to choose that same behavior in the future. But if a behavior results in less pleasant outcomes, then employees are less likely to choose that behavior in the future.

Therefore, if an employee works hard and as a direct result of that hard work receives a reward such as a pay increase or praise from the supervisor in charge, then the individual is more likely to work hard in the future. But if the employee works hard and receives no additional reward or no praise from the supervisor and really has only fatigue and stress to show for her or his hard work, then that individual is less likely to work hard in the future. Obviously, this behavior does not sound very different from the situation for expectancy theory, described above. In fact, although the details of the theories differ as to the mechanisms underlying decisions to work hard on the job, in practice, the two theories bring us to the same conclusion: how hard people will work is based on the strength of the link they see between that hard work and obtaining desired outcomes.

Another important perspective on reward and motivation is a relatively new approach to understanding organizations called agency theory. **Agency theory** is concerned with the diverse interests and goals that are held by the organization's stakeholders, including its employees and managers, and the methods through which the organization's reward system can be used to align these diverse interests and goals. Agency theory derives its name from the fact that those in control of most modern corporations (that is, the managers who run the company) are not the principal owners of the organization, but are instead agents that presumably represent the owners' interests.

Agency theory highlights three fundamental differences that may exist and helps explain how managers approach compensation, as opposed to how the

■ **Agency theory** is concerned with the diverse interests and goals that are held by the organization's stakeholders, including its employees and managers, and the methods through which the organization's reward system can be used to align these diverse interests and goals.

owners of a corporation might approach compensation.[2] For one thing, the owners of a corporation might be more inclined to focus on minimizing cost as a way of maximizing their personal wealth. But their agents, or the managers who are running the business, might be more inclined to spend a larger percentage of the organization's resources on activities that do not directly contribute to owner wealth.

A second point derived from agency theory has to do with risk. Since managers depend on the success of their organization for their income, they may be less inclined to accept risk. And finally, the agents of an organization may have a fundamentally different time horizon than the owners of the firm have. These agents, for example, may tend to focus more on the short run because it is easier to maximize performance over a shorter period of time than it is over a longer period of time and because their tenure with the organization may also involve a shorter period of time. We further consider the role of agency theory and employee compensation at several later points in this chapter.

Rewards and Performance

Rewards in an organization may also have a direct impact on performance not only at the individual level but also at the group and organizational level.[3] This relates primarily to the relationship between performance and motivation. Most people suggest that performance in an organization is determined by three things: the ability to perform, the environmental context of performance, and the motivation to perform. Rewards and performance from this perspective are highlighted in Figure 12.2.

Ability to perform is handled primarily through the organization's selection and training mechanisms. That is, the organization should ensure that it hires only people who have the ability to perform at the expected level. And for those individuals who may be deficient in ability, training and development activities may be undertaken to improve their ability. The environmental context includes such things as equipment, machinery, materials, information, and other support factors. For example, individuals who are required as part of their work to perform spreadsheet calculations need to have computers with adequate memory and software to allow them to actually engage in spreadsheet analyses.

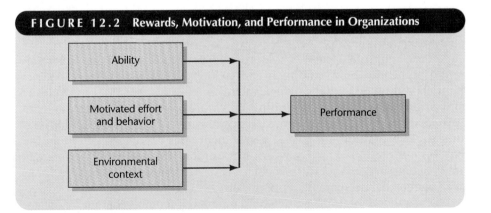

FIGURE 12.2   Rewards, Motivation, and Performance in Organizations

Pay for Morale?

Linking pay to performance is a long-standing practice in many organizations. Compensation programs based on this linkage generally measure performance from a relatively objective perspective, such as sales or revenues, stock price, productivity gains, and so forth. But this practice may be ending—or least broadening in scope to include "softer" and more subjective indexes of performance. The most significant example of this effort in recent times is embedded in labor contracts recently negotiated at United Airlines (UAL). The unions were able to push for a major new approach in part because they own 60 percent of UAL's stock.

Under terms of the agreement, more than half of the bonus pay received by the top 625 UAL managers will be determined by three new criteria—on-time performance, customer satisfaction, and employee satisfaction. While on-time performance is clearly an objective—and standard in the airline industry—measure of performance, customer and employee satisfaction are just as clearly both less objective and more unusual. Indeed, only a small handful of other firms use satisfaction to determine

"I don't think most managements would be enthusiastic about giving employees a chance to say anything about them."

(Graef Crystal, compensation expert)*

executive pay. For example, at Eastman Kodak employee satisfaction determines 20 percent of executive bonuses.

Of course, satisfaction has to be measured and evaluated in order to implement the new plan at UAL. Under terms of the agreement, an outside survey firm will be hired to perform the annual attitude surveys for both customers and employees. The results of these surveys will be widely shared throughout the company. Thus, everyone will know how customers and employees feel about the airline. And the firm's top managers will see their own personal compensation directly affected as a result! Meanwhile, the same labor unions own significant portions of Northwest Airlines and Trans World Airlines stock and indicate that they hope to implement the same kind of satisfaction-based incentive systems in those firms as well. Will this trend continue and become widely used, or will it remain the exception? Only time, of course, will tell.

Sources: "UAL: Labor Is My Co-Pilot," *Business Week*, March 1, 1999, p. 38 (*quote on p. 38); *Hoover's Handbook of American Business 1999* (Austin, Texas: Hoover's Reference Press, 1999), pp. 1420–1421.

Thus motivation remains as the third important ingredient in performance. As described in the preceding section, properly designed incentive and performance-based reward systems can be significant contributors to employee motivation. Thus managers who truly want to motivate people to perform at their highest level should structure a reward system that rewards people who engage in such behavior. "Human Resources Fad, Fashion, or Fact?" describes an interesting new approach to linking rewards and performance at United Airlines. The most significant element of this plan is the way in which performance is being assessed.

Rewards and Other Employee Behaviors

Rewards can also be used to influence other kinds of employee behaviors as well. One of the most significant such behaviors is turnover. If employees believe that their basic compensation is adequate and that their performance is recognized and rewarded beyond the basic compensation levels, then they are likely to want to remain a member of the organization. On the other hand, if employees believe that their performance is not recognized or has no impact on the rewards that they receive from the organization, then these individuals may be more likely to leave the organization and seek a more attractive job elsewhere.

Incentives and performance-based rewards also affect absenteeism and attendance. One strategy an organization can use to improve attendance among its employees is to tie some form of reward to high levels of attendance. For example, some companies provide people with a financial bonus if they exceed certain minimal levels of attendance expectations. A company using this strategy might reward employees who miss only one or two days per year with, say, an extra day's pay. A related strategy is to provide premium pay to people who do not use their sick pay. For example, some companies pay individual employees time and a half for unused sick time that is "turned in" at the end of the year.

THE BOTTOM LINE Performance-based pay can affect employee behavior in various ways. Managers need to have a clear understanding of how rewards relate to motivation, performance, and other employee behaviors. Such an understanding can better enable managers to structure reward systems in ways to enhance organizational effectiveness.

MERIT COMPENSATION SYSTEMS

Merit compensation systems are one of the most fundamental forms of performance-based rewards. In this section we examine merit pay plans and some of their limitations.

Merit Pay Plans

■ **Merit pay** is awarded to employees on the basis of the relative value of their contributions to the organization.

■ **Merit pay plans** are compensation plans that formally base at least some meaningful portion of compensation on merit.

Merit pay generally refers to pay awarded to employees on the basis of the relative value of their contributions to the organization. Employees who make greater contributions are given higher pay than those who make lesser contributions. **Merit pay plans**, then, are compensation plans that formally base at least some meaningful portion of compensation on merit.

The most general form of merit pay plan is to provide annual salary increases to individuals in the organization based on their relative merit. Merit, in turn, is usually determined or defined based on the individual's performance and overall contributions to the organization. In Chapter 8, for example, we discussed various methods for evaluating the performance of individuals. We noted that performance appraisal had the most meaning to employees if it was subsequently connected with a reward such as a salary increase.

For example, an organization using such a traditional merit pay plan might instruct its supervisors to give all their employees an average pay raise of, say, 4 percent. But the individual supervisor is further instructed to differentiate among high, average, and low performers. Under a simple system, for example, a manager might give the top 25 percent of her or his employees a 6 percent pay raise, the middle 50 percent a 4 percent or average pay raise, and the bottom 25 percent a 2 percent pay raise.

Of course, the organization must have valid and reliable measures of what merit entails. Although *merit* generally refers to performance, for the plan to ac-

Performance-based reward systems are intended to recognize and reward an organization's most valuable employees. Bob Thompson, shown in the center of this photograph, recently rewarded his key employees in a most unusual way. Thompson sold the asphalt company he had founded over forty years ago for $422 million. Instead of sticking the money in his own pockets, though, he first paid all the taxes and then divided up $128 million among his 550 employees. He allocated the money based on a combination of their contributions to the firm and seniority. More than eighty workers received at least $1 million each. Thompson's rationale was that they had helped build the business, so they deserved a share of the rewards.

tually have motivation and performance effects, people throughout the organization must have a clear understanding of what the firm means by merit. In addition, the organization's performance management systems must be rigorous enough to validly and appropriately differentiate among various levels of performance. For example, if the system does not really break out very many performance classifications, it may be difficult to distribute merit raises in any sort of meaningful way.

Limitations of Merit Compensation Systems

Merit compensation systems are very widely used and serve a number of valuable purposes in organizations but also suffer from some relatively important limitations. One major limitation of most merit pay systems is that they focus almost exclusively on individual performance. But in some cases an individual's performance might be determined by factors beyond her or his control. For example, coworkers, resources, and information may all play a role in determining whether or not an employee is able to perform at a high level.

Another basic limitation of merit systems is that they are primarily based on performance appraisal systems, which may themselves be subject to error and mistakes. Again, in our earlier discussion of performance management in Chapter 8, we noted many of the drawbacks and shortcomings that might be associated with performance appraisal techniques. As a result, it is not unusual for employees to disagree with performance ratings given (even when they are accurate). These problems are magnified when pay increases are being based on the ratings given, which has led some scholars to recommend that merit pay plans be abandoned completely.[4]

Another important limitation of merit pay systems is that they may be prone to focusing on too broad a period of performance. That is, individual performance might vary significantly from day to day, from week to week, and from month to month. The merit systems award salary increases on the basis of overall performance spanning a full year. Thus they may fail to account for short-term variation and fluctuations in individual performance.

Finally, merit systems are also subject to considerable disagreement among employees and may very well lead to perceptions of favoritism and unfairness. Stated differently, to the extent that people in an organization disagree with their supervisor as to the relative merits of the performance of different individuals, they will similarly disagree with rewards accorded to individuals on the basis of that level of performance.

A final limitation of merit compensation systems is that under most such arrangements, the increases given to individuals become a permanent part of their base pay. For example, an individual who performs at an exceptionally strong level in a year that the organization has a lucrative salary increase budget might receive a significant merit pay raise of, say, 10 percent or higher. That increase, however, becomes a part of the individual's base pay for the rest of her or his career with the organization. Thus the individual might reflect a much more average level of performance for the next several years but still maintain the 10 percent pay increase based on the one especially strong year. Over the course of a twenty-, thirty-, or forty-year career, merit pay increases given during the early years of a person's tenure with the organization accumulate to very substantial amounts of money.

Skill- and Knowledge-Based Pay Systems and Merit

Although these systems are usually not viewed as merit-pay or incentive-pay systems, it is worth noting how skill-based or knowledge-based pay systems, discussed in Chapter 11, focus employee attention in different areas but still use similar motivational processes. These systems reward employees for the acquisition of more skills or knowledge, instead of for increased performance. More traditional merit-pay systems reward employees for achieving some level of performance. But this performance is defined by what the organization needs (or wants) right now. In the future different types of performance may be needed, requiring effort focused in other areas. Changing the requirements for merit pay could be confusing or even demoralizing.

Skill-based pay systems reward employees not for any specific level of performance, but for the acquisition of job-related skills. Presumably, as the employee acquires more and more of these skills, he or she becomes more valuable to the organization. Furthermore, since the focus is on skill acquisition rather than performance, it should be easier for the organization to shift directions or focus without causing problems for the employee. In fact, since the employee now has these additional skills, he or she should be able to adapt to a wider variety of situations and demands, increasing the organization's flexibility.

Although problems are associated with these systems and their administration,[5] they offer an alternative to more traditional merit-pay systems and provide a longer-term, more strategic focus for the organization. In addition, they allow the organization to move employees toward focusing on more than just basic productivity.[6]

THE BOTTOM LINE   All managers should understand the basic concepts of merit and merit pay plans. They should know how such plans work, as well their basic limitations. In addition, managers should see how skill- and knowledge-based pay systems differ from traditional merit systems but rely on similar motivational processes.

INCENTIVE COMPENSATION SYSTEMS

Incentive compensation systems are among the oldest forms of performance-based rewards. For example, as noted earlier some companies were using individual piece-rate incentive plans more than a hundred years ago.[7] Under a **piece-rate incentive plan**, the organization pays an employee a certain amount of money for every unit she or he produces. For example, an employee might be paid one dollar for every dozen units of product that are successfully completed. But these simplistic systems fail to account for such factors as minimum wage levels and rely very heavily on the assumptions that performance is totally under an individual's control and that the individual employee does a single task continuously throughout his or her work time. Thus most organizations today that try to use incentive compensation systems use more sophisticated methodologies.

▨ A **piece-rate incentive plan** involves the organization paying an employee a certain amount of money for every unit she or he produces.

Incentive Pay Plans

Generally speaking, **individual incentive plans** reward individual performance on a real-time basis for meeting a goal or hitting a target. That is, rather than increasing a person's base salary at the end of the year, an individual receives some level of salary increase or financial reward in conjunction with demonstrated outstanding performance in close proximity to when that performance occurred. Individual incentive systems are most likely to be used when performance can be objectively assessed in terms of number of units of output or similar measures, rather than on a subjective assessment of performance by a superior.

▨ **Individual incentive plans** reward individual performance on a real-time basis for meeting a goal or hitting a target.

Some variations on a piece-rate system are still fairly popular. Although many of these still resemble the early plans in most ways, a well-known piece-rate system at Lincoln Electric illustrates how an organization can adapt the traditional model to achieve better results. For years Lincoln's employees were paid individual incentive payments based on their performance. However, the amount of money shared (or the incentive pool) was based on the company's profitability. Lincoln also had a well-organized system whereby employees could make suggestions for increasing productivity. There was motivation to make suggestions because the employees received one-third of the profits (another third went to the stockholders, and the last share was retained for improvements and seed money). Thus the pool for incentive payments was determined by profitability, and an employee's share of this pool was a function of his or her base pay and rated performance based on the piece-rate system. Lincoln Electric was most famous, however, because of the stories (which were apparently typical) of production workers receiving a year-end bonus payment that equaled their yearly base pay.[8] In recent years, Lincoln has partially abandoned its famous system for business reasons but still serves as a benchmark for other companies seeking innovative piece-rate-type pay systems.

Perhaps the most common form of individual incentive is **sales commissions** that are paid to people engaged in sales work. For example, sales representatives for consumer products firms and retail sales agents may be compensated under this type of commission system. In general, the person might receive a percentage of the total volume of attained sales as her or his commission for a period of time. Some sales jobs are based entirely on commission, whereas others use a combination of base minimum salary with additional commission as an incentive. Notice that these plans put a considerable amount of the salespersons' earnings "at risk." That is, although organizations often have drawing accounts to allow the salesperson to live during lean periods (the person then "owes" this money to the organization), sales representatives who do not perform well will not be paid much. The portion of salary based on commission is not guaranteed and is paid only if sales reach some target level.

■ A **sales commission** is an incentive paid to people engaged in sales work.

Other Forms of Incentives

Occasionally, organizations use nonmonetary incentives such as additional time off or another special perk to motivate people. For example, a company might establish a sales contest in which the sales group that attains the highest level of sales increase over a specified period of time will receive an extra week of paid vacation, perhaps even at an arranged place such as a tropical resort or a ski lodge.[9] "The Lighter Side of HR" provides a humorous example of how such incentives might be used to attract new employees.

A major advantage of incentives relative to merit systems is that incentives are typically a one-shot reward and do not accumulate by becoming a part of the individual's base salary. Stated differently, an individual whose outstanding performance entitles him or her to a financial incentive gets the incentive only one time, based on that level of performance. If the individual's perform-ance begins to erode in the future, then the individual may receive a lesser incentive or perhaps no incentive. As a consequence, base salary remains the same or is perhaps increased at a relatively moderate pace. Furthermore, since these plans, by their very nature, focus on one-time events, it is much easier for the organization to change the focus of the incentive plan. At a simple level, for example, an organization can set up an incentive plan for selling one product during one quarter but then shift the incentive to a different product the next quarter as the situation requires. Automobile companies like Ford and GM routinely reduce sales incentives for

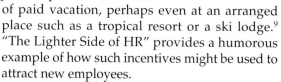

Incentive pay plans reward individual performance. Many professional athletes such as these have incentive clauses in their contracts based on statistical performance and/or external recognition. Football players, for example, may receive financial incentives based on yards gained (running backs), passing yards (quarterbacks), sacks (defensive linemen), or designation as an All-Pro. Baseball players may receive financial incentives for home runs (fielders), victories (pitchers), or being voted to the All-Star team.

models that are selling very well and increase sales incentives for models that are selling below expectations or are about to be discontinued.

Limitations of Incentive Compensation Systems

As with merit systems incentive compensation systems have some shortcomings and weaknesses. One major shortcoming is that they are practical for use only when performance can be easily and objectively measured. Most managerial work does not fit this pattern and, in fact, is often characterized by very ambiguous and difficult-to-assess performance indicators. Thus providing valid and appropriate incentive for these individuals may be difficult. Another important limitation of incentive systems is that they are often administratively burdensome. That is, it may be a major challenge for the organization to continuously evaluate performance, to recognize the level of performance that warrants additional rewards, and to then provide those rewards on a fair and timely basis.

Another problem with individual incentives is that they may be likely to focus attention only on a narrow range of behaviors, perhaps at the expense of other behaviors. Consider, for example, a sales representative in a department store. One of the ways such a sales representative could maximize his or her pay is to aggressively greet every customer, to try to sell things that the customer may not need, and to overlook deficiencies or shortcomings in the product being purchased. In such cases, for instance, sales representatives sometimes make grandiose claims that have no basis in reality and may stretch the truth to the point of creating totally inaccurate expectations. Thus the individual sales representative may be maximizing her or his income in the short term but at the cost of poor morale among less aggressive salespeople and increasingly dissatisfied customers.

THE BOTTOM LINE | Incentives can be an effective and powerful way to reward employees and motivate their behavior. Thus managers need to understand how incentive systems work and be sure that any such system they adopt is well matched to their own particular situation. At the same time, managers should be aware of the various limitations of incentive compensation systems.

TEAM AND GROUP INCENTIVE REWARD SYSTEMS

The merit compensation and incentive compensation systems described in the preceding sections deal primarily with performance-based reward arrangements for individuals. A different set of performance-based reward programs is targeted for teams and groups. These programs are particularly important for managers to understand given the widespread trend toward team and group-based methods of work.[10] "Point/Counterpoint" underscores some of the basic issues between individual and team-based incentives systems.

Team and Group Pay Systems

■ **Gainsharing** is a team and group-based incentive system designed to share with employees the cost savings from productivity improvements.

There are two commonly used types of team and group reward systems. One type used in many organizations is an approach called gainsharing. **Gainsharing programs** are designed to share with employees the cost savings from productivity improvements. The underlying assumption of gainsharing is that employees and the employer have the same goals and thus should appropriately share in incremental economic gains.[11]

In general, organizations that use gainsharing start by measuring team- or group-level productivity. This measure must be valid, reliable, and truly reflective of current levels of performance. The team or work group itself then is given the charge of attempting to lower costs and otherwise improve productivity through any measures that its members develop and its manager approves. Any cost savings or productivity gains that result are quantified and translated into dollar values, and predetermined formula is used to allocate these dollar savings between the employer and the employees. A typical formula for distributing gainsharing savings is to provide 25 percent to the employees and 75 percent to the company.

■ The **Scanlon plan** is a type of gainsharing plan in which the distribution of gains is tilted toward employees and across the entire organization.

One specific type of gainsharing plan is called the Scanlon plan. This approach was developed by Joseph Scanlon in 1927. The **Scanlon plan** has the same basic strategy as gainsharing plans in that teams or groups of employees are encouraged to suggest strategies for reducing cost. However, the distribution of these gains is usually tilted much more heavily toward employees, with employees usually receiving between two-thirds and three-fourths of the total cost savings that the plan achieves. Furthermore, the distribution of cost savings resulting from the plan are not given just to the team or group that suggested and developed the ideas, but are instead distributed across the entire organization.

POINT/COUNTERPOINT   Team versus Individual Incentives

 Incentives are meant to shape employee behavior in some desired direction. So, for example, if we want employees to produce more units, we would pay them for each additional unit (over some minimum) they produce. Under such a system employees learn to maximize their rewards by behaving in a way desired by the organization. But as organizations increase the extent to which work is done by teams, the incentive situation becomes more complex. Should we reward the behavior of individual team members as if they were independent employees, or should we focus on team behaviors instead? In the latter situation we would reward behaviors exhibited by the team as a whole, rather than behaviors exhibited by any individual team member.

POINT . . . **We should base incentives on individual behavior because . . .**	COUNTERPOINT . . . **We should base incentives on team behavior because . . .**
Individual effort is the easiest to monitor, and the individual behaviors are the easiest to specify.	When work is done by teams, we are ultimately interested in changing the behavior of the team.
Any team performance must be a function of the effort and performance of individual team members.	Team effectiveness requires more than just the efforts of individuals to perform their own jobs. It also requires people to be concerned with team spirit and communications.
If individuals are not rewarded for their efforts, they will be less motivated to exert effort.	If team members are rewarded for individual performance, each member will seek to maximize his or her own performance, even if it must be at a cost to team effectiveness.
If individuals are not responsible for achieving performance goals, there is a good chance that no one will feel responsible.	Individuals will not exert effort to maintain effective team functioning unless they are rewarded, and this effort can only be rewarded at the team level.
There will always be free riders who will not exert effort if the job is being done by others, and anything but individual-based incentives will unjustly reward these individuals.	The free-rider problem can be addressed by the rest of the team, which can exert group pressure on nonperforming members.

So . . .   As we move more toward team work, we must establish incentives so that team-level goals and objectives are accomplished. Efforts to do so by implementing individual-based incentives will almost certainly fail, since individual goals may be independent of, or even in conflict with, team goals. Nonetheless, if we ignore rewards for individual efforts, team performance levels are likely to drop. The key, then, is to combine the two. One possibility is to implement team-level incentives and then to allow the team, as a group, to provide incentives to individual team members for their individual efforts.

Other Types of Team and Group Rewards

Whereas gainsharing and Scanlon type plans are among the most popular group incentive reward systems, other systems are also used. Some companies, for example, have begun to use true incentives at the team or group level. Just as with individual incentives, team or group incentives tie rewards directly to

As more and more businesses adopt team- and group-based methods of work and organization, new and creative methods for rewarding performance continue to be developed as well. Stock options are one popular approach to rewarding people based on the performance of the overall organization. Robert Flores, for example, is a manufacturing associate at Dell Computer. He and his co-workers all participate in a stock option plan that has provided them with significant financial rewards.

performance increases. And like individual incentives, team or group incentives are paid as they are earned rather than being added to employees' base salaries. The incentives are distributed at the team or group level, however, rather than at the individual level. In some cases the distribution may be based on the existing salary of each employee with incentive bonuses being given on a proportionate basis. In other settings each member of the team or group receives the same incentive pay.

Some companies also use nonmonetary rewards at the team or group level. These are most commonly in the form of prizes and awards. For example, a company might designate the particular team in a plant or subunit of the company that achieves the highest level of productivity increase, the highest level of reported customer satisfaction, or similar index of performance. The reward itself might take the form of additional time off, as described earlier in this chapter, or be a tangible award such as a trophy or a plaque. In any event the reward is at the team level and serves as recognition of exemplary performance by the entire team.

Other kinds of team- or group-level incentives go beyond the contributions of a specific work group. These are generally organizationwide kinds of incentives. One longstanding method for this approach is **profit sharing.** In a profit-sharing approach, at the end of the year some portion of the company's profits is paid into a profit-sharing pool, which is then distributed to all employees. This amount is either distributed at that time or put into an escrow account, in the latter case payment is deferred until the employee retires.

The basic rationale behind profit-sharing systems is that everyone in the organization can expect to benefit when the company does well. But on the other side of the coin, during bad economic times when the company is perhaps achieving low or perhaps no profits, then no profit sharing is paid out. This situation sometimes results in negative reactions from employees, who perhaps believe that the profit sharing is really a part of their annual compensation.

Employee stock ownership plans (ESOPs) also represent a group-level reward system that some companies use. Under an ESOP employees are gradually given a major stake in ownership of a corporation. The typical form of this plan involves the company taking out a loan that it uses to buy a portion of its own stock in the open market. Over time, company profits are then used to pay off this loan. Employees, in turn, receive a claim on ownership of some portion of the stock held by the company, based on seniority and perhaps performance. Eventually, each individual becomes an owner of the company.

■ **Profit sharing** is an incentive system in which, at the end of the year, some portion of the company's profits is paid into a profit-sharing pool, which is then distributed to all employees.

■ **Employee stock ownership plans (ESOPs)** are a group-level reward system in which employees are gradually given a major stake in ownership of a corporation.

Limitations of Team and Group Reward Systems

Although group reward systems can be very effective in some situations, they can be subject to difficulties as well. For example, in many cases not every member of a group contributes equally to the group's performance. But if the group incentive system distributes rewards equally to all members of the group, then people may feel that some factors beyond individual performance are dictating the distribution of rewards. Also, for incentive plans based on firm profitability, employees may not see how their efforts will lead to increased profits (often referred to as a "line of sight" problem). In fact, many factors that are beyond the employees' control can affect profitability. Thus the links between effort, performance, and outcomes, specified by expectancy theory, are often quite weak, resulting in little motivation. Finally, a limitation noted earlier in our discussion on profit sharing is that employees may come to view the group-level incentive as a normal part of their compensation and consequently will be unhappy or dissatisfied if that reward is withheld one year.

THE BOTTOM LINE Because teams and groups are becoming increasingly popular in organizations today, managers must have a solid understanding of how incentives and similar rewards can and cannot be used effectively for teams ands groups. The human resource function in an organization is often asked to play a critical role as a center of expertise in developing and/or adapting reward systems to team- or group-level settings.

EXECUTIVE COMPENSATION

The top level executives of most companies have separate compensation programs and plans. These are intended to reward these executives for their performance and for the performance of the organization. In this section we describe both standard and special forms of executive compensation and note some of the current criticisms of executive compensation.

Standard Forms of Executive Compensation

Most senior executives receive their compensation in two forms. One form is a **base salary.** As with the base salary of any staff member or professional member of an organization, the base salary of an executive is a guaranteed amount of money that the individual will be paid. For example, the last year Chrysler was an independent corporation, its chairman and CEO, Robert Eaton, earned $1,612,500 in base salary.[12]

Above and beyond this base salary, however, most executives also receive one or more forms of incentive pay. The traditional method of incentive pay for executives is the bonus. Bonuses, in turn, are usually determined by the performance of the organization. Thus at the end of the year, some portion of a corporation's profits may be diverted into a pool. Senior executives then receive a bonus expressed as a percentage of this pool. The chief executive officer and president are obviously likely to get a larger percentage bonus than a vice president. The exact distribution of the bonus pool is usually specified ahead of time in the individual's employment contract. Some organizations intentionally leave the distribution unspecified so that the board of directors has the flexibility to give larger rewards to individuals deemed to be most deserving. The same year Chrysler's Eaton was paid $1,612,500 in base salary, he also earned a $3,000,000 bonus.

■ The **base salary** of an executive is a guaranteed amount of money that the individual will be paid.

Special Forms of Executive Compensation

Beyond base salary and bonuses, many executives receive other kinds of compensation as well. A form of executive compensation that has received a lot of attention in recent years is various kinds of stock options. A **stock option plan** gives senior managers the option to buy the company stock in the future at a predetermined fixed price. The basic idea underlying stock option plans is that if the executives contribute to higher levels of organizational performance, the value of company stock should increase. Then the executive will be able to purchase the stock at the predetermined price, which, theoretically, should be lower than its future market price. The difference then becomes profit for the individual. Chrysler's Eaton also earned more than $10,000,000 in stock options.

▪ A **stock option plan** is an incentive plan established to give senior managers the option to buy the company stock in the future at a predetermined fixed price.

Stock options continue to grow in popularity as a means of compensating top managers. Options are seen as a means of aligning the interests of the manager with those of the stockholders, and, given that they don't cost the organization much (other than some possible dilution of stock values), they will probably be even more popular in the future. In fact, a recent study by KPM Peat Marwick indicates that for senior management whose salary exceeds $250,000, stock options represent the largest share of the salary mix (relative to salary and other incentives). Furthermore, when we consider all of top management (annual salary over $750,000), stock options are a full 60 percent of their total compensation. The report also indicates that, even among exempt employees at the $35,000-a-year level, stock options represent 13 percent of total compensation. "Human Resources Legal Brief" notes some of the legal and regulatory issues surrounding stock option plans.

Agency theory arguments are often cited as the rationale for these stock option plans. The owners of the firm (typically the stockholders) want to increase firm profitability, but there is not necessarily an incentive for the CEO to work toward maximizing profits. However, by making a considerable portion of the CEO's compensation reliant upon stock, the interests of the CEO are presumably more closely aligned with the interests of the owners, and everyone works in the same direction. According to some critics, however, these interests are not really aligned until the CEO or executive actually exercises the option. Up to that point the executive might actually have an incentive to lower stock prices in the short run, in the hopes of being offered more options on the lower-priced stock.[13]

Aside from stock option plans, other kinds of executive compensation are also used by some companies. Among the more popular are perquisites such as memberships in private clubs, access to company recreational facilities, and similar kinds of considerations. Some organizations also make available to senior executives low- or no-interest

Top-level executive compensation packages are a complex—and sometimes controversial—set of incentive and performance-based rewards. When Carly Fiorina was recently appointed as president and CEO of Hewlett-Packard, she attracted national headlines because she was the first female executive in the United States to head a firm of HP's size. Her compensation package includes $1 million in base salary and a bonus arrangement that will pay her between $1.25 and $3.75 million in additional compensation based on firm performance. In addition, she received a "signing bonus" of $3 million and a very attractive stock option plan. Finally, she also will receive several lucrative perquisites and relocation expenses.

Stock Options as Incentives

 Given the recent interest in stock options, it is perhaps not surprising that the government pays close attention to them. Indeed, the federal government actually started passing legislation regulating the use of stock options as part of compensation in the 1920s and has been at it ever since. Although a more detailed review of these efforts is beyond the scope of this discussion, several points are worth noting.

The government first regulated stock options as compensation in 1923. That year the U.S. Treasury ruled that when an employee exercised a stock option, the value of the option exercised would be taxed as income. Specifically, the employee would be taxed on an amount equal to the value of the stock at the time the option is exercised, less the cost of the option. Interestingly, in 1939, the IRS modified this view somewhat, stating that stock options would be treated as income only if the company *intended* the option to be compensation at the time it was issued. Stock options intended as gifts, on the other hand, would be treated as such. By 1945, however, the IRS dropped this distinction and taxed options regardless of the intent of the parties involved.

In 1934 the Securities Exchange Act required "insiders" to reveal information about their stockholdings and also restricted profits that were based on privileged information. The Revenue Act of 1950 first recognized the nature of "restricted" options that could be sold only after a certain period of time had elapsed. In deciding that profits from the sale of these restricted stocks would not be taxed as regular income, but as long-term capital gains, Congress was lining up in favor of stock options as a form of managerial compensation. Nonetheless, over the next two decades Congress began to reverse its position, and by 1969 all stock options would be treated the same for tax purposes, and all profits would be taxed as income.

But as the government was tightening legislation regulating stock options, the stock market itself had become stagnant. By 1970 long-term incentives (such as stock options) accounted for only about 15 percent of executive compensation, and as the market remained sluggish through 1980 stock options lost their popularity. But

> *"There are a number of CEOs who underperformed the market and yet made $20 million or $30 million from options."*
>
> (Graef Crystal, compensation expert)*

when the stock market began to regain its vitality in 1981, stock options began to be an important part of compensation once more. Both the Economic Recovery Act of 1981 and the Tax Reform Act of 1986 included major provisions regulating stock options.

Stock options became even more popular in the 1990s, and legislation through the 1990s lowered many tax rates. Nonetheless, in 1994, while the average compensation for a worker in the United States increased by 2.0 percent, the average compensation for a *Fortune* 100 firm increased by 16 percent. Congress again became very interested in executive compensation and, as a result, in stock options. Consequently, from 1994 until 1996 a series of laws reduced some of the benefits of stock options for both the manager and the organization. That trend ended in 1996, however, as Republicans took control of both houses of the Congress. Legislation since that time has made it easier for companies to give stock options to their employees (since these transactions were no longer subject to as many regulations) and reduced the maximum tax rate on long-term capital gains to 20 percent.

Thus the legislative environment today is very favorable to stock options, which, along with the recent performance of the stock market, helps explain their popularity. It is important to remember, though, that Congress has reversed itself in these matters in the past, and as new elections are held and the balance of power might shift in Congress, we must assume that Congress will again impose stiffer taxes on stock options in the future. It will be interesting to see how any such changes in legislation will affect the popularity of stock options. It will be equally interesting to see how organizations might respond to any such changes and what new types of compensation will come into the mix if stock options start to fade.

References: "Corporate Coffers Gush with Currency of an Opulent Age," *Wall Street Journal*, August 10, 1998, pp. B1, B8; "CEO Pay Outpaces Companies' Performance," *USA Today*, March 30, 1998, p. 1B (*quote on p. 1B); Wayne Grossman and Robert Hoskisson, "CEO Pay at the Crossroads of Wall Street and Main: Toward the Strategic Design of Executive Compensation," *Academy of Management Executive*, Vol. 12, No. 1, 1998, pp. 43–52.

loans. These are often given to new executives that the company is hiring from other companies and serve as an incentive for the individual to leave his or her current job to join a new organization. One of the special incentive plans set up for Chrysler's Eaton was a plan wherein the company matched his annual personal savings.

Criticisms of Executive Compensation

In recent years executive compensation has come under fire for a variety of reasons. One major reason is that the levels of executive compensation attained by some managers simply seem to be too large for the average shareholder to understand. It is not uncommon, for instance, for a senior executive of a major corporation to earn a total annual income from his or her job well in excess of a million dollars, and sometimes the income of CEOs can be substantially more. In 1997, for example, Chrysler's Eaton earned a total of $16,131,105 from the company. Thus just as the typical person has difficulty comprehending the astronomical salaries paid to some movie stars and sports stars, so too would the average person be aghast at the astronomical salaries paid to some senior executives. Table 12.1 summarizes the compensation packages for the ten highest-paid CEOs in the United States in 1997.

Executive compensation in the United States also seems far out of line with that paid to senior executives in other countries. For example, the same year that Chrysler paid Robert Eaton more than $16 million, the CEO of Daimler-Benz AG, the German firm that recently acquired Chrysler, earned slightly less than $2 million. The specific breakdown for this individual, Juergen Schrempp,

TABLE 12.1 The Highest-Paid CEOs						
Company	Executive	Salary & Bonus	Gain on Option Exercise	Restricted Stock Grants	Long-Term Incentive Payouts	Total Direct Compensation
Travelers Group Inc.	Sanford I. Weill	$ 9,525.000	$220,162,892	$ 777,322	$ 0	$230,465,214
Morgan Stanley Dean Witter & Co.	Philip J. Purcell	10,473,750	36,397,538	3,135,577	0	50,006,865
Monsanto Co.	Robert B. Shapiro	1,765,000	46,741,110	0	750,365	49,256,475
General Electric Co.	John F. Welch Jr.	8,000,000	31,825,020	0	0	39,825,020
American Express Co.	Harvey Golub	3,200,000	27,132,498	0	2,856,231	33,188,729
Bristol-Myers Squibb Co.	Charles A. Heimbold Jr.	2,802,635	25,286,763	0	1,121,900	29,211,298
AlliedSignal Inc.	Lawrence A. Bossidy	5,150,000	23,082,225	0	0	28,232,225
Pfizer Inc.	William C. Steere Jr.	3,861,800	15,402,984	0	8,837,500	28,102,284
Colgate-Palmolive Co.	Reuben Mark	3,846,555	18,164,302	704,769	2,674,716	25,390,342
Merrill Lynch & Co.	David H. Komansky	7,728,863	14,398,750	1,524,325	0	23,651,938

Source: The Wall Street Journal Almanac 1999, p. 237; study conducted by William M. Mercer Inc. for the Wall Street Journal. Based on an analysis of proxy statements from 350 of the largest U.S. businesses in 1997. Reprinted by permission of Dow Jones, Inc. via Copyright Clearance Center, Inc. © 1999 Dow Jones and Company, Inc. All Rights Reserved.

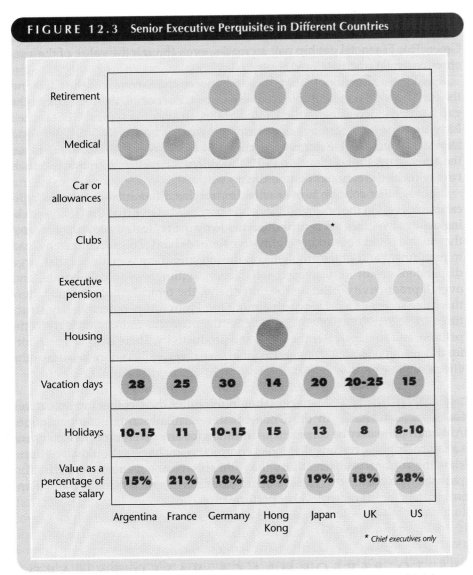

FIGURE 12.3 Senior Executive Perquisites in Different Countries

	Argentina	France	Germany	Hong Kong	Japan	UK	US
Retirement			●	●	●	●	●
Medical	●	●	●	●		●	●
Car or allowances	●	●	●	●	●	●	
Clubs				●	●*		
Executive pension		●				●	●
Housing				●			
Vacation days	28	25	30	14	20	20-25	15
Holidays	10-15	11	10-15	15	13	8	8-10
Value as a percentage of base salary	15%	21%	18%	28%	19%	18%	28%

* Chief executives only

Source: "How Perks Stack Up," *Forbes*, May 19, 1997, p. 162; Watson Wyatt Worldwide Survey. Reprinted by permission of *Forbes* Magazine © Forbes, Inc., 1997.

was salary of $1,137,300 plus $796,100 in stock options. But looking at the total package clouds the compensation comparisons a bit. For example, Figure 12.3 shows the complete package of executive perquisites in seven countries. Although U.S. executives still top the list, their counterparts tend to get more vacation and sick time, plus a car or car allowance.

Compounding the problem created by perceptions of executive compensation is that often little or no relationship seems to exist between the performance of the organization and the compensation paid to its senior executives.[14] Certainly if an organization is performing at an especially high level and its stock price is increasing consistently, then most observers would agree that the senior executives responsible for this growth should be entitled to attractive rewards.[15] However, it is more difficult to understand cases where executives are paid huge salaries and other forms of rewards when their

13

Employee Benefits and Services

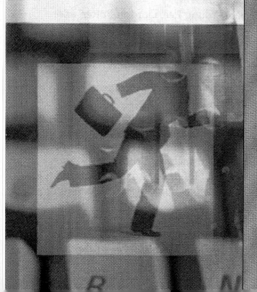

CHAPTER OUTLINE

Basic Considerations in Indirect Compensation and Benefits
Purposes of Indirect Compensation and Benefit Programs
Legal Considerations

Mandated Protection Plans
Unemployment Insurance
Social Security
Workers' Compensation

Optional Protection Plans
Insurance Coverage
Private Pension Plans

Paid Time Off
Other Types of Benefits
Cafeteria-Style Benefit Plans
Evaluating Indirect Compensation and Benefit Plans

CHAPTER OBJECTIVES

After studying this chapter you should be able to:

■ Identify and discuss basic considerations in indirect compensation.

■ Discuss legally mandated protection plans as employee benefits.

■ Describe various optional protection plans as employee benefits.

■ Discuss paid time off as an employee benefit.

■ Identify and discuss various other benefits that some organizations provide for their employees.

■ Describe cafeteria-style approaches to benefits.

■ Discuss how organizations evaluate indirect compensation and benefit plans.

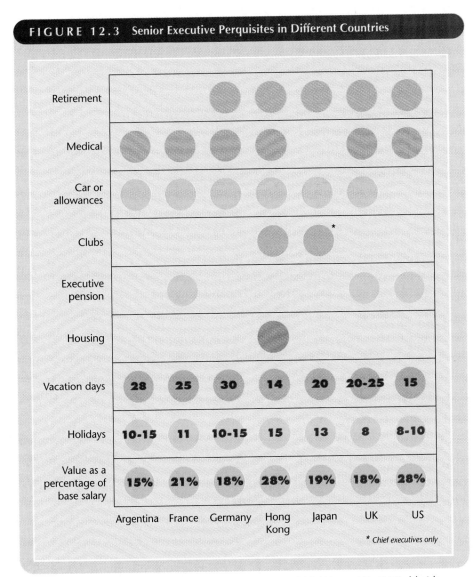

FIGURE 12.3 Senior Executive Perquisites in Different Countries

	Argentina	France	Germany	Hong Kong	Japan	UK	US
Vacation days	28	25	30	14	20	20-25	15
Holidays	10-15	11	10-15	15	13	8	8-10
Value as a percentage of base salary	15%	21%	18%	28%	19%	18%	28%

* Chief executives only

Source: "How Perks Stack Up," *Forbes*, May 19, 1997, p. 162; Watson Wyatt Worldwide Survey. Reprinted by permission of *Forbes* Magazine © Forbes, Inc., 1997.

was salary of $1,137,300 plus $796,100 in stock options. But looking at the total package clouds the compensation comparisons a bit. For example, Figure 12.3 shows the complete package of executive perquisites in seven countries. Although U.S. executives still top the list, their counterparts tend to get more vacation and sick time, plus a car or car allowance.

Compounding the problem created by perceptions of executive compensation is that often little or no relationship seems to exist between the performance of the organization and the compensation paid to its senior executives.[14] Certainly if an organization is performing at an especially high level and its stock price is increasing consistently, then most observers would agree that the senior executives responsible for this growth should be entitled to attractive rewards.[15] However, it is more difficult to understand cases where executives are paid huge salaries and other forms of rewards when their companies are performing only at marginal levels, and yet this situation is fairly common today. For example, in 1997 the CEOs at Reebok, 3M, and Green Tree Financial got big pay increases, even though the value of their respective firms' stock declined.[16]

Finally, we should note that the gap between the earnings of the CEO and the earnings of a typical employee is enormous. First of all, the very size of the gap has been increasing in the United States. In 1980 the typical CEO earned forty-two times the earnings of an ordinary worker, but by 1990 this ratio had increased to eighty-five times the earnings of an ordinary worker. In Japan, on the other hand, the relationship in 1990 was that a typical CEO made less than twenty times the earnings of an ordinary worker.[17]

But the other concern is over what impact this differential has for the typical employee. On the one hand, he or she may not believe that the CEO is making eighty-five times the contribution made by the typical employee, or at least that no one could be working eighty-five times as hard. This situation may lead to resentment and other problems on the job, and there is evidence that large dispersions result in decreased satisfaction, willingness to collaborate, and overall productivity.[18] But on the other hand, the typical employee may view this huge salary as a prize worth aiming for. From this perspective pay structures are seen as tournaments; the bigger the prize, the more intense the competition, and so the greater the effort and productivity. There is, in fact, support for this position as well,[19] suggesting that managers really cannot be sure of the effects of these gaps.

THE BOTTOM LINE   Managers should recognize the fact that top executives in the United States earn substantial compensation. Although there may be complete justification for any given executive compensation package—even one that looks enormous—managers should also appreciate the concern and sensitivity that others have about these compensation packages and ensure that to the extent possible everyone is being rewarded appropriately for his or her level of performance.

NEW APPROACHES TO PERFORMANCE-BASED REWARDS

Some organizations have started to recognize that they can leverage the value of the incentives they offer to their employees and to groups in their organization by allowing those individuals and groups to have a say in how rewards are distributed. For example, a company could grant salary-increase budgets to work groups and then allow the members of those groups to determine how to allocate the rewards. This strategy would appear to hold considerable promise if everyone understands the performance arrangements that exist in the work group and everyone is committed to being fair and equitable. Unfortunately, it can also create problems if people in a group feel that rewards are not being distributed fairly.

Organizations are also getting increasingly innovative in their incentive programs. For example, some now offer stock options to all their employees, rather than just to top executives. Regardless of the method used, however, it is also important that managers in an organization effectively communicate what rewards are being distributed and the basis for that distribution. That is, if incentives are being distributed on the basis of perceived individual contributions to the organization, then members of the organization should be informed of that fact. This information will presumably help them to understand the basis on which pay increases and other incentives and performance-based rewards have been distributed.

THE BOTTOM LINE Because so many organizations are continuing to seek new kinds of incentives to use to attract and reward talented employees, all managers need to stay abreast of new approaches as they emerge. Awareness of new development will serve two purposes. First, it will allow managers to have more information as they develop new incentives for their won organization. And second, it will help prevent an organization from falling too far behind other firms as they compete for the best employees.

Chapter Summary

Performance-based rewards play a number of roles and address a variety of purposes in organizations. The major purposes involve the relationship of rewards to motivation and to performance. Rewards can be used to influence other kinds of employee behaviors as well, such as turnover, absenteeism, and attendance.

Merit compensation systems are one of the most fundamental forms of performance-based rewards. Merit pay generally refers to pay awarded to employees on the basis of the relative value of their contributions to the organization. The most general form of merit pay plan is to provide annual salary increases to individuals in the organization based on their relative merit. Of course, it is very important for the organization to have valid and reliable measures of what merit entails. While merit compensation systems are very widely used and serve a number of valuable purposes in organizations, they also suffer from some relatively important limitations.

Individual incentive plans reward individual performance on a real-time basis. Some variations on a piece-rate system are still fairly popular. Perhaps the most common form of individual incentive is sales commissions that are paid to people engaged in sales work. Occasionally, organizations also use other forms of incentives to motivate people. A major advantage of incentives relative to merit systems is that incentives are typically a one-shot reward and do not accumulate by becoming a part of the individual's base salary. As with merit systems incentive compensation systems also have some shortcomings and weaknesses.

Another set of performance-based reward programs is targeted for teams and groups. These programs are particularly important for managers to understand today given the widespread trends toward team and group-based methods of work. There are two commonly used types of team and group reward systems. One approach is called gainsharing. Another is the Scanlon plan. Whereas gainsharing and Scanlon-type plans are among the most popular group incentive reward systems, other systems are also in use. Profit sharing is used in many organizations, and employee stock ownership plans are growing in popularity. Group reward systems can be very effective in some situations but can also be subject to difficulties.

The top level executives of most companies have separate compensation programs and plans. Most senior executives receive their compensation in two forms. One form is a base salary. Above and beyond this base salary, however, most executives receive one or more forms of incentive pay. The traditional method of incentive pay for executives is the bonus. Bonuses, in turn, are usually determined by the performance of the organization. A form of executive compensation that is receiving a lot of attention is stock options. In recent years executive compensation has come under fire for a variety of reasons.

Review and Discussion Questions

1. Explain the relationships among rewards, motivation, and performance.

2. Putting yourself in the role of an employee, either in your present job or the next job you anticipate having, identify the rewards that are most important to you and how you think you can most likely attain them.

3. How do you think incentives and other rewards might affect your own personal absenteeism and attendance?

4. Compare and contrast merit and incentive compensation systems.

5. Can merit and incentive compensation be used together? Why or why not?

6. Should all compensation be based on merit or performance? Why or why not?

7. What are the basic differences between incentive systems for individuals and incentive systems for teams and groups?

8. Is one harder to use than the other? Which one? Why?

9. What are your views on very high levels of executive compensation?

10. Assume you are head of public relations for a big company that just gave its CEO a huge bonus. Outline a plan for justifying the bonus to the press.

Closing Case

Continental's Remarkable Turnaround

In 1994 Continental Airlines posted net losses (pretax) of $202 million, was ranked last among all major airlines in customer satisfaction (according to J.D. Powers and Associates), scored below its competitors on all major performance factors (such as load factor and revenue per mile flown), and had a market value of only $175 million. The firm had virtually no cash reserves, and its creditors closely scrutinized every move the company made. Moreover, its employees were demoralized, and few expected to remain with the company for long—even if it survived. In 1999 Continental was consistently posting big profits, had twice been rated *first* in customer satisfaction by J.D. Powers, had a cash balance in excess of $1 billion, and had a market value in excess of $4 billion. In addition, Continental scored above industry averages on every important performance indicator and actually led the industry on several indicators. Moreover, Continental was rated among the one hundred best companies to work for by *Fortune* magazine and had a motivated, loyal, and committed workforce.

How did Continental accomplish such a dramatic turnaround in only five years? Many factors helped, but one that was clearly critical was Chairman Gordon Bethune's belief that "what gets measured and rewarded gets done." As a result, shortly after Bethune took over in 1994, Continental introduced a series of incentives for employees who helped the airline meet critical goals. For example, the "old" Continental had one of the worst on-time records in the industry. A new incentive plan rewarded employees for on-time performance. The plan was actually very simple. Bethune calculated what the airline saved (in hotels, meals, and rebooking charges) when flights were on time. He divided this amount by the number of employees. The total was about $100. Bethune then announced that every month that Continental was in the top five in the industry in on-time performance, all employees would receive $65, and they would receive a check for $100 any month that Continental was in the top three. Continental has now distributed more than $100 million in on-time bonuses.

Continental also realized that employee absenteeism was costly, both in terms of overtime payments and in terms of peak service. Therefore, every employee who has a perfect performance record for six months is entered in a drawing for eight Eddie Bauer Edition Ford Explorers (plus a check to cover the taxes). Since the program began in 1996, the company has given away thirty-eight Explorers worth $1.5 million. Also, since the program began, the number of eligible employees (with perfect attendance for six months) has more than doubled, and overall absenteeism has dropped 31 percent.

In addition, the airline reports a reduction in turnover (since 1994) of 52 percent and a drop in on-the-job injuries of 48 percent. Clearly, then, the incentive programs seem to be achieving the desired goals. Furthermore, as profits have risen, so has the price of Continental's stock ($3.25 a share in January 1995 to more than $48 a share by the beginning of 1999), and as a result, the airline has been able to buy new planes, dropping the average fleet age of Continental's planes to 7.2 years, one of the lowest anywhere.

Finally, to be certain that Continental's employees are fully recognized for their contributions to the airline's recovery, the company has announced plans for bringing salaries up to the industry standard in 1999. And in 1998 Continental distributed $105 million in profit sharing to its employees—a figure representing 7 percent of total annual wages. Again, a number of factors have contributed to Continental's improved performance, but the fact that the airline decided to target specific behaviors for incentives must be seen as one of the most important and successful parts of that turnaround.

Case Questions

1. What role have incentives played in Continental's success?

2. What problems or roadblocks might arise in the future to limit Continental's continued success and effectiveness?

3. Why don't more companies use Continental's approach?

Sources: "Continental Is Winning the Battle for Share in New York Market," *Wall Street Journal*, January 9, 1999, pp. A1, A11; *Hoover's Handbook of American Business 1999* (Austin, Texas: 1999), pp. 426–427; "Explorer Possibilities," *Continental Magazine*, October 1997, p. 19.

Building Human Resource Management Skills

Purpose: The purpose of this exercise is to help you better understand the opportunities and limitations in using performance-based rewards in organizations.

Step 1: Form small groups with three or four of your classmates.

Step 2: Select three different jobs with which people in your group have some familiarity. These might be jobs that people in the group perform and/or jobs that you come into contact with on a regular basis (for example, retail sales clerk, bus driver, fast-food clerk).

Step 3: Develop a performance-based reward system for each job you select. For each job specify the precise behaviors that you want to reward and the types of rewards you propose to link to those behaviors.

Step 4: Compare and contrast the three different models, looking for similarities and differences.

Step 5: Respond to the following questions:

1. How easy or difficult is it to tie performance-based rewards to various kinds of jobs?

2. What are the major challenges in developing performance-based rewards?

3. What job characteristics or attributes make some jobs easier than others to reward on the basis of performance?

4. Are there some jobs that simply do not accommodate a performance-based reward system?

Ethical Dilemmas in Human Resource Management

Assume that you are a senior manager in a regional warehouse and distribution center for a large national retailer. Since the center opened several years ago, everyone working there has been paid on either a straight hourly basis or a standard salary basis. This year, however, corporate management has unveiled a sweeping new compensation system for the entire firm. Under the terms of this plan, all employees will be eligible for annual bonuses based on unit performance. All of the employees at the center are very excited about this new plan, and it seems that everyone is committed to working harder to help the center's workforce get a big bonus.

Today is January 5, and the new system has just been announced and implemented. Unfortunately, you have some serious concerns. Specifically, you have heard some rumors that sometime during the next nine months the firm is likely to either sell the distribution center to a competitor or else close it down altogether. Since the center is not unionized, you suspect that if the center is closed, all lower-level workers will simply be terminated and none of them will receive any sort of bonus. Although you are reasonably certain that you and the other senior managers will be transferred to another location, you don't know whether you will be involved in the new bonus system since the center will not have any year-end performance statistics on which to base a bonus.

You have tried to broach this subject with the center's general manager on several occasions but have only received vague answers. For example, she has said things like "Don't worry, the company will take care of everyone," "No one really knows what might happen, so we shouldn't get too worked up about it," "No decisions have been made about anything yet, so we should stop trying to guess what's going to happen," and "Even if that were to happen, I'm sure we managers would be taken care of." You also suspect that her next move will be to a corporate-level job. You are really troubled about things, though. If you tell too many people about your concerns and rumors start flying, morale will plummet, and even if the center remains open, performance will not improve. But if you remain silent and the center does close, your conscious will bother you.

Questions

1. What are the ethical issues in this situation?

2. What are the basic arguments for and against keeping quiet versus continuing to ask questions?

3. What do you think most managers would do? What would you do?

Human Resource Internet Exercise

 Put yourself in the role of a manager contemplating the implementation of a new incentive system for a major corporation. Do a Web search, looking for topics such as *incentives, merit compensation,* and *gainsharing.* Then respond to the following questions.

Questions

1. How useful is the Internet in this situation?

2. What are the advantages and disadvantages of using the Internet for this kind of activity?

3. What advice would you give to other managers interested in the same questions?

Notes

1. For a review, see Gregory Moorhead and Ricky W. Griffin, *Organizational Behavior,* 6th ed. (Boston: Houghton Mifflin, 2001).

2. Matt Bloom and George Milkovich, "Relationships among Risk, Incentive Pay, and Organizational Performance," *Academy of Management Journal,* Vol. 41, No. 3, 1998, pp. 283–297.

3. Matt Bloom, "The Performance Effects of Pay Dispersion on Individuals and Organizations," *Academy of Management Journal,* Vol. 42, No. 1, 1999, pp. 25–40.

4. Edward E. Lawler, *Strategic Pay: Aligning Organizational Strategies and Pay Systems* (San Francisco: Jossey-Bass, 1990).

5. G. D. Jenkins, Gerald E. Ledford, Nina Gupta, and D. Harold Doty, *Skill-Based Pay* (Scottsdale, Ariz.: American Compensation Association, 1992).

6. John L. Morris, "Lessons Learned in Skill-Based Pay," *HRMagazine,* June 1996, pp. 136–142.

7. Daniel Wren, *The Evolution of Management Theory,* 4th ed. (New York: Wiley, 1994).

8. Carol Wiley, "Incentive Plan Pushes Production. *Personnel Journal,* August 1993, p. 91.

9. "When Money Isn't Enough," *Forbes,* November 18, 1996, pp. 164–169.

10. Jacquelyn DeMatteo, Lillian Eby, and Eric Sundstrom, "Team-Based Rewards: Current Empirical Evidence and Directions for Future Research," in L. L. Cummings and Barry Staw (eds.), *Research in Organizational Behavior,* Vol. 20 (Greenwich, Conn.: JAI Press, 1998), pp. 141–183.

11. Theresa M. Welbourne and Luis R. Gomez-Mejia, "Gainsharing: A Critical Review and a Future Research Agenda," *Journal of Management,* Vol. 21, No. 3, 1995, pp. 559–609.

12. "Chrysler Pay Draws Fire Overseas," *Wall Street Journal,* May 26, 1998, pp. B1, B12.

13. T. A. Steward, "The Trouble with Stock Options," *Fortune,* January 1, 1990, pp. 93–95; See also "To a Pile of CEO Perks, Add the 'Special' Bonus," *Wall Street Journal,* April 28, 1999, pp. B1, B12.

14. Harry Barkema and Luis Gomez-Mejia, "Managerial Compensation and Firm Performance: A General Research Framework," *Academy of Management Journal,* Vol. 41, No. 2, 1998, pp. 135–145.

15. Rajiv D. Banker, Seok-Young Lee, Gordon Potter, and Dhinu Srinivasan, "Contextual Analysis of Performance Impacts of Outcome-Based Incentive Compensation," *Academy of Management Journal,* Vol. 39, No. 4, 1996, pp. 920–948.

16. "CEOs' Pay Outpaces Companies' Performance," *USA Today,* March 30, 1998, p. 1B.

17. M. Blair, "CEO Pay: Why Such a Contentious Issue? *Brookings Review,* Winter 1994, pp. 23–27.

18. Jeffrey Pfeffer and Nancy Langton, "The Effects of Wage Dispersion on Satisfaction, Productivity and Working Collaboratively: Evidence from College and University Faculty," *Administrative Science Quarterly,* Vol. 38, 1993, pp. 382–407.

19. Ronald G. Ehrenberg and Mario L. Bognanno, "The Incentive Effects of Tournaments Revisited: Evidence from the European PGA Tour," *Industrial and Labor Relations Review,* Vol. 43, 1990, pp. 74–88.

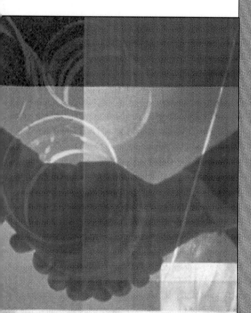

13

Employee Benefits and Services

CHAPTER OUTLINE

Basic Considerations in Indirect Compensation and Benefits
Purposes of Indirect Compensation and Benefit Programs
Legal Considerations

Mandated Protection Plans
Unemployment Insurance
Social Security
Workers' Compensation

Optional Protection Plans
Insurance Coverage
Private Pension Plans

Paid Time Off
Other Types of Benefits
Cafeteria-Style Benefit Plans
Evaluating Indirect Compensation and Benefit Plans

CHAPTER OBJECTIVES

After studying this chapter you should be able to:

■ Identify and discuss basic considerations in indirect compensation.

■ Discuss legally mandated protection plans as employee benefits.

■ Describe various optional protection plans as employee benefits.

■ Discuss paid time off as an employee benefit.

■ Identify and discuss various other benefits that some organizations provide for their employees.

■ Describe cafeteria-style approaches to benefits.

■ Discuss how organizations evaluate indirect compensation and benefit plans.

When most people think of employee benefits, they think of insurance, vacation days, and sick time. But how about an artificial rock-climbing wall? or aerobic classes? or free spa weekends? These are just some of the innovative—and expensive—benefits provided by Clif Bar, Inc., a San Francisco Bay Area company that makes high-powered snacks for athletes.

Clif Bar started out in 1986 as a bakery called Kali Sport Naturals. But one day cofounder Gary Erickson decided that there was a market for good-tasting snack foods after eating bad-tasting alternative products during a 175-mile bike ride. Erickson and his partner decided to change their product mix—and the firm's name—and have enjoyed tremendous success ever since. But from the beginning Clif Bar has offered its employees an impressive array of both standard and innovative benefits.

There are actually two very different reasons for the impressive array of benefits the firm offers. One is that the firm's benefits mesh nicely with Clif Bar's emphasis on

> *"[Climbing the rock wall] is a relaxing way to separate myself from everything that's going on in the office."*
>
> (Tom Richardson, Clif Bar marketing coordinator)*

health. For example, Erickson installed the $20,000 climbing wall in part because he wanted to use it. All employees, however, are encouraged to climb the wall, use other exercise equipment, attend aerobics classes, and participate in stress-reduction seminars. And on-site personal trainers make it even easier. Erickson and others at the firm think these are all great ways to reduce stress and help people lead a better-balanced life.

But Clif Bar has another reason for providing these benefits. The Bay Area is filled with worker—and family—friendly businesses competing for scarce labor. By providing unusual but attractive benefits, employers stand a better chance of getting the workers they want and then keeping them. Indeed, Clif Bar has lost only five employees since 1992.

"Climbing Walls on Company Time," *Wall Street Journal*, December 1, 1998, pp. B1, B14 (*quote on p. 1); "Bonanza of Job Benefits," *USA Today*, August 3, 1998, p. B2; "Fringe Benefits on the Rise," *USA Today*, October 8, 1997, pp. 1B, 2B.

Most employees are accustomed to receiving more than just a paycheck from their employer. Indeed, almost as important as their pay to many employees are the additional benefits that their employer provides. And although companies have a long history of providing certain "standard" benefits such as insurance and vacation time, some organizations, like Clif Bar, are finding that it also pays off to continue to provide new and unusual benefits as well.

In the last two chapters we discussed basic compensation issues as well as various merit-based and incentive pay systems. The remaining part of most employees' total compensation consists of indirect compensation and benefits. Although some of these benefits are mandated by law, modern organizations are increasingly looking to indirect compensation and benefits as a means of attracting certain groups of employees. We first review the legal considerations in the administration of benefit programs and then discuss the most common types of benefits and the features of each. Next we discuss variable benefit programs where the actual benefits given to an employee can be tailored to his or her needs. Finally, we discuss some issues associated with the evaluation of benefit and indirect compensation programs.

BASIC CONSIDERATIONS IN INDIRECT COMPENSATION AND BENEFITS

■ **Benefits** generally refer to various rewards, incentives, and other things of value that an organization provides to its employees beyond their wages, salaries, and other forms of direct financial compensation.

In addition to wages and salaries, most organizations provide their employees with an array of indirect compensation and benefits as well. **Benefits** generally refer to various rewards, incentives, and other things of value that an organization provides to its employees beyond their wages, salaries, and other forms of direct financial compensation. Because these benefits have tangible value but are generally not expressed in financial terms, they essentially represent a meaningful, albeit indirect, form of compensation. Strategically, benefits should be more than just a laundry list of specific benefit entitlements. Ideally, they should be well-developed packages of benefits and benefit options that best serve the needs and preferences of employees and the organization.

In earlier times these benefits were often called "fringe benefits," and a few people still use this expression. However, as managers began to realize that they were spending perhaps more than a third of wages and salaries in additional expenses on benefits, they decided that the word *fringe* might have been understating to employees the true value of these benefits. Hence most organizations no longer use the term *fringe benefits,* but instead refer to *employee benefits* or simply just *benefits.*

In fact, data from the U.S. Chamber of Commerce provides some insights into the composition of the total compensation paid to a typical employee in the United States. According to these figures, the typical employee costs the company almost $47,000 a year in total compensation. Of this amount, roughly $32,000 is paid for time worked, whereas the remaining $15,000 is paid for other than time worked and includes vacation time, mandated benefits, pensions, insurance, and so on.[1]

It is therefore quite clear that organizations are spending huge amounts of money on benefits. It appears that many organizations are trying to hold the tide, or even reverse it, by asking employees to bear some of the costs of these benefits, but surely benefit costs will continue to be a large part of labor costs in the United States. "The Lighter Side of HR" illustrates this point—at the extreme! It is also interesting to note in this context that, despite these figures, the United States actually ranks rather low in terms of the relative costs of benefits around the world.

These differences are due almost entirely to the number of mandated benefits in the different countries based on the different social contracts (guarantees made by the government in return for higher taxes) in place there, and they are substantial. For example, the German workweek is 37.6 hours (on average), the German worker works 1,499 hours per year, has forty-two days off, and has mandated benefit costs *alone* that equal almost 30 percent of wages. (For comparison purposes the average U.S. worker spends 40 hours a week at work, 1,847 hours a year working, has twenty-three days off a year, and has mandated benefit costs equal to about 10 percent of wages.)

The Lighter Side of HR

Many human resource managers are studying ways to lower the costs of the benefits they provide to their employees and/or to improve the effectiveness of the benefits they currently provide for the same costs. Although few managers would resort to the level of cost reduction illustrated by this particular human resource manager, it nevertheless demonstrates the basic idea that some managers adopt!

"Before I forget, Detrick, here's the dental plan."

Indeed, when Ford recently announced its purchase of the Swedish automobile maker Volvo, that firm's workers immediately started to express their concerns about the potential loss of their relatively lavish benefits. For example, Volvo's main manufacturing plant in Gothenburg has a sprawling health complex including an Olympic-size swimming pool, tanning beds, and tennis courts. The firm spends more than $600,000 a year to maintain the center. Although Ford's U.S. workers enjoy a strong benefit program, it pales in comparison to that at Volvo and cutbacks may be imposed.[2] "Human Resources Around the Globe" sheds additional light on some of the issues associated with benefits in international companies.

As can be seen, the exact benefits offered differ substantially from one country to the next, but in each case the benefits are designed to meet the specific needs (relative to balancing work and family) in the host country. For example, in Egypt resorts are quite expensive and offering short vacations for the family to spend together is a much-appreciated benefit. AMOCO will pay for the pilgrimage to Mecca (haj) if the employee hasn't already gone. Since all Muslims are expected to make the haj at least once during their life (if at all possible), this is a very valuable benefit. In Norway, Trinidad, and the United Kingdom, oil operations tend to be offshore and in rather remote regions of the country. As a result, employees do not see their families every day and do not generally

Global Benefits: Similarities and Differences

Even before its recent merger with BP, Amoco was a major multinational firm with operations in dozens of other countries. One of the more challenging issues that Amoco's human resource executives have long had to confront, therefore, has been juggling the legal, cultural, and social forces dictating and reinforcing the needs for different benefit programs.

For example, in the United States Amoco offers insurance, vacation and sick leave, alternative work schedules, childcare centers, employee assistance programs, and referral services. And indeed, its array of benefits is strong enough for Amoco to be the only oil company on *Working Mother*'s list of the best companies for working mothers.

In Egypt, though, Amoco offers some different benefits. Among the more prominent of these is a one-time haj pilgrimage allowance and two annual subsidized trips to Egyptian resorts. In the Netherlands the emphasis is on flexibility—parents can take up to three months of unpaid

> *"You have to tailor your benefits to the unique situation in each country where you do business."*
>
> (Amoco executive)*

leave after their child is born, and all employees can opt for part-time employment anytime they want, for as long as a year at a time.

Amoco's U.K. employees get many of the same benefits as their U.S. counterparts get but also receive five bereavement days per year following the death of a family member and two days a year if they need to move their residence. In Norway fathers of newborns get five days of paid leave. In addition, Amoco employees in Norway also get perhaps the most unusual benefits of all: because the country has an especially high marginal tax rate, employees are often looking for things companies can provide that are not subject to taxation. Those who work for Amoco, therefore, get seven free magazine subscriptions a year—the most allowed under Norwegian law!

References: James Yates, "Work-family Practices at Amoco," Presentation at the Texas A&M University Center for Human Resource Management Conference, *The Family-Friendly Organization,* October 24, 1997.

live at home. Under these circumstances, compressed workweeks are extremely important to employees, as are other benefits such as "family days," where families are brought to work sites for visits at company expense.

Purposes of Indirect Compensation and Benefit Programs

So even though U.S. companies spend a great deal of money on benefits, they are nowhere near the top in this area relative to the rest of the world, and especially relative to European countries. Nonetheless, U.S. companies *do* spend a great deal of money on benefits, so there must be a reason for this expense. Why are these companies willing to spend this money on benefits? As Figure 13.1 illustrates, indirect compensation and benefits serve a variety of basic purposes.

First, there is a belief that organizations that spend more money on compensation are able to attract "better" people and/or are able to convince employees to work harder. The general concept underlying this approach is known as *efficiency wage theory.* This theory suggests that firms can actually save money and become more productive if they pay more because they attract employees who are better or who would be willing to work hard. Very little data actually support or refute this position, but some organizations appear to view wages and benefits as a means of attracting better applicants.

Most organizations would also argue that money spent on benefits will have an impact on job satisfaction and subsequent turnover. That is, even if employees will not work harder in response to better benefits, they will be more likely to remain with a firm that provides better benefits and will be more satisfied with that firm. In part an employee's reactions to specific benefit programs will reflect that individual's belief about the value of benefits at the present company as compared with the value of benefits at other companies. As a result, the need to remain competitive with other firms in an industry is a major force driving up the price of benefits. Much the same as when one airline in a market lowers fares and all others must follow suit, once one visible organization in an industry starts offering a given benefit, it is usually not long until its competitors offer similar benefits.

In addition, various social, cultural, and political forces may facilitate the introduction of new and broader benefits programs. For example, increases in the number of women in the workforce and the rising costs of health care have each affected benefit program in recent times. Because of the growth in numbers of female workers, for instance, more and more companies offer on-site daycare, dual parental maternity leave, and other benefits that help people to work and have productive careers. Likewise, the health-care environment has prompted growth in benefit programs that provide HMOs, managed health care, and so forth.

Finally, employee expectations are a driving force in determining what benefits a firm must offer. For example, there is no legal requirement that an organization offer *any* vacation time. But because this benefit is so desirable and has become so common, virtually every person who accepts a new job expects that he or she will be given some vacation time. Indeed, most people today would be unlikely to accept a permanent full-time job that did not include this basic benefit. A major implication of these issues, then, is the strategic importance of employee benefits. Their costs are high, and their impact is great. Thus careful planning, monitoring, and communication about benefits is of paramount importance.

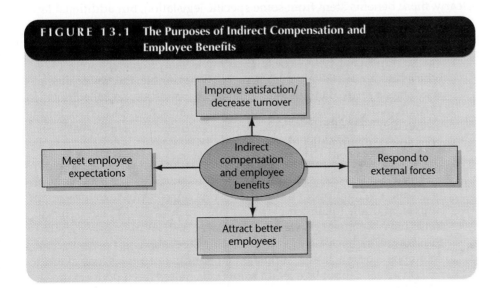

FIGURE 13.1   The Purposes of Indirect Compensation and Employee Benefits

One of the key reasons organizations should pay careful attention to the benefits they provide for their employees relates to turnover and retention. That is, a good benefits program will make it more likely that valued employees will remain with an organization, and this is one of the reasons SAS Institute subsidizes high-quality daycare for its employees. These children, for example, are enrolled in the firm's on-site daycare center; their parents pay only $250 a month for this benefit. SAS, in turn, enjoys exceptionally high retention rates, generally exceeding 95 percent a year.

Legal Considerations

Although vacation time is not mandated in the United States, a number of other benefits are actually mandated by law, and we discuss those shortly. Clearly, those benefits stem from some specific legislation, but additional laws govern various aspects of benefit administration without actually mandating a specific benefit. The major laws are

1. Tax Reform Act of 1997—The law has numerous provisions, some of which directly affect employee benefits. For example, the law created a special new form of individual retirement account (the so-called Roth IRA). In addition, this act increased the amount self-employed individuals can deduct for health insurance premiums and relaxed the rules for home-office deductions.

2. Tax Reform Act 1986 and Revenue Reconciliation Act of 1993—Both of these legislative acts have basically the same purpose. They set limits on how much an employee (and an employer) can contribute to tax-exempt retirement funds (qualified pension plans) such as 401(k) plans. Theses limits have the intent of insuring that lower-paid employees are treated the same as higher-paid employees relative to tax-exempt pension contributions. These acts also stipulate that, for top executives, pay over $1 million a year cannot be exempt from taxes unless it is a performance-related bonus.

3. Family and Medical Leave Act of 1993—This act requires all organizations (with at least fifty employees) to grant any employee (who has worked for the organization for at least one year) an *unpaid* leave of up to twelve weeks for childbirth, for the adoption of a child, to care for any family member with a serious health problem, or because of a health problem the employee has. All health benefits must remain intact, and the employee must return to the same or an equivalent job after the leave.

4. Economic Recovery Tax Act of 1981—This is the act that first allowed employees to make a tax-deductible contribution of up to $2,000 to a pension, savings, or individual retirement account. The act also provides mechanisms that made it easier for companies to finance employee stock ownership plans (ESOPs).

5. Pregnancy Discrimination Act of 1978—This act protects a woman from being fired for being pregnant. It has been reported that about eight thousand women a year (about 4 percent of the workforce that becomes pregnant) are fired for that reason.[3] Recent court decisions have also suggested that all related health benefits must be extended to the spouse of male employees as well.

6. Employee Retirement Income Security Act of 1974—This act does *not* require companies to set up pension funds for employees. If a firm does elect to have a pension fund and wishes to deduct contributions to that fund, it must follow certain guidelines. These guidelines restrict the company's freedom to take money out of pension funds as needed, restrict how those pension funds might be invested, and generally attempt to ensure that an employee will have money to retire on when the time comes. The act also provides formulas for vesting (when the employee has a right to the employer's contributions to the fund) and portability (the employee's ability to transfer funds to a different retirement account).

Clearly, then, the legal context plays a major role in how organizations structure the benefits programs and options they offer to their employees.

THE BOTTOM LINE All managers should understand and be knowledgeable about the benefits their organization provides to its members. In addition, they should be familiar with the costs of benefits, the legal context of benefits, and the purposes that benefits can play in organizational effectiveness. The human resource function can also play a special role as a center of expertise vis-à-vis managing and administering benefit programs and components.

M A N D A T E D   P R O T E C T I O N   P L A N S

Protection plans are benefits designed to protect employees when their income is threatened or reduced by illness, disability, unemployment, or retirement. A number of these benefits are required by law, but others are optional. We will first discuss those plans that are required, or mandated, by law.

■ **Protection plans** protect employees when their income is threatened or reduced by illness, disability, unemployment, or retirement.

Unemployment Insurance

One mandated benefit is unemployment insurance. Unemployment insurance was created in the United States as a part of the Social Security Act of 1935. The rationale for the act was to protect people who were experiencing the very high levels of unemployment that pervaded the United States during the 1930s.

■ **Unemployment insurance**,
a mandated protection plan,
is intended to provide a basic subsistence payment to
employees who are between
jobs.

Unemployment insurance is intended to provide a basic subsistence payment to employees who are between jobs. That is, it is intended for people who have stopped working for one organization but who are assumed to be actively seeking employment with another organization. Employers pay premiums to the unemployment insurance fund. In addition, in the states of Alabama, Alaska, and New Jersey, employees also contribute to the fund. The premium payment is increased if more than an average or designated number of employees from the organization are drawing from the fund at any given time.

Unemployment insurance and related systems for certain former government workers cover almost sixty-five million employees in the United States. Major categories that are excluded from coverage include self-employed workers, employees of very small firms with fewer than four employees, domestic employees, farm employees, state and local government employees, and employees of nonprofit organizations such as hospitals.

To be covered by unemployment insurance, an individual must have worked a minimum number of weeks, must now be without a job, and must be willing to accept a suitable position if one is found through the State Unemployment Compensation Commission. A critical variable in determining when an employee is qualified for receipt of benefits is the circumstances under which he or she became unemployed. In general, if the employee is out of work through no fault of his or her own, then benefits start almost immediately. For example, if an employee is laid off because the organization cuts back its workforce or shuts down operations altogether, then the employee really isn't to blame for this circumstance.

On the other hand, if the employee quits of his or her own free will or is fired because of poor performance or other legitimate circumstances, then states might mandate a somewhat longer period of time before the individual becomes qualified for benefits. Regardless of the starting time, however, compensation is only available for a limited period of time. This period of time is usually twenty-six weeks, although some states will extend this term in an emergency situation, such as high unemployment rates.

The payment that is provided is intended to represent around half of what individuals might have been earning had they retained their former job, although there is an upper limit on the benefit that is paid. As noted above, this program is funded through employer contributions. The tax for this is 6.2 percent on the first $7,000 earned by each employee. However, each state administers this program in its own fashion, and there is considerable variation in how the laws and provisions are interpreted.

■ **Social security** (officially
the **Old Age Survivors and
Disability Insurance Program**),
another mandated program,
was designed to provide limited income to retired individuals to supplement their own
personal savings, private
pensions, part-time work, and
so forth.

Social Security

A second mandated benefit is **social security**. The social security system was also established in 1935. What most people think of as social security is officially the **Old Age Survivors and Disability Insurance Program**. The initial purpose of this program was to provide some limited income to retired individuals to supplement their own personal savings, private pensions, part-time work, and so forth. The program is funded through employee and employer taxes that are withheld on a payroll basis.

The current tax is 7.65 percent of earnings on the first $72,600 of a person's annual income. Individuals are eligible for partial benefits when they reach the age of 62 or full benefits when they reach the age of 65. However, effective in the year 2027, individuals will not be able to retire with full benefits until they reach age 67. If an employee dies before reaching retirement age, a family with children under 18 receives survival benefits regardless of the employee's age at the time of her or his death. In addition, an employee who becomes totally disabled before the age of 65 is also eligible to receive insurance benefits, and in fact, Medicare benefits are provided under this act as well.

The amount of money any given individual is eligible to be paid from the social security system is a function of the average monthly wage that individual earned, weighted toward the later years of a person's career. In addition, an individual has to have worked a minimum period of time and made a minimum amount of contributions to the system in order to be able to draw full benefits.

In recent years considerable concern has been raised in the United States about the long-term future viability of the social security system. In particular, with longer life expectancies and increased risk of suffering disability in older age, new work patterns, and new family norms, the demands being placed on the social security system have increased significantly. Indeed, the system is paying out more money than it is taking in. Thus there continues to be a frequent need for the government to intervene and make some manipulation or adjustment in the system to maintain its viability. In 1998 President Clinton vowed to use any budget surplus money to strengthen the social security system and so ensure its viability for years to come.

Workers' compensation is a mandated benefit that provides insurance coverage for individuals who suffer a job-related illness or accident. This worker, for example, is part of a large team of construction workers completing a massive highway, tunnel, and bridge project through the heart of Boston. During the course of the project, reported injuries have included 155 strains, 191 bruises, 94 sprains, 64 lacerations, 71 eye problems, 26 burns, 21 punctures, and 32 miscellaneous injuries ranging from fractures to hernias to infections. In each instance, workers' compensation covered all of the health recovery expenses.

Workers' Compensation

A final mandated benefit is workers' compensation. **Workers' compensation** is insurance that covers individuals who suffer a job-related illness or accident. Employers pay the cost of workers' compensation insurance. The exact premium that is paid is a function of each employer's past experience with job-related accidents and illnesses. Almost ninety million workers in the United States are protected under the Workers' Compensation Insurance Program.[4]

■ **Workers' compensation**, another mandated protection program, is insurance that covers individuals who suffer a job-related illness or accident.

THE BOTTOM LINE All managers should be familiar with the three forms of mandated employee protection: unemployment insurance, social security, and workers' compensation. However, it is generally the responsibility of an organization's human resource function to administer these mandated benefits.

O P T I O N A L   P R O T E C T I O N   P L A N S

Another major category of employee benefits consists of various optional protection plans. These plans provide protection in the same areas as those discussed above but are not mandated. It is therefore the organization's option whether or not to offer the specific benefit. As noted in the section on legislation, though, in some cases an organization that elects to offer the benefit must follow certain guidelines.

Insurance Coverage

Perhaps the most common optional protection plan that many organizations provide to their full-time employees is insurance coverage. Insurance coverage is not mandated but has become such a standard benefit that, as noted, most organizations elect to provide it. In some cases the organization pays all or at least a major portion of the insurance premiums. However, it is also not uncommon for employees to bear a considerable portion of the load themselves.

Many kinds of insurance are available. Health insurance, of course, is the most common. Because of the dramatic escalation of medical costs over the last several years, health insurance has become an increasingly expensive and complicated benefit for many organizations to provide and to maintain. It is

Private pension plans are a popular optional benefit many companies provide to their employees. For example, while working as a materials manager for Fisher Berkeley Corporation in San Leandro, California, Francisco Moreno systematically compiled a 401(k) retirement account of $100,000. But complexities in pension plan law can create problems for employees. Under one provision of federal tax laws, Moreno borrowed $30,000 from his account for a down payment on a home and agreed to repay the money through payroll deductions. But after Fisher Berkeley was sold to new owners, Moreno was fired and ordered to repay the money in six months. While he managed to do this, it created some hardships for him and his family.

estimated that in the United States between 85 and 90 percent of all health insurance coverage is purchased by employers as group plans covering their employees.[5]

In recent years health-care coverage has been expanded by many organizations to include such things as special programs for prescription drugs, vision-care products, mental health services, and dental care. For example, today about one-fourth of all employees in the United States at least have the opportunity to purchase dental insurance through their employers. **Health maintenance organizations**, or **HMOs**, are also a growing trend in health insurance coverage. An HMO is a medical organization that provides medical and health services on a prepaid basis. That is, rather than billing patients or companies for specific services rendered, the initial premium that is paid to the HMO provides the employee with prepaid coverage of all expenses he or she might incur for health care.

■ **Health maintenance organizations**, or **HMOs**, are medical organizations that provide medical and health services on a prepaid basis.

There is also a growing trend toward cost-containment strategies by organizations to reduce the huge outflow of funds for medical benefits. These strategies include such things as coordinating benefits across plans and cost sharing. Unfortunately for the employee, cost sharing simply means that he or she will have to bear a greater part of the cost of the insurance.

In addition, some organizations have become self-funded or self-insured. In most such cases an organization actually contracts with an insurance company to provide health benefits, but some companies have been trying to fund their own health insurance plans. These firms believe that this approach will give them better control over costs and avoid state insurance regulations.

Other kinds of insurance coverage include life insurance and long-term disability insurance. Life insurance, of course, provides a payment to the survivors of an individual who has died or been killed. Disability insurance is designed to supplement workers' compensation insurance and provide continued income in case the employee becomes disabled.

Private Pension Plans

In addition to the pension benefits that are guaranteed under the Social Security Act, many companies elect to establish **private pension plans** for their employees. These prearranged plans, administered by the organization, provide income to the employee upon her or his retirement. Contributions to the retirement plan may come from either the employer or the employee but in most cases are actually supported by contributions from both parties. A variety of retirement plans are available, including individual retirement accounts or IRAs and employee pension IRAs. In addition, a 401(k) plan allows employees to save money on a tax-deferred basis by entering into salary-deferral agreements with their employer. "Human Resources in the Twenty-first Century" discusses the details of a new model currently being adopted for private pension plans.

■ **Private pension plans** are administered by the organization and provide income to employees upon retirement.

There are two basic types of pension plans: **defined benefit plans** and **defined contribution plans**. Under defined benefit plans the size of the benefit is precisely known and is usually based on a simple formula using such input as years of service. This type of plan is often favored by unions and is closely monitored under ERISA (ERISA was discussed in Chapter 3). Although the employee may contribute to these plans, the amount of the contribution has no bearing on the benefits. Under defined contribution plans the size of the

■ **Defined benefit plans** are private pension plans in which the size of the benefit is precisely known and is usually based on a simple formula, using input such as years of service.

■ **Defined contribution plans** are private pension plans in which the size of the benefit depends on how much money is contributed to the plan.

Taking It with You

Traditional pension plans were basically set up to reward workers who stayed with the same employer for their entire career—thirty-, forty-, or even fifty-year veterans. Workers who left after only a few years had typically not accumulated a substantial balance and had to wait until at least age fifty-five—and usually age sixty-five—before they could start drawing a pension check.

The 401(k) retirement plan has made portability much easier. The employer and the employee each make contributions to an investment account, often on a pretax basis, and the employee can move the account to a new employer whenever necessary. But the risk to the employee is much greater, since her or his pension balance is usually invested in securities markets.

But some big employers have begun offering a hybrid pension called a "cash-balance plan." Under this

"With cash-balance accounts, not only do they know what they have, they're not in pension jail until 65."

(Michael Gulotta, president of ASA, a benefits management and consulting firm)*

arrangement the employer pays a set amount, usually 5 percent to 7 percent of the employee's gross pay, into the individual's cash-balance account. The account itself has a guaranteed growth rate of around 6 percent a year. The employee gets quarterly statements showing the account value. And if the individual leaves, usually after a vesting period averaging about five years, the account goes with the departing employee.

For companies, this plan serves as a good recruiting tool for new employees, cuts record keeping for long-term workers, and limits liability. Little wonder, then, that companies such as AT&T, Bell Atlantic, Cigna, Cincinnati Bell, and Xerox have moved to this system. Indeed, cash-balance plans look like the model pension program for the twenty-first century.

References: "Companies Switching to Portable Cash Pensions," *USA Today,* July 20, 1998, p. B1 (*quote on p. B1).

benefit depends on how much money is contributed to the plan. This money can be contributed either by the employer alone (noncontributory plans) or by the employer and the employee (contributory plans). Most new pension plans are contributory, defined contribution plans.

THE BOTTOM LINE Optional protection plans have become near-standard benefits. As such, managers should generally be familiar with the options provided by their particular organization. Human resource managers in particular should closely monitor the costs of these programs so as to most effectively balance the quality of the benefit relative to its cost.

P A I D   T I M E   O F F

Many organizations also provide their employees with some amount of time off with pay. Although, again, no laws in the United States mandate this type of benefit, most employees have come to expect it. One major type of paid time off is paid holidays. Most full-time employees receive around ten paid holidays per year. The most common holidays for which workers are paid without having to work include New Year's Day, Memorial Day, Independence Day, Labor Day, Thanksgiving Day, and Christmas. In addition, many other holidays are purposefully scheduled to abut a weekend so that people can have three days off. These include Martin Luther King, Jr. Day in January, President's Day in February, Memorial Day in May, and Columbus Day in October.

Religious holidays are also often given (in addition to Christmas). Organizations have to be careful with this practice, however, because the growing diversity in the workplace is accompanied by an increasingly diverse set of religions and thus religious holidays. An organization has to be sensitive to the fact that it can create problems if it gives time off for some religions but not others. For example, Christianity is the most common religion in the United States. Judaism is second, but Islam is on track to soon become number two. Each of these three religions, though, has different holidays, both in terms of numbers and dates. An organization that seeks to accommodate members of one or two religions but not all is asking for problems. But accommodating all religions creates other complications. Thus organizations need to have clear policies and to enforce those policies in a fair and equitable manner.[6]

Paid vacations are also common, but are, likewise, not required by law. Paid vacations are usually a period of one, two, or more weeks when an employee can take time off from work and continue to be paid. Most organizations vary the amount of paid vacation with an individual's seniority with the organization. For example, it might be typical to give employees one week of paid vacation a year if they have three or less years' service with the organization. Following a third-year anniversary, however, the vacation benefit may increase to two weeks a year. At a later point, perhaps after ten years, it might increase to three weeks of vacation a year. A firm's most senior employees, such as those with perhaps twenty or twenty-five years of experience, may enjoy four weeks of paid vacation a year.[7]

Organizations administer vacation pay in very different ways. Some require employees to take their accumulated vacation time each year. Others are willing to pay employees time and a half if they continue to work instead of taking the time off. Some also allow employees to roll vacation time over into the next year (that is, to save it for at least some period of time).

Earlier in the chapter we mentioned that German workers had more extensive benefits than the typical U.S. employee. One area where there is a considerable difference is in the number of days off per year. Although there are no mandated number of days off in the United States (or in the United Kingdom), many European countries *do* mandate a minimum annual vacation. Table 13.1 lists the annual vacation policies in various countries.

Yet another common paid time-off plan is sick leave. This benefit is provided when an individual is sick or otherwise physically unable to perform his or her job duties. Most organizations allow an individual to accumulate sick time on the basis of some schedule, such as one sick day per month. Some organizations require that employees submit a doctor's note verifying illness in the event the employee wants to draw sick pay. Other organizations take a more egalitarian approach, however, and require no such documentation, relying instead simply on the honesty of the employee. One interesting wrinkle on sick-leave policies is that some organizations require employees to use their allocation of sick days or lose them. Under such a system it would seem illogical for an employee to *not* take all the sick days allocated during the year.

A final common method of paid time off is personal leave. Sometimes an organization will allow an employee to take a few days off simply for "personal business." Examples might include funerals, religious observances, a marriage, a birthday, or a personal-choice holiday.

TABLE 13.1 Minimum Annual Vacation by Law in Different Countries	
Country	**Minimum Vacation**
Belgium	4 weeks
Denmark	36 days
France	36 days
Greece	4 weeks
Ireland	3 weeks
Italy	National Collective Bargaining Agreement
The Netherlands	4 weeks
Portugal	21–30 days

Source: Reprinted from G. Milkovich and J. Newman, *Compensation,* 5th ed. (Chicago: Richard D. Irwin, 1996). Copyright © 1996 by The McGraw-Hill Companies. Reprinted with the permission of The McGraw-Hill Companies.

THE BOTTOM LINE Paid time off is a very common benefit in organizations. Managers should be sensitive to the various kinds of paid time off their organization allows so as to avoid misunderstandings or other problems.

OTHER TYPES OF BENEFITS

In addition to protection plans and paid time off, many organizations also offer a growing array of other kinds of benefit programs. For example, the climbing wall at Clif Bar is clearly seen as an employee benefit, albeit a very unusual one. In this section we describe several of the more common of these kinds of benefits. Figure 13.2 also illustrates recent trends among some of the more intriguing new benefits.

As noted earlier, many organizations have been struggling with ways to reduce health-care costs. In addition to the attempts described earlier, these efforts have resulted in a new type of benefit known as **wellness programs**. These programs concentrate on keeping employees from becoming sick, rather than simply paying expenses when they become sick.[8] In some organizations these programs may be simple and involve little more than organized jogging or walking during lunch breaks. More elaborate programs might include smoking cessation programs, high blood pressure and cholesterol screening, and stress management programs. Some organizations actually have full-fledged health clubs on site and provide counseling and programs for fitness and weight loss. Although these programs typically take place after work hours (or before), the companies often provide the services either for free or at cost.

■ **Wellness programs** are special benefits programs that concentrate on keeping employees from becoming sick, rather than simply paying expenses when they become sick.

These plans not only are attractive to employees who appreciate the ease and low costs but also are usually seen as an excellent investment by the organization. Specifically, many case studies indicate that these programs reduce sick days, reduce medical costs, and actually improve productivity as the organization gains a more physically fit workforce.[9]

An additional group of benefits is often referred to collectively as **life cycle benefits**. The most common of these are childcare and elder-care benefits. Thus they are targeted at different stages in an employee's life.

▨ **Life cycle benefits** are based on a person's stage of life and include childcare and elder-care benefits.

Childcare   Childcare benefits are becoming extremely popular. In fact, any organization that wants to be considered a "family-friendly organization" must have some type of childcare benefits at a minimum, and the ability to claim that a firm is family friendly is increasingly viewed as being a competitive advantage.[10] These plans might include scheduling help, referrals to various types of services, or reimbursement accounts for childcare expenses, but in many cases they actually include company-paid daycare. For example, AMOCO International's headquarters in Houston has an on-site, but freestanding, daycare facility. The building had been intended for some other use and had been abandoned. The management at AMOCO purchased the building and contracted with an outside firm to provide daycare services, which are provided at heavily discounted rates to employees. Programs such as this have a strong impact on employee attitudes and job performance.[11]

Elder care   Unlike childcare, it would be unusual for an organization to have on-site elder-care facilities. Instead, these benefits tend to take the form of referrals, which are especially useful for the employee with a disabled parent or one needing constant care. The employee is saved the time and effort of locating these resources, and the resources provided by the organization have presumably been checked first. Long-term health-care insurance is also becoming a more common benefit, and these plans provide for nursing homes or at-home care. The premium is typically paid fully by the employee and, at least for now, these benefits are for the employee or the employee and spouse only.

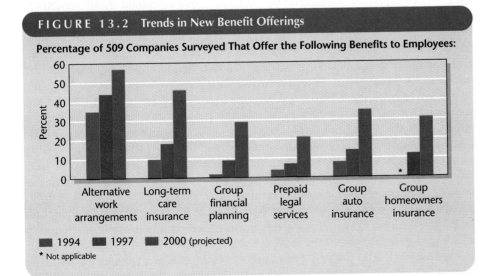

FIGURE 13.2   **Trends in New Benefit Offerings**

Percentage of 509 Companies Surveyed That Offer the Following Benefits to Employees:

■ 1994   ■ 1997   ■ 2000 (projected)
* Not applicable

Source: "What about benefits?" *Time,* November 9, 1998. © 1998 Time Inc. Reprinted by permission.

HUMAN RESOURCES Legal Brief

Legislating Domestic Partner Benefits?

 It has long been customary for firms to extend benefits such as insurance coverage to an employee's husband or wife. But what if the employee is not married to her or his domestic partner? Or if they are the same sex? More and more companies are extending benefits to their employees' unmarried and/or gay partners, sometimes because of legal pressure, sometimes because of competitive pressure, and sometimes both. (Of course, some firms have adopted this practice just because they think it's the right thing to do!)

One major impetus for the growth in partner benefits is an ordinance passed by the city of San Francisco. The ordinance simply says that any business doing business with the city has to extend benefits to unmarried and/or gay partners. Oil giant Chevron is headquartered in San Francisco. It changed its policies to be compliant with the ordinance but did so nationwide for all twenty-six thousand of its employees. Shortly thereafter, both Shell and Amoco followed suit—not because they do business in San Francisco, but to remain competitive with Chevron in a tight labor market.

"The market is very, very tight for good people, and we want to do anything we can to attract and retain them."

(Alison Jones, Chevron spokesperson)*

Sometimes, unfortunately, this practice can have unexpected repercussions. For example, one major factor cited in a religious boycott of Disney was that the entertainment giant extended benefit coverage to its employees' unmarried and/or gay partners. Although Disney may have multiple reasons for its practices, one major factor was that competitors such as Universal, Paramount, Sony, and Warner Bros. had already done so.

Interestingly, this practice has also not increased costs for insurers. For one thing, these couples tend to be younger and thus in better health. And for another, pregnancy rates are also lower. Over a quarter of U.S. companies with more than five thousand employees have revised their benefits to include unmarried and/or gay domestic partners. And if a few more cities follow the lead of San Francisco, this percentage will certainly take a big jump.

References: "Domestic Partner Benefits on Rise," *USA Today,* October 14, 1997, p. 8B (*quote on p. 8B).

One of the most controversial issues for benefit programs involves the question of whether to extend benefits to same-sex partners. Most organizations offer benefits to spouses of employees, but the move to extend these benefits to life partners or spousal equivalents is slower in coming.[12] Obviously, there are different bases for objecting to such a plan, but more organizations are coming to the view that this policy is simply the "fair" thing to do. Chevron's corporate headquarters is located in San Francisco and, in an attempt to be fair and to remain competitive for employees in the local market, the company decided to extend all health and insurance benefits to same-sex partners. Although this move was applauded in San Francisco, employees at headquarters for the firm's production company (located in Houston) were less enthusiastic. The company made it clear, however, that Chevron believed that gay and lesbian employees deserved equal treatment on the job and invited employees who could not live with this policy to seek employment elsewhere. "Human Resources Legal Brief" discusses this issue in more detail.

In addition, sometimes organizations provide a variety of services for their employees. These may include relocation services and help with mortgage financing, although these are typically available for senior-level employees only. In the late 1970s IBM preferred managers to retire earlier than at sixty-five. The company realized, in turn, that one constraint many people faced when thinking about early retirement was money. IBM therefore offered estate-planning and wealth-accumulation programs for its management employees. All of these services are such that an employee might pay for them him- or herself if they were not provided, so they are rather attractive benefits.

A somewhat different type of service is contained in what are referred to as **employee assistance plans** (or EAPs). These programs are designed to assist employees who have chronic problems with alcohol or drugs or serious domestic problems, although there is an increase in such programs for mental problems and stress, as well as for bereavement.[13] These programs are typically voluntary, and referrals are confidential. Yet there is also a need to balance the needs of the organization (especially when the personal problem is causing performance problems on the job) and the needs of the individual to avoid any stigmas attached to the specific problem.[14]

Finally, employee perquisites are also sometimes provided. A **perquisite**, or a perk, as it is more informally known, is an extra benefit that may or may not have any direct financial value but is considered to be an important reward by the employees. A perk might include a bigger office, a company car, a membership in a country club, stock purchase options, premium insurance coverage, and similar kinds of things. Perquisites are usually made available only to members of top management or to certain especially valuable professionals within the organization.

However, sometimes organizations provide special perquisites to all employees. For example, some firms might provide the cost of uniforms for a company softball team, an on-site health club that all members of the organization can use, car-pooling van service for employees who live some distance from work, and similar kinds of amenities.

■ **Employee assistance plans** (or EAPs) are designed to assist employees who have chronic problems with alcohol or drugs or serious domestic or personal problems.

■ A **perquisite**, or a perk, as it is more informally known, is an extra benefit that may or may not have any direct financial value but is considered to be an important reward by the employees.

Employers continue to seek new and innovative perquisites to reward their employees. This is especially important in industries where talented workers are in short supply. QUALCOMM, a wireless technology company, for example, offers several novel benefits to its employees. One perk, shown here, is a sand volleyball court right outside the firm's San Diego headquarters. Another is its policy allowing the unlimited accumulation of unused vacation time. Because competition for top-quality workers in the high-tech environment in which QUALCOMM competes is so intense, it must provide these kinds of benefits to attract and retain workers.

Managers need to understand the array of benefits that might be potentially provided to employees, as well as the precise benefits their own organization has chosen to provide. Human resource managers in particular should also be attuned to market forces that affect benefit options and the human resource role in helping administer diverse benefit options.

C A F E T E R I A - S T Y L E   B E N E F I T   P L A N S

■ **Cafeteria-style benefit plans** allow employees to choose the benefits they really want.

Most benefit programs are designed for all the employees in an organization. Although the exact benefits may vary as a function of level in the organization, within those levels the plans are generally "one size fits all." **Cafeteria-style benefit plans** allow employees to choose the benefits they really want. Thus under these plans the organization typically establishes a budget, indicating how much it is willing to spend, per employee, on benefits.[15] Employees are presented with a list of possible benefits and the cost of each and are free to put them together in any combination. Such an approach should maximize the effectiveness of the benefit program for achieving the organizational goals we discussed at the beginning of the chapter, and some evidence suggests that cafeteria-style programs can lead to increased satisfaction and reduced turnover.[16]

There are, not surprisingly, variations in how these plans are designed. In some cases the cafeteria menu includes only basic levels of coverage, and the employee must pay (or sacrifice other types of coverage) for enhanced coverage. In other cases the employee is allowed to keep the money not spent on benefits. In yet other plans the cost to the employee of each benefit is structured so that the employee is rewarded for choosing more cost-effective benefits (for example, HMO versus more traditional medical plans).

Two serious problems limit the willingness of organizations to adopt these plans, however. The first is the cost of administration. Since every employee potentially has a unique set of benefits, someone has to keep track of what benefits each employee has chosen. Furthermore, since it is typical for the employee to be able to change his or her choices, this task is further complicated by the fact that the package of benefits will change.

The second problem stems from the presumably rational choices an employee will make. For example, if an employee has children who are at an age when children typically get dental braces, the employee will most likely select a dental plan that includes such coverage. Because the adopters of this plan are those most likely to use it, the provider will charge relatively high prices to both the individual and the organization. And since the individual will probably drop this coverage for some different benefit when the children get older, the costs of coverage cannot be amortized across less-intense users. This problem, known as *adverse selection*, can be very costly for the organization.

One final consideration in the design of cafeteria-style plans is that employees are not always rational in their choices. A younger employee may elect to contribute less to his or her retirement because it is so far away and wait until later before increasing the contribution. But given the power of compounding, a larger contribution early on, followed by a smaller contribution later, will actually be worth much more at retirement age than the reverse approach. It is therefore extremely important for employees to have full information about the available benefits, and the organization may need to mandate minimum benefit levels in some areas.

THE BOTTOM LINE Managers should understand the basic advantages and disadvantages of cafeteria-style benefit plans. Human resource managers in particular should be sure that the cafeteria "menu" is appropriate and that employees have full and complete information to enable them to make the most-informed choices.

EVALUATING INDIRECT COMPENSATION AND BENEFIT PLANS

Given the enormous cost to an organization of benefit packages, managers must carefully assess the benefit that accrues to the organization from those packages. On the one hand, the organization must provide appropriate benefits to its employees. At the same time, the best interest of stockholders and other constituents of the organization requires the firm to manage its resources wisely. Thus it is important to periodically assess the extent to which costs are in line. One way of doing so is through the use of the wage surveys, discussed in Chapter 10. Although these surveys typically ask about wages for specific jobs, questions about benefits can be included as well. Any organization, for example, can learn the average insurance premium costs that other organizations are paying, and even if it cannot match these premiums, the company can nevertheless get a better feel for how close its costs are to those of other firms.

Likewise, some organizations might audit their benefit programs to determine whether or not they are providing a competitive package. As a part of the recruiting process, of course, the organization wants to be seen as an attractive employer so that it can hire high-quality human resources. Thus if other organizations in the labor market are providing special benefits that the organization is not providing, it might have to reconsider this policy. On the other hand, the organization may be providing more benefits than its competitors are providing and might be able to scale back in some areas as a way of controlling cost.

There is one final issue to consider relative to evaluating benefit programs. In many cases these programs are not as effective as they might be simply because the organization has not effectively communicated with the employees about those benefits. As Figure 13.3 shows, some employees are not totally knowledgeable about their benefits. Evidence suggests that awareness about benefits can be increased through communication via several media and that, as awareness increased, so did satisfaction with benefits.[17] The reason for this relationship is underscored by the results of another study that asked employees to estimate the value of the employer's contribution to their benefits. When asked about family coverage, the average estimate was only 38 percent of the actual cost of those benefits to the employer.[18] An organization can never expect to gain the full advantage of its benefit program when employees underestimate the cost of their benefits by such a large degree.

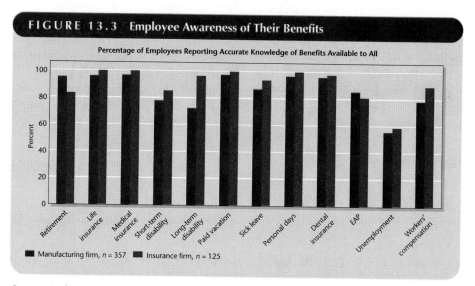

FIGURE 13.3 Employee Awareness of Their Benefits

Source: Andrew Muonio, "How Aware Are Employees of Their Benefits?" *HRMagazine,* May 1997, p. 53; Danehower and Lust, *Benefits Quarterly,* Fourth Quarter 1996.

THE BOTTOM LINE Given the cost and significance of benefits, organizations must do a thorough job of evaluating the effectiveness and costs of the benefits they are providing to their employees. As a center of expertise, the human resource function should take the lead role in evaluating the effectiveness of the organization's benefit program as well as in communicating the significance of those benefits to all employees in the organization.

Chapter Summary

Benefits are costing employers an ever-larger portion of their total labor costs. Organizations sustain these costs because they believe that competitive benefit packages will attract better applicants and help the company retain the employees they have. Although benefit costs are high in the United States, levels of mandated benefits are much higher in Europe and elsewhere. Furthermore, the kinds of benefits that are attractive or appropriate to employees around the world differ considerably. A number of laws provide guidelines for how benefit plans should be administered

Additional laws mandate that all employees must have certain benefits, such as social security, unemployment insurance, and workers' compensation. In addition, many organizations offer optional protection plans such as health and dental insurance coverage and private pension plans.

Paid time off is another important benefit. The most common forms of paid time off are vacation time, holidays, religious days, sick leave, and personal time. This benefit, in particular, varies widely in different parts of the world.

Organizations are also becoming more likely to offer benefits in areas such as wellness programs, childcare, elder care, and employee assistance programs. Finally, some benefits are in the form of services that the employee would otherwise have to pay for and others are true perks.

Because needs and preferences differ, some organizations offer cafeteria-style benefits, where the employee gets to pick and choose the benefits desired. These programs are expensive to run, but they result in employees getting exactly what they want, which makes the benefit program more cost-effective.

Given the enormous cost to an organization of compensation and benefit packages, it is clearly important that managers carefully assess the benefit that accrues to the organization from those packages. One key factor in the administration of benefit programs is communications. Employees often underestimate the cost of the benefits provided to them, and this misperception will reduce the effectiveness of any benefit package.

Review and Discussion Questions

1. What are the basic purposes of indirect compensation and benefit programs?

2. How and in what ways do legal considerations impinge on benefit programs in organizations?

3. What are the three basic mandated protection plans? Summarize each one.

4. What are the more common forms of optional protection plans? Summarize each one.

5. What are the basic forms of paid time off provided by some organizations?

6. What are some of the important issues associated with managing paid time off?

7. Identify and summarize four other kinds of basic benefits.

8. What is an employee assistance program?

9. What is a cafeteria-style benefit plan? What are its strengths and weaknesses?

10. Why is it especially important to evaluate the effectiveness of an organization's indirect compensation and benefit plans?

Closing Case

Flexible Benefits Are All the Rage

Whereas most benefits packages once all looked about the same, in today's competitive business climate flexible benefit programs are all the rage. By flexible, experts mean that companies are giving employees more choices about their benefits and/or providing benefits that add flexibility to the daily lives of employees.

For example, take the case of Katherine Lechler, a young graphics designer for a trade publication. Her employer provides high-quality on-site childcare for her two children. She pays about 20 percent less than she would for commercial childcare, has lunch with her children each day, and knows that she can be at their side at a moment's notice. For its part the company gets a higher percentage of Ms. Lechler's work time plus makes it more difficult for her to look for a job with some other company that might not provide the same benefits.

Another increasingly popular benefit is on-site counseling of various types. ATS, for instance, a large telecommunications firm, provides psychological counseling for its employees. People use the service to work through personal and/or family problems, career issues, or just about anything else where a trained psychologist can be of help. Again, the firm benefits as well. The part-time psychologist costs about one-fifth of what ATS saves on hiring new people—the turnover is one-third of its industry average.

Similarly, Marriott International provides a twenty-four-hour toll-free hotline for its employees staffed by social workers. Employees can call for advice on everything from setting up a family budget to dealing with a child's problems at school to selecting the best automobile insurance policy. Marriott spends about $1 million annually to operate the service but estimates that it saves $4 million in reduced absenteeism and lower turnover.

Small businesses are getting in on the act as well. Russell, Karsh, & Hagen, an eleven-person public relations firm in Denver, allows its employees to donate public relations work—on company time—to their favorite charity. Although this type of donation might not be a benefit per se, it nevertheless helps employees see that the firm is interested in supporting activities they value.

Another small public relations firm in New Jersey, Daly Gray, allows staffers to tack on a couple of extra vacation days whenever they travel on company business. The president even donates some of his own frequent flyer miles to make it easier for his employees to travel. And again, both the firm and its employees benefit.

Indeed, these and other kinds of benefits continue to grow in popularity. One recent survey, for example, found that human resource managers expect part-time work options, telecommuting, and flexible work hours to grow significantly by the year 2001. In addition, the same survey found rapid and continuing growth in other benefit options as well, including long-term care insurance, group financial planning, prepaid legal services, group auto insurance, and group homeowners insurance.

Case Questions

1. What do you see as the pluses and minuses for the growing array of benefits for employees? for employers?

2. What circumstances, if any, might prompt a reversal of this trend?

3. What benefits appeal most to you personally?

Sources: "Perks That Work," *Time,* November 9, 1998, pp. 126–130; "Fringe Benefits on the Rise," *USA Today,* October 8, 1997, pp. 1B, 2B; "Bonanza of Job Benefits," *USA Today,* August 3, 1998, p. B2.

Building Human Resource Management Skills

Purpose: The purpose of this exercise is to help you better assess the issues associated with cafeteria-style benefit programs.

Step 1: Assume that you are the human resource manager of a medium-size manufacturing company. Your company currently offers a relatively traditional benefits program. The specifics are as follows:

1. Health insurance: the organization contributes $250 per employee per month, which covers the cost for the employee; employees pay an additional $50 per month per covered dependent.

2. Dental insurance: the organization contributes $50 per month, which covers the cost for the employee; employees pay an additional $10 per month per covered dependent.

3. Life insurance: the organization contributes $20 per month for $40,000 in term life insurance; employees can buy additional units of coverage as a function of annual salary.

4. Vacation: everyone gets two weeks per year.

5. Holidays: everyone gets ten paid holidays per year.

6. Sick time: everyone gets ten sick days per year.

Step 2: Your boss has indicated that the firm wants to go to a cafeteria-style plan, and you are to devise a plan for doing this. Outline as many options as you can think of for such a plan, given the above set of benefits as a starting point.

Ethical Dilemmas in Human Resource Management

 You are the human resource manager for a service organization. Your boss recently read that most employees underestimate the value of the benefits provided to them by their employer and has instructed you to develop a plan for communicating the costs of benefits to your employees. The boss has also instructed you to actually manipulate the information so that it looks better than it really is.

For example, although your firm offers ten sick days per year, the average employee takes only eight days per year and forfeits the unused portion. Your boss, however, wants you to show the value of this benefit as though everyone took the full allotment. Similarly, your firm offers two health insurance options, a standard plan and a premium plan. Both the company and the individual pay more if the premium plan is chosen. Your boss wants you to quote only the cost for the more expensive plan, even though more than half of your workers have chosen the standard plan.

When you questioned these ideas, the boss simply said, "These are the potential costs that we could incur for everyone. Just because someone doesn't take all of his or her sick days or selects the basic insurance, that's the person's choice. The company is willing to pay for ten sick days and for the high-end insurance. So we should get the credit for being generous."

Questions

1. What are the ethical issues in this situation?

2. What are the basic arguments for and against what your boss is instructing you to do?

3. What do you think most managers would do? What would you do?

Human Resource Internet Exercise

 Many companies today post information about their benefits on their Web site. Select any five companies in which you have a personal interest. Visit their Web sites and learn about their benefits. If any of them don't list benefits on their Web sites, continue exploring until you obtain information on five different companies.

Questions

1. Compare and contrast the different benefit packages.

2. What are the advantages and disadvantages of posting information about benefits on a Web site?

3. How effective do you think each site is in terms of actually communicating information about its benefits?

Notes

1. Bureau of National Affairs, U.S. Chamber of Commerce data, January 5, 1995.

2. "Detroit Meets a 'Worker Paradise,'" *Wall Street Journal*, March 3, 1999, pp. B1, B4.

3. Randall S. Schuler and Susan E. Jackson, *Human Resource Management: Positioning for the 21st Century*, 6th ed. (Minneapolis: West Publishing Company, 1996), p. 309.

4. Fran Lipson, "How to Cut the Waste from Workers' Compensation," *HRMagazine*, June 1993, pp. 83–87.

5. Richard Wolfe and Donald Parker, "Employee Health Management: Challenges and Opportunities," *Academy of Management Executive*, Vol. 8, No. 2, 1994, pp. 22–31.

6. For a recent discussion of these issues, see Maureen Minehan, "Islam's Growth Affects Workplace Policies," *HRMagazine*, November 1998, p. 216.

7. Mina Westman and Dov Eden, "Effects of Respite from Work on Burnout: Vacation Relief and Fade-Out," *Journal of Applied Psychology*, August 1997, pp. 516–527.

8. "Employer Benefit Surveys Target Unhealthy Habits," *USA Today*, May 28, 1998, p. 1B.

9. S. Caudron, "The Wellness Pay Off," *Personnel Journal*, July 1990, pp. 55–60.

10. Shirley Hand and Robert Zawacki, "Family-Friendly Benefits: More Than a Frill," *HRMagazine*, October 1994, pp. 79–84.

11. Ellen E. Kossek and V. Nichol, "The Effects of On-Site Child Care on Employee Attitudes and Performance," *Personnel Psychology*, Vol. 45, 1992, pp. 485–509.

12. "Gay Employees Win Benefits for Partners at More Corporations," *Wall Street Journal*, March 18, 1994, p. A1.

13. Rudy Yandrick, "The EAP Struggle: Counselors or Referrers?" *HRMagazine*, August 1998, pp. 90–91.

14. W. J. Sonnenstuhl and Harrison M. Trice, *Strategies for Employee Assistance Programs: The Crucial Balance* (Ithaca, N.Y.: Cornell University ILR Press, 1990).

15. Melissa Barringer and George Milkovich, "A Theoretical Exploration of the Adoption and Design of Flexible Benefit Plans: A Case of Human Resource Innovation," *Academy of Management Review*, April 1998, pp. 305–324.

16. Alison E. Barber, Randall B. Dunham, and R. A. Formisano, "The Impact of Flexible Benefits on Employee Satisfaction: A Field Study," *Personnel Psychology*, Vol. 45, 1992, pp. 55–57.

17. H. W. Hennessey, Pamela L. Perrewe, and W. A. Hochwarter, "Impact of Benefit Awareness on Employee and Organizational Outcomes: A Longitudinal Field Experiment," *Benefits Quarterly*, Vol. 8, No. 2, 1992, pp. 90–96.

18. M. Wilson, Gregory B. Northcraft, and Margaret A. Neale, "The Perceived Value of Fringe Benefits," *Personnel Psychology*, Vol. 38, 1985, pp. 309–320.

PART SIX

Managing the Existing Workforce

CHAPTER 14
Managing Labor Relations

CHAPTER 15
Managing the Work
Environment

CHAPTER 16
Managing the Diverse
Workforce

CHAPTER 17
Managing New
Employment Relationships

14

Managing Labor Relations

CHAPTER OUTLINE

The Role of Labor Unions in Organizations
Historical Development of Unions
Legal Context of Unions
Union Structures

Trends in Unionization
Trends in Union Membership
Trends in Union-Management Relations
Trends in Bargaining Perspectives

The Unionization Process
Why Employees Unionize
Steps in Unionization
Decertification of Unions

The Collective Bargaining Process
Preparing for Collective Bargaining
Setting Parameters for Collective Bargaining

Negotiating Labor Agreements
The Negotiation Process
Barriers to Effective Negotiation
Resolving Impasses

Administering Labor Agreements

CHAPTER OBJECTIVES

After studying this chapter you should be able to:

■ Describe the role of labor unions in organizations.

■ Identify and summarize trends in unionization.

■ Discuss the unionization process.

■ Describe the collective bargaining process.

■ Discuss how labor agreements are negotiated.

■ Summarize how labor agreements are administered.

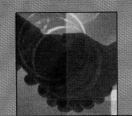

It's Sunday, Memorial Day weekend, in Flint, Michigan. A line of big flatbed trucks pulls up to the delivery doors of the General Motors Flint Metal Center. Drivers and crew members get out and look around nervously. A few minutes later the big doors are open and more than a dozen two-ton metal dies, valued at over $300,000 each, are loaded on the trucks. When all the dies are loaded and tied down, the men again look around nervously, get back into the trucks, and drive off.

Was this a serious case of industrial espionage? After all, these dies are used to turn sheets of steel into the hoods and fenders of the new GMC Sierra pickup trucks and are extremely valuable. Or perhaps this was the work of the United Auto Workers (UAW). After all, the union had been feuding with GM over the new trucks, with GM trying to cut labor costs by reducing the workforce and the union fighting to save jobs and keep the company from moving jobs to Mexico. In truth the real culprits were neither the competition nor the union. GM itself actually "stole" the dies from a plant that was being threatened with a strike.

In June 1998 the UAW had threatened to shut down the metal-stamping plant. This action represented a major concern for GM because this particular plant was being set up to make fenders and bumpers for a new truck model with the potential to be the best-selling and highest profit margin vehicle in GM's 1999 lineup. GM could simply not risk losing production time because of a strike and was taking extreme measures to protect itself.

> *". . . moving these dies is a slap in the union's face . . . and we're not going to tolerate it. The risk, frankly, is on (GM's) side."*
>
> (Reuben Burks, UAW official)*

The dies and other key components for the new trucks were secretly stored in old factories, and even a few bowling alleys, in the area and were then shipped to a stamping plant in Mansfield, Ohio. That plant's contract with GM prohibited a strike at that critical time, and so the Mansfield facility could produce the needed parts if the Flint plant was closed. GM later justified its actions on the grounds that the Sierra truck, the company's most promising new product in a long time, had to be available at the start of the new model year. The UAW, on the other hand, felt it was fighting for jobs for its workers and against trends by GM to move auto jobs outside the United States.

GM did get the trucks out on time, but it also endured one of the costliest strikes in its history. The dispute was so bitter, the loss of jobs so substantial, and the concessions made by GM so sweeping that it is not clear who ultimately "won" the battle. Thus despite predictions that unions were slowly dying in the United States or calls for a new unionism where cooperation replaced conflict and both sides would win, the harsh reality of union-management relationships remains for the most part. Painful, costly strikes are not a thing of the past at all, and management operating under collective bargaining agreements must still find ways to deal with and live with a labor union.

"Automaker's Stealth Move Heightens Labor Tensions," *USA Today,* June 4, 1998, pp. 1B, 2B (*quote on p. 2B); "What's Really behind GM's Strike? A Battle over a Hot New Truck," *Wall Street Journal,* July 28, 1998, pp. A1, A5.

General Motors and its managers have had to contend with one of the most significant challenges facing many businesses today—dealing with organized labor in ways that optimize the needs and priorities of both the business and its employees. When this is done effectively and constructively, both sides benefit. But when relationships between an organization and its unions turn sour, both sides can suffer great costs. While Ford has enjoyed relatively positive relationships with its unions in recent years, GM has not fared as well. And the costs have been enormous.

In this part of the book, we focus on the fundamental issues and challenges associated with managing a workforce. The proceeding parts have dealt with entry-level processes based on the mechanisms of staffing and strategies and techniques used to enhance motivation and performance among workers. By definition, then, these subjects have focused on dynamic, changing, and evolutionary processes. But organizations must also attend to the management of an existing and ongoing workforce. These issues, then, are the focus of this part.

In Chapter 15 we examine the management of the organizational work environment. Managing a diverse workforce is the subject of Chapter 16. And Chapter 17 concludes this part with a discussion of managing new employment relationships. This chapter focuses on the management of labor relations. We start by assessing the role of labor unions in organizations and then examine trends in unionization and the unionization process itself. Collective bargaining is then discussed, followed by a description of the issues involved in negotiating labor agreements. A discussion of the administration of labor agreements concludes this chapter.

THE ROLE OF LABOR UNIONS IN ORGANIZATIONS

- **Labor relations** is the process of dealing with employees who are represented by a union.

- A **labor union** is a legally constituted group of individuals working together to achieve shared job-related goals, including higher pay and shorter working hours.

- **Collective bargaining** is the process by which managers and union leaders negotiate acceptable terms and conditions of employment for workers represented by the unions.

Labor relations is the process of dealing with employees who are represented by a union. A **labor union,** in turn, is a legally constituted group of individuals working together to achieve shared job-related goals, including items such as higher pay, shorter working hours, enhanced benefits, and/or better working conditions. **Collective bargaining,** a specific aspect of labor relations discussed more fully later in this chapter, is the process by which managers and union leaders negotiate acceptable terms and conditions of employment for workers represented by the unions.[1] Although collective bargaining is a term that technically and properly is applied only in settings where employees are unionized, similar processes, of course, often exist in nonunionized settings as well. In these cases, however, they are likely to be labeled as *employee relations* rather than labor relations.

Historical Development of Unions

Figure 14.1 shows the major historical events in the emergence and growth of labor unions in the United States. Indeed, the historical formation of labor unions closely parallels the history of the country itself. For example, the earliest unions in the United States emerged during the Revolutionary War. These unions were called craft unions, meaning that each such union limited itself to representing groups of workers who performed common and specific skilled jobs. For example, one of the first unions was formed by shoemakers in Philadelphia in 1794 (the Journeyman Cordwainers Society of Philadelphia). The union's goal was to enhance the pay and working conditions of all shoemakers.

Many of the earliest unions were local and often confined their activities to a single setting. But in 1834 the first national unions in the United States began to emerge. Throughout the remainder of the nineteenth century, one major union after another began to appear. Among the most significant were the National Typographical Union in 1852, the United Cigarmakers in 1856, and the National Iron Molders in 1859. As the nineteenth century ended, there were thirty national unions with a combined membership of around three hundred thousand individuals.

The first major union to have a significant impact in the United States, however, was the **Knights of Labor,** founded in 1869. Like most other unions, the knights originally represented crafts and sought to improve the lot of its members. But unlike most other national unions, which restricted their organizing activities to a single craft or job, the Knights of Labor expanded its goals and its membership to include workers in numerous fields. The union's objective was quite simple—the leaders of the Knights of Labor believed that if they could control (or represent) the entire supply of skilled labor in the United States, their ability to negotiate favorable wages would be significantly enhanced. Members would actually join the knights directly, as opposed to a later model where they would join a separate union that was affiliated with other more specific unions under an umbrella organization.

The Noble and Holy Order of the Knights of Labor (the union's full name) admitted anyone to membership, regardless of race or creed (which typically

■ **Knights of Labor** was an important early union that expanded its goals and its membership to include workers in numerous fields rather than a single one.

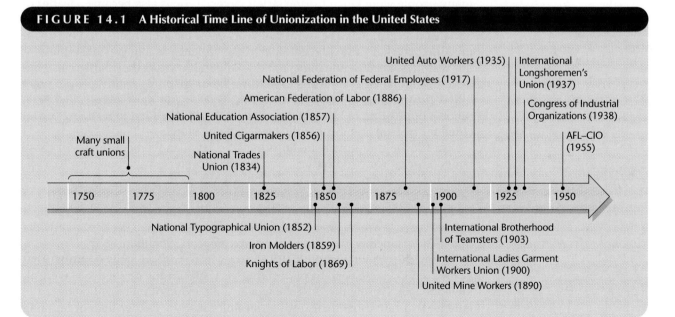

FIGURE 14.1 A Historical Time Line of Unionization in the United States

Source: Ricky Griffin and Ronald Ebert, *Business,* 3rd ed., © 2000. Reprinted by permission of Prentice-Hall, Inc., Upper Saddle River, N.J.

were important considerations for membership in unions at the time) except for those they considered to be "social parasites" (such as bankers). In addition to improving wages, the Knights of Labor sought to replace capitalism with worker cooperatives. The union enjoyed incredible growth for several years, growing from fifty-two thousand members in 1883 to seven hundred thousand members in 1886. But internal strife, disagreement about goals, and disagreement over what should replace the capitalist model all led to the eventual demise of the Knights of Labor. However, the single event that contributed most to this demise was a mass meeting in Chicago's Haymarket Square protesting some earlier violence that stemmed from an attempt to establish an eight-hour workday. When the May 4 meeting was over, further violence left two hundred wounded and resulted in the hanging of several leaders of the knights. By the end of the century, the Knights of Labor had all but disappeared from the labor scene.

Even as the Knights of Labor was dying, however, its replacement was already beginning to gather strength. The **American Federation of Labor,** or **AF of L,** was founded in 1886 by Samuel Gompers. Like the Knights of Labor, the American Federation of Labor comprised various craft unions. But unlike the Knights of Labor, the AF of L sought not to get involved in legislative and political activities, but instead focused its efforts on improved working conditions and better employment contracts. Also unlike the Knights of Labor, the AF of L served as an umbrella organization, with members joining individual unions that were affiliated with the AF of L, as opposed to directly joining the AF of L itself.

While the AF of L focused exclusively on the "business" of unions, a number of other more radical and violent union movements developed in the wake of the demise of the Knights of Labor. For example, under the leadership of Eugene V. Debs the American Railway Union (ARU) battled the railroads (especially the Pullman Company of Pullman car fame) mostly over wages, and many people were killed during strike violence. Debs also became a leader of the Socialist Party and actually ran for president of the United States on the Socialist ticket in 1920. The Industrial Workers of the World consisted mostly of unskilled workers and advocated extreme violence as a means of settling labor disputes. Because the miners and textile mill owners they battled also believed in violence as a means of settling labor disputes, many people were killed during strikes organized by the *Wobblies,* as they were called. The union's opposition to U.S. involvement in World War I led to its being prosecuted for treason and most of the leaders being jailed.

But for the more mainstream organized labor movement, many of these fringe groups were too radical, and workers preferred the business-like approach of the AF of L. As a result, the AF of L grew rapidly throughout the early decades of the twentieth century. Indeed, by the end of World War I, it had a total membership of more than five million individuals. Over the next several years, however, membership in the AF of L began to decline, and by the mid-1930s its membership stood at approximately 2.9 million.

One of the weaknesses of the AF of L was its continued focus on crafts. That is, only skilled craftspersons performing very specifically defined jobs were allowed to join. During the 1930s, however, a new kind of unionization began to emerge that had as its focus industrial unionization. Rather than organizing workers across companies or across industries based on their craft, this new

◾ The **American Federation of Labor,** or **AF of L,** was another early union; it sought not to get involved in legislative and political activities, but instead focused its efforts on improved working conditions and better employment contracts.

type of union activity focused on organizing employees by industry, regardless of their craft or skills or occupation.

In the late 1930s, John L. Lewis of the United Mine Workers led a dissenting faction of members of the AF of L to form a new labor organization called the **Congress of Industrial Organizations,** or **CIO.** The CIO was the first major representative of the new approach to unionization noted above. The CIO quickly began to organize the automobile, steel, mining, meatpacking, paper, textile, and electrical industries. By the dawn of the early 1940s, CIO unions had almost five million members.

In the years following World War II, union memberships in the AF of L and the CIO, as well as other unions, was gradually increasing. However, a series of bitter strikes during that same era also led to public resentment and calls for union reform. And Congress did indeed intervene to curtail the power of unions. The AF of L and the CIO then began to contemplate a merger as a way of consolidating their strength. Eventually, in 1955, the AFL-CIO was formed, with a total membership of around fifteen million employees. Union membership since that time, however, has been quite erratic, a fact that we discuss more fully in the next section. "Point/Counterpoint" highlights some of the basic arguments for and against the viability of unions today. It sheds some light on the question of whether or not unions still have a role in contemporary society. First, however, we examine the legal context of unions and common union structures.

■ Another important early union was the **Congress of Industrial Organizations,** or **CIO,** which focused on organizing employees by industry, regardless of their craft, skills, or occupation.

Legal Context of Unions

Owing in part to the tumultuous history of labor unions in the United States, a variety of laws and other regulations have been passed, some of which are intended to promote unionization and union activities, whereas others are intended to limit or curtail them. As early as 1806 the local courts in Philadelphia declared the cordwainers to be, by its very existence, in restraint of trade, and so illegal. The *Cordwainer Doctrine,* as it became known, dominated the law's view of unions until 1843 when the Massachusetts Supreme Court, in *Commonwealth v. Hunt,* ruled that unions were not by their very nature in restraint of trade, but that this charge had to be proven in each individual case. This decision led to increased union activity, but organizations responded by simply firing union organizers. Further, after the Sherman Antitrust Act was passed in 1890, business once again sought (successfully) court injunctions against unions for restraint of trade. By the 1920s organizations also sought to identify union leaders as communists in order to reduce public sympathy and give the government an excuse to move on the unions.

By the end of the 1920s, the country was in the grips of the Great Depression, and the government soon intervened in an attempt to end work stoppages and start the economy on the road to recovery. The first significant piece of legislation was the **National Labor Relations Act** passed in 1935. This act is more commonly referred to as the **Wagner Act** and still forms the cornerstone of contemporary labor relations law. The basic purpose of the Wagner Act was to grant power to labor unions and to put unions on a more equal footing with managers in terms of the rights of employees. Among its most important provisions are that it gives workers the legal right to form unions, the legal right to bargain collectively with management, and the legal right to engage in group activities such as strikes to accomplish their goals. Moreover, this act

■ The **National Labor Relations Act,** passed in 1935 and more commonly referred to as the **Wagner Act,** granted power to labor unions and put unions on a more equal footing with managers in terms of the rights of employees.

POINT/COUNTERPOINT   Are Labor Unions Still Needed?

 Labor unions were initially formed to try to equalize the power between labor and management. Since management controlled more resources, labor could have power only if individual workers united in some concerted effort. This approach would allow workers to enjoy the rights they deserved and to deal with management as equals. But, over time, some people have claimed that unions have become too powerful and too interested in political agendas that were not always in the country's best interests. Others simply argue that labor is now the equal to management, and because effective management requires granting workers power and discretion, unions are simply no longer needed.

POINT . . . Labor unions are no longer needed in the United States because . . .	COUNTERPOINT . . . But labor unions still serve important functions and so are needed because . . .
Employees already have clear rights, and nonunion companies often offer better pay and conditions than do unionized companies.	Employees without unions only have the rights management chooses to grant, rather than those the workers might actually deserve. Would nonunion companies offer those levels of pay and benefits without the continued threat of unionization?
Unions raise pay without regarding costs and so hurt U.S. competitiveness.	What is the good of improving competitive position if it comes at the cost of jobs and fair pay for U.S. employees?
Unions are largely corrupt.	There is a history of corruption in many unions, but there have been extensive efforts aimed at cleaning up this problem.
Union leaders pursue political agendas that are at odds with the interests of their members.	Individual workers often see only what is in their own best interests, without seeing how some policies can hurt other workers and, in the long run, hurt themselves as well.
Unions interfere with more progressive management efforts aimed at improving competitiveness in international markets.	Union-management cooperation has led to situations where competitive advantage has been gained. Saturn (the auto company) claims that cooperation with the UAW has led to lower production costs and better quality—sources of competitive advantage. The key is to get unions involved in decision making.

So . . .   It is reasonable to suggest that unions still have a function, and the threat of unionization probably continues to play a role in management decisions to implement more "enlightened" policies. But the role of unions will probably need to change (and already is changing). Unions need to become strategic partners with management to help ensure that U.S. companies survive and prosper—which is in everyone's best interests. But unions must continue to fight for employee rights and to serve as the voice of employees who believe they have been wronged by management. It will be interesting to see how unions manage to change, or whether they even manage to do so. If they do not, they may well become "obsolete."

The legal context of labor unions is an important backdrop for all labor relations. Moreover, this context is strongly rooted in the historical evolution of labor relations. For example, the Taft-Hartley Act (more formally known as the Labor Management Relations Act) was passed in 1947 to curtail and limit certain union practices. These protesters are members of the International Ladies' Garment Workers Union. They are picketing nonunion garment shops in downtown Los Angeles in 1948 as a demonstration of their strength. Some of their signs are clearly directed at the Taft-Hartley Act and Taft himself. But the law remains intact and still plays an important role in labor relations today.

also forces employers to bargain with properly elected union leaders and prohibits employers from engaging in certain unfair labor practices such as discriminating against union members in hiring, firing, and promotion.

The Wagner Act also established the **National Labor Relations Board,** or **NLRB,** to administer its provisions. Today the NLRB still administers most labor law in the United States. For example, the board defines the units with which managers much collectively bargain, and it oversees most elections held by employees that will determine whether or not they will be represented by a union.

In the previous section, we noted congressional activity in the years following World War II that curtailed union power. The most important piece of legislation in this era was the **Labor Management Relations Act,** also know as the **Taft-Hartley Act,** passed in 1947. This act was passed in response to public outcries against a wide variety of strikes in the years following World War II. The basic purpose of the Taft-Hartley Act was to curtail and limit union practices. For example, the Taft-Hartley Act specifically prohibits such practices as requiring extra workers solely as a means to provide more jobs and refusing to bargain with management in good faith. It also outlawed an arrangement called the **closed shop,** which refers to a workplace where only workers who are already union members may be hired by the employer.

▨ The **National Labor Relations Board,** or **NLRB,** administers most labor law in the United States.

▨ The **Labor Management Relations Act,** also known as the **Taft-Hartley Act,** was passed in 1947 in response to public outcries against a wide variety of strikes in the years following World War II; it curtailed and limited union powers.

▨ A **closed shop** refers to a workplace in which only workers who are already union members may be hired by the employer.

■ A **union-shop agreement** allows an employer to hire a nonunion member but requires the new employee to join the union within a specified time to keep his or her job.

Section 7 of the Taft-Hartley Act also allows states, if they wish, to further restrict union security clauses, such as closed-shop agreements. Roughly twenty states took advantage of this opportunity and have passed laws that also outlaw **union-shop agreements** (where a nonunion member can be hired but must join the union within a specified time to keep his or her job) and various other types of union security agreements. These laws are known as "right to work" laws, and the states that have adopted them (which are predominantly in the southeast) are known as right-to-work states.*

The Taft-Hartley Act also established procedures for resolving strikes that are deemed threatening to the national interest. For example, the president of the United States has the authority under the Taft-Hartley Act to request an injunction that prohibits workers from striking for sixty days. The idea is that during this so-called cooling-off period labor and management stand a greater chance of being able to resolve their differences. For example, in February 1997 the union representing the pilots at American Airlines announced that its members had voted to strike. Within minutes of this announcement, President Clinton invoked the Taft-Hartley Act ordering the union to cancel its strike. His argument was that since American is the nation's largest air carrier, a shutdown would be extremely detrimental to national interests. In addition, the Taft-Hartley Act extended the powers of the NLRB. For example, the act empowered the NLRB to regulate unfair union practices.

■ The **Landrum-Griffin Act** (officially called the **Labor Management Reporting and Disclosure Act**) was passed in 1959 and focused on eliminating various unethical, illegal, and undemocratic union practices.

A final significant piece of legislation affecting labor relations is the **Landrum-Griffin Act** passed in 1959. Officially called the **Labor Management Reporting and Disclosure Act,** this law focused on eliminating various unethical, illegal, and undemocratic union practices. For instance, the Landrum-Griffin Act requires national labor unions to elect new leaders at least once every five years and states that convicted felons cannot hold national union office (which is

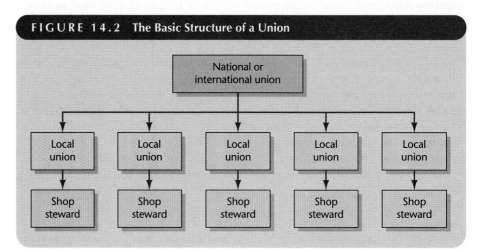

FIGURE 14.2   The Basic Structure of a Union

Source: Ricky Griffin and Ronald Ebert, *Business,* 3rd ed. © 2000. Reprinted by permission of Prentice-Hall, Inc.

* Alabama, Arkansas, Florida, Georgia, Iowa, Kansas, Kentucky, Louisiana, Mississippi, Nebraska, Nevada, North Carolina, North Dakota, South Carolina, South Dakota, Tennessee, Texas, Utah, Virginia, and Wyoming are right-to-work states, although a state can change its status on this issue at any time.

why Jimmy Hoffa was removed as the president of the teamsters). It also requires unions to file annual financial statements with the Department of Labor. And finally, the Landrum-Griffin Act stipulates that unions provide certain information regarding their internal management and finances to all members.

Union Structures

Large labor unions, like all organizations, have unique structures. But most unions have some basic structural characteristics in common. Figure 14.2 shows the basic structure of most unions. The cornerstone of most labor unions, regardless of their size, is local unions, more frequently referred to as "locals." **Locals** are unions that are organized at the level of a single company, plant, or small geographic region. Each local elects its own **shop steward.** The shop steward is a regular employee who functions as a liaison between union members and supervisors.

Local unions are usually clustered by geographic region and coordinated by a regional officer. These regional officers, in turn, report to and are a part of a national governing board of the labor union. The national affairs of a large union are generally governed by an executive board and a president, who are usually elected by the union members. This election takes place at an annual national convention that all union members are invited to and are encouraged to attend.

The president is almost always a full-time union employee and may earn as much money as a senior manager of a business. The executive board functions much more like a board of directors and is generally composed of individuals who serve on the board in addition to their normal functions as employees of an organization. And just as a large business has various auxiliary departments such as public relations and a legal department, large national unions have auxiliary departments as well. These auxiliary departments may handle such things as legal affairs of the union, oversee collective bargaining issues, and provide various assistance and service to the local unions as requested and needed.

> ■ **Locals** are unions that are organized at the level of a single company, plant, or small geographic region.
>
> ■ The **shop steward,** an elected position in a local union, is a regular employee who functions as a liaison between union members and supervisors.

THE BOTTOM LINE All managers need to have a basic understanding of the legal context of labor unions and the relevant structural dimensions of unions with which they interact. The human resource function, in particular, can serve as a critical center of expertise in providing more detailed and technical assistance and information regarding both legal issues and structural characteristics that may be relevant to individual managers.

T R E N D S   I N   U N I O N I Z A T I O N

Although understanding the historical, legal, and structural context of labor unions is important, so too is an appreciation of other trends regarding factors such as union membership, union-management relations, and bargaining perspectives. These topics are discussed in the sections that follow. "Human Resources in the Twenty-first Century" describes some other interesting trends in unionization.

Emerging Trends in Unionization

As noted in the text, unionization among U.S. workers has been on the decline for some time and will probably continue in that direction for the foreseeable future. Although there is clearly an increase in unionization in the service sector of the economy, this gain has been more than offset in the rest of the economy. Will unions disappear? Probably not, but they may look different in the next century than they have looked in the past. For example, some experts suggest that a basic transformation in unionism and the relationship between unions and management is already taking place. A key component of this transformation is an end to the adversarial relationship between labor and management.

The Saturn plant in Tennessee is often pointed to as an example of how such a system can work. Saturn was created several years ago by General Motors as a new kind of U.S. car company modeled on the Japanese system of cooperation between management and workers. To understand how this model works, consider an event at the Saturn plant a few years ago: GM instructed Saturn management to increase its production quotas, and the UAW registered its strong opposition to the proposed change. Since workers in general have long resisted management's efforts to boost productivity, this response may not sound so unusual on the surface. But the basis for resistance was very unusual in this instance—employees were concerned that increased production would have to come at the price of decreased quality, and they believed that producing high-quality automobiles was the more important goal. Eventually, GM management agreed and dropped its insistence on higher production! And while labor relations at Saturn aren't perfect, they are generally far better than throughout the rest of GM.

A related trend in unionization is an increase in concessionary bargaining. This type of bargaining, which gained popularity in the 1980s, involves unions making concessions in areas such as wages and work rules in order to help firms survive. In return, unions obtained greater job security for their members. There has been debate, though, as to whether this trend represented a

"I think she's going to be good for Saturn."

(Saturn union leader Mike Bennett, referring to new Saturn president Cynthia Trudell)*

real shift in the way unions and management worked or was simply a "blip" caused by hard economic times. But it has been widely argued that the only real future for unions in the United States lies with their working together with management to improve competitive position and to increase productivity.

Finally, some recent research sheds additional light on unionization trends. For example, research has found that bargaining relationships may be becoming *either* more cooperative or more contentious than they have been in the past, that strikes may become less common, and that concessions involving benefits (rather than wages or work rules) are becoming more common. Thus there is some reason to believe that the basic nature of the relationship between unions and management has already begun changing and will likely continue to change in the same direction.

But notice that the results of this study also point out that bargaining relationships that are not becoming more cooperative are becoming more contentious. That is, the disparity between more and less positive relationships between unions and management may be growing. As a result, the future may bring many instances where the "new" industrial relations model is firmly in place but many others where hostilities are as strong (or stronger) than in the past. Perhaps firms that cannot establish more cooperative relationships with unions will be less likely to prosper in the future, but that remains to be seen. In any case it is interesting to note that the same company that has entered into a new type of agreement with its major unions—General Motors—was also described in the opening case as engaging in less-than-cooperative behavior.

References: "She's Jump-Starting Saturn," *USA Today,* February 19, 1999, p. 3B (*quote on p. 3B); "Union Battles," *Wall Street Journal,* January 11, 1999, p. R27; Charles C. Heckscher, *The New Unionism: Employee Involvement in the Changing Corporation* (New York: Basic Books, 1988); Joel Cutcher-Gershenfeld, Patrick McHugh, and Donald Power, "Collective Bargaining in Small Firms: Preliminary Evidence of Fundamental Change," *Industrial and Labor Relations Review,* Vol. 49, 1996, pp. 195–212; "Cooperation Keeps Saturn Plant Working," *USA Today,* June 24, 1998, p. 1B.

FIGURE 14.3 Trends in Union Membership

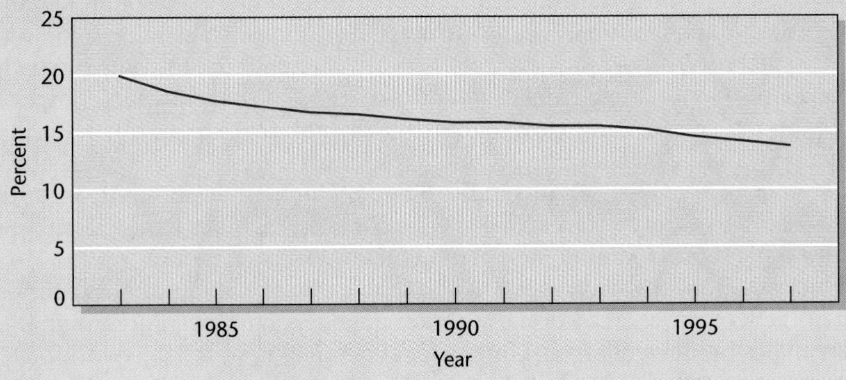

Year	Union or Employee Association Members (thousands)	Union or Association Members as Percent of Wage and Salary Employment (percent)
1983	17,717	20.1
1984	17,340	18.8
1985	16,996	18.0
1986	16,975	17.5
1987	16,913	17.0
1988	17,002	16.8
1989	16,960	16.4
1990	16,740	16.1
1991	16,568	16.1
1992	16,390	15.8
1993	16,598	15.8
1994	16,748	15.5
1995	16,360	14.9
1996	16,269	14.5
1997	16,110	14.1

Source: Wall Street Journal Almanac 1999, p. 248. Reprinted by permission of Dow Jones, Inc. via Copyright Clearance Center, Inc. © 1999 Dow Jones and Company, Inc. All Rights Reserved.

Trends in Union Membership

Since the mid-1950s labor unions in the United States have experienced increasing difficulties in attracting new members. As a result, although millions of U.S. workers still belong to labor unions, union membership as a percentage of the total workforce has continued to decline at a very steady rate. For example, in 1977 more than 26 percent of U.S. wage and salary employees belonged to labor unions. But today that figure is about 14 percent of those workers. Moreover, if government employees are excluded from consideration, then only around 11 percent of wage and salary employees in private industry currently belong to labor unions. These membership trends are shown in Figure 14.3.

Furthermore, just as union membership has continued to decline, so has the percentage of successful union-organizing campaigns. In the years immediately following World War II, for instance, and continuing on through the mid-1960s, most unions routinely won certification elections. (When the union wins such an election, it becomes the sole bargaining agent for the employees involved and they are then considered "unionized.") In recent years, however, labor unions are winning certification fewer than 50 percent of the time in which workers are called upon to vote. From most indications then, the power and significance of labor unions in the United States, while still quite formidable, is also significantly lower than it was just a few decades ago. A number of factors explain the declining membership in labor unions today.

One reason for the decline in union membership is changes in the composition of the workforce. Traditionally, union members have been predominantly white males in blue-collar jobs. But as most people know, today's workforce is increasingly composed of women and ethnic minorities, and these groups have a much weaker tradition of union affiliation. A corollary to these trends has to do with the fact that much of the workforce has shifted toward geographic areas in the south and toward occupations in the service sector in the economy that have also traditionally been less heavily unionized than the manufacturing sector or the economy in general.

A second reason for the decline in union membership in the United States is more aggressive, anti-unionization strategies undertaken by businesses.[2] Although the National Labor Relations Act and other forms of legislation specify strict practices of management vis-à-vis labor unions, companies are still free to pursue certain strategies intended to eliminate or minimize unionization. For example, both Motorola and Procter & Gamble now offer no layoff guarantees for their employees and have created a formal grievance system for all workers. These arrangements were once available only through unions. But because these firms offer them aside from any union contract, employees are likely to see less benefit from a potential union.

Some companies have also worked to create a much more employee-friendly work environment and strive to treat all employees with respect and dignity. One goal of this approach is to minimize the attractiveness of labor unions for employees. And many Japanese manufacturers that have set up shop in the United States have successfully avoided unionization efforts by the United Auto Workers by providing job security, better wages, and a work environment in which employees are allowed to participate and be actively involved in the management of the facilities.

Trends in Union-Management Relations

Some significant trends in union management relations have accompanied the gradual decline in unionization in the United States. In some sectors in the U.S. economy, perhaps most notably the automobile and steel industries, labor unions still remain very strong. In these areas unions have a large membership and considerable power vis-à-vis the organizations in which they work. The United Auto Workers, for example, is still one of the strongest unions in the United States today.

But in most sectors of the economy, labor unions are clearly in a weakened position, and as a result, many have had to take a much more conciliatory stance in their relations with managers and organizations.[3] This attitude con-

Union-management relations continue to change constantly. Consider, for example, the relationship between LTV, a major steel company, and the United Steel Workers (USW). During a period of economic decline in the late 1980s and early 1990s, the USW agreed to absorb pay cuts and to loosen work rules to help LTV become more competitive with the growing number of mini-mills. But when LTV tried to get around some technical agreements with the USW in a joint venture with British and Japanese partners, the union's leadership decided that it had had enough. The USW launched both public relations campaigns, such as these picketing workers, and legal challenges. As a result, LTV's CEO ended up retiring early, and the firm gave in to most of the union's demands.

trasts sharply with the more adversarial relationship that once dominated labor relations in this country. Increasingly, for instance, unions recognize that they don't have as much power as they once held and that it is in their own best interests, as well as the best interests of the workers they represent, to work with, not against, management. Hence union-management relations are in many ways better today than they have been in many years. Admittedly, this improvement is attributable in large part to a weakened power of unions; nevertheless, most experts would agree that union-management relations have indeed improved. "Human Resources Fad, Fashion, or Fact?" discusses some other interesting issues associated with union-management relationships.

Trends in Bargaining Perspectives

Building on the trends identified in the two previous sections, it also follows that bargaining perspectives have changed in recent years. For example, in the past union demands for dramatic increases in wages and salaries characterized most union-management bargaining situations. A secondary issue was usually increased benefits for union members. But now unions often bargain for different kinds of things, such as job security. Of special interest in this area is the trend toward moving jobs to other countries to take advantage of lower labor costs. Thus unions might want to restrict job movement, whereas companies might want to maximize their flexibility vis-à-vis moving jobs to other countries.[4]

HUMAN RESOURCES Fad, Fashion, or Fact?

Changing Relationships between Management and Labor

The opening case of this chapter describes a series of events that took place at General Motors involving its need to bring a new truck on-line in time for 1999 model year while facing possible strikes or slowdowns by the United Auto Workers. Unfortunately for the company, however, its problems escalated rather than improved. On June 5, 1998, twenty-five thousand workers from the firm's Flint, Michigan, plants went on strike. The strike spread quickly and lasted until July 28. By the time the strike was settled, GM estimated that it lost $2.2 billion in sales and even more in terms of lost market share, making it the costliest battle in decades.

How could this happen, and what were the issues behind this costly strike? Can the two sides ever get back together to work cooperatively under a more enlightened industrial relations system? The causes behind the strike were noted earlier: GM was trying to launch a redesigned pickup truck to boost volume and increase profit margins. The company saw the project as critical for maintaining a competitive position in the truck market and, in fact, saw it as having the potential to take over an even bigger share of that market. After years of shrinking market share and profits, then, this new product was critical for the future of GM.

But although the project would result in twenty thousand new jobs in five plants, accompanying efficiencies and automation could also result in the long-term reduction of fifty thousand workers and even more jobs moving to Mexico and Asia. Furthermore, the UAW alleged that GM had not followed through on promises to spend millions on modernizing U.S plants because the company, the union claimed, was planning to shift more production to other countries. Therefore, the UAW was opposing GM at every step along the way. In fact, strikes the previous year had been called in reaction to this plan.

There is an interesting side note to one of these earlier strikes at a Pontiac, Michigan, plant. A union official there commented that, in order to settle the strike, the union made a number of concessions, including agreeing to have repair persons fix problems with the trucks while they were still on the assembly line instead of at the end. Although this move was termed a *concession,* it sounds exactly like the more enlightened employee-involvement systems described earlier, since this arrangement would give the workers more say on when repairs were needed and what types of repairs were needed. But the union claimed that these systems were not working at GM be-

"You pull that stop-line chord twice and you won't be pulling it a third time."

(Ken Summers, UAW official)*

cause of a lack of trust. As the official put it, stopping the line by pulling the "stop-line chord" to make repairs often got workers in trouble with management.

GM was trying to circumvent these labor problems by shifting production to sites less likely to be disrupted by work stoppages. The company finally returned the dies it had spirited away on July 26. But by then the strike had been going on for some time, and things had become ugly. During the strike GM attempted to have the strike declared illegal and, when that failed, threatened to stop medical benefits for striking workers—an unheard of move!

When the fifty-four-day strike finally ended, it was difficult to see what GM had won. The union did agree to new work rules that would increase productivity at the Flint stamping plant and also agreed to settle several other disputes, which should assure labor peace until the national contract expires. But in return GM had to agree to invest some $180 million in plant modernization and to hold onto several plants that were planned for divestiture. Perhaps more critically, the relationship between the UAW and GM has been damaged. Can it be improved? That is not yet clear, although the UAW vice president, William Shoemaker, urged cooperation in a speech he made before two thousand GM managers. On the other hand, employees at the Lordstown, Ohio, GM plant have complained that they are being pressured to increase productivity or else GM will move most of the jobs from that plant to Mexico.

The real issue, then, is whether the relationship between unions and management is really changing. There have clearly been cases of increased cooperation and partnering, but as union membership dwindles and as jobs are shifted to other countries, unions are unlikely to view the situation as one where "everyone wins." In the coming years GM will have to reduce its workforce and cut labor costs if it is to retain its leadership in the auto industry, since both Ford and Daimler-Chrysler are already way ahead in modernization. If GM can accomplish this goal with the cooperation of the UAW, it will truly signal the beginning of a new era in union-management relations, but for now, it may just be business as usual.

References: "What's Really behind GM's Strike? A Battle over a Hot New Truck," *Wall Street Journal,* July 28, 1998, pp. A1, A5 (*quote on p. A5); "What Price Peace?" *Business Week,* August 10, 1998, pp. 24–25; "GM Might Stop Benefits for Workers," *USA Today,* June 26, 1998, p. B1; "Rivals Make Strides after Nasty Strike," *USA Today,* December 16, 1998, pp. B1, B2.

As a result of organization downsizing and several years of relatively low inflation in this country, many unions today opt to fight against wage cuts instead of striving for wage increases. Similarly, organizations might be prone to argue for lower health-care benefits and other benefits for workers, and a common union strategy today is simply to attempt to preserve what currently exists. Unions also place greater emphasis on improved job security for their members. An issue that has become especially important in recent years has been to focus on improved pension programs for employees.

THE BOTTOM LINE   Managers need to understand that although union membership has been declining in recent years, unions are nevertheless still very important in many sectors of the economy. Thus managers should be cognizant of trends in membership, as well as union-management relations and bargaining perspectives.

THE UNIONIZATION PROCESS

The laws discussed earlier, as well as various associated regulations, prescribe a very specific set of steps that employees must follow if they want to establish a union. These laws and regulations also dictate what management can and cannot do during an effort by employees to form a union.

Why Employees Unionize

Why do employees choose to join labor unions? The simplest answer is very straightforward: they believe that they are somehow better off as a result of joining a union than they would be by not joining a union.[5] More precisely, employees are more likely to unionize when they are dissatisfied with some aspect of their job, believe that a union could help make this aspect of the job better, and are not philosophically opposed to unions or to collective action.[6]

But the real answer is much more complex. In the early days of labor unions, people chose to join them because working conditions were in many cases so unpleasant. In the eighteenth and nineteenth centuries, for example, in their quest to earn ever-greater profits some business owners treated their workers with no respect. For example, they often forced their employees to work long hours, there were no minimum wage laws or other controls, and there were no safety standards. As a result, many employees worked twelve, fifteen, or eighteen hours a day and sometimes were forced to work seven days a

Employees choose to join unions for a variety of reasons. For example, many of the workers in the major casinos, hotels, and restaurants in Las Vegas are represented by unions. They elected to first form and then join unions as a way of forcing these businesses to provide them with higher wages and better benefits. Indeed, one labor economist has stated that Las Vegas is the only place in the United States where a "chamber maid or bus boy can make a decent enough living to buy a house." Their income is high enough to do this because of the unions that represent them. Hattie Cantry, shown here, is president of the Culinary Workers Union Local. Her union has over 50,000 members and is one of the fastest-growing locals in the United States.

week. The pay was sometimes just pennies a day, and they received no vacation time or other benefits. Moreover, they worked totally at the whim of their employer, and if they complained about working conditions, they were dismissed. Thus people initially chose to join labor unions because of the strength that lay in the numbers associated with the large-scale labor unions.

In many parts of the United States and in many industries, these early pressures for unionization became an ingrained part of life. Union values and union membership expectations were passed down from generation to generation. This trend typified many industrialized northern cities such as Pittsburgh, Cleveland, and Detroit. In general, parents' attitudes toward unions are still an important determinant of whether an employee will elect to join a union.[7] And as noted earlier, strong unionization pressures still exist in some industries, such as the automobile industry, the steel industry, and other economic sectors that rely on heavy manufacturing.

Steps in Unionization

A number of prescribed steps must be followed if employees are to form and join a labor union. These general steps are shown in Figure 14.4 and described in more detail below.

First, employees must have some interest in joining a union. In some cases this interest may arise because current employees are dissatisfied or unhappy with some aspects of the employment relationship. In other instances existing labor unions may send professional union organizers to nonunionized plants or work facilities to create interest in unionization.[8]

If interest exists in forming a union, the National Labor Relations Board is asked to define the bargaining unit. The **bargaining unit** refers to the specifically defined group of employees who will be eligible for representation by the union. For example, a bargaining unit might be all nonmanagement employees in an organization or perhaps all clerical workers at a specific site within the organization.

Once the bargaining unit has been defined, organizers must then strive to get 30 percent of the eligible workers within the bargaining unit to sign authorization cards requesting a certification election (see Figure 14.5). Signing an authorization card does not necessarily imply that the individual signing the card wants to join a union. Rather, the authorization card simply indicates the individual's belief that an election should be held. If organizers cannot get 30 percent of the workers to sign authorization cards, then the process ends.

But if the required number of signatures is obtained, the next step in forming a union is for organizers to petition the National Labor Relations Board to conduct an election. The board sends one or more representatives, depending on the size of the bargaining unit, to the facility and conducts an election. The election is always conducted via secret ballot. If a simple majority of those voting approve union certification, then the union becomes the official bargaining agent of eligible employees. But if a majority fails to approve certification, the process ends. In this instance organizers cannot attempt to have another election for at least one year.[9]

If, however, the union becomes certified, then its organizers create a set of rules and regulations that will govern the conduct of the union. The organizers also elect officers, establish a meeting site, and began to recruit members from the labor force in the bargaining unit to join the union. Thus the union comes

■ The **bargaining unit** refers to the specifically defined group of employees who will be eligible for representation by the union.

into existence as a representative of the organization's employees who fall within the boundaries of the bargaining unit.

Decertification of Unions

Just because a union becomes certified, however, does not necessarily mean that it will exist in perpetuity. Indeed, under certain conditions an existing labor union may be *decertified*. A company's workers, for example, might become disillusioned with the union and may even come to feel that they are being hurt by the presence of the union in their organization. For example, they may believe that management of the organization is trying to be cooperative and to bargain in good faith but that the union itself is refusing to cooperate.

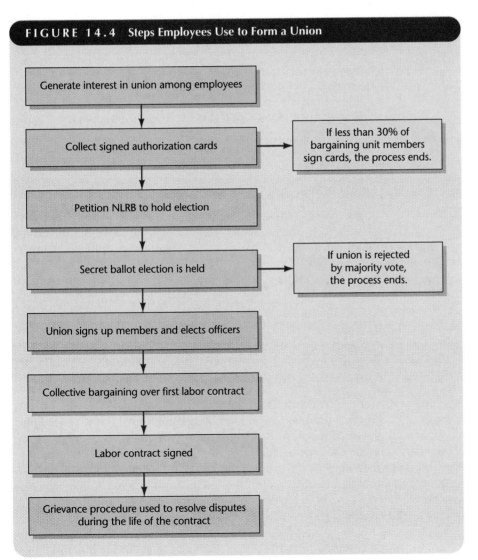

FIGURE 14.4 Steps Employees Use to Form a Union

Generate interest in union among employees

↓

Collect signed authorization cards → If less than 30% of bargaining unit members sign cards, the process ends.

↓

Petition NLRB to hold election

↓

Secret ballot election is held → If union is rejected by majority vote, the process ends.

↓

Union signs up members and elects officers

↓

Collective bargaining over first labor contract

↓

Labor contract signed

↓

Grievance procedure used to resolve disputes during the life of the contract

Source: Ricky Griffin, *Management,* 6th ed. (Boston: Houghton Mifflin, 1999), p. 439. Copyright © 1999 by Houghton Mifflin Company. Reprinted with permission.

FIGURE 14.5 Sample Union Authorization Card

UAL PASSENGER SERVICE AND RESERVATION AGENTS ORGANIZING CAMPAIGN

A-CARD

YES, I want the IAM

I, the undersigned, an employee of United Airlines do hereby authorize the International Association of Machinists and Aerospace Workers (IAM) to act as my collective bargaining agent with the company for wages, hours, and working conditions.

Name (print) _____ **Date** _____

Address (print) _____

City _____ **State** ____ **Zip** _____

Dept _____ **Shift** _____ **Phone** _____

Job Title _____ **Employee #** _____

Sign Here X _____

NOTE: The authorization to be SIGNED and DATED in EMPLOYEE's OWN HAND-WRITING. YOUR RIGHT TO SIGN THIS CARD IS PROTECTED BY FEDERAL LAW.

Make sure your card counts, SIGN and DATE the card before you return it.

These cards will not be disclosed to United Airlines at any time. For further information about how cards are used in the representation process see "How to Win Representation Under the Railway Labor Act."

Please print this page. Once you have completed, signed, and dated your A-card, please mail it to:

UAL Organizing Campaign
IAMAW Lodge 1886
5621 Bowen Ct.
Commerce City, CO 80022-9917

If you have questions or need additional cards, contact campaign headquarters at 1-800-411-6069.

Source: UAL Organizing Campaign http://www.iamnoworg/special/acard.htm

For decertification to occur, two conditions must be met. First, a labor contract cannot be in force (that is, the previous agreement must have expired and a new one not yet approved). And second, the union must have served as the official bargaining agent for the employees for at least one year. If both of these conditions are met, employees or their representatives can again solicit signatures on decertification cards. As with the certification process, if 30 percent of the eligible employees in the bargaining unit sign, then the National Labor Relations Board conducts a decertification election. And again, a majority decision determines the outcome. Thus if a majority of those voting favor decertification, the union is removed as the official bargaining agent for the unit. Once a union has been decertified, a new election cannot be requested for certification for at least one additional year.

Managers need to understand the basic reasons that might motivate their employees to form a union. Managers should also know the basic steps in unionization, as well as the mechanisms through which unions may be decertified.

THE COLLECTIVE BARGAINING PROCESS

When a union has been legally certified, it becomes the official bargaining agent for the workers that it represents. Collective bargaining is generally an ongoing process that includes both the drafting and the administration of a labor agreement.

Preparing for Collective Bargaining

By definition, collective bargaining involves two sides: management representing the employing organization and the labor union representing its employees. The collective bargaining process is aimed at agreement on a binding labor contract that will define various dimensions of the employment relationship for a specified period of time. Thus both management and union leaders must be adequately prepared for a bargaining and negotiation period, since the outcome of a labor negotiation will have long-term effects on both parties.

Management can prepare for collective bargaining in a number of ways. For example, the firm can look closely at its own financial health to provide a realistic picture of what it can and cannot do in terms of wages and salaries for its employees. Management can also do comparative analysis to see what kinds of labor contracts and agreements exist in similar companies and can also research what this particular labor union has been requesting—and settling for—in the past.

The union can and should also undertake a number of actions to prepare for collective bargaining. It, too, should examine the financial health of the company through public financial records and other such sources. And like management, labor can also carefully determine what kinds of labor agreements have been reached in other parts of the country and what kinds of contracts other divisions of the company or other businesses owned by the same corporation may have negotiated in recent times.

Setting Parameters for Collective Bargaining

Another part of preparing for collective bargaining is prior agreement on the parameters that the bargaining session will encompass. In general, two categories of items may be dealt with during labor contract negotiations. One set of items, as defined by law, are **mandatory items.** Mandatory items include wages, working hours, and benefits. If either party expresses a desire to negotiate over one or more of these items, the other party has to agree.

Beyond these mandatory items, however, almost any other aspect of the employment relationship is also subject to negotiation as long as both sides agree. These items are called **permissive items.** For example, if the union expresses an interest in having veto power over the promotion of certain man-

■ **Mandatory items,** including wages, working hours, and benefits, must be included as part of collective bargaining if either party expresses a desire to negotiate over one or more of them.

■ **Permissive items** are items that may be included in collective bargaining if both parties agree.

agers to higher-level positions and if for some reason the company is willing to agree to this item as a point of negotiation, then it would be permissible to enter this issue into negotiations.

But some items are not permissible for negotiation under any circumstances. For example, in a perfect world, management might want to include a clause in the labor contract specifying that the union promises to not strike. However, legal barriers prohibit such clauses from being installed in labor contracts, and therefore this clause would not be permissible.

THE BOTTOM LINE Managers should know both the steps and the importance of thorough preparation for a collective bargaining session with labor representatives. Moreover, managers should also understand the mandatory, permissive, and prohibited items than can and cannot be included in collective bargaining.

NEGOTIATING LABOR AGREEMENTS

After appropriate preparation by both parties, the actual negotiation process itself begins. Of course, barriers may also arise during this phase, and bargaining impasses may result in strikes or other actions.

The Negotiation Process

Generally speaking, the negotiation process involves representatives from management and the labor union meeting at agreed-upon times and at agreed-upon locations and working together to attempt to reach a mutually acceptable labor agreement. In some instances, the negotiation process might be relatively brief and cordial. But in other instances it might be very lengthy, spanning weeks or perhaps even months, and also be quite acrimonious. For example, the labor agreement reached between the owners and the union representing the professional baseball players in late 1996 took several years to negotiate, and the negotiations were interrupted by a players' strike.

A useful framework for understanding the negotiation process refers to the bargaining zone,[10] as shown in Figure 14.6. During their preparations for negotiation, both sides are likely to attempt to define three critical points. For the organization the bargaining zone and its three intermediate points include the employer's maximum limit, the employer's expectation, and the employer's desired result on items being negotiated. For example, the organization might have as a desired result a zero increase in wages and benefits (also known as management's "target point"). But the organization also recognizes that this outcome is very unlikely and actually expects to provide a modest increase in wages and benefits totaling perhaps 4 to 5 percent. But if preparations are done thoroughly, managers also know the maximum amount they are willing to pay, which might be as high as 7 or 8 percent (management's "resistance point"). Note that in this example management would rather suffer through a strike than agree to more than an 8 percent pay increase.

Negotiating labor contracts is one of the most important parts of labor relations. When Daimler-Benz merged with Chrysler to form the new DaimlerChrysler, the firm found it necessary to carefully review all of its existing labor contracts and take steps to create more standardization and equity among them. These Detroit workers, for example, build the Jeep Grand Cherokee and Dodge Viper. They are listening intently as their union leaders present a proposed new contract just negotiated with the company. And as they left the meeting they voted overwhelmingly to approve the new four-year contract.

On the other side of the table, the labor union also defines a three-point bargaining zone for itself. These three points cover the union's minimum acceptable limit on what it will take from management (union resistance point; the settlement level below which the union will strike), its own expectations as to what management is likely to agree to, and the most it can reasonably expect to get from management (union target point). For instance, the labor union might feel that it has to provide a minimum increase in wages and benefits to its members of 2 to 3 percent. The union expects a settlement of around 5 percent but would realistically like to get 9 or 10 percent. Furthermore, in the spirit of bargaining it may well make an opening demand to management as high as 12 percent.

Hence during the opening negotiation session, labor might inform management that it demands a 12 percent wage and benefit increase. And the employer might begin by stating emphatically that no increases should be expected. Assuming, however, that there is some overlap between the organization's and the union's demands and expectations in the bargaining zone (a positive settlement zone) and assuming that both sides are willing to compromise and work hard to reach an agreement, it is likely that an agreement will, in fact, be attained. Where exactly the final agreement falls depends on the relative bargaining power of the two parties. This power is a function of many factors such as negotiating skills, data on other settlements, and the financial resources needed to either call for (for the union) or survive (for management) a strike.

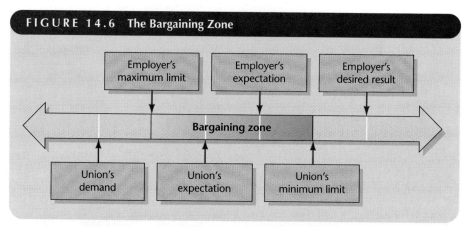

FIGURE 14.6 The Bargaining Zone

Source: Ricky Griffin and Ronald Ebert, *Business,* 5th ed. Reprinted by permission of Prentice-Hall, Inc., Upper Saddle River, N.J.

Much of the actual negotiation process revolves around each party trying to discover the other's resistance point without revealing its own. Since this point represents the least favorable settlement the party is willing to accept, the opponent who discovers that point makes a "final" offer exactly at the resistance point. So, for example, if the union discovered that management was willing to go as high as 8 percent before breaking off negotiations (and facing a strike), the union would then make an offer at 8 percent and indicate that it was their final offer. Since, by definition, management would rather pay 8 percent than have a strike, the parties should settle at 8 percent, which is actually the most favorable contract the union could have possibly won. Incidentally, once a party makes a true "final offer," it cannot back away from that position without losing face in the negotiations. As a result, parties usually leave themselves some room for further negotiations and use phrases such as "I cannot imagine our members accepting anything less than an 8 percent raise," and "I'm sure they would walk out on strike if we came back with less."

The resulting agreement is not necessarily the end of the bargaining process. First, the union membership must ratify the new contract agreement. If the membership votes to reject the contract (which typically reflects internal union politics more than anything else), the parties must return to the bargaining table. But even before union members vote, a final step in the bargaining process must be followed. As soon as an agreement is reached, both parties begin to make public statements about how tough a negotiator the other party was. Both acknowledge that they really wanted a lot more but that the other party was so good that this agreement was the best they could come up with and they hope their constituents can live with it. This posturing is to help both parties "sell" the agreement to their constituencies and also to allow both parties to maintain their image as strong negotiators no matter how one-sided the final agreement might be. Once ratified, this agreement then, in turn, forms the basis for a new labor contract.

Barriers to Effective Negotiation

The foremost barrier to effective negotiation between management and labor is when the bargaining zones of the respective sides do not coincide (that is, there is a negative settlement zone). For example, if management's upper limit for a wage increase is 3.5 percent and the union's minimum limit for what it is willing to accept is 5 percent, then there is no overlap in bargaining zones and the two sides will almost certainly be unable to reach agreement. Beyond such differences in bargaining zones, however, other barriers to effective negotiation can also come into play.

For example, sometimes a long history of acrimonious relationships between management and labor makes it difficult for the two sides to negotiate in good faith. If, for example, the labor union believes that management has a history of withholding or distorting information and that management therefore approaches negotiation from the standpoint of distrust and manipulation, then the union will be very suspicious of any proposal made by management and may be unwilling to accept almost any suggestion made by management. Of course, the same pattern can hold from the other side as well, with management being extremely distrustful of the labor union.

Negotiations can also be complicated by inept negotiators and poor communication between negotiators. Effective negotiation is a truly critical skill and one that not everyone possesses. Thus if managers select as a representative someone who doesn't understand the negotiation process very well, difficulties are likely to arise.

Hopefully, however, as a result of diligent negotiation, management and labor will be able to agree on a mutually acceptable labor contract. On the other hand, if after a series of bargaining sessions, management and labor cannot agree on a new contract or a contract to replace an existing contract, then either or both sides might declare that they have reached an impasse. An **impasse** is simply a situation in which one or both parties believe that reaching an agreement is not imminent.

Resolving Impasses

If labor and management have reached an impasse, either or both sides can do a number of things in an attempt to break the impasse. The basic objective of most of these tactics is to force the other side to alter or redefine its bargaining zone so that an accord can be reached.

The most potent weapon that the union holds is the potential for a strike. A **strike** occurs when employees walk off their jobs and refuse to work. In the United States most strikes are called economic strikes because they are triggered by impasses over mandatory bargaining items such as salaries and wages. During a strike workers representing the union frequently march at the entrance to the employer's facility with signs explaining their reasons for striking. This action is called **picketing** and is undertaken to elicit sympathy for the union and to intimidate management.

Two less extreme tactics that unions sometimes use are boycotts and slowdowns. A **boycott** occurs when union members agree not to buy the products of a targeted employer. A **slowdown** occurs when instead of striking, workers perform their jobs at a much slower pace than normal. A variation on the slowdown occurs when union members agree, sometimes informally, to call in sick in large numbers on certain days. Pilots at American Airlines engaged in a massive "sick out" in early 1999, causing the airline to cancel thousands of flights before a judge ordered the pilots back to work.

Some kinds of strikes and labor actions are illegal. Foremost among these is the so-called **wildcat strike.** A wildcat strike occurs during the course of a

▪ An **impasse** is a situation in which one or both parties believe that reaching an agreement is not imminent.

▪ A **strike** occurs when employees walk off their jobs and refuse to work.

▪ **Picketing** occurs when workers representing the union march at the entrance to the employer's facility with signs explaining their reasons for striking.

▪ A **boycott** occurs when union members agree not to buy the products of a targeted employer.

▪ A **slowdown** occurs when instead of striking, workers perform their jobs at a much slower pace than normal.

▪ A **wildcat strike** occurs during the course of a labor contract and is usually undertaken in response to a perceived injustice on the part of management.

labor contract and is usually undertaken in response to a perceived injustice on the part of management. Because strikes are not legal during the course of a binding labor agreement, a wildcat strike is also, at least theoretically, unauthorized by the strikers' union.

Management also has certain tactics that it may employ in its efforts to break an impasse. One possibility is called a lockout. A **lockout** occurs when the employer denies employees access to the workplace. Managers must be careful when they use lockouts, however, because the government closely regulates this practice. A firm cannot lock out its employees simply to deprive them of wages in an effort to gain power during the labor negotiation. But suppose, however, the employer has a legitimate business need for locking out its employees. If this business need can be carefully documented, then a lockout might be legal. For example, in 1998 ABC locked out its off-camera employees because they staged an unannounced one-day strike during a critical broadcasting period.[11] Similarly, almost half of the 1998–99 NBA season was lost when team owners locked out their players over contract issues.[12] Management also occasionally uses temporary workers or replacements for strikers. These individuals are called strikebreakers. Conflict sometimes erupts between strikebreakers attempting to enter an employer's workplace and picketers representing the interest of the union at the employer's gates.

Sometimes the various tactics described above are successful in resolving the impasse. For instance, after workers have gone out on strike, the organization may change its position and indeed modify its bargaining zone to accommodate potentially larger increases in pay. After experiencing a strike, the organization may realize that the costs of failing to settle are greater than it believed and so is willing to give more to avoid a longer strike (in other words, the company's resistance point has shifted). But in many situations other alternatives to resolve an impasse, such as the use of mediation and arbitration, are also available.

In **mediation** a neutral third party, called the mediator, listens to and reviews the information presented by both sides. The mediator then makes an informed recommendation and provides advice to both parties as to what she or he believes should be done. For example, suppose the impasse centers around wage increases, with the union demanding 8 percent and the company willing to pay 5 percent. The mediator may listen to both sides and review all the evidence and may subsequently conclude that because of the financial profile of the company and because of other labor negotiations in other industries, 5 percent is both fair and all the organization can afford to pay. This advice is then provided to both sides. However, the union doesn't have to accept this information and can continue its efforts to obtain a higher wage increase from the employer.

Yet another alternative to resolving impasses is arbitration. In **arbitration** both sides agree in advance that they will accept the recommendations made by an independent third-party arbitrator. Like the mediator, this individual listens to both sides of the picture and presents and reviews all the evidence. But in arbitration the information that results is placed in the form of a proposed settlement agreement that the parties have agreed in advance to accept. Thus the arbitrator imposes a settlement on the parties, and the impasse ends.

But there is some belief that arbitrators tend to impose settlements that "split the difference." If the parties believe that, they will have an incentive to stick to their original positions and not move toward a settlement, since each such move shifts the middle further away from their target point.[13] As such, the threat of arbitration might "chill" the negotiation process and actually make a negotiated

■ A **lockout** occurs when the employer denies employees access to the workplace.

■ In **mediation** a neutral third party, called the mediator, listens to and reviews the information presented by both sides and then makes an informed recommendation and provides advice to both parties as to what she or he believes should be done.

■ In **arbitration** both sides agree in advance that they will accept the recommendations made by an independent third-party arbitrator.

settlement *less* likely. An alternative form of arbitration has therefore been proposed that, it is argued, should increase the parties' willingness to negotiate a settlement by potentially imposing "strikelike" costs on the parties.[14]

Under **final-offer arbitration** the parties bargain until impasse. At that point the two parties submit their final offers to the arbitrator. Under traditional arbitration the arbitrator is then free to impose a settlement at any point he or she wishes. But under final-offer arbitration the arbitrator has only two choices for the imposed settlement—the two parties' final offers. That is, the arbitrator must select either one or the other final offer *as the imposed settlement.* Thus the party that does not bargain in good faith may get everything it wants in the arbitrator's decision but may just as easily lose everything. Under such a system the parties are more willing to try to reach a settlement on their own rather than go to the arbitrator. Professional baseball uses final-offer arbitration to resolve contract disputes between individual players and owners.

■ Under **final-offer arbitration** the parties bargain until impasse and then submit their final offers to the arbitrator.

THE BOTTOM LINE   Managers should understand the basic issues and processes involved in negotiating labor agreements. In particular, they need to be familiar with the negotiation process and barriers to effective negotiation. Moreover, they should also understand the various ways through which impasses get resolved.

ADMINISTERING LABOR AGREEMENTS

Another key clause in the labor contracts that are negotiated between management and labor is precise agreements as to how the labor agreement will be enforced. In some cases enforcement is, of course, very clear. If the two sides agree that the company will increase the wages it pays to its employees 2 percent a year over the next three years according to a prescribed increase schedule, then there is little opportunity for disagreement. Wage increases can be mathematically calculated, and union members will see the effects in their paychecks. But other provisions of many labor contracts are much more subjective and thus are more prone to misinterpretation and different perceptions.

For example, suppose a labor contract specifies how overtime assignments are to be allocated in the organization. Such allocation strategies are often relatively complex and suggest that the company may have to take into account a variety of factors such as seniority, previous overtime allocations, the hours or days in which the overtime work is needed, and so forth. Now suppose that a supervisor in the factory is attempting to follow the labor contract and offers overtime to a certain employee. This employee, however, wants to check with his or her spouse or partner before accepting the overtime offer. The supervisor, however, may feel a time crunch and be unable to wait as long as the employee would like and, as a result, may end up awarding the overtime opportunity to another employee. The first employee may feel aggrieved by this course of action and elect to protest.

When there are differences of opinions about issues such as overtime, the individual labor union member takes the complaint to the shop steward, a union officer described earlier in this chapter. The shop steward listens to the complaint, forms an initial impression, and has the option of advising the employee that the supervisor handled things appropriately. But other appeal mechanisms are available if the shop steward refutes the employee.

And, of course, if the shop steward agrees with the employee, she or he may also follow prescribed methods for dealing with this situation. The prescribed methods might include starting with the supervisor to listen to his or her side of the story and in continued lines of appeal on up the hierarchy of both the labor union and the company. In some cases mediation and arbitration may also be called into play at this stage, as well in an effort to resolve the agreement. For example, one potential resolution to this particular aggrievement would be to reassign the overtime opportunity to the original employee. Or the overtime opportunity may stay with the second employee with the first employee still receiving pay.

THE BOTTOM LINE   All managers need to have a complete and thorough understanding of how relevant labor contracts are administered. A lack of understanding, for example, can result in strained labor-management relations, lawsuits, and more acrimonious bargaining processes for future contracts.

Chapter Summary

Labor relations is the process of dealing with employees who are represented by a union. A labor union is a legally constituted group of individuals working together to achieve shared job-related goals. Collective bargaining is the process by which managers and union leaders negotiate acceptable terms and conditions of employment for those workers represented by the unions. The historical formation of labor unions in the United States closely parallels the history of the country. A variety of laws and other regulations have been passed, some of which are intended to promote unionization and union activities, whereas others are intended to limit or curtail union activities. And like any large organization, labor unions also have structures that facilitate their work.

Since the mid-1950s labor unions in the United States have experienced increasing difficulties in attracting new members. Indeed, while millions of U.S. workers still belong to labor unions, union membership as a percentage of the total workforce has continued to decline at a very steady rate. Increasingly, unions recognize that they don't have as much power as they once held and that it is in their own best interests, as well as the best interests of the workers they represent, to work with, not against,

management. Bargaining perspectives have also altered in recent years.

Employees must follow a very specific set of steps if they want to establish a union. First, employees must be interested in joining a union. If interest exists in forming a union, the National Labor Relations Board is asked to define the bargaining unit. Once the bargaining unit has been defined, organizers strive to get 30 percent of the eligible workers within the bargaining unit to sign authorization cards requesting a certification election. If organizers cannot get 30 percent of the workers to sign authorization cards, the process ends. But if the required number of signatures is obtained, the next step in forming a union is for organizers to petition the National Labor Relations Board to conduct an election. If the union becomes certified, then its organizers create a set of rules and regulations that will govern the conduct of the union. Under certain conditions an existing labor union may be decertified.

Collective bargaining involves management representing the employing organization and the labor union representing its employees. The collective bargaining process is aimed at agreement on a binding labor contract that will define various dimensions of the employment relationship for a specified period of time. One important part of preparing for collective bargaining is prior agreement on the parameters that the bargaining session will encompass.

Generally speaking, the negotiation process involves representatives from management and the labor union meeting at agreed-upon times and at agreed-upon locations and working together to attempt to reach a mutually acceptable labor agreement. A useful framework for understanding the negotiation process is the bargaining zone. Of course,

numerous barriers exist to effective negotiation, and several methods are available for both management and labor to use in their attempts to overcome an impasse.

A key clause in the labor contracts that are negotiated between management and labor is precise agreement as to how the terms of the contract will be enforced. Although some enforcement issues are relatively straightforward, others may rely heavily on a formal grievance procedure.

Review and Discussion Questions

1. Discuss the evolution of labor unions in the United States.

2. Identify and briefly explain each of the major laws affecting unionization in the United States.

3. What is a shop steward?

4. Is your state a right-to-work state? What are your personal opinions about this?

5. Discuss trends in unionization.

6. If you wanted to increase union membership, what steps might you take?

7. Summarize the basic steps employees must follow to create a union.

8. What is the bargaining zone?

9. Identify and describe the three general areas that relate to collective bargaining.

10. Identify and discuss the major techniques used to resolve impasses.

Closing Case

AMR and Its Pilot Problems

When labor unions and company management fail to resolve disputes, observers often think that a strike (or the threat of a strike) will follow. But strikes are often costly to the union and, in some cases, collective bargaining agreements allow strikes as a means of resolving only some kinds of disputes. There are, however, other ways for a union to express dissatisfaction over a management decision, and some of these can be as costly and problematic as a strike for the management. A recent conflict involving AMR (the holding company for American Airlines) and the Allied Pilots Association (APA) illustrates one such possibility.

In November 1998 AMR announced that it planned to acquire Reno Air. The deal was to be a friendly takeover and would allow American Airlines to increase its presence in the critical West Coast market much more quickly than any other option. The major stumbling block in the deal, it turned out, was the attempt to integrate the three hundred pilots from Reno Air into the ninety-two-hundred-pilot American Airlines system.

In a nutshell the problem was that Reno Air pilots earned almost 60 percent less than American pilots. But why should this issue concern American pilots more than it concerned Reno Air pilots? In fact, the American pilots were concerned that the company would perhaps drop some existing American routes and replace them with Reno routes to lower labor costs. Further, AMR was also concerned that the company would give preferential treatment for promotions to Reno pilots based on their seniority with Reno rather than with American. The American pilots thus demanded faster promotions to captain for themselves, retroactive pay increases, and faster integration of the Reno pilots into the American system, including bringing their pay up to 100 percent of the American pilots' pay. There were also some problems with the way in which seniority would be determined.

AMR, for its part, stated that the full integration of Reno pilots would take place within eighteen months (which management argued was a remarkably short period for full integration) at which time Reno pilots would be paid at 100 percent the rate for American pilots. Furthermore, AMR stated that 150 additional American Airline pilots would have the opportunity to be promoted to captain within one year, instead of the two- to three-year wait they would have faced under current conditions.

The two sides met and talked, but nothing was settled. Faced with an impasse, the APA walked away from the bargaining table and took action. But rather than call for a strike, or even threaten a strike, the union called for a sick-out. On February 6 American pilots began calling in sick. That day the airline was forced to cancel more than one thousand flights; over the next ten days, the airline was forced to cancel more than six thousand flights. By February 17 an American spokesperson said the sickout had cost the company more than $150 million, and by March 17 AMR chairman and CEO Donald Carty reported that the final impact of the job action was between $200 and $225 million.

But AMR had not sat idly by and watched the sickout. On February 10 the firm sought and received a temporary restraining order in federal court. The airline argued that it had made several good-faith proposals to the union but the union had not responded. Therefore, there was no reason for this dispute to continue, and so the job action was illegal. The court agreed with the airline and ordered the pilots back to work. The next day the APA sent out e-mail messages to its members stating that if they did not feel better (and that they probably did not), they should not go back to work. Later that day AMR filed a motion for contempt of court, arguing that the union was not complying with the court orders.

On February 13 a judge indeed found the union in contempt of court and eventually imposed financial penalties on the order of several hundred thousand dollars a day. By February 16 the two sides were back in negotiations. There was still no resolution, and the airline argued the union still refused to bargain in good faith. Finally, on February 24 the two sides announced they would submit the dispute to a mediator and would continue to meet until it was resolved.

Both sides made concessions (for example, the Reno Air pilots received an immediate 56 percent pay hike), but there was no clear winner in the dispute. Nevertheless, the case illustrates the effectiveness of a work slowdown, such as a sickout, as a means of pressuring management to come to a settlement. Although strikes and lockouts get a lot of media attention, more limited job actions such as this one are far more common and, in many cases, are equally effective.

Case Questions

1. Which side do you think had a better argument for its position, the APA or AMR? Why?

2. Which side do you think won? Why? Do you agree or disagree with the judge's ruling forcing the pilots back to work?

3. What general insights can be gleaned from this case regarding labor-management relations?

Sources: "At American Airlines, Pilots Trace Grievances to Deals in Lean Years," *Wall Street Journal,* February 11, 1999, pp. A1, A10; "Will Fine Divide or Solidify Pilots?" *USA Today,* February 15, 1999, p. 1B.

Building Human Resource Management Skills

Purpose: The purpose of this exercise is to help you understand both the bargaining process as well as how the bargaining-zone model can help facilitate negotiating and bargaining.

Step 1: Your instructor will divide the class into an even number of small groups. Half the groups will be designated as management and the other half as labor. Assume that you are about to negotiate and bargain over a potential wage increase.

Step 2: Your instructor will provide each set of groups with information that corresponds to the three parts of the bargaining-zone model as it applies to your role.

Step 3: Your group should spend a few minutes discussing the best way to handle negotiations so as to meet or exceed your expectations.

Step 4: Your instructor will pair teams of labor negotiators with teams of management negotiators. Within a time limit specified by your instructor, engage in bargaining until you reach an agreement (if possible).

Step 5: Each group should share its negotiated agreement on the wage increase with the rest of the class.

Step 6: Respond to the following questions:

1. Explain differences and/or similarities in negotiated agreements.

2. How useful did you find the bargaining-zone model? Without using this model, would your bargaining have been more or less difficult?

3. Can you think of other areas of applicability (besides collective bargaining) for the bargaining-zone model?

Ethical Dilemmas in Human Resource Management

Assume that you work for a medium-size nonunion company. The firm is facing its most serious union organizing campaign in years, however, and your boss is determined to keep the union out. He has just given you a list of things to do to thwart the organizers. For example, he has suggested each of the following steps:

- Whenever you learn about a scheduled union information meeting, you should schedule a "worker appreciation" event at that same time. He wants you to offer free pizza and barbecue and to give cash prizes (with the winners having to be present to get their prize).

- He wants you to look at the most recent performance evaluations of the key union organizers and to terminate the one with the lowest overall evaluation.

- He also wants you to announce that the firm is seriously considering new benefits such as on-site childcare, flexible work schedules, telecommuting options, exercise facilities, and several others. Although you know the firm is indeed looking into these benefits, you also know that ultimately what is provided will be far less lavish than your boss wants you to intimate.

When you questioned the ethics and legality of these practices, he responded by saying, "Look, all's fair in love and war, and this is war." He went on to explain that he was seriously concerned that if the union wins, the company might actually shut down its domestic operations altogether, moving all of its production capacities to lower-cost foreign plants. He concluded by saying that he was really only looking out for the benefit of the employees, even if he had to play hard ball to help them. And indeed, while you easily see through his hypocrisy, you also recognize some potential truth in his warning—if the union wins, jobs may actually be lost.

Questions

1. What are the ethical issues in this situation?

2. What are the basic arguments for and against extreme measures to fight unionization efforts?

3. What do you think most managers would do in this situation? What would you do?

Human Resource Internet Exercise

Both the AFL-CIO and the NLRB maintain Web sites to help explain what they do, how, and why. Visit each of their Web sites at these addresses:

http://www.aflcio.org/
http://www.nlrb.gov/

Questions

1. What specific information can you find on each site that might be of benefit to you as a manager?

2. What specific information can you find on each site that might be of benefit to you as an individual worker interested in forming a union?

3. What improvements might you suggest to make each Web site more effective for its intended audience?

Notes

1. David Lipsky and Clifford Donn, *Collective Bargaining in American Industry* (Lexington, Mass.: Lexington Books, 1981).
2. "Companies Counter Unions," *USA Today,* September 1997, pp. 1B, 2B. See also "Unions on the Ropes," *Forbes,* April 19, 1999, pp. 170–171.
3. Edward E. Lawler III and Susan A. Mohrman, "Unions and the New Management," *Academy of Management Executive,* Vol. 1, No. 3, 1987, pp. 65–75.
4. "Why Mexico Scares the UAW," *Business Week,* August 3, 1998, pp. 37–38.
5. Clive Fullagar, Paul Clark, Daniel Gallagher, and Michael E. Gordon, "A Model of the Antecedents of Early Union Commitment: The Role of Socialization Experiences and Steward Characteristics," *Journal of Organizational Behavior,* Vol. 15, 1994, pp. 517–533.
6. Stuart Youngblood, Angelo DeNisi, Julie Molleston, and William Mobley, "The Impact of Worker Attachment, Instrumentality Beliefs, Perceived Labor Union Image, and Subjective Norms on Voting Intentions and Union Membership," *Academy of Management Journal,* Vol. 27, 1984, pp. 576–590.
7. Julian Barling, E. Kevin Kelloway, and Eric H. Bremermann, "Preemployment Predictors of Union Attitudes: The Role of Family Socialization and Work Beliefs," *Journal of Applied Psychology,* Vol. 75, 1991, pp. 725–731.
8. "Some Unions Step Up Organizing Campaigns and Get New Members," *Wall Street Journal,* September 1, 1995, pp. A1, A2.
9. See Jeanette A. Davy and Frank Shipper, "Voter Behavior in Union Certification Elections: A Longitudinal Study," *Academy of Management Journal,* Vol. 36, No. 1, 1993, pp. 187–199 for a discussion of some of the determinants of individual voting behavior in union elections.
10. Adapted from Richard E. Walton and Robert B. McKersie, *A Behavioral Theory of Labor Negotiations* (New York: McGraw-Hill, 1965).
11. "ABC Locks Out Striking Employees," *USA Today,* November 3, 1998, p. B1.
12. Phil Taylor, "To the Victor Belongs the Spoils," *Sports Illustrated,* January 18, 1999, pp. 48–52.
13. Henry S. Farber and Harry C. Katz, "Interest Arbitration, Outcomes, and the Incentive to Bargain," *Industrial and Labor Relations Review,* Vol. 33, 1979, pp. 55–63.
14. Peter Feuille, "Final Offer Arbitration and the Chilling Effect," *Industrial Relations,* Vol. 14, 1975, pp. 302–310.

15

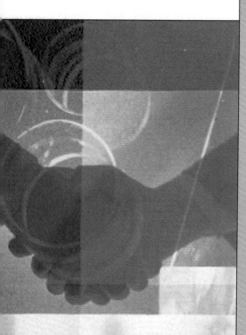

Managing the Work Environment

CHAPTER OUTLINE

Employee Rights in the Workplace
The Meaning of Employee Rights
Preserving Employee Rights

The Role of Discipline in Organizations
Discipline, Punishment, and Development
The Dysfunctional Employee

Managing the Discipline System
Documenting Disciplinary Actions
Approaches to Discipline

The Physical Environment
Hours of Work
Illumination, Temperature, and Office and Work Space Design

Employee Safety and Health
Common Workplace Hazards and Threats
Organizations and OSHA
Controlling Accidents at Work
Controlling Occupational Diseases

Job Design in the Workplace
Health and Stress Management Programs
Causes of Stress at Work
Consequences of Stress at Work
Wellness Programs in Organizations
AIDS in the Workplace

CHAPTER OBJECTIVES

After studying this chapter you should be able to:

- Describe employee rights in the workplace.

- Discuss the role of discipline in organizations and describe how organizations manage their discipline systems.

- Discuss the physical environment at work.

- Discuss employee safety and health.

- Discuss the meaning of and options for job design.

- Describe health and stress management programs in organizations.

Once upon a time, around the middle of the twentieth century, experts were forecasting a utopian society where leisure time was abundant and people had little hard work to do. When was this supposed to happen? Just about now. But in reality, of course, almost the opposite has happened. Many people report that they work longer hours than ever before, worry about job security, and feel an array of workplace pressures ranging from stress to tension to anxiety.

These circumstances have been brought about by a variety of factors. For one thing, in this age of doing more with less, managers are sometimes simply pressuring their employees to work harder and/or longer hours. Similarly, because people can no longer expect to work for one employer for their entire careers, they may focus more attention on the possibilities of layoffs and/or outright job loss. And the proliferation of demographic changes such as dual-career couples and single-parent families makes it harder for people to find time to attend to normal activities like banking, exercise, and so forth. In 1973 the median number of hours of work per week in the United States was 40.6, and the median number of hours of leisure was 26.2. By 1997, however, the median number of hours of work per week had increased to 50.8, and the median number of hours of leisure had declined to 19.5 hours per week.

So what are the effects of these trends? For one thing, employers may be getting more work out of their employees. But on the other hand, some experts suggest that stress and stress-related problems cost U.S. companies more than $200 billion annually. These costs include higher health-care costs, turnover, unscheduled absenteeism, and declining morale. And, in particular, more workers are filing stress-related claims under workers' compensation programs. These claims have increased in number from 911 in 1981 to 4,997 in 1996.

How are companies responding to this evnironment? Increasingly, more and more companies and their managers are recognizing both the organizational and the human costs of excess stress. As a result, many are now actively seeking ways to lower stress by reducing job demands and/or by offering stress-reduction benefits. For example, Public Service Electric & Gas, a New Jersey firm, offers yoga and stress management classes to its employees. Rourke, MS&L, a Boston-based public relations firm, gives its employees $75 a quarter to spend on exercise classes, massages, and similar stress-reduction activities. Indeed, these kinds of programs are proliferating rapidly. At the same time, though, stress is still a major problem in many companies and to many workers.

"You could feel the tension. It wasn't anything to see somebody cry over stress. When a job gets you to that point, it's not worth it."

(Teresa Williford, former customer service representative at BellSouth)*

"Workplace Hazard Gets Attention," *USA Today*, May 5, 1998, pp. 1B, 2B (*quote on p. 1B); *The Wall Street Journal Almanac 1999* (New York: Ballantine Books, 1999), p. 231; "The New Paternalism," *Forbes*, November 2, 1998, pp. 68–70.

The "good life" has always been just around the corner. But as illustrated in the opening vignette, that "corner" never seems to get any closer. Indeed, the pace and pressures of life appear to be increasing for many people, not decreasing. Work hours are getting longer, not shorter, and people everywhere seem to be facing more and more pressure and anxiety. But some enlightened companies today are seeking to reduce the stress they impose on their workers. And many workers themselves are taking greater responsibility for reducing the stress they allow to be placed on them and/or better managing that stress so as to avoid the dysfunctional consequences that may accompany excessive stress. And managing stress is just one of the many contemporary challenges that human resource managers face today as they attempt to more effectively manage their workplaces.

This chapter identifies and describes a variety of issues and challenges associated with managing the workplace in modern organizations. We first introduce and describe the fundamental premises of employee rights in the workplace. Next we discuss the role of discipline in organizations and describe how organizations go about managing discipline. Issues associated with the physical environment at work are discussed next, and this topic leads to a discussion of employee safety and health. Then we examine job design programs and conclude by looking at various health and stress management programs.

E M P L O Y E E   R I G H T S   I N   T H E   W O R K P L A C E

The view that many people in the United States hold toward the concept of "individual rights" is derived from the U.S. Constitution, which guarantees certain fundamental rights to everyone—the rights to free speech and freedom of religion, for example. But there are also rights that are unique to the workplace. This section introduces the concept of workplace rights and then discusses the preservation of employee rights at work.

The Meaning of Employee Rights

The foundation of workplace rights is the employment-at-will doctrine, as discussed in a slightly different context in Chapter 17. The concept of **employment-at-will** suggests that people work at the sole discretion of their employer and thus can be terminated at any time for any reason. This viewpoint, however, represents one extreme perspective on employee rights in the workplace. Essentially, the employment-at-will doctrine suggests that individuals have relatively few rights.

■ The concept of **employment-at-will** suggests that people work at the sole discretion of their employer and thus can be terminated at any time for any reason.

In fact, however, many of the laws and regulations governing human resource management that were described earlier, most notably in Chapter 3, have been created to help define, maintain, and preserve various employee rights. For example, discrimination law essentially gives people the right to work without being evaluated on the basis of non-job-relevant factors such as sex or race. Similarly, minimum wage legislation gives people the right to expect a certain base level of compensation for their work. And labor law gives employees the right to organize and join a labor union under certain prescribed circumstances.

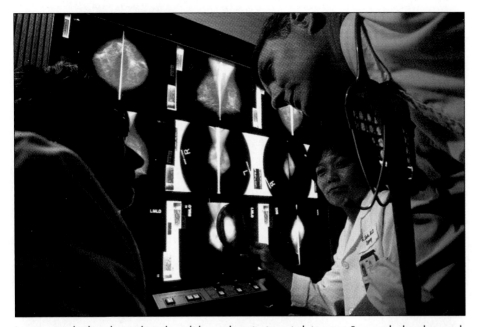

Issues associated with employee rights in the workplace are becoming increasingly important. For example, these doctors and this patient are reviewing his x-rays. Later, the films will be digitized and stored as electronic data files. On the plus side, this allows health-care providers to retrieve records more quickly, to more efficiently transfer them between care facilities, and to more effectively match multiple records from different medical problems. On the other hand, it also increases the risks that the patient's x-rays and other records might be obtained by unauthorized people, used for unintended purposes, and end up creating unanticipated problems or embarrassment for the individual. An unethical manager, for instance, might use confidential patient records to illegally discriminate against someone in a hiring or promotion decision because of a medical condition that is actually unrelated to the job.

More recently, various other rights-related issues have arisen. One very important rights issue today is the employee's right to privacy. This issue centers around such things as access to e-mail and voice mail in a job location. For instance, what rights does the employee have to maintain privacy of e-mail? Does the employer, who perhaps owns the computer and the computer system that the employee is using, have the right to enter the employee's computer without the employee's knowledge or consent and review whatever e-mail lies within? This emerging legal question is not likely to be resolved for at least a few more years.

What about an employee's private life? Is it truly private, or does the organization have a right to monitor and be concerned about how employees spend their personal time? Some have argued that employees, especially higher-ranking and more visible employees, are *always* representatives of the company, and so the company always has a right to monitor and deal with their behavior. Obviously, others would disagree with this viewpoint and argue that behavior that does not affect performance on the job is the employee's own business. Wal-Mart once had a policy of not hiring divorced persons, since its executives believed divorce clashed with the company's "family oriented" image. But a court in New York ruled that Wal-Mart could not discharge an employee who obtained a divorce. Clearly, then, there will also continue to be debates and concerns over the extent to which an employee really has rights to privacy.

Preserving Employee Rights

As noted above, various laws and regulations are intended to preserve employee rights. Beyond the legal context, however, some organizations go further in their efforts to preserve employee rights. For example, many firms have relatively formalized grievance systems wherein employees who believe that they have been improperly or unjustly punished or sanctioned can appeal any actions that have been taken against them. In unionized companies such systems are almost always spelled out as a part of the labor contract.

THE BOTTOM LINE   All managers need to have a fundamental understanding of both individual and organizational rights. The human resource function in an organization can serve as an effective center of expertise in helping to identify these rights and interpret the extent to which they have or have not been preserved or violated.

THE ROLE OF DISCIPLINE IN ORGANIZATIONS

A second important part of the workplace is discipline.[1] Although some people equate discipline with punishment, these are actually two distinct concepts. And they should be applied differently, depending in part on the nature of the circumstances and the organization's intent.

Discipline, Punishment, and Development

■ **Discipline** is a formal organizational action taken against an employee as a result of a rules violation, subpar performance, or other dysfunctional behavior.

■ **Punishment** is any behavior or action, formal or informal, that results in unpleasant effects or consequences for someone else.

Organizations and human resource managers must pay careful attention to issues associated with discipline in the workplace. **Discipline** is a formal organizational action taken against an employee as a result of a rules violation, subpar performance, or similar dysfunctional behavior. It is important to understand the distinction, however, among discipline, punishment, and development. Discipline is a formal process that follows prescribed rules and steps within the organizational context. **Punishment**, however, is a broader concept that includes both formal and informal dimensions. Specifically, it is any behavior or action that results in unpleasant effects or consequences for someone else.

For example, if a supervisor chastises an employee for not exerting effort on the job and does so casually and informally, this action may have a punishing effect on the employee. However, if the incident is not documented and made a part of the organization's discipline system, then problems may arise in the future. And regardless of whether the focus is on discipline or punishment, either serves its intended purpose only to the extent that it is seen as punishing by the employee. For example, suppose an employee is planning to quit his or her job and, as the date of resignation comes closer, begins to exert less effort on the job. Reprimanding this employee for poor performance may not be punishing whatsoever, given that the individual is planning to leave soon anyway. At the extreme, the individual may actually take pleasure from the fact that the supervisor can do nothing of consequence.

The distinction between discipline and punishment as opposed to development is also an important one. The basic distinction usually depends on the employee's intent. Assume, for example, that an employee clearly has the skills

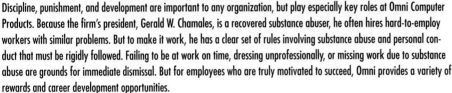

Discipline, punishment, and development are important to any organization, but play especially key roles at Omni Computer Products. Because the firm's president, Gerald W. Chamales, is a recovered substance abuser, he often hires hard-to-employ workers with similar problems. But to make it work, he has a clear set of rules involving substance abuse and personal conduct that must be rigidly followed. Failing to be at work on time, dressing unprofessionally, or missing work due to substance abuse are grounds for immediate dismissal. But for employees who are truly motivated to succeed, Omni provides a variety of rewards and career development opportunities.

and the resources necessary to do the job, but does not perform at an acceptable level because she or he simply doesn't want to try hard. In this instance performance is at the discretion of the individual employee, and the manager may choose to use discipline or punishment in an effort to get the employee to work harder. Indeed, the manager may even desire to terminate the employee and hire someone else who is willing to work harder.

On the other hand, consider the case of the employee who no longer has the skills necessary to perform the job. For example, the job may have been redefined and new technology brought to bear in ways that render the employee's existing skills obsolete. Thus the employee may be trying very hard to perform at an acceptable level, but may be unable to do so simply because she or he does not have the skills. In this case punishing the individual would not appear to be an equitable option. Instead, perhaps the organization should focus its efforts on attempting to help the employee learn the new skills necessary to perform at a higher level again. Thus, rather than discipline or punishment, training and development might be more properly called for.

The Dysfunctional Employee

Various kinds of employee behaviors can result in problems for the organization. As noted above, for example, some employees may be in need of discipline or punishment because of their unacceptable performance. Again, it is important to keep in mind that this response is appropriate only when the employee has the skills and resources necessary to do the job but simply chooses to not perform at an acceptable level. In this instance discipline may be called for in the short term, with a longer-term option being to terminate the employee.

Another category of employee who might be subject to discipline or punishment is a substance-abusing employee. Employees who drink on the job, for example, or who drink off the job but bring the effects of their alcohol indulgence to work may create problems in the workplace.[2] Similarly, employees who use and abuse drugs such as cocaine and heroin on the job are also clear candidates for discipline and punishment. In cases such as these, there is no question about rights to privacy, since the substance abuse has affected the job or is actually taking place on the job. In some organizations and in some industries, alcohol and drug abuse can be especially critical. For example, individuals who are operating heavy equipment or who are engaged in transportation-related activities may potentially be endangering customers, passengers, and fellow employees as a result of illicit drug use or alcoholism.[3] The Exxon *Valdez* disaster of several years ago was allegedly caused in part because the ship's captain had been drinking.

Yet another category of employee who is subject to disciplinary issues is someone who participates in illegal activities such as theft or crime. Sometimes individuals may engage in criminal activities that are directly related to the organization. For instance, they may use company telephones or credit cards for their personal use or steal company materials to take home. Other forms of criminal activity may be more subtle. For example, embezzlement of company resources or selling important company secrets might be significant legal violations.

A final type of employee who may be in need of discipline or punishment is the rule violator. In this instance the employee may not be breaking the law, but may be violating a rule that the company considers to be very important. For example, consider employees who are constantly interfacing with the general public, such as hotel clerks, retail clerks, and so forth. A company might appropriately require such individuals to maintain reasonable grooming standards and personal hygiene. If an employee in such a position repeatedly comes to work wearing dirty clothes or not having bathed for several days, she or he is clearly breaking company rules and is jeopardizing the company's image in the eyes of the consuming public. Thus the organization might reasonably undertake disciplinary or punishing actions against this individual.

THE BOTTOM LINE Managers need to understand the distinctions among discipline, punishment, and development. Moreover, they should also be familiar with the various kinds of dysfunctional behaviors that an employee can engage in and the organization's policies and procedures for dealing with such behaviors.

MANAGING THE DISCIPLINE SYSTEM

Given that discipline and punishment may have to be used in organization, it follows that these activities should be closely managed in order to maximize their potential impact. The process of managing discipline starts with the need for documentation.

Documenting Disciplinary Actions

We earlier noted that the distinction between discipline and punishment may reside on documentation. Indeed, effective and appropriate documentation can and should be the cornerstone of an effective disciplinary system. Suppose, for instance, that a company does not document any of its disciplinary actions. After the third or fourth instance of unacceptable behavior by an employee, the organization might want to terminate that individual. But if the individual is a member of a protected class, she or he may be able to claim discrimination if the prior disciplinary problems have not been adequately and appropriately documented.

Typically, organizations that want to effectively manage their discipline systems do so by following a certain well-defined model. First the organization must establish rules and goals. Next it must clearly communicate those rules and goals to all employees. That is, people need to know what they can and can't do and why such behaviors are deemed important by the organization. There must also be an assessment mechanism through which managers and others in the organization observe instances of inappropriate or unacceptable behavior and then initiate the proper disciplinary action. But as noted, this action should be well documented.

For example, if the appropriate first action is a verbal reprimand by the supervisor, the supervisor should nevertheless write up the details of this reprimand—why it was necessary, what behavior was observed, precisely when it was given, and so forth. And these details should be placed in the employee's personal file in the human resource office. By following this procedure, the organization establishes the premise for future disciplinary actions on the basis of this initial rules violation.

As part of this documentation procedure, organizations generally specify degrees of severity or seriousness. For example, while all stealing is, of course, unacceptable, an employee who takes home a company note pad or pen for personal use is not committing an act that is as serious as one who steals a personal computer from the company. Table 15.1 identifies several examples of criteria that an organization can use to define problem behavior and provides examples of each, varying from minor to moderate to serious.[4]

Approaches to Discipline

Organizations can undertake a variety of disciplinary approaches. Some managers prefer to use what has traditionally been called the *hot stove rule* of discipline. As the term suggests, this approach to discipline is analogous to what happens when people touch a hot stove. As their hand gets close to it, they experience increased warmth emanating from the stove. When they touch it, they suffer an immediate burn, and everyone who touches the stove receives the same burn. In the case of discipline, a manager using the hot stove rule will have a very clearly articulated set of rules and a system whereby employees should be clearly aware of an approaching rules violation. When a rule is broken and discipline is necessary, it occurs immediately after the unacceptable behavior is observed. And everyone is treated exactly the same—a rules violation by anyone will result in consistent and immediate response.

Unfortunately, the hot stove rule, while very popular, has some significant drawbacks. For one thing, the warning system is often not as good as the

TABLE 15.1	Criteria for Assesssing the Seriousness of Problem Behaviors		
Criterion	**Violation Category**		
	Minor	**Moderate**	**Serious**
1. Disruption to the workflow.	Little or no disruption to the workflow.	Disruption to workflow that required changes in production or personnel scheduling.	Severe and expensive disruption to the workflow that resulted in shutdown of a facility.
2. Damage to products and equipment.	No damage to products or equipment.	Damage to products and equipment (e.g., less than $1,000).	Severe and expensive damage to products and equipment (e.g., more than $1,000).
3. Safety hazard created (even though no one was injured).	Inconsequential safety hazard.	Persons were exposed to a definite risk of bodily injury.	Persons were placed in a potentially life-threatening situation.
4. Bodily injury to customers or employees.	Bodily injury requiring no medical treatment.	Bodily injury that required less than 48 hours of hospitalization.	Bodily injury that required more than 48 hours of hospitalization or resulted in a death.
5. Acceptability of conduct given the professional or organizational level of the employee.	Conduct lacked good taste or judgment but was not grossly out of line.	Conduct was definitely unacceptable, and the employee knew such actions were wrong.	Conduct was outside what is expected of a prudent, rational person or conduct was clearly a major violation of the employee's professional code of ethics.
6. Violation of a federal or state law.	No state or federal law was violated, but the act could be regarded as unethical.	The employee committed a misdemeanor on the job or violated a civil law.	The employee committed a felony on the job or violated a civil law that could create a major liability for the employer.
7. Extent to which organizational resources were misappropriated by an employee.	An insignificant misappropriation of resources (less than $100) resulting in no personal gain to the employee.	A small misappropriation of resources that provided a personal gain to the employee (less than $100).	A larger misappropriation of resources (more than $100) or multiple misappropriations of resources (of any amount) regardless of whether the the employee personally gained.

(continued)

TABLE 15.1 *(continued)*

Criterion	Violation Category		
	Minor	**Moderate**	**Serious**
8. Impact on the morale and welfare of co-workers and customers.	Morale and welfare were not disrupted significantly.	Morale and welfare could be disrupted for a short period of time.	Morale and welfare could be disrupted for a long period of time (or damaged irreparably).
9. Correctability of the employee's behavior.	Employee's behavior can be corrected simply by discussing the incident with him or her.	Employee's behavior may be corrected through further training or counseling.	Employee's behavior may be uncorrectable or correctable only through extensive training or psychiatric counseling.
10. Degree to which minor incidents might be a signal for more serious problems.	Employee's behavior is of minor consequence and is not likely to be repeated.	Employee's behavior is of minor consequence but indicates deeper problems that could have serious consequences at a later time.	Employee's behavior, though minor, is a signal of potentially dangerous or violent behavior at a later time.
11. Extent to which an employee's actions damage the reputation of the organization.	Employee's actions did little damage to the firm's reputation but did create an unfavorable impression among potential customers.	Employee's actions created adverse prublicity among a small number of business associates, although there was little or no damage to the firm's business or relationships with customers or suppliers.	Employee's actions created widespread adverse publicity for the organization or caused it to lose valued customers or suppliers.
12. Extent to which the disciplinary incident undermined management's authority to maintain discipline and decorum in the workplace.	Management's authority was challenged, but its ability to maintain discipline and decorum was not compromised.	Management's authority was damaged on a temporary or limited basis.	Management's authority was damaged irreparably throughout a large part of the organization.

Source: Terry L. Leap and Michael Crino, "How Serious Is Serious," *HRMagazine*, May 1998, p. 47, Volume 43, Issue 6. Reprinted with permission of *HRMagazine* published by the Society for Human Resource Management, Alexandria, Va.

manager really believes it to be. Thus the manager believes that she or he has established a clearly articulated and well-understood set of rules and regulations and that people will know when they are in violation of those regulations. But employees may feel that the rules are not nearly as objective and clear as the manager thinks they are. Similarly, it would also seem unreasonable to truly treat everyone exactly the same.

Consider, for example, three employees guilty of a rules violation. One employee is brand new to the firm, having worked there only a few weeks. Thus this individual might reasonably be expected to be unfamiliar with the rules. Another employee might be someone with fifteen or twenty years of experience with the firm. This situation is considerably more complex. On the one hand, it might be argued that this individual should know all the rules and thus should be afforded very little consideration. On the other hand, if the employee has a long and attractive work record with no previous instances of rules violation, the manager might be advised to carefully determine whether or not there might be extenuating circumstances. A final scenario might be the employee who has been on the job for perhaps a year and who is known to be a consistent rules violator. Most managers will probably agree that this third employee is a much clearer candidate for strict disciplinary action.

More typically, organizations that create discipline systems attempt to provide what is called progressive discipline. In a **progressive discipline system**, the organization defines a sequence of penalties, each somewhat more severe than the previous, and a time frame across which an individual's continued rules violations will escalate to higher levels of discipline. Texas Instruments, Kroger, and Pizza Hut are among the businesses that use a progressive discipline system. For example, an organization might have a set of rules and regulations regarding tardiness or unexcused absenteeism from work. It might subsequently develop a progressive disciplinary system of the type that follows:

1. If the employee is absent or tardy for work without satisfactory explanation, the supervisor will verbally reprimand the employee for the first offense and this reprimand is noted in the employee's file.

2. If within sixty days of the first reprimand, the employee breaks the rule again, he or she will be subject to a more serious verbal reprimand and a formal reprimand is written up and placed in the human resource file.

3. If the rule is broken again within sixty days of the second offense, the employee will be suspended for three days without pay.

4. If the employee breaks the rule again within sixty days of the third offense, then the employee is subject to dismissal.

The logic behind such progressive systems is that they may gradually shape the employee's behavior in ways that are more acceptable and desirable to the organization. They are also seen as relatively equitable, given that the employee has multiple chances to redeem him- or herself in the eyes of the organization. Of course, in some instances additional flexibility may very well be necessary. For example, in the case of the tardy or absent employee, if the individual is very tardy or absent from work without satisfactory reason three or four days in a row, the organization might choose to sanction the individual more severely and to do so immediately. Similarly, if an employee commits a significant theft or engages in very unacceptable behavior, such as sexual harassment or striking a supervisor, immediate dismissal may be warranted.

■ In a **progressive discipline system**, the organization defines a sequence of penalties, each somewhat more severe than the previous, and a time frame across which an individual's continued rules violations will escalate to higher levels of discipline.

Wal-Mart uses a very interesting approach to its progressive disciplinary system. After going through several steps of the type described above, a Wal-Mart employee who is on the verge of being dismissed is instructed by his supervisor to take the next day off with full pay. This day is known informally at Wal-Mart as the *day of decision*. The individual is supposed to spend the day thinking about whether or not he is willing to make the commitment to following Wal-Mart's rules and regulations and changing the behaviors that have resulted in his being in a difficult spot to begin with. The company reports that the decision day concept seems to work pretty effectively. Occasionally, the employee will decide that no, she is not willing to do what is necessary to meet Wal-Mart's expectations and so will instead leave the employment of the firm. In many other cases, however, the employee does recognize the gravity of the situation and at that point does indeed alter her behavior and become a much more valuable and contributing member of the organization.

THE BOTTOM LINE   Human resource managers need to ensure that the organization has a well-conceived and defensible discipline system. All managers need to make sure they understand the discipline system and that they clearly follow the prescribed steps in dealing with problem employees.

THE PHYSICAL ENVIRONMENT

The actual physical environment in which an employee works is also extremely important. Later in the chapter, we discuss issues of safety and health, but aspects of the physical environment can also clearly influence how pleasant or unpleasant a work setting might be. Many aspects of the physical environment may affect an employee's attitudes and behavior on the job, but we discuss just a few of these.

Hours of Work

In Chapter 17 we discuss new trends toward nontraditional workweeks, such as the compressed workweek. But, although working four long days for three days off a week may be attractive, there is evidence that this schedule can be problematic as well. Also, it may not be equally attractive to all employees. For example, one study found that young males were much more receptive to compressed workweeks than were any other workers.[5] But preferences aside, studies of compressed work schedules have found evidence of accidents later in the day (which would be ten hours long) due to fatigue on construction jobs and generally mixed results relative to the effects of compressed work schedules on productivity.[6]

In many industries the problems of shift work present another challenge to effectively managing the work environment. All human beings are subject to **circadian rhythms**, which tell our bodies when to eat and sleep. When employees are placed on a night shift, their bodies must adapt to having to sleep in the day and be awake at night. Although this change is disruptive, the body adapts and learns to switch day and night. But employees who must work on rotating

■ **Circadian rhythms** are natural cycles that indicate when a body needs to eat or sleep.

HUMAN RESOURCES **in the Twenty-first Century**

Building the Perfect Work Environment

One of the more interesting changes sweeping corporate America today involves architecture. Specifically, many companies are seeking new and innovative designs for the workplace to make their facilities more interesting and appealing and to promote interaction and spontaneity. Traditionally, offices were arrayed down long corridors; the further up the hierarchy a manager moved, the bigger the office until the ultimate prize was obtained—the corner office.

The next major trend was toward cubicles. These modular constructions afforded only a modicum of privacy but still defined a specific work space for each employee. Moreover, workplace arrangements could be dismantled and/or rearranged with minimal hassle. But cubicles also reduce individuality and interaction, partially explaining why they became the object of derision in *Dilbert* and other cartoons. So today many firms are moving in new and nontraditional ways as they seek to redefine their physical environment.

Several characteristics generally are reflected in how companies structure their space today. For one thing, there is a clear movement toward large, well-lit open spaces, where people can gather, talk, and interact. Designers

"Before, we were in a typical office. Nothing stood out about the space. We wanted an atmosphere that was comfortable, untraditional, and more open."

(Debbie Shecterle, director of human resources, Doane Pet Care Company)*

often hope that such features promote greater interaction among employees. Further, whereas workplaces used to be developed around straight lines, squares, and rectangles, today they are more likely to feature curves, circles, and other oblique lines and spaces. Right angles are avoided whenever possible, ceilings rise and fall, and bright colors mix with more somber wood tones.

Of course, such designs have problems as well. For one thing, furniture may not fit into a round office as well as in a square one. And if a design is too idiosyncratic, landlords may worry that if the current tenant leaves, it may be difficult to find a new one. But still, many companies are attracted to the benefits of this new model. Doane Pet Care, for example, eliminated all of its cubicles and redesigned its work space with curved walls; few interior walls; and gold, brown, and green colors. First Bank Systems, in Minneapolis, Sears, Roebuck & Co., and Gap, Inc., are also adopting this new approach.

References: "Pride of Place," *Business Week*, November 2, 1998, pp. 61–81; Dominic Bencivenga, "A Humanistic Approach to Space," *HRMagazine*, March 1998, pp. 68–74; "Curves Ahead," *Wall Street Journal*, March 10, 1999, pp. B1; B10 (*quote on p. B1).

---

shifts are never quite able to establish a new rhythm. As a result, employees on rotating shifts are more likely to have ulcers than are other employees, as their bodies struggle to find an equilibrium.[7] Nonetheless, other research has indicated that some workers, especially older, more experienced employees, may actually like the variety and are able to cope with the changes in biological rhythms.[8]

Illumination, Temperature, and Office and Work Space Design

Recall that one phase of the Hawthorne studies, conducted in 1924 in a Western Electric plant outside of Chicago, was concerned with the effects of illumination on productivity. The results indicated that changes in the level of illumination were *not* responsible for the changes observed in productivity. This failure discouraged scholars from examining the effects of illumination on workplace behavior for quite some time. Yet, there is considerable evidence that extremes of temperature (in either direction) can affect both attitudes and decision making on the job,[9] and it has even been suggested that ambient temperature helps explain national differences in stress on the job.[10] In a similar fashion research has shown that optimal lighting is different for different tasks and that employees who perceive their work environments as being "dark" are generally less satisfied with their jobs.[11]

Other aspects of the physical work environment that have received attention over the years include the use of music in the workplace. These studies, many of them going back more than fifty years, have indicated that almost any type of background music can improve employee attitudes and performance on the job,[12] and a recent study found that the use of personal stereos on the job improved both attitudes and performance, especially on relatively simple jobs.[13] Also, the physical layout of office space and the use of dividers and cubicles have been found to influence attitudes and behavior at work.[14] "Human Resources in the Twenty-first Century" explores some modern twists on workplace design.

It is interesting to note that, although many of these studies found that changes in the physical environment affected performance, the physical environment seems to have a stronger effect on attitudes. That is, even when light, heat, or office layout didn't influence performance, these factors were associated with differences in how employees felt about their jobs and where they worked. It is clear, however, that some aspects of the environment can influence employee safety and health, which we discuss in the next section.

THE BOTTOM LINE Managers should appreciate the impact of hours of work, as well as illumination, temperature, and work space design on the organization. The human resource function can play a key role in setting work hours and other characteristics of the workplace so as to satisfy the needs of individuals and the organization itself.

E M P L O Y E E   S A F E T Y   A N D   H E A L T H

Another important part of managing a work environment deals with employee safety and health. As we will see, employee safety and health, in general, and the impact of the Occupational Safety and Health Act of 1970, in particular, have had a significant impact on human resource management. Basic issues involve actions that the organization can and should take to control or eliminate safety hazards and health hazards.

Safety hazards refer to those things in the work environment that have the potential to cause harm to an employee. **Health hazards**, on the other hand, are those characteristics of the work environment that more slowly and systematically, and perhaps cumulatively, result in damage to an employee's health. Thus a poorly connected string of wiring that might result in electrical shock to an employee poses a safety hazard, whereas continuous and ongoing exposure to chemicals that may increase the risk of cancer represents a health hazard.

Table 15.2 lists several of the most injury-prone businesses and occupations in the United States. For example, hospitals reported 300,200 nonfatal injuries in 1996, representing about ten injuries for every one hundred employees. Among those injuries were things like puncture wounds from needles or scalpels, pulled muscles from lifting patients, and burns from caustic chemicals, as well as more

■ **Safety hazards** refer to those things in the work environment that have the potential to cause harm to an employee.

■ **Health hazards** are those characteristics of the work environment that slowly and systematically, and perhaps cumulatively, result in damage to an employee's health.

generalizable events like slips and falls. Similarly, among the most dangerous occupations was timber cutting. In 1996, for example, 118 timber cutters lost their lives, most (about 76 percent) from being struck by objects (such as falling trees and heavy tree limbs).

TABLE 15.2 Injury-Prone Businesses and Dangerous Occupations

Injury-Prone Businesses
Nonfatal Occupational Injuries: Number of Cases and Incidence Rates per 100 Full-Time Workers, for Industries with 100,000 or More Injury Cases, 1996

Industry	Total Cases (Thousands)	Incidence Rate
Eating and drinking places	309.7	6.1
Hospitals	300.2	10.0
Nursing and personal care facilities	221.9	16.2
Grocery stores	211.6	9.7
Department stores	172.8	9.8
Trucking and courier services, except air	153.3	10.2
Motor vehicles and equipment	148.9	14.9
Air transportation, scheduled	148.4	18.6
Hotels and motels	118.3	8.9

Dangerous Occupations
Index of Relative Risk and Number of Occupational Fatalities Resulting from 1996 Injuries, for 10 High-Risk Occupations (Index for All Workers = 1.0)

Occupation	Index of Relative Risk	Number of Fatalities	Major Deadly Event
Fishers	37.5	66	Drowning (74%)
Timber cutters	33.1	118	Struck by object (76%)
Airplane pilots	18.5	100	Airplane crash (100%)
Structural metal workers	17.9	52	Fall (77%)
Extractive jobs	14.1	87	Vehicular (26%)
Water transportation jobs	12.8	42	Fall from ship (36%)
Garbage collectors	10.3	21	Vehicular (81%)
Public transportation attendants	8.4	38	Airplane crash (92%)
Construction laborers	7.5	291	Vehicular (29%)
Taxicab drivers and chauffeurs	6.7	65	Homicide (71%)

Common Workplace Hazards and Threats

We first address some of the more frequent causes of accidents and then describe some of the more pervasive health hazards. Various characteristics of the physical environment are a major cause of accidents in the workplace. At a general level, of course, accidents can happen anywhere. People can slip on wet flooring or a loose piece of carpeting or can drop something heavy on their foot in virtually any setting. But in manufacturing settings, a number of specific conditions of the work environment might prove to be potentially dangerous. Among the more common are unguarded or improperly guarded machines (in this instance "guarding" refers to a shield of other piece of equipment to keep body parts from coming in contact with moving machine parts, such as gears or conveyor belts).

Defective equipment and tools can also cause accidents. Similarly, poor lighting and poor or improper ventilation can also be dangerous. Improper dress also poses a hazard. For example, if a person wears overly loose clothing, she or he runs a risk that the clothing might get caught in a moving part of the machine. Sharp edges around machinery can also be a hazard. And finally, poor housekeeping resulting in avoidably dirty or wet floors, improperly stacked materials, and congested storage areas can also result in accidents. Of course, hazards are not restricted to manufacturing settings; they can occur at virtually any work setting. Increasingly, for example, as we noted in Chapter 3, home office safety is becoming a concern for businesses that allow telecommuting.[15]

Personal actions of individual employees also represent a common workplace hazard. Among the more frequently described and identified personal actions that result in accidents are behaviors such as taking unnecessary risks, failing to wear protective equipment such as goggles or gloves, using improper tools and equipment for specific jobs, taking unsafe shortcuts, and simply engaging in foolish horseplay. Any of these characteristics has the potential to quickly and without warning bring harm or injury to people in the workplace. These are the primary kinds of things that had for years caused excessive injuries at Georgia-Pacific, as detailed in this chapter's closing case.

But there remains a separate set of workplace factors whose effects may appear much more gradually. Chemicals, toxic fumes, and similar workplace factors may fall into this category. Secondary smoke may also be a factor. And some buildings themselves have relatively unsafe characteristics, for example, asbestos insulation and carpeting that has been treated with improper combinations of chemicals and dyes.

In many cases these sorts of health hazards are occupational. For example, people who work in coal mines and pesticide plants may be especially prone to coming into contact with potential health hazards. The U.S. Department of Labor has identified seven major categories of occupational illnesses. These categories are

1. Occupational skin diseases or disorders
2. Dust diseases of the lungs
3. Respiratory conditions due to toxic agents
4. Poisoning
5. Disorders due to physical agents
6. Disorders associated with repeated trauma
7. Other categories of occupational illness

Organizations and OSHA

■ **OSHA** authorized the U.S. government to create and enforce various standards regarding occupational safety and health.

Widespread concern about employee safety and health led to the passage in 1970 of the most comprehensive law ever passed regarding worker safety. This act is technically known as the Occupational Safety and Health Act of 1970 but is most frequently referred to simply by the initials **OSHA**. At the time OSHA was passed, there were approximately fifteen thousand work-related deaths in the United States every year.

OSHA authorized the U.S. government to create and enforce various standards regarding occupational safety and health. The responsibility for enforcing the provisions of OSHA was assigned to the Department of Labor. In concert with the Department of Labor, the Department of Health was also given the task of sponsoring research to establish the criteria for various task and occupations and for training employees to comply with the act. Most of this work is conducted by an agency called the National Institute for Occupational Safety and Health. A sample of guidelines developed from this work is shown in Table 15.3.

Through research and analysis of workplace statistics, OSHA has created various safety standards. These standards are defined as "practices, means, operations, or processes, reasonably necessary to provide safe . . . employment." The various standards that OSHA creates are regularly published and disseminated to employers across the country. Organizations are responsible for being completely aware of all current OSHA standards. This undertaking often becomes very difficult because of the length and volume of the various sets of regulations and standards. Each year OSHA issues new standards, extends and revises old standards, and reinterprets various existing standards in volumes that total hundreds of pages. Thus there is little wonder that managers frequently feel that OSHA represents unnecessary regulation of their activities.

To ensure compliance with OSHA, inspectors from the U.S. Department of Labor visit places of employment, either on a random basis or by invitation of an employer, an employee, or a union. If an employee requests an OSHA inspection, her or his identity is kept confidential. If the OSHA inspector determines that the employer is guilty of major violations, significant penalties can result. For example, an employer can be fined $10,000 per violation for willful or repeated major violations. In addition, company officials may be personally fined for failure to comply with OSHA regulations and can conceivably be sentenced to serve jail time.

OSHA also requires employers to keep highly specific and very standardized records of illnesses and injuries that occur in the workplace. These records must be produced and shown to any OSHA compliance officer who requests them. Moreover, in addition to routine record keeping, employers must also report directly and immediately to OSHA all accidents and illnesses that result in deaths in the workplace or that pose a serious health hazard to all employees in the organization. Of course, employers have some avenue for appeal. For example, if they disagree with the recommendations of an OSHA compliance officer, they can turn to the Occupational Safety and Health Review Commission. Alternatively, they can pursue their claim through federal courts.

Unfortunately, most people believe that OSHA has not been terribly effective. They argue, for example, that the standards are too comprehensive, too technical, and oftentimes too arbitrary. Critics also point out that enforcement of OSHA standards is still relatively uneven. And even in terms of actual measurable effects, OSHA has been less than successful. While awareness of safety issues has undoubtedly been increased, the number of occupational accidents and occupational illnesses has not been significantly diminished.[16]

Controlling Accidents at Work

Regardless of whether OSHA is involved or not, organizations can do a number of things to create a safer, less accident prone, work environment. One very important approach is to design more safety into the workplace through a

---

TABLE 15.3 **Some Sample General Industry Safety and Health Regulations from OSHA**

For drinking water . . .

- Potable water shall be provided in all places of employment.

- The nozzle of a drinking fountain shall be set at such an angle that the jet of water will not splash back down the nozzle; and the end of the nozzle shall be protected by a guard to prevent a person's mouth or nose from coming in contact with the nozzle.

- Portable drinking water dispensers shall be designed and serviced to ensure sanitary conditions, shall be capable of being closed, and shall have a tap. Unused disposable cups shall be kept in a sanitary container, and a receptacle shall be provided for used cups. The "common drinking cup" is prohibited.

For fire protection . . .

- Portable fire extinguishers, suitable to the conditions and hazards involved, shall be provided and maintained in effective operating condition.

- Portable fire extinguishers shall be given maintenance service at least once a year. A durable tag must be securely attached to show the maintenance or recharge date.

- In storage areas, clearance between sprinkler systems deflectors and the top of storage varies with the type of storage. For combustible material, stored over 15 feet, but not more than 21 feet high, in solid piles, or over 12 feet, but not more than 21 feet, in piles that contain horizontal channels, the minimum clearance shall be 36 inches. The minimum clearance for smaller piles, or for noncombustible materials, shall be 18 inches.

And for portable ladders . . .

- The maximum length for portable wooden ladders shall be as follows: step, 20 feet; single straight ladders, 30 feet; sectional ladders, 60 feet; trestle ladders, 20 feet; platform stepladders, 20 feet; painter's stepladders, 12 feet; mason's ladders, 40 feet.

- Non-self-supporting ladders shall be erected on a sound base at a 4 to 1 pitch, and placed to prevent slippage.

- The top of a ladder used to gain access to a roof should extend at least 3 feet above the point of contact.

Source: General Industry Standards and Interpretations, U.S. Department of Labor, OSHA. (Vol. 1, Revised 1989, Part 1910).

Controlling accidents at work is an especially important part of enhancing employee safety and health. Consider, for example, the dangers and risks inherent in working on an oil rig in icy waters. To help minimize these risks, workers in such settings frequently engage in safety exercises and training. These rig workers, for example, are from the Hibernia oil rig, a joint venture involving Mobil, Chevron, Petro-Canada, and the Canadian government. In the event of a drifting iceberg threatening to hit the rig, they would be sent out to shove it away with water cannons or tow it off course. The crew members here are attaching a line to an iceberg to practice towing.

■ **Safety engineers** are experts who carefully study the workplace, try to identify and isolate particularly dangerous situations, and recommend solutions for dealing with those situations.

process called safety engineering. **Safety engineers** are experts who carefully study the workplace, try to identify and isolate particularly dangerous situations, and recommend solutions for dealing with those situations.

In addition, organizations can sometimes help control accidents at work by providing protective clothing and related devices to employees. Among the more common kinds of protective clothing and devices are various types of head protection, eye goggles and face shields, hearing protection for loud-noise environments, gloves for hand protection, safety shoes for foot protection, back-support belts for people who lift heavy objects, and belts and lifelines for employees who work in high places. And in today's technology-driven workplaces, the focus of safety engineers also includes wrist and elbow support and screen filters for people who work at keyboards several hours a day and properly designed chairs and desk surfaces for people who sit for most of their day.

In addition, employee training is also a very important ingredient in attempts to control accidents at work. Employees should be taught to follow the safest work procedures that the organization can identify and to report unsafe conditions to managers. Finally, providing safety incentives and behavior modification training to employees is another effective way to reduce the number of accidents on the job.[17]

Controlling Occupational Diseases

Controlling occupational diseases is a bit more complex. Given that the effects of occupational diseases are often observable only after extended periods of time, it may be difficult for the organization to know how effectively it is really dealing with occupational diseases. For example, several years ago Amoco was determined that a disproportionate number of workers at one of its research facilities had contracted brain cancer. Experts have been studying the problem for more than ten years. Although some observers theorize that chemicals at the work site are responsible, neither the independent researchers or the company have been able to pinpoint the problem or to even establish conclusively that the work site is to blame.[18]

Nevertheless, the organization should be thoroughly familiar with all hazardous circumstances in the work environment that might bring about occupational diseases. To the extent that these hazards can be eliminated or minimized, then the organization should attempt to do so. In the event that there is no choice but to deal with the hazardous environment, the organization can still take certain actions.

For example, all employees should be clearly informed of the various risks and hazards that they are associated with. This information should enable employees to take a larger role in protecting their own health. And again in many cases, proper equipment might be helpful. Respiratory shields for breathing, pressurized or rubberized body suits, and appropriate safety materials and equipment such as gloves and masks might also be helpful.

THE BOTTOM LINE   All managers should be thoroughly familiar with OSHA regulations as well as the potential hazards and safety risks they and their employees might face. The human resource function will generally take a lead role in this area and is almost always seen as the center of expertise on health and safety issues, especially those that relate to OSHA.

JOB DESIGN IN THE WORKPLACE

Aside from activities to minimize problems at work—discipline and safety and health management, for example—some organizations attempt to go further and create better jobs for their employees. Indeed, job design is one of the more popular strategies for improving the quality of employee work life. **Job design** is the determination of an individual's work-related responsibilities. For a machinist at Caterpillar, job design might specify what machines are to be operated, how they are to be operated, and what performance standards are expected. For a manager at Caterpillar, job design would involve defining areas of decision-making responsibility, identifying goals and expectations, and establishing appropriate indicators of success. The natural starting point for designing jobs is determining the level of desired specialization.

■ **Job design** is the determination of an individual's work-related responsibilities.

Job specialization is the degree to which the overall task of the organization is broken down and divided into smaller component parts. Job specialization evolved from the concept of *division of labor*. Adam Smith, an eighteenth-century economist, described how division of labor was used in a pin factory to improve productivity. One man drew the wire, another straightened it, a third cut it, a fourth ground the point, and so on. Smith claimed that ten men working in this fashion were able to produce forty-eight thousand pins in a day, whereas each man working alone would have been able to produce only twenty pins per day. More recently, the best example of the impact of specialization is the automobile assembly line pioneered by Henry Ford and his contemporaries. Mass-production capabilities stemming from job specialization techniques have had a profound impact throughout the world. High levels of low-cost production transformed U.S. society during the first several decades of this century into one of the strongest economies in the history of the world.

■ **Job specialization** is the degree to which the overall task of the organization is broken down and divided into smaller parts.

Job specialization provides four benefits to organizations.[19] First, workers performing small, simple tasks will probably become very proficient at that task. Second, transfer time between tasks may decrease. If employees perform several different tasks, some time may be lost as they stop doing the first task and start doing the next. Third, the more narrowly defined a job is, the easier it may be to develop specialized equipment to assist with that job. Fourth, when an employee who performs a highly specialized job is absent or quits, the manager should be able to train someone new at relatively low cost. Although specialization is generally thought of in terms of operating jobs, many organizations have extended the basic elements of specialization to managerial and professional levels as well.

On the other hand, job specialization can have negative consequences. The foremost criticism is that workers who perform highly specialized jobs may become bored and dissatisfied. The job may be so specialized that it offers no challenge or stimulation. Boredom and monotony set in, absenteeism rises, and the quality of the work may suffer. Furthermore, the anticipated benefits of specialization do not always occur. For example, an early study conducted at Maytag found that the time spent moving work-in-process from one worker to another was greater than the time needed for the same individual to change from job to job. Thus although some degree of specialization is necessary, it should not be carried to extremes because of the negative consequences that might result. Managers should be sensitive to situations where extreme specialization should be avoided. And indeed, several alternative approaches to designing jobs have been developed in recent years.

To counter the problems associated with specialization, managers have sought other approaches to job design that achieve a better balance between organizational demands for efficiency and productivity and individual needs for creativity and autonomy. Five alternative approaches are job rotation, job enlargement, job enrichment, the job characteristics approach, and work teams.

Job rotation involves systematically moving employees from one job to another. A worker in a warehouse might unload trucks on Monday, carry incoming inventory to storage on Tuesday, verify invoices on Wednesday, pull outgoing inventory from storage on Thursday, and load trucks on Friday. Thus the jobs do not change, but instead, workers move from job to job. Unfortunately, for this very reason job rotation has not been very successful in enhancing employee motivation or satisfaction. Jobs that are amenable to rotation tend to be relatively standard and routine. Workers who are rotated to a "new" job may be more satisfied at first, but this soon wanes. Although many companies (among them American Cyanamid, Bethlehem Steel, Ford, Prudential Insurance, TRW, and Western Electric) have tried job rotation, it is most often used today as a training device to improve worker skills and flexibility.

On the assumption that doing the same basic task over and over is the primary cause of worker dissatisfaction, **job enlargement** was developed to increase the total number of tasks workers perform. As a result, all workers perform a wide variety of tasks, presumably reducing the level of job dissatisfaction. Many organizations have used job enlargement, including IBM, Detroit Edison, AT&T, the U.S. Civil Service, and Maytag. At Maytag, for example, the assembly line for producing washing-machine water pumps was systematically changed so that work that had originally been performed by six workers, who passed the work sequentially from one person to another, was performed by four workers, each of whom assembled a complete pump. Unfortunately, al-

■ **Job rotation** involves systematically moving employees from one job to another.

■ **Job enlargement** was developed to increase the total number of tasks workers perform on the assumption that doing the same basic task over and over is the primary cause of worker dissatisfaction.

though job enlargement does have some positive consequences, they are often offset by several disadvantages: (1) Training costs usually rise. (2) Unions have argued that pay should increase because the worker is doing more things. (3) In many cases the work remains boring and routine even after job enlargement.

A more comprehensive approach, **job enrichment**, assumes that increasing the range and variety of tasks is not sufficient by itself to improve employee motivation.[20] Thus job enrichment attempts to increase both the number of tasks a worker does and the control the worker has over the job. To accomplish this goal managers remove some controls from the job, delegate more authority to employees, and structure the work in complete, natural units. These changes increase the subordinates' sense of responsibility. Another part of job enrichment is to continually assign new and challenging tasks, thereby increasing the employees' opportunity for growth and advancement.

> ■ **Job enrichment** attempts to increase both the number of tasks a worker does and the control the worker has over the job.

AT&T was one of the first companies to try job enrichment. In one experiment eight typists in a service unit prepared customer service orders. Faced with low output and high turnover, management determined that the typists felt little responsibility to clients and received little feedback. The unit was changed to create a typing team. Typists were matched with designated service representatives, the task was changed from ten specific steps to three more general steps, and job titles were upgraded. As a result, the frequency of order processing increased from 27 percent to 90 percent, the need for messenger service was eliminated, accuracy improved, and turnover became practically nil.[21] Other organizations that have tried job enrichment include Texas Instruments, IBM, and General Foods. Problems have also been found with this approach, however. For example, analysis of work systems before enrichment is needed but seldom performed, and managers rarely deal with employee preferences when enriching jobs.

The **job characteristics approach** is an alternative to job specialization that does take into account the work system and employee preferences.[22] As illustrated in Figure 15.1, the job characteristics approach suggests that jobs should be diagnosed and improved along five core dimensions:

> ■ The **job characteristics approach** is an alternative to job specialization that takes into account the work system and employee preferences; it suggests that jobs should be diagnosed and improved along five core dimensions.

1. *Skill variety*: the number of things a person does in a job
2. *Task identity*: the extent to which the worker does a complete or identifiable portion of the total job
3. *Task significance*: the perceived importance of the task
4. *Autonomy*: the degree of control the worker has over how the work is performed
5. *Feedback*: the extent to which the worker knows how well the job is being performed.

The higher a job rates on those dimensions, the more employees will experience various psychological states. Experiencing these states, in turn, presumably leads to high motivation, high-quality performance, high satisfaction, and low absenteeism and turnover. Finally, a variable called growth-need strength is presumed to affect how the model works for different people. People with a strong desire to grow, develop, and expand their capabilities (indicative of high growth-need strength) are expected to respond strongly to the presence or absence of the basic job characteristics; individuals with low growth-need strength are expected not to respond as strongly or consistently.

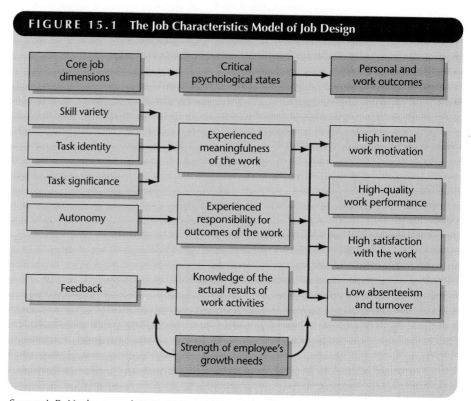

FIGURE 15.1 The Job Characteristics Model of Job Design

Source: J. R. Hackman and G. R. Oldham, "Motivation through the Design of Work: Test of a Theory," *Organizational Behavior and Human Performance*, Vol. 16, 1976, pp. 250–279. Republished by permission of Academic Press via Copyright Clearance Center, Inc. © 1976 by Academic Press, Inc.

Numerous studies have been conducted to test the usefulness of the job characteristics approach. The Southwestern Division of Prudential Insurance, for example, used this approach in its claims division. Results included moderate declines in turnover and a small but measurable improvement in work quality. Other research findings have not supported this approach as strongly. Thus, although the job characteristics approach is one of the most promising alternatives to job specialization, it is probably not the final answer.

Another alternative to job specialization is **work teams**, where a group is given responsibility for designing the work system to be used in performing an interrelated set of jobs. In the typical assembly-line system, the work flows from one worker to the next, and each worker has a specified job to perform. In a work team, however, the group itself decides how jobs will be allocated. For example, the work team assigns specific tasks to members, monitors and controls its own performance, and has autonomy over work scheduling.

■ **Work teams** are an arrangement in which a group is given responsibility for designing the work system to be used in performing an interrelated set of jobs.

THE BOTTOM LINE Managers need to understand the role that job design plays in their organization. They should be especially familiar with the advantages and disadvantages of various alternative approaches to job design and understand why they and their organization have chosen a particular approach to job design. The human resource function may need to play an important role if the organization intends to alter the design of its jobs.

HEALTH AND STRESS MANAGEMENT PROGRAMS

Finally, organizations today are increasingly getting involved in health and stress management programs for their employees.[23] For such programs to be effective, it is first necessary to understand the causes and consequences of stress at work. Figure 15.2 notes the major causes and consequences.

Causes of Stress at Work

We define **stress** as a person's adaptive response to a stimulus that places excessive psychological or physical demands on him or her. The stimuli that cause stress are called *stressors*. Organizational stressors are various factors in the workplace that can cause stress. Four general sets of organizational stressors are task demands, physical demands, role demands, and interpersonal demands.

Task demands are stressors associated with the specific job a person performs. Some occupations are by nature more stressful than others. The jobs of a surgeon, air traffic controller, and professional football coach obviously are more stressful than those of a general practitioner, airplane baggage loader,

■ **Stress** is a person's adaptive response to a stimulus that places excessive psychological or physical demands on him or her.

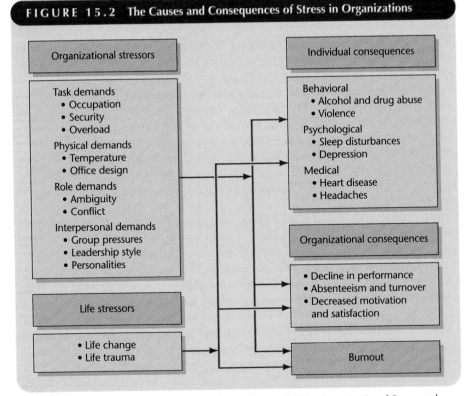

FIGURE 15.2   The Causes and Consequences of Stress in Organizations

Organizational stressors

Task demands
- Occupation
- Security
- Overload

Physical demands
- Temperature
- Office design

Role demands
- Ambiguity
- Conflict

Interpersonal demands
- Group pressures
- Leadership style
- Personalities

Life stressors
- Life change
- Life trauma

Individual consequences

Behavioral
- Alcohol and drug abuse
- Violence

Psychological
- Sleep disturbances
- Depression

Medical
- Heart disease
- Headaches

Organizational consequences
- Decline in performance
- Absenteeism and turnover
- Decreased motivation and satisfaction

Burnout

Source: Reprinted from James C. Quick and Jonathan D. Quick, *Organizational Stress and Preventive Management,* McGraw-Hill, 1984, pp. 19, 44, and 76. Copyright © 1984 by The McGraw-Hill Companies. Reprinted with the permission of The McGraw-Hill Companies.

and football team equipment manager. Beyond specific task-related pressures, other task demands may pose physical threats to a person's health. Such conditions exist in occupations like coal mining, toxic-waste handling, and so forth. Job security is another task demand that can cause stress. Someone in a relatively secure job is not likely to worry unduly about losing that position. On the other hand, if job security is threatened, stress can increase dramatically. For example, stress generally increases throughout an organization during a period of layoffs or immediately following a merger with another firm. Such a phenomenon has been observed at a number of organizations, including AT&T, Safeway, and Digital Equipment.

A final task demand stressor is overload. Overload occurs when a person simply has more work to do than he or she can handle. The overload can be either quantitative (the individual has too many tasks to perform or too little time in which to perform them) or qualitative (the person may believe she or he lacks the ability to do the job). More managers than ever before report having to go to their office on the weekends to get their job done, a direct result of overload.[24] We should also note that the opposite of overload may also be undesirable— low task demands can result in boredom and apathy just as overload can cause tension and anxiety. Thus a moderate degree of workload-related stress is optimal because it leads to high levels of energy and motivation. "Human Resources Tech Talk" discusses how electronic communication may result in information overload, causing heightened stress for managers.

Physical demands relate to the setting of the job. Many of the physical aspects of the work environment we discussed earlier have been associated with stress on the job, such as the requirement that an employee work in extreme temperatures. Also, office design can be related to stress resulting either from isolation or boredom or from too much interaction with coworkers. Strenuous labor such as loading heavy cargo or lifting packages can also lead to stress, as can poor lighting or inadequate work surfaces.

Role demands can also cause stress. A role is a set of expected behaviors associated with a position in a group or organization. Stress can result from either role ambiguity or role conflict that people can experience in groups. For example, an employee who is feeling pressure from her boss to work longer hours while also being asked by her family for more time at home will almost certainly experience stress. Similarly, a new employee experiencing role ambiguity because of poor orientation and training practices by the organization will also suffer from stress.

Yet another set of organizational stressors consists of group pressures, leadership style, and personality conflicts. Group pressures include pressure to restrict output and pressure to conform to the group's norms. For instance, as we have noted before, it is quite common for a work group to arrive at an informal agreement about how much each member will produce. The group may pressure individuals who produce much more or much less than this level to get back in line. An individual who feels a strong need to vary from the group's expectations (perhaps to get a pay raise or promotion) will experience a great deal of stress, especially if acceptance by the group also is important to him or her.

Leadership style also may cause stress. Suppose an employee needs a great deal of social support from his leader. The leader, however, is quite brusque and shows no concern or compassion for him. This employee will likely feel stressed. Similarly, assume an employee feels a strong need to participate in decision making and to be active in all aspects of management. Her boss is very

Too Much Technology?

Information and communication lie at the heart of what most human resource managers do. Finding out what's going on, thinking about what it means and what else is going on, and then telling others what's going on are constant rituals that define much of a manager's work. Today's cutting-edge information technology enables many managers to keep in constant touch with all of their information contacts at all times, regardless of time or location. Need to get a quick message to someone? Send an e-mail. Need an important document from the office? Have it faxed. Need to talk to some right away? Use the cell phone.

Are all these high-tech devices good things? Certainly, new information technology has enabled many human resource managers to make decisions better and faster than ever before. And this technology also promotes more frequent communication among people, resulting in improved coordination and enhanced organizational flexibility and response times. Managers can keep in constant touch with others, and a manager's boss, colleagues, and subordinates can reach the manager at any time.

But there are also trouble spots to be wary of as well. For example, information technology makes it easier than ever before for human resource managers to suffer from information overload. One recent survey, for example, found that managers in typical large corporations send or receive an astonishing 177 messages each day. The form of these messages run the gamut from e-mail to sticky notes. And

"Critical thinking and analysis get lost in an interrupt-driven workplace."

(Nancy Ozawa, consultant)*

many human resource managers fall into the trap of thinking that because they *can* always be in touch, they *must* always be in touch. Thus they check their e-mail constantly, carry their cell phones on vacation or to the golf course, and keep a pager strapped around their waist at all times.

Left unchecked, these managers risk a variety of problems. From an organizational perspective, for example, people may begin to spend so much time communicating that other parts of their work suffer. And instant access to information and the pressure that accompanies modern technology may lead managers to make decisions too rapidly, without taking proper time to reflect and consider all alternatives. Just from an information processing perspective alone, a single daily issue of the *New York Times* contains more information than an average person in the seventeenth century would have encountered in a lifetime!

And the pressure itself can carry dire consequences for individuals. They risk losing balance in their lives, for example, and may be so "connected" that they are never away from their work. As a result, they become prime candidates for burnout and end up falling behind others who take a more ordered and balanced approach not only to their work but also to their lives.

References: Gina Imperato, "The E-mail Prescription," *Fast Company*, May 1999, pp. 90–92; "Drowning in Data," *Newsweek*, April 28, 1997, p. 85; "Memo 4/8/97, FYI: Messages Inundate Offices," *Wall Street Journal*, April 8, 1997, pp. B1, B10 (*quote on p. B1).

autocratic and refuses to consult subordinates about anything. Once again stress is likely to result.

In addition, conflicting personalities and behaviors may cause stress. Conflict can occur when two or more people must work together even though their personalities, attitudes, and behaviors differ. For example, a person with an internal locus of control—that is, who always wants to control how things turn out—might get frustrated working with a person who likes to wait and just let things happen. Likewise, a smoker and a nonsmoker who are assigned adjacent offices obviously will experience stress. Table 15.4 provides a subjective list of the most and least stressful jobs, based on factors such as quotas and deadlines, long work weeks, and various other problem areas. Finally, it is important to note that all of the stressors mentioned here exist against a background of general life events that cause stress as well.

TABLE 15.4 Most and Least Stressful Jobs

The most and least stressful jobs, based on such factors as quotas and deadlines, long work weeks, the hazards involved, level of competitiveness, physical demands, environmental conditions, contact with the public, need for precision, and amount of stamina required.

Most Stressful Jobs	Least Stressful Jobs
1. U.S. president	1. Medical records technician
2. Firefighter	2. Janitor
3. Senior corporate executive	3. Forklift operator
4. Race car driver (Indy class)	4. Musical instrument repairer
5. Taxi driver	5. Florist
6. Surgeon	6. Actuary
7. Astronaut	7. Appliance repairer
8. Police officer	8. Medical secretary
9. Football player (NFL)	9. Librarian
10. Air traffic controller	10. Bookkeeper
11. Highway patrol officer	11. File clerk
12. Public relations executive	12. Piano tuner
13. Mayor	13. Photographic process worker
14. Jockey	14. Dietitian
15. Basketball coach (NCAA)	15. Paralegal assistant
16. Advertising account executive	16. Vending machine repairer
17. Real estate agent	17. Bookbinder
18. Photojournalist	18. Barber
19. Member of Congress	19. Medical laboratory technician
20. Stockbroker	20. Electrical technician
21. Fisherman	21. Typist/Word processor
22. Airplane pilot	22. Broadcast technician
23. Lumberjack	23. Mathematician
24. Emergency medical technician	24. Dental hygienist
25. Architect	25. Jeweler

Source: The Wall Street Journal Almanac 1999, p. 232. Republished by permission of Dow Jones, Inc. via Copyright Clearance Center, Inc. © 1999 Dow Jones and Company, Inc. All Rights Reserved.

Consequences of Stress at Work

Stress can have a number of consequences. If the stress is positive, the result may be more energy, enthusiasm, and motivation. Of more concern, of course, are the negative consequences of stress. Three sets of consequences that can result from stress are individual consequences, organizational consequences, and burnout.[25]

Stress is a major problem in many organizational settings. As illustrated in this cartoon, people often bring their work-related problems home with them. Although doing so is generally unavoidable, if carried to excess, this practice can result in sleep disturbances, depression, and similar problems. One method for helping counter stress is to have a good support network. A partner and friends, for example, can help people cope with stress, keep things in perspective, and take their minds off work.

Behavioral consequences of stress are responses that may harm the person under stress or others. One such behavior is smoking. Research has clearly documented that people who smoke tend to smoke more when they experience stress. Other possible behavioral consequences of stress are accident proneness, violence, and appetite disorders. Psychological consequences of stress relate to an individual's mental health and well-being. When people experience too much stress at work, they may become depressed or find themselves sleeping too much or not enough. Stress may also lead to family problems and sexual difficulties. The medical consequences of stress affect a person's physical well-being. Heart disease and stroke, among other illnesses, have been linked to stress. Other common medical problems resulting from too much stress include headaches, backaches, ulcers and related stomach and intestinal disorders, and skin conditions like acne and hives. The "Lighter Side of HR" illustrates how these consequences can occur.

Clearly, any of the individual consequences just discussed can also affect the organization. Still other consequences of stress have even more direct consequences for organizations. One clear organizational consequence of too much stress is a decline in performance. For operating workers such a decline can translate into poor-quality work or a drop in productivity. For managers it can mean faulty decision making or disruptions in working relationships as people become irritable and hard to get along with.

Withdrawal behaviors also can result from stress. For the organization the two most significant forms of withdrawal behavior are absenteeism and quitting. People who are having a hard time coping with stress in their jobs are more likely to call in sick or consider leaving the organization for good. And indeed, many organizations today report increased absenteeism among their most overworked staff members.[26] Other, more subtle forms of withdrawal also can result from stress. A manager may start missing deadlines or taking longer lunch breaks. An employee may withdraw psychologically by ceasing to care about the organization and the job. Employee violence, noted above as a potential individual consequence of stress, also has obvious organizational implications, especially if the violence is directed at an employee or at the organization in general.

Wellness programs are a common component of many organizational health and stress management initiatives. These employees, for example, work for Autodesk, a firm specializing in computer-aided design software. Because the workers sit for long periods with little motion, the company sponsors such wellness activities as this yoga class. By providing employees with opportunities to both stretch and exercise their bodies plus get their minds off work for a while, the firm feels that it is helping them lead healthier and more balanced lives.

Another direct organizational consequence of employee stress relates to attitudes. As we just noted, job satisfaction, morale, and organizational commitment can all suffer, along with motivation to perform at high levels. As a result, people may be more prone to complain about unimportant things, do only enough work to get by, and so forth. Burnout, another consequence of stress, has clear implications for both people and organizations. **Burnout** is a general feeling of exhaustion that develops when an individual simultaneously experiences too much pressure and too few sources of satisfaction.

■ **Burnout** is a general feeling of exhaustion that develops when an individual simultaneously experiences too much pressure and too few sources of satisfaction.

■ **Institutional programs** for managing stress are undertaken through established organizational mechanisms.

Wellness Programs in Organizations

Two basic organizational strategies for helping employees manage stress are institutional programs and collateral programs. **Institutional programs** for managing stress are undertaken through established organizational mechanisms. For example, properly designed jobs and work schedules, as discussed earlier, can help ease stress. Shift work, in particular, can cause major problems for employees, as they constantly have to adjust their sleep and relaxation patterns. Thus the design of work and work schedules should be a focus of organizational efforts to reduce stress.

The organization's culture also can be used to help manage stress. In some organizations, for example, there is a strong norm against taking time off or going on vacation. In the long run such norms can cause major stress. Thus the organization should strive to foster a culture that reinforces a healthy mix of work and nonwork activities. Finally, supervision can play an important institutional role in managing stress. A supervisor is a potential major source of overload. If made aware of their potential for assigning stressful amounts of work, supervisors can do a better job of keeping workloads reasonable.

In addition to their institutional efforts aimed at reducing stress, many organizations are turning to collateral programs. A **collateral stress program** is specifically created to help employees deal with stress. Organizations have adopted stress management programs, health promotion programs, and other kinds of programs for this purpose. More and more companies are developing their own programs or adopting existing programs of this type. For example, Lockheed Martin offers screening programs for its employees to detect signs of hypertension, and Hospital Corporation of America offers its employees four cents a mile for cycling, sixteen cents a mile for walking or jogging, and sixty-four cents a mile for swimming.

Many firms today also have employee fitness programs. These kinds of programs attack stress indirectly by encouraging employees to exercise, which in turn is presumed to reduce stress. On the negative side, this kind of effort costs considerably more than stress management programs because the firm must invest in physical facilities. Still, more and more companies are exploring this option. Both Tenneco and L.L. Bean, for example, have state-of-the-art fitness centers available for their employees to use.

Finally, organizations try to help employees cope with stress through other kinds of programs. For example, existing career development programs, like that at General Electric, are used for this purpose. Other companies use programs promoting everything from humor to massage as antidotes for stress. Of course, there is little or no research to support some of the claims made by advocates of these programs. Thus managers must take steps to ensure that any organizational effort to help employees cope with stress is at least reasonably effective.

> ■ **Collateral stress programs** are organizational programs specifically created to help employees deal with stress.

AIDS in the Workplace

Everyone recognizes that acquired immune deficiency syndrome, or AIDS, has become a major problem in the world today. AIDS is relevant to employers for a variety of reasons. First of all, if an employee has AIDS, in addition to that being a serious issue for the individual, it is also important to that individual's coworkers. Unfortunately, there is no clear-cut solution for how to deal with this problem. Individuals who publicly disclose their illness increase the potential for retaliation from coworkers—many people fear the disease and may shun those who have it. And the organization faces a variety of privacy-related issues.

In general, an organization that wants to truly deal with this issue must start by developing and implementing a comprehensive AIDS policy. As a premise for developing a policy, however, all employers must keep in mind certain things. First of all, it is illegal to ask an applicant whether she or he has AIDS. Some states allow organizations to require applicants to take an AIDS test, whereas other states do not. But regardless of the outcome, an employee can be denied employment on the basis of AIDS only if it is determined that the applicant cannot perform the job. Similarly, as long as the individual is capable of performing the job, he or she cannot be terminated or placed on leave. All medical information regarding the individual and her or his condition must also be treated in absolute confidence.

In general, organizations can follow three approaches in trying to deal with AIDS from a management perspective. One strategy is to categorize AIDS under a comprehensive life-threatening-illness policy. In this instance the organization treats AIDS just like terminal cancer or any other life-threatening illness and applies the same sorts of insurance coverage provisions, early retirement and leave provisions, and so forth.

Another strategy is to form an AIDS-specific policy. Contemplating this type of policy is a completely legal action, as long as neither the intent nor the implementation of the policy results in discrimination against people on the basis of AIDS. In general, most companies that form an AIDS-specific policy do so in an affirmative way. That is, the essence of the policy is to affirm the organization's stance that employees with AIDS are still entitled to work, receive benefits, and be treated comparably to all other employees.

Finally, the third approach that some companies take is to have no policy at all. Unfortunately, far too many companies take this approach. The problem here is that the organization doesn't want to confront the necessity for having an AIDS policy, is afraid to confront the need for such a policy, or doesn't know how to approach such a policy. In any of these events, managerial ignorance can potentially result in serious problems for both the employer and the employees of an organization.

THE BOTTOM LINE   All managers should be well versed in the basic issues of health and stress management in organizations. Since stress affects both managers and their employees, they should have a clear understanding of its causes and consequences. Managers should also be familiar with relevant details about any wellness programs supported by their organization. And finally, managers need to have an understanding of AIDS, both at a general level as well as specific policy-related details.

Chapter Summary

The foundation of workplace rights is the employment-at-will doctrine. Many of the laws and regulations governing human resource management have been created to help define, maintain, and preserve various employee rights. The rights to privacy and the protection of employees' personal lives are major issues today.

Organizations and human resource managers must pay careful attention to issues associated with discipline in the workplace. Discipline is a formal organizational action taken against an employee as a result of a rules violation, subpar performance, or similar dysfunctional behavior. Punishment, however, is any behavior or action that results in unpleasant effects or consequences for someone else. Various kinds of employee behaviors can result in problems for the organization.

Given that organizations may have to use discipline and punishment, it follows that these activities should be closely managed to maximize their potential

impact. Appropriate documentation is the cornerstone of an effective disciplinary system. Organizations can undertake a variety of disciplinary approaches. Some managers prefer to use what has traditionally been called the hot stove rule of discipline. More typically, organizations that create discipline systems attempt to provide what is called progressive discipline.

The actual physical environment in which an employee works is also extremely important. Many aspects of the physical environment may affect an employee's attitudes and behavior on the job. Hours of work reflect one such aspect. Illumination, temperature, and office and workspace design are also important.

Another important part of managing a work environment deals with employee safety and health. Basic issues involve actions that the organization can and should take to control or eliminate safety hazards and health hazards. Safety hazards are factors in the work environment that have the potential to cause harm to an employee. Health hazards are those characteristics of the work environment that more slowly and systematically, and perhaps cumulatively, result in damage to an employee's health. OSHA authorized the U.S. government to create and enforce various standards regarding occupational safety and health.

Job design is the determination of an individual's work-related responsibilities. Job specialization is the degree to which the overall task of the organization is broken down and divided into smaller component parts. Job rotation involves systematically moving employees from one job to another. On the assumption that doing the same basic task over and over is the primary cause of worker dissatisfaction, job enlargement was developed to increase the total number of tasks workers perform. A more comprehensive approach, job enrichment, assumes that increasing the range and variety of tasks is not sufficient by itself to improve employee motivation. The job characteristics approach is an alternative to job specialization that takes into account the work system and employee preferences. Another alternative to job specialization is work teams.

Stress is a person's adaptive response to a stimulus that places excessive psychological or physical demands on him or her. The stimuli that cause stress are called stressors. Organizational stressors are various factors in the workplace that can cause stress. Four general sets of organizational stressors are task demands, physical demands, role demands, and interpersonal demands. If the stress is positive, the result may be more energy, enthusiasm, and motivation. Three other sets of consequences that can result from stress are individual consequences, organizational consequences, and burnout. Two basic organizational strategies for helping employees manage stress are institutional programs and collateral programs. Dealing with AIDS is also important to employers for a variety of reasons.

Review and Discussion Questions

1. What are your personal opinions regarding the privacy of e-mail and the private lives of employees?

2. Distinguish between discipline and punishment.

3. What are the basic differences between hot stove and progressive discipline systems?

4. Describe the kind of physical environment in which you would most like to work.

5. What are the differences between safety hazards and health hazards?

6. Review the list of injury-prone jobs and dangerous occupations in Table 15.2. Identify five other jobs that you think might also belong on each list.

7. Research the OSHA guidelines and regulations that most directly relate to your current or anticipated job.

8. What are the advantages and disadvantages of job specialization?

9. Identify and summarize the various alternatives to job specialization.

10. What are the primary causes and consequences of stress in organizations?

Closing Case

Safety Comes to Georgia-Pacific

Georgia-Pacific Corporation is the world's largest distributor of building products (such as wood panels, lumber, and gypsum products) and among the five largest manufacturers of packaging materials, correspondence paper (such as office printing products and stationery), wood pulp, and tissue paper. The Atlanta-based firm has more than one hundred distribution centers scattered across North America and controls more than six million acres of timberland in the United States and Canada. Its annual revenues generally run around $13 to $14 billion.

Forest-products businesses have never been known for their safe, pleasant, and comfortable work environments. Paper mills, sawmills, and plywood factories, for example, are generally characterized by constant deafening noise, huge razor-toothed blades, shredders and grinders, long chutes loaded with rumbling tons of lumber, and giant vats full of boiling water and caustic chemicals. The products they make are awkward in size, heavy, and often full of painful splinters, and the machinery used to make them requires frequent maintenance and close contact with sharp edges and dangerous moving parts.

Throughout much of its history, Georgia-Pacific had an unenviable safety record even for what experts see as a highly dangerous and hazardous industry. For example, between 1986 and 1990 the firm averaged nine serious injuries per year per one hundred employees, and twenty-six workers lost their lives on the job. Two factors contributing to these statistics were unrelenting pressure to keep productivity high and a macho organization culture that promoted risk taking and bravado.

For example, top management continually reinforced the importance of keeping production lines moving, no matter what. As a result, workers would often attempt to perform routine maintenance or repair broken equipment parts without shutting down the line. And if they didn't have a pair of safety gloves handy, they would carry around heavy—and sharp—saw blades with their bare hands rather than "waste" an extra few minutes to take appropriate safety cautions. Indeed, one observer noted that you weren't considered a real Georgia-Pacific "mill guy" unless you were missing a finger or two!

But this culture started to change about ten years ago when a new top management team came in. The new managers were appalled at the firm's poor safety record and vowed to make it a source of pride rather than a source of embarrassment. The starting point was to create a task force charged with learning more about operating practices that contributed to accidents and then figuring out how to change those practices. The next step was to alter the firm's basic culture so as to reinforce safe rather than risky practices and behaviors. And finally, Georgia-Pacific implemented an array of new rules and regulations that explicitly promote safe work and punish those responsible for unnecessarily hazardous or dangerous actions.

So far, the results have been impressive. Accident rates dropped consistently every year in the 1990s, for example, and very few workers lose their lives anymore. At one of the firm's most hazardous plants, injuries run about 0.7 per 100 workers annually. OSHA indicates that this figure is about one-third the injury rate at the average bank! And the company has realized that being more cautious and following safer work procedures has actually boosted its productivity. Clearly, stopping a production line to correct a problem usually takes only a few minutes, whereas stopping it because of an accident or injury might shut down production for hours—or even days.

Injury rates now play a major role in the performance evaluation and compensation for all supervisors and managers at Georgia-Pacific. And safety equipment is an absolute requirement. One top manager, for example, happily tells the story of how he was recently chewed out by an hourly worker for carelessly stepping too close to a dangerous piece of equipment while visiting a sawmill. And all employees in the mills have to wear earplugs, hardhats, goggles, gloves, and steel-toed shoes at all times. Failure to follow these regulations can result in immediate dismissal. And indeed, Georgia-Pacific is so proud of its achievements in this area that it's working to extend the same principles used to make these changes to other areas of its business, including quality and customer service.

Case Questions

1. Why do you think Georgia-Pacific has been so successful in reducing its accident and injury rates?

2. What other industries and businesses might benefit from the same kind of approach?

3. Research Georgia-Pacific's most recent safety statistics and see whether the firm is still doing as well.

Sources: Anne Fisher, "Danger Zone," *Fortune*, September 8, 1997, pp. 165–167; *Hoover's Handbook of American Business 1999* (Austin, Texas: Hoover's Business Press, 1999), pp. 660–661.

Building Human Resource Management Skills

Purpose: The purpose of this exercise is to help you understand the motivational properties of jobs and the possibilities and constraints that exist with regard to improving them.

Step 1: Begin by identifying three jobs with which you have some basic familiarity. Select one job that you would imagine to be extremely boring and routine, one that you would imagine to be wildly exciting and enjoyable, and one somewhere in between these two extremes.

Step 2: Using the job dimensions reflected in the job characteristics approach, figure out how to change the design of each job to make it more enriched, enjoyable, and motivating. For example, suggest ways to add variety and feedback to the jobs in as realistic a way as possible.

Step 3: Identify the constraints and limitations that are likely to exist if an organization wanted to make the changes you have identified.

Step 4: Respond to the following questions:

1. What job qualities make some jobs easier to enrich than others?

2. Can all jobs be enriched?

3. Even if a particular job should be enriched, does that always mean that it should be enriched?

4. Under what circumstances might an individual prefer to have a routine and unenriched job?

Ethical Dilemmas in Human Resource Management

You are the owner/manager of a small software enterprise. You employ 150 people, all of whom have stock options in the business. Working in consultation with several of your designers, you are closing in on a major breakthrough with a software product that can dramatically reduce manufacturing costs for firms in several industries. Several larger competitors are working hard to develop the same basic technology. If your firm is to achieve the breakthrough first, a major push is needed.

You are sitting in your office weighing the following basic facts:

1. All of your employees are on the verge of exhaustion; they have each been putting in sixty to eighty hours per week for the last four months, and no one ever takes a day off. You know that a couple of employees are drinking more than normal, and at least three are reportedly having marital difficulties.

2. You estimate that another six to eight weeks of intense work and long hours should allow your firm to get the new product up and running first.

3. If your firm is, in fact, first to get the new software finished, everyone in the firm will reap a big financial reward. The most senior employees (and you, of course) will probably become millionaires; even the newest employees should see their stock options increase in value to near $100,000 more than their current value.

4. It will take an all-or-nothing effort if you are to succeed. That is, if you cut back on work schedules or give people time off, you will fall behind your competitors. Every single worker will need to go all out until the project is finished, or you might as well give up now.

So you have two options. On the one hand, you could cut back on the workload and reduce the stress and pressure on your employees. Although your firm would almost certainly lose the race for the software breakthrough, the company is nevertheless quite profitable and your employees earn an above-market income. Moreover, there may be other opportunities for major breakthroughs in the future. On the other hand, you could keep things going as they are. After all, its only for a few more weeks, and then everyone will share in what promises to be a major reward.

Questions

1. What are the ethical issues in this situation?

2. What are the basic arguments for and against continuing an all-out push to achieve the breakthrough?

3. What do you think most owner/managers would do? What would you do?

Human Resource Internet Exercise

The Occupational Safety & Health Administration (OSHA), a part of the U.S. Department of Labor, maintains a very extensive Web site. Start by visiting the site at the address below:

http://www.osha.gov/

Now assume that you have just been placed in charge of workplace safety for a medium-size manufacturing firm plagued by a high rate of injuries and accidents. Based on your review of the OSHA Web site, respond to these questions:

1. How helpful do you think the OSHA Web site might be to you in working to lower your plant's accident and injury rate?

2. What parts of the site do you think are most and least helpful?

3. Do you think a manager in your position can rely solely on the OSHA Web site to deal with problems, or is other information required?

Notes

1. Brian S. Klaas and Daniel C. Feldman, "The Impact of Appeal System Structure on Disciplinary Decisions," *Personnel Psychology*, 1994, pp. 91–103.

2. Jonathan A. Segal, "Alcoholic Employees and the Law," *HRMagazine*, December 1993, pp. 87–92.

3. Bill Oliver, "How to Prevent Drug Abuse in Your Workplace," *HRMagazine*, December 1993, pp. 78–82.

4. Terry L. Leap and Michael D. Crino, "How Serious IS Serious?" *HRMagazine*, May 1998, pp. 43–48.

5. Myron D. Fottler, "Employee Acceptance of a Four Day Work Week," *Academy of Management Journal*, Vol. 20, 1977, pp. 656–668.

6. Simca Ronen and Sophia B. Primpts, "The Compressed Work Week as Organizational Change: Behavioral and Attitudinal Outcomes," *Academy of Management Review*, Vol. 6, 1981, pp. 61–74.

7. A. Purach, "Biological Rhythm Effects of Night Work and Shift Changes on the Health of Workers," *Acta Medica Scandanvia*, Vol. 152, 1973, pp. 302–307.

8. Sheldon Zedeck, Susan E. Jackson, and Elizabeth S. Marca, "Shift Work Schedules and Their Relationship to Health, Adaptation, Satisfaction, and Turnover Intentions," *Academy of Management Journal*, Vol. 26, 1983, pp. 297–310.

9. G. B. Meese, M. I. Lewis, D. P. Wyon, and R. Kok, "A Laboratory Study of the Effects of Thermal Stress on the Performance of Factory Workers," *Ergonomics*, Vol. 27, 1982, pp. 19–43.

10. E. VanDeVliert and N. W. Van Yperen, "Why Cross National Differences in Role Overload? Don't Overlook Ambient Temperature," *Academy of Management Journal*, Vol. 39, 1996, pp. 986–1004.

11. D. G. Hayward, "Psychological Factors in the Use of Light and Lighting in Buildings," in J. Lang, C. Burnette, W. Moleski, and D. Vachon (eds.), *Designing for Human Behavior: Architecture and the Behavioral Sciences* (Stroudsburg, Penna.: Dowden, Hutchinson, & Ross, 1974), pp. 120–129.

12. R. I. Newman, D. L. Hunt, and F. Rhodes, "Effects of Music on Employee Attitude and Productivity in a Skateboard Factory," *Journal of Applied Psychology*, Vol. 50, 1956, pp. 493–496.

13. Gregory R. Oldham, Anne Cummings, L. J. Mischel, J. Marshall Scmidtke, and Jing Zhou, "Listen While You Work? Quasi-Experimental Relations between Personal Stereo Headset Use and Employee Work Responses," *Journal of Applied Psychology*, Vol. 80, 1995, pp. 547–564.

14. Gregory R. Oldham, "Effects of Changes in Workspace Partitions and Spatial Density on Employee Reactions: A Quasi-Experiment," *Journal of Applied Psychology*, Vol. 73, 1988, pp. 253–258.

15. "Working at Home Raises Job Site Safety Issues," *USA Today*, January 29, 1998, p. 1A.

16. "Labor Secretary's Bid to Push Plant Safety Runs into Skepticism," *Wall Street Journal*, August 19, 1994, pp. A1, A5.

17. Robert S. Haynes, Randall C. Pine, and H. Gordon Fitch, "Reducing Accident Rates with Organizational Behavior Modification," *Academy of Management Journal*, Vol. 25, 1982, pp. 407–416.

18. "In an Amoco Lab, Researchers Hunt for Colleagues' Killer," *USA Today*, April 13, 1999, p. 8D.

19. Ricky W. Griffin, *Task Design* (Glenview, Ill.: Scott, Foresman, 1982).

20. Frederick Herzberg, *Work and the Nature of Man* (Cleveland: World Press, 1966).

21. Robert Ford, "Job Enrichment Lessons from AT&T," *Harvard Business Review*, January–February 1973, pp. 96–106.

22. J. Richard Hackman and Greg R. Oldham, *Work Redesign* (Reading, Mass.: Addison-Wesley, 1980).

23. Karen Danna and Ricky W. Griffin, "Health and Well-Being in the Workplace," *Journal of Management*, Vol. 25, 1999, pp. 357–384.

24. "Workplace Demands Taking up More Week-Ends," *USA Today*, April 24, 1998, p. 1B.

25. Richard S. DeFrank and John M. Ivancevich, "Stress on the Job: An Executive Update," *Academy of Management Executive*, Vol. 12, No. 3, 1998, pp. 55–65.

26. "Overloaded Staffers Are Starting to Take More Time off Work," *Wall Street Journal*, September 23, 1998, p. B1.

16

Managing the Diverse Workforce

CHAPTER OUTLINE

The Nature of Workforce Diversity
The Meaning of Workforce Diversity
Trends in Workforce Diversity

Diversity Management Versus Equal Employment Opportunity
Similarities among People at Work
Differences among People at Work
Identical Treatment versus Equitable Treatment

Basic Dimensions of Diversity
Age Distributions
Gender
Ethnicity
Disability
Other Dimensions of Diversity

The Impact of Diversity on Organizations
Diversity and Social Change
Diversity and Competitiveness
Diversity and Conflict

Managing Diversity in Organizations
Individual Strategies for Dealing with Diversity
Organizational Strategies for Dealing with Diversity

The Multicultural Organization

CHAPTER OBJECTIVES

After studying this chapter you should be able to:

■ Discuss the nature of diversity, including its meaning and associated trends.

■ Distinguish between diversity management and equal employment opportunity.

■ Identify and describe the major dimensions of diversity in organizations.

■ Discuss the primary impact of diversity on organizations.

■ Describe individual and organizational strategies and approaches to coping with diversity.

■ Discuss the six characteristics of the fully multicultural organization.

Diversity is a fact of life in organizations today. And although there are many benefits of diversity, the potential for conflict also increases significantly. Different backgrounds, perspectives, customs, and values combine to make it ever more likely that people will disagree and see things in different ways.

For example, take the Marriott Marquis Hotel near New York's Times Square. The hotel employs seventeen hundred people from seventy countries who speak a total of forty-seven languages. One major reason for the hotel's diversity is its labor pool—the area is populated by a diverse set of immigrants, and it is often these residents who apply for jobs. But the hotel managers also strongly believe that the diverse workforce is an asset, in part because it fits the hotel's multicultural clientele.

But managing diversity at the Marriott can be a challenge. For example, consider the case of Jessica Brown, an African-American quality-assurance manager responsible for housekeeping. Ms. Brown says that when she rewards other African-Americans, some of her Hispanic employees criticize her for playing favorites. But when she rewards

"... all you can really do is hope [the resentment] goes away eventually. And it usually does."

(Cynthia Keating, Marriott manager)*

the Hispanics, some African-Americans accuse her of ignoring them.

Balancing religious preferences is also complicated. One manager, Victor Aragona, recently sought out a room attendant to fix an overflowing bathtub. He found the attendant prostrate on a towel in the housekeeper's closet, bowing to Mecca and saying his daily Islamic prayers. Rather than disturb him, Aragona fixed the bathtub himself.

To help cope with these challenges, Marriott offers frequent training programs in multiculturalism and conflict management. These courses are required for all managers and are open to most other employees as well. Even so, the hotel still offers periodic and regular refresher courses to help people work together with a minimum of conflict.

"How One Hotel Manages Staff Diversity," *Wall Street Journal*, November 20, 1996, pp. B1, B11 (*quote on p. B11); *Hoover's Handbook of American Business 1999* (Austin, Texas: Hoover's Business Press, 1999), pp. 904–905; "In a Factory Schedule, Where Does Religion Fit In?" *Wall Street Journal*, March 4, 1999, pp. B1, B12; Roy Johnson, "The 50 Best Companies for Blacks & Hispanics," *Fortune*, August 3, 1998, pp. 94–106.

Managers at the Marriott Marquis Hotel face a complex set of challenges and opportunities. On the one hand, the diverse workforce that they oversee poses far more complications and complexities than would a more homogenous one. On the other hand, however, the diverse workforce employed at the hotel also provides competitive advantages and opportunities to better cater to the multinational clients who frequent the area. Balancing the complications and benefits of diversity is among the most important workplace issues facing managers and their organizations today.

This chapter is about workforce diversity in organizations. We begin by exploring the meaning and nature of diversity. We then distinguish between diversity management and equal employment opportunity. Next we identify and discuss several common dimensions of diversity and explore the impact of diversity on the organization. We then address how diversity can be managed for the benefit of both individuals and organizations. Finally, we characterize and describe the fully multicultural organization.

THE NATURE OF WORKFORCE DIVERSITY

Workforce diversity has become a very important issue in many organizations, both within the United States and abroad. A logical starting point in studying this phenomenon, then, is to establish the meaning of diversity and to then examine why such diversity is increasing today.

The Meaning of Workforce Diversity

■ **Diversity** exists in a group or organization when its members differ from one another along one or more important dimensions.

Diversity exists in a group or organization when its members differ from one another along one or more important dimensions.[1] If everyone in the group or organization is exactly like everyone else, diversity does not exist. But if everyone is different along every imaginable dimension, the situation is one of total diversity. In reality, of course, these extremes are more hypothetical than real. Most settings are characterized by a level of diversity somewhere between these extremes. Thus diversity is not an absolute phenomenon wherein a group or organization is or is not diverse. Instead, diversity should be conceptualized as a continuum. Therefore, diversity should be thought of in terms of degree or level of diversity along relevant dimensions.[2]

These dimensions of diversity might include gender, age, ethic origin, or any of several other characteristics. A group of five middle-age white male U.S. executives has relatively little diversity. If one member leaves and is replaced by a young white female executive, the group becomes a bit more diverse. If another member is replaced by an older African-American executive, diversity increases a bit more. And when a third member is replaced by a Japanese executive, the group becomes even more diverse.

Trends in Workforce Diversity

As we noted earlier, organizations today are becoming increasingly diverse along many different dimensions. Several factors have accounted for these trends and changes. One factor that has contributed to increased diversity is changing demographics in the labor force. As more women and minorities have entered the labor force, for example, the available pool of talent from which organizations hire employees has changed in both size and composition. If talent within each segment of the labor pool is evenly distributed (for example, if the number of very talented men in the workforce as a percentage of all men in the workforce is the same as the number of very talented women in the workforce as a percentage of all women in the workforce), it follows logically that, over time, an organization will hire proportionately more women and proportionately fewer men.

A related factor that has contributed to diversity is the increased awareness by organizations that they can improve the overall quality of their workforce by hiring and promoting the most talented people available, regardless of gender, race, or any other characteristics. By casting a broader net in recruiting and looking beyond traditional sources for new employees, organizations are finding more broadly qualified and better qualified employees from many different segments of society. Thus these organizations are finding that diversity can be a source of competitive advantage.

Another reason for the increase in diversity is legislation and legal actions that have forced organizations to hire more broadly. In earlier times organizations in the United States were essentially free to discriminate against women, blacks, and other minorities. Thus most organizations were dominated by white males. But over the last thirty years or so, various laws have outlawed discrimination against these and other groups. As we detailed in Chapter 3, organizations must hire and promote people today solely on the basis of their qualifications.

More and more organizations have come to realize that workforce diversity can be a significant source of competitive advantage. Consider, for example, Kellogg's and its new CEO, Carlos Gutierrez. Under Gutierrez's leadership, Kellogg's has made a major commitment to increasing the diversity in its workforce. As suggested by Kellogg's head of research and development, Donna Banks, "creativity comes with diversity." To help tap this diversity, Banks looks for new employees with exotic backgrounds. The research center she directs employs people from twenty-two different nationalities.

A final contributing factor to increased diversity in organizations has been the globalization movement. Organizations that have opened offices and related facilities in other countries have had to learn to deal with different customs, social norms, and mores. Strategic alliances and foreign ownership have also contributed as managers today are more likely to have job assignments in other countries and/or to work with foreign managers within their own countries. As employees and managers move from assignment to assignment across national boundaries, organizations and their subsidiaries within each country thus become more diverse. Closely related to this pattern is a recent increase in immigration into the United States. As illustrated in Figure 16.1, for example, immigration declined steadily from 1900 until around 1930 but has been increasing since that time.

THE BOTTOM LINE Managers need to clearly understand the meaning of diversity. It is also helpful to understand what the reasons are that underly a consistent increase in diversity in most organizations today.

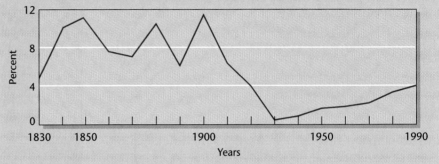

FIGURE 16.1   Immigration Trends into the United States

IMMIGRATION RATE RISES

The immigration rate reached a high just after the turn of the twentieth century, when 11 of every 100 U.S. residents were immigrants. Today the rate is higher than at any time since the 1910s. The immigration rate per 100 U.S. residents:

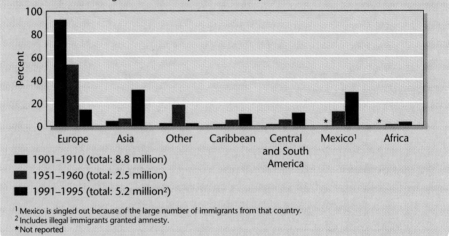

National origin of immigrants is changing. A hundred years ago, the greatest number of immigrants were Europeans. Now they are Asians and Latin Americans.

■ 1901–1910 (total: 8.8 million)
■ 1951–1960 (total: 2.5 million)
■ 1991–1995 (total: 5.2 million²)

¹ Mexico is singled out because of the large number of immigrants from that country.
² Includes illegal immigrants granted amnesty.
* Not reported

Source: USA TODAY, February 28, 1997, p. 7A. Copyright 1997, *USA Today*. Reprinted with permission.

■ **Equal employment opportunity** means treating people fairly and equitably and taking actions that do not discriminate against people in protected classes on the basis of some illegal criterion.

■ **Diversity management** places a much heavier role on recognizing and appreciating differences among people at work and attempting to provide accommodations for those differences to the extent that is feasible and possible.

DIVERSITY MANAGEMENT VERSUS EQUAL EMPLOYMENT OPPORTUNITY

Many managers assume that diversity and equal employment opportunity mean the same thing. In fact, they mean very different things. **Equal employment opportunity** means treating people fairly and equitably and taking actions that do not discriminate against people in protected classes on the basis of some illegal criterion. But **diversity management** places a much heavier role on recognizing and appreciating differences among people at work and attempting to accommodate those differences to the extent that is feasible and possible.

Similarities among People at Work

Regardless of how different people appear to be, virtually all employees share some fundamental similarities.[3] For example, most people work to satisfy some set of needs, almost always based on financial criteria. Further, most people have a fundamental and basic desire to be treated with respect and dignity by their employer. And third, most people have a capacity for being reasonable and understanding when confronted with reasonable behavior by others and when they recognize all the information relevant to a work setting.

Differences among People at Work

Despite the fact that people generally share some basic set of similar characteristics, various fundamental differences (treated more fully later in the chapter) also exist. Common differences include characteristics such as gender, ethnicity, and age. But the long list of differences among individuals ranges from factors such as religious beliefs to dietary preferences to political philosophies.

Identical Treatment versus Equitable Treatment

In the years immediately following the passage of Title VII of the 1964 Civil Rights Act, many human resource managers operated under the assumption that they were required by the law to treat everyone equally. But in reality, that was neither the intent of the law nor is it really even possible. The real essence, not only of Title VII but also of the more contemporary perspective on workforce diversity, is that it is appropriate to acknowledge differences among people just as long as people are treated fairly.

Consider religion, for example. A typical company in the United States routinely closes for major Christian holidays such as Christmas and Easter. However, people who have different religious beliefs may not acknowledge the sanctity of these days and instead have a different set of religious holidays. Thus an employer who provides Christian holidays off should also try to provide important religious holidays off for employees of other faiths. The Whirlpool appliance factory near Nashville, for example, employs about two hundred Muslims (about 10 percent of its workforce). Whirlpool offers its Muslim employees time off for their major religious holidays just as it does for its employees of different faiths and beliefs. Further, the factory found it necessary to adjust its daily work schedules, cafeteria menus, and dress codes to accommodate workers who need to pray

Managers need to remember that diversity management is not the same thing as equal employment opportunity. For example, firms who recruit a diverse set of employees like those shown here—vice presidents at No. 1-ranked Union Bank of California, whose stock has quadrupled in five years—must obviously use only job-related criteria in selection and other elements of the employment relationship. But they must also recognize that effectively utilizing a diverse workforce will mean allowing for equitable accommodation due to differences in religion, gender, age, and so forth.

several times a day; don't eat pork; and wear loose-fitting clothing, head covering, and sandals.[4]

Similarly, men and women are fundamentally different in various ways that cannot be ignored in the workplace. For example, on average men have greater muscle mass than do women and can therefore lift heavier weights. And it is women who have the biological capacity to bear children. Consequently, men and women may need fundamentally different treatment in work organizations. For example, women may need to be given longer periods of time off immediately preceding and after the birth of a child. Similarly, when a woman chooses to return to work, the organization may need to provide a transitional period during which her work-related demands gradually increase until she returns to her normal schedule.

The Americans with Disabilities Act (ADA) presents a serious challenge to managers who try to balance treating everyone the same with treating everyone equitably. The ADA specifically states that an organization cannot discriminate against a person with a disability as long as he or she can perform the essential functions of the job "with or without a reasonable accommodation." Therefore, an employee who requests such an accommodation must be accommodated. At first glance, this request may not seem very problematic, since the employee presumably needs this accommodation to perform his or her job. Furthermore, many of the accommodations requested and granted, such as large-print computer screens, allowances for guide dogs, wheelchair ramps, or amplified phones, don't usually present a problem.

But what about an accommodation requested by a person with a disability that would be desirable and/or useful to other employees who do not have a disability? An interesting example of this dilemma occurred in early 1998 when the Professional Golf Association (PGA) ruled that Casey Martin, whose serious circulatory disorder made walking a golf course dangerous, would be allowed to use a golf cart in tournament play. Many other golfers claimed that if they too were allowed to ride around the course, they would be less tired and so would play better. In this case other golfers believed that this accommodation gave Martin an unfair competitive advantage and wanted to have the same privilege for themselves.

Although this example may be particularly dramatic, we can easily imagine other accommodations requested by a person with a disability that would also be valued by other employees or that other employees might perceive as an unfair advantage. Even in classroom settings, students often perceive it as unfair when a student with a disability is granted extra time for a test. Coworker resentment over the granting of accommodations can be a problem for all concerned. For the able-bodied employee, these accommodations may be perceived as unjust, leading to dissatisfaction on the job. For the disabled employee, the anticipated resentment may discourage him or her from asking for the accommodation needed to perform the job effectively. And from the manager's perspective, of course, the problem becomes one of balancing the concerns of the different parties.[5]

Again, the important message is for managers to simply recognize that differences among people exist. It is important to first acknowledge and to then make reasonable accommodation to deal with these differences. The key thing, however, is to make sure that the acknowledgment and the accommodation are equitable—everyone needs to have an equal opportunity to contribute to and advance within the organization.

THE BOTTOM LINE All managers should understand and appreciate the differences between equal employment opportunity and diversity management. Moreover, they should also understand patterns of similarity and difference among people and the important differences between identical treatment and equitable treatment.

B A S I C   D I M E N S I O N S   O F   D I V E R S I T Y

As indicated earlier, many dimensions of diversity can be used to characterize an organization. In this section we discuss age, gender, ethnicity, disability, and other dimensions of diversity.

Age Distributions

One key dimension of diversity in any organization is the age distribution of its workers.[6] The average age of the U.S. workforce is gradually increasing and will continue to do so for the next several years. Several factors are contributing to this pattern. For one thing, the baby-boom generation (a term used to describe the unusually large number of people who were born in the twenty-year period following World War II) continues to age. Declining birth rates among the post-baby-boom generations simultaneously account for smaller percentages of new entrants into the labor force. Another factor that contributes to the aging trend in the workforce is improved health and medical care. As a result of these improvements, people are able to remain productive and active for longer periods of time. Combined with higher legal limits for mandatory retirement, more and more people are working beyond the age at which they might have retired just a few years ago.

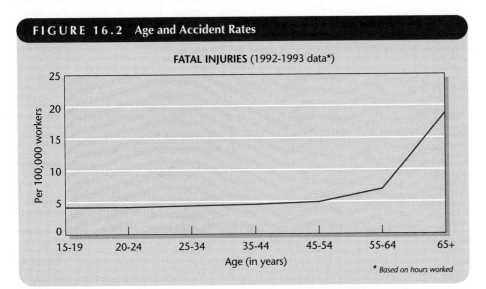

FIGURE 16.2 Age and Accident Rates

Source: Michael Moss, "For Older Employees, On-the-Job Injuries Are More Often Deadly," *Wall Street Journal,* June 17, 1997, pp. A1, A10. Reprinted by permission of Dow Jones Company via the Copyright Clearance Center.

How does this trend affect human resource management? For one thing, older workers tend to have more experience, may be more stable, and can make greater contributions to productivity. On the other hand, despite the improvements in health and medical care, older workers are nevertheless likely to require higher levels of insurance coverage and medical benefits. Similarly, as shown in Figure 16.2, accident rates increase substantially for older workers. After a person reaches the age of sixty-five, the likelihood of a fatal injury increases significantly.

Gender

As more and more females have entered the workforce, organizations have subsequently experienced changes in the relative proportions of male and female employees. Figure 16.3 highlights trends in gender composition (as well as ethnicity) in the workplace. As the figure clearly shows, the proportion of female employees to male employees has and will continue to gradually increase. For instance, projections are that by the year 2006 women will account for 47.4 percent of the workforce, up from 44.5 percent in 1986 and 46.2 percent in 1996.

■ The **glass ceiling** describes a barrier that keeps women from advancing to top management positions in many organizations.

These trends aside, a significant gender-related problem that many organizations face today is the so-called glass ceiling. The **glass ceiling** describes a barrier that keeps women from advancing to top management positions in many organizations. This ceiling represents a real barrier that is difficult to break but is also so subtle that it can be hard to see. Indeed, although almost 45 percent of all managers are women, there are only two female CEOs among the one thousand largest businesses in the United States. Similarly, the average pay of females in organizations is lower than that of males. While the pay gap is gradually shrinking, inequalities are still present.

Why does the glass ceiling exist? One reason is that some male managers are still reluctant to promote female managers. Another is that many talented women choose to leave their jobs in larger organizations and start their own businesses. Still another factor is that some women choose to suspend or slow their career progression in order to have children. "Human Resources in the Twenty-first Century" explores the glass ceiling in more detail.

Ethnicity

■ **Ethnicity** refers to the ethnic composition of a group or organization.

A third major dimension of cultural diversity in organizations is ethnicity. **Ethnicity** refers to the ethnic composition of a group or organization. Within the United States, most organizations reflect varying degrees of ethnicity composed of whites, African-Americans, Hispanics, and Asians. Figure 16.3 also shows trends in the ethnic composition of the U.S. workforce.

The biggest projected changes involve whites and Hispanics. In particular, the percentage of whites in the workforce is expected to drop to 72.7 percent by 2006, down from 79.8 percent in 1986 and 75.3 percent in 1996. At the same time, the percentage of Hispanics is expected to climb to 11.7 percent by 2006, up from 6.9 percent in 1986 and 9.5 percent in 1996. The percentage of blacks is expected to remain about stable (10.6 percent in 1986, 11.0 percent in 1996, and 10.7 percent in 2006). Finally, Asians and others are expected to represent 4.9 percent of the U.S. workforce in 2006, up from 2.8 percent in 1986 and 4.1 percent in 1996.

As with women, members of the African-American, Hispanic, and Asian groups are generally underrepresented in the executive ranks of most organizations today, as well as in several different occupational groups. And their pay is similarly lower than might be expected. As is the case for women, the differences are gradually disappearing as organizations fully embrace equal employment opportunity and recognize the higher overall level of talent available to them. Table 16.1 shows trends in different occupations for blacks and Hispanics. For example, the percentage of blacks and Hispanics in several kinds of business roles plus a variety of professional specialties increased substantially from 1983 to 1997. In only a few areas (management analysts; authors; engineers) were declines or no change registered.

FIGURE 16.3 Changing Composition of the U.S. Workforce

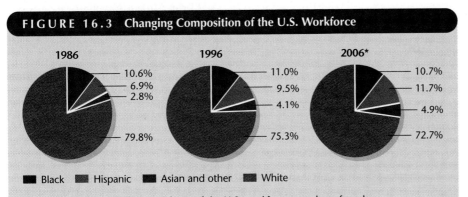

1986
- 10.6%
- 6.9%
- 2.8%
- 79.8%

1996
- 11.0%
- 9.5%
- 4.1%
- 75.3%

2006*
- 10.7%
- 11.7%
- 4.9%
- 72.7%

■ Black ■ Hispanic ■ Asian and other ■ White

The shifting racial and ethnic makeup of the U.S. workforce: number of workers by race and ethnic origin and their share of the total civilian labor force.

Numbers (thousands)	1986	1996	2006*	Percent	1986	1996	2006*
Total	117,834	133,944	148,847	Total	100.0	100.0	100.0
Men	65,422	72,087	78,226	Men	55.5	53.8	52.6
Women	52,412	61,857	70,620	Women	44.5	46.2	47.4
White, non-Hispanic	94,026	100,915	108,166	White, non-Hispanic	79.8	75.3	72.7
Men	52,442	54,451	56,856	Men	44.5	40.7	38.2
Women	41,583	46,464	51,310	Women	35.3	34.7	34.5
Black, non-Hispanic	12,483	14,795	15,983	Black, non-Hispanic	10.6	11.0	10.7
Men	6,279	7,091	7,347	Men	5.3	5.3	4.9
Women	6,204	7,704	8,636	Women	5.3	5.8	5.8
Hispanic origin	8,076	12,774	17,401	Hispanic origin	6.9	9.5	11.7
Men	4,948	7,646	10,235	Men	4.2	5.7	6.9
Women	3,128	5,128	7,166	Women	2.7	3.8	4.8
Asian and other, non-Hispanic	3,249	5,459	7,296	Asian and other, non-Hispanic	2.8	4.1	4.9
Men	1,753	2,899	3,788	Men	1.5	2.2	2.5
Women	1,496	2,561	3,508	Women	1.3	1.9	2.4

*Projection

Disability

Disability is another significant dimension of diversity. Disabilities can range from hearing impairment to missing fingers or limbs to blindness to paralysis. Not only does the presence of a disability represent another aspect of diversity in organizations, but among persons who have disabilities, there are some differences that are important as well. That is, unlike other dimensions of diversity, reactions to persons with disabilities vary dramatically as a function of several dimensions of the disability. One of these dimensions is termed *origin*. In this case coworkers are likely to react more negatively to a disability that is perceived as being avoidable (for example, someone who has been injured while driving drunk) than when the problem was unavoidable (for example, a person who was born blind).

Another dimension is the aesthetic aspect of the disability, with disabilities that are more disfiguring being perceived more negatively. A third—and critical—dimension refers to the nature of the disability itself. For example, although mental disabilities might be more easy to conceal than physical disabilities, they are also more frightening to coworkers. Furthermore, disabilities related to stress or to back injuries are not as physically obvious, and so, when individuals with these disabilities request and are granted an accommodation, resentment by coworkers is more likely.[7]

HUMAN RESOURCES in the Twenty-first Century

Will the Glass Ceiling Ever Be Shattered?

The executive ranks of America's largest companies have always been dominated by men. So scarce are female top executives that the recent ascension of Jill Barad to the top spot at Mattel—making her the first woman to be promoted to such a position at a major company—made national headlines. The unseen boundary that apparently keeps women from reaching the top has long been called the glass ceiling.

But there are clear signs that the glass ceiling is cracking, at least in some companies. A cadre of talented, skilled, and motivated women stand ready to move ever higher up the corporate ladder and are certain to join Jill Barad among the ranks of corporate leaders in the very near future. At Pitney Bowes, for example, five of the top eleven managers are women. Motorola has thirty-eight female vice presidents. And 44 percent of the top management positions at Avon are held by women.

Several women executives, in particular, are poised to compete for the top spot at their respective companies. Gail McGovern was recently named head of AT&T's $26 billion consumer business, perhaps the second most

> *"Women are in the pipeline in droves."*
>
> (James E. Preston, CEO, Avon)*;
>
> *"Progress is being made, but it's painfully slow."*
>
> (Rene Redwood, U.S. Labor Department official and former director of the Federal Glass Ceiling Commission)**

important job in the company. Lois Juliber runs Colgate-Palmolive's North American and European operations. Irene Rosenfeld is a top vice president at Kraft Foods. And Ellen Marram is executive vice president at Seagram and runs the company's $2-billion nonalcoholic beverage business.

The absolute numbers, however, are still sobering: only 10 percent of the top management jobs in the largest five hundred companies in the United States are held by women. But the middle ranks are more balanced. And as enlightened firms continue to seek the best people—not men, but people—to assume key leadership positions, more and more women are certain to make the move through the glass ceiling, perhaps one day leaving its remnants as only dim memories.

Sources: Janet Guyon, "The Global Glass Ceiling and the Ten Women Who Broke through It," *Fortune,* October 12, 1998, pp. 102–103; "Watershed Generation of Women Executives Is Rising to the Top," *Wall Street Journal,* February 10, 1997, pp. A1, A6 (**quote on p. A6); "Breaking Through," *Business Week,* February 17, 1997, pp. 64–70 (*quote on p. 64).

TABLE 16.1	Employment of Blacks and Hispanics in Selected Occupations, 1983 and 1997*			
	Blacks		**Hispanic Origin**	
Occupation	**1983**	**1997**	**1983**	**1997**
Total work force, 16 years and over	9.3%	10.8%	5.3%	9.3%
Executive, administrative, and managerial	4.7	6.9	2.8	5.4
Officials and administrators, public administration	8.3	11.9	3.8	5.6
Financial managers	3.5	5.6	3.1	5.1
Personnel and labor relations managers	4.9	7.5	2.6	2.9
Purchasing managers	5.1	6.4	1.4	4.6
Managers, marketing, advertising, and public relations	2.7	3.7	1.7	4.8
Managers, medicine and health	5.0	7.4	2.0	4.3
Accountants and auditors	5.5	7.9	3.3	5.0
Management analysts	5.3	3.6	1.7	3.0
Professional specialty	6.4	7.8	2.5	4.5
Architects	1.6	1.7	1.5	5.1
Engineers	2.7	3.9	2.2	3.8
Mathematical and computer scientists	5.4	7.5	2.6	3.1
Natural scientists	2.6	5.1	2.1	2.2
Physicians	3.2	4.2	4.5	4.8
Dentists	2.4	2.6	1.0	1.1
Teachers, college and university	4.4	6.5	1.8	3.4
Economists	6.3	6.6	2.7	3.7
Psychologists	8.6	9.2	1.1	4.5
Lawyers	2.6	2.7	0.9	3.8
Authors	2.1	1.7	0.9	2.1
Musicians and composers	7.9	10.5	4.4	9.3
Editors and reporters	2.9	4.8	2.1	1.7

*Data for 1983 and 1997 are not strictly comparable.
Minorities as a percentage of total employed.
Source: The Wall Street Journal Almanac 1999, p. 241. Republished by permission of Dow Jones, Inc. via Copyright Clearance Center, Inc. © 1999 Dow Jones and Company, Inc. All Rights Reserved.

Other Dimensions of Diversity

In addition to age, gender, ethnicity, and disability status, organizations are also confronting other dimensions of diversity. National origin is a dimension that can be important for global organizations. This can be particularly significant when different languages are involved. Single parents, dual-career couples, gays and lesbians, people with special dietary preferences (for example, vegetarians), and people with different political ideologies and viewpoints also represent significant dimensions of diversity.

Managers should be thoroughly aware of the various dimensions of diversity at a general level, as well as the specific dimensions that affect their work areas of responsibility. The organization's human resource function can play a significant role as a center of expertise in helping everyone in the organization better understand differences among people.

THE IMPACT OF DIVERSITY ON ORGANIZATIONS

There is no question that organizations are becoming ever more diverse. But what is the impact of this diversity on organizations? As we will see, diversity provides both opportunities and challenges for organizations. Diversity also plays a number of important roles in organizations today.

Diversity and Social Change

Diversity can have a significant impact on organizations as a force for social change. This generally occurs as the composition of an organization's workforce gradually comes to fully mirror the composition of its surrounding labor market. For example, if a manager in an organization learns to effectively interact with a diverse set of people at work, it follows logically that she or he will be better equipped to deal with a diverse set of people in other settings. And conversely, an individual who is comfortable interacting with diverse settings should have little problem in dealing with diversity at work. Thus diversity in organizations both facilitates and is facilitated by social change in the environment. Another way that organizations affect social change is through the images they use to promote themselves and their products. An organization that runs print ads showing only white male executives in its workplace conveys a certain image of itself. In contrast, an organization that uses diverse groups as representatives conveys a different image.

Diversity in organizations can be a significant force in facilitating social change. For example, Ralph Bazhaw leads an affinity group of Native Americans at Lucent Technology. He and a network of other Native Americans in professional positions are increasingly networking among themselves to raise the awareness of both other Native Americans and corporate recruiters about the mutual benefits that diversity can bring. That is, as more Native Americans seek and land professional positions they improve their standards of living considerably. Likewise, businesses also benefit as they recruit from a larger pool of talented employees.

Diversity and Competitiveness

Many organizations are also finding that diversity can be a source of competitive advantage in the marketplace. In general, six arguments have been proposed for how diversity contributes to competitiveness.[8] These are illustrated in Figure 16.4.

The *cost argument* suggests that organizations that learn to cope with diversity will generally have higher levels of productivity and lower levels of turnover and absenteeism. Those organizations that do a poor job of managing diversity, on the other hand, will suffer from

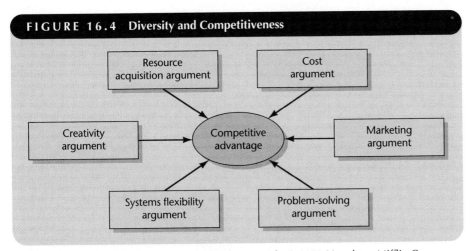

FIGURE 16.4 Diversity and Competitiveness

Source: Ricky W. Griffin, *Management,* 6th ed. Copyright © 1999 Houghton Mifflin Company, p. 181. Reprinted by permission.

problems of lower productivity and higher levels of turnover and absenteeism. Since each of these factors has a direct impact on costs, the former organization will remain more competitive than will the latter. Ortho Pharmaceuticals estimates that it has saved $500,000 by lowering turnover among women and ethnic minorities.

The *resource acquisition argument* for diversity suggests that organizations that manage diversity effectively will become known among women and minorities as good places to work. These organizations will thus be better able to attract qualified employees from among these groups. Given the increased importance of these groups in the overall labor force, organizations that can attract talented employees from all segments of society are likely to be more competitive.

The *marketing argument* suggests that organizations with diverse workforces will be better able to understand different market segments than will less diverse organizations. For example, a cosmetics firm like Avon that wants sell its products to women and blacks can better understand how to create such products and to effectively market them if women and black managers are available to provide inputs into product development, design, packaging, advertising, and so forth.

The *creativity argument* for diversity suggests that organizations with diverse workforces will generally be more creative and innovative than will less diverse organizations. If an organization is dominated by one population segment, it follows that its members will generally adhere to norms and ways of thinking that reflect that segment. Moreover, they will have little insight or stimulus for new ideas that might be derived from different perspectives. "Human Resources Around the Globe" explores this idea in more detail. The diverse organization, in contrast, will be characterized by multiple perspectives and ways of thinking and is therefore more likely to generate new ideas and ways of doing things.

Related to the creativity argument is the *problem-solving argument*. Diversity carries with it an increased pool of information. In virtually any organization there is some information that everyone has, and other information that is unique to each individual. In an organization with little diversity, the larger pool of information is common, and the smaller pool is unique. But in a more diverse organization, the pool of unique information is larger. Thus, because more information can be brought to bear on a problem, better solutions are more likely to be identified.[9]

HUMAN RESOURCES **Around the Globe**

Too Little Diversity?

It's no secret, of course, that many businesses from Japan and South Korea have been highly successful in recent years. But interestingly, some experts question whether or not the lack of diversity that exists in those firms will be an advantage or disadvantage in the future.

To see how little diversity exists in some of these businesses, consider the case of Samsung Electronics, a huge Korean business. The firm's board of directors consists of nineteen members, all male. Fifteen of them have worked for the firm for at least twenty years, and eight even attended the same university. Japan's Honda Motor Co. is quite similar—its board is all Japanese, as is every president of each Honda foreign subsidiary.

Executives at these firms defend their hiring and promotion practices. They argue, for example, that their lack of diversity reduces management conflict, smoothes decision making, and ensures that top management is both

"Cohesiveness of corporation is more important to Japanese. They are not well trained in managing different nationalities. They are more comfortable in [their own] group."

(Kaoru Kobayashi, Japanese professor)*

loyal to and knowledgeable about the business. It also enhances cohesiveness among key leaders, since they tend to see things in the same way and to have similar interests.

But critics point out that the lack of diversity also creates problems. For example, some experts contend that executives from Japan and Korea do not understand people from other cultures very well and thus treat them cavalierly and with disdain. By not relying more heavily on foreigners, Japanese and Korean firms may also be less knowledgeable about international laws and regulations. And some critics even predict that the lack of executive diversity may dampen creativity and innovation, potentially causing Japanese and Korean firms to be less competitive in the future.

Sources: "Men's Club," *Wall Street Journal,* September 26, 1996, pp. A1, A8 (*quote on p. A1); "Tight Little Island," *Forbes,* January 12, 1998, pp. 52–53; and "Seoul Is Still Teetering on the Edge," *Business Week,* January 5, 1998, pp. 56–57.

Finally, the *systems flexibility argument* for diversity suggests that organizations must become more flexible as a way of managing a diverse workforce. As a direct consequence the overall organizational system will also become more flexible. Organizational flexibility enables the organization to better respond to changes in its environment. Thus by effectively managing diversity within its workforce, an organization simultaneously becomes better equipped to address its environment.[10]

Diversity and Conflict

Unfortunately, diversity in an organization can also become a major source of conflict,[11] which can arise for various reasons. One potential avenue for conflict is when an individual thinks that someone has been hired, promoted, or fired because of her or his diversity status.[12] For example, suppose a male executive loses a promotion to a female executive. If he believes that she was promoted because the organization simply wanted to have more female managers rather than because she was the better candidate for the job, he will likely feel resentful toward both her and the organization. For example, there is apparent continuing conflict among whites and blacks within the ranks of the FAA. Some blacks have charged that they are subject to various subtle forms of discrimination and that their white supervisors are prejudiced. Some whites, however, believe that the government agency has hired some blacks who really aren't qualified for the job of air traffic controller because it cannot attract enough qualified black applicants.[13]

Another source of conflict stemming from diversity is through misunderstood, misinterpreted, or inappropriate interactions between people of different groups. For example, suppose a male executive tells a sexually explicit joke to a new female executive. He may intentionally be trying to embarrass her, he may be clumsily trying to show her that he treats everyone the same, or he may think he is making her feel like part of the team. Regardless of his intent, however, if she finds the joke offensive, she will justifiably feel anger and hostility. These feelings may be directed only at the offending individual or more generally toward the entire organization if she believes that its culture facilitates such behaviors. And of course, sexual harassment is both unethical and illegal.

Interestingly, some evidence suggests that conflict may be especially pronounced among older and younger women in the workplace. Older women may be more likely to have sacrificed family for career and to have faced higher obstacles to get ahead—they were in a sense trailblazers. Younger women, on the other hand, may find that organizational accommodations make it relatively easier for them to balance multiple roles and may also have a less pronounced sense of having to fight to get ahead.[14]

Conflict can also arise as a result of other elements of diversity. For example, suppose a U.S. manager publicly praises the work of a Japanese employee. The manager's action stems from the dominant cultural belief in the United States that such recognition is important and rewarding. But because Japanese culture places a much higher premium on group loyalty and identity than on individual accomplishment, the employee will likely feel ashamed and embarrassed. Thus a well-intentioned action may backfire and result in unhappiness.

Conflict may also arise as a result of fear, distrust, or individual prejudice. Members of the dominant group in an organization may worry that newcomers from other groups pose a personal threat to their own position in the organization. For example, when U.S. firms have been taken over by Japanese firms, U.S. managers have sometimes been resentful or hostile to Japanese managers assigned to work with them. People may also be unwilling to accept anyone they perceive as being different. And personal bias and prejudices are still very real among some people today and can lead to potentially harmful conflict. The "Lighter Side of HR" cleverly illustrates this point.

THE BOTTOM LINE Managers need to appreciate the numerous positive benefits of diversity. In addition, though, they should also recognize that it can be a serious source of conflict and must be prepared to address any and all diversity-related issues that might arise in the organization.

The Lighter Side of HR

While there are clearly any number of strong arguments—legal, moral, ethical, and economic—for increased diversity in organizations, there are also costs and/or inconveniences that must be borne. Among other things, differences among people may increase conflict and make it more complicated for them to work together. And as shown here, for example, sometimes individuals lament the "old days" when everyone they worked with was alike. Nevertheless, these arguments against diversity are extremely modest when set beside the myriad reasons for greater diversity in organizations.

"I think I preferred it before he became an equal-opportunity employer."

MANAGING DIVERSITY IN ORGANIZATIONS

Because of the tremendous potential that diversity holds for competitive advantage, as well as the possible consequences of diversity-related conflict, much attention has been focused in recent years on how individuals and organizations can better manage diversity. In the sections that follow, we first discuss individual strategies for dealing with diversity and then summarize organizational approaches to managing diversity.

Individual Strategies for Dealing with Diversity

One key element of managing diversity in an organization consists of concentrating on four basic things individuals can strive for: understanding, empathy, tolerance, and communication.

Understanding   The first of these is understanding the nature and meaning of diversity. Some managers have taken the basic concepts of equal employment opportunity to an unnecessary extreme. They know that, by law, they cannot discriminate against people on the basis of sex, race, and so forth. Thus in following this mandate, they come to believe that they must treat everyone the same.

But this belief can cause problems when it is translated into workplace behaviors among people after they have been hired. The fact is—as noted earlier—that people are not the same. While people need to be treated fairly and equitably, managers must understand that differences do exist among people. Thus any effort to treat everyone the same, without regard to their fundamental human differences, will only lead to problems. It is therefore important for managers to understand that cultural factors cause people to behave in different ways and that these differences should be accepted.

Empathy   Related to understanding is empathy. People in an organization should try to understand the perspective of others. For example, suppose that a female employee joins a group whose members have traditionally been white males. Each male may be a little self-conscious as how to act toward the new member and may be interested in making her feel comfortable and welcome. But the men may be able to welcome the new member even more effectively by empathizing with how she may feel. For example, she may feel disappointed or elated about her new assignment, she may be confident or nervous about her position in the group, and she may be experienced or inexperienced in working with male colleagues. By learning more about these and similar circumstances, the existing group members can further facilitate their ability to work together effectively.

Tolerance   A third related individual approach to dealing with diversity is tolerance. Even though managers learn to understand diversity and even though they may try to empathize with others, the fact remains that they may still not accept or enjoy some aspect of behavior on the part of others. For example, one organization recently reported that it was experiencing considerable conflict between its U.S. and Israeli employees. The Israeli employees seemed to want to argue about every issue that arose. The U.S. managers preferred a more harmonious way of conducting business and became uncomfortable with the conflict. Finally, after considerable discussion the U.S. employees learned that many Israelis simply enjoy arguing and just see it as part of getting work done. The firm's U.S. employees still do not enjoy the arguing, but are more willing to tolerate it as a fundamental cultural difference between themselves and their colleagues from Israel.

Communication   A final individual approach to dealing with diversity is communication. Problems often get magnified over diversity issues because people are afraid or otherwise unwilling to openly discuss issues that relate to diversity. For example, suppose a younger employee has a habit of making jokes about the age of an elderly colleague. Perhaps the younger colleague means no harm and is just engaging in what she sees as good-natured kidding. But the older employee may find the jokes offensive. If there is no communication between the two, the jokes will continue and the resentment will grow. Eventually, what started as a minor problem may erupt into a much bigger one.

For communication to work, it must be a two-way street. If a person wonders whether a certain behavior on her or his part is offensive to someone else, the curious individual should probably just ask. Similarly, if someone is offended by the behavior of another person, he or she should explain to the offending individual how the behavior is perceived and request that it be stopped. As long as such exchanges are handled in a friendly, low-key, and nonthreatening fashion, they will generally have a positive outcome. Of course, if the same message is presented in an overly combative manner or if a person continues to engage in offensive behavior after having been asked to stop, problems will only escalate. At this point third parties within the organization may have to intervene. And in fact, most organizations today have one or more systems in place to address questions and problems that arise as a result of diversity. We now turn our attention to various ways that organizations can indeed better manage diversity.

Organizational Strategies for Dealing with Diversity

Although individuals can play an important role in managing diversity, the organization must also play a fundamental role. An organization's various policies and practices show its people what behaviors are and are not appropriate. Diversity training is an even more direct method for managing diversity. The organization's culture is the ultimate context from which diversity must be addressed.

Organizational policies   The starting point in managing diversity is the policies that an organization adopts that directly or indirectly affect how people are treated. Obviously, for instance, the extent to which an organization embraces the premise of equal employment opportunity will to a large extent determine the potential diversity within an organization. But the organization that follows the law to the letter and still allows passive discrimination is very different from the organization that actively seeks a diverse and varied workforce.

Another aspect of organizational policies that affects diversity is how the organization addresses and responds to problems that arise from diversity. For example, consider the example of a manager charged with sexual harassment. If the organization's policies put an excessive burden of proof on the

Organizations sincerely interested in managing diversity need to ensure that their own practices and policies support diversity. Applied Materials, for example, is a leading recruiter and employer of minorities in the Silicon Valley. Glen Toney, group vice president of corporate affairs for the firm, routinely scrutinizes corporate policies to make sure that they are as inclusive and flexible as possible. Whenever he encounters some rule or regulation that might adversely affect an employee based on religion, ethnicity, gender, age, or other difference, he makes it his personal mission to change things.

individual being harassed and invoke only minor sanctions against the guilty party, that organization is sending a clear signal as to the importance of such matters. But the organization that has a balanced set of policies for addressing questions like sexual harassment sends its employees a different message as to the importance of diversity and individual rights and privileges.

Indeed, perhaps the major policy through which an organization can reflect its stance on diversity is its mission statement. If the organization's mission statement articulates a clear and direct commitment to diversity, everyone who comes into contact with that mission statement will grow to understand and accept the importance of diversity, at least to that particular organization.

Organizational practices   Organizations can also help manage diversity through a variety of ongoing practices and procedures. Avon's creation of networks for various groups represents one example of an organizational practice that fosters diversity. In general, the idea is that since diversity is characterized by differences among people, organizations can more effectively manage that diversity by following practices and procedures that are based on flexibility rather than rigidity.

Benefit packages, for example, can be structured so as to better accommodate individual situations. An employee who is part of a dual-career couple and who has no children may require relatively little insurance (perhaps because her spouse's employer provides more complete coverage) and would like to be able to schedule vacations to coincide with those of her spouse. Another employee, who happens to be a single parent, may need a wide variety of insurance coverage and prefer to schedule his vacation time to coincide with school holidays.

Flexible working hours are also a useful organizational practice to accommodate diversity. Differences in family arrangements, religious holidays, cultural events, and so forth may dictate that employees have some degree of flexibility in when they work. For example, a single parent may need to leave the office at 4:30 to pick up the children from their daycare center. An organization that truly values diversity will make every reasonable attempt to accommodate such a need.

Organizations can also facilitate diversity by making sure that there is diversity in its key committees and executive teams. Even if diversity exists within the broader organizational context, an organization that does not reflect diversity in groups like committees and teams implies that diversity is not a fully ingrained element of its culture. In contrast, if all major groups and related work assignments reflect diversity, the message is quite different.

Diversity training   Many organizations are finding that diversity training is an effective means for managing diversity and minimizing its associated conflict. More specifically, **diversity training** is designed to enable members of an organization to function in a diverse workplace. This training can take various forms.[15] As discussed in "Human Resources Legal Brief," all too often diversity training has to be undertaken to remedy specific problems or crises that have erupted. But many organizations find it useful to help people learn more about their similarities to and differences from others for other reasons as well.

Men and women can be taught to work together more effectively and can gain insights into how their own behaviors affect and are interpreted by others. In one organization a diversity-training program helped male managers understand how various remarks they made to one another could be interpreted as being sexist. In the same organization female managers learned how to point out their discomfort with those remarks without appearing overly hostile.

Similarly, white and black managers may need training to better understand each other. Managers at Mobil noticed that four black colleagues never seemed to eat lunch together. After a diversity-training program, the white managers came to realize that the black managers felt that if they ate together, their conversations would be a subject of much curiosity among their white colleagues. Thus the blacks avoided close associations with one another because they feared calling attention to themselves.

Some organizations even go so far as to provide language training for their employees as a vehicle for managing diversity. Motorola, for example, provides English language training for its foreign employees on assignment in the

■ **Diversity training** is specifically designed to enable members of an organization to function in a diverse workplace.

HUMAN RESOURCES Legal Brief

The Merits (?) of Diversity Training

Texaco executives made headlines a few years ago when a tape-recorded conversation in which they made racially insulting remarks was made public. About the same time, AT&T came under fire when a company newsletter used images of monkeys to represent people in Africa. And Denny's, the popular restaurant chain, attracted national attention over charges that it discriminated against minority customers and employees.

In each case company officials made public apologies and offered restitution to those who were most directly offended. Another response from each company was an announced requirement that key managers throughout the firm would need to participate in diversity training. Diversity training, as the term suggests, is an activity designed to help

"The objective is to help managers and supervisors to understand how unconscious behavior can impact employees, how differences can get in the way of productivity in the workplace, and how to leverage diversity as a competitive advantage."

(Edward N. Gadsden Jr., Texaco's diversity director)*

individuals better understand people who are different from themselves.

Such training is supposed to help people better understand the beliefs, values, and life styles of others and to make participants more tolerant and accepting of diverse points of view. Many experts believe that a well-planned and well-delivered diversity-training program can indeed help people become more tolerant. On the other hand, some critics believe that such training addresses only surface-level issues. For example, some of the terms the Texaco executives were using in a negative manner had actually been learned in a diversity program!

Sources: "A 3Com Factory Hires a Lot of Immigrants, Gets Mix of Languages," *Wall Street Journal,* March 30, 1998, pp. A1, A12; "Do Diversity Programs Make a Difference?" *Wall Street Journal,* December 4, 1996, p. B1 (*quote on p. B1).

United States. At Pace Foods in San Antonio, with a total payroll of 350 employees, staff meetings and employee handbooks are translated into Spanish for the benefit of the company's one hundred Hispanic employees.

Organizational culture   The ultimate test of an organization's commitment to managing diversity is its culture. Regardless of what managers say or put in writing, unless there is a basic and fundamental belief that diversity is valued, it cannot ever become truly an integral part of an organization. An organization that really wants to promote diversity must shape its culture so that it clearly underscores top management commitment to and support of diversity in all of its forms throughout every part of the organization. With top management support, however, and reinforced with a clear and consistent set of organizational policies and practices, diversity can become a basic and fundamental part of an organization.

THE BOTTOM LINE   Managers need to be fully aware of the various individual and organizational strategies that can help them and others better embrace diversity. The human resource function in an organization will often be asked to play a key role as a center of expertise in this regard, especially in areas related to organizational strategies.

THE MULTICULTURAL ORGANIZATION

■ The **multicultural organization** is one that has achieved high levels of diversity, is able to fully capitalize on the advantages of the diversity, and has few diversity-related problems.

Many organizations today are grappling with cultural diversity. While organizations are becoming ever more diverse, there are few truly multicultural organizations. The **multicultural organization** is one that has achieved high levels of diversity, one that is able to fully capitalize on the advantages of the diversity, and one that has few diversity-related problems.[16] One recent article described the six basic characteristics of such an organization.[17] These characteristics are illustrated in Figure 16.5.

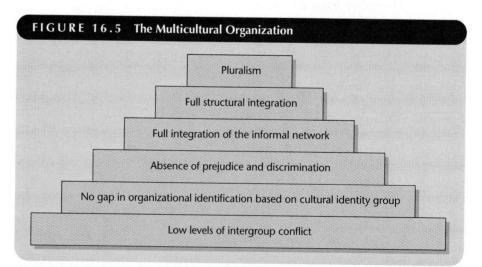

FIGURE 16.5   The Multicultural Organization

Pluralism

Full structural integration

Full integration of the informal network

Absence of prejudice and discrimination

No gap in organizational identification based on cultural identity group

Low levels of intergroup conflict

Source: Based on Taylor H. Cox, "The Multicultural Organization," *Academy of Management Executive,* May 1991, pp. 34–47. Reprinted by permission of the Academy of Management via the Copyright Clearance Center. All rights reserved.

First of all, the multicultural organization is characterized by pluralism; that is, every group represented in an organization will work to better understand every other group. Thus black employees will try to understand white employees, and white employees will try just as hard to understand their black colleagues. In addition, every group represented within an organization will have the potential to influence the organization's culture and its fundamental norms.

Second, the multicultural organization achieves full structural integration. Full structural integration suggests that the diversity within an organization will be a complete and accurate reflection of the organization's external labor market. If around half of the labor market is female, then about half of the organization's employees will be female. Moreover, this same proportion will be reflected at all levels of the organization. There will be no glass ceilings or other subtle forms of discrimination.

Third, the multicultural organization achieves full integration of the informal networks. This characteristic suggests that there will be no barriers to entry and participation in any organizational activity. For example, people will enter and exit lunch groups, social networks, communication grapevines, and other informal aspects of organizational activity without regard to age, gender, ethnicity, or other dimension of diversity.

Fourth, the multicultural organization is characterized by an absence of prejudice and discrimination. No traces of bias will exist, and prejudice will be eliminated. Discrimination will not be practiced in any shape, form, or fashion. And discrimination will be nonexistent not because it is illegal, but because of the lack of prejudice and bias. People will be valued, accepted, and rewarded purely on the basis of their skills and contributions to the organization.

Fifth, in the multicultural organization there is no gap in organizational identification based on cultural identity group. In many organizations today there is a tendency to make presumptions about organizational roles based on group identity. For example, many people walking into an office and seeing a male and female conversing tend to assume that the female is the secretary and the male is the manager. No such tendencies will exist in the multicultural organization. People will recognize that males and females are equally likely to be managers and secretaries.

Finally, the multicultural organization experiences low levels of intergroup conflict. We noted earlier that conflict is a likely outcome of increased diversity. The multicultural organization will have evolved beyond this point to a state of virtually no conflict among people who are members of different groups. People within the organization will fully understand, empathize with, have tolerance for, and openly communicate with everyone else. Values, premises, motives, attitudes, and perceptions will be so well understood by everyone that any conflict that does arise will be over meaningful and work-related issues as opposed to differences in age, gender, ethnicity, or other dimensions of diversity.

Chapter Summary

Diversity exists in a group or organization when its members differ from one another along one or more important dimensions. Diversity is increasing in organizations today because of changing demographics, the desire by organizations to improve their workforce, legal pressures, and increased globalization.

Diversity management and equal employment opportunity may appear to be the same thing but are, in fact, quite different. Whereas equal employment opportunity is intended to eliminate discrimination in the workplace, management diversity focuses on recognizing and accommodating differences among people.

Diversity has several key dimensions. Four of the more common dimensions are age, gender, ethnicity, and disability. The overall age of the workforce is increasing. More women are also entering the workplace, although there is still a perceived glass ceiling in many settings. In the United States, more Hispanics are entering the workplace, and the percentage of whites is gradually declining.

Diversity affects organizations in many ways and serves as a force for social change. Many organizations are realizing the diversity can also be a major force for competitive advantage. Finally, diversity can also be a significant source of conflict.

Both individuals and the organization can help to manage diversity in an organization. Individual approaches to dealing with diversity include understanding, empathy, tolerance, and communication. Major organizational approaches are through policies, practices, diversity training, and culture.

Few, if any, organizations have become truly multicultural. The key dimensions that characterize such organizations are pluralism, full structural integration, full integration of the informal network, an absence of prejudice and discrimination, no gap in organizational identification based on cultural identity group, and low levels of intergroup conflict attributable to diversity.

Review and Discussion Questions

1. What does diversity mean?

2. What are the basic trends in diversity in the United States today? What accounts for these trends?

3. Distinguish between identical treatment and equitable treatment in an organizational setting.

4. What are the four most common bases of diversity that are relevant to managers and their organizations?

5. What trends are apparent regarding age, gender, and ethnicity in the workplace?

6. How does diversity contribute to competitiveness?

7. How does diversity contribute to conflict?

8. Identify and discuss various individual strategies for dealing with diversity.

9. Identify and discuss various organizational strategies for dealing with diversity.

10. What is a "multicultural" organization? Do you think such a thing exists?

Closing Case

The Avon Way

Women have always played an important role at Avon, the largest cosmetics firm in the United States. Starting with the first Avon Lady in 1886, women have long been the foundation of the firm's marketing and sales efforts. And Avon has always employed a lot of women throughout its organization. But control always remained with the handful of men who ran the company. However, a series of disastrous decisions and setbacks in the 1980s caused the firm to rethink its philosophies and to promote its best middle managers, many of them women, into the executive ranks. And as a result, Avon has turned itself around. Today the firm is known for both its exemplary financial performance and its acceptance of all people, regardless of their gender, skin color, or age.

Avon's problems started in the 1970s when its top management team tried to change the firm's strategy. This group of predominantly male managers first ignored its own marketing research about women consumers and shifting career patterns, which indicated that more women were entering the workforce and seeking professional careers. In particular, the men failed to recognize that the personal care products preferred by women were also changing. Then, in the 1980s, they tried to buck emerging trends and to diversify with a number of ill-conceived acquisitions. Finally, as the firm was on the brink of bankruptcy, a new top management team was brought in. Led by CEO Jim Preston, Avon refocused itself on its roots and began to again market cosmetics to a still largely female, albeit very different, market.

But this time the firm adopted new approaches. For one thing, it decided to recognize and reward managerial talent rather than the gender of the individual manager. As a result, more women were quickly promoted into higher-level positions. In addition, Preston shifted the firm's organization culture to be more accommodating of all its employees—to value differences among people rather than to impose a rigid and controlling model for how things were to be done. For example, the firm dropped its season-ticket purchases to Knicks and Yankees games and replaced them with season tickets for the New York City Ballet and the New York Philharmonic. And the company eliminated its annual hunting retreat, a male bastion of drinking and card playing.

Avon is also moving aggressively into foreign markets. For example, Avon products are now sold in mature markets like Western Europe and Japan. But in addition, the firm also sells its products throughout China, Russia, and Eastern Europe. All told, Avon manufactures its products in 18 countries and sells them in 125. Preston credits several key female executives for championing the international push and for making sure that it was done right. And many new managers at the firm have come from international contacts, organizations, and networks that the firm did not previously see as a valuable source of executive talent.

But perhaps the biggest testament to the "new" Avon is its plans for executive succession. Four of the firm's eight top officers are women, for example, and more than 40 percent of its global managers are women. Almost half of the firm's board of directors is female. And among the six executives considered most likely to replace Preston when he retires, four are women. Clearly, then, Avon is a firm that has changed its own culture and that appreciates the power of diversity and multiculturalism.

Case Questions

1. What are the reasons for Avon's commitment to diversity?

2. Why don't more companies follow Avon's lead?

3. What, if anything, could derail Avon's success along dimensions of diversity?

Sources: Betsy Morris and Patricia Sellers, "*Fortune's* 50 Most Powerful Women in American Business," *Fortune,* October 25, 1999, pp. 103–106; "If Women Ran the World, It Would Look a Lot Like Avon," *Fortune,* July 21, 1997, pp. 74–79; *Hoover's Handbook of American Business 1999* (Austin, Texas: Hoover's Business Press, 1999), pp. 200–201; "Why Avon Called a 'Non-woman,'" *Business Week,* March 16, 1998, pp. 57–60.

Building Human Resource Management Skills

Purpose: The purpose of this exercise is to help develop increasingly important human resource skills as they relate to multicultural issues and challenges.

Step 1: Read and reflect on the scenario that follows:
Your firm has recently undergone a significant increase in its workforce. Many

of the new workers you have hired are immigrants from Eastern Europe and Asia. Several do not speak English very well, but all are hard workers who appear to be trying very hard to be successful and to fit in with their coworkers.

Recently, however, some problems have come to your attention. For one thing, several of your female workers have begun to complain about an increase in sexual harassment. For another, your supervisors have noticed an increase in tardiness and absenteeism among all of your workers.

You have decided that some action is clearly needed. However, you are unsure how to proceed. Consequently, you have decided to spend a few days thinking about what to do.

Step 2: Respond to the questions that follow:

1. Think of as many reasons as you can for each problem you are facing.

2. Determine how you might address each problem, given the potential array of contributing factors.

3. What role might organization culture be playing in this situation, apart from issues of multiculturalism?

4. What role might multiculturalism be playing in this situation, apart from issues of organization culture?

Ethical Dilemmas in Human Resource Management

Assume you are the senior human resource executive in your company. For years your firm had relatively little diversity. The one-thousand-member workforce was almost exclusively white and male. But in recent years you have succeeded in increasing diversity substantially. Almost 33 percent of your employees are now female, and more than 40 percent are Hispanic or African-American.

Unfortunately, your firm has recently met with some financial setbacks. You feel that you have no choice but to lay off about three hundred employees for a period of at least six months. If everything goes well, you also expect to be able to bring them back at that time.

You are currently puzzling over what criteria to use in selecting people for layoff. If you use strict seniority, women and ethnic minorities will bear the brunt of the layoffs, since they are almost all among the newest employees in the firm. If you use strict performance, however, your older and more senior (and predominately white male) workers will bear the brunt, since your newer employees have the most current training and up-to-date job skills. You also wonder what role loyalty should play in that many of your older workers could have left for higher-paying jobs a few years ago but chose to stay.

Questions

1. What are the ethical issues in this situation?

2. What are the basic arguments for the different criteria in selecting employees to be laid off?

3. What do you think most managers would do? What would you do?

Human Resource Internet Exercise

 One of the most important multicultural challenges facing managers today involves language skills. Assume you are the human resource manager for a large domestic company. Your firm has recently decided to enter into a joint venture with three foreign companies, one each from France, Germany, and Korea.

Under the terms of this joint venture, your three partners will each send a team of managers to your corporate headquarters for a period of two years. Your job is to make sure that your own top management team has basic language skills in the three other languages.

With the background information above as context, do the following:

Use the Internet to obtain information about language-training programs and methods.

Obtain information about one or more of each such program or method and make a decision about how you should proceed.

Notes

1. David A. Thomas and Robin J. Ely, "Making Differences Matter: A New Paradigm for Managing Diversity," *Harvard Business Review,* September–October 1996, pp. 79–90.

2. Dora C. Lau and J. Keith Murnighan, "Demographic Diversity and Faultlines: The Compositional Dynamics of Organizational Groups," *Academy of Management Review,* Vol. 23, No. 2, 1998, pp. 325–340.

3. Frances J. Milliken and Luis L. Martins, "Searching for Common Threads: Understanding the Multiple Effects of Diversity in Organizational Groups," *Academy of Management Review,* Vol. 21, No. 2, 1996, pp. 402–433.

4. "In a Factory Schedule, Where Does Religion Fit In?" *Wall Street Journal,* March 4, 1999, pp. B1, B12.

5. Adrienne Colella, "The Work Group Perspective: Co-Worker Responses to Group Member Accommodations," in D. Harrison (chair), *Implementing What Matters Most: Multiple Stakeholders in Accommodating People with Disabilities at Work.* All-Academy Symposium, presented at Annual Meetings of the Academy of Management, San Diego, August 1998.

6. Barbara L. Hassell and Pamela L. Perrewe, "An Examination of Beliefs about Older Workers: Do Stereotypes Still Exist?" *Journal of Organizational Behavior,* Vol. 16, 1995, pp. 457–468.

7. For a more complete discussion of these dimensions, see Diane L. Stone and Adrienne Colella, "A Model of Factors Affecting the Treatment of Disabled Individuals in Organizations," *Academy of Management Review,* Vol. 21, 1996, pp. 352–401.

8. Based on Taylor H. Cox and Stacy Blake, "Managing Cultural Diversity: Implications for Organizational Competitiveness," *Academy of Management Executive,* August 1991, pp. 45–56; see also Gail Robinson and Kathleen Dechant, "Building a Business Case for Diversity," *Academy of Management Executive,* August 1997, pp. 21–31.

9. C. Marlene Fiol, "Consensus, Diversity, and Learning in Organizations," *Organization Science,* August 1994, pp. 403–415.

10. Douglas Hall and Victoria Parker, "The Role of Workplace Flexibility in Managing Diversity," *Organizational Dynamics,* Summer 1993, pp. 5–14.

11. Janice R. W. Joplin and Catherine S. Daus, "Challenges of Leading a Diverse Workforce," *Academy of Management Executive,* August 1997, pp. 32–44. See also "Female Minorities Still Feel Left Behind," *USA Today,* July 14, 1999, p. 3B.

12. "As Population Ages, Older Workers Clash with Younger Bosses," *Wall Street Journal,* June 13, 1994, pp. A1, A8.

13. "Pursuit of Diversity Stirs Racial Tension at an FAA Center," *Wall Street Journal,* December 3, 1998, pp. A1, A8.

14. "Generational Warfare," *Forbes,* March 22, 1999, pp. 62–66.

15. Karen Hildebrand, "Use Leadership Training to Increase Diversity," *HRMagazine,* August 1996, pp. 53–57.

16. Patricia L. Nemetz and Sandra L. Christensen, "The Challenge of Cultural Diversity: Harnessing a Diversity of Views to Understand Multiculturalism," *Academy of Management Review,* Vol. 21, No. 2, 1996, pp. 434–462.

17. This discussion derives heavily from Taylor H. Cox, "The Multicultural Organization," *Academy of Management Executive,* May 1991, pp. 34–47.

17

Managing New Employment Relationships

CHAPTER OUTLINE

The Nature of Employment Contracts
Employment at Will
The Nature of Psychological
  Contracts
Psychological Contracts and
  Employee Rights
The Nature of Social Contracts

Managing Knowledge Workers
The Nature of Knowledge Work
Knowledge Worker Management
  and Labor Relations

Managing Low-Skill Workers
Outsourcing
Contingent and Temporary Workers
Trends in Contingent and Temporary
  Workers
Advantages and Disadvantages of
  Using Contingent and Temporary
  Workers
Managing Contingent and
  Temporary Workers

**Managing New Forms of Work
  Arrangements**
Managing Alternative Work
  Schedules
Managing Alternative Work Sites

CHAPTER OBJECTIVES

*After studying this chapter you should
be able to:*

■ Discuss the nature of employment
  contracts between organizations
  and employees.

■ Identify and describe the issues involved in managing knowledge
  workers.

■ Discuss management issues associated with low-skill workers.

■ Describe outsourcing and its relationship to managing new employment relations.

■ Discuss the use of contingent and
  temporary workers.

■ Describe new forms of work
  arrangements.

N o one argues with the fact that the fundamental relationship between employers and employees has changed dramatically over the last several years. As one case in point, consider the recent series of events that took place at Merrill Lynch. The firm recruited Alexander Lambros Jr. in 1989 to open a new office in Cape Coral, Florida, by giving him a $50,000 signing bonus, a 50 percent cut of commissions, and free rein to decorate and staff the office to his own tastes. He quickly became a company star, and his performance was never questioned.

Health problems subsequently forced him out of the branch manager position, but he stayed on with the office, maintaining a large and loyal client base with a sales base of $88 million. But Lambros began to question the ethics of some of his predecessor's business practices. Later still, Lambros was asked to fill in as branch manager during the holiday period so the official manager could take a vacation. While acting in that capacity one day, Lambros accepted an important document addressed to the branch manager. A sales assistant saw him take possession of the document and reported that to the real manager.

A few days later, the manager stormed into Lambros's office and fired him for "destroying company property." He claimed that the sales assistant supported his charges that Lambros had opened the envelope. A series of suits and countersuits have failed to uncover what really hap-

"The easiest way for managers of a firm to get new clients is to fire a broker and take his accounts. It's very common."

(Brad Hopper, brokerage executive)*

pened, however, and why. For his part Lambros argues that the firm wanted him out, in part so that other managers could divide up his customer base and in part because he had been so critical of certain business practices that he thought were unethical.

For its part, however, Merrill Lynch argues that neither of these things played a role in his departure. Company officials instead point out that there were concerns that Lambros was funneling business to his wife, who worked for a different brokerage company. They also charged that he was undermining the authority of the official branch manager in ways that were damaging morale in the Cape Coral office. Finally, they charged that he did, in fact, inappropriately "damage company property" by opening an envelope that was not really his and that there was the witness who observed this action. But in a bizarre turn, the sales assistant later claimed that she had never said she saw Mr. Lambros open the letter, merely that she saw it in his possession. She also charged that Merrill Lynch had tried to pressure her into lying so as to support its case. Ah, the tangled webs!

"Merrill Broker Protests Policies, Is Fired, Finds His Clients Divvied Up," *Wall Street Journal,* February 27, 1998, pp. A1, A8 (*quote on p. A1); *Hoover's Handbook of American Business 1999* (Austin, Texas: Hoover's Business Press, 1999), pp. 952–953.

The case involving Alexander Lambros Jr. and Merrill Lynch underscores a number of important issues regarding businesses today. Most important, it reflects the fundamental change in relationships between employers and employees that has taken place during the last several years. In many firms employees no longer trust their employer to treat them fairly and equitably. And employers often believe their employees act too much in their own self-interests. As a result, the fundamental nature of the employment relationship continues to change in a variety of ways.

Many Americans grew up with clear expectations concerning the relationship they would have with the organization where they worked. Traditional models of this relationship suggested that an employee could expect to have a job as long as he or she worked hard and followed the rules. For their part employees understood they were expected to exhibit loyalty and commitment to the organization. These contributions from the employee, along with these inducements from the organization, formed the basis of the relationship between the employee and the organization. But the nature of this relationship has been changing, and continues to change.

When we consider the relationship between the organization and the employee, we can talk about the basic legal employment contract, the psychological contract between employee and employer, or the social contract that involves both these parties plus the government. But in each case the nature of these contracts is not what many people today grew up to expect. As a result, many kinds of relationships between organization and employee are possible in today's workplace, and the nature of these varied relationships pose a new set of challenges for the human resource manager.

THE NATURE OF EMPLOYMENT CONTRACTS

When they begin a job today, many new employees sign a formal contract with the employing organization. These legal employment contracts usually set out each party's responsibilities and rights and specify the length of the contract terms. In some cases, although individuals do not sign the contract, the organization agrees to a legal contract called a **collective bargaining agreement** between the organization and an agent representing the employees as a group—typically a labor union. These contracts are legal documents and are enforceable in a court of law. Therefore, if either party fails to live up to its responsibilities, the other party can sue for breach of contract. Although we now turn our attention to one especially important issue related to legal employment contracts, there is actually more interest in the changing nature of a different kind of contract between employer and employee, and that is where we will focus most of our attention.

■ The **collective bargaining agreement** between the organization and an agent representing the employees precisely defines the nature of the employment relationship.

■ **Employment at will** is a nineteenth-century common-law rule that allows an employer to terminate any employee, at any time, for any reason (good or bad), or for no reason at all.

Employment at Will

One important part of a legal employment contract covers the conditions and terms under which an employee can be terminated. Although some people are surprised to learn this, the only real legal perspective on employee termination is a nineteenth-century common-law rule known as **employment at will.** Basically, this view asserts that since an employee can terminate an employment relationship at any time (that is, quit a job), the employer should have similar rights. Therefore, employment at will states that an employer can terminate any employee, at any time, for any reason (good or bad), or for no reason at all. This concept differs dramatically from the situation in many European countries where the only reason for termination is criminal behavior.[1]

In the United States companies are relatively free to terminate employees at any time, so that, in most cases, the employee has no legal recourse if he or she is terminated. There are a few important exceptions to the employment-at-will doctrine, however. These exceptions define situations in which an employee who was discharged would be able to sue for wrongful termination and so get his or her job back. The first exception is when a law forbids termination for a specific reason. For example, it is a violation of the Civil Rights Act to terminate an employee because he or she is an African-American, and it is a violation of the Taft-Hartley Act to terminate an employee because he or she advocates joining a labor union. There are other statutory exceptions as well.

Another exception exists when someone has a contractual right to his or her job. Therefore, an organization cannot terminate someone with a valid contract (unless the firm is willing to pay off the contract). Following this logic, in some cases courts have actually stated that some employees are protected because they have an "implied contract." Such a situation might exist, for example, if a contract employee had his or her contract renewed every year for the past twelve years, was told that his or her performance was good, and was still terminated.

A further exception exists when a person's rights to due process have been violated. For example, most organizations have progressive disciplinary programs in which termination can come only after other steps have been tried and failed. If these steps are not followed, but the employee is still terminated, the employer might be found guilty of violating due process rights. Finally, in some cases courts have identified a public policy exception. Several years ago, for example, a nurse at a plant in South Carolina was terminated because she complained that the company was pressuring her to send injured workers back to work before they were ready. The court found that this behavior was a public policy violation in that it would be better for society if organizations did not try to force injured workers back to work prematurely.

These exceptions vary a great deal from state to state to the point where it is easier for employers to terminate employee in some states than in others. It is important to note, however, that even with these exceptions, employers can always terminate employees for cause. That is, if the employee violates some rule or is a poor performer (and this claim can be documented), he or she can always be terminated. Outside these exceptions, however, the employer does not need any reason. Therefore, unless an employee has an explicit contract, his or her rights to a job are extremely limited.

The Nature of Psychological Contracts

A **psychological contract**, illustrated in Figure 17.1, is the set of expectations an employee holds concerning what he or she will contribute to the organization (referred to as **contributions**) and what the organization, in return, will provide to the employee (referred to as **inducements**). Thus psychological contracts define the most basic relationship we expect to have with an organization.

■ A **psychological contract** is the set of expectations an employee holds concerning what he or she will contribute to the organization (referred to as **contributions**) and what the organization, in return, will provide to the employee (referred to as **inducements**).

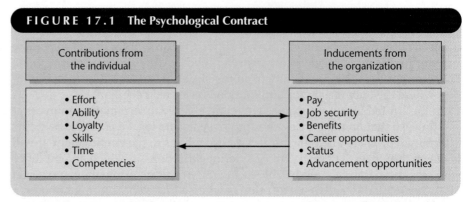

Source: Adapted from Gregory Moorhead and Ricky W. Griffin, *Organizational Behavior,* 5/e. Copyright © 1998 Houghton Mifflin Company, p. 89. Reprinted with permission.

These contracts are typically not written, so they are not formal contracts in any legal sense and are not enforceable in court. Nonetheless, an organization that believes an employee has violated his or her commitment and reduced contributions below an acceptable level will often discipline or terminate that employee. On the other hand, an employee who feels the organization has violated its commitment to provide inducements will either reduce contributions to the company or leave. Note that the employee's contributions include things such as loyalty, and so a reduction in contributions might not be simply a reduction in effort or output, but a basic change in attitude toward the organization.

Not all psychological contracts are the same, of course. Some experts, for example, have characterized these contracts as falling on a continuum from *transactional* to *relational.*[2] Contracts that are more transactional in nature typically involve a shorter time horizon, contain specific obligations, and stress financial inducements or inducements that can be converted into money (for example, salary, benefits). Contracts that are more relational in nature involve longer and indeterminate time horizons, have nonspecific and wide-ranging obligations, and stress nonfinancial (for example, socioemotional) inducements as well as financial inducements. These latter contracts are much more fluid and so are more likely to change over time.

Traditionally, one of the inducements offered by an organization was employment security. The basic understanding was that if an employee continued to contribute to the organization, he or she could expect to remain employed. Although some have argued (probably correctly) that U.S. corporations never really offered security as an inducement,[3] the fact that many employees perceived this to be the case is enough for it to become part of their view of the contract.

But as noted in earlier chapters, this inducement has not been available to employees over the last few years, as downsizing and layoffs have become common. In many cases organizations have tried to substitute training and development opportunities for job security. In other words, organizations were admitting that hard work no longer guaranteed a job, but if they were potentially going to lay off a worker who was productive, they would at least provide that employee with some skills and competencies that would make him or her more employable elsewhere. Thus even if the nature of the contract was not changed, the terms of the psychological contract often were.

But for many employees this shift represented a violation of the contract. As a result, employees felt they could reduce their contributions and their obligations to the organization.[4] As long as unemployment was rising, employees could not afford to reduce effort on the job or output for fear of being fired. Instead, they reduced contributions in the form of loyalty and commitment. To some extent this behavior made the terms of the contract less specific (and more transactional in nature), but again the real change was in the terms of the psychological contract. "Human Resources Fad, Fashion, or Fact?" explores some of the more unpleasant results that might occur as a consequence of this trend.

At the end of the 1990s, however, unemployment in the United States was at an all-time low. Employees no longer needed to fear losing their jobs because other jobs were available. Therefore, it would be possible to reduce effort and output on the job, but this possibility was not the worst of it for organizations. As unemployment shrank, organizations found they again had to compete for employees. Furthermore, the reduced rate of population growth began to play a role in further limiting the supply of workers in the economy (we discuss special problems with certain types of employees below). Instead of workforce reductions, organizations began to think about ways of retaining employees, and retention bonuses have become more popular, as have sign-on bonuses.

HUMAN RESOURCES Fad, Fashion, or Fact?

An Eye for an Eye . . .

 Going postal—an interesting phrase that has become all too common. Coined in response to several high-profile incidents in the U.S. Postal Service, the phrase is generally used when a worker or former employee takes violent action against a manager, coworker, or other employee in the organization. The highest-profile examples involve homicides in the workplace, something that is happening today with alarming regularity.

But while these homicides grab the headlines, some experts fear a growing epidemic of other forms of violence taken for purposes of revenge, retribution, or retaliation or to cause the company or its employees various kinds of problems. For example, among the more common acts of revenge reported in recent years are actions such as spitting in the boss's food, calling someone's spouse and hinting at an extramarital affair, and tampering with computers. Other common "pranks" include duplicating someone's car keys and moving the car to a different area of the parking lot, spreading malicious rumors, and leaking important confidential information.

A former broker at Smith Barney was recently arrested after eighteen months of e-mail and Internet mischief

> *"For some people, sabotage can give a feeling of fairness and closure."*
>
> (Daniel Levine, editor of Internet e-zine *Disgruntled*)*

aimed at company managers who he believed had wronged him in some way. A former worker at Omega Engineering has been charged with planting a software "bomb" in the firm's computer system, causing critical software to be erased and costing the company up to $10 million in sales. And a North Carolina theater worker has been charged with trying to blackmail his employer by threatening to tell people he had put the ashes of his recently cremated aunt into the popcorn! Because he did, in fact, have his aunt's ashes, the employee knew that part of his story, at least, would have credibility.

When will all this end? Unfortunately, many experts believe that these kinds of actions will increase. As the bond that once connected employers and their employees continues to weaken as a result of layoffs and other factors, some people will continue to feel cheated, misled, and/or shortchanged by their employers. And if these feelings become strong enough, some form of sabotage or revenge is increasingly likely.

Sources: "Employees, Ex-Workers Get Even," *USA Today,* August 20, 1998, pp. 1B, 2B (*quote on p. 2B).

Unfortunately, as we noted above, the terms of the psychological contract have already changed. As a result, employees feel less loyalty and attachment to an organization and so are quite willing to be lured away by competing offers. The changing terms of the psychological contract may now become a bigger problem for the organization than it was for the employees who had felt violated when they lost their jobs regardless of the levels of their contributions. These changes in the psychological contract will clearly be one of the major challenges facing organizations in the twenty-first century. This challenge will even be more difficult to meet as organizations come to realize that they can no longer offer "lifetime" employment as an inducement after employees experienced how empty an inducement that was a few years earlier.

Psychological Contracts and Employee Rights

One aspect of the psychological contract that is getting increasing attention is the issue of employee rights. That is, in addition to inducements offered by the organization, employees have certain expectations about their rights while at work. As we noted above, an employee's right to a job are rather limited in most cases, as he or she can be terminated at will. But beyond the right to a job, other employee rights might be challenged at work. An important part of the psychological contract involves expectations about these rights.

Freedom of speech is guaranteed by the first amendment to the U.S. Constitution. Many people are familiar with the limitation that suggests this freedom does not extend to someone's right to yell "fire" in a crowded movie theater, but at work there are often other limitations as well. Private sector employees who publicly disagree with management or who say something that damages the reputation of the company, for instance, can be disciplined for this behavior. The more visible the employee and the more the employee "represents" the organization (for example, someone in top management), the more this type of freedom of speech is limited. Even in the public sector, employees cannot use their position to endorse political candidates (although they can do so as private citizens).

Another area of employee rights that is often disputed is the right to privacy. These rights at work also vary considerably by state and even by sector. Thus, for example, public sector employers cannot search employee desks without some "probable cause" (that is, a real basis for suspecting wrongdoing), but private sector employers typically can do so with much less justification. Although most states outlaw an employer listening in on private phone conversations (or reading e-mail) without probable cause, not all do. Also, in some states random drug testing of employees (as opposed to applicants for jobs) is outlawed, but not in others.

New technology has also introduced new challenges to employee rights to privacy. Traditionally, employee personnel files contained paper records that were stored in one location and could easily be kept secure. However, many organizations now keep employee records electronically, and it is more difficult to keep these secure and confidential. In fact, many organizations design human resource information systems for *easy* access to information about employees. We discuss these systems and the problems they pose for privacy rights in more detail in Appendix 1.

In addition, in many organizations employees are under electronic surveillance to prevent theft—and many of these employees are not even aware of the surveillance. In fact, a report by the Office of Technology Assessment (conducted a number of years ago) reported that some ten million workers in the United States are being secretly monitored at work.[5] The purpose of this surveillance ranges from checking on unauthorized breaks to attempts to increase quality control. But whatever the purpose the threat of invasion of privacy from these programs is considerable.

One interesting application of electronic monitoring at work has been in the area of performance appraisal. These systems are usually quite widely publicized, so the issue is not clearly one of privacy rights. Organizations are now able to monitor the number of keystrokes entered by a data entry clerk or the number of calls handled by a reservations clerk. Many employees believe that electronic monitoring programs are an invasion of privacy, and as such cause increased stress and more work time lost due to stress-related pressure and illness.[6] Yet, some evidence suggests that computer-monitored performance can lead to fairer appraisals and can actually increase productivity. The success or failure of these systems seems to depend on the nature of the job, the way the monitoring is introduced, and whether individuals or groups are monitored.[7] Thus although the overall effects of computer-monitored appraisal systems are still unknown, they are likely to grow in popularity, and in controversy as well.

The Nature of Social Contracts

The notion of a **social contract** simply refers to expanding the relationship between employer and employee to include a third party—the government. This view recognizes that public policies such as minimum wage levels, taxes, union-management relations, and health-care provisions are an important part of the relationship between employer and employee. For example, we discussed in Chapter 13 that many employee benefits are, in fact, mandated by law and are an important part of a total benefits package. (We also noted that mandated benefits in the United States are relatively low compared to those in most European countries.) Therefore, employees should expect that, in exchange for their efforts and loyalty, organizations will provide, at a minimum, those benefits mandated by law.

> ■ A **social contract** model expands the relationship between employer and employee to include the government.

But the terms of the social contract are changing as well. Some of the nontraditional work relationships discussed below have resulted in more employees not having even basic benefits usually mandated by law. Years of organizational downsizing have led to many workers not having any type of health insurance (for example, people who have ultimately started their own businesses are less likely than traditional employees to be covered by health insurance plans). As a result, some groups believe that the government needs to do more to ensure a minimum safety net for all employees. President Clinton's attempt to provide minimum mandated health-care benefits was a concrete manifestation of this growing concern. Furthermore, the Dunlop Commission report, released in 1995, noted that workplace productivity and a hard-working workforce are important assets for any nation and the government should move to protect these assets, suggesting further government involvement.[8]

As the government gets more involved in providing benefits and guaranteeing worker rights, its actions will surely have implications for human resource managers. At the very least additional government involvement will require increased paperwork and record keeping and is also likely to increase restrictions on how employees can be treated at work. In fact, some critics say

Social contracts refer to the relationships among employers, employees, and the government. Social contracts are frequently defined by law, but then get reinterpreted as courts rule on various challenges. For example, during the years following the passage of the Americans with Disabilities Act, most judges interpreted its coverage as only applying to individuals with major handicaps. But Vaughn Murphy, shown here, recently filed a suit against his former employer, UPS, after the firm fired him because his blood pressure was higher than federal standards for safe driving. He argued that since his job involved driving only a small percentage of the time, the firm should have accommodated him by having someone else do the job. As more such suits are filed, judges may maintain their earlier strict interpretation or may take a more encompassing view. Either stance, in turn, will affect future social contracts.

that under the "new" social contract organizations should no longer compete on the basis of costs, but instead pursue a high-productivity, high-wage strategy that allows voice for all employees.[9] Such a strategy would surely change the nature of the human resource function in organizations.

THE BOTTOM LINE   All managers should have a fundamental understanding of any and all legal contracts affecting employment relationships in the organization. Managers should also understand the concept of psychological contracts, the manner in which organizations "create" such contracts, and the implications when such contracts are changed and/or "broken."

MANAGING   KNOWLEDGE   WORKERS

Traditionally, employees added value to organizations because of what they did or because of their experience. However, as we enter the information age in the workplace, many employees add value simply because of what they know.[10]

The Nature of Knowledge Work

Employees who add value simply because of what they know are usually referred to as **knowledge workers,** and how well these employees are managed has become a major factor in determining which firms will be successful in the future.[11] Knowledge workers include computer scientists, engineers, and physical scientists, and they provide special challenges for the human resource manager. They tend to work in high-technology firms and usually have a great deal of expertise in a rather narrow area. They often believe they have the right to work in an autonomous fashion and identify more strongly with their profession than with any organization—even to the extent of defining performance in terms recognized by other members of their profession.[12]

■ **Knowledge workers** add value simply because of what they know.

As the importance of information-driven jobs grows, the need for knowledge workers will grow as well. But these employees require extensive and very specialized training, and not everyone is willing to make the human capital investments necessary to move into these jobs. In fact, even after knowledge workers are on the job, retraining and training updates are critical so that their skills do not become obsolete. It has been suggested, for example, that the half-life for a technical education in engineering is about three years. Further, the failure to update the required skills will result not only in the organization losing competitive advantage but also in the increased likelihood that the knowledge worker will go to another firm that is more committed to updating these skills.[13]

Compensation and career development policies must also be specially tailored for knowledge workers. For example, in many high-tech organizations, engineers and scientists have the option of entering a technical career path that parallels a management career path. This opportunity allows the knowledge worker to continue to carry out specialized work and earn a manager's salary without taking on large management responsibilities. Also, in many high-tech organizations, within various classifications for management workers, salary adjustments are most frequently based on maturity curves rather than on performance. That is, since performance is difficult to quantify for these employees and since a great deal of research and development activity may not have an immediate payoff, salary is based on a worker's years of experience. The assumption is that, in a technical area, more experience makes the employee more valuable to the organization.[14]

But in other high-tech firms, the emphasis is on pay for performance, with profit sharing based on projects or products developed by the knowledge workers. In addition, in most firms employing these workers, there has been a tendency to reduce the number of levels of the

Knowledge work is becoming more and more central to what many organizations do. As a result, knowledge workers are also becoming increasingly important to these organizations. Consider, for example, these two physical scientists, experts on the geology of Antarctica. Because this knowledge is very important to their employer, Bell Geospace, and because relatively few individuals have this expertise, managers at the firm are very motivated to keep them happy and productive. As a result, the scientists receive larger-than-average salaries, comprehensive benefits, and ample opportunities to continue their education and to stay abreast of the latest developments in their field.

organization to allow the knowledge workers to react more quickly to the external environment and to reduce the need for bureaucratic approval.[15]

Knowledge Worker Management and Labor Markets

In recent years the demand for knowledge workers has been growing at a dramatic rate. As a result, organizations that hire these workers need to introduce regular market adjustments (upward) to pay in order to retain them. Such pay adjustments are especially critical in an area where demand is growing, since the entry-level wages for these employees are skyrocketing. Once an employee accepts a job with a firm, he or she is more subject to the internal labor market, which is not likely to be growing as quickly as the external market for the knowledge workers. As a result, the longer an employee remains with a firm, the further behind the market his or her pay falls unless it is regularly adjusted.

Of course, the growing demand for these workers also results in organizations going to rather extreme measures to attract them in the first place.[16] High starting salaries and sign-on bonuses are very common. British Petroleum Exploration was recently paying starting petroleum engineers with undersea-platform-drilling knowledge (not experience, just knowledge) salaries in the six figures, with sign-on bonuses of more than $50,000 and immediate profit sharing. Even with these incentives, human resource managers from the organization complained that in the Gulf Coast region they could not retain these specialists because, after a few months, the young engineer would leave to accept a sign-on bonus with a competitor.

But these phenomena occur in times when unemployment is relatively low, and the demand for certain types of knowledge workers is relatively recent. As time goes on and college students see the salaries paid to these specialists, more students will gravitate to programs in areas such as undersea drilling. More universities will respond with larger and larger programs in these and other areas to accommodate the new demand. As a result, in a few years there will be enough drilling specialists to meet the demand, and the frenzy over hiring and retaining these employees will subside.

This information takes time to filter down to new students, and many students will already be in the pipeline in these areas. Therefore, in the future we are likely to see a surplus of ocean-drilling engineers, for example. The over-supply will drive down salaries, which, in the long run, will discourage new students from making the human capital investments needed to perform these jobs. Then, just as we described the process above, a new shortage of these knowledge workers will trigger a new round of efforts to attract and retain those that are available. Although these patterns greatly complicate the lives of human resource professionals, to be competitive in the long run organizations are going to have to do better long-term planning so they can manage the supply and demand of knowledge workers rather than just react to the labor market conditions.

THE BOTTOM LINE Knowledge workers represent a special category of employees. All managers need to understand the peculiar motivational profiles that drive such workers. The human resource function can—and must—play an important role as a center of expertise in helping to manage knowledge workers in the organization.

M A N A G I N G   L O W - S K I L L   W O R K E R S

Although thinking about managing highly specialized knowledge workers may be interesting and exciting, organizations, of course, employ several other kinds of workers as well. Over the past several years, as highlighted in Figure 17.2, the greatest growth in jobs and employment has been in the service sector of the economy. Service jobs include such things as accounting, real estate, and other professional service functions. But many service jobs tend to be unglamorous, low paying, and low in skill requirement. What is most challenging about this trend is the shortage of employees for these jobs.

A great deal of this growth in this sector has been in areas such as counter workers at fast-food restaurants. These jobs typically do not pay much (if anything) above the minimum wage, and they typically offer no career paths or advancement opportunities. Thus workers in these jobs would have a great deal of trouble supporting a family, and they would not have particularly bright prospects. Pressures to raise the minimum wage are often aimed at making these jobs more attractive to potential employees and to position them as a meaningful alternative to welfare programs.

How does an organization manage workers on these jobs? Traditionally, these jobs were performed by teenagers who were working part-time while going to school. Thus although the jobs did not pay very much and lacked career opportunities, teenagers found the salaries adequate for their current needs and planned to seek careers elsewhere. But the slowing growth in the population has reduced the number of teenagers now in the labor market. The first problem, then, is to find other workers to fill these jobs.

There is some evidence that employers are seeking nontraditional employees as a potential alternative. While the number of teenagers is shrinking, the number of older workers is growing, and these workers have been hit disproportionately hard by downsizing activities in recent years.[17] These older employees, especially those nearing or at retirement age where they can collect pensions and social security, may well be willing to work for the wages offered on these jobs, and they do not need career opportunities at this point in their lives. Persons with disabilities may well serve as another alternative source of employees for these jobs, and both these groups are likely to include employees who are committed to the organization and who will be motivated to work hard.

But many low-skill jobs exist in other sectors of the economy as well. Maintenance workers and cleaning staffs are two groups of low-skill workers that might be found in a wide range of organizations. Older workers or workers with disabilities may fill some of these jobs, but there are simply not enough potential employees from these groups to fill all the jobs. Thus organizations still have problems of unemployment among younger able-bodied employees who simply do not have the education or training to perform higher-level jobs. Therefore, the problem of managing employees working in these low-skill jobs remains. Most of these employees are unlikely to develop loyalty and commitment to the organization. As a result, these employees may be relatively easy targets for unionization. Furthermore, the lack of career opportunities and the low levels of commitment tend to result in high levels of absenteeism and turnover on these jobs.

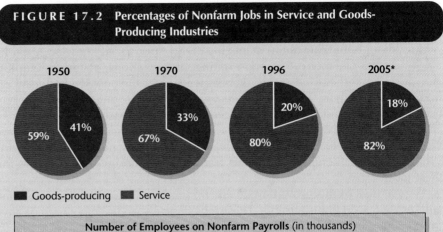

FIGURE 17.2 Percentages of Nonfarm Jobs in Service and Goods-Producing Industries

Number of Employees on Nonfarm Payrolls (in thousands)							
Annual Averages				Annual Averages			
Year	Total	Goods-producing	Service-producing	Year	Total	Goods-producing	Service-producing
1946	41,652	17,248	24,404	1988	105,209	25,125	80,084
1950	45,197	18,506	26,691	1989	107,884	25,254	82,631
1955	50,641	20,513	30,128	1990	109,403	24,905	84,497
1960	54,189	20,434	33,755	1991	108,249	23,745	84,504
1965	60,765	21,926	38,839	1992	108,601	23,231	85,370
1970	70,880	23,578	47,302	1993	110,713	23,352	87,361
1975	76,945	22,600	54,345	1994	114,163	23,908	90,256
1980	90,406	25,658	64,748	1995	117,191	24,265	92,925
1985	97,387	24,842	72,544	1996	119,523	24,431	95,092
1986	99,344	24,533	74,811	1997	112,259	24,739	97,520
1987	101,958	24,674	77,284	2005*	130,185	22,930	107,256

*Projection

Source: The Wall Street Journal Almanac 1999, p. 227. Republished by permission of Dow Jones, Inc. via Copyright Clearance Center, Inc. © 1999 Dow Jones and Company, Inc. All Rights Reserved.

In fact, rather than trying to manage these employees, many organizations have sought to simply avoid the problem completely. They have done so by establishing completely different types of relationships with employees, creating new "types" of employees. The remainder of this chapter is devoted to discussing some of the issues that arise from these new work relationships.

THE BOTTOM LINE   Most organizations have at least some low-skill workers. Human resource managers need to fully understand the limitations and constraints they face in managing such workers.

O U T S O U R C I N G

As we mentioned at the beginning of this book, there has been a great deal of interest in **outsourcing** certain functions in organizations today. In essence, outsourcing means that an organization "rents," rather than buys, help in a functional area. In fact, low-skill jobs, such as those we discussed above, are prime candidates for outsourcing. For example, if an organization contracts with an outside vendor to provide maintenance services, it does not need to worry about recruiting or retaining employees for those jobs. (However, if the vendor discriminates in employment practices, the organization may still be liable in some cases as well.) The organization is also no longer concerned about career paths or ways to motivate employees in what might not be the most attractive jobs. Finally, since these employees might otherwise be an excellent target for unionization activities, the organization also reduces its vulnerability in this area.

■ **Outsourcing** occurs when an organization "rents," rather than buys, help in a functional area.

The major issue for managers interested in this tactic is to decide what kinds of functions or activities are suitable for outsourcing. Maintenance, cleaning, and food service operations within large organizations are increasingly being outsourced with little evidence of problems. In some industries where the workforce has been steadily shrinking for years (such as steel), organizations can contract with outside vendors for a wide variety of functions and actually have their former employees working for them again. These employees, who may have lost their jobs in earlier periods of downsizing, may have subsequently been hired by a vendor to perform the same functions they did before for the steel company. Then, when the activity is outsourced, the company gets the same well-trained employee, at a lower wage, and without any responsibilities relative to job security or advancement.

But some organizations are also outsourcing higher-level functions. When IBM created a new organization called Workforce Solutions, for instance, it essentially "spun off" its human resource function to create a new firm. The new firm could perform human resource consulting activities for a variety of organizations, but, presumably, IBM would always be a large client. Thus IBM would be able to benefit from the training and experience it provided to its human resource managers when they still worked for that company.

These managers and the programs they install would no longer be a source of competitive advantage for IBM, however. Since Workforce Solutions can provide services for other firms as well, the new company is likely to sell the same programs to IBM and to other clients. In fact, many large management consulting

Outsourcing is a popular trend in many businesses today. For example, Razorfish is a high-tech firm that designs web sites for businesses. When Schwab decided it needed a new design for the firm's web site, managers turned to Razorfish for assistance. Two of Razorfish's employees, Hyo Yeon and Arun Bordoloi, took the lead on the project and designed a totally new look for Schwab's web site. By using this approach, Schwab avoided the costs of recruiting new web designers and developing a compensation package for them, as well as myriad other human resource issues. It also had to ensure that the outside designers worked with Schwab's in-house web staff that will be responsible for maintaining the site.

firms, which have been the beneficiaries of outsourcing, essentially sell similar programs to all their clients. Although they claim to do a separate needs analysis in each case, the recommended programs look very much the same from one organization to the next. Therefore, balancing the efficiencies that can come from outsourcing with the loss of competitive advantage in a given area must be the basis of any organization's decision on whether or not to outsource a given function.

THE BOTTOM LINE Managers should be fully aware of the advantages and disadvantages of outsourcing. Even if some or all of an organization's human resource functions are outsourced, a center of human resource expertise must remain as a core part of the organization. And the managers who are involved in the outsourced unit itself are clearly also a part of this center of expertise.

CONTINGENT AND TEMPORARY WORKERS

When an organization decides to outsource a function, the people who carry out that function are no longer employees of the organization, and so there is no psychological contract in place. Or, organizations may decide to employ the workers, but on a basis other than full-time or permanent status. As a result, we have seen an explosion in the use of contingent and temporary workers by organizations.[18] We turn now, to some trends as well as to some of the management issues associated with those workers.

Trends in Contingent and Temporary Workers

■ A **contingent worker** is a person who works for an organization on something other than a permanent or full-time basis.

In recent years the number of contingent workers in the workforce has increased dramatically. Table 17.1 summarizes recent statistics. A **contingent worker** as a person who works for an organization on something other than a permanent or full-time basis. Categories of contingent workers include independent contractors, on-call workers, temporary employees (usually hired through an outside agency), and contract and leased employees. Another category is part-time workers. For example, Citigroup is making extensive use of part-time sales agents to pursue new clients.[19] About 10 percent of the U.S. workforce currently has one of these alternative forms of employment relationships. Experts suggest, that this percentage is increasing at a consistent pace.

Advantages and Disadvantages of Using Contingent and Temporary Workers

There are a number of advantages and disadvantages to companies that choose to use contingent and temporary workers. The primary advantage that most companies seek to achieve with the use of contingent workers is cost savings. For the most part an organization that uses contingent workers does not have to pay for their benefits, such as health insurance, vacation time, and sick days. Usually the provider of the contingent workers absorbs these costs. And in some arrangements tax burdens can also be shifted to either the employee or the provider of the contingent worker.

Another major advantage that companies derive from the use of contingent workers is increased flexibility. Recruiting and hiring permanent workers is a costly proposition. And if the organization miscalculates its workforce needs and hires more employees than it can adequately support, it may then be faced with expensive and painful layoffs and downsizing efforts. But using contingent workers helps an organization address this problem more effectively. That is, the organization can maintain a permanent and full-time workforce of somewhat less than it really needs to conduct its business and then make up the difference with contingent workers. Then, as its demand for human resources increases or decreases, it can bring in more or fewer contingent workers.

One major disadvantage to the use of contingent workers is productivity. Although few studies have been conducted on this matter, the average contingent worker will probably not be as well versed in how the organization conducts its business as will a permanent and full-time employee. That is, the individual contingent worker may possess adequate generalized skills but may lack firm specific skills. Consequently, the contingent worker may not understand enough about specific organizational procedures and operations to be able to function efficiently, at least during the early period of work.

Organizations have often chosen to use contingent or temporary workers in order to realize some form of cost saving. But the outcome of a recent lawsuit against Microsoft may change all that. Jeff Nachtigal, shown here, is part of a class action lawsuit against his employer. He and his colleagues argue that because Microsoft has retained their services for an extended period (two years, in his case) they should receive the same benefits as the firm's permanent workers. These include health care, a stock purchase plan, paid vacation, and sick days. An early ruling in favor of Microsoft was overturned by a three-judge panel; Microsoft, meanwhile, has filed an appeal. The final results of the legal battle will have far-reaching implications for businesses and temporary workers in every sector of the economy.

Another disadvantage that firms confront when using contingent workers is decreased organizational commitment and loyalty. "The Lighter Side of HR" illustrates this situation. When a given employee is a permanent, full-time, and long-term member of a firm's staff, she or he is likely to develop a reasonably strong feeling of loyalty and commitment to the organization. This feeling is a function of well-established working relationships, common and shared experiences, and the security of employment. But none of these characteristics are likely to exist in the work relationship an organization has with contingent workers. Thus compared to traditional employees, contingent workers are almost surely going to be less committed and less loyal to the organization.

Another disadvantage is that if an organization relies too heavily on contingent workers, it may fail to develop a strong human resource base of its own. In today's environment an organization can staff virtually all skilled positions with contingent workers. But if it takes this course of action, it may end up with few or even no employees of its own who possess some of these fundamental skills. In the short run this situation might not be a particularly big problem. But longer term the organization may face at least some problems of decreased effectiveness as a result of a weaker human resource foundation of

TABLE 17.1 **Employed Workers with Alternative Work Arrangements by Occupation and Industry, 1997 (Percent Distribution)**

Characteristic	Workers with Alternative Arrangements			
	Independent Contractors	On-Call Workers	Temporary Help Agency Workers	Workers Provided by Contract Firms
Total, 16 years and over (thousands)	8,456	1,996	1,300	809
Occupation				
Executive, administrative, and managerial	20.7%	2.7%	6.9%	8.1%
Professional specialty	17.9	21.2	6.6	19.8
Technicians and related support	0.8	4.1	5.8	7.2
Sales occupations	17.9	6.7	1.7	2.8
Administrative support, including clerical	3.9	8.6	34.1	5.2
Services	9.1	20.4	9.0	27.7
Precision production, craft, and repair	17.9	14.7	5.2	19.8
Operators, fabricators, and laborers	6.8	18.8	29.1	9.2
Farming, forestry, and fishing	5.1	2.8	1.6	0.2
Industry				
Agriculture	5.7	3.4	—	0.2
Mining	0.2	0.4	0.6	2.1
Construction	20.7	14.4	2.2	4.6
Manufacturing	4.7	5.3	27.7	19.0
Transportation and public utilities	5.1	8.6	5.3	12.9
Wholesale trade	3.5	1.7	3.8	1.5
Retail trade	10.1	12.5	3.4	6.3
Finance, insurance, and real estate	8.4	1.5	7.4	7.5
Services	41.4	47.5	36.6	26.5
Public administration	0.2	4.0	—	13.1

About 10% of the American workforce is employed under an alternative arrangement, particularly as independent contractors.

Source: The Wall Street Journal Almanac 1999, p. 244. Republished by permission of Dow Jones, Inc. via Copyright Clearance Center, Inc. © 1999 Dow Jones and Company, Inc. All Rights Reserved.

its own. "Human Resources Legal Brief" summarizes another disadvantage, namely, the potential for legal complications if the firm mismanages its contingent workers.

Managing Contingent and Temporary Workers

Given the widespread use of contingent and temporary workers today, it follows logically that managers should understand how to more effectively manage these kinds of employees.

One key to the effective management of contingent and temporary workers is careful planning. Even though one of the presumed benefits of using contingent workers is flexibility, it still is important for managers to try to use such workers in a relatively smooth and coordinated fashion. Rather than having to call in contingent workers sporadically and with no prior notice, it is beneficial for the organization to be able to bring in specified numbers of contingent workers for well-defined periods of time. And the ability to do so comes from careful planning.

A second important part of managing contingent and temporary workers effectively is to understand and acknowledge the advantages and disadvantages described in the preceding section. That is, the organization needs to recognize what it can and can't achieve from the use of contingent and temporary workers. Expecting too much from such workers, for example, is a mistake that the manager should avoid.

Third, it is very important that managers carefully assess the real cost of using contingent workers. For example, we noted above that many firms adopt this course of action as a way of saving labor costs. And the organization should be able to document very precisely these savings. The firm can look at how much it would be paying people in wages and benefits if they were on permanent staff, compare this amount with how much it is paying the contingent worker provider, and assess the difference. But this difference might be misleading. For instance, we also noted above that contingent workers might not perform as effectively as permanent and full-time employees. So comparing employee for employee on a direct cost basis is not necessarily valid. Instead, the organization has to adjust the direct differences in labor costs for differences in productivity and performance.

Finally, managers need to articulate and fully understand their own strategies and decide in advance how they intend to manage their temporary workers, specifically focusing on how to integrate these workers into the organization. At a very simplistic level, for example, an organization with a large contingent workforce needs to make some decisions about the treatment of contingent workers relative to the treatment of permanent, full-time workers. Should contingent workers, for example, be invited to the company holiday party? Should contingent workers have the same access to employee auxiliary benefits such as counseling services or childcare facilities as do permanent and full-time employees? There are no clear right or wrong answers to these questions. The point simply is that managers need to understand that they need to develop a strategy for integrating contingent workers according to some sound logic and rationale and then follow that strategy consistently.

When Is Temporary Permanent?

For the last several years, more and more big companies have hired a growing number of temporary workers. And indeed, some companies rely so heavily on temporary workers that they almost become a permanent part of the organization. One of the primary reasons that employers hire temporary workers is because they are generally not covered under various benefits plans, especially pensions.

But what happens when a firm takes on temporary workers and then keeps them for an extended period? For example, more than 29 percent of the workers employed by temp agencies remain on their assignments for a year or longer. The question, then, is who is the primary employer: the temp agency that hired the individuals and then gave them an assignment or the firm that contracted for their services with the temp agency but that then keeps them on indefinitely?

It's just that circumstance that has prompted the courts to take a close look. For example, the Labor Department recently filed a lawsuit against Time Warner. The suit charges that some of its temp workers actually qualify now as permanent employees and thus should be covered by the same benefits that apply to other workers. An even more significant case, however, has been filed by

"Any company with any sense is going to be aware of these [new legal questions] and is talking to counsel about the potential liabilities."

(Ed Lenz, general counsel of the National Association of Temporary & Staffing Services)*

a group of Microsoft workers. About six thousand contract workers claim that they are essentially "common law" Microsoft employees and should have the same pension plan coverage as the firm's permanent employees. Other recent cases have involved Allstate and Pacific Gas & Electric.

The critical factor in determining which side is "right," so far at least, is the nature of the employment relationship. If the firm itself decides whom it will use, provides the same supervision for temp workers as for permanent workers, and uses its own payroll system to compensate them, the courts are generally finding that the workers qualify for all other benefits afforded regular employees. It's only when the temp agency makes the assignment decision, provides at least part of the supervision, and handles compensation that the individuals remain temp workers. But although a pattern seems to be emerging, more court decisions are no doubt on the horizon before these issues get settled once and for all.

Sources: "When Is a Temp Not a Temp?" *Business Week,* December 7, 1998, pp. 90–92 (*quote on p. 90); "Programmers of the World . . . ," *Business Week,* December 7, 1998, pp. 92–94; "Temping as a Career Choice," *Fortune,* December 6, 1999, pp. 350–351.

THE BOTTOM LINE   All managers need to be aware of the issues associated with managing contingent workers, especially their own organization's policies and procedures. Organizations that rely heavily on contingent workers will need to ensure that their human resource function is fully involved in planning and managing all facets of the contingent employment relationships.

MANAGING NEW FORMS OF WORK ARRANGEMENTS

Even when organizations continue to employ people on a permanent, full-time basis, the work schedules and arrangements for these employees are also changing rapidly. Traditionally, if employees worked forty hours a week, they were expected to be physically present at work five days a week, eight hours a day, unless the nature of the job was such that the employee was required to spend time on the road. In modern organizations, however, it is becoming increasingly common for people to work on a schedule other than five days/forty hours and/or to work at a place other than the office or place of business.

Managing Alternative Work Schedules

The two most common alternatives to the traditional workweek are programs known as flexible work hours and compressed workweeks. Employees working under **flexible work hour** plans usually must still work for a full forty hours, and typically they must work five days a week. The employees have control, however, over the starting and ending times for work on each day. In almost every case there is a *core time* each day when every employee must be at work. During these hours the organization can schedule meetings or any other activities that require coordination among employees. The remaining hours (*flex time*) can be made up in any way the employee prefers. For example, if a company's core time is from 10:00 until 2:00, everyone is expected to be at work during those hours. But starting times can be anywhere between 7:00 and 10:00, and quitting times can be anywhere between 2:00 and 7:00. Under this plan the core time represents twenty hours a week, and the employee is free to work the remaining twenty hours in any fashion within the stated constraints.

Figure 17.3 illustrates how an organization might function with one type of flexible work schedule. This organization has defined 6:00 a.m.–9:00 a.m., 11:00 a.m.–1:00 p.m., and 3:00 p.m.–7:00 p.m. as flexible time, and 9:00 a.m.–

■ In **flexible work hour** programs, employees work forty hours per week, five days a week, but have flexible starting and ending times.

FIGURE 17.3 Flexible Work Schedules

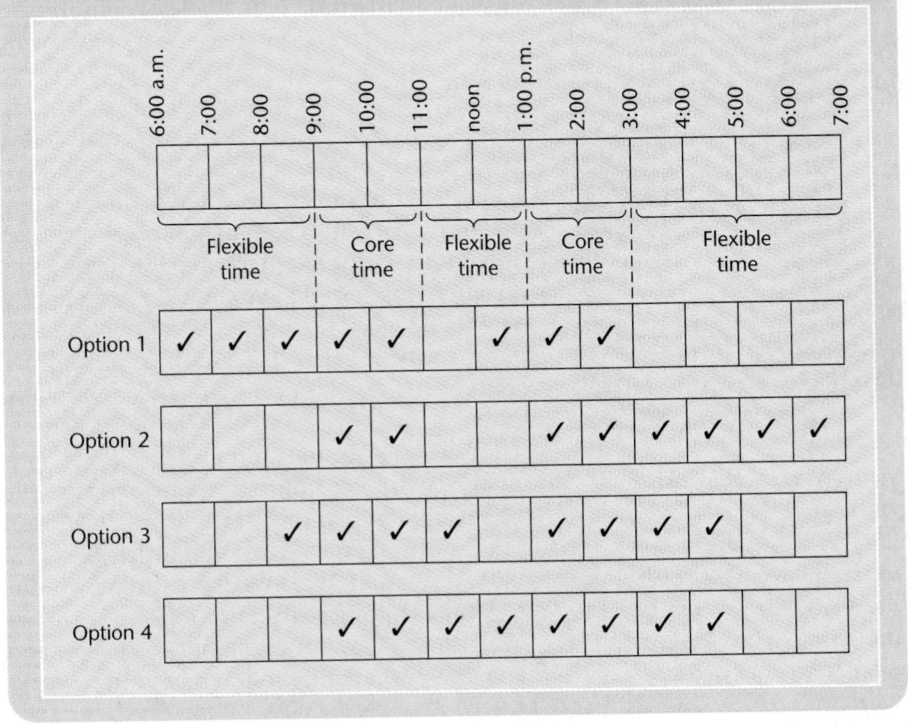

11:00 a.m. and 1:00 p.m.–3:00 p.m. as core time. A worker choosing option 1 (that is, the "early riser") comes to work at 6:00 a.m., takes an hour for lunch, and is finished for the day at 3:00 p.m. Option 2, perhaps more attractive for those who don't think of themselves as "morning people," involves starting work at 9:00 a.m., taking two hours for lunch, and working until 7:00 p.m. Option 3 is closest to a standard workday, starting at 8:00 a.m., taking an hour for lunch, and leaving at 5:00 p.m. Finally, option 4 involves starting at 9:00 a.m., taking no lunch, and finishing at 5:00. Note that all employees are working during the core time periods.

These plans are believed to reduce stress, since employees do not have to travel during peak commuting times and can have more control over the commute.[20] They are also believed to increase job satisfaction, since the employee is given more control over the work environment and a stronger feeling that he or she is trusted by the organization.[21] They are not as feasible in organizations that have a strong emphasis on teams, but otherwise there are no reports about serious problems associated with their use.

Compressed workweeks are arrangements in which employees work the required number of hours (typically forty), but do so in fewer than five days. For example, a four-day, ten-hour-a-day work schedule is fairly common. Employees gain the flexibility of three days off a week, presumably making it less likely that they will lose work time to deal with personal business. Schedules

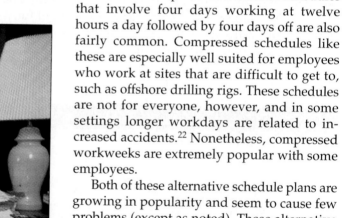

that involve four days working at twelve hours a day followed by four days off are also fairly common. Compressed schedules like these are especially well suited for employees who work at sites that are difficult to get to, such as offshore drilling rigs. These schedules are not for everyone, however, and in some settings longer workdays are related to increased accidents.[22] Nonetheless, compressed workweeks are extremely popular with some employees.

Both of these alternative schedule plans are growing in popularity and seem to cause few problems (except as noted). These alternative schedules present some unique challenges to the human resource manager, however. As noted above, for example, flexible schedules are often not feasible in organizations that rely heavily on teams. In fact, whenever one employee's work depends on input from another employee, these schedules may be a problem. Even when they are not a problem, flexible schedules reduce the amount of time that employees interact with their fellow employees, which makes it more difficult to develop a strong culture or even a strong esprit de corps.

Compressed workweeks present similar challenges because, although employees are at work the same number of hours as before and have the opportunity to interact with cowork-

■ **Compressed workweeks** are arrangements in which employees work the required number of hours (typically forty), but do so in fewer than five days.

Working at home has become a very popular new form of work arrangement. Under the right circumstances, it can give employees the flexibility to better juggle child care and other personal responsibilities with the demands of their job. It can also allow employers to maintain less physical workspace and to more effectively retain valuable employees. Kelly Ramsey-Dolson, for example, is an accountant employed by Ernst & Young. By working at home, she can spend more time with her son Jeffrey while maintaining a full-time work schedule. Both Ms. Ramsey-Dolson and her employer feel that this arrangement works to their mutual benefit.

TABLE 17.2 Number of People Doing Job-Related Work at Home

| Characteristic | Number (thousands) | Rate* | Wage & Salary | | Self-Employed | |
			Paid	Unpaid	Total	Home-Based Business
Total, 16 years and over	21,478	17.8%	17.0%	51.5%	30.1%	19.2%
With no children under 18	12,179	16.1	16.3	52.0	30.3	19.0
With own children under 18	9,299	20.5	17.8	50.9	29.9	19.5
With own children under 6	3,885	19.6	18.8	47.6	31.6	22.3
Men, 16 years and over	11,202	17.3	15.0	50.1	33.8	19.3
With no children under 18	6,259	15.4	16.0	47.1	35.8	21.3
With own children under 18	4,943	20.5	13.8	54.0	31.2	16.7
With own children under 6	2,118	18.8	14.2	55.5	28.7	16.3
Women, 16 years and over	10,275	18.3	19.1	53.1	26.2	19.2
With no children under 18	5,920	17.0	16.7	57.2	24.6	16.6
With own children under 18	4,356	20.4	22.4	47.4	28.3	22.7
With own children under 6	1,767	20.8	24.3	38.1	35.0	29.6

*Refers to the number of persons working at home as a percent of the total at work.

Source: *The Wall Street Journal Almanac 1999*, p. 246. Republished by permission of Dow Jones, Inc. via Copyright Clearance Center, Inc. © 1999 Dow Jones and Company, Inc. All Rights Reserved.

ers, the stress of longer hours may make that less likely. The greater number of days off may also affect some social aspects of the job. The human resource manager's job is to try to find ways to replace these socializing activities with other experiences so that employees, especially new employees, can learn more about their coworkers and can become more fully socialized into the organization.

Managing Alternative Work Sites

In addition to having employees work on alternative schedules, there is also a growing trend to have employees perform their work at somewhere other than the place of business, most likely at home. Home work and telecommuting are two popular variations on this theme. Table 17.2 shows the number and characteristics of people currently having one or the other of these options. **Home work programs** include arrangements that are often referred to as cottage industries. In the earliest days of the industrial revolution, before there were many factories, employees would take parts back home to their "cottages" and manufacture them, then returning them to a central point where they could be

■ **Home work programs** include arrangements that are often referred to as cottage industries.

■ **Telecommuters** do almost all of their work at home and perhaps even receive assignments electronically.

assembled. Similar types of cottage industries still exist for the manufacturing of small and not very complex items.

It is more common, however, to operate in what can be called an "electronic cottage." Employees take office work home with them and complete it on a home computer. They can then return to the "office" to collect more work and be connected to that office via a modem, fax machine, and e-mail. These arrangements can even result in a "virtual office" and are becoming especially popular with people who want (or need) to work, but do not wish to work full-time or who have other responsibilities such as childcare or elder care.[23]

Telecommuting is simply the logical extension of the electronic cottage. Under these arrangements, employees may do almost all of their work at home and even receive assignments electronically. This practice provides employees with the ultimate in flexibility as they can choose the hours they work and even the location. According to a growing body of evidence, telecommuting increases job satisfaction and even productivity, and it also allows organizations to have the services of individuals who may not be able to work at a given site.[24] For example, employees can live many hours from their office if they telecommute. Finally, larger organizations can save considerable amounts of money if they do not need large (or any) real office space. For example, Cisco Systems, a pioneer in telecommuting, estimates that by allowing employees to work at home it has boosted productivity by 25 percent, lowered its own overhead by $1 million, and retained key knowledge workers who might have left for other jobs without the flexibility provided by the firm's telecommuting options.[25]

Alternative work sites present a more serious challenge than some other nontraditional arrangements to the human resource manager. In the past the AFL-CIO has complained that home working arrangements allow management to impose unfair working conditions on employees. These plans also make it more difficult for unions to organize workers, and so they continue to oppose such arrangements. As with alternative work schedules, communications among employees are difficult under alternative work site arrangements, and it is extremely difficult for a new employee to become socialized. But, in fact, there may be little to become socialized into, since the organization may exist in virtual reality only.

In addition, some individuals may simply lack the self-discipline to get the work done in a completely unconstrained environment, although the available evidence suggests that this is not much of a problem. What does seem to be a problem is that these alternative work sites are likely to increase employee's sense of alienation at work.[26] Without connections and support from coworkers, there is likely to be little loyalty or commitment to the organization. Companies are trying, however, to overcome these problems. For example, Merrill Lynch allows potential telecommuters a two-week dry run to see how they like it. Aetna assigns each of its telecommuters an office "buddy" to help those working at home to stay in touch with what's going on at the office. And America West even arranges monthly potluck dinners to maintain social interaction among employees who work at home.[27]

THE BOTTOM LINE   Managers should understand the pluses and minuses involved in new forms of work arrangements. They should also recognize the need for such options in order to retain key workers. Human resources can play a key role as a center of expertise in helping managers create and manage new forms of work arrangements.

Chapter Summary

One important part of a legal employment contract covers the conditions and terms under which an employee can be terminated. Employment at will asserts that an employer can terminate any employee, at any time, for any reason, or for no reason at all. A psychological contract is the set of expectations an employee holds concerning what he or she will contribute to the organization and what the organization, in return, will provide to the employee. Because job security is less prevalent than in earlier times, many companies are finding that they must redefine the psychological contracts they have with their employees. One aspect of the psychological contract that is getting increasing attention is employee rights. The notion of a social contract simply refers to expanding the relationship between employer and employee to include the government.

As we enter the information age in the workplace, many employees add value simply because of what they know. These employees are usually referred to as knowledge workers, and how well these employees are managed is a major factor in determining which firms will be successful in the future. Compensation and career development policies must be specially tailored for knowledge workers.

Over the past several years, the greatest growth in jobs and employment has been in the service sector of the economy. Service jobs include such things as accounting, real estate, and other professional service functions. But many service jobs tend to be unglamorous, low paying, and low in skill requirements. A challenging aspect of this trend is the developing shortage of employees for these jobs.

There has been a great deal of interest in outsourcing certain functions in organizations today. The major issue for managers interested in this tactic is to decide what kinds of functions or activities are suitable for outsourcing. Although lower-level jobs are often outsourced first, some organizations are also outsourcing higher-level functions.

Recent years have seen an explosion in the use of contingent and temporary workers. Contingent workers work for an organization on something other than a permanent or full-time basis. Categories of contingent workers include independent contractors, on-call workers, temporary employees, contract and leased employees, and part-time workers. There are a number of advantages and disadvantages to companies that choose to use contingent and temporary workers.

Even when organizations continue to employ people on a permanent, full-time basis, the work schedules and arrangements for these employees are also changing rapidly. In modern organizations it is becoming increasingly common for people to work on a schedule other than five days/forty hours and/or to work at a place other than the office or traditional place of business.

Review and Discussion Questions

1. What is employment at will? Do you agree or disagree with its basic premise?

2. Distinguish between a psychological contract and a social contract.

3. What contributions and inducements typify a psychological contract in a class such as this one?

4. What are knowledge workers? What are the special challenges involved in managing knowledge workers?

5. What are the special challenges involved in managing low-skill workers?

6. Describe the various kinds of contingent workers that organizations use.

7. What are the primary advantages and disadvantages in using contingent and temporary workers?

8. What are the differences between flexible work schedules and compressed work schedules?

9. Which would you personally prefer, a flexible work schedule or a compressed work schedule?

10. Identify and discuss some of the major issues involved in allowing people to work at alternative work sites, such as a home office.

Closing Case

Temps, Temps, Temps Everywhere!

Charleston Naval Shipyard, Charleston, South Carolina: Like other pieces of complicated equipment, navy ships have to have regular maintenance and service work, as well as less-frequent major overhauls and upgrades. This work is usually done by one of several naval shipyards around the country. Whenever a ship is scheduled for service, each shipyard can bid for that work. The Charleston Naval Shipyard is one of these yards. Over the years it has specialized in working on nuclear missile submarines, although it also works on every type of ship. The civilian employees in Charleston, like those at other shipyards, work for the Department of Defense. But they are limited to one year of continuous employment. If they work for longer than one year, they attain certain status and privileges as government workers that the government does not wish to bestow.

Whenever the shipyard wins a bid, therefore, an interesting employment process begins. The shipyard immediately begins advertising for temporary (one year) employees who have the exact skills to perform the required maintenance work on the project. These skills will obviously vary from project to project. The shipyard can usually hire many of the workers it needs but may have to train others. In either case on the day the ship arrives for its maintenance work, the shipyard must have in place all the systems and the employees needed to carry out the work.

The fact that these temporary employees can work only for one year presents another interesting dilemma for the shipyard. What if the work takes longer than is anticipated? What if employees are needed for more than one year? The regulations say that employees cannot work for more than one year continuously. If they are needed longer, they are terminated. Then, after one week of not being employed, the shipyard can rehire them for another year. Of course, the shipyard always needs skilled workers, and so some people attain almost permanent employee status as they move from one project to another. Nonetheless, all the employees are officially classified as temporary, and all hiring is on an as-needed basis.

Macy's, Herald Square, New York City, New York: There are few more enduring symbols of the onset of Christmas season than the Macy's Thanksgiving parade. But when the parade is over and the official shopping season begins, it also signals the beginning of one of the largest programs of temporary hiring in the United States. Indeed, the process is repeated all over the country, as department and specialty stores get ready for the Christmas rush.

Every year stores such as Macy's hire hundreds of temporary employees to supplement the regular staff. Although the demands of the season are substantial, the Christmas season does not last long enough to justify hiring more full-time people. On the other hand, the amount of time required makes it unreasonable to try to meet this demand by extending overtime to existing employees. Instead, notices go out in early November, and the hiring process begins. Few applicants have had meaningful retail-selling experience, although a large cadre of people returns every year to Macy's to work during the holiday season.

What kind of person applies for and gets these temporary jobs? The most typical groups are retired persons, students, and housewives. These are people unwilling or unable to work full-time, but they tend to be hard-working and loyal employees. The temporary employees typically receive employee discounts of 10 to 15 percent—even off sale prices—as well as extra money for the holiday season. Macy's and similar stores are able to meet the demands of the holiday shopping period without increasing their basic payroll, and for all, another holiday tradition continues.

Collin Street Bakery, Corsicana, Texas: Although many people associate the holiday rush with retailing, many other kinds of employers also find it necessary to make seasonal workforce adjustments. For example, consider the Collin Street Bakery, a one-hundred-year-old firm in Corsicana, Texas, that for much of the year is a small, family-operated enterprise selling cookies, pies, cakes, and bread and employing fewer than fifty people. But fruitcakes, often the brunt of jokes, are serious business to the folks at the Collin Street Bakery.

As it turns out, the Collin Street Bakery sells more fruitcakes during the holiday season than any other producer in the world. All told, the firm sells about 1.5 million fruitcakes a year, with about a fourth of them being shipped to foreign countries. Starting in September the bakery expands its workforce, first for the preparation of fruitcakes and later for their mailing and shipping. By Thanksgiving the company has hired more than five hundred temporary workers.

But unlike Macy's in New York, the Collin Street Bakery has a much smaller labor pool to draw from—the local community only has about 23,000 residents! Therefore, rather than market its jobs to seasonal workers, the bakery instead promotes opportunities to employees with full-time jobs elsewhere who might want to supplement their income during the holiday season. The shipping jobs, for instance, can be performed at any hour, and most workers actually come in after their "day jobs," perhaps working from 7:00 (after dinner) or so until 11:00 two or three nights a week. This approach gives the bakery an ample supply of talent while enabling local residents to supplement their pay.

Case Questions

1. What are the similarities and differences among the temporary staffing situations faced by the shipyard, the department store, and the bakery?

2. Which of the three challenges is the biggest? Which is the smallest?

3. What forces might cause each of the three employers to have to change its temporary staffing strategy?

Sources: "Seasonal Businesses Bustle to Find Teen Workers," *USA Today,* May 15, 1997, p. B1; "Industries Crying Out for Help Wanted," *USA Today,* May 5, 1997, p. B1; "Worker Shortage Forces Small Business into Creative Hiring," *USA Today,* October 30, 1998, pp. B1, B2.

Building Human Resource Management Skills

Purpose: The purpose of this exercise is to help you understand the implicit and explicit elements of psychological contracts in an organization.

Step 1: Assume that you are the senior human resource executive of a large service company. Your firm has undergone three layoffs during the last five years, and your employees feel very little job security. While your pay and training opportunities are among the best in your industry, you can also foresee the possibility of further workforce reductions.

Step 2: Your boss, the CEO, has suggested that you develop what she calls a "new covenant" for your organization, something you see as really an explicit psychological contract. This document, to be committed to writing and shared throughout the organization, will outline exactly what the firm will offer to its employees and what it expects in return.

Step 3: Draft the new covenant for your organization.

Step 4: Repeat this process for each of the following scenarios:

1. Your firm is a medium-size distribution company; pay is slightly below industry averages, but you have never laid off anyone.

2. You are the company owner; you pay above-average wages and provide superior benefits. You also expect your employees to work long and hard and to exhibit unerring loyalty to you and to your firm.

3. You manage a large domestic subsidiary of a foreign corporation. Your parent company wants to instill its own values and corporate culture into your firm. These changes will include a more paternalistic approach, more job security, but lower pay and less lavish benefits.

Step 5: Form groups with your classmates and compare your responses. Then respond to the following questions:

1. What are the major similarities and differences in your new covenants for the three scenarios?

2. How similar or different were the various covenants developed by the members of your group?

3. What are the advantages and disadvantages of formal and written psychological contracts compared to informal and unwritten ones?

Ethical Dilemmas in Human Resource Management ━━━━━

 Your firm has a major telecommuting program. Under the terms of the program, employees are allowed to work at home two days a week. Because you prefer the structure and routine of a regular work schedule and workplace, you have elected to not participate. One of your best friends, however, was an early participant and is today one of its most outspoken advocates.

You have recently heard some things that are causing you distress. For one thing, you know from casual comments that your friend recently spent part of a "work at home" day on the golf course. You also know that your friend occasionally buys groceries and/or runs family errands during work-at-home time. You have just gently asked your friend about this. Your friend was clearly very uncomfortable and embarrassed by the question and mumbled that it was just "comp time" to offset some evening and weekend work and then quickly changed the subject.

Questions

1. What are the ethical issues in this situation?

2. What are the basic arguments for and against your friend's behavior?

3. What would you do in this situation? What do you think most people would do?

Human Resource Internet Exercise

 Assume that you are the human resources manager for a mid-size manufacturing company. Your firm has just gotten a big contract that will boost your human resource requirements for the next eighteen months or so. You will need new production workers, office/administrative workers, truck drivers and warehouse personnel, and sales support personnel. However, because the company is uncertain as to what might happen after the contract is over, you do not want to add permanent employees, although your permanent workforce might also grow.

Search the Internet to locate temporary employment agencies that might be of value. Review each site carefully and then prepare a memo to your boss outlining how you should proceed and your degree of comfort/discomfort with this approach.

Questions

1. Do you feel more comfortable working with a national agency or a smaller local one? Why?

2. Do you feel more comfortable working with one service for all your needs, or do you prefer to work with different agencies for each type of worker you need? Why?

3. What information was easiest to learn from the Web sites you visited? What information was the most difficult to find?

Notes

1. M. R. Buckley and W. Weitzel, "Employment at Will," *Personnel Administrator,* Vol. 33, 1988, pp. 78–80.
2. Denise M. Rousseau and Judi McLean Parks, "The Contracts of Individuals and Organizations," in L. L. Cummings and B. M. Staw (eds.), *Research in Organizational Behavior,* Vol. 15 (Greenwich, Conn.: JAI Press, 1993), pp. 1–43.
3. Douglas T. Hall and J. E. Moss, "The New Protean Career Contract: Helping Organizations and Employees Adapt," *Organizational Dynamics,* Winter 1998, pp. 22–37.
4. Sandra L. Robinson, Matthew S. Kraatz, and Denise M. Rousseau, "Changing Obligations and the Psychological Contract: A Longitudinal Study," *Academy of Management Journal,* Vol. 37, 1994, pp. 137–152. See also

"The Wild New Workforce," *Business Week,* December 6, 1999, pp. 38–44.
5. J. J. Laabs, "Surveillance: Tool or Trap?" *Personnel Journal,* Vol. 71, 1992, pp. 96–104.
6. B. Garson, *The Electronic Sweatshop: How Computers Are Transforming the Office of the Future into the Factory of the Past* (New York: Simon & Schuster, 1988).
7. John R. Aiello, "Computer-Based Work Monitoring: Electronic Surveillance and Its Effects," *Journal of Applied Social Psychology,* Vol. 23, 1993, pp. 499–507.
8. Commission on the Future of Worker-Management Relations, *Final Report* (Washington, D.C.: Department of Labor/Department of Commerce, 1995).
9. R. Marshall, "A New Social Contract," in J. Auerbach and J. Welsh (eds.), *Aging and Competition: Rebuilding*

the U.S. Workforce (Washington, D.C.: The National Planning Association, 1994), pp. 207–224.

10. Max Boisot, *Knowledge Assets* (Oxford, England: Oxford University Press, 1998).

11. Michael L. Tushman and Charles A. O'Reilly, *Winning through Innovation* (Cambridge, Mass.: Harvard Business School Press, 1996).

12. Mary Ann Von Glinow, *The New Professionals* (Cambridge, Mass.: Ballinger, 1988).

13. Thomas W. Lee and Steve D. Maurer, "The Retention of Knowledge Workers with the Unfolding Model of Voluntary Turnover," *Human Resource Management Review,* Vol. 7, 1997, pp. 247–276.

14. J. C. Kail, "Compensating Scientists and Engineers," in David B. Balkin, and Luis R. Gomez-Mejia (eds.), *New Perspectives on Compensation* (Englewood Cliffs, N.J.: Prentice-Hall, 1987), pp. 278–281.

15. George T. Milkovich, "Compensation Systems in High-Technology Companies," in A. Klingartner and C. Anderson (eds.), *High Technology Management* (Lexington, Mass.: Lexington Books, 1987).

16. Thomas Stewart, "In Search of Elusive Tech Workers," *Fortune,* February 16, 1998, pp. 171–172.

17. Michael Useem, "Business Restructuring and the Aging Workforce," in James Auerbach and Joyce Welsh (eds.), *Aging and Competition: Rebuilding the U.S. Workforce* (Washington, D.C.: National Planning Association, 1994), pp. 33–57.

18. Daniel C. Feldman, Helen I. Doerpinghaus, and William H. Turnley, "Managing Temporary Workers: A Permanent HRM Challenge," *Organizational Dynamics,* Autumn 1994, pp. 49–63.

19. "Citibank Hitches Itself to Primerica's Team to Peddle Accounts," *Wall Street Journal,* April 19, 1999, pp. A1, A6.

20. Avraham N. Kluger, "Commute Variability and Strain," *Journal of Organizational Behavior,* Vol. 19, 1998, pp. 147–166.

21. D. Denton, "Using Flextime to Create a Competitive Workforce," *Industrial Management,* January–February 1993, pp. 29–31.

22. Jon Pearce and Randall Dunham, "The 12-Hour Work Day: A 48-Hour, Eight-Day Week," *Academy of Management Journal,* Vol. 35, 1992, pp. 1086–1098.

23. S. Greengard, "Making the Virtual Office a Reality," *Personnel Journal,* September 1994, pp. 66–79.

24. S. Caudron, "Working at Home Pays Off," *Personnel Journal,* November 1992, pp. 40–49.

25. "Making Stay-at-Homes Feel Welcome," *Business Week,* October 12, 1998, pp. 155–156.

26. S. D. Atchison, "The Care and Feeding of 'Lone Eagles,'" *Business Week,* November 15, 1993, p. 58.

27. "Saying Adios to the Office," *Business Week,* October 12, 1998, pp. 152–153.

Human Resource Information Systems

OUTLINE

**What Are Human Resource
Information Systems?**
The Nature of Information
Technology
Human Resource Information
Systems

**Potential Uses of Human Resource
Information Systems**
Human Resource Functions
Record Keeping and Report
Generation

**Issues and Concerns in the Use of
Human Resource Information
Systems**
Legal Issues
Ethical Issues

Conclusions

The human resource manager's job requires a large number of decisions. These decisions, in turn, require access to a large amount of information. In simple cases we can imagine a human resource manager reading and analyzing the files for the ten applicants for a recent job opening and deciding who should receive an offer. Perhaps the position for which these applicants are applying is a new one within the organization, and so at some point the human resource manager must determine the appropriate compensation for this position relative to other jobs within the firm. Furthermore, this new position may be the result of a new strategic initiative that requires information about the kinds of skills and abilities available inside the organization.

Clearly, these decisions require that various kinds of information be available for the human resource manager. As we will see, there is also a fair amount of information that might be useful to new employees once they join the organization and to other individuals who may have to make very different kinds of decisions but might still need to know something about the current human resources in the organization. The need for this kind of information, in an easily accessible and ready to use form, is at the heart of human resource information systems.

WHAT ARE HUMAN RESOURCE INFORMATION SYSTEMS?

A human resource information system is a special form of a more general kind of information system. Thus we begin by briefly examining the nature of information technology in general, and then we focus more specifically on human resource information systems and their role in organizations.

The Nature of Information Technology

Information technology refers to the resources used by an organization to manage information that it needs to carry out its mission. Information technology is generally of two types—manual or computer based. All information technology, and the systems that it defines, has five basic parts. One part is the *input medium*, the device that is used to add data and information into the system. For example, an optical scanner at Kroger enters point-of-sale information. Likewise, someone can also enter data through a keyboard. And when people apply for jobs in an organization, their resumes and/or job applications might be scanned into the firm's information system.

The data that are entered into the system typically flow first to a processor. The *processor* is the part of the system that is capable of organizing, manipulating, sorting, or performing calculations or other transformations with the data. Most systems also have one or more *storage devices*—a place where data can be stored for later use. Floppy disks, hard drives, CD-ROMS, and optical disks are common forms of storage devices. As data are transformed into usable information, the resulting information must be communicated to the appropriate person by means of an *output medium*. Common ways to display output are video displays, printers, other computers, and facsimile machines.

Finally, the entire information technology system is operated by a *control system*—most often software of one form or another. Simple systems in smaller organizations can use off-the-shelf software. Microsoft Windows 98, DOS, and OS2 are general operating systems that control more specialized types of software. WordPerfect and Microsoft Word are popular systems for word processing. Lotus 1-2-3 and Excel are popular spreadsheet programs, and dBASE III is frequently used for database management. Of course, elaborate systems of the type used by large businesses require a special customized operating system. Some firms create their own information system for human resources, whereas others buy existing software commercial products.[1] And when organizations start to link computers together into a network, the operating system must be even more complex.

Human Resource Information Systems

A human resource information system, as noted above, is a special form of information system oriented directly at an organization's human resource management needs. That is, a **human resource information system** (or **HRIS**) is the entire set of people, procedures, forms, and data used to acquire, store, analyze, retrieve, distribute, and use information about an organization's human resources. The system is, therefore, much more than just computer hardware and software (although these components are critical to an effective HRIS). Finally, the major goal of the system is to provide needed information that is timely and accurate and to provide it in a way that it is useful to persons making human resource–related decisions.

In essence, the information contained in an HRIS is information that has always been available in books, reports, records, or forms. The key difference, though, is that the information is now computerized. There is no longer any need for paper forms or reports, for instance, and decision makers should be able to locate and access easily and exactly the information they need. For example, if there is a need to know exactly how many people are working in an area (the "head count"), when they began working with the company (perhaps to determine potential wage costs), or even the average number of dependents employees have (perhaps to project benefit costs), the person charged with obtaining the information should be able to access a computer database and retrieve the desired information.

Thus the specific nature of any HRIS will depend on the needs of the organization. Organizations will differ, for example, in terms of what information they actually need to retrieve, and therefore need to store, as part of the HRIS. Some organizations may focus on race and gender characteristics of the workforce, while others might be concerned about accidents and work days lost. Furthermore, organizations will differ in terms of how they need the information to be presented. Some may need information at the aggregate level, about the organization as a whole (numbers of employees, average wages, average hours, and so on), while others might need more information about individuals (a person's work history, skills profile, and so on). The remainder of this appendix discusses some specific uses of HRISs in organizations, as well as some specific ideas about the kinds of information that might be needed. Finally, we discuss some of the moral, ethical, and legal issues that are involved with setting up and using an HRIS.

■ A **human resource information system** (or **HRIS**) is the entire set of people, procedures, forms, and data used to acquire, store, analyze, retrieve, distribute, and use information about an organization's human resources.

POTENTIAL USES OF HUMAN RESOURCE INFORMATION SYSTEMS

Of course, the potential types of output from an HRIS depend on the nature of the input. But the decision concerning what information to input depends on how the system will be used. Ultimately, the HRIS should help the organization in its strategic planning process, but there are a number of other more-focused applications.

Human Resource Functions

At a very basic level, the HRIS can be used by the organization and its members to help them more effectively manage the employment relationship. For example, from the standpoint of the organization, the HRIS can be used in human resource planning. Job openings can be posted as part of its recruiting efforts. Applications can be scanned (as already noted) and stored. Performance appraisal information can also be stored, as can the employee's history of training and development activities. Career path, compensation, and benefit information can also be an integral part of the HRIS. Individual employees should be able to scan the HRIS for new job possibilities within the organization and be better informed about training opportunities and benefit options.

Record Keeping and Report Generation

Perhaps the most common application of an HRIS, however, involves the generation of reports, especially reports that must be prepared on a regular basis. A good example of this would be the EEO-1 report on current employees that many organizations are required to file with the government. Data must be presented for all jobs using the following categories: officials and managers, professionals, technicians, sales workers, office and clerical, (skilled) craft workers, (semiskilled) operatives, (unskilled) laborers, and service workers. For each job category the organization is required to report how many incumbents can be classified as white (not of Hispanic origin), black (not of Hispanic origin), Hispanic, Asian or Pacific Islander, and American Indian or Alaskan native. Furthermore, the organization must report numbers within these groups for male and female employees separately.

Also, many organizations are required to regularly submit "eight factor" reports, which indicate both the availability and utilization of employees within the same categories (for both jobs and employees) as in the EEO-1 report. These reports depend on the same types of information as the EEO-1 reports, and an HRIS is extremely useful in supplying that information. Other reports requiring HRIS input involve the evaluation of training programs. Computation of cost-benefit ratios for these programs require information about which training programs an employee has gone through and some evaluation of past and current levels of job performance, turnover, or absenteeism. In fact, virtually any evaluation that deals with absenteeism and turnover data, or with any type of productivity data, requires input from an HRIS.

But perhaps the area where the most report generation activity requiring an HRIS takes place is the compensation and benefits area. For example, to "price" jobs, an organization needs data on how the jobs score on various compensable factors, as well as data on what other organizations are paying. The results of the wage surveys for comparison data and the results of the job evaluation are likely to be kept in an HRIS and thus made available to compensation analysts. Also, once jobs are priced, an HRIS can provide the data needed to compare current compensation rates with those generated through the pricing process and to indicate which jobs should have their compensation adjusted. HRIS data are also used to determine withholdings and to generate rates of take-home pay for employees. In such cases the system must be flexible enough to deal with changes in the tax codes or in the number of dependents.

Similarly, recall that in Chapter 13 we discussed the idea of a cafeteria benefits program. These systems provide an allowance for benefits that employees can "spend" on any mix of benefits they want. It is virtually impossible to implement such a system and keep track of choices and changes in choices and allocations without an HRIS, and data from these systems are needed to provide reports to employees. Even without a cafeteria system, HRIS data are needed to generate annual reports informing employees of their present benefits and the value of those benefits. Here again, flexibility is vital, as choices and options are likely to change.

One final example of an area where an HRIS is critical is in the area of planning. Specifically, as an organization plans its human resource needs for the following year, it needs information about planned changes in operations and the implications of those changes for human resources. But the organization also needs to know about its available human resources and what types of skills and experiences the present workforce possesses. Inventories of skills and experience provide a challenge not only because of the amount of information required but also because of the way the information is encoded and used.

In most of the other examples we have discussed, the kind of data required for the system is pretty clear. That is, if managers need to know the number of women in a certain job, encoding this information is straightforward. However, to prepare an inventory of skills and experiences, managers need to first decide which skills and experiences are relevant for the decisions to be made. Then they must decide exactly what information about those skills and experiences to include. For example, a manager might simply want to note whether an employee has had a certain job assignment of not. Or the manager might want to know how long the assignment lasted and how successful the employee was on the job. In the area of skills, an organization might simply rely on self-reports that an employee can speak French, for example. But more complex systems might include information about scores on a French test or might indicate the level of speaking ability. Thus HRISs used for planning require the organization to make many more decisions than do systems used for other types of decisions.

These examples provide some idea of the range of information that might be included in an HRIS and what kinds of decisions this information might be used for. Nonetheless, the actual range of possibilities is almost endless, as organizations determine what kinds of information they need to have access to in order to make the decisions that need to be made. But regardless of the kinds of information included, a number of other issues must be considered as an organization designs and implements an HRIS.

ISSUES AND CONCERNS IN THE USE OF HUMAN RESOURCE INFORMATION SYSTEMS

Regardless of the exact information an organization retains in its HRIS and regardless of how that information is used, the fact that the organization collects and stores a large amount of information about its employees, and that this information can be easily retrieved, raises a number of issues and concerns. Some of these are related to legal questions concerning privacy and the invasion of privacy, whereas others are related to the ethics of storing and retrieving personal information about employees.

Legal Issues

Most of the legal issues concerning HRISs are related to privacy. The Fourth Amendment to the U.S. Constitution guarantees protection from unreasonable search and seizure. The ability of an organization (or its representatives) to search an employee's files without his or her permission might well violate that protection. In addition, the Fifth Amendment provides protection against self-incrimination, and if an organization searches through an employee's personnel files and finds incriminating information, this action could be viewed as a violation of that protection.

Most of the legislation in the privacy area has been enacted by states, but the Privacy Act of 1974 requires federal agencies to open their personnel files for employee inspection. Furthermore, the law enables the employee to correct any incorrect or misleading information in those files *and* allows the employee to prevent the use of the information in those files for anything other than its original intent. Several lawmakers have suggested that this protection be extended to employees in private industry, but such legislation has not yet been formally proposed. It seems clear, however, that in the future organizations might have more difficulty in deciding what kinds of information to keep about employees and how to use that information, which will have a substantial impact on the design of HRISs.

The Privacy Protection Study Commission was established in 1977 to determine which safeguards needed to be put in place to protect employee rights in this area. The commission has suggested a number of steps to help organizations protect employee rights as they set up HRIS systems. These include

1. Organizations should collect and store only job-relevant information in their information systems.

2. Organizations should limit or completely avoid storing subjective information about employees (such as appraisal information) in their information systems.

3. Organizations should provide employees with information about exactly how their records will be used.

4. Organizations should allow employees to access their records and files and to correct any incorrect information.

5. Organizations should strictly limit internal access to employee information.

6. Organizations should strictly limit and always document the release of information to anyone outside the organization without employee approval.[2]

Clearly, these suggestions would significantly limit the organization's ability to rely on information systems for decision making, and the potential conflicts between an employee's right to privacy and an organization's need to have information will continue to be an important issue.

Ethical Issues

Some legal restrictions already in place potentially limit the information an organization can store about employees and how that information is used. And these restrictions are likely to increase over time. But in addition to legal restrictions, a number of ethical considerations should guide the design and use of an HRIS.

For example, organizations are restricted in the information they can collect about an employee's health at the time of hiring. However, once a person is an employee, an organization might routinely collect and store information about insurance claims that possibly contain information about health issues. Likewise, organizations should not ask applicants (or even current employees) about any disabilities they might have. On the other hand, employees who have disabilities may be able to request certain accommodations in order to carry out their jobs. Furthermore, the organization would be likely to store information about these accommodations, especially if they dealt with hours or conditions of employment. But retaining such information in an employee's file could jeopardize opportunities in the future if some decision maker discovers the employee's "hidden" disability (for example, a learning disability).

Even if there were no tangible results of this information becoming known, coworkers might begin treating the employee differently. Therefore, the question arises of whether or not the organization should keep this kind of information. Clearly, there might be good reasons to keep such information, and doing so is probably legal, but the information could cause embarrassment or discomfort to the employee if it were known. Again, the solution to such dilemmas probably lies with tighter restrictions on who can access an employee's file. But of course, as these restrictions grow, the chances increase that someone who might need to have access to some information will be denied access because he or she would then also have access to more-sensitive information.

C O N C L U S I O N S

As organizations become more complex and as the amount of information they need increases, the need for automated information systems increases dramatically. The organization must determine what kinds of information it will need by deciding what kinds of decisions it will make based on the HRIS information and who will actually make the decisions. Because these needs are likely to change over time, it is also necessary to build in a certain amount of flexibility.

But the ultimate flexibility would involve having a maximum amount of information available for every employee and then making this information accessible by every employee. Such a system would almost certainly violate an employee's rights to privacy and may well cause the employee embarrassment. Weighing the present and future organizational needs for information against the employee's rights and well-being will remain a major challenge for designers of HRISs.

Notes

1. Bill Roberts, "Software Selection Made Easier," *HRMagazine*, June 1998, pp. 44–49.

2. Privacy Protection Study Commission, *Personal Privacy in an Information Society* (Washington, D.C.: Government Printing Office, 1977).

Appendix 2

Data and Research in Human Resource Management

OUTLINE

Determining Causal Relationships

Common Human Resource Research Issues
  Samples and Sampling
  Measurement Issues
  Statistical Issues

Other Technical Issues in Human Resource Research
  Validity Generalization
  Utility Analysis

Many aspects of the human resource manager's job require decisions to be made. Throughout this text we have tried to provide information about the nature of these decisions, as well insights into potential solutions. But even after a decision is made, the job is not complete—it is still necessary to evaluate the decision. That is, the human resource manager (or perhaps someone else in the organization) needs to determine whether the implemented decision or program worked as intended. To be able to evaluate the decision effectively, the human resource manager needs some appreciation and understanding of research, data, and data analysis. Note that in this day of computerization, human resource managers do not usually need to actually perform specific statistical tests, but they must be able to decide which data to collect and determine which tests to run; then they must be able to interpret the results.

This appendix provides an overview of some of these issues. Although the principles discussed here apply to a wide variety of settings, we place them in the context of human resource decisions and human resource programs. In addition, we discuss in some detail two human resource issues of a fairly technical nature that are also mentioned in the body of the text—validity generalization and utility analysis. First, though, we discuss a general issue that underlies all research in the social sciences, including human resource research: causality.

DETERMINING CAUSAL RELATIONSHIPS

When a human resource manager implements a new pay plan as a means of reducing turnover and then observes that turnover has, in fact, been reduced, the manager would probably like to believe that the new pay plan *caused* the reduction in turnover. This desire to believe the new pay plan was responsible for the change in turnover is especially true if the new pay plan was implemented in one division, perhaps as a pilot project, and the organization must now decide whether or not to implement the plan throughout the organization. At first glance the issue may seem to be quite simple. Turnover was high (say, 15 percent), a new pay plan was implemented, and turnover subsequently went down (perhaps to 8 percent). What else could have caused the drop in turnover?

This is exactly the right question to be asking, but the answer is not obvious. Any number of factors other than the new pay system could conceivably influence turnover in the organization. For example, when unemployment rates are high, turnover generally drops in all organizations as employees see few alternatives to their present jobs. When unemployment rates are lower, alternatives are available, and so an unhappy employee might feel more secure in acting on the basis of his or her dissatisfaction. Therefore, if the local unemployment rate increased around the time the new pay plan was implemented, reduced employment alternatives, rather than the new pay plan, may have caused the turnover rate to change. In fact, in this case, if the organization had done nothing, the turnover rate would still have gone down as a result of the rise in unemployment.

Another possibility is that disgruntled employees have been leaving the organization at a fairly constant rate. However, at some point all the disgruntled employees have already quit, and all that are left are the satisfied employees who are not likely to quit. Perhaps this point occurred at about the same time the new pay plan was implemented. Here again, the turnover rate would have dropped even if the organization did nothing.

In yet one more scenario, perhaps the employees believed that the management didn't really care much about them, and so their leaving was in response to a perceived neglect. When the organization introduced a new pay system, the management signaled to the employees that it did care about them. But the important thing was the fact that the management did *something* for the employees, rather than the specific nature of the new pay plan. Here, turnover would not have gone down if the organization did nothing, but a much less expensive intervention that communicated concern on the part of the management might have been equally effective.

To establish that a causal relationship exists, we must be able to effectively rule out all other rival plausible explanations for the changes we have observed. If any or all of the explanations discussed above (or some other explanation) are possible, we cannot say with certainty that the new pay plan caused the reduction in turnover. In fact, under such a set of circumstances we cannot say exactly what caused the reduction in turnover.

Many times, when we want to examine the impact of some program on an outcome of interest, we simply examine the relationship between a variable corresponding to the program and a variable corresponding to the outcome of interest. For example, if an organization is interested in training employees as a means of increasing satisfaction (since the employees would have more skills and be able to do a wider variety of jobs), a human resource manager might decide to correlate the amount of training employees have with their levels of satisfaction. This task would involve determining whether employees with more training were also more satisfied with their jobs. Assuming that the human resource manager would find such a relationship, she or he might conclude that training causes higher levels of satisfaction and so recommend companywide training programs. (We discuss correlations in more detail a bit later.)

But again, there would be problems with such a statement. Because the manager did not provide the training (and so had no control over who was trained or how much training a person received), many other factors could explain the relationship observed. Perhaps being more satisfied on the job leads an employee to make more investments for the sake of the company, including seeking training. Thus increased satisfaction caused increased training, rather than vice versa. Alternatively, perhaps more highly motivated employees were more likely to seek training and more likely to be happy on the job. In this case training would not have caused satisfaction, and satisfaction would not have caused employees to seek training. Instead, a third variable (the level of employee motivation) caused both, the seeking of training and the increase in satisfaction.

Therefore, we state again that we can make causal statements (changes in *a* caused changes in *b*) only when we have ruled out all plausible alternative explanations. Furthermore, we can never make causal statements when our conclusions are based on a correlation between two variables. Instead, if we wish to make causal statements, we need to be able to control for these alternative explanations. How do we do that? The simple answer is that we need to conduct an experiment in which two groups are equivalent on everything that might possibly be relevant, especially on levels of overall satisfaction. Then we introduce a treatment (for example, a new pay plan) to one group (at random), but not the other. After a suitable period of time, we measure the levels of satisfaction in the two groups. If the level of satisfaction (following the intervention) is higher in the group that received the new pay plan, we can be relatively sure that the new pay plan caused satisfaction to increase.

We have just described a true experiment that allowed us to make a causal statement. It is often difficult to conduct true experiments in organizational settings, but some variations are easier to carry out. The discussion of these different designs is beyond the scope of the present discussion. Nevertheless, without some type of experiment, we cannot make statements of the type that "*a* causes *b*."

COMMON HUMAN RESOURCE RESEARCH ISSUES

Whether or not some type of experiment will be conducted, a number of issues must be considered whenever an organization does human resource research. We will discuss sampling, measurement, and statistical issues in the context of various types of human resource research issues. Again, these subjects are complex, and we can provide only an introduction to them here. The interested reader is encouraged to look for additional material.[1]

Samples and Sampling

In Chapter 7 we introduced the idea of validation as it relates to selection—demonstrating that persons who scored higher on some test (or other selection devise) also performed better on the job. To demonstrate such a relationship (and so validate the test), we typically collect information on test scores and subsequent (or current) performance and then calculate a correlation to determine the extent of any relationship. Presumably, an organization could give this test to every employee and obtain performance information for every employee, but this process would be extremely time consuming. The organization would be more likely to collect these data from some subset of employees, which we call a "sample." The organization would then determine the extent of the relationship in the sample data and infer that the same relationship holds true for the rest of the population.

Before discussing any details about samples, we must point out that even if the organization decided to test and collect performance data from every employee, sampling would still be involved. That is, managers are not really interested in the relationship between test scores and job performance for current employees—the organization already knows how well they are performing. Instead, managers want to use any information about test scores and performance with future applicants. If a relationship exists between the two, managers would use the test scores of applicants to predict their later performance on the job and hire only those expected to perform well. Therefore, managers would be using the relationship between scores and performance in current employees and assume that the same relationship would hold for new applicants.

For this logic to work, the sample must be representative of the population of interest. If we use current employees to compute a relationship that we hope will apply to later applicants, our current employees must be representative of future applicants. If, for example, our present employees are mostly white males and we expect many future applicants to be either nonwhite and/or females, we can be pretty certain that our sample is not a good one for predicting performance of later applicants.

Effective sampling procedures allow television networks to predict the outcome of elections early in the evening. When network executives tell us that 75 million families watched the last Super Bowl, they base this statement on the viewing patterns of a small sample of "typical" families—referred to as "Nielsen families" because of the name of the firm that compiles the ratings.

One of the most famous blunders based on poor sampling occurred during the presidential election of 1948. Harry Truman was running against a Republican named Thomas Dewey. Pollsters conducted an opinion poll to try to predict the outcome of the election. They sought a "representative" sample of all Americans they could poll and decided to draw the sample from local phone directories. The polls indicated that Dewey would be the easy winner, and everyone was surprised when Truman won handily. The problem was with the sample used in the polls. In 1948 many Americans did not own a phone because they could not afford one. Therefore, the phone directory only provided information about phone owners—not the general population. People with more money were more likely to own phones, and traditionally people with more money are more likely to vote Republican. The sample was therefore biased in that it overrepresented Republicans. Had the sample been more representative, the outcome would have been different. Modern pollsters have become much more sophisticated about drawing samples, and in fact, the phone directory might provide a much more representative sample of Americans today than it did in 1948.

Measurement Issues

If we were interested in measuring someone's height, we could do so with a yardstick and be pretty sure that we got it right. We can measure time and distance with amazing precision as well. But when we try to measure someone's level of ability, or personality or intelligence, we begin to have difficulties. In addition to measuring the level of someone's conscientiousness (for example), we are also measuring a lot of other things we don't really want to measure. This is the problem of unreliability we discussed in Chapter 7. Eventually, we could be measuring so many of these unwanted things that we are not measuring conscientiousness at all. We discussed the validity problem in Chapter 7 as well.

If we are interested in seeing whether a test for conscientiousness is related to performance on the job, we have to be sure that we can measure both conscientiousness and performance in a meaningful way. If our test is somehow biased, or requires a high level of reading ability, for example, we will have problems, since the test is supposed to measure conscientiousness not reading ability. As a result, we might conclude that conscientiousness does predict job performance when we have really only found that reading ability predicts job performance. Likewise, if we do not have a good measure of job performance (see Chapter 8), we may conclude that our test predicts performance on the job when it really only predicts a person's gender, since men consistently are rated higher on our (flawed) performance measure even when they do not perform better than women. Using the test in this case would then result in selecting only men, which, in this case, would almost certainly be illegal.

Statistical Issues

Despite our discussion of causality, the single most common statistical test used in human resources is the correlation coefficient. A correlation coefficient indicates the degree of linear relationship between two sets of scores. When scores on, say, a test and job performance are correlated, we know that changes in test scores are associated with changes in job performance. If the correlation is positive, we further know that higher test scores are associated with higher levels of performance. The stronger the relationship, the higher the correlation and the closer changes in one are associated with changes in the other. Notice that we are not saying that the test scores *cause* the changes in performance. Instead, we simply note that those who score higher also tend to perform better. In fact, correlations are used in settings where we do not have experimental designs and so we cannot assess causality.

Correlations can also be negative. The sign (positive or negative) indicates nothing about the strength of the relationship, only the nature of the relationship. When a correlation is negative it means that higher scores on one variable are associated with lower scores on the other. For example, we know that employees who are more satisfied on their jobs should be absent less frequently. Therefore, if we took a sample of employees, measured their job satisfaction, and noted how many days they missed work in the past year, we should find that those with higher satisfaction scores were absent fewer days—a negative correlation.

The size of the correlation coefficient indicates the strength of the relationship between the two sets of scores. Correlations can range from –1.00 through 0 to +1.00. Because the sign of the correlation only tells us the direction of the relationship, we can see that a correlation of 0 indicates no relationship between the variables, whereas a correlation of 1.00 indicates the strongest relationship possible. In fact, a correlation of 1.00 is also referred to as a perfect correlation. It means that for every unit of change in one variable, there is exactly one unit of change in the other. Because the relationship is perfect, we can also perfectly predict the scores on one variable from the scores on the other vari-

---

FIGURE A.1   Diagrams Illustrating the Scatter Plots for Five Correlation Coefficients

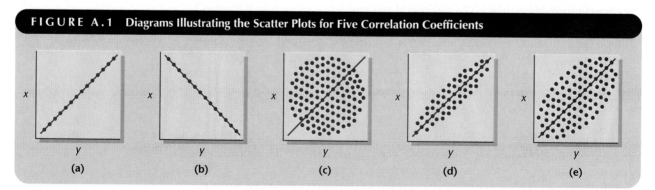

| (a) | (b) | (c) | (d) | (e) |

These diagrams illustrate correlations of 1.00 (a), –1.00 (b), zero (c), .80 (d), and .10 (e).

able. To help illustrate this principle and to help make the concept of correlations clearer, we have presented some correlation coefficients in Figure A.1.

The top three diagrams illustrate correlations that are either perfect or 0. Specifically, these are the scatter plots that would correspond to each correlation. A scatter plot is obtained by simply graphing each person's scores on the two variables x and y (where x might be scores on a test and y might be job performance). For example, we have indicated the point corresponding to a person who scored 80 on x and 90 on y. Every other point in the scatter plot was determined in exactly the same way. You may wonder why, if the correlation between the two variables is perfect, the person whose scores we have illustrated does not have exactly the same score on both variables. To explain that condition, we need one more piece of information that is presented in the figure.

Notice that in each case we draw a line, called the regression line, through the scatter plot. This represents the best straight-line fit to the information in the graph. The linear equations represented by those lines are always of the form: $y = bx + c$ where y is the score on variable y; x is the score on variable x; c is a constant; and b is the regression coefficient, or the *slope* of the line. The constant term simply allows the scores on the two variables to differ by some constant and is also referred to as the y *intercept*, since it marks the point at which the line crosses the vertical axis. The slope of the line is a ratio of the number of units of change in one variable to the number of units of change in the other. In all the examples provided here, the slope is equal to 1.0. This slope is simply the easiest to illustrate and indicates that in the best-fitting line one unit of change in x is associated with one unit of change in y. The y intercept, or constant, in each case is 10, indicating that the two variables change on different scales but that these scales differ by exactly ten units. Thus for each case except for the negative correlation, the equation for the best-fitting regression line would be equal to

$$y = 1.0 \, (x) + 10$$

In the first example, where there is a perfect and positive correlation, the best-fitting line fits the data perfectly—all the points on the scatter plot line up exactly on the regression line. Our equation would lead us to predict that for any value of x, if we simply add 10, we will get a corresponding value for y. In the first case our predictions are exactly right each time, since every point is on the line. So if we knew someone had a score on x of 30, we would predict a score on y of 40, and in the first case we would be exactly right. The nature of the equation and prediction are the same for the negative correlation, except that the equation would have a negative slope, but prediction would still be perfect.

The regression line for the third correlation is the same as for the first but here the correlation is 0. Thus knowing a score on x provides absolutely no help in predicting a score on y. In fact, we can see that someone scoring 50 on x could score anywhere from 0 to 100 on y. This same range of predicted values will be obtained for every value of x. Notice here that the points in the scatter plot form more of a circle and, in any case, deviate far from the straight line. The only predictions we can make in all cases are those based on the simple linear regression equation, and the further the points deviate from the straight line, the less accurate our predictions until we reach this case, where the correlation is 0, and our predictions are no better than we could obtain if we just chose random numbers.

The remaining two graphs illustrate correlations greater than 0 but less than 1.00. In both cases the points in the scatter plot deviate from our best-line regression line, but the degree of deviation is quite different. In the fourth illustration, the correlation is computed to be =.80. Although prediction is not perfect here, notice the points do not deviate much from the regression line. As in the other cases, if a person had a score of 50 on x, we would predict that he or she should score 60 on y. Because prediction cannot be perfect here, we are not always right. But notice that a person scoring 50 on x will score somewhere between 55 and 65 on y. We predicted a score of 60, and we were off, but not by much. Thus knowing someone's score on x does not perfectly predict the score on y, but it narrows things down considerably.

The final illustration involves a correlation of +.10. Here the points of the scatter plot deviate quite a bit from the regression line, and so we would expect predictions to be less accurate. The person scoring 50 on x would still be predicted to score 60 on y, but in fact, persons scoring 50 on x score anywhere from 10 to 90 on y. This is still better than the accuracy of prediction when the correlation is 0, but not by much, and we can predict very little about scores on y from scores on x.

Another statistical test that is encountered in human resources is known as a t-test. This test, which compares two groups in terms of their mean scores, may well be used in experimental designs as a means of determining causality. For example, if we were interested in whether a group that had received a training program produced more "units" than one that wasn't trained (but was otherwise comparable to aid in determining causality), we would use a t-test to compare the mean levels of output in the two groups. If the trained group produced more units and the difference was greater than we would expect by chance alone (determined by comparing our obtained t-value with some critical value from a table), we would conclude that the training did cause an increase in output.

If, instead, there were three groups, we would need to employ a related but slightly different statistical test. So if we wanted to compare the output of a group receiving traditional training, a group receiving computer-aided training, and a group receiving no training, we could compare the mean levels of output for the three groups simultaneously, using a statistical test called analysis of variance (ANOVA). This technique would be preferable to conducting a series of t-tests among all the possible pairs of groups for a number of reasons that are beyond the scope of this discussion. Suffice it to say, however, that in this case ANOVA would be the best test to use. If we determined that the means differed at a level beyond what we would expect by chance, we would still need to conduct some follow-up (post hoc) tests to determine exactly which means differed from which other means.

These, then, are the statistical tests basic to human resource operations. Using the right test, along with proper sampling techniques and sound measurement, allows human resource managers to answer the questions needed to carry out their job effectively. Many of these questions deal with the evaluation of programs or interventions. That is, if an organization introduces a new appraisal or compensation program, the firm wants to be sure that the new program is accomplishing what was intended. A human resource manager often deals with questions of this type, and the tools and techniques discussed here make it more likely that the manager can provide the organization with the answers it needs.

OTHER TECHNICAL ISSUES IN HUMAN RESOURCE RESEARCH

In addition to using statistics and research techniques to answer specific questions, there are also at least two areas in which a human resource manager needs some specialized technical expertise related to the treatment of data. We focus on the issues of validity generalization and utility analysis. In both cases the human resource manager needs to understand something about data and analysis to provide the best services possible to the organization.

Validity Generalization

When we discussed test validation in Chapter 7, we discussed it in terms of separate validation efforts for each test on each job. In fact, organizations and courts have traditionally viewed the validation process this way. Each test must be validated for each job. Yet, at some level we recognize that this approach may be unnecessary. For example, let us say that State Farm Insurance Company develops a test to select insurance agents and goes through the process of validating the test. Let us say further that State Farm relies on a test of clerical abilities that is generally available to any interested organization. Now if Allstate decides to use the same abilities test to select its insurance agents, does it need to conduct a separate validity study? It would seem reasonable to assume that if scores on the test were related to performance at State Farm, they should be related to performance at Allstate as well.

In fact, Allstate would be able to "borrow" State Farm's validity data, and even rely on it in court if necessary, as long as Allstate could demonstrate through job analysis that the job requirements and the settings in the two firms were the same. In fact, in the simplest and least controversial form of validity generalization, one firm uses the validity study results of another firm, but both firms are interested in using the same test to select persons for the same job.

An extension of this type of validity generalization involves the use of the Position Analysis Questionnaire (or PAQ), which was designed to describe a wide variety of jobs using a common set of job dimensions (see Chapter 5). The developers of the PAQ extended some earlier work on synthetic validity[2] and argued that it was possible to show relationships between tests and job dimensions, just as one usually demonstrated relationships between tests and the entire job. If one could establish such relationships (that is, performance on a test was related to performance on some aspect of a job) and if a general set of job dimensions could be used that were believed to underlay all jobs, it would be possible to "construct" validity data for any job. That is, it would be possible to then determine which job dimensions were important for a given job and then put together a selection battery by combining those tests that were related to performance on each dimension.

In fact, such a system has been developed for use with the PAQ and was introduced in Chapter 5. This system (which is referred to job component validity) allows an organization to conduct a job analysis of a job, using the PAQ, and then rely on the already established relationships to construct a recommended test battery for use in selecting persons for the job in question.

Although limited, the available information suggests that these recommendations, in fact, prove to be valid for the job in question when this is tested empirically.[3] Thus this approach would allow an organization to piece together validity information for a variety of jobs and tests and would require job analysis, rather than a formal validation study, to support the use of a test or tests in a selection setting. Whether the courts will accept this broader application is not clear.

The most far-reaching proposal for validity generalization, however, has been proposed by Schmidt and Hunter.[4] These authors and their associates have compiled an enormous amount of data clearly indicating that many of the differences we observe in the validity of a given test, across different jobs, can be attributed to problems of unreliability and measurement, rather than to true differences in the predictability of performance. In fact, these arguments even suggest that certain types of cognitive ability tests (such as intelligence tests), and certain other types of tests, are related to performance on *virtually all* jobs. Furthermore, these tests predict performance better than alternatives do, and so there is no need to conduct any validity studies. An organization can simply use these tests for selection and know it is selecting the best people.[5]

These arguments, although supported by a great deal of data, have not been completely accepted by the courts and are quite controversial. The controversy has been generated not only because these arguments obviate the need for separate validity studies but also because they propose tests such as intelligence tests, which tend to have adverse impact, as the best predictors of performance across a wide variety of jobs.

Utility Analysis

Test validation is concerned with demonstrating that persons who score higher on some test also perform better on some job. Once this relationship has been established, an organization can use the test to select applicants by hiring only those who score above a certain cutoff on the test. This approach will result in the organization hiring more people who are ultimately successful and fewer persons who would ultimately fail on the job. Therefore, the organization can be said to be improving its selection system and selecting better people. But how much better is the selection system, and how much better are the people selected? Utility analysis attempts to answer these critical questions.

For example, we do not need very sophisticated models to conclude that if 95 percent of the persons hired without the use of a test are successful, then even if the test is valid, if it improves the success rate to 96 percent but costs the firm hundreds of thousands of dollars to administer, it probably is not worth the additional cost. Over the years a number of approaches to assessing utility have been proposed. An early approach used a series of charts (the Taylor Russell tables) that indicate the improvement in the selection of successful applicants by using a test with specified validity, given the percentage of successful employees selected without using the test and the selection ratio (explained below).[6] But this approach failed to consider the costs associated with selection. Therefore, more complete utility models have been proposed that do consider the costs associated with selection, training, or whatever intervention is being evaluated.

An early utility model that considered costs was proposed by Brogden[7] and is presented below. The original model had a problem calculating one critical component, but subsequent versions, as well as other models that further refined the basic relationships,[8] could be used to express exactly how much (in dollars) a new selection system or training program was worth to an organization. Conceptually, the model is as follows (mathematically, the model must be expressed differently):

Savings per person selected = $z_y SD_y$ – Cost of selecting the person

The cost of selecting a person is the product of the cost of testing each applicant (which includes actual testing costs and recruiting costs) and the selection ratio, or the ratio of applicants per job opening. If there were ten applicants for each job opening, the selection ratio would be 1/10, or .10. The greater the selection ratio, the more applicants per job, which allows the organization to be more selective, but also increases the cost of testing. So if the cost to test each applicant is $10, and the selection ratio is .10, the cost to select an individual is $100 (plus recruiting costs). If the selection ratio goes to $i/100$, the cost to select an individual becomes $1,000 (plus recruiting costs).

The remaining terms in the expression require some explanation as well. The term z_y refers to the mean criterion score (in standard score units) of those selected. Basically, this value indicates how successful those selected with the test in question might be. The SD_y term refers to the variance in performance on the job, expressed in dollar terms. If this term is high, the performance, or output, of a high-performing individual is worth a lot more to the organization than is the performance of a low-performing individual. In such a case the value to the company of selecting high-performing individuals would go up. But in other cases the difference between the value of a high- and low-performing employee might not be so great. The value of the SD_y term would be reduced, and the utility of the test would be less. That is, in such a case, high-performing employees would be worth less to the organization relative to low-performing employees as compared to a case where the utility of the test was high. More complete illustrations of the use of utility analyses can be found elsewhere,[9] but these analyses are an important weapon for human resource managers who wish to demonstrate that their efforts yield financial returns to the organization.

Notes

1. For excellent overviews see Floyd J. Fowler Jr., *Survey Research Methods* (Beverly Hills, Calif.: Sage Publications, 1984) and Randall B. Dunham and Frank J. Smith, *Organizational Surveys* (Glenview, Ill.: Scott-Foresman, 1979).

2. M. J. Balma, "The Concept of Synthetic Validity," *Personnel Psychology*, Vol. 12, 1959, pp. 395–396; C. H. Lawshe and M. D. Steinberg, "Studies in Synthetic Validity I: An Exploratory Investigation of Clerical Jobs," *Personnel Psychology*, Vol. 8, 1955, pp. 291–301.

3. Ernest J. McCormick, Angelo S. DeNisi, and James B. Shaw, "The Use of the Position Analysis Questionnaire (PAQ) for Establishing the Job Component Validity of Tests," *Journal of Applied Psychology*, Vol. 64, 1979, pp. 51–56; John R. Hollenbeck and Ellen M. Whitener, "Criterion-Related Validity for Small Sample Context: An Integrated Approach to Synthetic Validity," *Journal of Applied Psychology*, Vol. 73, 1988, pp. 536–544.

4. Frank L. Schmidt and John E. Hunter, "Development of a General Solution to the Problem of Validity Generalization," *Journal of Applied Psychology*, Vol. 62, 1977, pp. 529–540.

5. Frank L. Schmidt, Deniz S. Ones, and John E. Hunter, "Personnel Selection," *Annual Review of Psychology*, Vol. 43, 1992, pp. 627–670.

6. H. C. Taylor and J. T. Russell, "The Relationship of Validity Coefficients to the Practical Effectiveness of Tests in Selection," *Journal of Applied Psychology*, Vol. 23, 1939, pp. 565–578.

7. Hubert E. Brogden, "When Testing Pays Off," *Personnel Psychology*, Vol. 2, 1949, pp. 171–185.

8. For example, see proposals by Wayne F. Cascio and Robert A. Ramos, "Development and Application of a New Method for Assessing Job Performance in Behavioral/Economic Terms," *Journal of Applied Psychology*, Vol. 71, 1986, pp. 20–28; or John W. Boudreau, "Utility Analysis for Decision Making in Human Resource Management," in Marvin D. Dunnette and Leaetta M. Hough (eds.), *Handbook of Industrial and Organizational Psychology*, Vol. 2 (Palo Alto, Calif.: Consulting Psychologists Press, 1991), pp. 621–745.

9. Wayne F. Cascio, *Costing Human Resources: The Financial Impact of Behavior in Organizations*, 2nd ed. (Boston, Mass.: PWS-Kent Publishing Co., 1987).

360-degree feedback an approach to performance appraisal that involves gathering performance information from people all around the manager—above, beside, below, and so forth in order to obtain multiple sources of ratings

ADA see Americans with Disabilities Act

adaptation model a popular approach to business strategy; describes different ways businesses can seek to adapt to their environment

ADEA see Age Discrimination in Employment Act

AF of L see American Federation of Labor

affirmative action represents a set of steps an organization takes to actively seek qualified applicants from groups underrepresented in the workforce

Age Discrimination in Employment Act (or **ADEA**) prohibits discrimination against employees over the age of forty

agency theory concerned with the diverse interests and goals that are held by the organization's stakeholders, including its employees and managers, and the methods through which the organization's reward system can be used to align these diverse interests and goals

American Federation of Labor (or **AF of L**) an early union federation; it sought not to get involved in legislative and political activities, but instead focused its efforts on improved working conditions and better employment contracts

Americans with Disabilities Act of 1990 (or **ADA**) prohibits discrimination based on disability in all aspects of the employment relationship such as job application procedures, hiring, firing, promotion, compensation, and training, as well as other employment activities such as advertising, recruiting, tenure, layoffs, leave, and fringe benefits

apprenticeship training method that combines on-the-job and classroom instruction

arbitration conflict resolution process in which both sides agree in advance to accept the recommendations made by an independent third-party arbitrator

assessment center an approach to selecting managers based on measuring and evaluating their ability to perform critical work behaviors

banding involves creating clusters of job applicants who do not differ substantially from one another, allowing an organization to select an applicant from some underrepresented group in the organization while still ensuring high-performance standards

bargaining unit refers to the specifically defined group of employees who will be eligible for representation by a union

BARS see behaviorally anchored rating scale

base salary a guaranteed amount of money that the individual will be paid

behavioral observation scales (or **BOS**) performance appraisal method developed from critical incidents like BARS but using substantially more critical incidents to specifically define all the measures that are necessary for effective performance

behaviorally anchored rating scales (or **BARS**) performance appraisal method representing a combination of the graphic rating scale and the critical incident method

benefits various rewards, incentives, and other things of value that an organization provides to its employees beyond wages, salaries, and other forms of direct financial compensation

BFOQ see bona fide occupational qualification

"big five" personality traits tend to be more behavioral than cognitive or emotional; are likely to be more important for job performance than are more traditional personality traits; are *neuroticism, extraversion, openness to experience, agreeableness,* and *conscientiousness*

biodata applications focus on the same type of information as found in a regular application but also go into more complex and detailed assessments about that background

bona fide occupational qualification (**BFOQ**) legal requirement for performing a particular job such that race, sex, or other personal characteristic legitimately affects a person's ability to perform the job

BOS see behavioral observation scale

boycott when union members agree not to buy the products of a targeted employer

burnout a general feeling of exhaustion that develops when an individual simultaneously experiences too much pressure and too few sources of satisfaction

business strategy deals with how the firm will compete in each market where it conducts business

cafeteria-style benefit plan allows employees to choose the benefits they really want

career the set of work-related experiences and activities that people engage in related to their job and livelihood over the course of their working life

career counseling involves interaction between an individual employee or manager in the organization and either a line manager or a human resource manager

center of expertise a perspective arguing that everyone in the organization should recognize human resource managers as the firm's most critical source of information about employment practices, employee behavior, labor relations, and the effective management of all aspects of human resources

CIO   see Congress of Industrial Organizations

circadian rhythms   natural cycles that indicate when a body needs to eat or sleep

Civil Rights Act of 1991   makes it easier for individuals who feel they had been discriminated against to take legal action against organizations and provides for the payment of compensatory and punitive damages in cases of discrimination under Title VII

classification system   a job evaluation method attempting to group sets of jobs into clusters, often called grades

closed shop   a workplace in which the employer can hire only workers who are already union members

cognitive ability test   measure of mental skills

collateral stress management programs   organizational programs specifically created to help employees deal with stress

collective bargaining   the process by which managers and union leaders negotiate acceptable terms and conditions of employment for those workers represented by the unions

collective bargaining agreement   formal and written agreement between the organization and a labor union precisely defining the nature of the employment relationship

compensable factors   in job evaluation, any aspect of a job for which an organization is willing to provide compensation

compensation   the set of rewards that organizations provide to individuals in return for their willingness to perform various jobs and tasks within the organization

competencies   vary from organization to organization but basically refer to relatively broad capabilities that are necessary for effective job performance

competitive strategies   framework suggesting that three basic strategies are appropriate for a wide variety of organizations in diverse industries

compressed workweeks   arrangements in which employees work the required number of hours (typically forty) but do so in fewer than five days

computer-assisted instruction   involves a trainee operating personal computer software that has been specifically developed to impart certain material

Congress of Industrial Organizations (or **CIO**)   an early union federation that focused on organizing employees by industry, regardless of their craft or skills or occupation

contextual performance   refers to things an employee does on the job that are not required as part of the job but still benefit the organization in some way

contingent worker   a person who works for an organization on something other than a permanent or full-time basis

contrast error   occurs when we compare people against one another instead of against an objective standard

corporate strategy   deals with determining how businesses will compete in the market

cost leadership strategy   one that focuses on minimizing costs as much as possible

country culture   the set of values, symbols, beliefs, and languages that guide behavior of people within a culture

critical incident approach   job analysis method focusing on those critical behaviors that distinguish between effective and ineffective performers

critical incident method   performance appraisal method relying on instances of especially good or poor performance on the part of the employee

culture   refers to the set of values that helps an organization's members understand what it stands for, how it does things, and what it considers important

defined benefit plan   private pension plan in which the size of the benefit is precisely known; is usually based on a simple formula that uses input such as years of service

defined contribution plan   private pension plan in which the size of the benefit depends on how much money is contributed to the plan

development   refers to teaching managers and professionals the skills needed for both present and future jobs

differentiation strategy   attempting to develop an image or reputation for products or services that set them apart from competitors

direct applicants   individuals who apply for a position with the organization without any proactive action from the organization

direct investment   occurs when a firm headquartered in one country builds or purchases operating facilities or subsidiaries in a foreign country

discipline   a formal organizational action taken against an employee as a result of a rules violation, subpar performance, or other dysfunctional behavior

disengagement   fourth stage of the traditional career model when the individual gradually begins to pull away from work in the organization, priorities change, and work may become less important

disparate impact discrimination   occurs when an apparently neutral employment practice disproportionately excludes a protected group from employment opportunities

disparate treatment discrimination   exists when individuals in similar situations are treated differently and when the differential treatment is based on the individual's race, color, religion, sex, national origin, age, or disability status

distributional error   occurs when the rater tends to use only one part of the rating scale

diversification strategy   used by companies that are adding new products, product lines, or businesses to their existing core products, product lines, or businesses

diversity   exists in a group or organization when its members differ from one another along one or more important dimensions

diversity management   places a much heavier role on recognizing and appreciating differences among people at work and attempting to provide accommodations for those differences to the extent that is feasible and possible

diversity training   training that is specifically designed to enable members of an organization to function in a diverse workplace

EAP   see employee assistance plan

economic communities   sets of countries that agree to reduce or eliminate trade barriers among their member nations

education formal classroom training an individual has received in public or private schools and colleges, universities, and/or technical schools

employee assistance plan (or **EAP**) designed to assist employees who have chronic problems with alcohol or drugs or who have serious domestic or personal problems

employee leasing an alternative to recruiting in which the organization pays a fee to a leasing company that provides a pool of employees to the first firm

Employee Retirement Income Security Act of 1974 (or **ERISA**) was passed to guarantee a basic minimum benefit that employees could expect to be paid upon retirement

employee stock ownership plan (or **ESOP**) a group-level reward system in which employees are gradually given a major stake in ownership of a corporation

employee training a planned attempt by an organization to facilitate employee learning of job-related knowledge, skills, and behaviors

employment application asks individuals for personal information

employment at will a nineteenth-century common-law rule that allows an employer to terminate any employee, at any time, for any reason (good or bad), or for no reason at all

employment test a device for measuring characteristics of an individual, such as personality, intelligence, or aptitude

equal employment opportunity means treating people fairly and equitably and taking actions that do not discriminate against people in protected classes on the basis of some illegal criterion

Equal Pay Act of 1963 requires that organizations provide the same pay to men and women who are doing equal work

ERISA see Employee Retirement Income Security Act

ESOP see employee stock ownership plan

establishment second stage of the traditional career model when the individual creates a meaningful and relevant role in the organization

ethics an individual's beliefs about what is right and wrong and what is good and bad

ethnicity refers to the ethnic composition of a group or organization

ethnocentric staffing model primarily uses parent-country nationals to staff higher-level foreign positions

Executive Order 11246 prohibits discrimination based on race, color, religion, sex, or national origin for organizations that are federal contractors and subcontractors

Executive Order 11478 requires the federal government to base all of its own employment policies on merit and fitness and specifies that race, color, sex, religion, and national origin should not be considered

executive succession involves systematically planning for future promotions into top management positions

expatriates employees who are sent by a firm to work in another country; may be either parent-country nationals or third-country nationals

experience the amount of time the individual may have spent working either in a general capacity or in a particular field of study

exploration first traditional career stage when the individual identifies interests and opportunities

exporting the process of making a product in the firm's domestic marketplace and then selling it in another country

external equity in compensation, refers to comparisons made by employees to others performing similar jobs in different organizations

external recruiting the process of looking to sources outside the organization for prospective employees

factor comparison method method of job evaluation that assesses jobs on a factor-by-factor basis, using a factor comparison scale as a benchmark

Fair Labor Standards Act passed in 1938; established a minimum hourly wage for jobs

Family and Medical Leave Act of 1993 requires employers having more than fifty employees to provide up to twelve weeks of unpaid leave for employees after the birth or adoption of a child; to care for a seriously ill child, spouse, or parent; or in the case of an employee's own serious illness

final offer arbitration conflict resolution process in which the parties bargain until impasse and then submit their final offers to the arbitrator

Fleishman job analysis system a job analysis procedure that defines abilities as enduring attributes of individuals that account for differences in performance; it relies on the taxonomy of abilities that presumably represents all the dimensions relevant to work

flexible work hours programs involve employees working forty hours per week, and working five days a week, but with the potential for flexible starting and ending times

focus strategy undertaken when an organization tries to target a specific segment of the marketplace for its products or services

forced distribution method performance appraisal method that groups employees into predefined frequencies of performance ratings

foreign service premium see hardship premium

four-fifths rule suggests that disparate impact exists if a selection criterion (such as a test score) results in a selection rate for a protected class that is less than four-fifths (80 percent) of the selection rate for the majority group

functional strategy deals with how the firm will manage each of its major functions, such as marketing, finance, and human resources

gainsharing a team and group-based incentive system designed to share with employees the cost savings from productivity improvements

general labor pool the local labor market from which a firm hires its employees

general training involves providing trainees with skills and abilities that can be applied in any organization

geocentric staffing model puts parent-country nationals, host-country nationals, and third-country nationals in the same category, with the firm attempting to always hire the best person available for a position

glass ceiling refers to a barrier that prevents women from advancing to top management positions in many organizations

goal-based system (or **management by objectives system**) performance appraisal method based largely on the extent to which individuals meet their personal perfomance objectives

grand strategy a single overall framework for action that the top management team develops at the corporate level

graphic rating scale performance appraisal method consisting of a statement or question about some aspect of an individual's job performance; the rater provides an evaluation on a numerical scale corresponding to his or her response or answer to the statement or question

halo error occurs when one positive performance characteristic causes the manager to rate all other aspects of performance positively

hardship premium (also called a **foreign service premium**) an additional financial incentive offered to individuals to entice them to accept a "less than attractive" international assignment

Hawthorne studies series of research studies that led to the human relations era

headhunter an individual working for an executive search firm that seeks out qualified individuals for higher-level positions

health hazards those characteristics of the work environment that slowly and systematically, and perhaps cumulatively, result in damage to an employee's health

health maintenance organization (or **HMO**) medical organization that provides medical and health services to employees on a prepaid basis

hierarchy of human needs theory of motivation based on differentially important needs; was developed during the human relations era by Abraham Maslow

high-performance work systems rely on a set of "best practices" to use human resources to gain a meaningful competitive advantage

HMO see health maintenance organization

home work programs include arrangements that are often referred to as cottage industries

horns error occurs when the manager downgrades other aspects of an employee's performance because of a single performance dimension

hostile work environment sexual harassment resulting from a climate or culture that is punitive toward people of a different gender

HRIS see human resource information system

human relations era supplanted scientific management as the dominant approach to management during the 1930s

human resource information system (or **HRIS**) the entire set of people, procedures, forms and data used to acquire, store, analyze, retrieve, distribute, and use information about an organization's human resources

human resource management the comprehensive set of managerial activities and tasks concerned with developing and maintaining a qualified workforce—human resources—in ways that contribute to organizational effectiveness

human resource management system an integrated and interrelated approach to managing human resources that fully recognizes the interdependence among the various tasks and functions that must be performed

human resource planning the process of forecasting the supply and demand for human resources within an organization and developing action plans for aligning the two

human resources the people an organization employs to carry out various jobs, tasks, and functions in exchange for wages, salaries, and other rewards

illegal discrimination results from behaviors or actions by an organization or managers within an organization that cause members of a protected class to be unfairly differentiated from others

impasse a situation in which one or both parties believe that reaching an agreement is not imminent

in-basket exercise special form of work simulation for prospective managers; consists of collections of hypothetical memos, letters, and notes that require responses

individual assessment phase part of career planning requiring individuals to carefully analyze what they perceive to be their own abilities, competencies, skills, and goals

individual incentive plans reward individual performance on a real-time basis

in-house training or **development program** one that is conducted on the premises of the organization primarily by the organization's own employees

institutional stress management programs for managing stress, are undertaken through established organizational mechanisms

instructional-based programs approach training and development from a teaching and learning perspective

integrity tests attempt to assess an applicant's moral character and honesty

internal equity in compensation, refers to comparisons made by employees to other employees within the same organization

internal recruiting the process of looking inside the organization for qualified employees who might be promoted to higher-level positions

interviews face-to-face conversations between prospective job applicants and representatives of the organization

job analysis the process of gathering and organizing detailed information about various jobs within the organization so that managers can better understand the processes through which they are most effectively performed

job analysts individuals who actually perform job analysis in an organization

job characteristics approach an alternative to job specialization that takes into account the work system and employee preferences; it suggests that jobs should be diagnosed and improved along five core dimensions

job description lists the tasks, duties, and responsibilities that a particular job entails and specifies the major job elements, provides examples of job tasks, and provides some indication of the relative importance of each task in the effective conduct of the job

job design the determination of an individual's work-related responsibilities

job enlargement increases the total number of tasks workers perform on the assumption that doing the same basic task over and over is the primary cause of worker dissatisfaction

job enrichment attempts to increase both the number of tasks a worker does and the control the worker has over the job

job evaluation a method for determining the relative value or worth of a job to the organization so that individuals who perform that job can be adequately and appropriately compensated

job families groups of jobs that have similar task and KSA requirements

job posting a mechanism for internal recruiting in which the organization publicizes vacancies through various media such as company newsletters, bulletin boards, internal memos, and the firm's intranet

job ranking a job evaluation method requiring the manager to order jobs based on their relative importance to the organization from most important to least important

job rotation involves systematically moving employees from one job to another

job specialization the degree to which the overall task of the organization is broken down and divided into smaller component parts

job specification focuses on the individual who will perform the job and indicates the knowledge, abilities, skills, and other characteristics that an individual must have to be able to perform the job

joint venture two or more firms cooperate in the ownership and/or management of an operation on an equity basis

Knights of Labor an important early union that expanded its goals and its membership to include workers in numerous fields rather than a single one

knowledge, skills, and abilities (or **KSA**) the fundamental requirements necessary to be able to perform a job

knowledge workers add value simply because of what they know

KSA see knowledge, skills, and abilities

Labor Management Relations Act (or **Taft-Hartley Act**) passed in 1947 in response to public outcries against a wide variety of strikes in the years following World War II; curtailed and limited union powers; specified steps and procedures by which a union can represent employees

Labor Management Reporting and Disclosure Act (or **Landrum-Griffin Act**) passed in 1959; focused on eliminating various unethical, illegal, and undemocratic union practices; regulates union actions and their internal affairs in a way that puts unions on an equal footing with management and organizations

labor relations the process of dealing with employees who are represented by a union

labor union a legally constituted group of individuals working together to achieve shared job-related goals, including higher pay and shorter working hours

Landrum-Griffin Act see Labor Management Reporting and Disclosure Act

learning a relatively permanent change in behavior or behavioral potential that results from direct or indirect experience

learning curve a sophisticated elaboration of basic forecasting methods that considers increases in productivity that might be expected as employees gain experience and learn more effective ways of performing their job

learning organization one whose employees continuously attempt to learn new things and to use what they learn to improve product or service quality

lecture or discussion approach involves a trainer presenting the training material in a descriptive fashion

licensing involves one company permitting a company in a foreign country to manufacture and/or market the first company's products in the second company's local market

life cycle benefits benefits based on life cycle events; common examples include childcare and elder-care benefits

line managers those directly responsible for creating goods and services

locals unions that are organized at the level of a single company, plant, or small geographic region

lockout when the employer denies employees access to the workplace

maintenance third stage of the traditional career model; involves optimizing talents or capabilities

management by objectives system see goal-based system

mandatory items must be included as part of collective bargaining if either party expresses a desire to negotiate over one or more of them; common examples are wages, working hours, and benefits

manufacturing a form of business that combines and transforms resources into tangible outcomes that are then sold to others

maturity curve a schedule specifying the amount of annual increase a person will receive

mediation conflict resolution process in which a neutral third party, called the mediator, listens to and reviews the information presented by both sides, makes an informed recommendation, and provides advice to both parties as to what she or he believes should be done

merit pay pay awarded to employees on the basis of the relative value of their contributions to the organization

merit pay plans compensation plans that formally base at least some meaningful portion of compensation on merit

midcareer plateau a point many people reach when they no longer receive promotions or advancement opportunities in the organization

mission a statement of how an organization intends to fulfill its purpose

multicultural organization one that has achieved high levels of diversity, is able to fully capitalize on the advantages of the diversity, and has few diversity-related problems

multiple regression a complex mathematical forecasting technique that relies on multiple correlation indices

National Labor Relations Act (or **Wagner Act**) was passed in 1935; an effort to control and legislate collective bargaining between organizations and labor unions; granted power to labor unions and put them on a more equal footing with managers in terms of the rights of employees

National Labor Relations Board (or **NLRB**)   administers most labor law in the United States

needs analysis   the assessment of the organization's job-related needs and the capabilities of the current workforce

NLRB   see National Labor Relations Board

Occupational Safety and Health Act of 1970 (or **OSHA**) grants the federal government the power to establish and enforce occupational safety and health standards for all places of employment directly affecting interstate commerce

Old Age Survivors and Disability Insurance Program see social security

on-the-job training   the most common and popular method of work-based training, involves having employees learn their job while they are actually performing it

operating managers   an increasingly popular term for those previously called line managers

organization design   refers to the framework of jobs, positions, clusters of positions, and reporting relationships among positions that are used to construct an organization

organization development   system-wide effort, managed from the top of the organization, to increase the organization's overall performance through planned interventions relying heavily on behavioral science technology

orientation   the process of introducing new employees to the organization so that they can more quickly become effective contributors

OSHA   see Occupational Safety and Health Act

outsourced training or **development program**   one that involves having people from outside the organization perform the training

outsourcing   the practice of hiring external vendors to provide basic human resource management services for an organization based on their ability to perform them more efficiently than the organization itself

overtime   an alternative to recruiting in which current employees are asked to work extra hours

paired-comparison method   performance appraisal method that involves comparing each employee with every other employee, one at a time

PAQ   see Position Analysis Questionnaire

part-time workers   individuals who routinely expect to work less than forty hours a week

pattern or practice discrimination   similar to disparate treatment but occurs on a classwide basis

pay compression   a circumstance in which individuals with substantially different levels of experience and/or performance abilities are being paid wages or salaries that are relatively close together

pay for knowledge   involves compensating employees for learning specific material

pay secrecy   refers to the extent to which an individual's compensation in an organization is secret or formally made available to other individuals

pay surveys   surveys of compensation paid to employees by other employers in a particular geographic area, an industry, or an occupational group

performance appraisal   the specific and formal evaluation of an employee to determine the degree to which the employee is performing his or her job effectively

performance management   the general set of activities carried out by the organization to change (improve) employee performance

perk   see perquisite

permissive items   items that may be included in collective bargaining if both parties agree

perquisite (or **perk**)   an extra benefit that may or may not have any direct financial value but is considered to be an important reward by employees

personality tests   measure traits, or tendencies to act, that are relatively unchanging in a person

personnel departments   original name for specialized organizational units for hiring and administering human resources; became popular during the 1930s and 1940s

personnel management   original name for human resource management; grew from the recognition that human resources needed to be managed

picketing   when workers representing a striking union march at the entrance to the employer's facility with signs explaining their reasons for striking

piece-rate incentive plan   involves the organization paying an employee a certain amount of money for every unit she or he produces

point manual   used to implement the point system of job evaluation; carefully and specifically defines the degrees of points from first to fifth

point system   a job evaluation method requiring managers to quantify in objective terms the value of the various elements of specific jobs

polycentric staffing model   calls for heavy use of host-country nationals throughout the organization

Position Analysis Questionnaire (or **PAQ**)   a standardized job analysis instrument consisting of 194 items reflecting work behavior, working conditions, or job characteristics that are assumed to be generalizable across a wide variety of jobs

Pregnancy Discrimination Act of 1978   protects pregnant women from discrimination in the workplace

private pension plan   prearranged plan administered by the organization that provides income to the employee upon her or his retirement

productivity   an economic measure of efficiency that summarizes and reflects the value of the outputs created by an individual, organization, industry, or economic system relative to the value of the inputs used to create them

productivity ratio   the average number of units produced per direct labor employee per year

profit sharing   an incentive system in which, at the end of the year, some portion of the company's profits is paid into a profit-sharing pool, which is then distributed to all employees

programmed instruction   training method wherein the material that is to be learned is prepared in a manual or training booklet; the individual studies the manual or booklet at his or her own pace

progressive discipline system   system in which the organization defines a sequence of penalties, each somewhat more severe than the previous, and a time frame across which an individual's continued rules violations will escalate to higher levels of discipline

projection   occurs when we see in others characteristics that we ourselves have that we think contribute to effectiveness

projective technique   involves showing an individual an ambiguous stimulus, such as an inkblot or a "fuzzy" picture, and then asking what he or she "sees"

protected class   consists of all individuals who share one or more common characteristic as indicated by that law

protection plans   benefits designed to provide protection to employees when their income is threatened or reduced by illness, disability, unemployment, or retirement

psychological contract   the set of expectations an employee holds concerning what he or she will contribute to the organization (referred to as **contributions**) and what the organization, in return, will provide to the employee (referred to as **inducements**)

psychomotor ability tests   measure physical abilities such as strength, eye-hand coordination, and manual dexterity

punishment   any behavior or action, formal or informal, that results in unpleasant effects or consequences for someone else

purpose   an organization's basic reason for existence

quality   the total set of features and characteristics of a product or service that bears on its ability to satisfy stated or implied needs

quid pro quo harassment   sexual harassment when the harasser offers to exchange something of value for sexual favors

quota   a limit on the number or value of goods that can be traded

realistic job preview   ensuring that job seekers understand the actual nature of the jobs available to them

recruiting   the process of developing a pool of qualified applicants who are interested in working for the organization and from which the organization might reasonably select the best individual or individuals to hire for employment

referral   an individual who is prompted to apply for a position by someone else within the organization

regression-based system   method of job evaluation that utilizes a statistical technique called multiple regression to develop an equation that establishes the relationship between different dimensions of the job and compensation

reliability   the consistency of a particular selection (measurement) device

reverse discrimination   refers to any practice that has disparate impact on members of nonprotected classes

safety engineers   experts who carefully study the workplace, try to identify and isolate particularly dangerous situations, and recommend solutions for dealing with those situations

safety hazards   those things in the work environment that have the potential to cause harm to an employee

salary   income that is paid to an individual not on the basis of time, but on the basis of performance

sales commission   an incentive paid to people engaged in sales work

Scanlon plan   a type of gainsharing plan in which the distribution of gains is tilted much more heavily toward employees and across the entire organization than it is in other profit sharing or gain sharing plans

scientific management   one of the earliest approaches to management; was concerned with how to structure individual jobs so as to maximize efficiency and productivity

selection process   concerned with identifying the best candidate or candidates for jobs from among the pool of qualified applicants developed during the recruiting process

self-report inventory   a paper-and-pencil measure in which applicants respond to a series of statements that might or might not apply to them

service organization   one that transforms resources into an intangible output and creates time or place utility for its customers

shop steward   elected position in a local union; is a regular employee who functions as a liaison between union members and supervisors

simple ranking method   performance appraisal method in which the manager simply orders from top to bottom or best to worst all members of a particular work group or department

skill-based pay   rewards employees for acquiring new skills

skills and abilities   relate precisely to the specific qualifications and capabilities of an individual to perform a specific job

slowdown   when instead of striking, workers perform their jobs at a much slower pace than normal

SMEs   see subject matter experts

social contract model   expands the relationship between employer and employee to include the government

social security (officially the **Old Age Survivors and Disability Insurance Program**)   a mandated program originally designed to provide limited income to retired individuals to supplement their personal savings, private pensions, part-time work, and so forth

specific training   provides the trainee with skills or information that are of use only to the current organization

staff managers   responsible for an indirect or support function that has costs but whose bottom-line contributions are sometimes less direct

staffing   the process of determining the organization's current and future human resource needs and then taking steps to ensure that those needs are effectively met

staffing ratio   used to calculate the number of individuals required in other jobs in the organization aside from those directly involved in the production of actual products

stock option plan   an incentive plan established to give managers the option to buy the company stock in the future at a predetermined fixed price; was once reserved for senior managers only but is increasingly offered to other managers as well

strategic alliance   two or more firms cooperate in the ownership and/or management of an operation

stress   a person's adaptive response to a stimulus that places excessive psychological or physical demands on him or her

strike occurs when employees walk off their jobs and refuse to work

subject matter experts (or **SME**s) individuals presumed to be highly knowledgeable about jobs and who provide data for job analysis; may be incumbents, supervisors, or other knowledgeable employees

SWOT analysis conceptual framework useful in formulating strategies; SWOT is an acronym for strengths, weaknesses, opportunities, and threats

systematic job rotations and transfers involves the employee being systematically rotated or transferred from one job to another

Taft-Hartley Act see Labor Management Relations Act

tariff a tax that is collected on goods that are shipped across national boundaries

task analysis inventory a family of job analysis methods, each with unique characteristics; each focuses on analyzing all the tasks performed in the focal job

telecommuting involves employees doing almost all of their work at home, perhaps even receiving assignments electronically

temporary employees used as an alternative to recruiting; these employees join the organization to work for a specific period of time, rather than with the expectation of permanent or continued employment

Theory X and **Theory Y** important framework reflecting different ways managers can see employees; developed by Douglas McGregor during the human relations movement

Title VII of the Civil Rights Act states that it is illegal for an employer to fail or refuse to hire or to discharge any individual or to in any other way discriminate against any individual with respect to any aspect of the employment relationship on the basis of that individual's race, color, religious beliefs, sex, or national origin

top-down forecasting involves the use of experienced and skilled executives and top managers to forecast the future supply and demand for labor

top management team the group of senior executives responsible for the overall strategic operation of the firm

unemployment insurance a mandated protection plan intended to provide a basic subsistence payment to employees who are between jobs

union-shop agreement includes a requirement that a nonunion member can be hired but must join the union within a specified time to keep his or her job, as well as various other types of union security agreements

unit, or **bottom-up**, **forecasting** involves allowing individual units, branches, departments, or line managers to predict their own future needs for employees

utilization analysis a comparison of the racial, gender, and ethnic composition of the employer's workforce compared to that of the available labor supply

validity the extent to which a measure or indicator is in fact a real reflection of what it was intended to measure

vestibule training involves a work simulation situation in which the job is performed under a condition that closely simulates the real work environment

Vietnam Era Veterans' Readjustment Act of 1974 requires that federal contractors and subcontractors take affirmative action toward employing Vietnam-era veterans

Vocational Rehabilitation Act of 1973 requires that executive agencies and subcontractors and contractors of the federal government receiving more than $2,500 a year from the government engage in affirmative action for disabled individuals

wage and salary administration the ongoing process of managing a wage and salary structure

wages generally refers to hourly compensation paid to operating employees; the basis for wages is time

Wagner Act see National Labor Relations Act

weighted application blank relies on the determination of numerical indices to indicate the relative importance of various personal factors for predicting a person's ability to perform a job effectively

wellness programs special benefit programs that concentrate on keeping employees healthy, rather than simply paying expenses when they become sick

wildcat strike strike that occurs during the course of a labor contract (and which is therefore generally illegal) and is usually undertaken in response to a perceived injustice on the part of management

word-of-mouth recruiting when the organization encourages present employees to refer friends, family, or neighbors to apply for available jobs

work-based programs tie the training and development activities directly to performance of the task

work simulation involves asking the prospective employee to perform tasks or job-related activities that simulate or represent the actual work for which the person is being considered

work teams an arrangement in which a group is responsible for designing the work system to be used in performing an interrelated set of jobs

workers' compensation a mandated protection program; insurance that covers individuals who suffer a job-related illness or accident

Chapter 1: Page 4: Gregory Foster. Used by permission. Page 6: Corbis Images. Used by permission. Page 7: Courtesy Ford Motor Company. Page 18: Michael Abramson. Used by permission. Page 21: Thomas Sandberg. Used by permission.

Chapter 2: Page 39: Brian Smith. Used by permission. Page 42: Greg Smith/Saba. Used by permission. Page 43: The New Yorker Collection. Copyright 1990 by Peter Steiner, from *cartoonbank.com.* All rights reserved. Page 52: Mark Richards/PhotoEdit. Used by permission. Page 57: Burk Uzzle. Used by permission.

Chapter 3: Page 71: Danny Shanahan. Used by permission. Page 78: Tom Herde/*The Boston Globe.* Used by permission. Page 88: Dan Lamont/Matrix. Used by permission. Page 92: Greg Miller. Used by permission.

Chapter 4: Page 109: Peter Obe/AP Wide World Photos. Used by permission. Page 116: *Dilbert* reprinted by permission of United Feature Syndicate, Inc. Page 118: Greg Girard/ Contact Press Images. Used by permission. Page 121: AP/Wide World Photos. Used by permission. Page 124: Jurgen Bindrim/LAIF. Used by permission.

Chapter 5: Page 141: Jeffery MacMillan for USN&WR. Used by permission. Page 146: AP/Wide World Photos. Used by permission. Page 153: Mark Richards. Used by permission.

Chapter 6: Page 171: Rex Rystedt. Used by permission. Page 175: Warren Denning. Used by permission. Page 181: Amy Etra/PhotoEdit. Used by permission. Page 184: *Dilbert* reprinted by permission of United Feature Syndicate, Inc. Page 186: Mark Richards. Used by permission.

Chapter 7: Page 197: Courtesy of Monster.com. Page 200: T. Michael Keza. Used by permission. Page 205: Arnold Adler. Used by permission. Page 208: 1998 Thaves/ Reprinted with permission. Newspaper dist. by NEA, Inc. Page 221: Greg Miller. Used by permission.

Chapter 8: Page 233: Agence France-Presse. Used by permission. Page 238: *Dilbert* reprinted by permission of United Feature Syndicate, Inc. Page 241: Spencer Grant/ Stock Boston. Used by permission. Page 254: Courtesy of Lansdale, Inc. Page 257: Michael Newman/PhotoEdit. Used by permission.

Chapter 9: Page 274: Jay Reed. Used by permission. Page 278: Mike Greenlar. Used by permission. Page 280: Bob Daemmrich/Stock Boston. Used by permission. Page 284: *Dilbert* reprinted by permission of United Feature Syndicate, Inc. Page 285: Mark Richards. Used by permission.

Chapter 10: Page 305: Mike Malone/Malone & Co. Photography. Used by permission. Page 309: Blake Little/Corbis/Sygma. Used by permission. Page 313: Suzanne Kreitner/ *The Boston Globe.* Used by permission. Page 314: Najlah Feanny/SABA. Used by permission.

Adams, J. Stacey, 352n
Ahlstrand, Bruce, 67n
Aiello, John R., 527n
Aley, James, 132
Allen, L., 322n
Allen, Oliver E., 32n
Alvares, Kenneth M., 263n
Andrews, Kenneth, 67n
Ankeny, David C., 101n
Antonioni, David, 231
Aragona, Victor, 475
Arbittier, Lauren, 265
Arthur, Winfred, Jr., 134n
Arvey, Richard D., 295n
Atchison, S. D., 528n
Atkinson, Marcia, 294n
Atwater, D., 228n
Atwater, Leanne, 231, 263n

Bailyn, Lotte, 32n
Balma, M. J., 547n
Bamberger, Peter, 67n
Banker, Rajiv D., 379n
Banks, Donna, 477
Barad, Jill, 297, 298, 299, 484
Barber, Alison E., 193n, 404n
Bargerstock, Andy, 193n
Barkema, Harry G., 66n, 379n
Barling, Julian, 437n
Barney, Jay, 67n
Barrick, Murray, 228n
Barringer, Melissa, 404n
Bazhaw, Ralph, 486
Beatty, Richard W., 263n
Becherer, Hans, 164, 165
Becker, Brian, 32n, 67n
Bedrosian, Kathy, 214
Behling, Orlando, 228n
Bennett, Craig, 160
Bennett, Winston, Jr., 134n
Bernardin, H. John, 263n
Bernstein, Mark, 282
Best, Patty, 98
Bethune, Gordon, 376
Binet, Alfred, 7
Bishko, Michael J., 134n
Black, James Stewart, 134n, 307

Blair, M., 379n
Blake, Robert R., 32n
Blake, Stacy, 67n, 499n
Blencoe, Allyn G., 263n
Bloch, Gerald D., 101n
Bloom, Matt, 352n, 379n
Bognanno, Mario L., 379n
Boisot, Max, 528n
Bolino, Mark C., 101n
Borman, Walter C., 262n, 263n
Bossidy, Lawrence A., 372
Boudreau, John W., 548n
Boyacigiller, Nakiye, 134n
Boyle, Susan K., 322n
Bracker, Jeffrey S., 193n
Brauch, Shelly, 66n
Bray, Douglas, 228n
Breaugh, James A., 193n
Breen, Bill, 301
Bremermann, Eric H., 437n
Bretz, Robert D., Jr., 193n
Brodzinski, James D., 101n
Brogden, Hubert E., 546–547, 548n
Brooks, Susan, 32n
Brousseau, Kenneth R., 322n
Brown, Ed, 294n
Brown, Jessica, 475
Brugger, John, 193n
Buchner, Stefan, 124
Buckley, M. R., 527n
Burgum, Doug, 50
Burks, Reuben, 407
Burns, R. K., 263n
Bynum, Robert and Benjamin, 345

Cafferty, Thomas P., 262n, 263n
Callender, John, 228n
Campbell, John P., 295n
Campbell, Richard, 228n
Campion, Michael, 228n
Cantry, Hattie, 421
Caplan, R. D., 322n
Cappelli, Peter, 32n
Cardy, Robert L., 67n
Carty, Donald, 434
Cascio, Wayne F., 548n
Case, John, 64

Caudron, S., 404n, 528n
Chaddock, Paul, 294n
Chamales, Gerald W., 443
Chambers, John, 169
Chase, Richard B., 67n
Cherniss, Cary, 288
Chowanec, Gregory D., 134n
Christensen, Sandra L., 499n
Church, Allan H., 263n
Clark, J. P., 228n
Clark, Paul, 437n
Clements, Christine, 295n
Cleveland, Jeanette N., 241, 262n
Clinton, Bill, 389, 414, 507
Cochrane, Marilyn, 146
Colella, Adrienne, 193n, 262n, 499n
Collins, Bobbie, 91
Collins, Eileen, 233
Collins, Judith, 353n
Commission on the Future of
      Worker-Management Relations,
      527n
Condon, Marilyn, 312
Conway, James M., 263n
Cox, Taylor H., 67n, 494, 499n
Crable, Elaine A., 101n
Crino, Michael D., 473n
Crocker-Hefter, Anne, 32n
Crystal, Graef, 359, 371
Cummings, Anne, 473n
Cutcher-Gershenfeld, Joel, 416

Daft, Richard L., 67n
Daily, Catherine M., 66n
Danna, Karen, 473n
Darwin, Charles, 7
Daugherty, Mark, 122
Daus, Catherine S., 499
Davie, Bob, 69
Davis, Herbert J., 134n
Davy, Jeanette A., 437n
De La Torre, Phillip, 263n
Deal, Terrence E., 67n
Dean, R. A., 193n
Debs, Eugene V., 410
Dechant, Kathleen, 499n
Deere, John, 164

DeFrank, Richard S., 473n
Delery, John E., 32n
DeMatteo, Jacquelyn, 379n
DeNisi, Angelo S., 67n, 166n, 167n, 193n, 262n, 263n, 437n, 547n
Denton, D., 528n
Devlin, S. E., 228n
Dewey, Thomas, 541
Disney, Walt, 52
Dobbins, Gregory H., 67n
Doby, V. J., 322n
Doeringer, Peter B., 322n
Doerpinghaus, Helen I., 528n
Donn, Clifford, 437n
Dorf, Paul R., 101n
Dorsey, David W., 263n
Doty, D. Harold, 32n, 379n
Dougherty, Thomas, 228n
Driver, Michael J., 322n
Dulebohn, James H., 32n
Dumaine, Brian, 64
Dunham, Randall B., 404n, 528n, 547n
Dunn, Wendy, 228n
Dunnette, Marvin D., 295n
Dutt, James, 40
Dyer, Lee, 167n

Eaton, Robert, 369, 370, 372
Ebert, Ronald J., 64, 409, 414, 428
Eby, Lillian, 379n
Eden, Dov, 404n
Ehrenberg, Ronald G., 379n
Eisenstat, Russell A., 32n, 67n
Elliott, Mary Ann, 200
Ely, Robin J., 499n
Eneroth, Kristina, 322n
Engel, Hank, 193n
Erickson, Gary, 381
Erikson, Warren J., 67n
Etzold, Madeline, 314
Ezer, Alan, 160

Falcone, Paul, 228n
Farber, Henry S., 437n
Farley, William, 137
Fay, Charles H., 263n
Feldman, Daniel C., 322, 322n, 473n, 528n
Feldman, Jack M., 262n
Fennell, Frank, 355
Fenster, J. M., 32n
Ferber, M., 322n
Ferris, Gerald R., 32n
Festa, R. M., 262n
Fetterolf, Cynthia, 134n
Feuille, Peter, 437n
Fiegenbaum, Avi, 67n

Fine, Sidney A., 167n
Finney, Martha I., 32n, 59, 134n
Fiol, C. Marlene, 499n
Fiorina, Carly, 370
Fischtal, Allison, 263n
Fisher, Anne, 160, 301, 471
Fisher, George, 180
Fitch, H. Gordon, 473n
Flanagan, John C., 167n, 263n
Flanders, Ethel P., 101n
Fleishman, E. A., 166n
Flores, Robert, 368
Follette, Mary Parker, 5
Ford, Henry, 7, 457
Ford, Kevin, 262n
Ford, Robert, 473n
Formisano, R. A., 404n
Forward, Gordon, 63
Fottler, Myron D., 473n
Fowler, Floyd J., Jr., 547n
Frazier, John, 325
Freivalds, John, 277
Fullagar, Clive, 437n

Gadsden, Edward N., Jr., 493
Gagne, Robert M., 277, 279, 295n
Gallagher, Daniel, 437n
Gallup, Patricia, 39
Garson, B., 527n
Gaugler, Barbara B., 228n
Geffen, David, 309
Geiger-DuMond, Adrianne H., 322n
Gerhart, Barry, 32n, 67n, 193n
Gerstner, Louis, 299
Ghoshal, Sumantra, 66n
Gifford, Kathy Lee, 112
Gilbreth, Frank and Lilian, 5
Gilliland, S. W., 228n
Glass, David, 40
Goleman, Daniel, 288
Golub, Harvey, 372
Gomez-Mejia, Luis R., 66n, 379n
Gompers, Samuel, 410
Gordon, Michael E., 437n
Graves, Samuel B., 32n
Gray, Patricia, 59
Greengard, S., 528n
Greer, Charles R., 32n, 66n, 166n, 262n, 294n, 353n
Gregersen, Hal B., 134n, 307
Griffeth, Rodger, W., 193n
Griffin, Ricky W., 64, 67n, 103, 134n, 379n, 409, 414, 423, 428, 473n, 487, 504
Grossman, Wayne, 371
Gulotta, Michael, 392
Gupta, Nina, 353n, 379n

Gutek, Barbara, 262n
Gutierrez, Carlos, 477
Guyon, Janet, 484

Hackman, J. Richard, 460, 473n
Hall, Douglas T., 299, 302, 322n, 499n, 527n
Hall, Elizabeth L., 101n
Hall, Francine S., 101n
Hamel, Gary, 265
Hand, Shirley, 404n
Handley, Nancy, 350
Hanson, Robert, 164
Hardiek, Bernard, 164
Harding, Robert, 278
Harrison, David, 134n
Harshbarger, Scott, 10
Hassell, Barbara L., 499n
Haworth, Susan, 263n
Haynes, Robert S., 473n
Hayward, D. G., 473n
Heath, Chip, 263n
Heckscher, Charles C., 416
Heimbold, Charles A., Jr., 372
Hennessey, H. W., 404n
Herzberg, Frederick, 473n
Higgins, Kitty, 160
Hildebrand, Karen, 499n
Hill, Charles W. L., 66n, 67n
Hochwarter, W. A., 404n
Hodgetts, Richard M., 134n
Hoekenga, Craig, 225
Hoffa, Jimmy, 415
Hollenbeck, John R., 547n
Hollinger, R. C., 228n
Holt, Paul, 274
Hom, Peter W., 193n
Hopper, Brad, 501
Hopper, Mark, 214
Hoskisson, Robert, 371
Hossain, Sakhawat, 134n
Hough, Leaetta M., 228n
Hunsaker, Karen, 35
Hunt, D. L., 473n
Hunter, John E., 228n, 546, 547n, 548n
Hunter, R. F., 228n
Huselid, Mark A., 67n

Iacocca, Lee, 299
Ilgen, Daniel R., 262n
Imperato, Gina, 463
Isabella, Lynn A., 322n
Israel, David, 101n
Ivancevich, John M., 473n

Jackson, Susan E., 404n, 473n
Jeffrey, Jeff, 153

Jenkins, G. Douglas, 353n, 379n
Jensen, Arthur R., 228n
Johnson, Carla, 193n, 228n, 320
Johnson, Lyndon, 77
Johnson, Ross, 32n
Johnson, Roy, 475
Joinson, Carla, 167n
Jones, Alison, 396
Jones, Gareth R., 66n, 67n
Joplin, Janice R. W., 499
Jordan, Michael, 112
Jourden, Forest J., 263n
Judge, Timothy A., 193n
Juliber, Lois, 484

Kail, J. C., 528n
Kane, Jeffrey S., 263n
Katz, Harry C., 437n
Kaufman, Bruce, 32n
Keating, Cynthia, 475
Kelleher, Herb, 3, 4, 40, 272
Kelloway, E. Kevin, 437n
Kelly, Mary L., 228n
Kendall, L. M., 263n
Kendrick, John W., 32n
Kennedy, Allan A., 67n
King, Albert S., 101n
Kirkpatrick, S. A., 66n
Klaas, Brian S., 353n, 473n
Kluger, Avraham N., 528n
Kobayashi, Kaoru, 488
Kok, R., 473n
Komansky, David H., 372
Korndorf, Ferdinand, 164
Kossek, Ellen E., 404n
Kraatz, Matthew S., 67n, 527n
Kraiger, Kurt, 262n
Kupfer, Andrew, 169

Laabs, J. J., 527n
Labig, Chalmer E., Jr., 193n
Lambros, Alexander, Jr., 501–502
Landy, Frank, 166n
Lane, Robert, 164
Langton, Nancy, 379n
Larsson, Rikard, 322n
LaShells, M. B., 263n
Latham, Gary P., 263n
Lau, Dora C., 499n
Lawler, Edward E., III, 353n, 437n
Lawshe, C. H., 547n
Leap, Terry L., 473n
Lechler, Katherine, 401
Ledford, Gerald E., 379n
Lee, Seok-Young, 379n
Lee, Thomas W., 528n
Legler, Ken, 225

Lenz, Ed, 518
Leonard, Bill, 193n
Lepak, David P., 66n
Leroy, Pierre, 164
Levering, Robert, 3
Levine, Daniel, 505
Lewis, John L., 411
Lewis, M. I., 473n
Lieber, Ron, 29
Liemandt, Joe, 265, 266
Limao de Mello, Raimundo, 114
Ling, Dan, 171
Lipsky, David, 437n
Lipson, Fran, 404n
Locke, Edwin A., 66n
Lockwood, Ginny, 92
London, Manuel, 322n
Ludeman, Kate, 263n
Luthans, Fred, 134n

McClendon, John A., 353n
McCormick, Ernest J., 148, 166n, 167n, 547n
McDaniel, Michael, 228n
McGovern, Gail, 484
McGregor, Douglas, 8, 32n
McHugh, Patrick, 416
MacKenzie, Jerold, 98–99
McKersie, Robert B., 437n
McManus, Margaret A., 228n
Mahoney, Thomas A., 32n
Maltby, Lewis, 214
Manson, JoAnn, 313
Marca, Elizabeth S., 473n
Mark, Reuben, 372
Marram, Ellen, 484
Marshall, R., 527n
Martin, Casey, 480
Martin, Justin, 228n
Martinez, Michelle Neely, 32n, 101n
Martins, Luis L., 499n
Martocchio, Joseph J., 295n
Maslow, Abraham, 8, 32n
Matsumae, Modoka, 336
Mattdson, J., 228n
Maurer, Steven D., 32n, 228n, 528n
Mayo, Elton, 8, 32n
Meese, G. B., 473n
Meglino, Bruce M., 193n, 262n
Mendenhall, Mark E., 134n, 307
Mercer, William M., 372–373
Mero, Neal P., 263n
Miles, Raymond E., 67n
Milkovich, George T., 353n, 379n, 394, 404n, 528n
Miller, Harris, 160
Milliken, Frances J., 499n

Minehan, Maureen, 404n
Mintzberg, Henry, 67n
Mischel, L. J., 473n
Mobley, William, 437n
Mohrman, Susan A., 437n
Molleston, Julie, 437n
Montemayor, Edilberto F., 67n
Montgomery, L., 262n
Montoya, John, 101n
Moore, Joe, 69
Moorhead, Gregory, 379n, 504
Moravec, Milan, 167n
Morgan, H., 322n
Morin, Bill, 301
Morris, Betsy, 497
Morris, John L., 379n
Morrison, Elizabeth Wolfe, 67n
Morsh, Joseph, 167n
Mosier, K. L., 322n
Moskowitz, Milton, 3
Moss, J. E., 527n
Moss, Michael, 481
Motowidlo, Stephan J., 262n, 263n
Mount, Michael K., 228n
Muchinsky, Paul, 353n
Munsterberg, Hugo, 5
Muonio, Andrew, 400
Murdick, R. G., 167n
Murnighan, J. Keith, 499n
Murphy, Kevin R., 241, 262n
Murphy, Vaughn, 508

Nachtigal, Jeff, 515
Nahapiet, Janine, 66n
Nakache, Patricia, 169
Nasser, Jacques, 298–299
Neale, Margaret A., 404n
Nemetz, Patricia L., 499n
Newman, Jerry, 353n, 394
Newman, R. I., 473n
Newstrom, Charles N., 134n
Nichol, V., 404n
Nielson, Jeff, 195
Nieva, V. F., 262n
Nixon, Richard, 77
Northcraft, Gregory B., 404n

O'Farrell, B., 322n
Oldham, Gregory R., 460, 473n
Oliver, Bill, 473n
O'Meara, Daniel P., 228n
O'Neil, Sandra, 353n
Ones, Deniz S., 228n, 548n
O'Reilly, Brian, 29, 67n
O'Reilly, Charles A., 528n
Organ, Dennis W., 262n
Ornstein, Suzyn, 322n

Overman, Stephanie, 32n, 182, 193n
Owen, Robert, 5
Ozawa, Nancy, 463

Palich, Leslie E., 193n
Parker, Donald, 404n
Parker, Victoria, 499n
Parks, Judi McLean, 527n
Parvin, David, 259
Paterson, Paul, 160
Pattison, Patricia, 101n
Pavlovic, Emily, 353n
Pearce, Jon, 528n
Pearlman, Kenneth, 166n
Perrewe, Pamela L., 404n, 499n
Peters, Lawrence H., 262n
Peyrefitte, Joseph, 263
Pfeffer, Jeffrey, 32n, 352n, 379n
Philbrick, Tim, 349–350
Phillion, Lee, 193n
Pine, Randall C., 473n
Pinheiro, Marcio, 174
Pohley, Katja, 228n
Porter, Lyman, 299
Porter, Michael, 67n
Potter, Gordon, 379n
Powell, Douglas, 160
Power, Donald, 416
Prensky, Marc, 282
Preston, James E., 484, 497
Primpts, Sophia B., 473n
Pritchard, Bill, 175
Privacy Protection Study Commis-
  sion, 536n
Purach, A., 473n
Purcell, John, 67n
Purcell, Philip J., 372
Pustay, Michael W., 103, 134n

Quick, James C., 461
Quick, Jonathan D., 461
Quinones, Miguel A., 228n

Ramos, Robert A., 548n
Randolph, W. Alan, 263n
Ravlin, Elizabeth C., 193n
Redwood, Rene, 484
Reese, Jennifer, 35
Rhodes, F., 473n
Richards, Lynette and Mike, 224
Richardson, Tom, 381
Robbins, Tina, 263n
Roberts, Bill, 536n
Robertson, Ivan, 228n
Robinson, Charles, 103
Robinson, Gail, 499n
Robinson, Sandra L., 67n, 527n

Roche, Gerald, 180
Roehling, Mark, 193n
Roethlisbeger, Fritz J., 8
Roland, Christopher C., 295n
Ronen, Simca, 134n, 473n
Rosenbaum, Diane, 331
Rosenfeld, Irene, 484
Rothfeder, Jeffrey, 282
Roush, Paul, 263n
Rousseau, Denise M., 67n, 527n
Russell, Craig J., 228n
Russell, J. T., 548n
Ryan, K., 262n
Rynes, Sara L., 193n

Saari, Lisa M., 263n
Sackett, Paul R., 228n, 295n
Saks, Adam, 193n
Sampler, Jeff, 265
Samuels, Howard, 78
Sanchez, Juan I., 263n
Scanlon, Joseph, 366
Schein, Edgar H., 322n
Scherer, Robert F., 101n
Schmidt, Frank L., 228n, 546, 547n,
  548n
Schmidtke, J. Marshall, 473n
Schmitt, Neal, 228n
Schrempp, Juergen, 372–373
Schuler, Randall S., 32n, 404n
Schultz, Howard, 35, 36
Schuster, F., 167n
Schweiger, David M., 67n
Schwenk, Charles, 66n
Segal, Jonathan A., 91, 101n, 473n
Seinfeld, Jerry, 98
Sellers, Patricia, 497
Shaffer, Margaret, 134n
Shapiro, Robert B., 372
Sharp, Allen, 69
Shaw, James B., 167n, 547n
Shecterle, Debbie, 450
Shipper, Frank, 437n
Shoemaker, William, 420
Siegel, Matt, 132
Simon, Theophile, 7
Sisson, E. D., 263n
Sizemore, Joe, 186
Sklover, Alan, 95
Smith, Adam, 457
Smith, Frank J., 547n
Smith, Patricia C., 263n
Smith, Teresa L., 295n
Snell, Scott A., 66n
Snow, Charles C., 67n
Sonnenstuhl, W. J., 404n
Spielberg, Steven, 309

Spychalski, Annette C., 228n
Srinivasan, Dhinu, 379n
Stack, Jack, 295n
Stahl, Steve, 206
Starkweather, Richard A., 32n
Steere, William C., Jr., 372
Steers, Richard M., 134n
Steffy, Brian D., 32n
Steinbacher, Cheryl L., 32n
Steinberg, M. D., 547n
Stephens, Gregory K., 322
Stephenson, Debra, 182
Stevens, Michael, 228n
Steward, T. A., 379n
Stewart, Thomas A., 32n, 528n
Stodd, James T., 32n
Stone, Diane L., 499n
Stone, Thomas, 193n
Stroh, Linda K., 307
Suhl, Sean, 329
Summers, Ken, 420
Sundstrom, Eric, 379n
Swamidass, Paul M., 67n

Taylor, Frederick W., 5, 32n, 356
Taylor, H. C., 548n
Taylor, Jack, 28
Taylor, Jeff, 197
Taylor, Phil, 437n
Thomas, Clarence, 93
Thomas, David A., 499n
Thompson, Bob, 361
Thompson, Marcia, 221
Thornburg, Linda, 206
Tinney, Ruth, 225
Tompkins, Neville C., 101n
Toney, Glen, 492
Torres, Jorge, 10
Tracey, J. Bruce, 294n
Tracey, William R., 101n
Trice, Harrison M., 404n
Trudell, Cynthia, 416
Truman, Harry, 541
Tucker, K., 322n
Tucker, Robert, 167n
Turban, Daniel, 228n
Turnley, William H., 528n
Tushman, Michael L., 528n
Tyler, Kathryn, 134n, 294n, 295n,
  352n
Tylo, Hunter, 80

Ulrich, Dave, 32n
U.S. Bureau of National Affairs,
  404n
U.S. Department of Labor, 166n
Useem, Michael, 528n

Van Yperen, N. W., 473n
Vanderbroeck, Paul, 134n
VanDeVliert, E., 473n
Varca, Philip E., 101n
Varma, Arup, 262n
Vasey, Joseph, 166n
Villanova, Peter, 263n
Von Glinow, Mary Ann, 528n

Waddock, Sandra A., 32n
Wagner, Richard J., 295n
Waldman, David, 231
Walsh, James P., 67n
Walter, C. S., 263n
Walton, Richard E., 437n
Walton, Sam, 40, 52
Wanous, John P., 193n
Ward, Lloyd, 305

Weaver, W. Timothy, 262n
Webster, Jane, 295n
Weill, Sanford I., 372
Weiss, Alan, 288
Weitzel, W., 527n
Welbourne, Theresa M., 379n
Welch, John F., Jr., 306, 372
Werner, Jon M., 101n, 262n
Westman, Mina, 404n
Whetzel, Deborah, 228n
White, Leonard A., 263n
Whitener, Ellen M., 547n
Whitney, John O., 67n
Wick, James, 160
Wiley, Carol, 379n
Wiley, W. W., 167n
Williams, Charles R., 193n
Williams, Kevin J., 193n

Williford, Teresa, 439
Wilson, M., 404n
Winchell, William O., 32n
Wolfe, Richard, 404n
Wren, Daniel, 32n, 379n
Wyon, D. P., 473n

Yandrick, Rudy M., 32n, 404n
Yang, Hyuckseung, 295n
Yates, James, 384
Young, Andrew, 47
Youngblood, Stuart A., 193n, 437n

Zawacki, Robert, 404n
Zedeck, Sheldon, 322n, 473n
Zhou, Jing, 473n

ABC, 42, 44, 430
Abercrombie & Fitch, 44
Aetna, 522
A F of L, *see* American Federation of
    Labor
AFL-CIO
    alternative work sites and, 522
    formation of, 409, 411
    see also American Federation of
        Labor; Congress of Industrial
        Organizations
Albertson, 325
Allied Pilots Association (APA),
    433–435
AlliedSignal Inc.
    executive compensation and, 372
    360-degree feedback and, 231
American Airlines, 4
    labor unions and, 429, 433–435
    strategic alliance and, 119
    strikes and, 414
    training and development and,
        291–292
American Civil Liberties Union, 214
American Cyanamid, 458
American Express Co.
    executive compensation and, 372
    as service organization, 53
American Federation of Labor
    (AF of L), 409, 410, 411
American Railway Union, 410
American Trucking Association, 146
AMOCO International, 130
    career planning and development
        and, 308
    childcare and, 395
    employee benefits and services
        and, 383–384, 396
    merger and, 131
AMR, 433–435
Analog Devices, 78
Andersen Consulting
    management development and, 290
    recruiting from abroad and, 174
Apple Computer, 285
Applied Materials, 492
Arrowhead Space and Telecommuni-
    cations, Inc., 200

ASA, 392
ATS, 401
AT&T
    assessment centers and, 215–216
    diversity and, 493
    expatriate failure and, 125
    job enlargement and, 458
    job enrichment and, 459
    overtime and, 325
    pension plans and, 392
    safety for telecommuters and, 91
    stress and, 462
    360–degree feedback and, 231
    women in workforce and, 484
Attorneys@Work.net, 182
Autodesk, 466
Avis, 28, 29, 206
Avon
    diversity and, 487, 492, 496–497
    women in workforce and, 484

Bankers Trust, 282, 288
Barbie, 297
Barnes & Noble, 244
Bath & Body Works, 44
Bayer AG, 95, 105
Bean, L.L., 467
Beatrice Foods, 40
Bechtel, 39
Bell Atlantic, 392
Bell Geospace, 509
BellSouth, 439
Bethlehem Steel, 62
    hiring in early days of, 6
    job rotation and, 458
BMW
    differentiation strategy and, 46
    direct investment and, 118–119
    incentives and, 113
Boeing
    hiring in early days of, 6
    360–degree feedback and, 231
    training and development and,
        291–292
Brave New World, 345
Brigham and Women's Hospital, 313
Bristol-Myers Squibb Co., 372
British Airways, 119

British Petroleum (BP), 130
    career planning and development
        and, 308
    merger and, 131
British Petroleum Exploration, 510
Bryan-College Station Eagle, 179
Burger King, 283
Business Week, 334

Campbell Soup, 95
Candleworks, 224–225
Capital Records, 35
Career Path, 182
Career Television Network, 182
CareerMosaic, 182
Caterpillar, 457
CBS, 44, 309
Chaparral Steel Corporation
    selection and, 198, 201
    strategic human resource manage-
        ment and, 62–64
Charleston Naval Shipyard, 524
Chevron, 456
    employee benefits and services
        and, 396
Chili's, 242
Chrysler, 299
    employment tests and, 209
    executive compensation and, 369,
        370, 372
    human resource planning for re-
        ductions in, 161
Cigna, 392
Cincinnati Bell, 392
CIO, *see* Congress of Industrial Orga-
    nizations
Cisco Systems
    compensation and, 330
    management development and,
        285
    recruiting and, 169–170
    telecommuting and, 522
Citigroup, 514
Clif Bar, 381–382, 394
CNA, 189–190
Coca-Cola, 206
Cognex, 214
    recruiting and, 190

Colgate-Palmolive Co.
   executive compensation and, 372
   women in workforce and, 484
Collin Street Bakery, 525
Compaq Computer
   mission statement of, 39
   recruiting and, 175
Conference Board, 288
Congress of Industrial Organizations
   (CIO), 409, 411. See also AFL-CIO
Continental Airlines
   performance-based rewards and,
      376–377
   training and development and,
      291–292
Control Data, 160
Corning, 186
Coty Cosmetics, 297
Cougar Mountain Software, 259
Culinary Workers Union Local, 421

Daimler-Benz AG, 105
   executive compensation and,
      372–373
DaimlerChrysler AG, 427
   international transfers and assign-
      ments and, 124
   merger and, 130–131
Dalton, B., 244
Daly Gray, 402
Deere & Company, 164–165
Dell Computer
   direct investment and, 118
   stock options and, 368
Delphi Automotive Systems, 103
Delta Airlines, 4
   Position Analysis Questionnaire
      and, 150
   training and development and,
      291–292
Denny's, 493
Detroit Edison, 458
Digital Equipment, 462
Disney, Walt, Company
   analyzer strategy and, 46
   direct investment and, 118
   employee benefits and services
      and, 396
   founder's influence on culture
      and, 52
   growth strategy and, 42
   realistic job previews and, 183
Doane Pet Care Company, 450
Dow Chemical, 95
DreamWorks, 309
Dreyer's, 35
Dupont, 231

Eastman Kodak
   compensation and, 359
   direct investment and, 118
   employee knowledge and, 95
   management development and, 285
   Position Analysis Questionnaire
      and, 150
   recruiting and, 180
Eddie Bauer, 198
Electronic Data Systems (EDS)
   career planning and development
      and, 319
   recruiting from abroad and, 174
Enterprise Rent-A-Car, 28–29
Excite, 52
Express, 44
   selection and, 198
Exxon, 131
   international human resources
      and, 307
   training and development and, 275
   Valdez and, 444

FedEx, 231
Fennell Promotions, 355
Fiesta Mart, 47
Fighter Pilots USA, 355
First Bank Systems, 450
Foot Locker, 198
Ford Motor Company, 13, 52, 305
   career planning and development
      and, 298–299
   direct investment and, 119
   employee benefit and services and,
      383
   employment tests and, 209
   hiring in early days of, 6–7
   human resource planning and, 139
   incentives and, 355, 364–365
   job rotation and, 458
   labor unions and, 333, 408
   personnel department in, 7
   selection and, 199
Fortune, 334
Frito-Lay, 305
Fruit of the Loom, 137–138
Fuji Film, 95

Gap
   human resource function and, 23
   work space design and, 450
Gateway Computers, 50
Geffen Records, 309
Genentech, 283
General Electric Co., 160
   career planning and development
      and, 305, 306, 467

compensation and, 44
   diversification strategy and, 43–44
   employee knowledge and, 95
   executive compensation and, 372
   international human resources
      and, 306
   management development and,
      290
   prospector strategy and, 45
General Foods
   job enrichment and, 459
   training and development and, 283
General Motors (GM), 299
   compensation and, 349–350
   expatriate failure and, 125
   hiring in early days of, 6
   human resource planning for re-
      ductions in, 161
   incentives and, 364–365
   internal recruiting and, 177
   labor unions and, 333, 407–408,
      416, 420
   manufacturing and, 53
   manufacturing in Mexico and, 103
   strikes and, 55
Georgia-Pacific Corporation, em-
      ployee safety and health and,
      453, 467–469
Great Plains Software, 50
Green Tree Financial, 374
Greyhound, 42

Handwriting Research, 214
Hanes, 138
Harvard Medical School, 313
Harvard University, 275–276
Heinz, H. J., 95
Herman Miller, 18
Hershey Foods, 45
Hertz, 28, 29
Hewlett-Packard
   executive compensation and, 370
   orientation and, 272
Hibernia oil rig, 456
Hilton, 121
Home Depot, 41
Honda Motor Co.
   diversity and, 488
   quotas and, 113
Honeywell, 231
Hoover's Online, 182
Hospital Corporation of America, 467
Houston Community College, 17
Houston Wire Works, 225
Human Resource Certification Insti-
      tute (HRCI), 26
Hyundai, 46

IBM, 299
  human resource planning for reductions in, 161
  job enlargement and, 458
  job enrichment and, 459
  outsourcing and, 513
  recruiting and, 190
  selection process and, 206
Ideo U., 285
IG Metall, 131
Incentive Federation, 355
Industrial Workers of the World, 410
Information Technology Association, 160
Intel, 39, 231
International Association of Machinists and Aerospace Workers (IAM), 424
International Brotherhood of Teamsters, 114, 409
International Harvester, 43
International Ladies' Garment Workers Union, 409, 413
International Longshoremen's Union, 409
IRMCO Manufacturing, 153

Jaguar, 119
JAI, 291–292
Journeyman Cordwainers Society of Philadelphia, 409

Kellogg's, 477
Kmart
  compensation and, 330
  reactor strategy and, 46
Knights of Labor, 409–410
Korean Air Service Academy, 121
Korn/Ferry, 334
KPM Peat Marwick, 370
Kraft Foods, 484
Kroger, 530
  disciplinary system and, 448

Las Vegas, unions and, 421
Lemonpop.com, 329
Levi Strauss, 161
Limited, The
  human resource function in, 23
  related diversification and, 44
Lincoln Electric, 363–364
Lockheed Martin, 467
Long Beach Convention & Entertainment Center, 257
Love Cosmetics, 297
LTV, 419

Lucent Technologies
  diversity and, 486
  incentive compensation systems and, 355
Lufthansa Airlines, 291–292

Macy's, 524–525
Marriott International
  diversity and, 475–476
  employee counseling and, 401
Mattel Inc., 297, 299
  women in workforce and, 484
Mayo Clinic, 17
Maytag, 44, 305, 458
Mazda, 336
McDonald's, 23
MCI WorldCom, 221
Medtronic, 182
Mercedes, 113. *See also* Daimler-Chrysler AG; Daimler-Benz AG
Merck, 241, 314
Merrill Lynch & Co.
  executive compensation and, 372
  new employment relationships and, 501–502
  telecommuting and, 91, 522
Mervyn, 325
Michigan, recruiting and, 190
Michigan, University of, 275–276
Microboard Processing, 225
Microsoft
  career planning and development and, 319
  competitiveness and, 17
  contingent or temporary workers and, 515
  human resource planning and, 153
  licensing and, 118
  recruiting and, 171, 181
  selection and, 206, 220–221
Miller Brewing Company, 98–99
MindSpring Enterprises, 4
Minute Maid, 114
Mitsubishi, 105
Mobil, 456
Monsanto Co., 372
Monster.com, 197
Morgan Stanley Dean Witter & Co., 372
Morton International, 10
Motorola
  diversity and, 493–494
  labor unions and, 418
  management development and, 290
  recruiting and, 180
  women in workforce and, 484
MS&L, 439

National Airlines, 291–292
National Association of Temporary & Staffing Services, 518
National Education Association, 409
National Federation of Federal Employees, 409
National Institute for Occupational Safety and Health, 454
National Iron Molders, 409
National Trades Union, 409
National Typographical Union, 409
Nations Business, 334
NationsBank, 206
Navistar, 43
NBA, 430
NBC, 44
NEC, 105
Nestlé
  child labor and, 114
  competitiveness and, 17
  geocentric staffing model and, 108
  international transfers and assignments and, 124
  Position Analysis Questionnaire and, 150
Nike
  global human resource management and, 47
  wages and conditions in foreign plants and, 112
Noble and Holy Order of the Knights of Labor, *see* Knights of Labor
Northwest Airlines
  compensation and, 359
  strikes and, 55
Northwestern University, 275–276
Notre Dame, University of, 69–70

Ohio State University, 17
Omni Computer Products, 443
Online Career Center, 182
Ortho Pharmaceuticals, 487
Outward Bound, 283

Pace Foods, 494
Paine Webber, 206
Pan American Airlines, 291–292
Paramount, 396
PC Connection, 39
PeopleSoft, 190
PepsiCo, 95, 305
Petro-Canada, 456
Pfizer Inc.
  executive compensation and, 372
  selection process and, 206
Philadelphia, revitalization of, 345
Pitney Bowes, 484

Pizza Hut, 448
PriceWaterhouseCoopers, 178
Procter & Gamble, 305
  executive succession and, 155
  labor unions and, 418
  management development and,
    285
Professional Golf Association (PGA),
    480
Prudential Insurance
  international training and develop-
    ment and, 126
  job characteristics approach and,
    460
  job rotation and, 458
Public Service Electric & Gas, 439

Quaker Oats, 95
QUALCOMM, 397

Red Cross, 141
Red Lobster, 242
Redhook Brewery, 35
Reebok, 374
Reno Air, 433–435
RJR Nabisco, 299
Rolex, 46
Rourke, 439
Royal Dutch/Shell, 131, 139
Russell, Karsh, & Hagen, 402
Rutgers University, 288

Safeway, 462
St. Louis Independent School
    District, 17
Samsung Electronics, 488
Sara Lee Corporation, 138
SAS Institute, 386
Saturn, 416
Schwinn, 52–53
Seagram, 484
Sears, Roebuck & Co.
  employment application and,
    204
  work space design and, 450
Seinfeld, 98–99
Shell Oil, 39
  career planning and development
    and, 305
  employee benefits and services
    and, 396
  selection process and, 206
Shoney's, 75
Siemens, 105
Smith Barney, 505
Society for Human Resource Man-
    agement (SHRM), 26, 334

Sony Corporation, 13
  employee benefits and services
    and, 396
  ethnocentric staffing model and,
    108
  selection process and, 206
South Texas Veterans' Health Sys-
    tems, 319
Southwest Airlines
  career planning and development
    and, 319
  culture and, 53
  human resource management and,
    3–4
  mission statement of, 39
  no-layoff policy and, 11
  orientation and, 272
  recruiting and, 190
  top human resource executive
    and, 11
  top management team and, 40
  training and development and, 281
Spring Paranet, 288
Sprint Corporation, 190
Starbucks Coffee Company
  culture and, 53
  growth strategy and, 41
  mission statement of, 38
State Farm Insurance, 190
State Street Corporation, 189
State Unemployment Compensation
    Commission, 388
Steelcase, 285
Structure, 44
Subway, 23

Taco Bell, 325
Tenneco, 467
Texaco
  diversity and, 493
  360–degree feedback and, 231
Texas, recruiting and, 190
Texas A&M University, 280
Texas Instruments
  disciplinary system and, 448
  human resource function and, 24
  job enrichment and, 459
  recruiting from abroad and, 174
  training and development and, 275
3Com, 285
3M Corporation
  executive compensation and, 374
  performance appraisals and, 241
Thunderbird, 52
Time Warner, 518
Timex, 46
Toshiba, 139

Toyota, 105
  competitiveness and, 17
  international training and develop-
    ment and, 121, 122
Trammell Crow Real Estate Investors,
    198
Trans World Airlines, 359
Travelers Group Inc., 372
Trilogy Software, Inc., 265–266
Tropicana, 114
TRW, 458

Unilever, 13
  geocentric staffing model and, 108
United Airlines (UAL), 4
  age discrimination and, 234
  compensation and, 359
  labor unions and, 424
United Auto Workers (UAW), 7, 418
  compensation and, 333, 349
  formation of, 409
  manufacturing in Mexico and, 103
  mergers and, 131
  strikes and, 407, 420
United Cigarmakers, 409
United Mine Workers, 409
United Parcel Service (UPS)
  human resource planning for
    growth and, 161
  social contracts and, 508
  strikes and, 55
  360–degree feedback and, 231
U.S. Army, 185
U.S. Bureau of Labor Statistics, 334
U.S. Bureau of National Affairs, 334
U.S. Civil Service Commission
  equal employment opportunity
    and, 85, 87
  job enlargement and, 458
U.S. Department of Health, 90
U.S. Department of Justice
  equal employment opportunity
    and, 86, 87
  selection and, 85
U.S. Department of Labor
  employee safety and health and,
    90, 91, 453, 454
  equal employment opportunity
    and, 87
  functional job analysis and, 148
  regulations and, 71
  selection and, 85
  temporary workers and, 518
U.S. Department of Transportation,
    281
U.S. Employment Service, 179
U.S. Marine Corps, 185

U.S. Office of Personnel Management, 338
U.S. Postal Service (USPS), 17
   classification system and, 337
   violence in workplace and, 505
U.S. Steel, 62. *See also* Bethlehem Steel
United Steel Workers (USW), 419
United Way, 17
Universal, 396
USX, 62

Victoria's Secret, 44
Volvo, 119
   employee benefits and services
      and, 383

Wal-Mart, 46
   career planning and development
      and, 313

compensation and, 330, 349, 350
competitiveness and, 17
disabled employees and, 92
disciplinary system and, 449
employee rights and, 441
founder's influence on culture
      and, 52
global environment and, 21
human resource planning and, 139
initial job assignment and, 222
mission statement of, 39
top human resource executive at, 11
top management team and, 40
Warmdaddy's, 345
Warner Bros., 396
Wells Fargo Bank, 283
Western Electric Company, 450
   Hawthorne studies and, 8
   job rotation and, 458

Whirlpool, 44
   diversity and, 479–480
Wichita Tool Company, 175
Willemina, 345
William Morris Agency, 309
Wrigley, 45

Xerox Corporation
   job posting at, 176
   pension plans and, 392
   training and development and, 283

Abilities, *see* Knowledge, skills, and abilities
Absenteeism
  compensation and, 360
  diversity and, 486–487
  low-skilled jobs and, 511
  stress and, 465
Achievement tests, 208
Acquisitions, *see* Mergers and acquisitions
Activity, learning and, 268
ADA, *see* Americans with Disabilities Act of 1990
Adaptation model, 45–46
ADEA, *see* Age Discrimination and Employment Act
Advertisements, recruiting from, 178–179
Affirmative action, 77, 79, 85–87
African-Americans
  disparate impact and, 74
  diversity and, 487, 488, 493
  pattern or practice discrimination and, 75
  in workforce, 482–483, 485
  see also Equal employment opportunity
Age, of workforce, 54
Age discrimination, 69, 78–79, 88, 234
Age Discrimination and Employment Act (ADEA), 69, 78–79, 234
Agencies, regulations and, 70–72
Agency theory, 357–358
Agreeableness, selection considering, 201
AIDS, 93, 467–468
Alcoholism
  discipline and, 444
  employee assistance plans and, 397
Alternative-form reliability, 217
Americans with Disabilities Act (ADA) of 1990, 19, 78, 80–81, 82, 85, 92–93, 140, 213, 480, 508
Analysis of variance (ANOVA), 544
Analyzer strategy, 45–46
Annual review, *see* Performance appraisal
ANOVA, *see* Analysis of variance

Applications, *see* Employment applications
Apprenticeship training, 280–281
Aptitude tests, 208
Arbitration, labor relations and, 430–431
Asians, in workforce, 482, 483
Assembly line, 5, 457
Assessment center, managers selected with, 215–216
Attendance, compensation and, 360
Attitudes, human resource strategy implementation and, 56
Attrition, human resource reduction with, 161–162
Audits, of employee benefits and services, 399
Automation, strategic human resource management and, 53–54

Background checks, for selection, 203–205
Banding, selection and, 220
Bangladesh, international business and, 110
Bargaining, 422
BARS, *see* Behaviorally Anchored Rating Scales
Base salary, of executives, 369
Behavioral Observation Scale (BOS), 249
Behaviorally Anchored Rating Scales (BARS), 248–249
Belgium, international business and, 107
Benchmarking, job evaluation and, 339–340
Benefits, *see* Employee benefits and services
Bennet Mechanical Comprehension Test, 207
BFOQ, *see* Bona fide occupational qualification
"Big five" personality traits, 201, 209–210
Biodata applications, 205
Blue-collar workers, public employment agencies and, 180

Bona fide occupational qualification (BFOQ), 73–74
Bonuses, executives and, 359, 369
BOS, *see* Behavioral Observation Scale
Bottom-up forecasting, demand for human resources forecasted with, 157
Boycotts, 429
Brazil
  high-tech workers hired from, 174
  international business and, 114, 117
Bridge jobs, 317
Britain
  Darwin and, 7
  employee benefits and service and, 383–384, 393
  international business and, 105, 109–110, 117, 121, 122
  labor unions in, 129
Burnout, stress and, 464, 466
Business schools, training and development programs run by, 275–276
Business strategy, 41–42, 45–47
  adaptation model and, 45–46
  competitive strategies and, 46–47
  cost leadership strategy and, 46–47, 49
  differentiation strategy and, 46, 49
  focus strategy and, 47
  see also Strategic human resource management

Cafeteria-style benefit plans, 398–399, 533
California Psychological Inventory (CPI), 209
Canada, international business and, 104, 107
Career counseling, 305, 315–316
  for late-career problems, 315
  for midcareer problems, 311–312
Career planning and development, 14, 19, 49, 296–322
  alternative paths in, 319–320
  case on, 319–320
  consequences of, 306–307

Career planning and development
(*continued*)
discipline and punishment *versus*,
442–443
dual-career families and, 54,
316–317, 485
emerging career stages and,
300–302
evaluation of, 317
importance of, 304–306
individual assessment stage of, 305
individual perspectives on, 303,
304
international human resource management and, 125–126, 306–307
job families and, 141–142
for late-career employees, 313–315
limitations and pitfalls in, 307–308
meaning of career and, 298–299
for midcareer employees, 310–313
for new entrants, 308–310
organizational perspectives on,
302–303
performance appraisal and, 234
steps in, 304, 305
stress management and, 467
traditional career stages and,
299–300
work-family issues and, 316–317
see also Career counseling
Careers, in human resource
management, 27
Cash-balance plan, 392
Causal relationships, 538–540
Center of expertise, human resource
management as, 24–25
Central tendency distributional error,
performance appraisal and, 251
Child labor, international human resource management and,
110–111, 113, 114
Childcare, 395, 396, 401
China, international business and, 107
Circadian rhythms, 449–450
Civil Rights Act of 1964, 9, 19
Civil Rights Act of 1991 and, 80
termination and, 503
Title VII of, 74, 75, 77, 82, 83, 93,
479
Civil Rights Act of 1991, 80, 82, 116
Civil Rights Acts of 1866 and 1871,
72–73
Classification system, for job
evaluation, 337–338
Closed shop, 413–414
Cognitive ability tests, 208–209, 210
Collateral stress programs, 467

Collective bargaining, 54, 55, 89–90,
408, 411, 425–426, 502
Colleges, recruiting through, 181
Color, legal environment and, 77, 80.
See also African-Americans;
Equal employment opportunity
Commonwealth v. Hunt, 411
Communication
career planning and development
and, 305
diversity management and, 491
of employee benefits and services,
399–400
human resource strategy implementation and, 58–59
learning and, 269
Compensable factors, for job
evaluation, 339
Compensation, 14, 21, 325
above-market, 329–330
below-market, 330–331
department for, 23
early, 6, 7
evaluation of, 347–348
executives and, 334, 359, 369–374
external equity and, 327
human resource information systems for, 532–533
human resource managers and, 26
internal equity and, 326–327
international human resource management and, 108, 111, 112, 117,
122–123, 126–128, 372–373
Internet and, 334
job analysis and, 140–141
knowledge workers and, 509–510
labor unions and, 328, 333, 349,
350, 359, 421
legal environment and, 78, 87–89,
325, 331, 333
management of, 344–345
market rate and, 331–332
merit, 360–362
negotiation and, 221
organization's ability to attract and
retain employees and, 332–333
organization's ability to pay and,
333
outsourcing of, 24
overall strategy of organization
and, 333
pay surveys and, 333–335, 348
performance appraisal and, 233
purposes of, 326–328
seniority and, 328–329, 345
skill- and knowledge-based pay
and, 289, 328, 342–344, 362

strategic options for, 328–333
strategy and, 48, 49, 50
total, 87–88
women and, 327, 482
workers', 389, 391, 439
see also Employee benefits and services; Incentives; Performance-
based rewards; Salaries; *under*
Wages
Compensation administration, *see*
Wage and salary administration
Competencies, selection and, 199
Competitiveness, 10–11
diversity and, 486–488
facilitation of as human resource
management goal, 17–18
strategy and, 46–47
Compliance, evaluation of, 96
Compressed workweeks, 520–521
Computer-assisted instruction,
281–282
Confidentiality, executive search
firms and, 180–181
Conflict, diversity and, 488–489
Conglomerate organization design, 51
Conscientiousness
measurement of, 541
selection and, 201
Consent decree, 82
Construct validity, 218
Contacts, selection and, 216
Content validity, 218
Contextual performance, perfor-
mance appraisals and, 240–241
Contingent workers, 514–518
case on, 524–525
Contrast error
interviews and, 212
performance appraisal and, 251
Contributions, psychological con-
tracts and, 503–504
Contributory pension plans, 392
Control systems, in information
systems, 531
Cooking classes, for training and
development, 283
Cordwainer Doctrine, 411
Core time, 519
Corporate culture, *see* Culture
Corporate strategy, 41–45
diversification strategy and,
43–45, 49
grand strategy and, 41–43
see also Strategic human resource
management
Correlation coefficient, 542–544
Cost argument, for diversity, 487–488

Cost cutting, systems approach to, 16
Cost leadership strategy, 46–47, 49
Cottage industries, 521–522
Counseling, as employee benefit, 401
Country of national origin
    diversity and, 54, 485, 488
    legal environment and, 77, 80,
        see also Equal employment
        opportunity
Country's culture, international human resource management and, 109–111
CPI, see California Psychological Inventory
Craft unions, 408–409, 410. See also Labor unions
Creativity argument, for diversity, 487, 488
Crime, discipline and, 444
Criterion-related validity, 218–219
Critical-incident method
    for job analysis, 150–151
    for performance appraisal, 247–248
Culture
    diversity and, 494
    international human resource management and, 109–111
    orientation and, 272
    strategic human resource management and, 51–53
    stress and, 466–467
    top management team and, 39
Customers, performance appraisal and, 242

Decertification, of labor unions, 423–424
Decision making, performance appraisal and, 235
Defender strategy, 45
Defined contribution plans, 391–392
Delphi technique, demand for human resources forecasted with, 157
Design, stress and, 462
Development, 266, 267–268
    strategy and, 48, 49, 50
    see also Career planning and development; Management development; Performance management; Training and development
Diagnostic OD, 286
Dictionary of Occupational Titles (DOT), 145
Dietary preferences, diversity and, 54, 485
Differentiation strategy, 46, 49

Direct applicants, recruiting from, 178
Direct investment, international business and, 118–119
Disability insurance, 391
Disabled employees
    diversity and, 54, 480
    human resource information systems and, 535
    job analysis and, 140
    legal environment and, 19, 78, 79, 80–81, 82, 85, 92–93, 140, 213, 480, 508
    low-skilled jobs and, 511
Discipline, 442–449
    approaches to, 445, 448–449
    documentation and, 445, 446–447
    dysfunctional employee and, 443–444
    grievance systems and, 21
    hot stove rule of, 445, 448
    progressive, 448–449
    punishment versus, 442–443
    substance abuse and, 444
Discrimination, 72, 73–75
    employment agencies and, 181
    employment tests and, 195, 208–209
    Equal Employment Opportunity Commission and, 77, 79, 81, 82–85, 92–93
    illegal, 72, 73–75, 82–83, 84–85
    international human resource management and, 80, 115–116
    performance appraisal and, 233–244
    physical examinations and, 213
    selection and, 195, 203, 208–209, 216
    see also Equal employment opportunity
Discussion approach, to training and development, 281
Disengagement, as career stage, 299, 300
Disparate impact discrimination, 74
Disparate treatment discrimination, 73–74, 75
Distributional error, performance appraisal and, 251
Diversification strategy, 43–45, 49
Diversity, 15, 54, 474–499
    age and, 54
    case on, 496–497
    communication and, 491
    competitiveness and, 486–488
    conflict and, 488–489

country of national origin and, 54, 485, 489
    culture and, 494
    definition of, 476
    dietary preferences and, 54, 485
    disabled employees and, 54, 480
    diversity training and, 493–494
    dual-career couples and, 54
    empathy and, 490
    equal employment opportunity versus, 478–481
    ethnicity and, 54, 482–483, 485, 487, 488, 493, 494
    gays and lesbians and, 54, 485
    immigration and, 477, 478
    individual strategies for dealing with, 490–491
    international human resource management and, 477, 478, 487, 488, 490–491, 493–494
    legal environment and, 477, 479, 480
    management of, 490–495
    multicultural organization and, 494–495
    older employees and, 481–482, 491
    organizational policies and, 491–492
    organizational practices and, 492
    organizational strategies for dealing with, 491–493
    political ideologies and, 54
    religion and, 393, 479–480
    single-parent status and, 54, 316, 485
    social change and, 486
    tolerance and, 490–491
    trends in, 476–477
    understanding and, 490
    see also Women in workforce
Diversity management, equal employment opportunity versus, 478–481
Diversity training, 493–494
Division of labor, 5, 457
Divisional organization design, 51
Documentation, of disciplinary actions, 445, 446–447
Domestic partner benefits, 396
Domestic problems, employee assistance plans and, 397
Downsizing, 11, 42–43, 300
    health insurance and, 507
    low-skilled jobs and, 511
    midcareer employees and, 313
    overtime and, 325
    recruiting and, 177

Downward transfers, for midcareer employees, 313
Drop-ins, *see* Direct applicants
Drug tests, 214. *See also* Substance abuse
Dual-career families, 54, 316–317, 485
Due process, termination and, 503
Dunlop Commission, 507
Dysfunctional employee, 443–444

EAPs, *see* Employee assistance plans
Early retirement, 162, 314–315, 396–397
Eastern Europe, international business and, 121
Economic communities, international human resource management and, 113–114
Economic Recovery Tax Act of 1981, 371, 387
Economies of scale, 5
Education, selection and, 196, 199
EEO-1 report, 532
EEOC, *see* Equal Employment Opportunity Commission
Efficiency wage theory, employee benefits and service and, 384
Egypt, employee benefits and service and, 383, 384
Eight factor reports, 532
Elder care, referrals for, 395
Electronic cottage, 522
Electronic employment screening, 204, 206
E-mail, 58
    privacy of, 441
    stress and, 463
Empathy, diversity management and, 490
Employee appraisal, *see* Performance appraisal
Employee assistance plans (EAPs), 397
Employee benefits and services, 14, 21, 49, 380–404
    adverse selection and, 398
    cafeteria-style, 398–399, 533
    case on, 401–402
    childcare, 386, 395, 401
    communication of to employees, 399–400
    contingent workers and, 514, 515
    cost of, 382–383
    defined benefit plans and, 391–392
    definition of, 382
    diversity and, 492
    for domestic partners, 396

early retirement and, 162, 396–397
efficiency wage theory and, 384
elder care, 395
employee assistance plans, 397
employers' expectations and, 385
evaluation of, 399–400
flexible, 401–402
health care, 385, 507
holidays, 392–393
human resource information systems for, 532–533
insurance, 390–391, 507, 535
international human resource management and, 127
international human resources and, 383, 384, 393, 394
job satisfaction and turnover and, 385
labor unions and, 419, 421
legal aspects of, 386–389, 507
management of, 344
mandated protection plans, 387–389
negotiation and, 221–222
optional protection plans, 390–392
paid time off, 392–394
pensions, 88–89
perquisites, 397
personal leave, 393
private pension plans, 391–392
psychological counseling, 401
purposes of, 384–385
relocation services, 396
sick leave, 393
social security, 388–389
unemployment insurance, 388
vacations, 393, 394
wellness programs, 394–395, 466–467
women in workforce and, 385
workers' compensation, 389, 391, 439
Employee evaluation, *see* Performance appraisal
Employee knowledge, legal issues in, 94–95
Employee leasing, 187
Employee Retirement Income Security Act (ERISA) of 1974, 88, 387, 391
Employee rights, 430–432
    privacy and, 506–507, 534–535
    psychological contracts and, 506–507
Employee safety and health, 451–457
    accident control and, 455–456
    case on, 467–469

common hazards and threats, 453–454
criminal liability and, 10
legal issues in, 9–10, 90–91, 451, 454–455
occupational disease control and, 456–457
Occupational Safety and Health Act of 1970 and, 451, 454–455
safety engineers and, 456
Employee stock ownership plans (ESOPs), 368, 387
Employee training, 266–267. *See also* Training and development
Employment agencies
    executive search firms, 180–181
    private, 180
    public, 179–180
Employment applications, 203–205, 206
Employment contracts, 502–508
    employee rights and, 506–507
    employment-at-will and, 94, 440, 502–503
    psychological contracts and, 503–507
    social contracts and, 507–508
Employment tests, 205–210
    achievement tests, 208
    aptitude tests, 208
    cognitive ability tests, 208–209, 210
    discrimination and, 195, 208–209
    integrity tests, 210
    intelligence tests, 208–209
    personality tests, 209
    psychomotor ability tests, 209
    self-report inventory, 209
    validity and reliability of, 217–219
    see also specific tests
Employment-at-will, 94, 440, 502–503
Equal employment opportunity, 71, 72–87
    affirmative action and, 77, 79, 85–87
    age and, 69, 78–79, 88, 234
    Age Discrimination and Employment Act and, 78–79, 88, 234
    Americans with Disabilities Act of 1990 and, 19, 78, 80–81, 82, 85, 92–93, 140, 213, 480, 508
    bureaucratic complexity and, 82, 83
    case on, 98–99
    Civil Rights Act of 1964 and, 9, 19, 74, 75, 77, 80, 82, 83, 93, 479, 503
    Civil Rights Act of 1991 and, 80, 82, 116
    Civil Rights Acts of 1866 and 1871 and, 72–73

color and, 77, 80

country of national origin and, 77, 80

disabled employees and, 19, 78, 79, 80–81, 82, 85, 92–93, 140, 213, 480, 508

diversity management *versus*, 478–481

employee rights and, 440

enforcement of, 82–87, 92–93

Equal Employment Opportunity Commission and, 77, 79, 81, 82–85, 92–93

Equal Pay Act of 1963 and, 78, 82, 327

Executive Order 11246 and, 77

Executive Order 11478 and, 77

Family and Medical Leave Act of 1993 and, 81–82, 387

historical aspect of, 72–73

international human resource management and, 80, 115–116

Office of Federal Contract Compliance Procedures and, 77, 79, 82, 85–87

Pregnancy Discrimination Act of 1978 and, 79–80, 387

protected classes in workforce and, 73, 75–87

race and, 77, 80

religion and, 77, 80, 479–480

Title VII of Civil Rights Act of 1964 and, 74, 75, 77, 82, 83, 93, 479

Vietnam Era Veterans' Readjustment Act of 1974 and, 79

Vocational Rehabilitation Act of 1973 and, 79

women and, 77, 78, 79–80, 81, 98–99

see also Discrimination

Equal Employment Opportunity Commission (EEOC), 77, 79, 81, 82–85, 92–93

Equal Pay Act of 1963, 78, 82, 327

Equity, internal, 326–327

Equity theory, of motivation, 57

ERISA, *see* Employee Retirement Income Security Act

ESOPs, *see* Employee stock ownership plans

Establishment, as career stage, 299, 300

Ethics, 95–96

human resource information systems and, 535

international human resource management and, 111, 112

Ethnicity

diversity and, 54, 482–483, 485, 487, 488, 493, 494

mentoring and, 19

Ethnocentric staffing model, 107–108

EU, *see* European Union

Europe

employee benefits and services and, 393, 394

headhunting in, 124

international business and, 125

see also specific countries

European Union (EU), 113–114

Evaluation

of career planning and development, 317

of compensation, 347–348

of employee benefits and services, 399–400

human resource information systems for, 532

of human resource management, 60–61

of human resource planning process, 162–163

of legal compliance, 96

of recruiting process, 188

of selection process, 222–223

of training and development, 287–288, 532

see also Performance appraisal

Executive compensation, 334, 359, 369–374

Executive Order 11246, 77

Executive Order 11478, 77

Executive search firms, 180–181

Executive succession, 155–156, 164–165

Expatriates, 123. *See also* International human resource management

Expectancy theory, of motivation, 57, 356–357

Experience(s)

human resource information system for inventory of, 533

selection and, 196, 200

Exploration, as career stage, 299–300

Exporting, international business and, 117, 119

External equity, 327

External recruiting, 173–175, 177–182

Extraversion, selection considering, 201

Factor comparison method, for job evaluation, 339–340

Fair Labor Standards Act of 1938 (FLSA), 7, 87–88, 186, 325, 333

Family and Medical Leave Act of 1993, 81–82, 387

Federal Register, 85

Feedback

performance appraisal and, 252–253, 257

360–degree, 231–232, 242–244

Fifth Amendment, 534

Final-offer arbitration, 431

First-impression error, interviews and, 212

First-line employees, *see* Foremen

Fit

culture and, 53

as selection strategy, 201–202, 220, 303

Fitness centers, 467. *See also* Wellness and fitness programs

Flat organization, 51

Fleishman job analysis system, 147

Flex time, 519

Flexible work hour plans, 519–520

FLSA, *see* Fair Labor Standards Act

Focus strategy, 47

Follow-up plans

for human resource planning, 159–162

for performance appraisal, 255–256

Forced-distribution method, for performance appraisal, 245–246

Forecasting

demand for human resources and, 155–158, 159

supply of human resources and, 152–155, 156, 159

top-down, 157

Foreign service premium, *see* Hardship premium

Foremen

hiring by, 6–7

personnel management hiring, 8

Founder of organization, culture and, 52

Four-fifths rule, 74

401(k) plans, 386, 391, 392

Fourteenth Amendment, 72

Fourth Amendment, 534

Frame-of-reference training, *see* Rater-accuracy training

France

Binet and Simon and, 7

international business and, 105, 118

labor unions in, 129

Franchises, human resources in, 23

Freedom of speech, as employee right, 506
Fringe benefits, 382. *See also* Employee benefits and services
Functional job analysis, 148
Functional organization design, 50–51
Functional strategies, 40, 41, 42, 48. *See also* Strategic human resource management

Gainsharing, 366
Gays and lesbians
 diversity and, 54, 485
 employee benefits and services for partners and, 396
Gender differences in workforce, *see* Women in workforce
General Aptitude Test Battery (GATB), 150, 179
General Duty Clause, 90
General labor pool, 177
General training, 289
Geocentric staffing model, 108–109
Germany
 employee benefits and services and, 393
 international business and, 104, 105, 122
Glass ceiling, 54, 482, 484
Globalization, diversity and, 477, 478. *See also* International business; International human resource management
Goals, *see* Human resource management, goals of; Management by objectives
Government
 international human resource management and stability of, 111–113
 social contracts and, 507–508
 see also Legal environment
Grand strategy, 41–43
Graphic rating scale, for performance appraisal, 246–247
Great Depression, 411
Grievance systems, 21
Griggs v. Duke Power, 74
Group pressures, as stressors, 462
Groups, *see* Self-directed work teams; Teams
Growth
 human resource planning for, 160–161
 promotion of as human resource management goal, 19

strategy and, 41–42, 48, *see also* Mergers and acquisitions
see also Career planning and development; Training and development

Halo error, performance appraisal and, 251
Handwriting analysis, selection and, 214
Hardship premium, international human resource management and, 127
Hawthorne studies, 8, 450
Headhunters, 124, 180–181
Health care, 461–468
 AIDS in workplace and, 467–468
 employee benefits and services and, 385, 390–391, 507
 insurance, 390–391, 507, 535
 labor unions and, 421
 long-term insurance and, 395
 wellness programs and, 394–395, 466–467
 see also Employee safety and health; Stress
Health hazards, 451. *See also* Employee safety and health
Health insurance, 390–391, 507, 535
Health maintenance organizations (HMOs), 391
H-form organization design, *see* Conglomerate organization design
Hierarchy of human needs, 8
High-performance work systems, 60
High-tech industry, location and, 50
Hiring, *see* Selection
Hispanics, in workforce, 482, 483, 485, 494
HMOs, *see* Health maintenance organizations
Holidays, 392–393
Home office, human resources in, 23
Home work programs, 521–522
Horizontal corporation, *see* Flat organization
Horns error, performance appraisal and, 251
Hostile work environment, sexual harassment and, 93
Hot stove rule, of discipline, 445, 448
Hours of work, 449–450. *See also* Work schedules
HRIS, *see* Human resource information systems
Human relations era, 8

Human resource department
 job analysis done by, 144
 in larger organizations, 23–24
Human resource function, evolution of, 5–9
 origins, 6–8
 personnel management, 8–9
Human resource information systems (HRIS), 159–160, 529–536
 definition of, 531
 ethics and, 535
 human resource functions and, 532
 information technology and, 530–531
 legal issues and, 534–535
 record keeping and report generation by, 532–533
Human resource management, 27
 careers in, 27
 case on, 28–29
 as center of expertise, 24–25
 definition of, 4
 evaluation of, 60–61
 importance of, 9–11
 line *vs.* staff management perspectives of, 20–23, 27
 professionalism and, 26–27
 smaller *versus* larger organization perspectives of, 23–24
 tasks and functions of, 10–15
Human resource management, goals of, 17–20
 complying with legal and social obligations, 19
 enhancing productivity and quality, 18–19
 facilitating organizational competitiveness, 17–18
 promoting individual growth and development, 19
Human resource management system, 15–17
Human resource managers
 prerequisites for, 26–27
 professionalism of, 26–27
 salary for, 26
 selection by, 198
 strategic human resource management and, 36
 see also Top human resource executives
Human resource planning, 14, 152–163
 case on, 164–165
 evaluation of, 162–163

executive succession and, 154–155,
164–165
follow-up action plans and,
159–162
forecasting demand of human resources and, 155–158, 159
forecasting supply of human resources and, 152–155, 156, 159
for growth, 160–161
human resource information systems for, 159–160, 533
job analysis and, 139–142
performance appraisal and,
234–235
for reductions, 161–162
for stability, 161
strategic importance of, 138–139
supply and demand compared for,
159
see also Job analysis
Human resource research, 536–548
causal relationships and, 538–540
measurement issues and, 541–542
samples and sampling and,
540–541
statistics and, 542–544
utility analysis and, 546–547
validity generalization and,
545–546
Human resources, definition of, 4
Hungary, high-tech workers hired
from, 174

Illegal discrimination, 72, 73–75
Equal Employment Opportunity
Commission and, 82–83, 84–85
see also Equal employment
opportunity
Illumination, of work environment,
450–451
Immigration, diversity and, 477, 478
Impasses, labor relations and,
429–431
In baskets
for management development, 285
as work simulations, 211
Incentives, 14, 21, 49, 355, 359,
363–366, 374–375
early-retirement plans and,
314–315
executives and, 359, 369–374
individual, 363–364, 367
international human resource management and, 113
limitations of, 365–366
piece-rate, 363

sales commissions, 364
stock options, 368, 370, 371, 374
time off, 364
India, high-tech workers hired from,
174
Indirect compensation, *see* Employee
benefits and services
Individual assessment phase, of career planning and development,
305
Individual incentive plans, 363–364,
367
Individual retirement accounts
(IRAs), 386, 387, 391
Inducements, psychological contracts
and, 503–504
Industrial Revolution, 5
cottage industries and, 521–522
Information technology, 530–531. *See
also* Human resource information systems
In-house training or development
programs, 275
Initial job assignment, 222
Input medium, in information
systems, 530
Institutional programs, for stress
management, 466–467
Instructional-based programs, for
training and development,
281–283
Insurance, 390–391
disability, 391
health, 390–391, 507, 535
life, 391
long-term health-care, 395
unemployment, 388
Integrity tests, 210
Intelligence tests, 7, 208–209, 210
Interactive video, for training and
development, 283
Internal consultants, technical employees as, 312
Internal equity, 326–327
Internal recruiting, 172–173,
174–177
International business, growth of,
104–107. *See also* International
human resource management
International human resource
management, 13–14, 21,
102–134
career planning and development,
125–126, 306–307
case on, 130–132
child labor and, 110–111, 113, 114

compensation and, 108, 111, 112,
117, 122–123, 126–128, 372–373
cost reduction and, 47
country's culture and, 109–111
direct investment and, 118–119
discrimination and, 80, 115–116
diversity and, 477, 478, 487, 488,
490–491, 493–494
employee benefits and services
and, 383, 384, 393, 394
ethics and, 111, 112
executive compensation and,
372–373
expatriate compensation and, 108,
126–128
expatriate selection and, 107–108,
123–125
expatriate training and development and, 108, 125–126
exporting and, 117, 119
human resource strategy and,
107–109
job movement to other countries
and, 419
joint ventures/strategic alliances
and, 119
labor relations and, 114, 128–129
language training and, 277,
493–494
licensing and, 117–118, 119
local compensation and, 122–123
local recruiting and selection and,
108, 120
local training and development
and, 121–122
political and legal environment
and, 80, 111–114
selection and, 107–108, 116, 120,
123–125
strategy and, 107–109
systems approach to, 16–17
training and development and,
108, 116–117, 121–122, 125–126,
277
working conditions and, 112, 117
see also specific countries
Internet
compensation and, 334
recruiting and, 182
selection and, 197
Interviews, 211–213
feedback, 252–253
for job analysis, 143–144
Intranet, communication and, 58–59
Italy, international business and, 117,
122

Japan
  diversity and, 487
  headhunting in, 124
  international business and, 104,
    105, 108, 110, 113, 116, 117, 118,
    121, 122, 125, 127
  job differentiation and, 336
  labor unions in, 129
  World War II and, 104
Job analysis, 14, 139–152, 336
  collecting job analysis data and,
    145–147
  consultants for, 144–145
  critical incidents approach and,
    150–151
  determining information needs
    and, 142–143
  Dictionary of Occupational Titles
    for, 145
  Fleishman job analysis system and,
    147
  functional job analysis and, 148
  human resource planning, 139–142
  interviews for, 143–144
  job analysis for, 143–145, 147, 148,
    150
  job analysis methods and, 143–152
  job component validity and,
    545–546
  job descriptions and, 151–152
  job specifications and, 151–152
  knowledge, skills, and abilities
    and, 141, 146–147, 148, 150
  narrative job analysis and, 147
  O*NET for, 145
  Position Analysis Questionnaire
    and, 144, 148–150
  process of, 142–145
  purposes of, 139–141
  responsibilities for job analysis
    and, 144–145
  subject matter experts and,
    145–146, 147
  task analysis inventory and,
    147–148
  technology and, 147
  see also Human resource planning
Job analysts, 143–145, 147, 148, 150
Job characteristics approach, 459–460
Job classes, for wage and salary
  structure, 341, 342
Job component validity, 545–546
Job descriptions, 151–152
Job design, 457–460
  job characteristics approach,
    459–460
  job enlargement and, 458–459

job enrichment and, 459
  job rotation and, 458
  job specialization and, 457–458
  see also Self-directed work teams
Job enlargement, 458–459
Job enrichment, 459
Job evaluation, 336–340
  classification system and, 337–338
  factor comparison method and,
    339–340
  frequency of, 344–345
  human resource information
    systems for, 533
  job ranking and, 337
  point system and, 338–339
  regression-based system and, 340
Job fairs, 181
Job families, job analysis and,
  141–142
Job movement, to other countries,
  419
Job offer, 220–222
Job performance, measurement of,
  541–542. See also Performance
  appraisal
Job posting, 175–177
Job preview, see Realistic job preview
Job ranking, job evaluation and, 337
Job rotation, see Systematic job rotations and transfers
Job satisfaction, 10
  as early-career problem, 309
  employee benefits and services
    and, 385
  flexible work hour plans and, 520
  stress and, 466
Job security
  labor unions and, 419, 421
  psychological contract and,
    504–506
  stress and, 462
Job specialization, 457–458
Job specifications, 151–152
Job worth, see Job evaluation
Joint ventures, international business
  and, 119

Knowledge, skills, and abilities
  (KSAs)
  interviews and, 212
  job analysis and, 141, 146–147, 148,
    150
  selection and, 196, 200–201, 216,
    220
Knowledge workers, 508–510
Knowledge-based pay, see Pay for
  knowledge

Korea, diversity and, 487
KSAs, see Knowledge, skills, and
  abilities

Labor Management Relations Act, 89,
  413–414, 503
Labor Management Reporting and
  Disclosure Act, 89, 414–415
Labor relations, 14–15, 54–55, 408
  collective bargaining and, 54, 55,
    89–90, 408, 411, 425–426, 502
  department for, 21, 24
  international human resource man-
    agement and, 128–129
  legal issues in, 89–90
  see also Labor unions
Labor shortage, 160
  hiring from abroad and, 174
Labor unions, 54–55, 408–437
  arbitration and, 430–431
  authorization card and, 422, 424
  bargaining and, 416, 419, 421, see also
    collective bargaining and, below
  bargaining unit and, 423
  boycotts and, 429
  case on, 433–435
  closed shop and, 413–414
  collective bargaining and, 54, 55,
    89–90, 408, 411, 425–426, 502
  compensation and, 328, 333, 349,
    350, 359, 421
  concessionary bargaining and, 416
  decertification of, 423–425
  defined contribution plans and,
    391–392
  emergence of, 7
  employee benefits and services
    and, 419, 421
  employee rights and, 440, 442
  employment-at-will and, 94
  final-offer arbitration and, 431
  formation of, 422–423, 424
  historical development of, 408–411,
    421–422
  human resource management
    slowing growth of, 8
  impasses and, 429–431
  international human resource man-
    agement and, 129
  job movement to other countries
    and, 419
  labor agreements and, 426–432
  legal issues and, 89, 411, 413–415
  locals, 415
  lockouts and, 430
  low-skilled jobs and, 511
  mediation and, 430

membership in, 411, 417–418

negotiation process and, 426–429

orientation and, 272

picketing and, 429

reasons for joining, 421–422

shop stewards and, 415, 431–432

slowdowns and, 429

strikes and, 55, 89, 129, 407–408, 410, 411, 414, 420, 429–430

structure of, 414, 415

trends in, 415–421

union-management relations and, 418–419, 420

union-shop agreement and, 414

viability of, 411, 412

wildcat strikes and, 429–430

Landrum-Griffin Act, *see* Labor Management Reporting and Disclosure Act

Language, international human resource management and, 110

Language training, diversity and, 493–494

Late-career employees, career management for, 313–315

Lateral transfers, for midcareer employees, 312–313

Layoffs, 300, 462. *See also* Downsizing

Leaderless group exercise, for management development, 285

Leadership, human resource strategy implementation and, 58

Leadership style, as stressor, 462–463

Learning curve, demand for human resources forecasted with, 157

Learning organization, 268

Learning theory, employee training and, 268–270

Leave

Family and Medical Leave Act of 1993 and, 81–82, 387

personal, 393

sick, 393

Lebanon, international business and, 112

Lecture approach, to training and development, 281

Legal environment, 9–10, 12–13, 68–101

AIDS and, 93

case on, 98–99

compensation and, 78, 87–89, 325, 331, 333

compliance and, 19, 20–21, 22, 96

contingent and temporary workers and, 518

diversity and, 477, 479, 480

employee benefits and services and, 386–389, 507

employee knowledge and, 94–95

employee rights and, 440–442

employee safety and health and, 9–10, 90–91, 451, 454–455

employment-at-will and, 94

human resource information systems and, 534–535

international human resource management and, 80, 111–114

labor unions and, 89, 411, 413–415

pensions and, 386, 387

performance appraisal and, 233–244

recommendations and, 213

regulations, 70–72, 83

sexual harassment and, 93–94

smaller organizations and, 23

social contracts and, 507–508

stock options and, 371

see also Collective bargaining; Employment contracts; Equal employment opportunity; Ethics; *specific laws*

Leniency distributional error, performance appraisal and, 251

Lesbians, *see* Gays and lesbians

Licensing, international business and, 117–118, 119

Life cycle benefits, 395

Life insurance, 391

Line managers, 20–23, 27

job analysis and, 141, 144

see also Operating manager

Local unions, 415

Location, as human resource management strategy, 50

Lockouts, 430

Long-term health-care insurance, 395

Low-skill workers, 511–512, 513

Maintenance, as career stage, 299, 300

Malaysia, international business and, 107, 121, 127

Management by objectives (MBO), for performance appraisal, 249–250

Management development, 267, 276, 284–287, 288–289

business schools providing, 275–276

evaluation of, 288–290

international human resources and, 276–277

organization development and, 285–286

other firms providing, 290

see also Training and development

Managers, selection methods for, 215–216

Mandatory items, in collective bargaining, 425

Manila, high-tech workers hired from, 174

Manufacturing, strategic human resource management and, 53

Marketing argument, for diversity, 487

Mass production, 457

Maturity curve, 329

Meaningful, learning and, 268–269

Measurement issues, 541–542

Mediation, labor relations and, 430

Mentors

early-career problems and, 310

for women and minorities, 19

Mergers and acquisitions, 11, 42, 43

career planning and development and, 308

international business and, 130–132

stress and, 462

Merit pay plans, 360–362

Mexico

international business and, 107, 121

production in, 103, 122–123

M-form organization design, *see* Divisional organization design

Midcareer employees, career management for, 310–313

Midcareer plateau, 310–311

Middle East, international business in, 110, 113

Minimum wage, 330, 331, 333, 511

Fair Labor Standards Act and, 7, 440

legal issues in, 87–88

Minnesota Clerical Test, 207

Minnesota Multiphasic Personality Inventory, The (MMPI), 209

Minorities, *see* Ethnicity

Mission statement

diversity and, 492

strategic human resource management and, 38–39

MMPI, *see Minnesota Multiphasic Personality Inventory*

Motivation, 14

agency theory and, 357–358

compensation and, 327

equity theory and, 57

expectancy theory and, 57, 356–357

external recruiting and, 174

human resource strategy implementation and, 56–57

Motivation *(continued)*
  internal recruiting and, 172–173
  learning and, 268
  performance appraisal and, 234, 235
  performance-based rewards and, 356–358
  reinforcement and, 57–58, 357
  see also Performance feedback; Performance management; Training and development
Multicultural organization, 494–495. *See also* Diversity
Multinational firms, 106. *See also* International business; International human resource management
Multiple regression
  demand for human resources forecasted with, 157
  for job evaluation, 340

NAFTA, *see* North American Free Trade Agreement
Narrative job analysis, 147
National Labor Relations Act of 1935, 7, 89, 411–412, 418
National Labor Relations Board (NLRB), 413, 414, 422, 424
National origin, *see* Country of national origin
Nationalization, international business and, 113
Needs
  analysis of for training and development, 273–274
  hierarchy of, 8
Negative transfer, learning and, 270
Negotiation
  job offer and, 220–222
  labor agreements and, 426–429
Networks, selection and, 216
Neuroticism, selection considering, 201
New employees, 500–528
  alternative work schedules and, 519–521
  alternative work sites and, 521–522
  career management for, 308–310
  case on, 524–525
  contingent and temporary workers and, 514–518, 524–525
  knowledge workers and, 508–510
  low-skill workers and, 511–512, 513
  orientation for, 270–272
  outsourcing and, 513–514
  see also Employment contracts

Newspaper advertisements, recruiting from, 178–179
NLRB, *see* National Labor Relations Board
Noncontributory pension plans, 392
Nonrelevancy, interviews and, 212
North American Free Trade Agreement (NAFTA), 114
Norway, employee benefits and services and, 383–384

Occupational diseases, control of, 456–457
Occupational Safety and Health Act (OSHA) of 1970, 90–91, 451, 454–455
O'Connor Tweezer Dexterity test, 209
OD, *see* Organization development
OFCCP, *see* Office of Federal Contract Compliance Procedures
Office managers, hiring by, 6–7
Office of Federal Contract Compliance Procedures (OFCCP), 77, 79, 82, 85–87
Old Age Survivors and Disability Insurance Program, *see* Social security
Older employees
  diversity and, 481–482, 491
  low-skilled jobs and, 511
O*NET, 145
On-the-job training, 280
Openness to experience, selection considering, 201
Operating managers, 21–23
  selection by, 198
  strategic human resource management and, 36
Operation systems, in information systems, 531
Organization culture, *see* Culture
Organization design, strategic human resource management and, 50–51
Organization development, 285–286
Organizational citizenship behaviors, 241
Organizational culture, diversity and, 494
Orientation, for new employees, 270–272
OSHA, *see* Occupational Safety and Health Act of 1970
Outdoor training exercises, 283
Output medium, in information systems, 530

Outsourcing, 11–12, 21, 22, 513–514
  human resources overseeing, 24–25
  of training and development, 275–276
Overlearning, learning and, 268
Overload, stress and, 462, 463
Overtime, 325
  as alternative to recruiting, 185–186

Paired-comparison method, for performance appraisal, 245
PAQ, *see* Position Analysis Questionnaire
Part-time workers, 187
Pattern or practice discrimination, 75
Pay compression, 347
Pay for knowledge, 289, 328, 342–344, 362
Pay secrecy, 346
Pay structure, for wage and salary structure, 341–342
Pay surveys, 333–335, 348, 399, 533. *See also* Compensation; *under* wage
Peers, performance appraisals and, 241–242
Pension plans, 88–89, 387
  cash-balance plans, 392
  defined contribution plans, 391–392
  Employee Retirement Income Security Act of 1974 and, 88, 387, 391
  401(k) plans, 386, 391, 392
  individual retirement accounts, 386, 387, 391
  legal aspects of, 386, 387
  private, 390, 391–392
  qualified, 386
Performance, rewards and, 358–359
Performance appraisal, 21, 60–61, 231–255
  appraisers of, 239–243
  archiving results of, 253–255
  case on, 258–260
  contextual performance and, 240–241
  customers and, 242
  as early-career problem, 309
  electronic monitoring and, 507
  evaluation of, 256–258
  feedback and, 252–253, 257
  follow-up plan and, 255–256
  goals of, 235
  importance of, 232–235
  job analysis and, 140–141
  limitations of, 250–252
  managerial training for, 251

merit pay and, 360, 361
methods for, 244–250
objective, 244–245
organization's role in, 236–238
peers and, 241–242
process, 236–244
ranking methods for, 245–246
ratee's role in, 239
rater's role in, 238–243
rating errors and, 250–251
rating methods for, 246–250
reason for, 232–236
self-evaluation and, 242
sources of information for, 239–244
standards for, 238
subjective, 244–245
subordinates and, 242
supervisors and, 238–241
360–degree feedback and, 231–232,
      242–244
timing of, 236, 238, 258–260
Performance evaluation, *see* Perfor-
      mance appraisal
Performance feedback, 14
Performance management, 14, 21, 49,
      232, 239
   career planning and development
      and, 305
   see also Performance appraisal
Performance review, *see* Performance
      appraisal
Performance-based rewards, 329,
      345–346, 354–379
   absenteeism and, 360
   attendance and, 360
   case on, 376–377
   employee stock ownership plans,
      368, 387
   executive compensation, 334, 359,
      369–374
   individual, 363–364, 367
   merit compensation systems and,
      360–362
   motivation and, 356–358
   pay-for knowledge, 289, 328,
      342–344, 362
   performance and, 358–359
   profit-sharing, 368, 369, 509
   purpose of, 356–360
   skill-based pay, 343, 344, 362
   stock options, 368, 370, 371, 374
   team and group pay systems,
      366–369, 374
   turnover and, 359–360
   see also Incentives
Permissive items, in collective bar-
      gaining, 425–426

Perquisites, 397
   executives and, 370, 373
Personal characteristics, selection
      and, 196–197, 201–202
Personal financial planning, 19
Personal interviews, *see* Interviews
Personal leave, 393
Personality
   "big five" traits, 201, 209–210
   handwriting analysis and, 214
   tests of, 209
Personality conflicts, as stressors, 463
Personality traits, human resource
      strategy implementation and, 56
Personnel departments, 8–9
   origin of, 7
Personnel Management (Scott and
      Clothier), 7
Personnel management, evaluation
      of, 8–9
Personnel manager, 8, 9
Philippines, international business
      and, 112
Physical demands, as stressors, 462
Physical examinations, for selection,
      213–214
Picketing, 429
Piece-rate incentive plan, 363
Placement, *see* Selection
Planning, *see* Human resource
      planning
Point manual, for job evaluation, 339
Point system, for job evaluation,
      338–339
Police departments, selection by,
      195–196
Political ideologies, workforce diver-
      sity and, 54
Politics, international human re-
      source management and,
      111–114
Polycentric staffing model, 108
Position Analysis Questionnaire
      (PAQ), 144, 148–150, 340, 545
Practice, learning and, 268
Pregnancy, equal employment oppor-
      tunity and, 79–80, 81, 387
Pregnancy Discrimination Act of
      1978, 79–80, 387
President, regulations and, 70
Prima facie case, of discrimination, 74
Privacy
   as employee right, 441, 506–507,
      534–535
   human resource information sys-
      tems and, 534–535
Privacy Act of 1974, 534

Privacy Protection Study Commis-
      sion, 434–435
Private employment agencies, 180
Private pension plans, 390, 391–392
Problem-solving argument, for
      diversity, 487
Process consultation, 286
Processor, in information systems,
      530
Productivity, 10, 18
   contingent workers and, 515
   diversity and, 486–487
   enhancement of as human resource
      management goal, 18–19
Productivity ratio, demand for hu-
      man resources forecasted with,
      157
Professionalism, human resource
      management and, 26–27
Profit sharing, 368, 369
   knowledge workers and, 509
Programmed instruction, 282–283
Progressive discipline system,
      448–449
Projection, performance appraisal
      and, 250
Projective technique, 209–210
Prospector strategy, 45
Protected classes, in workforce, 73,
      75–78. *See also* Equal employ-
      ment opportunity
Protection plans, 387
   mandated, 387–389
   optional, 390–392
Psychological contracts, 503–507
   downsizing and, 43
   human resource management
      strategy implementation and,
      55–56, 57
Psychomotor ability tests, 209
Public employment agencies, 179–180
Punishment, 442–443. *See also* Disci-
      pline
Purpose of organization, strategic
      human resource management
      and, 38

Qualified pension plans, 386
Quality, 18, 21
   enhancement of as human resource
      management goal, 18–19
   systems approach to, 16
Quality of work life, 10
Quid pro quo harassment, 93
Quitting, stress and, 465
Quotas, international business and,
      113

Race, legal environment and, 77, 80. *See also* Equal employment opportunity

Radio, recruiting via, 182

Ranking methods, for performance appraisal, 245–246

Rater-accuracy training, performance appraisal and, 251

Rating error, performance appraisal and, 250–251

Rating methods, for performance appraisal, 246–250

Reactor strategy, 46

Realistic job preview, 171, 183
early-career problem and, 309
orientation and, 271

Recommendations, for selection, 213

Record keeping, by human resource information systems, 532–533

Recruiting, 14, 21, 168–193
from abroad, 174
advertisements and, 178–179
alternatives to, 185
case on, 189–191
college placement offices and, 181
department for, 23
direct applicants and, 128
employee leasing *versus*, 187
evaluation of, 188
executive search firms and, 180–181
external, 173–175, 177–182
general labor pool and, 177
goals of, 170–172
internal, 172–173, 174–177
international human resource management and, 120, 123–124
Internet and, 182
job posting and, 175–177
methods of, 175–182
organization's goals in, 170–171
outsourcing of, 24
overtime *versus*, 185–186
part-time workers *versus*, 187
performance appraisal and, 232
private employment agencies and, 180
prospective employee's goals in, 171–172
prospective employee's perspective and, 171–172, 184–185
public employment agencies and, 179–180
radio and television and, 182
realistic job previews and, 171, 183
referrals and, 177–178
sources for, 172–175, 177–178

supervisory recommendations and, 177
temporary workers *versus*, 186–187, 524–525
union halls and, 177
word-of-mouth, 178
see also Selection

Reductions, human resource planning for, 161–162

Reengineering, 11

References, for selection, 213

Referral, recruiting from, 177–178

Regression coefficient, 543

Regression line, 543–544

Regression-based system, for job evaluation, 340

Regulations, 70–72. *See also* Legal environment

Reinforcement
learning and, 268
motivation and, 57–58, 357

Related diversification, 44, 49

Reliability, 541
of selection technique, 217

Religious beliefs
diversity and, 393, 479–480
international human resource management and, 110
legal environment and, 77, 80, 479–480, *see also* Equal employment opportunity

Religious holidays, 393

Relocation services, 396

Report generation, by human resource information systems, 532–533

Research, *see* Human resource research

Resource acquisition argument, for diversity, 487

Retaliation, as illegal discrimination, 75

Retention, employee benefits and services and, 386

Retirement, 314–315
early, 162, 314–315, 396–397
individual retirement accounts and, 386, 387, 391
mandatory, 54, 481
new-employee orientation and, 272
social security and, 388–389
success in, 317
see also Pension plans

Retrenchment strategy, 42–43, 48

Revenue Act of 1950, 371

Revenue Reconciliation Act of 1993, 386

Reverse discrimination, 72, 87

Revised Minnesota Paper Form Board, 207

Rewards, *see* Compensation

Right to work laws, 414

Rightsizing, *see* Downsizing

Ripple effect, internal recruiting and, 173

RJP, *see* Realistic job preview

Role demands, stress and, 462

Roles, international human resource management and, 110

Rorschach inkblot test, 210

Roth IRA, 386

Rowe vs. General Motors, 177

Rule violators, discipline and, 444, 448

Russia
high-tech workers hired from, 174
international business and, 117

Safety, *see* Employee safety and health

Safety engineers, 456

Safety hazards, 451. *See also* Employee safety and health

Salaries, 328. *See also* Compensation; *under wage*

Sales commission, 364

Sampling, 540–541

Saudi Arabia, international business and, 110, 115, 116, 117

Scanlon plan, 366

Scatter plots, 542, 543–544

Scholastic Aptitude Test (SAT), 208

Scientific management, 5–6, 356

Screening, 21

Securities Exchange Act, 371

Selection, 14, 194–228
applications for, 203–205, 206
assessment centers for, 215–216
background checks for, 203–205
banding and, 220
case on, 224–226
competencies and, 199
contacts for, 216
criteria for, 197, 199–202
culture and, 53
decision and, 197–198, 220–222
department for, 23
discrimination and, 195, 203, 208–209, 216
education requirements for, 196, 199
electronic screening and, 204, 206
Equal Employment Opportunity Commission and, 84, 85

evaluation of, 222–223
experience criteria for, 196, 200
for fit *versus* skill, 201–202, 220, 303
four-fifths rule and, 74
handwriting analysis for, 214
high-risk employees and, 224–226
initial job assignments and, 222
international human resource management and, 107–108, 116, 120, 123–125
interviews for, 211–213
job analysis and, 139–140
job families and, 142
job offer and negotiation and, 220–222
knowledge, skills, and abilities and, 196, 200–201, 202, 216, 220
of managers, 215–216
networks for, 216
outsourcing of, 24
performance appraisal and, 232
personal characteristics for, 196–197, 201–202
physical examination for, 213–214
productivity and quality and, 18
references and recommendations for, 213
reliability and, 217
responsibilities for, 198
single- *versus* multiple-predictor approaches to, 219
steps in, 196–198
techniques for, 202–216
validity and, 217–219
work simulations for, 210–211
see also Employment tests
Self-directed work teams, 460
culture and, 52
human resource management and, 22
improved firm performance and, 61
selection and, 198, 201
see also Teams
Self-evaluation, performance appraisal and, 242
Self-report inventory, 209
Semistructured employment interview, 211
Seniority, compensation and, 328–329, 345
Service jobs, 511, 512
Service organization, strategic human resource management and, 53
Severity distributional error, performance appraisal and, 251
Sex, *see* Gays and lesbians; Women in workforce

Sexual harassment, 93–94, 98–99, 489, 491–492
Sherman Antitrust Act, 411
Shift work, 449–450, 466
Shop stewards, 415, 431–432
Sick leave, 393
Similarity error, interviews and, 212
Simple ranking method, for performance appraisal, 245
Singapore, international business and, 107
Single-parent employment, 54, 316, 485
Skill-based pay, 289, 328, 343, 344, 362
Skills, human resource information system for inventory of, 533
Skills and abilities, *see* Knowledge, skills, and abilities
Slope of the line, 543
Slowdowns, 429
Small independent business, human resources in, 23
Small organizations
human resources in, 23
selection and, 198
SMEs, *see* Subject matter experts
Smoking, stress and, 463, 465
Social change, diversity and, 486
Social contracts, 507–508
Social obligations, compliance with as human resource management goal, 19
Social security, 388–389, 391
Social Security Act of 1935, 388, 391
public employment agencies and, 179
South Africa, high-tech workers hired from, 174
South America, international business and, 113, 114
Spain, international business and, 105
Specific training, 289
Speech, freedom of as employee right, 506
Stability
human resource planning for, 161
strategy and, 43
Staff managers, 20–23
Staffing, 14, 138
strategy for, 48, 49, 50, *see also* Human resource planning; Job analysis; Recruiting; Selection
Staffing models
ethnocentric, 107–108
geocentric, 108–109
polycentric, 108

Staffing ratio, demand for human resources forecasted with, 157
Statistical methods
human resource demand forecasted with, 155, 157, 542–544
human resource supply forecasted with, 154
Stock options, 368, 370, 371, 374
Storage devices, in information systems, 530
Strategic alliance, international business and, 119
Strategic human resource management, 12, 21, 34–67
case on, 62–64
competitiveness and, 18
culture and, 51–53
evaluation of human resource function and, 60–61
formulation of, 48–55
implementation of, 55–59
individual processes and, 55–58
interpersonal processes and, 58–59
mission of organization and, 38–39
organization design and, 50–51
outsourcing and, 25
purpose of organization and, 38
SWOT analysis and, 40–41
technology and, 53–54
top management team and, 39–40
workforce and, 54–55
see also Business strategy; Corporate strategy; Functional strategies
Stress, 439–440, 461–466
causes of, 461–464
consequences of, 464–466
flexible work hour plans and, 520
human resource strategy implementation and, 56
institutional programs managing, 19, 466–467
Stress management programs, 19, 466–467
Stressors, 461–462
Strikebreakers, 430
Strikes, 55, 89, 407–408, 410, 411, 414, 420, 429–430
international human resource management and, 129
Structured employment interview, 211, 212
Subject matter experts (SMEs), job analysis and, 145–146, 147
Subordinates, performance appraisals and, 242

Substance abuse
  discipline and, 444
  employee assistance plans and, 397
Sudan, international business and, 110
Supervisors
  internal recruiting through recommendations of, 177
  performance appraisal conducted by, 238–241
Surveillance, privacy and, 506–507
Survey feedback OD, 286
Sweden, employee benefits and services and, 383–384
SWOT analysis, 40–41
Systematic job rotations and transfers, 281, 458
Systems approach, to human resource management, 15–17
Systems flexibility argument, for diversity, 488

Taft-Hartley Act, *see* Labor Management Relations Act
Taiwan, international business and, 107
Tariff, international business and, 113
Task analysis inventory, 147–148
Task demands, as stressors, 461–462
Tax Reform Act of 1986, 371, 386
Tax Reform Act of 1997, 386
Tax-equalization system, international human resource management and, 127
Teams
  diversity and, 492
  flexible work hour plans and, 520
  pay system based on, 366–369, 374
  for training and development, 283, 284
  see also Self-directed work teams
Technical employees, as internal consultants, 312
Technology
  job analysis and, 147
  labor shortage in, 174
  strategic human resource management and, 53–54
  stress and, 463
Telecommuting, 522
  home office safety and, 91, 453
Television, recruiting via, 182
Temperature, of work environment, 450–451, 462
Temporary employees, 186–187
  case on, 524–525
Termination, *see* Employment-at-will

Test-retest reliability, 217
Tests, *see* Employment tests
Theft
  discipline and, 444
  electronic surveillance and, 506
Thematic Apperception Test, 210
Theory X, 8
Theory Y, 8
Third-party peacemaking, 286
Thirteenth Amendment, 72
360-degree feedback, 231–232, 242–244
Time off, as incentive, 364
Title VII of Civil Rights Act of 1964, 74, 75, 77, 82, 83, 93, 479
Tolerance, diversity management and, 490–491
Top human resource executives
  prerequisites for, 26–27
  professionalism of, 26–27
  salary for, 26
  status of, 11
Top level managers, executive search firms and, 180–181
Top management team, strategic human resource management and, 39–40
Top-down forecasting, demand for human resources forecasted with, 157
Trade controls, international human resource management and, 113
Training, *see* Employee training; Training and development
Training and development, 14, 19, 21, 49, 264–295
  apprenticeship training and, 280–281
  assessing needs of, 273–276
  case on, 291–292
  computer-assisted instruction and, 281–282
  content of, 276–278, 279, 289
  department for, 23
  design of, 276–279
  development and, 266, 267–268
  evaluation of, 287–290, 532
  general, 289
  goals of, 274
  in-house, 275
  instructional-based programs and, 281–283
  instructors for, 278–279
  international human resource management and, 108, 116–117, 121–122, 125–126, 277
  job analysis and, 140

  knowledge workers and, 509
  learning theory and, 268–270
  management development and, 267, 276, 284–287
  needs analysis for, 273–274
  new-employee orientation and, 270–272
  on-the-job training and, 280
  organization development and, 285–286
  outline of, 276
  outsourcing, 275–276
  performance appraisal and, 233
  productivity and quality and, 18
  programmed instruction and, 282–283
  psychological contract and, 504
  purposes of, 266–270
  specific, 289
  systematic job rotation and transfers and, 281
  team-based activities for, 283, 284
  techniques and methods for, 279–284
  technology for, 283
  training and, 266–267
  vestibule training and, 281
  work-based programs and, 279–281
  see also Career planning and development; Management development
Transfer, learning and, 269–270
Trinidad, employee benefits and services and, 383–384
T-test, 544
Turnaround strategy, *see* Retrenchment strategy
Turnover
  compensation and, 359–360
  diversity and, 486–487
  employee benefits and services and, 385, 386
  low-skilled jobs and, 511

U-form organization, *see* Functional organization design
Understanding, diversity management and, 490
Unemployment insurance, 388
Union halls, internal recruiting through, 177
Unions, *see* Labor unions
Union-shop agreements, 414
Unit forecasting, *see* Bottom-up forecasting
Unrelated diversification, 44, 49

Unstructured employment interview, 211–212
Utilization analysis, 546–547
  affirmative action and, 86

Vacations, 393, 394
Validity, 541
  of selection technique, 217–219
Validity generalization, 545–546
Vestibule training, 281
Vesting, 387
Video teleconferencing, for training and development, 283
Vietnam Era Veterans' Readjustment Act of 1974, 79
Vietnam-era veterans, equal employment opportunity and, 79
Violence, in workplace, 465, 505
Vocational Rehabilitation Act of 1973, 79

Wage and salary administration
  case on, 349–356
  individual wages and, 345–346
  managing compensation and, 344–345
  pay compression and, 344–347
  pay secrecy and, 346
Wage and salary structure
  equity and, 57
  job classes and, 341, 342
  pay for knowledge and, 289, 328, 342–344, 362
  pay structure for, 341–342
  skill-based pay and, 343, 344, 362
  see also Job evaluation
Wage surveys, 333–335, 348, 399, 533
Wages, 328. See also Compensation; Employee benefits and services; Minimum wage; Wage and

salary administration; Wage and salary structure
Wagner Act, see National Labor Relations Act
Walk-ins, see Direct applicants
Weighted application blank, 205
Wellness and fitness programs, 19, 394–395, 466–467
White-collar workers, private employment agencies and, 180
Wildcat strikes, 429–430
Wobblies, 410
Women in workforce, 54, 477
  compensation and, 327, 482
  conflict and, 488
  diversity and, 480, 482, 483, 487, 496–497
  diversity training and, 493
  dual-career and work-family issues and, 316–317
  empathy and, 490
  employee benefits and services and, 385
  glass ceiling and, 54, 482, 484
  human resource planning and, 154
  international human resource management and, 110, 115–116
  legal environment and, 77, 78, 79–80, 81, 98–99, see also Equal employment opportunity
  mentoring programs for, 19
  pregnancy and, 79–80, 81, 387
  sexual harassment and, 93–94, 98–99, 489, 491–492
Word-of-mouth recruiting, 178
Work environment, 15, 439–473
  hours of work and, 449–450, see also Work schedules
  illumination and, 450–451
  temperature and, 450–451, 462

work space design and, 450, 451, 462
  see also Discipline; Employee rights; Employee safety and health; Health care; Job design; Stress
Work samples, see Work simulations
Work schedules
  compressed workweeks, 520–521
  diversity and, 492
  flexible work hour plans, 519–520
  hours of work and, 449–450
  stress and, 466
Work simulations, 210–211
Work sites, alternative, 521–522
Work space design, of work environment, 450, 451, 462
Work teams, see Self-directed work teams
Work-based programs, for training and development, 279–281
Workers' compensation, 389, 391, 439
Work-family issues, 316–317
Workforce analysis, for training and development, 273
Working conditions, international human resource management and, 112, 117
Workweeks, 449–450
World War I, intelligence tests and, 7
World War II, 104–105
  personnel management and, 8–9

Y intercept, 543